Introduction to

Java™

Programming

Fourth Edition

Y. Daniel Liang
School of Computing
Armstrong Atlantic State University

Prentice Hall

Prentice Hall
Upper Saddle River, New Jersey 07458
http://www.prenhall.com

Library of Congress Cataloging-in-Publication Data
CIP data on file.

Vice President and Editorial Director, ECS: *Marcia Horton*
Publisher: *Alan R. Apt*
Associate Editor: *Toni D. Holm*
Editorial Assistant: *Patrick Lindner*
Vice President and Director of Production and Manufacturing, ESM: *David W. Riccardi*
Executive Managing Editor: *Vince O'Brien*
Assistant Managing Editor: *Camille Trentacoste*
Production Editor: *Irwin Zucker*
Manufacturing Manager: *Trudy Pisciotti*
Manufacturing Buyer: *Lisa McDowell*
Director of Creative Services: *Paul Belfanti*
Creative Director: *Carole Anson*
Art Editor: *Xiaohong Zhu*
Cover Designer: *Geoffrey Cassar*
Cover Art: *Photo of circular Aztec carved stone, National Museum of the American Indian/Smithsonian Institution*
Executive Marketing Manager: *Pamela Shaffer*
Marketing Assistant: *Barrie Reinhold*

© 2003, 2001, 1999, 1998 by Pearson Education, Inc.
Pearson Education, Inc.
Upper Saddle River, New Jersey 07458

The author and publisher of this book have used their best efforts in preparing this book. These efforts include the development, research, and testing of the theories to determine their effectiveness. The author and publisher make no warranty of any kind, expressed or imiplied, with regard to these programs or the documentation contained in this book. The author and publisher shall not be liable in any event for incidental or consequential damages in connection with, or arising out of, the furnishing, performance, or use of these programs.

Java is a trademark of Sun Microsystems, Inc.

Printed in the United States of America
10 9 8 7 6 5 4 3 2 1

ISBN 0-13-100225-2

Pearson Education Ltd., *London*
Pearson Education Australia Pty. Ltd., *Sydney*
Pearson Education Singapore, Pte. Ltd.
Pearson Education North Asia Ltd., *Hong Kong*
Pearson Education Canada, Inc., *Toronto*
Pearson Educacíon de Mexico, S.A. de C.V.
Pearson Education—Japan, *Tokyo*
Pearson Education Malaysia, Pte. Ltd.
Pearson Education, *Upper Saddle River, New Jersey*

To Samantha, Michael, and Michelle

PREFACE

To the Instructor

Java Teaching Strategies

There are three popular strategies in teaching Java. The first, known as *GUI-first*, is to mix Java applets and GUI programming with object-oriented programming concepts. The second, known as *object-first*, is to introduce object-oriented programming from the start. The third strategy, known as *fundamentals-first*, is a step-by-step approach, first laying a sound foundation on programming concepts, control statements, and methods, then introducing object-oriented programming, and then moving on to graphical user interface (GUI), applets, and finally to exception handling, I/O, data structures, internationalization, multithreading, multimedia, and networking.

The GUI-first strategy, starting with GUI and applets, seems attractive, but requires substantial knowledge of object-oriented programming and a good understanding of the Java event-handling model; thus, students may never fully understand what they are doing.

The object-first strategy is based on the notion that objects should be introduced first because Java is an object-oriented programming language. This notion, however, overlooks the importance of the fundamental techniques required for writing programs in any programming language. Furthermore, this approach inevitably mixes static and instance variables and methods before students can fully understand classes and objects and use them to develop useful programs. Students are overwhelmed by object-oriented programming and basic rules of programming simultaneously in the early stage of learning Java. This is a common source of frustration for freshmen learning object-oriented programming.

From my own experience, confirmed by the experiences of many colleagues, I have found that learning basic logic and fundamental programming techniques like loops is a struggle for most freshmen. *Students who cannot write code in procedural programming are not able to learn object-oriented programming.* A good introduction on primitive data types, control statements, methods, and arrays prepares students to learn object-oriented programming. Therefore, this text adopts the fundamentals-first strategy, proceeding at a steady pace through all the necessary and important basic concepts, then moving to object-oriented programming, and then to using the object-oriented approach to build interesting GUI applications and applets with exception handling, I/O, data structures, internationalization, multithreading, multimedia, and networking.

Selection of Java Subjects

Many introductory Java texts lack sufficient breadth and do not cover all the core Java knowledge that is needed to develop useful projects. Some authors over ambitiously mix too many topics, such as Java database programming, Remote Method

Invocation, JavaBeans and rapid application development, servlets, and JSP, into one introductory Java text. With this approach the coverage of programming principles tends to lose coherence. What is the basis for deciding that one approach is too light and the other too heavy? I believe that the best yardstick is the Level 1 Java Certification Exam (http://www.jcert.org/level1.html) initiated by a consortium of leading IT companies, including Sun Microsystems, IBM, Oracle, Hewlett-Packard, BEA Systems, and Sybase. The Level 1 Certification Exam tests core Java knowledge and fundamental programming skills.

This book gives a comprehensive introduction on the fundamentals of programming in Chapters 1–5, an in-depth treatment of object-oriented programming in Chapters 6–9, extensive examples of GUI programming in Chapters 10–12, and appropriate coverage of advanced Java topics in Chapters 13–19. The book covers all the subjects required for the Level 1 Java Certification Exam.

Audience of This Book

The book is suited for both beginning and advanced students, depending on how it is used. It has been used in two-semester freshman programming courses and one-semester courses in Java as a second language. It has also been used in short training courses for experienced programmers. Computer science departments, engineering departments, and management information systems departments around the world have used this book at various levels.

Use of This Book

Every school is different. Some schools have used the book in one semester, and some have used it in a two-semester or three-semester sequence. The computer science curriculum has two important objectives: (1) to prepare students for immediate employment by teaching them marketable skills; (2) to teach students how to learn on their own. This book is designed to foster self-teaching with many complete examples, notes, tips, and cautions. Students should be able to learn on their own after mastering the first ten chapters. For students with no programming experience, an entire semester of four credit hours could be spent just on the first five chapters of the book, as we do in the first semester of the programming course at Armstrong Atlantic State University. In the second semester, we cover chapters 6–13, 17, and 19. In the first semester, students are new to programming. It takes time and patience to help them get into the mood of programming. In the second semester, we cover Chapters 6–13, 17, and 19. In the first semester, students are new to programming. It takes time and patience to help them get into the mood of programming. In the second semester, we cover Chapters 6, 7, part of 8 (up to Abstract Classes), part of 10 (up to Case Studies), 8 (Polymorphism, Dynamic Binding, and Interfaces), 10 (Event-driven programming), 11, part of 12 (just on applets), 13, part of 17 (just on file IO), 9 and 19, in this sequence (see Chapter Dependency Chart for other possible sequences). Students are capable of learning all the materials after Chapter 10 through self-teaching. The important part of the second semester is to guide the students to learn by themselves.

Interactive Lectures

Over the years, I have tried many ways of teaching Java. The most effective approach is to teach it using the slides and writing, running and testing programs in the class interactively. Using the slides, you don't have to write on the board. It saves valuable lecture time. Writing, running, and testing programs in the class can hold students' attention and give them instantaneous feedback on how to program.

Instructor Resources

The Instructor's Resource CD-ROM is available for instructors using this book. It contains the following resources:

- Microsoft PowerPoint slides for lectures, with interactive buttons to view syntax-highlighted source code and to run programs without leaving the slides.

- Twelve sample exams. In general, each exam has four parts: (1) multiple-choice questions or short questions; (2) correct programming errors; (3) trace programs; (4) write programs.

- Solutions to all the exercises. Students will have access to the solutions of even-numbered exercises in the book's companion CD-ROM.

- More than forty supplemental exercises and their solutions.

- Suggested syllabi for teaching Java to freshmen, for teaching Java as a second language, and for teaching Java to corporate employees.

- Lecture notes. A number of suggested teaching strategies and activities are presented to help you in the delivery of the course.

To obtain the Instructor's Resource CD-ROM, contact your Prentice Hall sales representative. Some students have requested the solutions to the odd-numbered programming exercises. Please understand that these are for instructors only. Such requests will not be answered.

Microsoft PowerPoint slides are also available at the book's Companion Website at http://www.prenhall.com/liang/intro4e.html. The Web site also contains interactive online self-tests and other supplemental materials.

Pedagogical Features of the Book

The philosophy of the Liang Java Series is *teaching by example and learning by doing*. Basic features are explained by example so that you can learn by doing. The book uses the following elements to get the most out of the material:

- **Objectives** list what students should have learned from the chapter. This will help them to determine whether they have met the objectives after completing the chapter.

- **Introduction** opens the discussion with a brief overview of what to expect from the chapter.

■ Programming concepts are taught by representative **Examples**, carefully chosen and presented in an easy-to-follow style. Each example has the problem statement, solution steps, complete source code, sample run, and review. The source code of the examples is contained in the companion CD-ROM.

■ **Chapter Summary** reviews the important subjects that students should understand and remember. It helps them to reinforce the key concepts they have learned in the chapter.

■ **Review Questions** help students to track their progress and evaluate their learning.

■ **Programming Exercises** at the end of each chapter provide students with opportunities to apply the skills on their own. The trick of learning programming is practice, practice, and practice. To that end, the book provides a large number of exercises.

■ **Interactive Self-Test** helps students to test their knowledge interactively online. The Self-Test is accessible from the book's Companion Website at `www.prenhall.com/liang/intro4e.html`. It provides more than six hundred multiple-choice and true/false questions organized by chapters.

■ **Notes**, **Tips**, and **Cautions** are inserted throughout the text to offer valuable advice and insight on important aspects of program development.

NOTE
Provides additional information on the subject and reinforces important concepts.

TIP
Teaches good programming style and practice.

CAUTION
Helps students steer away from the pitfalls of programming errors.

What's New in This Edition

This book expands and improves upon *Introduction to Java Programming, Third Edition*. The major changes are as follows:

■ The proprietary `MyInput` class for getting input from the console is replaced by the standard `JOptionPane` class. Students don't have to learn a proprietary class that is not used in the workplace.

■ Part II, "Objected-Oriented Programming," is expanded into four chapters to provide an in-depth introduction to object-oriented programming and design. Strings are now in a separate chapter, and Chapter 9, "Object-Oriented Software Development," covers class design techniques.

■ Every chapter is thoroughly revised and improved. Chapter 9, "Object-Oriented Software Development," is partly new; it now introduces object-oriented development using the UML approach and fosters the concept of developing reusable components. Chapter 19, "Java Data Structures" is brand-new; it introduces the Java collections framework.

■ The book has been reorganized to provide flexible ordering of chapters so that instructors can easily customize their use of it. Arrays are treated in Chapter 5, but can be covered after Chapter 8. The book provides flexible ordering of chapters. You may cover Chapter 6, "Objects and Classes," after Chapter 4, "Methods." You may cover Chapter 13, "Exception Handling," after class inheritance is introduced in Chapter 8, "Class Inheritance and Interfaces." Chapter 19, "Java Data Structures," can be covered after Chapter 9, "Object-Oriented Software Development."

■ Several new appendices provide readers with additional background information and supplemental material.

■ The comprehensive Companion Website at `www.prenhall.com/liang/intro4e.html` includes an interactive self-test for each chapter. There are more than six hundred questions in the self-test. This site also contains new supplements on computer basics that introduce the terms CPU, memory, hard disk, operating systems, and programming languages.

To the Student

There is nothing more important to the future of computing than the Internet. There is nothing more exciting on the Internet than Java. A revolutionary programming language developed by Sun Microsystems, Java has become the de facto standard for cross-platform applications and programming on the World Wide Web.

Java is a full-featured, general-purpose programming language that is capable of developing robust mission-critical applications. In recent years, Java has gained enormous popularity and has quickly become the most popular and successful programming language. Today, it is used not only for Web programming, but also for developing standalone applications across platforms on servers, desktops, and mobile devices. Many companies that once considered Java to be more hype than substance are now using it to create distributed applications accessed by customers and partners across the Internet. For every new project being developed today, companies are asking how they can use Java to make their work easier.

Java is now taught in every university. This book teaches you how to write Java programs from beginning.

Java's Design and Advantages

■ **Java is an object-oriented programming language**. Object-oriented programming is a favored programming approach that has replaced traditional procedure-based programming techniques. An object-oriented language uses abstraction, encapsulation, inheritance, and polymorphism to provide great flexibility, modularity, and reusability for developing software.

- **Java is platform-independent.** Its programs can run on any platform with a Java Virtual Machine, a software component that interprets Java instructions and carries out associated actions.

- **Java is distributed.** Networking is inherently built-in. Simultaneous processing can occur on multiple computers on the Internet. Writing network programs is treated as simple data input and output.

- **Java is multithreaded.** Multithreading is the capability of a program to perform several tasks simultaneously, such as downloading a video file while playing the video at the same time. Multithreading is particularly useful in graphical user interfaces (GUI) and network programming. Multithread programming is smoothly integrated in Java. In other languages, you can only enable multithreading by calling procedures that are specific to the operating system.

- **Java is secure.** Computers become vulnerable when they are connected to other computers. Viruses and malicious programs can damage your computer. Java is designed with multiple layers of security that ensure proper access to private data and restrict access to disk files.

Java's Versatility

Stimulated by the promise of writing programs once and running them anywhere, Java has become the most ubiquitous programming language. Java programs run on full-featured computers, and also on consumer electronics and appliances such as Palm and mobile phones.

Because of its great potential to unite existing legacy applications written on different platforms so that they can run together, Java is perceived as a universal front-end for the enterprise database. The leading database companies, IBM, Oracle, and Sybase, have extended their commitment to Java by integrating it into their products. Oracle, for example, enables Java applications to run on its server and to deliver a complete set of Java-based development tools supporting the integration of current applications with the Web.

Learning Java

To first-time programmers, learning Java is like learning any high-level programming language. The fundamental point in learning programming is to develop the critical skills of formulating programmatic solutions for real problems and translating the solutions into programs using selection statements, loops, and methods.

Once you acquire the basic skills of writing programs using loops, methods, and arrays, you can start to learn object-oriented programming. You will learn to develop object-oriented software using class encapsulation and class inheritance.

Applying the concept of abstraction in the design and implementation of software projects is the key to developing software. The overriding objective of this book, therefore, is to teach students to use many levels of abstraction in solving problems and to see problems in small and in large. *The examples and exercises throughout the book foster the concept of developing reusable components and using them to create projects.*

Students with no programming experience should take a slow-paced approach in Part I of the book. I recommend that you complete all the exercises in Part I before moving to Chapter 6. Students new to object-oriented programming may need some time to become familiar with the concepts of objects and classes. Once the principles are mastered, programming in Java is easy and productive. Students who know object-oriented programming languages such as C++ and Smalltalk will find it easier to learn Java. In fact, Java is simpler than C++ and Smalltalk in many aspects.

Organization of the Book

This book is divided into four parts that, taken together, form a comprehensive introductory course on Java programming. Because knowledge is cumulative, the early chapters provide the conceptual basis for understanding Java and guide students through simple examples and exercises; subsequent chapters progressively present Java programming in detail, culminating with the development of comprehensive Java applications. The appendixes contain a mixed bag of topics, including an HTML tutorial.

Part I: Fundamentals of Programming

The first part of the book is a stepping stone that will prepare you to embark on the journey of learning Java. You will begin to know Java, and will learn how to write simple Java programs with primitive data types, control statements, methods, and arrays.

Chapter 1, "Introduction to Java," gives an overview of the major features of Java: object-oriented programming, platform-independence, Java bytecode, security, performance, multithreading, and networking. The chapter also shows how to create, compile, and run Java applications and applets. Simple examples of writing applications are provided, along with a brief anatomy of programming structures.

Chapter 2, "Primitive Data Types and Operations," introduces primitive data types, operators, and expressions. Important topics include identifiers, variables, constants, assignment statements, assignment expressions, primitive data types, operators, and shortcut operators. Java programming style and documentation are also addressed.

Chapter 3, "Control Statements," introduces decision and repetition statements. Java decision statements include various forms of `if` statements and the `switch` statement. Java repetition statements include the `while` loop, the `do-while` loop, and the `for` loop. The keywords `break` and `continue` are discussed.

Chapter 4, "Methods," introduces method creation, calling methods, passing parameters, returning values, method overloading, scope of local variables, and recursion. Applying the concept of abstraction is the key to developing software. The chapter also introduces the use of method abstraction in problem-solving. The `Math` class for performing basic math operations is introduced.

Chapter 5, "Arrays," explores an important structure: arrays for processing data in lists and tables. You will learn how to declare, initialize, and copy arrays. Examples of using two-dimensional arrays for matrix operations are provided. This chapter also introduces popular search and sorting methods.

Part II: Object-Oriented Programming

In the book's second part, object-oriented programming is introduced. Java is a class-centric, object-oriented programming language that uses abstraction, encapsulation, inheritance, and polymorphism to provide great flexibility, modularity, and reusability in developing software. You will learn programming with objects and classes, class inheritance, interfaces, polymorphism, and developing software using the object-oriented approach.

Chapter 6, "Objects and Classes," begins with objects and classes. The important topics include defining classes, creating objects, using constructors, passing objects to methods, instance and class variables, and instance and class methods, scope of variables in the context of a class, the keyword `this`, and using the UML graphical notations to describe classes. Several examples are provided to demonstrate the power of the object-oriented programming approach. Students will learn the benefits (abstraction, encapsulation, and modularity) of object-oriented programming from these examples.

Chapter 7, "Strings," introduces the classes `String`, `StringBuffer`, and `StringTokenizer` for storing and processing strings. There are more than fifteen hundred predefined Java classes grouped in several packages. Starting with this chapter, students will gradually learn how to use Java classes to develop their own programs. The classes on strings are fine examples to demonstrate the concept of objects and classes.

Chapter 8, "Class Inheritance and Interfaces," teaches how an existing class can be extended and modified as needed. Inheritance is an extremely powerful programming technique, further extending software reusability. Java programs are all built by extending predefined Java classes. The major topics include defining subclasses, using the keyword `super`, using the modifiers `protected`, `final`, and `abstract`, polymorphism and dynamic binding, and casting objects. This chapter introduces the `Object` class, which is the root of all Java classes. You will also learn how to use abstract classes and interfaces.

Chapter 9, "Object-Oriented Software Development," focuses on class design. You will learn how to analyze relationships among objects and to design classes with the relationships association, aggregation, composition, strong inheritance, and weak inheritance. This chapter gives the guidelines for class design with several examples. The wrapper classes for primitive data types are introduced to encapsulate primitive data type values as objects. Finally, two examples of designing generic classes for matrix operations and linked lists are introduced.

Part III: GUI Programming

The third part of the book introduces Java GUI programming. Major topics include event-driven programming, creating graphical user interfaces, and writing applets. You will learn the architecture of Java GUI programming API and use the user interface components to develop GUI applications and applets.

Chapter 10, "Getting Started with GUI Programming," introduces the concepts of Java GUI programming using Swing components. Topics include the Swing class hierarchy, frames, panels, and simple layout managers (FlowLayout, GridLayout, and BorderLayout). The chapter introduces drawing geometric figures in the graphics context. The concept and techniques for Java event-driven programming are presented.

Chapter 11, "Creating User Interfaces," introduces the user interface components: buttons, labels, text fields, text areas, combo boxes, lists, check boxes, radio buttons, menus, scrollbars, and scroll panes. Today's client/server and Web-based applications use a graphical user interface. Java has a rich set of classes to help you build GUIs.

Chapter 12, "Applets and Advanced GUI," takes an in-depth look at applets, discussing applet behavior and the relationship between applets and other Swing classes. Applets are a special kind of Java class that can be executed from the Web browser. Students will learn how to convert applications to applets, and vice versa, and how to run programs both as applications and as applets. The chapter also introduces two advanced layout mangers (CardLayout and GridBagLayout) and the use of no layout. Advanced examples of handling mouse and keyboard events are provided.

Part IV: Developing Comprehensive Projects

The book's final part is devoted to several advanced features of Java programming. You will learn how to use these features to develop comprehensive programs; for example, using exception handling to make your program robust, using multithreading to make your program more responsive and interactive, incorporating sound and images to make your program user-friendly, using input and output to manage and process a large quantity of data, creating client/server applications with Java networking support, and using the classes in the Java Collections Framework to build data structures in Java.

Chapter 13, "Exception Handling," teaches students how to define exceptions, throw exceptions, and handle exceptions so that their programs can either continue to run or terminate gracefully in the event of runtime errors. The chapter discusses predefined exception classes, and gives examples of creating user-defined exception classes.

Chapter 14, "Internationalization," introduces the development of Java programs for international audiences. You will learn how to format dates, numbers, currencies, and percentages for different regions, countries, and languages. You will also learn how to use resource bundles to define which images and strings are used by a component depending on the user's locale and preferences.

Chapter 15, "Multithreading," introduces threads, which enable the running of multiple tasks simultaneously in one program. Students will learn how to use the `Thread` class and the `Runnable` interface to launch separate threads. The chapter also discusses thread states, thread priority, thread groups, and the synchronization of conflicting threads.

Chapter 16, "Multimedia," teaches how to incorporate sound and images to bring live animation to Java applets and applications. Various techniques for smoothing animation are introduced.

Chapter 17, "Input and Output," introduces input and output streams. Students will learn the class structures of I/O streams, byte and character streams, file I/O streams, data I/O streams, print streams, object streams, random file access, delimited I/O, and interactive I/O.

Chapter 18, "Networking," introduces network programming. Students will learn the concept of network communication, stream sockets, client/server programming, and reading data files from the Web server.

Chapter 19, "Java Data Structures," introduces the Java Collections Framework. Students will learn to use classes and interfaces such as `Collection`, `Set`, `HashSet`, `TreeSet`, `Iterator`, `List`, `ArrayList`, `LinkedList`, `Vector`, `Stack`, `Map`, `HashMap`, `TreeMap`, `Collections`, and `Arrays` to build projects.

Appendixes

This part of the book covers a mixed bag of topics. Appendix A lists Java keywords. Appendix B gives tables of ASCII characters and their associated codes in decimal and in hex. Appendix C shows the operator precedence. Appendix D summarizes Java modifiers and their usage. Appendix E introduces number systems and conversions among binary, decimal, and hex numbers. Bitwise operations are also introduced in this appendix. Appendix F introduces HTML basics. Appendix G lists UML Graphical Notations for describing classes and their relationships. Appendix H introduces package-naming conventions, creating packages, and using packages. Appendix I discusses special floating-point values. Finally, Appendix J provides a glossary of key terms used in the text.

Chapter Dependency Chart

The book provides flexible ordering of chapters. You may cover Chapter 6, "Objects and Classes," after Chapter 4, "Methods." You may cover Chapter 17, "Input and Output," after exception handling is introduced in Chapter 13. Chapter 19, "Java Data Structures," can be covered after Chapter 9, "Object-Oriented Software Development."

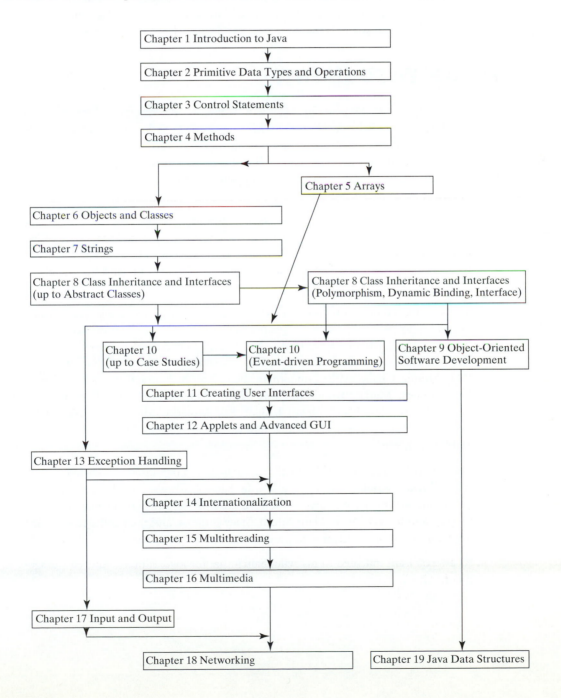

ABOUT THE AUTHOR

Y. Daniel Liang is the author and editor of the Prentice Hall Liang Java Series. His innovative Java texts have been adopted by many universities throughout the world.

Dr. Liang is currently a Yamacraw professor of software engineering in the School of Computing at Armstrong Atlantic State University, Savannah, Georgia. He can be reached at liang@armstrong.edu.

ACKNOWLEDGMENTS

I would like to thank Ray Greenlaw and Armstrong Atlantic State University for enabling me to teach what I write and for supporting me in writing what I teach. Teaching is the source of inspiration for continuing to revise the book. I am grateful to the students and instructors who offered comments, suggestions, bug reports, and praise. Their enthusiastic support contributed to the success of my books.

This book was greatly improved thanks to outstanding reviews by Yang Ang of the University of Wollongong (Australia), James Chegwidden of Tarrant County College (Texas), Harold Grossman of Clemson University, Ron Hofman of Red River College (Canada), Nana Kofi of Langara College (Canada), Gavin Osborne of the University of Saskatchewan, and Kent Vidrine of George Washington University.

This edition has benefited from the previous editions of all my Java books. I would like to acknowledge the following people who contributed to the previous editions: Bill Morrison, Hao Wu, Greg Geller, Ben Page, Michael Willig, Russell Minnich, Balaram Nair, Ben Stonebraker, C-Y Tang, Bertrand I-P Lin, Maw-Shang Chang, Ruay-Shiung Chang, Mike Sunderman, Fen English, James Silver, Mark Temte, Bob Sanders, Marta Partington, Tom Cirtin, Songlin Qiu, Tim Tate, Carolyn Linn, Alfonso Hermida, Nathan Clement, Eric Miller, Chris Barrick, John Etchison, Louisa Klucznik, Angela Denny, Randy Haubner, Robin Drake, Betsy Brown, and Susan Kindel.

For this edition, I would like to thank Alan Apt, Toni Holm, Patrick Lindner, Irwin Zucker, Xiaohong Zhu, Jake Warde, Sarah Burrows, Pamela Shaffer, Barrie Reinhold, and their colleagues at Prentice Hall for organizing and managing this project, and Robert Milch, Dana Smith, Stacy Proteau, and their colleagues at Pine Tree Composition for helping to produce the book.

As always, I am indebted to my wife, Samantha, for love, support, and encouragement.

Companion Website for the Book

The Companion Website for the book can be accessed at

www.prenhall.com/liang/intro4e.html

or

www.cs.armstrong.edu/liang/intro4e .html.

The Web site contains the following resources:

- Interactive Self-Test for every chapter
- Installing JDK from the book CD-ROM
- Java Programming Style and Documentation Guidelines
- Computer Basics (introducing CPU, cache, memory, hard disk, floppy disk, CD-R/W, programming languages, and operating systems)
- Java Supplements (HTML Converter and Java Plug-In, and Java Coding Guidelines)
- Microsoft PowerPoint slides for lectures
- Errata
- FAQs

Student CD-ROM

The student CD-ROM comes with the book. The contents of the CD-ROM are listed below:

- Java 2 Standard Development Kit 1.4.1_02 for Windows
- TextPad 4.5.0 Editor
- Answers to review questions
- Solutions to even-numbered programming exercises
- Source code for the examples in the book
- WinZip 8.1 Shareware Evaluation Version

CONTENTS AT A GLANCE

TABLE OF CONTENTS

FUNDAMENTALS OF PROGRAMMING

By now you have heard a lot about Java and are anxious to start writing Java programs. The first part of the book is a stepping stone that will prepare you to embark on the journey of learning Java. You will begin to know Java and will develop fundamental programming skills. Specifically, you will learn how to write simple Java programs with primitive data types, control statements, methods, and arrays.

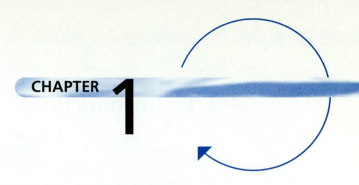

CHAPTER 1

INTRODUCTION TO JAVA

Objectives

- To learn about Java and its history.
- To understand the relationship between Java and the World Wide Web.
- To create, compile, and run Java programs.
- To understand the Java runtime environment.
- To write a simple Java application.
- To display output on the console and on the dialog box.

1.1   Introduction

By now you have heard quite a lot about the exciting Java programming language. It must seem as if Java is everywhere! Your local bookstores are filled with Java books. There are articles about Java in every major newspaper and magazine. It is impossible to read a computer magazine without coming across the magical word *Java*. You must be wondering why Java is so hot. The answer is that it enables users to deploy applications on the Internet for servers, desktop computers, and small hand-held devices. In fact, this is its main distinguishing characteristic. The future of computing will be profoundly influenced by the Internet, and Java promises to remain a big part of that future. Java is *the* Internet programming language.

You are about to begin an exciting journey, learning a powerful programming language. Java is cross-platform, object-oriented, network-based, and multimedia-ready. After its inception in May 1995, Java quickly became an attractive language for developing Internet applications. This chapter introduces Java and its programming features, followed by a simple example of Java applications.

NOTE

The book assumes that you are computer-literate. If you are not familiar with such terms as CPU, memory, hard disk, operating systems, and programming language, please see "Computer Basics" on the companion Web site.

1.2   The History of Java

Java was developed by a team led by James Gosling at Sun Microsystems, a company best known for its Sun workstations. Originally called *Oak*, it was designed in 1991 for use in embedded consumer electronic applications. In 1995, renamed *Java*, it was redesigned for developing Internet applications. Java programs can be embedded in HTML pages and downloaded by Web browsers to bring live animation and interaction to Web clients.

The power of Java is not limited to Web applications, for it is a general-purpose programming language. It has full programming features and can be used to develop standalone applications. Java is inherently object-oriented. Although many object-oriented languages began strictly as procedural languages, Java was designed from the start to be object-oriented. Object-oriented programming (OOP) is a popular programming approach that is replacing traditional procedural programming techniques.

NOTE

One of the central issues in software development is how to reuse code. Object-oriented programming provides great flexibility, modularity, clarity, and reusability through encapsulation, inheritance, and polymorphism—all of which you will learn about in this book.

1.3   Characteristics of Java

Java has become enormously popular. Java's rapid rise and wide acceptance can be traced to its design and programming features, particularly its promise that you can write a program once and run it anywhere. As stated in the Java-language white paper by Sun, Java is *simple, object-oriented, distributed, interpreted, robust, secure, architecture-neutral, portable, high-performance, multithreaded,* and *dynamic.* Let's analyze these often-used buzzwords.

1.3.1   Java Is Simple

No language is simple, but Java is a bit easier than the popular object-oriented programming language C++, which was the dominant software-development language before Java. Java is partially modeled on C++, but greatly simplified and improved. For instance, pointers and multiple inheritance often make programming complicated. Java replaces the multiple inheritance in C++ with a simple language construct called an *interface*, and eliminates pointers.

Java uses automatic memory allocation and garbage collection, whereas C++ requires the programmer to allocate memory and collect garbage. Also, the number of language constructs is small for such a powerful language. The clean syntax makes Java programs easy to write and read. Some people refer to Java as "C++--" because it is like C++ but with more functionality and fewer negative aspects.

1.3.2   Java Is Object-Oriented

Computer programs are instructions to computers. You tell a computer what to do through a program. Without programs, a computer is an empty machine. Computers do not understand human languages, so you need to use computer languages to communicate with them. There are more than one hundred programming languages. The most popular language of them are:

COBOL (COmmon Business Oriented Language)
FORTRAN (FORmula TRANslation)
BASIC (Beginner All-purpose Symbolic Instructional Code)
Pascal (Named for Blaise Pascal)
Ada (Named for Ada Lovelace)
C (So named because its developer designed B first)
Visual Basic (Basic-like visual language developed by Microsoft)
Delphi (Pascal-like visual language developed by Borland)
C++ (an object-oriented language, based on C)

Each of these languages was designed with a specific purpose. COBOL was designed for business applications and now is used primarily for business data processing. FORTRAN was designed for mathematical computations. BASIC, as its name suggests, was designed to be learned and used easily. Pascal was designed to be a simple structural programming language. Ada was developed at the direction of the Department of Defense, and is mainly used in defense projects. C is popular for system software projects, such as writing compilers and operating systems. Visual Basic and Delphi are for rapid application development. C++ is the C language with object-oriented features.

All of these languages except C++ are *procedural programming languages.* Software systems developed using procedural programming languages are based on the paradigm of procedures. Object-oriented programming models the real world in terms of objects. Everything in the world can be modeled as an object. A circle is an object, a person is an object, and a window's icon is an object. Even a mortgage can be perceived as an object. A Java program is object-oriented because programming in Java is centered on creating objects, manipulating objects, and making objects work together.

Part I, "Fundamentals of Programming," introduces primitive data types and operations, control statements, methods, and arrays. These are the fundamentals for all programming languages. You will learn object-oriented programming in Part II, "Object-Oriented Programming." Object-oriented programming provides great flexibility, modularity, and reusability. For years, object-oriented technology was perceived as elitist, requiring a substantial investment in training and infrastructure. Java has helped object-oriented technology enter the mainstream of computing. Its simple, clean syntax makes programs easy to write and read. Java programs are quite *expressive* in terms of designing and developing applications.

1.3.3   Java Is Distributed

Distributed computing involves several computers working together on a network. Java is designed to make distributed computing easy. Since networking capability is inherently integrated into Java, writing network programs is like sending and receiving data to and from a file. As an example, Figure 1.1 shows three programs running on three different systems; the three programs communicate with one other to perform a joint task.

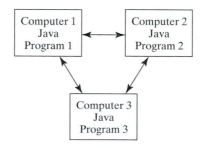

Figure 1.1   *Java programs can run on different systems that work together.*

1.3.4   Java Is Interpreted

You need an interpreter to run Java programs. The programs are compiled into the Java Virtual Machine code called *bytecode*. The bytecode is machine-independent and can run on any machine that has a Java interpreter, as shown in Figure 1.2.

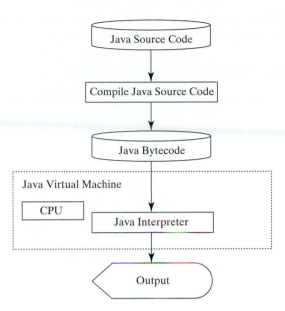

Figure 1.2   *The Java interpreter executes Java bytecode.*

Usually, a compiler, such as a C++ compiler, translates a program in a high-level language to machine code. The code can only run on the native machine. If you run the program on other machines, it has to be recompiled on the native machine. For instance, if you compile a C++ program in Windows, the executable code generated by the compiler can only run on the Windows platform. With Java, you compile the source code once, and the bytecode generated by a Java compiler can run on any platform with a Java interpreter. The Java interpreter translates the bytecode into the machine language of the target machine.

1.3.5   Java Is Robust

Robust means *reliable*. No programming language can ensure complete reliability. Java puts a lot of emphasis on early checking for possible errors, because Java compilers can detect many problems that would first show up at execution time in other languages. Java has eliminated certain types of error-prone programming constructs found in other languages. It does not support pointers, for example, thereby eliminating the possibility of overwriting memory and corrupting data.

Java has a runtime exception-handling feature to provide programming support for robustness. Java forces the programmer to write the code to deal with exceptions. Java can catch and respond to an exceptional situation so that the program can continue its normal execution and terminate gracefully when a runtime error occurs.

1.3.6   Java Is Secure

As an Internet programming language, Java is used in a networked and distributed environment. If you download a Java applet (a special kind of program) and run it on your computer, it will not damage your system because Java implements several security mechanisms to protect your system against harm caused by stray programs. The security is based on the premise that *nothing should be trusted*.

1.3.7   Java Is Architecture-Neutral

Java is interpreted. This feature enables Java to be *architecture-neutral*, or to use an alternative term, platform-independent. With a Java Virtual Machine (JVM), you can write one program that will run on any platform, as shown in Figure 1.3.

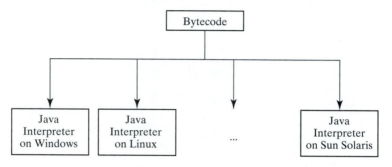

Figure 1.3   *Java bytecode can be executed on any platform that has a JVM.*

Java's initial success stemmed from its Web programming capability. You can run Java applets from a Web browser, but Java is for more than just writing Web applets. You can also run standalone Java applications directly from operating systems, using a Java interpreter. Today, software vendors usually develop multiple versions of the same product to run on different platforms (Windows, OS/2, Macintosh, and various UNIX, IBM AS/400, and IBM mainframes). Using Java, developers need to write only one version that can run on every platform.

1.3.8   Java Is Portable

Java is architectural neutral. This feature enables Java programs to be portable because they can be run on any platform without being recompiled. Moreover, there are no platform-specific features in the Java language. In some languages, such as Ada, the largest integer varies on different platforms. But in Java, the range of the integer is the same on every platform, as is the behavior of arithmetic. The fixed range of the numbers makes the program portable.

The Java environment is portable to new hardware and operating systems. In fact, the Java compiler itself is written in Java.

1.3.9   Java's Performance

Java's performance is sometimes criticized. The execution of the bytecode is never as fast as it would be with a compiled language, such as C++. Because Java is interpreted, the bytecode is not directly executed by the system, but is run through the interpreter. However, its speed is more than adequate for most interactive applications, where the CPU is often idle, waiting for input or for data from other sources.

CPU speed has increased dramatically in the past few years, and this trend will continue. There are many ways to improve performance. Users of the earlier Sun Java Virtual Machine have certainly noticed that Java is slow. However, the new JVM is significantly faster. The new JVM uses the technology known as *just-in-time compilation*, as shown in Figure 1.4. It compiles bytecode into native machine code, stores the native code, and reinvokes the native code when its bytecode is executed. Sun recently developed the Java HotSpot Performance Engine, which includes a compiler for optimizing the frequently used code. The HotSpot Performance Engine can be plugged into a JVM to dramatically boost its performance.

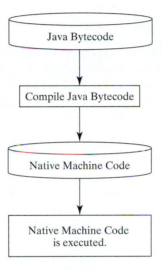

Figure 1.4 *The just-in-time compiler compiles bytecode to the native machine code.*

1.3.10 Java Is Multithreaded

Multithreading is a program's capability to perform several tasks simultaneously. For example, downloading a video file while playing the video would be considered multithreading. Multithread programming is smoothly integrated in Java, whereas in other languages you have to call procedures specific to the operating system to enable multithreading.

Multithreading is particularly useful in graphical user interface (GUI) and network programming. In GUI programming, there are many things going on at the same time. A user can listen to an audio recording while surfing a Web page. In network programming, a server can serve multiple clients at the same time. Multithreading is a necessity in multimedia and network programming.

1.3.11 Java Is Dynamic

Java was designed to adapt to an evolving environment. New code can be loaded on the fly without recompilation. There is no need for developers to create, and for users to install, major new software versions. New features can be incorporated transparently as needed.

1.4   World Wide Web, Java, and Beyond

The World Wide Web is an electronic information repository that can be accessed on the Internet from anywhere in the world. You can use the Web to book a hotel room, buy an airline ticket, register for a college course, download the *New York Times*, chat with friends, or listen to live radio. There are countless activities you can do on the Internet. Many people spend a good part of their computer time surfing the Web for fun and profit.

The Internet is the infrastructure of the Web. The Internet has been around for more than thirty years, but has only recently become popular. The colorful World Wide Web and sophisticated Web browsers are the major reason for its popularity.

The primary authoring language for the Web is the Hypertext Markup Language (HTML). HTML is a markup language: a simple language for laying out documents, linking documents on the Internet, and bringing images, sound, and video alive on the Web. However, it cannot interact with the user except through simple forms. Web pages in HTML are essentially static and flat.

Java was attractive initially because Java programs can be run from a Web browser. Java programs that run from a Web browser are called *applets*. Applets use a modern graphical user interface with buttons, text fields, text areas, radio buttons, and so on, to interact with users on the Web and process users' requests. Applets make the Web responsive, interactive, and fun to use. Figure 1.5 shows an applet running from a Web browser. To run applets from a Web browser, you need to use Netscape 6 or Internet Explorer 6.

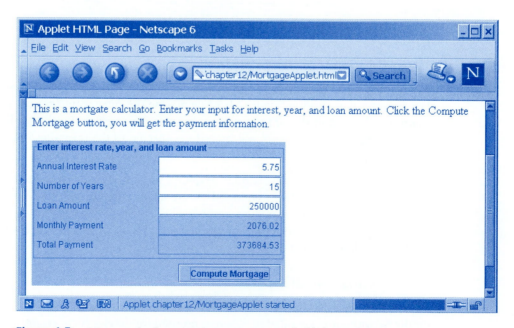

Figure 1.5   *A Java applet for computing mortgages is embedded in an HTML page. The user can use the applet to compute the mortgage payment.*

■ TIP

For a demonstration of Java applets, visit `java.sun.com/applets/`. This site provides a rich Java resource as well as links to other cool applet demo sites. `java.sun.com/` is the official Sun Java Web site.

Java can also be used to develop applications on the server side. These applications are called *Java servlets* or *Java ServerPages*, which can be run from a Web server to generate dynamic Web pages. The Self-Test Website for this book, as shown in Figure 1.6, was developed using Java servlets. The Web pages for the questions and answers are dynamically generated by the servlets.

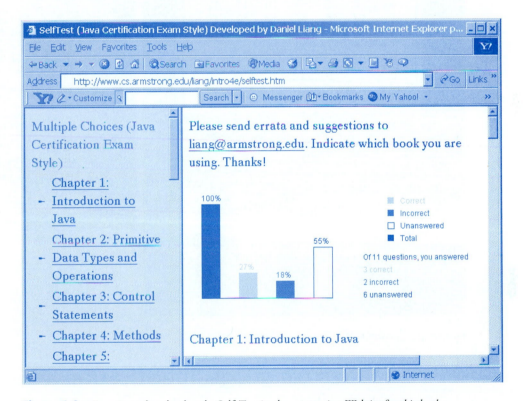

Figure 1.6   *Java is used to develop the Self-Test in the companion Website for this book.*

Java is a versatile programming language. You can use it to develop applications on your desktop and on the server. You can also use it to develop applications for small hand-held devices such as Palm and cell phones. Figure 1.7 shows a Java program that displays the calendar on a Palm and on a cell phone.

Figure 1.7 *Java is used to develop applications for hand-held and wireless devices.*

1.5   The Java Language Specification

Computer languages have strict rules of usage. If you do not follow the rules when writing a program, the computer will be unable to understand it. Sun Microsystems, the originator of Java, intends to retain control of this important new computer language—and for a very good reason: to prevent it from losing its unified standards. The complete reference of Java standards can be found in *Java Language Specification,* second edition, by James Gosling, Bill Joy, and Guy Steele (Addison-Wesley, 2000).

The Java language specification is a technical definition of the language that includes syntax, constructs, and the *application program interface* (API), which contains predefined classes. The Java language syntax and constructs are stable, but the API is still expanding. At the Sun Java Web site (java.sun.com/), you can view the language specification and the latest version and updates to the Java API.

Sun releases each version of Java with a Java Development Toolkit (JDK). This is a primitive command-line tool set that includes software libraries, a compiler for compiling Java source code, an interpreter for running Java bytecode, and an applet viewer for testing Java applets, as well as other useful utilities.

> **NOTE**
> Sun announced the Java 2 name in December 1998, just as it released JDK 1.2. Java 2 is the overarching brand that applies to the latest Java technology. JDK 1.2 was the first version of the Java Development Toolkit that supported the Java 2 technology. The official name for JDK 1.2 is Java 2 SDK v 1.2. SDK stands for Software Development Toolkit. Since most Java programmers are familiar with the name JDK, this book uses the names Java SDK and JDK interchangeably. There are not many differences among JDK 1.2, 1.3, and 1.4. The latest version is JDK 1.4. As far as this book is concerned, you can use either JDK 1.3 or 1.4.

> **NOTE**
> Java is a full-fledged and powerful language that can be used in many ways. There are three editions of Java: *Java Standard Edition (J2SE)*, *Java Enterprise Edition (J2EE)*, and *Java Micro Edition (J2ME)*. J2SE can be used to develop client-side standalone applications or applets. J2EE can be used to develop server-side applications, such as Java servlets and Java ServerPages. J2ME can be used to develop applications for mobile devices, such as cell phones. This book uses J2SE to introduce Java programming.

1.6   Java Development Tools

JDK consists of a set of separate programs for developing and testing Java programs, each of which is invoked from a command line. Besides JDK, there are more than a dozen Java development packages on the market today. The major development tools are:

JBuilder by Borland (`www.borland.com/`)

Visual Café by WebGain (`www.webgain.com/`)

Sun ONE Studio by Sun (`www.sun.com/`)

Visual Age for Java by IBM (`www.ibm.com/`)

These tools provide an *integrated development environment* (IDE) for rapidly developing Java programs. Editing, compiling, building, debugging, and online help are integrated in one graphical user interface. Just enter source code in one window or open an existing file in a window, then click a button, menu item, or function key to compile the source code.

The use of development tools makes it easy and productive to develop Java programs. However, you have to devote considerable time to learn how to use a development tool. The advantage of learning Java with JDK command-line tools is that you can completely concentrate on the Java language, and not be intimidated by the sophisticated tools.

1.7   A Simple Java Program

A Java program can be written in many ways. This book introduces Java applications and applets. *Applications* are standalone programs. This includes any program written with a high-level language. Applications can be executed from any computer with a Java interpreter. *Applets* are special kinds of Java programs that can run directly from a Java-compatible Web browser. Applets are suitable for deploying Web projects. Applets will be introduced in Chapter 12, "Applets and Advanced GUI."

Let us begin with a simple Java application to demonstrate how to write a Java application.

Example 1.1 A Simple Application

Problem

Write a program that displays the message "Welcome to Java!" on the console.

Solution

The following code gives the solution to the problem.

```
// Welcome.java: This application program prints Welcome to Java!
public class Welcome {
  public static void main(String[] args) {
    System.out.println("Welcome to Java!");
  }
}
```

Comments → (points to comment line)
Class heading → (points to public class line), *Class name* (points to Welcome)
Main method signature → (points to main method), *String* (points to "Welcome to Java!")

Review

Every Java program must have at least one class. Each class begins with a class declaration that defines data and methods for the class. In this example, the class name is Welcome.

The class contains a method named main. The main method in this program contains the println statement. The main method is invoked by the interpreter.

In this program, println("Welcome to Java!") is actually the statement that prints the message. So why use the other statements in the program? Because Java, like any other programming language, has its own syntax, and you need to write code that obeys the syntax rules. The Java compiler will report syntax errors if your program violates the syntax rules.

NOTE

You are probably wondering about such points as why the main method is declared this way and why System.out.println(. . .) is used to display a message to the console. Your questions cannot be fully answered yet. For the time being, you will just have to accept that this is how things are done. You will find the answers in the coming chapters.

1.8   Creating, Compiling, and Executing a Java Program

You have to create your program and compile it before it can be executed. This process is iterative, as shown in Figure 1.8. If your program has compilation errors, you have to fix them by modifying the program, then recompile it. If your program has runtime errors or does not produce the correct result, you have to modify the program, recompile it, and execute it again.

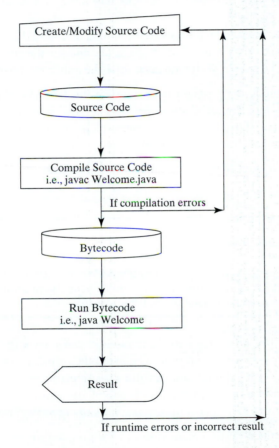

Figure 1.8   *The Java programming-development process consists of creating/modifying source code, compiling, and executing programs.*

You can use any text editor to create and edit a Java source code file. Figure 1.9 shows how to use the NotePad to create and edit the source code file. For information on using TextPad, JBuilder, and Sun ONE Studio, please see www.cs.arm-strong.edu/liang/intro4e/JavaIDE.html.

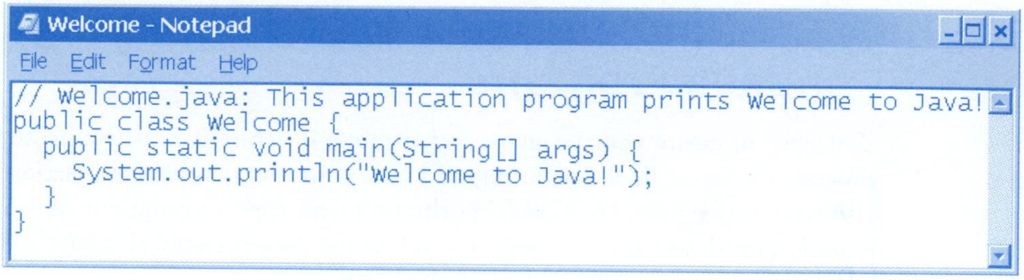

```
// Welcome.java: This application program prints Welcome to Java!
public class Welcome {
  public static void main(String[] args) {
    System.out.println("Welcome to Java!");
  }
}
```

Figure 1.9 *You can create the Java source file using Windows NotePad.*

This file must end with the extension .java and should have the exact same name as the public class name. For example, the file for the source code in Example 1.1 should be named **Welcome.java**, since the public class name is Welcome.

To compile the program is to translate the Java source code into Java bytecode using a software called the *compiler*. The Java compiler is a bundled in JDK 1.4. To install JDK 1.4 on your system, please refer to the companion Web site at www.prenhall.com/liang/intro4e.html.

The following command compiles **Welcome.java:**

```
javac Welcome.java
```

> **NOTE**
>
> Java source programs are case-sensitive. It would be wrong, for example, to re-place main in the program with Main. Program filenames are case-sensitive on UNIX and generally not case-sensitive on PCs, but JDK treats filenames as case-sensitive on any platform. If you try to compile the program using javac welcome.java, you will get a file-not-found error.

If there are no syntax errors, the *compiler* generates a file named **Welcome.class**. This file is called the *bytecode*. The bytecode is similar to machine instructions, but is architecture-neutral and can run on any platform that has the Java interpreter and runtime environment. This is one of Java's primary advantages: *Java bytecode can run on a variety of hardware platforms and operating systems.*

To execute a Java program is to run the program's bytecode. You can execute the bytecode on any platform with a Java interpreter.

The following command runs the bytecode:

```
java Welcome
```

Figure 1.10 shows the **javac** command for compiling **Welcome.java**. The compiler generated the **Welcome.class** file. This file is executed using the **java** command.

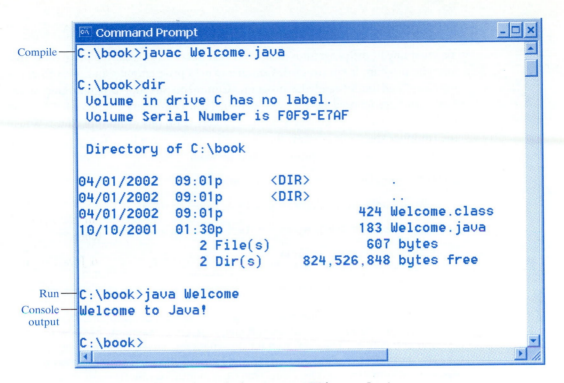

Compile — `C:\book>javac Welcome.java`

```
C:\book>dir
 Volume in drive C has no label.
 Volume Serial Number is F0F9-E7AF

 Directory of C:\book

04/01/2002  09:01p     <DIR>          .
04/01/2002  09:01p     <DIR>          ..
04/01/2002  09:01p              424 Welcome.class
10/10/2001  01:30p              183 Welcome.java
               2 File(s)            607 bytes
               2 Dir(s)     824,526,848 bytes free
```

Run — `C:\book>java Welcome`
Console output — `Welcome to Java!`

`C:\book>`

Figure 1.10   *The output of Example 1.1 displays a message: Welcome to Java!*

> **NOTE**
> Do not use the extension .class in the command line when executing the program. The Java interpreter assumes that the first argument in the command is the filename and then fetches filename.class to execute. It would fetch filename.class.class if you used Java filename.class in the command line.

1.9   Anatomy of the Application Program

The application program in Example 1.1 has the following components:

Comments
Reserved words
Modifiers
Statements
Blocks
Classes
Methods
The main method

To build a program, you need to understand these basic elements. They are explained in the sections that follow.

1.9.1   Comments

The first line in the program is a *comment* that documents what the program is and how the program is constructed. Comments help programmers and users to communicate and understand the program. Comments are not programming statements and are ignored by the compiler. In Java, comments are preceded by two slashes (//) on a line or enclosed between /* and */ on one or multiple lines. When the compiler sees //, it ignores all text after // on the same line. When it sees /*, it scans for the next */ and ignores any text between /* and */.

Here are examples of the two types of comments:

```
// This application program prints Welcome to Java!

/* This application program prints Welcome to Java! */

/* This application program
   prints Welcome to Java! */
```

■■ **NOTE**

In addition to the two comment styles, // and /*, Java supports comments of a special type, referred to as *javadoc comments*. javadoc comments begin with /** and end with */. They are used for documenting classes, data, and methods. They can be extracted into an HTML file using JDK's javadoc command. For more information, visit java.sun.com/j2se/javadoc/index.html.

1.9.2   Reserved Words

Reserved words, or *keywords,* are words that have a specific meaning to the compiler and cannot be used for other purposes in the program. For example, when the compiler sees the word class, it understands that the word after class is the name for the class. Other reserved words in Example 1.1 are public, static, and void. Their use will be introduced later in the book.

■■ **TIP**

Because Java is case-sensitive, public is a reserved word, but Public is not. Nonetheless, for clarity and readability, it would be best to avoid using reserved words in other forms. (See Appendix A, "Java Keywords.")

1.9.3   Modifiers

Java uses certain reserved words called *modifiers* that specify the properties of the data, methods, and classes and how they can be used. Examples of modifiers are public and static. Other modifiers are private, final, abstract, and protected. A public datum, method, or class can be accessed by other classes. A private datum or method cannot be accessed by other classes. Modifiers are discussed in Chapter 6, "Objects and Classes."

1.9.4   Statements

A *statement* represents an action or a sequence of actions. The statement `println("Welcome to Java!")` in the program in Example 1.1 is to display the greeting "Welcome to Java!" Every statement in Java ends with a semicolon (;).

1.9.5   Blocks

The braces in the program form the *block* that groups the components of the program. In Java, each block begins with an open brace ({) and ends with a closing brace (}). Every class has a *class block* that groups the data and methods of the class. Every method has a *method block* that groups the statements in the method. Blocks can be *nested*, meaning that one block can be placed within another, as shown in the following code.

```
public class Test {
   public static void main(String[] args) {
      System.out.println("Welcome to Java!");
   }
}
```

Class block

Method block

1.9.6   Classes

The *class* is the essential Java construct. To program in Java, you must understand classes and be able to write and use them. The mystery of classes will be unveiled throughout the book. For now, though, it is enough to know that a program is defined by using one or more classes. Every Java program has at least one class, and programs are contained inside a class definition enclosed in blocks. The class can contain data declarations and method declarations.

1.9.7   Methods

What is `System.out.println`? `System.out` is known as the *standard output object*. `println` is a method in the object, which consists of a collection of statements that performs a sequence of operations to display a message to the standard output device. If you run the program from the command window, the output from the `System.out.println` is displayed in the command window. The method can be used even without fully understanding the details of how it works. It is used by invoking a statement with a string argument. The string argument is enclosed in parentheses. In this case, the argument is `"Welcome to Java!"` You can call the same `println` method with a different argument to print a different message.

1.9.8   The *main* Method

You can create your own method. Every Java application must have a user-declared `main` method that defines where the program begins. The `main` method provides the control of program flow. The Java interpreter executes the application by invoking the `main` method.

The main method looks like this:

```
public static void main(String[] args) {
  // Statements;
}
```

1.10   Displaying Text in a Message Dialog Box

Example 1.1 displays the text in the command window, as shown in Figure 1.10. You can rewrite the program to display the text in a message dialog box. To do so, you need to use the showMessageDialog method in the JOptionPane class. JOptionPane is one of the many predefined classes in the Java system that can be reused rather than "reinventing the wheel." You can use the showMessageDialog box to display any text in a message dialog box (or simply dialog).

Example 1.2 Using Message Dialog Boxes

Problem

Write a program that displays text in a message dialog box.

Solution

The following code gives the solution to the problem. Figure 1.11 shows the text "Welcome to Java" displayed in a message dialog box.

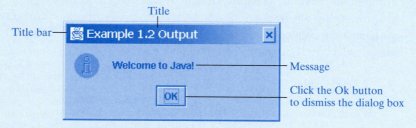

Figure 1.11   *The string Welcome to Java! is displayed in a message dialog box.*

```
1    /* WelcomeInMessageDialogBox.java:
2       This application program displays Welcome to Java!
3       in a message dialog box. */
4    import javax.swing.JOptionPane;
5
6    public class WelcomeInMessageDialogBox {
7      public static void main(String[] args) {
8        // Display Welcome to Java! in a message dialog box
9        JOptionPane.showMessageDialog(null, "Welcome to Java!",
10         "Example 1.2 Output", JOptionPane.INFORMATION_MESSAGE);
11
12       // Exit the program
13       System.exit(0);
14     }
15   }
```

Review

The line numbers are not part of the program, but are displayed for reference purposes.

This program uses two Java classes: JOptionPane (Line 9) and System (Line 13). Java's predefined classes are grouped into packages. JOptionPane is in the javax.swing package, and System is in the java.lang package. JOptionPane is imported to the program using the import statement in Line 4 so that the compiler can locate the class. The System class is not imported because it is in the java.lang package. All the classes in the java.lang package are implicitly imported in every Java program.

The showMessageDialog method is known as a *static* method. Such a method should be invoked by using the class name followed by a dot operator (.) and the method name with arguments. Static methods will be introduced in Chapter 4, "Methods." The showMessageDialog method can be invoked with four arguments, as in Lines 9-10.

```
JOptionPane.showMessageDialog(null, "Welcome to Java!",
    "Example 1.2", JOptionPane.INFORMATION_MESSAGE));
```

The first argument can always be null. null is a Java keyword that will be fully introduced in Part II, "Object-Oriented Programming." The second argument can be a string for text to be displayed. The third argument is the title of the message box. The fourth argument can be JOptionPane.INFORMATION_MESSAGE, which causes the icon (🛈) to be displayed in the message box.

NOTE

There are several ways to use the showMessageDialog method. For the time being, all you need to know is how to invoke the showMessageDialog method to display text, using a statement like this one:

```
JOptionPane.showMessageDialog(null, x,
    y, JOptionPane.INFORMATION_MESSAGE));
```

where x is a string for the text to be displayed, and y is a string for the title of the message dialog box.

The exit method in the System class is invoked as follows in Line 13.

```
System.exit(0);
```

Like the showMessageDialog method, exit is also a static method. Invoking this method terminates the program. The argument 0 indicates that the program is terminated normally. In the preceding example, you did not use the exit method, and the program terminates at the end of the main method. Why do you have to use the exit method in this program? The next note explains the reason.

continues

Example 1.2 continued

> **NOTE**
>
> When your program starts, a thread is spawned to run the program. When the `showMessageDialog` is invoked, a separate thread is spawned to run this method. The thread is not terminated even after you close the dialog box. To terminate the thread, you have to invoke the `exit` method. Threads will be introduced in Chapter 15, "Multithreading." If you run the program without invoking the `exit` method in Line 13, the thread is not terminated. You have to press CTRL+C in the command window to stop the thread.

Chapter Summary

In this chapter, you learned about Java and the relationship between Java and the World Wide Web. Java is an Internet programming language, and since its inception in 1995, it has quickly become a premier language for building software.

Java is platform-independent, meaning that you can write a program once and run it anywhere. Java is a simple, object-oriented programming language with built-in graphics programming, input and output, exception handling, networking, and multithreading support.

Java source files end with the .java extension. Every class is compiled into a separate file called a bytecode that has the same name as the class and ends with the .class extension.

Every Java program is a set of class definitions. The keyword `class` introduces a class definition. The contents of the class are included in a block. A block begins with an opening brace ({) and ends with a closing brace (}). Methods are contained in a class. A Java application must have a `main` method. The `main` method is the entry point where the application program starts when it is executed.

You learned how to create, compile, and run Java programs.

Review Questions

1.1 Briefly summarize the history of Java.

1.2 Java is object-oriented. What are the advantages of object-oriented programming?

1.3 Can Java run on any machine? What is needed to run Java on a computer?

1.4 What are the input and output of a Java compiler?

1.5 List some Java development tools. Are tools like Sun ONE Studio and JBuilder different languages from Java, or are they dialects or extensions of Java?

1.6 What is the relationship between Java and HTML?

1.7 Explain the Java keywords. List some Java keywords you learned in this chapter.

1.8 Is Java case-sensitive? What is the case for Java keywords?

1.9 What is the Java source filename extension, and what is the Java bytecode filename extension?

1.10 What is a comment? What is the syntax for a comment in Java? Is the comment ignored by the compiler?

1.11 What is the statement to display a string on the console? What is the statement to display the message "Hello world" in a message dialog box?

1.12 Identify and fix the errors in the following code:

```
public class Welcome {
  public void Main(String[] args) {
    System.out.println('Welcome to Java!);
  }
)
```

Programming Exercises

1.1 Create a source file containing a Java program. Perform the following steps to compile the program and run it (see Section 1.8, "Creating, Compiling, and Executing a Java Program")

1. Create a file named **Welcome.java** for Example 1.1. You can use any editor that will save your file in text format.

2. Compile the source file.

3. Run the bytecode.

4. Replace "Welcome to Java" with "My first program" in the program; save, compile, and run the program. You will see the message "My first program" displayed.

5. Replace main with Main, and recompile the source code. The compiler returns an error message because the Java program is case-sensitive.

6. Change it back, and compile the program again.

7. Instead of the command javac Welcome.java, use javac welcome.java. What happens?

8. Instead of the command java Welcome, use java Welcome.class. What happens? (The interpreter searches for Welcome.class.class.)

PRIMITIVE DATA TYPES AND OPERATIONS

Objectives

- To write Java programs to perform simple calculations.

- To understand identifiers, variables, and constants.

- To use assignment statements and assignment expressions.

- To know Java primitive data types: `byte`, `short`, `int`, `long`, `float`, `double`, `char`, and `boolean`.

- To use Java operators and write Java expressions.

- To know the rules governing operand evaluation order, operator precedence, and operator associativity.

- To obtain input from the keyboard using the dialog boxes.

- To become familiar with Java documentation, programming style, and naming conventions.

- To understand syntax errors, runtime errors, and logic errors.

2.1   Introduction

In the preceding chapter, you learned how to create, compile, and run a Java program. In this chapter, you will be introduced to Java primitive data types and related subjects, such as variables, constants, data types, operators, and expressions. You will learn how to write programs using primitive data types, input and output, and simple calculations.

2.2   Writing Simple Programs

To begin, let's look at a simple program that computes the area of a circle. The program reads in the radius of the circle and displays its area. The program will use variables to store the radius and the area, and will use an expression to compute the area.

Writing this program involves designing algorithms and data structures, as well as translating algorithms into programming codes. An *algorithm* describes how a problem is solved in terms of the actions to be executed, and it specifies the order in which the actions should be executed. Algorithms can help the programmer plan a program before writing it in a programming language. The algorithm for this program can be described as follows:

1. Read in the radius.

2. Compute the area using the following formula:

   area = radius × radius × π

3. Display the area.

Many of the problems you will meet when taking an introductory course in programming using this text can be described with simple, straightforward algorithms. As your education progresses, and you take courses on data structures or on algorithm design and analysis, you will encounter complex problems that require sophisticated solutions. You will need to design accurate, efficient algorithms with appropriate data structures in order to solve such problems.

Data structures involve data representation and manipulation. Java provides data types for representing integers, floating-point numbers (i.e. decimal numbers with optional fractional part), characters, and Boolean types. These types are known as *primitive data types*. Java also supports array and string types as objects. Some advanced data structures, such as stacks, sets, and lists, have built-in implementation in Java.

To novice programmers, coding is a daunting task. When you *code*, you translate an algorithm into a programming language understood by the computer. You already know that every Java program begins with a class declaration in which the keyword `class` is followed by the class name. Assume that you have chosen `ComputeArea` as the class name. The outline of the program would look like this:

```
public class ComputeArea {
  // Data and methods to be given later
}
```

As you know, every application must have a `main` method that controls the execution of the program. So the program is expanded as follows:

```
public class ComputeArea {
  public static void main(String[] args) {
    // Step 1: Read in radius

    // Step 2: Compute area

    // Step 3: Display the area
  }
}
```

The program needs to read the radius entered by the user from the keyboard. This raises two important issues:

- Reading the radius.

- Storing the radius in the program.

Let's address the second issue first. In order to store the radius, the program needs to declare a symbol called a *variable* that will represent the radius. Variables are used to store data and computational results in the program.

Rather than using x and y, choose descriptive names: in this case, `radius` for radius, and `area` for area. Specify their data types to let the compiler know what `radius` and `area` are, indicating whether they are integer, float, or something else. Declare `radius` and `area` as double-precision floating-point numbers. The program can be expanded as follows:

```
public class ComputeArea {
  public static void main(String[] args) {
    double radius;
    double area;

    // Step 1: Read in radius

    // Step 2: Compute area

    // Step 3: Display the area
  }
}
```

The program declares `radius` and `area` as double-variables. The reserved word `double` indicates that `radius` and `area` are double-precision floating-point values stored in the computer.

The first step is to read in `radius`. Reading a number is not a simple matter. For the time being, let us assign a fixed number to `radius` in the program. In Section 2.13, "Getting Input from Input Dialogs," you will learn how to obtain a numeric value from an input dialog.

The second step is to compute area by assigning the expression `radius * radius * 3.14159` to `area`.

In the final step, print area on the console by using the `System.out.println` method.

The program is completed in Example 2.1.

Example 2.1 Computing the Area of a Circle

Problem

Write a program that assigns a radius and computes the area. It concludes by displaying the area.

Solution

The following code gives the solution to the problem.

Comments ➔
```
// ComputeArea.java: Compute the area of a circle

    public class ComputeArea {        Class name

        /** Main method */
Main method
signature  ➔ public static void main(String[] args) {

    Data Type ➔ double radius;    ⟵ Variable
                double area;

                // Assign a radius
                radius = 20;

                // Compute area
                area = radius * radius * 3.14159;    ⟵ Expression

                // Display results
                System.out.println("The area for the circle of radius " +
                    radius + " is " + area);
            }
        }
```

Review

Compile the programs and fix any errors. A sample run of the program is shown in Figure 2.1.

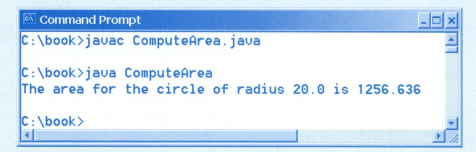

Figure 2.1   *The program displays the area of the circle.*

The plus sign (+) in the `System.out.println("The area for the circle of ra-dius " + radius + " is " + area)` statement means to concatenate strings if one of the operands is a string. If both operands are numbers, the + operator will add them.

Suppose that `i = 1` and `j = 2`, what is the output of the following statement?

```
System.out.println("i + j is " + i + j);
```

The output is "i + j is 12" because `"i + j is "` is concatenated with `i` first. To force `i + j` to be executed first, enclose `i + j` in the parentheses, as follows:

```
System.out.println("i + j is " + (i + j));
```

CAUTION

A string constant should not cross lines in the source code. Thus the following statement would result in a compilation error.

```
System.out.println("Introduction to Java Programming, Fourth
    Edition, by Y. Daniel Liang");
```

To fix the error, break the string into substrings, and use the concatenation operator (+) to combine them:

```
System.out.println("Introduction to Java Programming, " +
    "Fourth Edition, by Y. Daniel Liang");
```

2.3   Identifiers

Just as every entity in the real world has a name, so you need to choose names for the things you will refer to in your programs. Programming languages use special symbols called *identifiers* to name such programming entities as variables, constants, methods, classes, and packages. Here are the rules for naming identifiers:

- An identifier is a sequence of characters that consists of letters, digits, underscores (_), and dollar signs ($).

- An identifier must start with a letter, an underscore (_), or a dollar sign ($). It cannot start with a digit.

- An identifier cannot be a reserved word. (See Appendix A, "Java Keywords," for a list of reserved words.)

- An identifier cannot be `true`, `false`, or `null`.

- An identifier can be of any length.

For example, `$2`, `ComputeArea`, `area`, `radius`, and `showMessageDialog` are legal identifiers, whereas `2A` and `d+4` are illegal identifiers because they do not follow the rules. The Java compiler detects illegal identifiers and reports syntax errors.

NOTE

Since Java is case-sensitive, `X` and `x` are different identifiers.

TIP

Identifiers are used for naming variables, constants, methods, classes, and packages. Descriptive identifiers make programs easy to read. Besides choosing descriptive names for identifiers, there are naming conventions for different kinds of identifiers. Naming conventions are summarized in Section 2.15, "Programming Style and Documentation."

2.4   Variables

Variables are used to store data input, data output, or intermediate data. In the program in Example 2.1, `radius` and `area` are variables of double-precision, floating-point type. You can assign any numerical value to `radius` and `area`, and the values of `radius` and `area` can be reassigned. For example, you can write the code shown below to compute the area for different radii:

```
// Compute the first area
radius = 1.0;
area = radius * radius * 3.14159;
System.out.println("The area is " + area + " for radius " + radius);

// Compute the second area
radius = 2.0;
area = radius * radius * 3.14159;
System.out.println("The area is " + area + " for radius " + radius);
```

2.4.1   Declaring Variables

Variables are for representing data of a certain type. To use a variable, you declare it by telling the compiler the name of the variable as well as what type of data it represents. This is called a *variable declaration*. Declaring a variable tells the compiler to allocate appropriate memory space for the variable based on its data type. Here is the syntax for declaring a variable:

```
datatype variableName;
```

Here are some examples of variable declarations:

```
int x;              // Declare x to be an integer variable;
double radius;      // Declare radius to be a double variable;
double interestRate; // Declare interestRate to be a double variable;
char a;             // Declare a to be a character variable;
```

The examples use the data types `int`, `double`, and `char`. Later in this chapter you will be introduced to additional data types, such as `byte`, `short`, `long`, `float`, `char`, and `boolean`.

If variables are of the same type, they can be declared together using a short-hand form, as follows:

```
datatype variable1, variable2, . . ., variablen;
```

The variables are separated by commas.

NOTE

By convention, variable names are in lowercase. If a name consists of several words, concatenate all of them and capitalize the first letter of each word except the first. Examples of variables are `radius` and `interestRate`.

2.5   Assignment Statements and Assignment Expressions

After a variable is declared, you can assign a value to it by using an *assignment statement*. The syntax for assignment statements is as follows:

```
variable = expression;
```

An *expression* represents a computation involving values, variables, and operators that evaluates to a value. For example, consider the following code:

```
int x = 1;                  // Assign 1 to variable x;
double radius = 1.0;        // Assign 1.0 to variable radius;
a = 'A';                    // Assign 'A' to variable a;
x = 5 * (3 / 2) + 3 * 2;    // Assign the value of the expression to x;
x = y + 1;                  // Assign the addition of y and 1 to x;
area = radius * radius * 3.14159; // Compute area
```

The variable can also be used in the expression. For example,

```
x = x + 1;
```

In this assignment statement, x + 1 is assigned to x. If x is 1 before the statement is executed, then it becomes 2 after the statement is executed.

To assign a value to a variable, the variable name must be on the left of the assignment operator. Thus, 1 = x would be wrong.

In Java, an assignment statement can also be treated as an expression that evaluates to the value being assigned to the variable on the left-hand side of the assignment operator. For this reason, an assignment statement is also known as an *assignment expression*, and the symbol = is referred to as the *assignment operator*. For example, the following statement is correct:

```
System.out.println(x = 1);
```

which is equivalent to

```
x = 1;
System.out.println(x);
```

The following statement is also correct:

```
i = j = k = 1;
```

Which is equivalent to

```
k = 1;
j = k;
i = j;
```

NOTE

In an assignment statement, the data type of the variable on the left must be compatible with the data type of the value on the right. For example, int x = 1.0 would be illegal because the data type of x is int. You cannot assign a double value (1.0) to an int variable without using type casting. Type casting is introduced in Section 2.8, "Numeric Type Conversions."

CAUTION

Java assignment statements use the equals sign (=), not :=, which is often used in other languages.

2.5.1   Declaring and Initializing Variables in One Step

Variables often have initial values. You can declare a variable and initialize it in one step. Consider, for instance, the following code:

```
int x = 1;
```

This is equivalent to the next two statements:

```
int x;
x = 1;
```

You can also use a shorthand form to declare and initialize variables of the same type together. For example,

```
int i = 1, j = 2;
```

TIP

A variable must be declared before it can be assigned a value. A variable declared in a method must be assigned a value before it can be used.

Whenever possible, declare a variable and assign its initial value in one step. This will make the program easy to read and avoid programming errors.

2.6   Constants

The value of a variable may change during the execution of the program, but a *constant* represents permanent data that never change. In our `ComputeArea` program, π is a constant. If you use it frequently, you don't want to keep typing 3.14159; instead, you can define a constant for π. Here is the syntax for declaring a constant:

```
final datatype CONSTANTNAME = VALUE;
```

The word `final` is a Java keyword which means that the constant cannot be changed. For example, in the `ComputeArea` program, you could define π as a constant and rewrite the program as follows:

```
// ComputeArea.java: Compute the area of a circle
public class ComputeArea {
  /** Main method */
  public static void main(String[] args) {
    double radius;
    double area;
    final double PI = 3.14159; // Declare a constant

    // Assign a radius
    radius = 20;

    // Compute area
    area = radius * radius * PI;
```

```
      // Display results
      System.out.println("The area for the circle of radius " +
        radius + " is " + area);
    }
  }
```

CAUTION

A constant must be declared and initialized before it can be used. You cannot change a constant's value once it is declared. By convention, constants are named in uppercase: PI, not pi or Pi.

NOTE

There are three benefits of using constants: (1) you don't have to repeatedly type the same value; (2) the value can be changed in a single location, if necessary; (3) the program is easy to read.

2.7   Numeric Data Types

Every data type has a range of values. The compiler allocates memory space to store each variable or constant according to its data type. Java provides several primitive data types for numeric values, characters, and Boolean values. In this section, numeric data types are introduced.

Java has six numeric types: four for integers and two for floating-point numbers. Table 2.1 lists the six numeric data types, their ranges, and their storage sizes.

TABLE 2.1   Numeric Data Types

Name	Range	Storage Size
byte	-2^7 (-128) to 2^7-1 (127)	8-bit signed
short	-2^{15} (-32768) to $2^{15}-1$ (32767)	16-bit signed
int	-2^{31} (-2147483648) to $2^{31}-1$ (2147483647)	32-bit signed
long	-2^{63} to $2^{63}-1$ (i.e., -9223372036854775808 to 9223372036854775807)	64-bit signed
float	−3.4E38 to 3.4E38 (6 to 7 significant digits of accuracy)	32-bit IEEE 754
double	−1.7E308 to 1.7E308 (14 to 15 significant digits of accuracy)	64-bit IEEE 754

■ NOTE

IEEE 754 is a standard approved by the Institute of Electrical and Electronics Engineers for representing floating-point numbers on computers. The standard has been widely adopted. Java has adopted 32-bit **IEEE 754** for the `float` type and the 64-bit **IEEE 754** for the `double` type. The **IEEE 754** standard also defines special values and operations in Appendix I, "Special Floating-Point Values."

2.7.1   Numeric Operators

The arithmetic operators for numeric data types include addition (+), subtraction (-), multiplication (*), division (/), and remainder (%). For examples, see the following code:

```
int i1 = 34 + 1;            // i1 becomes 35
double d1 = 34.0 - 0.1;     // d1 becomes 33.9
long  i2 = 300 * 30;        // i2 becomes 9000
double d2 = 1.0 / 2.0;      // d2 becomes 0.5
int i3 = 1 / 2;             // i3 becomes 0; Note that the result is
                            // the integer part of the division
byte i4 = 20 % 3;           // i4 becomes 2; Note that the result is
                            // the remainder after the division
```

The result of integer division is an integer. The fractional part is truncated. For example, 5 / 2 = 2, not 2.5, and –5 / 2 = -2, not –2.5.

The % operator yields the remainder after division. Therefore 7 % 3 yields 1, and 20 % 3 yields 2. This operator is often used for integers but also can be used with floating-point values.

The + and - operators can be both unary and binary. A *unary* operator has only one operand; a *binary* operator has two operands. For example, the - operator in -5 can be considered as a unary operator to negate number 5, whereas the - operator in 4 - 5 is a binary operator for subtracting 5 from 4.

■ NOTE

Calculations involving floating-point numbers are approximated because these numbers are not stored with complete accuracy. For example,

```
System.out.println(1 - 0.1 - 0.1 - 0.1 - 0.1 - 0.1);
```

displays 0.5000000000000001, not 0.5, and

```
System.out.println(1.0 - 0.9);
```

displays 0.09999999999999998, not 0.1. Integers are stored precisely. Therefore, calculations with integers yield a precise integer result.

2.7.2   Numeric Literals

A *literal* is a constant value that appears directly in the program. For example, 34, 1,000,000, and 5.0 are literals in the following statements:

```
int i = 34;
long k = 1000000;
double d = 5.0;
```

2.7.2.1   Integer Literals

An integer literal can be assigned to an integer variable as long as it can fit into the variable. A compilation error would occur if the literal were too large for the variable to hold. The statement `byte b = 1000`, for example, would cause a compilation error, because 1000 cannot be stored in a variable of the `byte` type.

An integer literal is assumed to be of the `int` type, whose value is between -2^{31} (-2147483648) and $2^{31}-1$ (2147483647). To denote an integer literal of the `long` type, append the letter `L` or `l` to it. `L` is preferred because `l` (lowercase L) can easily be confused with 1 (the digit one).

NOTE

Integer literals can also be represented in octal (base 8) and hexadecimal (base 16) number systems using the prefixes 0 and 0x, respectively. For more information, see Appendix E, "Number Systems and Bit Manipulations."

2.7.2.2   Floating-Point Literals

Floating-point literals are written with a decimal point. By default, a floating-point literal is treated as a `double` type value. For example, 5.0 is considered a `double` value, not a `float` value. You can make a number a `float` by appending the letter `f` or `F`, and you can make a number a `double` by appending the letter `d` or `D`. For example, you can use `100.2f` or `100.2F` for a `float` number, and `100.2d` or `100.2D` for a `double` number.

2.7.2.3   Scientific Notations

Floating-point literals can also be specified in scientific notation; for example, 1.23456e+2, the same as 1.23456e2, is equivalent to $1.23456 \times 10^2 = 123.456$, and 1.23456e-2 is equivalent to $1.23456 \times 10^{-2} = 0.0123456$. E (or e) represents an exponent and can be either in lowercase or uppercase.

2.7.3   Arithmetic Expressions

Writing numeric expressions in Java involves a straightforward translation of an arithmetic expression using Java operators. For example, the arithmetic expression

$$\frac{34x}{5} - \frac{19(y-5)(a+b+c)}{x} + 9\left(\frac{4}{x} + \frac{9+x}{y}\right)$$

can be translated into a Java expression as:

```
(3 + 4 * x) / 5 - 19 * (y - 5) * (a + b + c) / x +
   9 * (4 / x + (9 + x) / y)
```

The numeric operators in a Java expression are applied exactly as in an arithmetic expression. Operators contained within pairs of parentheses are evaluated first. Parentheses can be nested, in which case the expression in the inner parentheses is executed first. Multiplication, division, and remainder operators are applied next. If an expression contains several multiplication, division, and remainder operators, they are applied from left to right. Addition and subtraction operators are applied last. If an expression contains several addition and subtraction operators, they are applied from left to right.

CAUTION

Be careful when applying division. Division of two integers yields an integer in Java. For example, the formula for converting a Fahrenheit degree is

$$\text{celsius} = \left(\frac{5}{9}\right)(\text{fahrenheit} - 32)$$

Because 5 / 9 yields 0 in Java, the preceding formula should be translated into the Java statement shown below:

```
celsius = (5.0 / 9) * (fahrenheit - 32)
```

2.7.4   Shortcut Operators

Very often the current value of a variable is used, modified, and then reassigned back to the same variable. For example, consider the following code:

```
i = i + 8;
```

This statement is equivalent to

```
i += 8;
```

The += is called a *shortcut operator*. The common shortcut operators are shown in Table 2.2.

TABLE 2.2   Shortcut Operators

Operator	Name	Example	Equivalent
+=	Addition assignment	i += 8	i = i + 8
-=	Subtraction assignment	f -= 8.0	f = f - 8.0
*=	Multiplication assignment	i *= 8	i = i * 8
/=	Division assignment	i /= 8	i = i / 8
%=	Remainder assignment	i % = 8	i = i % 8

There are two more shortcut operators for incrementing and decrementing a variable by 1. This is handy because that's often how much the value needs to be changed. These two operators are ++ and --. They can be used in prefix or suffix notation. For example,

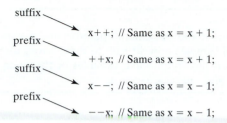

suffix — x++; // Same as x = x + 1;

prefix — ++x; // Same as x = x + 1;

suffix — x--; // Same as x = x − 1;

prefix — --x; // Same as x = x − 1;

If the operator is prefixed to the variable, the variable is first incremented or decremented by 1, then used in the expression. If the operator is a suffix to the variable, the variable is used in the expression first, then incremented or decremented by 1. Therefore, the prefixes ++x and --x are referred to, respectively, as the *preincrement operator* and the *predecrement operator*; and the suffixes x++ and x-- are referred to, respectively, as the *postincrement operator* and the *postdecrement operator*. The prefix form of ++ (or --) and the suffix form of ++ (or --) are the same if they are used in isolation, but they cause different effects when used in an expression. The following code illustrates this:

```
int i = 10;
int newNum = 10 * i++;
```
Equivalent to
```
int newNum = 10 * i;
i = i + 1;
```

In this case, the current value of i is used in the expression, and i is then incremented by 1. So newNum becomes 100. If i++ is replaced by ++i as follows:

```
int i = 10;
int newNum = 10 * (++i);
```
Equivalent to
```
i = i + 1;
int newNum = 10 * i;
```

i is incremented by 1, and the new value of i is used in the expression. Thus newNum becomes 110.

Here is another example:

```
double x = 1.0;
double y = 5.0;
double z = x-- + (++y);
```

After all three lines are executed, y becomes 6.0, z becomes 7.0, and x becomes 0.0.

The increment operator ++ and the decrement operator -- can be applied to all integer and floating-point types. These operators are often used in loop statements. A loop statement is a structure that controls how many times an operation or a sequence of operations is performed in succession. This structure, and the subject of loop statements, is introduced in Chapter 3, "Control Statements."

■ TIP

Using increment and decrement operators makes expressions short, but it also makes them complex and difficult to read. Avoid using these operators in expressions that modify multiple variables or the same variable multiple times, such as this one: int k = ++i + i.

■ NOTE

Like the assignment operator (=), the operators (+=, -=, *=, /=, %=, ++, and --) can be used to form an assignment statement as well as an expression. Prior to Java 2, all expressions could be used as statements. Since Java 2, only the following types of expressions can be statements:

```
variable op= expression; // Where op is +, -, *, /, or %
++variable;
variable++;
--variable;
variable--;
```

The following code has a compilation error in Java 2:

```
public static void main(String[] args) {
   3 + 4; // Correct prior to Java 2, but wrong in Java 2
}
```

■ CAUTION

There are no spaces in the shortcut operators. For example, + = should be +=.

2.8   Numeric Type Conversions

Sometimes it is necessary to mix numeric values of different types in a computation. Consider the following statements:

```
byte i = 100;
long k = i * 3 + 4;
double d = i * 3.1 + k / 2;
```

Are these statements correct? Java allows binary operations on values of different types. When performing a binary operation involving two operands of different types, Java automatically converts the operand of a smaller range type to the larger range type of the other operand. For example, if one operand is int and the other is float, the int operand is converted to float, since the range of the float type is larger than that of the int type. If one of the operands is of the double type, the other is converted to double, since the range of double is the largest of all the numeric types. Thus the result of 1 / 2 is 0, and the result of 1.0 / 2 is 0.5.

You can always assign a value to a numeric variable whose type supports a larger range of values; thus, for instance, you can assign a long value to a float variable. You cannot, however, assign a value to a variable of a type with smaller range unless you use *type casting*. Casting is an operation that converts a value of one data type into a value of another data type. Casting a variable of a type with a small range to a variable of a type with a larger range is known as *widening a type*. Casting a variable of a type with a large range to a variable of a type with a smaller range is known as *narrowing a type*. Widening a type can be performed automatically without explicit casting. Narrowing a type must be performed explicitly.

The syntax for casting gives the target type in parentheses, followed by the variable's name or the value to be cast. The code that follows is an example.

```
float f = (float)10.1;
int i = (int)f;
```

In the first line, the double value 10.1 is cast into float. In the second line, i has a value of 10; the fractional part in f is truncated. Be careful when using casting. Lost information might lead to inaccurate results, as shown in this example:

```
int i = 256; // i has 32 bits
byte b = (byte)i; // b has 8 bits
```

What is b? Numbers are represented in binary in a computer. Appendix E, "Number Systems and Bit Manipulations," introduces number representations in the computer. The binary representation for i ($256 = 2^8$) is 100000000. An integer has four bytes, and the last byte of i is 00000000, which is assigned to b, as shown in Figure 2.2. Thus, b becomes 0, which is totally distorted. To ensure correctness, you can use an if statement to test whether the value is in the correct target type range (see Table 2.1) before performing casting. The subject of if statements will be introduced in Chapter 3, "Control Statements."

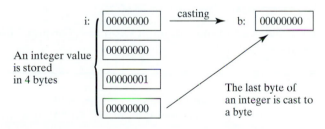

Figure 2.2   *An integer i is cast into a byte b.*

■ CAUTION

Casting is necessary if you are assigning a value to a variable of a smaller type range, such as assigning a double value to an int variable. A compilation error will occur if casting is not used in situations of this kind.

■ NOTE

Casting does not change the variable being cast. For example, d is not changed after casting in the following code:

```
double d = 4.5;
int i = (int)d;   // d is not changed
```

■■■ NOTE

To assign a variable of the int type to a variable of the short or byte type, explicit casting must be used. For example, the following statements have a syntax error:

```
int i = 1;
byte b = i; // Error because explicit casting is required
```

However, so long as the integer literal is within the permissible range of the target variable, explicit casting is not needed to assign an integer literal to a variable of the short or byte type. Please refer to Section 2.7.2.1, "Integer Literals."

2.9   Character Data Type

The character data type, char, is used to represent a single character.

A character literal is enclosed in single quotation marks. Consider the following code:

```
char letter = 'A';
char numChar = '4';
```

The first statement assigns character A to the char variable letter. The second statement assigns the numeric character 4 to the char variable numChar.

The char type only represents one character. To represent a string of characters, use the data type called String. For example, the line of code below declares the message to be a string that has an initial value of "Welcome to Java!"

```
String message = "Welcome to Java!";
```

String is discussed in more detail in Chapter 7, "Strings." From now on, you can use String to declare a string variable.

■■■ CAUTION

A string must be enclosed in quotation marks. A literal character is a single character enclosed in single quotation marks. So "A" is a string and 'A' is a character.

Java characters use *Unicode*, a 16-bit encoding scheme established by the Unicode Consortium to support the interchange, processing, and display of written texts in the world's diverse languages. (See the Unicode Web site at www.unicode.org/ for more information.) Unicode takes two bytes, preceded by \u, expressed in four hexadecimal numbers that run from '\u0000' to '\uFFFF'. For example, the word "coffee" is translated into Chinese using two characters. The Unicodes of these two characters are "\u5496\u5561". The following statement displays some Greek letters, as shown in Figure 2.3.

Figure 2.3 *You can use Unicode to represent international characters.*

```
JOptionPane.showMessageDialog(null, "\u03b1 \u03b2 \u03b3",
   "Display Greek Letters", JOptionPane.INFORMATION_MESSAGE);
```

Most computers use ASCII code. Unicode includes ASCII code, with `'\u0000'` to `'\u007F'` corresponding to the 128 ASCII characters. (See Appendix B, "The ASCII Character Set," for a list of ASCII characters and their decimal and hexadecimal codes.) You can use ASCII characters like `'X'`, `'1'`, and `'$'` in a Java program as well as Unicodes. Thus, for example, the following statements are equivalent:

```
char letter = 'A';
char letter = '\u0041';
```

Both statements assign character A to char variable `letter`.

Java allows you to use an escape sequence for special characters. An escape sequence begins with the backslash character (\) followed by a character that has a special meaning to the compiler. Some of the commonly used special characters are listed in Table 2.3.

TABLE 2.3   Examples of Special Characters

Description	Character Escape Sequence	Unicode
Backspace	\b	\u0008
Tab	\t	\u0009
Linefeed	\n	\u000A
Carriage Return	\r	\u000D
Backslash	\\	\u005C
Single Quote	\'	\u0027
Double Quote	\"	\u0022

NOTE

The increment and decrement operators can also be used on char variables to get the next or preceding Unicode character. For example, the following statements

```
char ch = 'a';
System.out.println(++ch);
```

display b.

Suppose you want to print the quoted message shown below:

```
He said "Java is fun"
```

Here is how to write the statement:

```
System.out.println("He said \ "Java is fun \");
```

2.9.1   Casting between char and Numeric Types

A char can be cast into any numeric type, and vice versa. When an integer is cast into a char, only its lower sixteen bits of data are used; the other part is ignored. When a floating-point value is cast into a char, the floating-point value is first cast into an int, which is then cast into a char. When a char is cast into a numeric type, the character's Unicode is cast into the specified numeric type.

Implicit casting can be used if the result of a casting fits into the target variable. Otherwise, explicit casting must be used. For example, since the Unicode of '0' is 48, which is within the range of a byte, the following implicit castings are fine:

```
byte b = '0';
int i = '0';
```

But the following castings are incorrect, because the Unicode \uFFF4 cannot fit into a byte.

```
byte b = '\uFFF4';
```

To force a casting, use explicit casting, as follows:

```
byte b = (byte)'\uFFF4';
```

Any positive integer between 0 and FFFF in hexadecimal can be cast into a character implicitly. Any number not in this range must be cast into a char explicitly.

NOTE

The + operator can be applied to char operands. If one or two operands are characters, the character is cast into a number. If one operand is a string, the character is combined with the other string. For example, the following statements

```
int i = '1' + '2'; // (int)'1' is 49 and (int)'b' is 50
System.out.println("i is " + i);
String s = "Chapter " + '2';
System.out.println("s is " + s);
```

display

```
i is 99
s is Chapter 2
```

2.10   *boolean* Data Type

Often in a program you need to compare two values, such as whether i is greater than j. Java provides six *comparison operators* (also known as *relational operators*) in Table 2.4 that can be used to compare two values. The result of the comparison is a Boolean value: true or false.

TABLE 2.4   Comparison Operators

Operator	Name	Example	Answer
<	less than	1 < 2	true
<=	less than or equal to	1 <= 2	true
>	greater than	1 > 2	false
>=	greater than or equal to	1 >= 2	false
==	equal to	1 == 2	false
!=	not equal to	1 != 2	true

NOTE

You can also compare characters. Comparing characters is the same as comparing the Unicode of the characters. For example, 'a' is larger than 'A' because the Unicode of 'a' is larger than the Unicode of 'A'.

CAUTION

The equality comparison operator is two equals signs (==), not a single equals sign (=). The latter symbol is for assignment.

For example, the following statement displays true.

```
System.out.println(1 < 2);
```

A variable that holds a Boolean value is known as a *Boolean variable*. The boolean data type is used to declare Boolean variables. The domain of the boolean type consists of two literal values: true and false. For example, the following statement assigns true to the variable lightsOn.

```
boolean lightsOn = true;
```

Boolean operators, also known as *logical operators*, operate on Boolean values to create a new Boolean value. Table 2.5 contains a list of Boolean operators.

TABLE 2.5   Boolean Operators

Operator	Name	Description
!	not	logical negation
&&	and	logical conjunction
||	or	logical disjunction
^	exclusive or	logical exclusion

These operators are demonstrated by the examples that follow. In the examples, the variables width and height contain the values of 1 and 2, respectively.

Table 2.6 defines the not (!) operator. The not (!) operator negates true to false and false to true. For example, !(width == 3) is true because (width == 3) is false.

TABLE 2.6   Truth Table for Operator !

Operand	!Operand
true	false
false	true

Table 2.7 defines the and (&&) operator. The and (&&) of two Boolean operands is true if and only if both operands are true. For example, (width == 1) && (height > 1) is true because (width == 1) and (height > 1) are both true.

TABLE 2.7   Truth Table for Operator &&

Operand1	Operand2	Operand1 && Operand2
false	false	false
false	true	false
true	false	false
true	true	true

Table 2.8 defines the or (¦¦) operator. The or (¦¦) of two Boolean operands is true if at least one of the operands is true. For example, (width > 1) ¦¦ (height == 2) is true because (width == 2) is true.

TABLE 2.8   Truth Table for Operator ¦¦

Operand1	Operand2	Operand1 ¦¦ Operand2
false	false	false
false	true	true
true	false	true
true	true	true

Table 2.9 defines the exclusive or (^) operator. The exclusive or (^) of two Boolean operands is true if and only if the two operands have different Boolean values. For example, (width > 1) ^ (height == 2) is true because (width > 1) is false and (height == 2) is true.

TABLE 2.9   Truth Table for Operator ^

Operand1	Operand2	Operand1 ^ Operand2
false	false	false
false	true	true
true	false	true
true	true	false

Here are some more examples that show the use of Boolean operators:

```
System.out.println("Is " + num + " divisible by 2 and 3? " +
  ((num % 2 == 0) && (num % 3 == 0)));

System.out.println("Is " + num + " divisible by 2 or 3? " +
  ((num % 2 == 0) || (num % 3 == 0)));

 System.out.println("Is " + num +
    " divisible by 2 or 3, but not both? " +
    ((num % 2 == 0) ^ (num % 3 == 0)));
```

2.10.1 Unconditional vs. Conditional Boolean Operators

When evaluating p1 && p2, Java first evaluates p1 and then evaluates p2 if p1 is true; if p1 is false, it does not evaluate p2. When evaluating p1 || p2, Java first evaluates p1 and then evaluates p2 if p1 is false; if p1 is true, it does not evaluate p2. Therefore, && is referred to as the *conditional* or *short-circuit AND* operator, and || is referred to as the *conditional* or *short-circuit OR* operator.

Java also provides the & and | operators. The & operator works exactly the same as the && operator, and the | operator works exactly the same as the || operator with one exception: the & and | operators always evaluate both operands. Therefore, & is referred to as the *unconditional and* operator, and | is referred to as the *unconditional or* operator. In some rare situations, you can use the & and | operators to guarantee that the right-hand operand is evaluated regardless of whether the left-hand operand is true or false. For example, the expression (width < 2) & (height-- < 2) guarantees that (height-- < 2) is evaluated. Thus, the variable height will be decremented regardless of whether width is less than 2 or not.

TIP
Avoid using the & and | operators. The benefits of the & and | operators are marginal. Using them will make the program difficult to read and could cause errors. For example, the expression (x != 0) & (100 / x) results in a runtime error if x is 0. However, (x != 0) && (100 / x) is fine. If x is 0, (x != 0) is false. Since && is a short-circuit operator, Java does not evaluate (100 / x) and evaluate the result as false for the entire expression (x != 0) && (100 / x).

NOTE
The & and | operators can also apply to bitwise operations. See Appendix E, "Number Systems and Bit Manipulations," for details.

NOTE
As shown in the preceding section, a char value can be cast into an int value, and vice versa. A Boolean value, however, cannot be cast into a value of other types, and vice versa.

NOTE

true and false are literals, just like a number such as 10, so they are not key-words, but you cannot use them as identifiers, just as you cannot use 10 as an identifier.

2.11   Operator Precedence and Associativity

Operator precedence and associativity determine the order in which operators are evaluated. Suppose that you have this expression:

```
3 + 4 * 4 > 5 * (4 + 3) - ++i
```

What is its value? How does the compiler know the execution order of the operators? The expression in the parentheses is evaluated first. (Parentheses can be nested, in which case the expression in the inner parentheses is executed first.) When evaluating an expression without parentheses, the operators are applied according to the precedence rule and the associativity rule. The precedence rule defines precedence for operators, as shown in Table 2.10, which contains the operators you have learned in this chapter. Operators are listed in decreasing order of precedence from top to bottom. Operators with the same precedence appear in the same group. (See Appendix C, "Operator Precedence Chart," for a complete list of Java operators and their precedence.)

TABLE 2.10   Operator Precedence Chart

Precedence	Operator
Highest Order	var++ and var-- (postincrement and postdecrement)
	+, - (Unary plus and minus), ++var and --var (prefix)
	(type) (casting)
	! (Not)
	*, /, % (Multiplication, division, and remainder)
	+, - (Binary addition and subtraction)
	<, <=, >, >= (Comparison)
	==, != (Equality)
	& (Unconditional AND)
	^ (Exclusive OR)
	¦ (Unconditional OR)
	&& (Conditional AND)
	¦¦ (Conditional OR)
Lowest Order	=, +=, -=, *=, /=, %= (Assignment operator)

When two operators with the same precedence are evaluated, their *associativity* determines the order of evaluation. All binary operators except assignment operators are *left-associative*. For example, since + and – are of the same precedence and are left-associative, the expression

```
a - b + c - d
```

is equivalent to

```
((a - b) + c) - d
```

Assignment operators are *right-associative*. Therefore, the expression

```
a = b += c = 5
```

is equivalent to

```
a = (b += (c = 5))
```

Suppose a, b, and c are 1 before the assignment; after the whole expression is evaluated, a becomes 6, b becomes 6, and c becomes 5.

 TIP

You can use parentheses to force an evaluation order as well as to make a program easy to read. Use of redundant parentheses does not slow down the execution of the expression.

2.12   Operand Evaluation Order

The precedence and associativity rules specify the order of the operators but not the order in which the operands of a binary operator are evaluated. Operands are evaluated from left to right in Java. *The left-hand operand of a binary operator is evaluated before any part of the right-hand operand is evaluated.* This rule takes precedence over any other rules that govern expressions. Consider this expression:

```
a + b * (c + d) / e
```

a, b, c, d, and e are evaluated in this order. If no operands have *side effects* that change the value of a variable, the order of operand evaluation is irrelevant. Interesting cases arise when operands do have a side effect. For example, x becomes 1 in the following code because a is evaluated to 0 before ++a is evaluated to 1.

```
int a = 0;
int x = a + (++a);
```

But x becomes 2 in the following code because ++a is evaluated to 1, then a is evaluated to 1.

```
int a = 0;
int x = ++a + a;
```

The order for evaluating operands takes precedence over the operator precedence rule. In the former case, (++a) has higher precedence than addition (+), but since a is a left-hand operand of the addition (+), it is evaluated before any part of its right-hand operand (i.e., ++a in this case).

2.13   Getting Input from Input Dialogs

In Example 2.1, the radius is fixed in the source code. To use a different radius, you have to modify the source code and recompile it. Obviously, this is not convenient. You can use the showInputDialog method in the JOptionPane class to get input at runtime. When this method is executed, a dialog is displayed to enable you to enter an input, as shown in Figure 2.4. After entering a string, click OK to accept the input and dismiss the dialog box. The input is returned from the method as a string.

Figure 2.4   *The input dialog box enables the user to enter a string.*

You can invoke the method with four arguments, as follows:

```
String input = JOptionPane.showInputDialog(null,
  "Enter an input", "Input Dialog Demo",
  JOptionPane.QUESTION_MESSAGE);
```

The first argument can always be null. The second argument is a string that prompts the user. The third argument is the title of the input box. The fourth argument can be JOptionPane.QUESTION_MESSAGE, which causes the icon ( ) to be displayed in the input box.

NOTE

There are several ways to use the showInputDialog method. For the time being, you only need to know how to invoke the showInputDialog method like this:

```
String string = JOptionPane.showInputDialog(null, x,
  y, JOptionPane.QUESTION_MESSAGE));
```

where x is a string for the prompting message, and y is a string for the title of the input dialog box.

2.13.1   Converting Strings to Numbers

The input returned from the input dialog box is a string. If you enter a numeric value such as 123, it returns "123". You have to convert a string into a number to obtain the input as a number.

To convert a string into an `int` value, use the `parseInt` method in the `Integer` class, as follows:

```
int intValue = Integer.parseInt(intString);
```

where `intString` is a numeric string such as "123".

To convert a string into a `double` value, use the `parseDouble` method in the `Double` class, as follows:

```
double doubleValue = Double.parseDouble(doubleString);
```

where `doubleString` is a numeric string such as "123.45".

The `Integer` and `Double` classes are both included in the `java.lang` package. These classes will be further discussed in Chapter 9, "Object-Oriented Software Development."

> **NOTE**
>
> You can also convert a string into a value of the `byte` type, `short` type, `long` type, `float` type, `char` type, or `boolean` type. You will learn the conversion methods later in the book.

Example 2.2   Entering Input from Dialog Boxes

Problem

This example shows you how to enter input from dialog boxes. As shown in Figure 2.5, the program prompts the user to enter a year as an `int` value and checks whether it is a leap year; then it prompts the user to enter a double value and checks whether it is positive. A year is a leap year if it is divisible by 4 but not by 100 or if it is divisible by 400. The source code of the program is given below.

Solution

The following code gives the solution to the problem.

```
1    // InputDialogDemo.java: Entering input from input dialog boxes
2    import javax.swing.JOptionPane;
3
4    public class InputDialogDemo {
5      /** Main method */
6      public static void main(String args[]) {
7        // Prompt the user to enter a year
8        String yearString = JOptionPane.showInputDialog(null,
9          "Enter a year", "Example 2.2 Input (int)",
10         JOptionPane.QUESTION_MESSAGE);
11
```

continues

Example 2.2   continued

```
12          // Convert the string into an int value
13          int year = Integer.parseInt(yearString);
14
15          // Check if the year is a leap year
16          boolean isLeapYear =
17            ((year % 4 == 0) && (year % 100 != 0)) || (year % 400 == 0);
18
19          // Display the result in a message dialog box
20          JOptionPane.showMessageDialog(null,
21            year + " is a leap year? " + isLeapYear,
22            "Example 2.2 Output (int)", JOptionPane.INFORMATION_MESSAGE);
23
24          // Prompt the user to enter a double value
25          String doubleString = JOptionPane.showInputDialog(null,
26            "Enter a double value", "Example 2.2 Input (double)",
27            JOptionPane.QUESTION_MESSAGE);
29          // Convert the string into a double value
30          double doubleValue = Double.parseDouble(doubleString);
31
32          // Check if the number is positive
33          JOptionPane.showMessageDialog(null,
34            doubleValue + " is positive? " + (doubleValue > 0),
35            "Example 2.2 Output (double)",
36            JOptionPane.INFORMATION_MESSAGE);
37
38          System.exit(0);
39        }
40      }
```

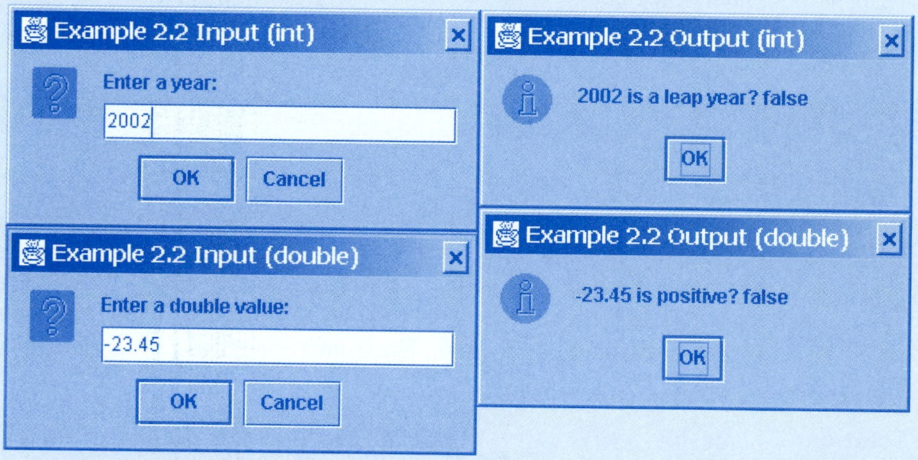

Example 2.2 Input (int)
Enter a year:
2002
OK   Cancel

Example 2.2 Output (int)
2002 is a leap year? false
OK

Example 2.2 Input (double)
Enter a double value:
-23.45
OK   Cancel

Example 2.2 Output (double)
-23.45 is positive? false
OK

Figure 2.5   *The input dialog box enables the user to enter a string.*

Review

The showInputDialog method in Lines 8–10 displays an input dialog box titled "Example 2.2 Input (int)." Enter a year as an integer and click OK to accept the input. The integer is returned as a string that is assigned to the String variable yearString. The Integer.parseInt(yerString) (Line 13) is used to convert the string into an `int` value. If you entered an input other than an integer, a run-time error would occur. In Chapter 13, "Exception Handling," you will learn how to handle the exception so that the program can continue to run.

The `showMessageDialog` method in Lines 20–22 displays the output in a message dialog box titled "Example 2.2 Output (int)."

The `showInputDialog` method in Lines 25–27 displays an input dialog box titled "Example 2.2 Input (double)." Enter a floating-point value and click OK to accept the input. The floating-point value is returned as a string that is assigned to the `String` variable `doubleString`. The `Double.parseInt(doubleString)` (Line 30) is used to convert the string into an `int` value. If you entered a non-numeric value, a runtime error would occur.

As explained in Example 1.2, for every program that creates dialog boxes using the methods in `JOptionPane`, you need to use `System.exit(0)` (Line 38) to terminate the program properly.

NOTE

If you click *Cancel* in the input dialog box, no string is returned. A runtime error would occur.

2.14   Case Studies

In the preceding sections, you learned about variables, constants, primitive data types, operators, and expressions. You are now ready to use them to write interesting programs. This section presents two examples: computing mortgage payments, and breaking a sum of money down into smaller units.

Example 2.3   Computing Mortgages

Problem

This example shows you how to write a program that computes mortgage payments. The program lets the user enter the interest rate, number of years, and loan amount, and then computes the monthly payment and the total payment. It concludes by displaying the monthly and total payments.

Solution

The formula to compute the monthly payment is as follows:

$$\frac{loanamount \times monthlyInterestRate}{1 - \dfrac{1}{(1 + monthlyInterestRate)^{numOfYears \times 12}}}$$

continues

Example 2.3 continued

You don't have to know how this formula is derived. Nonetheless, given the monthly interest rate, number of years, and loan amount, you can use it to compute the monthly payment.

Here are the steps in developing the program:

1. Prompt the user to enter the annual interest rate, number of years, and loan amount.

2. Obtain the monthly interest rate from the annual interest rate.

3. Compute the monthly payment using the preceding formula.

4. Compute the total payment, which is the monthly payment multiplied by 12 and multiplied by the number of years.

5. Display the monthly payment and total payment in a message dialog.

The mortgage calculation program follows, and the output is shown in Figure 2.6.

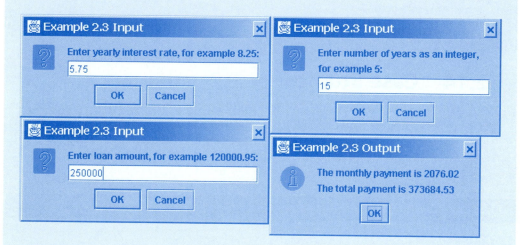

Figure 2.6   *The program accepts annual interest rate, number of years, and loan amount, then displays the monthly payment and total payment.*

```
1    // ComputeMortgage.java: Compute mortgage payments
2    import javax.swing.JOptionPane;
3
4    public class ComputeMortgage {
5      /** Main method */
6      public static void main(String[] args) {
7        double annualInterestRate;
8        int numOfYears;
9        double loanAmount;
10
11       // Enter yearly interest rate
12       String annualInterestRateString = JOptionPane.showInputDialog(
13         null, "Enter yearly interest rate, for example 8.25:",
```

```
14        "Example 2.3 Input", JOptionPane.QUESTION_MESSAGE);
15
16      // Convert string to double
17      annualInterestRate =
18        Double.parseDouble(annualInterestRateString);
19
20      // Obtain monthly interest rate
21      double monthlyInterestRate = annualInterestRate/1200;
22
23      // Enter number of years
24      String numOfYearsString = JOptionPane.showInputDialog(null,
25        "Enter number of years as an integer, \nfor example 5:",
26        "Example 2.3 Input", JOptionPane.QUESTION_MESSAGE);
27
28      // Convert string to int
29      numOfYears = Integer.parseInt(numOfYearsString);
30
31      // Enter loan amount
32      String loanString = JOptionPane.showInputDialog(null,
33        "Enter loan amount, for example 120000.95:",
34        "Example 2.3 Input", JOptionPane.QUESTION_MESSAGE);
35
36      // Convert string to double
37      loanAmount =  Double.parseDouble(loanString);
38
39      // Calculate payment
40      double monthlyPayment = loanAmount * monthlyInterestRate /
41        (1 - 1 / Math.pow(1 + monthlyInterestRate, numOfYears * 12));
42      double totalPayment = monthlyPayment * numOfYears * 12;
43
44      // Format to keep two digits after the decimal point
45      monthlyPayment = (int)(monthlyPayment * 100) / 100.0;
46      totalPayment = (int)(totalPayment * 100) / 100.0;
47
48      // Display results
49      String output = "The monthly payment is " + monthlyPayment +
50        "\nThe total payment is " + totalPayment;
51      JOptionPane.showMessageDialog(null, output,
52        "Example 2.3 Output", JOptionPane.INFORMATION_MESSAGE);
53
54      System.exit(0);
55    }
56  }
```

Review

Each new variable in a method must be declared once and only once. Choose the most appropriate data type for the variable. For example, numOfYears is best declared as int (Line 8), although it could be declared as long, float, or double.

The method for computing b^p in the Math class is pow(b, p) (Lines 40–41). The Math class, which comes with the Java runtime system, is available to all Java programs. The Math class is introduced in Chapter 4, "Methods."

The statements in Lines 45–46 are for formatting the number to keep two digits after the decimal point. For example, if monthlyPayment is 2076.0252175, (int)(monthlyPayment * 100) is 207602. Therefore, (int)(monthlyPayment * 100) / 100.0 yields 2076.02.

The strings are concatenated into output in Lines 49–50. The linefeed escape character '\n' is in the string to display the text after '\n' in the next line.

Example 2.4 Computing Change

Problem

This example shows you how to write a program that classifies a given amount of money into smaller monetary units. The program lets the user enter an amount as a `double` value representing a total in dollars and cents, and outputs a report listing the monetary equivalent in dollars, quarters, dimes, nickels, and pennies.

Your program should report the maximum number of dollars, then the maximum number of quarters, and so on, in this order.

Solution

Here are the steps in developing the program:

1. Prompt the user to enter the amount as a decimal number such as 11.56.

2. Convert the amount (e.g., 11.56) into cents (1156).

3. Divide the cents by 100 to find the number of dollars. Obtain the remaining cents using the cents *remainder* 100.

4. Divide the remaining cents by 25 to find the number of quarters. Obtain the remaining cents using the remaining cents *remainder* 25.

5. Divide the remaining cents by 10 to find the number of dimes. Obtain the remaining cents using the remaining cents *remainder* 10.

6. Divide the remaining cents by 5 to find the number of nickels. Obtain the remaining cents using the remaining cents *remainder* 5.

7. The remaining cents are the pennies.

8. Display the result.

The program follows, and the output is shown in Figure 2.7.

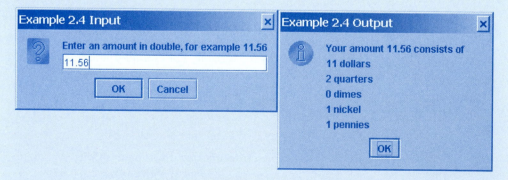

Figure 2.7   *The program receives an amount in decimals and breaks it into singles, quarters, dimes, nickels, and pennies.*

```
1     // ComputeChange.java: Break down an amount into smaller units
2     import javax.swing.JOptionPane;
3
4     public class ComputeChange {
5       /** Main method */
6       public static void main(String[] args) {
7         double amount; // Amount entered from the keyboard
8
9         // Receive the amount entered from the keyboard
10        String amountString = JOptionPane.showInputDialog(null,
11          "Enter an amount in double, for example 11.56",
12          "Example 2.4 Input", JOptionPane.QUESTION_MESSAGE);
13
14        // Convert string to double
15        amount = Double.parseDouble(amountString);
16
17        int remainingAmount = (int)(amount * 100);
18
19        // Find the number of one dollars
20        int numOfOneDollars = remainingAmount / 100;
21        remainingAmount = remainingAmount % 100;
22
23        // Find the number of quarters in the remaining amount
24        int numOfQuarters = remainingAmount / 25;
25        remainingAmount = remainingAmount % 25;
26
27        // Find the number of dimes in the remaining amount
28        int numOfDimes = remainingAmount / 10;
29        remainingAmount = remainingAmount % 10;
30
31        // Find the number of nickels in the remaining amount
32        int numOfNickels = remainingAmount / 5;
33        remainingAmount = remainingAmount % 5;
34
35        // Find the number of pennies in the remaining amount
36        int numOfPennies = remainingAmount;
37
38        // Display results
39        String output = "Your amount " + amount + " consists of \n" +
40          numOfOneDollars + " dollars\n" +
41          numOfQuarters + " quarters\n" +
42          numOfDimes + " dimes\n" +
43          numOfNickels + " nickel\n" +
44          numOfPennies + " pennies";
45        JOptionPane.showMessageDialog(null, output,
46          "Example 2.4 Output", JOptionPane.INFORMATION_MESSAGE);
47
48        System.exit(0);
49      }
50    }
```

Review

The variable amount stores the amount entered from the input dialog box (Lines 7–15). This variable is not changed because the amount has to be used at the end of the program to display the results. The program introduces the variable remainingAmount (Line 17) to store the changing remainingAmount.

The variable amount is a double decimal representing dollars and cents. It is converted to an int variable remainingAmount, which represents all the cents. For

continues

Example 2.4 continued

instance, if amount is 11.56, then the initial `remainingAmount` is 1156. The division operator yields the integer part of the division. So 1156 / 100 is 11. The remainder operator obtains the remainder of the division. So 1156 % 100 is 56.

The program extracts the maximum number of singles from the total amount and obtains the remaining amount in the variable `remainingAmount` (Lines 20–21). It then extracts the maximum number of quarters from `remainingAmount` and obtains a new `remainingAmount` (Lines 24–25). Continuing the same process, the program finds the maximum number of dimes, nickels, and pennies in the remaining amount.

One serious problem with this example is the possible loss of precision when casting a `double` amount to an `int remainingAmount`. This could lead to an inaccurate result. If you try to enter the amount 10.03, you will find that the program displays 10 dollars and 2 pennies. There are two ways to fix the problem. One is to enter the amount as an `int` value representing cents (see Exercise 2.4); the other is to read the decimal number as a string and extract the dollars part and the cents part separately as `int` values. Processing strings will be introduced in Chapter 7, "Strings."

As shown in Figure 2.7, 0 dimes, 1 nickels, and 1 pennies are displayed in the result. It would be better not to display 0 dimes, and to display 1 nickel and 1 penny using the singular forms of the words. You will learn how to use selection statements to modify this program in the next chapter (see Exercise 3.1).

2.15   Programming Style and Documentation

Programming style deals with what programs look like. A program can compile and run properly even if written on only one line, but writing it all on one line would be bad programming style because it would be hard to read. *Documentation* is the body of explanatory remarks and comments pertaining to a program. Programming style and documentation are as important as coding. Good programming style and appropriate documentation reduce the chance of errors and make programs easy to read. So far you have learned some good programming styles. This section summarizes them and gives several guidelines. More details can be found in the Java supplements in `www.prenhall.com/liang/intro4e.html`.

2.15.1   Appropriate Comments and Comment Styles

Include a summary at the beginning of the program to explain what the program does, its key features, its supporting data structures, and any unique techniques it uses. In a long program, you should also include comments that introduce each major step and explain anything that is difficult to read. It is important to make comments concise so that they do not crowd the program or make it difficult to read.

Use javadoc comments (/** . . . */) for commenting on an entire class or an entire method. These comments must precede the class or the method header, and can be extracted in a javadoc HTML file. For commenting on steps inside a method, use line comments (//).

2.15.2 Naming Conventions

Make sure that you choose descriptive names with straightforward meanings for the variables, constants, classes, and methods in your program. Names are case-sensitive. Listed below are the conventions for naming variables, methods, and classes.

■ Always use lowercase for variables and methods. If a name consists of several words, concatenate them into one, making the first word lowercase and capitalizing the first letter of each subsequent word; for example, the variables `radius` and `area` and the method `showInputDialog`.

■ Capitalize the first letter of each word in a class name; for example, the class names `ComputeAre`, `Math`, and `JOptionPane`.

■ Capitalize every letter in a constant, and use underscores between words; for example, the constant `PI` and constant `MAX_VALUE`.

TIP

It is important to become familiar with the naming conventions. Understanding them will help you to understand Java programs. If you stick with the naming conventions, other programmers will be more willing to accept your program.

CAUTION

Do not choose class names that are already used in the Java library. For example, since the `Math` class is defined in Java, you should not name your class `Math`.

2.15.3 Proper Indentation and Spacing

A consistent indentation style makes programs clear and easy to read. *Indentation* is used to illustrate the structural relationships between a program's components or statements. Java can read the program even if all of the statements are in a straight line, but it is easier to read and maintain code that is aligned properly. Indent each subcomponent or statement *two* spaces more than the structure within which it is nested.

A single space should be added on both sides of a binary operator, as shown in the following statement:

```
boolean b = 3 + 4 * 4 > 5 * (4 + 3) - ++i;
```

A single space line should be used to separate segments of the code to make the program easier to read.

2.15.4   Block Styles

A block is a group of statements surrounded by braces. There are two popular styles, *next-line* style and *end-of-line* style, as shown in Figure 2.8. Both are acceptable block styles. You can use either the next-line style or the end-of-line style as long as it is used consistently. This book uses the *end-of-line* style to be consistent with the Java API source code.

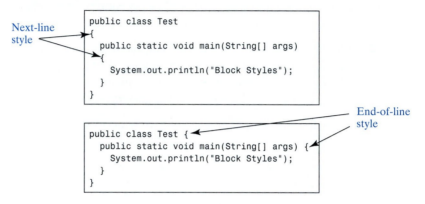

Figure 2.8   *The opening brace is placed at the end of line for end-of-line style and at the beginning of a new line for next-line style.*

2.15.5   Code Style Examples

Here is a coding style example:

```
/**
 * Course title: Introduction to Programming Principles
 * Course number: CSCI 1301-03
 * Instructor: Dr. Y. Daniel Liang
 * Description: Example 2.1, "Computing the Area of a Circle"
 *   This class is for computing the area of a circle given the
 *   radius. The radius is entered from the keyboard.
 * Copyright: Copyright (c) 2000
 * Company: Armstrong Atlantic State University
 * @author John F. Smith
 * @version 1.0, 11/30/2001
 */
public class ComputeArea {
  public static void main(String[] args) {
    double radius;
    double area;

    // Assign a radius
    radius = 20;

    // Compute area
    area = radius * radius * 3.14159;

    // Display results
    System.out.println("The area for the circle of radius " +
      radius + " is " + area);
  }
}
```

The javadoc comment for this example is quite long. To save space, the javadoc comments for the other examples in this book will be omitted.

2.16 Programming Errors

Programming errors are unavoidable, even for experienced programmers. Errors can be categorized into three types: syntax errors, runtime errors, and logic errors.

2.16.1 Syntax Errors

Errors that occur during compilation are called *syntax errors* or *compilation errors*. Syntax errors result from errors in code construction, such as mistyping a keyword, omitting some necessary punctuation, or using an opening brace without a corresponding closing brace. These errors are usually easy to detect, because the compiler tells you where they are and the reasons for them. For example, compiling the following program results in a syntax error, as shown in Figure 2.9.

```java
// ShowSyntaxErrors.java: The program contains syntax errors
public class ShowSyntaxErrors {
  public static void main(String[] args) {
    i = 30;
    System.out.println(i + 4);
  }
}
```

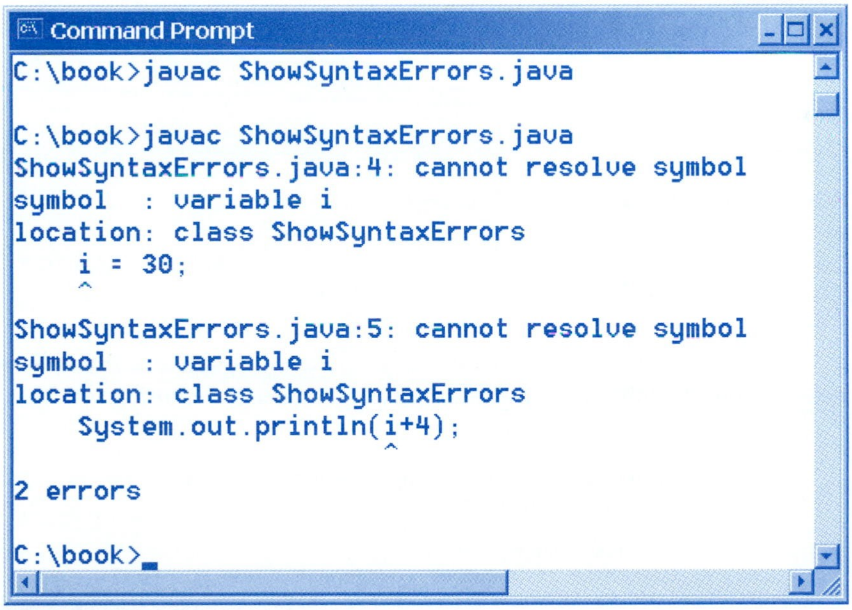

```
Command Prompt                                    _ □ ×

C:\book>javac ShowSyntaxErrors.java

C:\book>javac ShowSyntaxErrors.java
ShowSyntaxErrors.java:4: cannot resolve symbol
symbol  : variable i
location: class ShowSyntaxErrors
    i = 30;
    ^

ShowSyntaxErrors.java:5: cannot resolve symbol
symbol  : variable i
location: class ShowSyntaxErrors
    System.out.println(i+4);
                       ^

2 errors

C:\book>_
```

Figure 2.9 *The compiler reports syntax errors in the Command window.*

Two errors are detected. Both are the result of not declaring variable i. Since a single error will often display many lines of compilation errors, it is a good practice to start debugging from the top line and work downward. Fixing errors that occur earlier in the program may also fix cascading errors that occur later.

2.16.2   Runtime Errors

Runtime errors are errors that cause a program to terminate abnormally. Runtime errors occur while an application is running if the environment detects an operation that is impossible to carry out. Input errors are typical runtime errors.

An *input error* occurs when the user enters an unexpected input value that the program cannot handle. For instance, if the program expects to read in a number, but instead the user enters a string, this causes data-type errors to occur in the program. To prevent input errors, the program should prompt the user to enter the correct type of values. It may display a message like "Please enter an integer" before reading an integer from the keyboard.

Another common source of runtime errors is division by zero. This happens when the divisor is zero for integer divisions. For instance, the following program would cause a runtime error, as shown in Figure 2.10.

```java
// ShowRuntimeErrors.java: Program contains runtime errors
public class ShowRuntimeErrors {
  public static void main(String[] args) {
    int i = 1 / 0;
  }
}
```

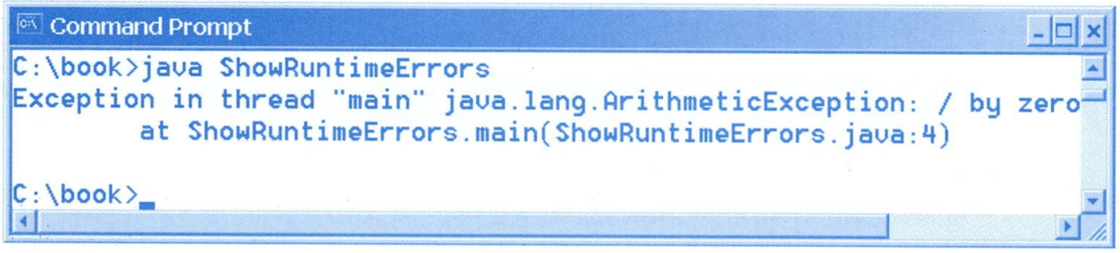

Figure 2.10   *The runtime error causes the program to terminate.*

2.16.3   Logic Errors

Logic errors occur when a program does not perform the way it was intended to. Errors of this kind occur for many different reasons. For example, suppose you wrote the following program to display a message reporting whether a number is between 1 and 100, inclusively.

```java
// ShowLogicErrors.java: program contains a logic errors
import javax.swing.JOptionPane;

public class ShowLogicErrors {
  // Determine if a number is between 1 and 100 inclusively
  public static void main(String[] args) {
    // Prompt the user to enter a number
    String input = JOptionPane.showInputDialog(null,
      "Please enter an integer:",
      "ShowLogicErrors", JOptionPane.QUESTION_MESSAGE);
    int number = Integer.parseInt(input);
```

```
          // Display the result
          System.out.println("The number is between 1 and 100, " +
            "inclusively? " + ((1 < number) && (number < 100)));

          System.exit(0);
      }
   }
```

The program does not have syntax errors or runtime errors, but it does not print the correct result for the number 100, as shown in Figure 2.11.

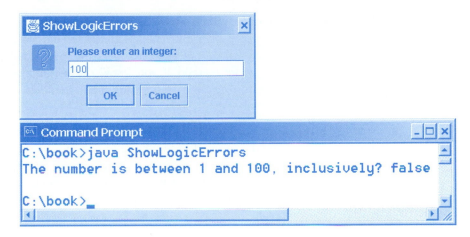

Figure 2.11   *The logic error causes the program to produce an incorrect result.*

The error is in the Boolean expression in the `println` statement. It should be as follows:

```
((1 <= number) && (number <= 100))
```

2.17   Debugging

In general, syntax errors are easy to find and easy to correct because the compiler gives indications as to where the errors came from and why they are there. Runtime errors are not difficult to find either, since the Java interpreter displays them on the console when the program aborts. Finding logic errors, on the other hand, can be very challenging.

Logic errors are called *bugs*. The process of finding and correcting errors is called *debugging*. A common approach to debugging is to use a combination of methods to narrow down to the part of the program where the bug is located. You can *hand-trace* the program (i.e., catch errors by reading the program), or you can insert print statements in order to show the values of the variables or the execution flow of the program. This approach might work for a short, simple program. But for a large, complex program, the most effective approach for debugging is to use a debugger utility.

JDK includes a command-line debugger (jdb), which is invoked with a class name. jdb is itself a Java program, running its own copy of Java interpreter. All the Java IDE tools like JBuilder, Sun ONE Studio, Visual J++, and Visual Café include integrated debuggers. The debugger utilities let you follow the execution of a program. They vary from one system to another, but they all support most of the following helpful features:

- **Executing a single statement at a time:** The debugger allows you to execute one statement at a time so that you can see the effect of each statement.

- **Tracing into or stepping over a method:** If a method is being executed, you can ask the debugger to enter the method and execute one statement at a time in the method, or you can ask it to step over the entire method. You should step over the entire method if you know the method works. For example, always step over the system-supplied methods, such as `System.out.println`.

- **Setting breakpoints:** You can set a breakpoint at a specific statement. Your program pauses when it reaches a breakpoint and displays the line with the breakpoint. You can set as many breakpoints as you want. Breakpoints are particularly useful when you know where your programming error starts. You can set a breakpoint at that line and have the program execute until it reaches the breakpoint.

- **Displaying variables:** The debugger lets you select several variables and display their values. As you trace through a program, the content of a variable is continuously updated.

- **Using call stacks:** The debugger lets you trace all of the method calls and lists all pending methods. This feature is helpful when you need to see a large picture of the program-execution flow.

- **Modifying variables:** Some debuggers enable you to modify the value of a variable when debugging. This is convenient when you want to test a program with different samples but do not want to leave the debugger.

NOTE

The debugger is an indispensable, powerful tool that boosts your programming productivity. However, it could take some time to become familiar with it. I recommend that beginning Java programmers using this book insert the print statements to trace the programs.

Chapter Summary

In this chapter, you learned about data representation, operators, and expressions. These are the fundamental elements needed to construct Java programs. You also learned about programming errors, debugging, and programming styles. These are all important concepts and should be fully understood before you apply them.

Identifiers are used for naming programming entities, such as variables, constants, methods, classes, and packages. Variables are symbols that represent data. The value of a variable can be changed with an assignment statement. All variables must be declared with an identifier and a type before they can be used. An initial value must be assigned to a variable before it is referenced.

The equals sign (=) is used to assign a value to a variable. A statement with an equals sign is called an assignment statement. When a value is assigned to a variable, it replaces the previous value of the variable, which is destroyed.

A constant is a symbol representing a value in the program that is never changed. You cannot change a constant once it is declared.

Java provides four integer types (byte, short, int, long) that represent integers of four different sizes, and two floating-point types (float, double) that represent floating-point numbers of two different precisions. Character type (char) represents a single character, and boolean type represents a true or false value. These are called primitive data types. Java's primitive types are portable across all computer platforms. They have exactly the same values on all platforms. When they are declared, the variables of these types are created and assigned memory space.

Java provides operators that perform numeric operations: + (addition), - (subtraction), * (multiplication), / (division), and % (remainder). Integer division (/) yields an integer result. The remainder operator (%) yields the remainder of the division.

The increment operator (++) and the decrement operator (--) increment or decrement a variable by 1. If the operator is prefixed to the variable, the variable is first incremented or decremented by 1, then used in the expression. If the operator is a suffix to the variable, the variable is used in the expression first, then incremented or decremented by 1.

The Boolean operators &&, &, |, |, !, and ^ operate with Boolean values and variables. The relational operators (<, <=, ==, !=, >, >=) work with numbers and characters, and yield a Boolean value.

You can use casting to convert a value of one type into another type. Casting a variable of a type with a small range to a variable of a type with a larger range is known as *widening a type*. Casting a variable of a type with a large range to a variable of a type with a smaller range is known as *narrowing a type*. Widening a type can be performed automatically without explicit casting. Narrowing a type must be performed explicitly.

The operands of a binary operator are evaluated from left to right. No part of the right-hand operand is evaluated until all the operands before the binary operator are evaluated. The operators in arithmetic expressions are evaluated in the order determined by the rules of parentheses, operator precedence, and associativity. Parentheses can be used to force the order of evaluation to occur in any sequence. Operators with higher precedence are evaluated earlier. The associativity of the operators determines the order of evaluation for operators of the same precedence. All binary operators except assignment operators are left-associative, and assignment operators are right-associative.

Part I Fundamentals of Programming

Review Questions

2.1 Are the following identifiers valid?

```
applet, Applet, a++, --a, 4#R, $4, #44, apps
```

2.2 Declare the following:

- An `int` variable with an initial value of `0`.
- A `long` variable with an initial value of `10000`.
- A `float` variable with an initial value of `3.4`.
- A `double` variable with an initial value of `34.45`.
- A `char` variable with an initial value of `4`.
- A `boolean` variable with an initial value of `true`.

2.3 Assume that `int a = 1` and `double d = 1.0`, and that each expression is independent. What are the results of the following expressions?

```
a = 46 / 9;
a = 46 % 9 + 4 * 4 - 2;
a = 45 + 43 % 5 * (23 * 3 % 2);
a = 45 + 45 * 50 % a--;
a = 45 + 1 + 45 * 50 % (++a + 1);
d += 1.5 * 3 + (++d);
d -= 1.5 * 3 + d++;
a %= 3 / a + 3;
```

2.4 Find the largest and smallest `byte`, `short`, `int`, `long`, `float`, and `double`. Which of these data types requires the least amount of memory?

2.5 Can different types of numeric values be used together in a computation?

2.6 Describe Unicode and ASCII code.

2.7 Can the following conversions involving casting be allowed? If so, find the converted result.

```
char c = 'A';
i = (int)c;

boolean b = true;
i = (int)b;

float f = 1000.34f;
int i = (int)f;

double d = 1000.34;
int i = (int)d;

int i = 97;
char c = (char)i;

int i = 1000;
boolean b = (boolean)i;
```

64

2.8 What is the result of 25 / 4? How would you rewrite the expression if you wished the result to be a floating-point number?

2.9 Are the following statements correct? If so, show the output.

```
System.out.println("the output for 25/4 is " + 25 / 4);
System.out.println("the output for 25/4.0 is " + 25 / 4.0);
```

2.10 What does an explicit conversion from a double to an int do with the fractional part of the *double* value? Does casting change the variable being cast?

2.11 How would you write the following arithmetic expression in Java?

$$\frac{4}{3(r + 34)} - 9(a + bc) + \frac{3 + d(2 + a)}{a + bd}$$

2.12 List six comparison operators.

2.13 Assume that x is 1, show the result of the following Boolean expressions if the result can be determined.

```
(true) && (3 > 4)
!(x > 0) && (x > 0)
(x > 0) || (x < 0)
(x != 0) || (x == 0)
(x >= 0) || (x < 0)
(x != 1) == !(x == 1)
```

2.14 Write a Boolean expression that evaluates to true if the number is between 1 and 100.

2.15 Write a Boolean expression that evaluates to true if the number is between 1 and 100 or the number is negative.

2.16 Assume that x and y are int type. Which of the following expressions are correct?

```
x > y > 0
x = y && y
x /= y
x or y
x and y
(x != 0) || (x = 0)
```

2.17 How do you denote a comment line and a comment paragraph?

2.18 Describe syntax errors, runtime errors, and logic errors.

2.19 What are the naming conventions for class names, method names, constants, and variables? Which of the following items can be a constant, a method, a variable, or a class according to the Java naming conventions?

```
MAX_VALUE, Test, read, readInt
```

2.20 Suppose that x is 1. What is x after the evaluation of the following expression?

```
(x > 1) & (x++ > 1)
```

2.21 Suppose that x is 1. What is x after the evaluation of the following expression?

```
(x > 1) && (x++ > 1)
```

2.22 List the precedence order of the Boolean operators. Evaluate the following expressions:

```
true | true && false
true || true && false
true | true & false
```

2.23 Evaluate the following expression:

```
1 + "Welcome " + 1 + 1
1 + "Welcome " + (1 + 1)
1 + "Welcome " + ('\u0001'  + 1)
1 + "Welcome " + 'a'  + 1
```

2.24 Which of these statements are true?
  a. Any expression can be used as a statement.
  b. The expression x++ can be used as a statement.
  c. The statement x = x + 5 is also an expression.
  d. The statement x = y = x = 0 is illegal.
  e. All the operators of the same precedence are evaluated from left to right.

2.25 Show and explain the output of the following code:

```
int i = 0;
System.out.println(--i + i + i++);
System.out.println(i + ++i);
```

2.26 Which of the following are correct literals for floating-point numbers?
  a. 12.3;
  b. 12.3e+2;
  c. 23.4e-2;
  d. −334.4

2.27 Which of the following are correct literals for characters?
  a. '1';
  b. \u345d;
  c. '\u3fFa';
  d. '\b'

2.28 What is the command to compile a Java program?

2.29 What is the command to run a Java application?

2.30 If the exception NoClassFoundError is raised when you run a program from the DOS prompt, what is wrong?

2.31 If the exception "NoSuchMethodError: main" is raised when you run a program from the DOS prompt, what is wrong?

2.32 Identify and fix the errors in the following code:

66

```
public class Test {
  public void main(string[] args) {
    int i;
    int k = 100.0;
    int j = i + 1;

    System.out.println("j is " + j + " and
      k is " + k);
  }
}
```

2.33 Show the output of the following program:

```
public class Test {
  public static void main(String[] args) {
    char x = 'a';
    char y = 'c';
    System.out.println(++y);
    System.out.println(y++);
    System.out.println(x > y);
    System.out.println(x - y);
  }
}
```

2.34 Reformat the following program according to the programming style and documentation guidelines proposed in Section 2.15. Use the next-line brace style.

```
public class Test
{
  // Main method
  public static void main(String[] args) {
  /** Print a line */
  System.out.println("2 % 3 = " 2%3);
  }
}
```

Programming Exercises

2.1 Write a program that converts Fahrenheit to Celsius. The formula for the conversion is as follows:

celsius = (5 / 9) * (fahrenheit – 32)

Your program reads a Fahrenheit degree in double from the input dialog box, then converts it to Celsius and displays the result in a message dialog box.

HINT
In Java, 5 / 9 is 0, so you need to write 5.0 / 9 in the program to obtain the correct result.

2.2 Write a program that computes the volume of a cylinder. The program should read in radius and length, and compute volume using the following formulas:

```
area = radius * radius * π
volume = area * length
```

2.3 Write a program that displays "Welcome to Java!" in large block letters, each letter made up of the same character it represents. The letters should be six printed lines each. For example, *W* is displayed as follows:

2.4 Rewrite Example 2.4, "Computing Changes," to fix the possible loss of accuracy when converting a `double` value to an `int` value. Enter the input as an integer whose last two digits represent the cents. For example, the input 1156 represents 11 dollars and 56 cents.

2.5 Write a program that reads an integer between 0 and 1000 and summarizes all the digits in the integer. For example, if an integer is 932, the sum of all its digits is 14.

HINT

Use the % operator to extract digits and use the / operator to remove the extracted digit. For instance, 932 % 10 = 2 and 932 / 10 = 93.

2.6 Write a program that reads a double number and checks whether the number is between 1 and 1000. If your input is 5, your output should be:

The number 5 between 1 and 1000 is true.

If your input is 2000, your output should be:

The number 2000 between 1 and 1000 is false.

2.7 Write a program that reads an integer and checks whether it is even. If your input is 25, your output should be:

Is 25 even? false

If your input is 2000, your output should be:

Is 2000 even? true

2.8 Write a program that converts pounds into kilograms. The program prompts the user to enter a number in pounds, converts it to kilograms, and displays the result. One pound is 0.454 kilograms.

2.9 Write a program that computes future investment value at a given interest rate for a specified number of years. The future investment is determined using the following formula:

```
futureInvestmentValue =
    investmentAmount x (1 + monthlyInterestRate)^(numOfYears*12)
```

Your program should prompt the user to enter investment amount, annual interest rate, and number of years, and should display the future investment value.

HINT

Use the `Math.pow(a, b)` method to compute a raised to the power of b.

2.10 Write a program that converts an uppercase letter to a lowercase letter. The character is typed in the source code. In Chapter 7, "Strings," you will learn how to enter a character from the input dialog box.

HINT

In the ASCII table (see Appendix B), uppercase letters appear before lowercase letters. The offset between any uppercase letter and its corresponding lowercase letter is the same. So you can find a lowercase letter from its corresponding uppercase letter, as follows:

```
int offset = (int)'a' - (int)'A';
char lowercase = (char)((int)uppercase + offset);
```

2.11 Write a program that receives an ASCII code (an integer between 0 and 128) and displays its character. For example, if the user enters 97, the program displays character a.

2.12 Write a program that calculates tips and total amount. The program prompts the user to enter the subtotal and the gratuity rate, and computes the gratuity and total. For example, if the user enters 10 for subtotal and 15 percent for gratuity rate, the program displays $1.5 as gratuity and $11.5 as total.

2.13 Write a program that converts feet into meters. The program prompts the user to enter a number in feet, converts it to meters, and displays the result. One foot is 0.305 meters.

CONTROL STATEMENTS

Objectives

- To understand the concept of program control.
- To use selection statements to control the execution of programs.
- To use loop statements to control the repetition of statements.
- To understand and use the keywords `break` and `continue`.

3.1   Introduction

Program control specifies the order in which statements are executed in a program. The programs that you have written so far execute statements in sequence. Often, however, you are faced with situations in which you must provide alternative steps.

In Chapter 2, "Primitive Data Types and Operations," if you assigned a negative value for radius in Example 2.1, "Computing the Area of a Circle," for instance, the program would print an invalid result. If the radius is negative, you don't want the program to compute the area. Like all high-level programming languages, Java provides selection statements that let you choose actions with two or more alternative courses. You can use selection statements in the following pseudocode to rewrite Example 2.1:

```
if the radius is negative
  the program displays a message indicating a wrong input;
else
  the program computes the area and displays the result;
```

Like other high-level programming languages, Java provides iteration structures in order to control the repeated execution of statements. Suppose that you need to print the same message a hundred times. It would be tedious to have to write the message over and over again. Java provides a powerful control structure called a *loop*, which controls how many times an operation or a sequence of operations is performed in succession. Using a loop statement, you simply tell the computer to print the message a hundred times without having to code the print statement a hundred times. Java has three types of loop statements: while loops, do-while loops, and for loops.

In this chapter, you will learn various selection and loop control statements.

3.2   Selection Statements

This section introduces selection statements. Java has several types of selection statements: simple if statements, if . . . else statements, nested if statements, switch statements, and conditional expressions.

3.2.1   Simple *if* Statements

A simple if statement executes an action only if the condition is true. The syntax for a simple if statement is shown below:

```
if (booleanExpression) {
  statement(s);
}
```

The execution flow chart is shown in Figure 3.1.

If the booleanExpression evaluates as true, the statements in the block are executed. As an example, see the following code:

```
if (radius >= 0) {
  area = radius * radius * PI;
  System.out.println("The area for the circle of radius " +
    radius + " is " + area);
}
```

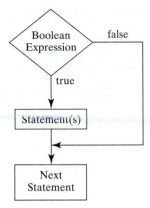

Figure 3.1 *An* if *statement executes statements if the* booleanExpression *evaluates as* true.

If the value of radius is greater than or equal to 0, then the area is computed and the result is displayed; otherwise, the two statements in the block will not be executed.

CAUTION

Adding a semicolon at the end of an if clause is a common mistake. For example,

```
if (radius >= 0);   ←─────── Logic Error
{
  area = radius * radius * PI;
  System.out.println("The area for the circle of radius " +
    radius + " is " + area);
}
```

This mistake is hard to find, because it is not a compilation error or a run-time error, it is a logic error. The preceding statement is equivalent to

```
if (radius >= 0) { };
area = radius * radius * PI;
System.out.println("The area for the circle of radius " +
  radius + " is " + area);
```

This error often occurs when you use the next-line block style. Using the end-of-line block style will prevent this error.

NOTE

The booleanExpression is enclosed in parentheses for all forms of the if statement. Thus, for example, the outer parentheses in the following if statement are required.

```
if ((i > 0) && (i < 10)) {
  System.out.println("i is an integer between 0 and 10");
}
```

The braces can be omitted if they enclose a single statement. For example:

```
if ((i > 0) && (i < 10))
  system.out.println("i is an integer between 0 and 10");
```

> **CAUTION**
>
> Forgetting the braces when they are needed for grouping multiple statements is a common programming error. If you modify the code by adding new statements in an `if` statement without braces, you will have to insert the braces if they are not already in place.

The following statement determines whether a number is even or odd:

```
// Prompt the user to enter an integer
String intString = JOptionPane.showInputDialog(null,
  "Enter an integer:", "Example", JOptionPane.QUESTION_MESSAGE);

// Convert string into int
int number = Integer.parseInt(intString);

if (number % 2 == 0)
  System.out.println(number + " is even.");

if (number % 2 != 0)
  System.out.println(number + " is odd.");
```

3.2.2   if . . . else Statements

A simple `if` statement takes an action if the specified condition is `true`. If the condition is `false`, nothing is done. But what if you want to take alternative actions when the condition is `false`? You can use an `if . . . else` statement. The actions that an `if . . . else` statement specifies differ based on whether the condition is `true` or `false`.

Here is the syntax for this type of statement:

```
if (booleanExpression) {
  statement(s)-for-the-true-case;
}
else {
  statement(s)-for-the-false-case;
}
```

The flow chart of an the statement is shown in Figure 3.2.

If the `booleanExpression` evaluates as `true`, the `statement(s)` for the true case is executed; otherwise, the `statement(s)` for the false case is executed. For example, consider the following code:

```
if (radius >= 0) {
  area = radius * radius * PI;
  System.out.println("The area for the circle of radius " +
    radius + " is " + area);
}
else {
  System.out.println("Negative input");
}
```

If `radius >= 0` is true, `area` is computed and displayed; if it is `false`, the message `"Negative input"` is printed.

As usual, the braces can be omitted if there is only one statement within them. The braces enclosing the `System.out.println("Negative input")` statement can therefore be omitted in the preceding example.

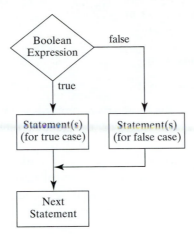

Figure 3.2 *An* if . . . else *statement executes statements for the* true *case if the* boolean *expression evaluates as* true; *otherwise, statements for the* false *case are executed.*

Using the if … else statement, you can rewrite the code for determining whether a number is even or odd in the preceding section, as follows:

```
if (number % 2 == 0)
    System.out.println(number + " is even.");
else
    System.out.println(number + " is odd.");
```

This is more efficient because whether number % 2 is 0 is tested only once.

3.2.3   Nested *if* Statements

The statement in an if or if . . . else statement can be any legal Java statement, including another if or if . . . else statement. The inner if statement is said to be *nested* inside the outer if statement. The inner if statement can contain another if statement; in fact, there is no limit to the depth of the nesting. For example, the following is a nested if statement:

```
if (i > k) {
    if (j > k)
        System.out.println("i and j are greater than k");
}
else
    System.out.println("i is less than or equal to k");
```

The if (j > k) statement is nested inside the if (i > k) statement.

The nested if statement can be used to implement multiple alternatives. The statement given below, for instance, assigns a letter grade to the variable grade according to the score, with multiple alternatives.

```
if (score >= 90.0)
    grade = 'A';
else
    if (score >= 80.0)
        grade = 'B';
    else
```

```
if (score >= 70.0)
  grade = 'C';
else
  if (score >= 60.0)
    grade = 'D';
  else
    grade = 'F';
```

The execution of this if statement proceeds as follows. The first condition (score >= 90.0) is tested. If it is true, the grade becomes 'A'. If it is false, the second condition (score >= 80.0) is tested. If the second condition is true, the grade becomes 'B'. If that condition is false, the third condition and the rest of the conditions (if necessary) continue to be tested until a condition is met or all of the conditions prove to be false. If all of the conditions are false, the grade becomes 'F'. Note that a condition is tested only when all of the conditions that come before it are false.

The preceding if statement is equivalent to the following:

```
if (score >= 90.0)
  grade = 'A';
else if (score >= 80.0)
  grade = 'B';
else if (score >= 70.0)
  grade = 'C';
else if (score >= 60.0)
  grade = 'D';
else
  grade = 'F';
```

In fact, this is the preferred writing style for multiple alternative if statements. This style avoids deep indentation and makes the program easy to read.

NOTE

The else clause matches the most recent if clause in the same block. For example, the following statement

```
int i = 1;
int j = 2;
int k = 3;

if (i > j)
  if (i > k)
    System.out.println("A");
else
  System.out.println("B");
```

is equivalent to

```
int i = 1;
int j = 2;
int k = 3;

if (i > j)
  if (i > k)
    System.out.println("A");
  else
    System.out.println("B");
```

Nothing is printed from the preceding statement. To force the else clause to match the first if clause, you must add a pair of braces:

```
int i = 1;
int j = 2;
int k = 3;

if (i > j) {
  if (i > k)
    System.out.println("A");
}
else
  System.out.println("B");
```

This statement prints B.

TIP

Often your program assigns a test condition to a `boolean` variable like this:

```
if (number % 2 == 0)
  even = true;
else
  even = false;
```

Avoid using `if` statements to assign test values to `boolean` variables. Instead, assign the test values directly to the variables, as follows:

```
boolean even = number % 2 == 0;
```

CAUTION

To test whether a `boolean` variable is `true` or `false` in a test condition, it is redundant to use the equality comparison operator like this:

```
if (even == true)
  System.out.println("It is even.");
```

Instead, it is better to use the `boolean` variable directly, as follows:

```
if (even)
  System.out.println("It is even.");
```

Another good reason to use the `boolean` variable directly is to avoid potential errors that are difficult to detect. It is a common error to use the = operator instead of the == operator to compare equality of two items in a test condition. This could lead to the following erroneous statement:

```
if (even = true)
  System.out.println("It is event.");
```

This statement does not have syntax errors. It assigns `true` to `even` so that `even` is always `true`.

Example 3.1 Using Nested `if` Statements

Problem

In Example 2.3, "Computing Mortgages," you built a program that reads annual mortgage interest rate, number of years, and loan amount and computes mortgage payments. In this example, assume that the annual interest rate depends on the number of years.

Suppose that you have three different interest rates: 7.25 percent for seven years, 8.5 percent for fifteen years, and 9 percent for thirty years. The program prompts the user to enter a loan amount and the number of years for the mortgage, then finds the annual interest rate according to the number of years. The program concludes by displaying the monthly payment and the total payment.

Solution

The following code gives the solution to the problem. Figure 3.3 shows a sample run of the program.

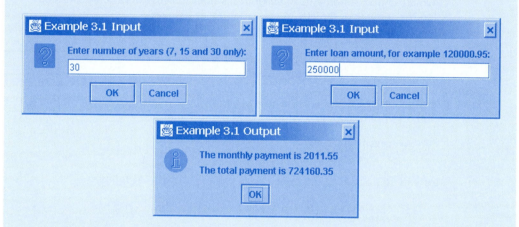

Figure 3.3   *The program validates the input year, obtains the interest rate according to the number of years, receives the loan amount, and displays the monthly payment and the total payment.*

```
1     // TestIfElse.java: Test if-else statements
2     import javax.swing.JOptionPane;
3
4     public class TestIfElse {
5       /** Main method */
6       public static void main(String[] args) {
7         double annualInterestRate = 0;
8         int numOfYears;
9         double loanAmount;
10
11        // Prompt the user to enter number of years
12        String numOfYearsString = JOptionPane.showInputDialog(null,
13          "Enter number of years (7, 15 and 30 only):",
14          "Example 3.1 Input", JOptionPane.QUESTION_MESSAGE);
15
16        // Convert string into int
17        numOfYears = Integer.parseInt(numOfYearsString);
18
```

```
19        // Find interest rate based on year
20        if (numOfYears == 7)
21          annualInterestRate = 7.25;
22        else if (numOfYears == 15)
23          annualInterestRate = 8.50;
24        else if (numOfYears == 30)
25          annualInterestRate = 9.0;
26        else {
27          JOptionPane.showMessageDialog(null,
28            "Wrong number of years",
29            "Example 3.1 Output", JOptionPane.INFORMATION_MESSAGE);
30          System.exit(0);
31        }
32
33        // Obtain monthly interest rate
34        double monthlyInterestRate = annualInterestRate / 1200;
35
36        // Prompt the user to enter loan amount
37        String loanAmountString = JOptionPane.showInputDialog(null,
38          "Enter loan amount, for example 120000.95:",
39          "Example 3.1 Input", JOptionPane.QUESTION_MESSAGE);
40
41        // Convert string into double
42        loanAmount = Double.parseDouble(loanAmountString);
43
44        // Compute mortgage
45        double monthlyPayment = loanAmount*monthlyInterestRate / ( 1 -
46          (Math.pow(1 / (1 + monthlyInterestRate), numOfYears * 12)));
47        double totalPayment = monthlyPayment * numOfYears * 12;
48
49        // Format to keep two digits after the decimal point
50        monthlyPayment = (int)(monthlyPayment * 100) / 100.0;
51        totalPayment = (int)(totalPayment * 100) / 100.0;
52
53        // Display results
54        String output = "The monthly payment is " + monthlyPayment +
55          "\nThe total payment is " + totalPayment;
56        JOptionPane.showMessageDialog(null, output,
57          "Example 3.1 Output", JOptionPane.INFORMATION_MESSAGE);
58
59        System.exit(0);
60      }
61    }
```

Review

The import statement (Line 2) makes the class javax.swing.JOptionPane available for use in this example.

The program receives the number of years (Lines 12–17) and assigns the annual interest rate: 7.25 percent for seven years, 8.5 percent for fifteen years, and 9 percent for thirty years. If the number of years is not seven, fifteen, or thirty, the program displays Wrong number of years (Lines 27–29).

Note that an initial value of 0 is assigned to annualInterestRate (Line 7). A syntax error would occur if it had no initial value because all of the other statements that assign values to annualInterestRate are within the if statement. The compiler thinks that these statements may not be executed and therefore reports a syntax error.

3.2.4   *switch* Statements

The `if` statement in Example 3.1 makes selections based on a single `true` or `false` condition. There are three cases for assigning interest rates, which depend on the number of years. To fully account for all the cases, nested `if` statements were used. Overuse of nested `if` statements makes a program difficult to read. Java provides a `switch` statement to handle multiple conditions efficiently. You could write the following `switch` statement to replace the nested `if` statement in Example 3.1:

```java
switch (numOfYears) {
  case 7:   annualInterestRate = 7.25;
            break;
  case 15:  annualInterestRate = 8.50;
            break;
  case 30:  annualInterestRate = 9.0;
            break;
  default:  System.out.println("Wrong number of years");
            System.exit(0);
}
```

The flow chart of the preceding `switch` statement is shown in Figure 3.4.

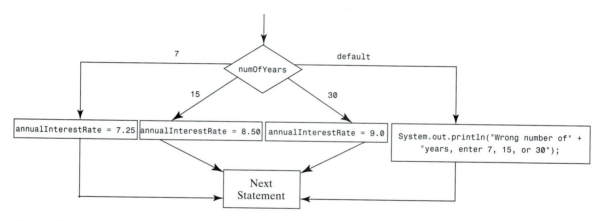

Figure 3.4   *The* `switch` *statement obtains the interest rate according to the number of years.*

This statement checks to see whether the number of years matches the value 7, 15, or 30, in that order. If matched, the corresponding statement is executed; if not matched, a message is displayed. Here is the full syntax for the `switch` statement:

```java
switch (switch-expression) {
  case value1: statement(s)1;
               break;
  case value2: statement(s)2;
               break;
  …
  case valueN: statement(s)N;
               break;
  default:     statement(s)-for-default;
}
```

The switch statement observes the following rules:

- The switch-expression must yield a value of char, byte, short, or int type and must always be enclosed in parentheses.

- The value1, . . ., and valueN must have the same data type as the value of the switch-expression. The resulting statements in the case statement are executed when the value in the case statement matches the value of the switch-expression. (The case statements are executed in sequential order.)

- The keyword break is optional, but it should be used at the end of each case in order to terminate the remainder of the switch statement. If the break statement is not present, the next case statement will be executed.

- The default case, which is optional, can be used to perform actions when none of the specified cases matches the switch-expression.

- The order of the cases (including the default case) does not matter. However, it is good programming style to follow the logical sequence of the cases and place the default case at the end.

CAUTION

Do not forget to use a break statement when one is needed. The following code, for example, always displays Wrong number of years regardless of what numOfYears is. Suppose the numOfYears is 15. The statement annualInterestRate = 8.50 is executed, then the statement annualInterestRate = 9.0, and finally the statement System.out.println("Wrong number of years").

```
switch (numOfYears) {
   case 7:  annualInterestRate = 7.25;
   case 15: annualInterestRate = 8.50;
   case 30: annualInterestRate = 9.0;
   default: System.out.println("Wrong number of years");
}
```

TIP

To avoid programming errors and improve code maintainability, it is a good idea to put a comment in a case clause if break is purposely omitted.

3.2.5 Conditional Expressions

You might want to assign a value to a variable that is restricted by certain conditions. For example, the following statement assigns 1 to y if x is greater than 0, and -1 to y if x is less than or equal to 0.

```
if (x > 0)
   y = 1
else
   y = -1;
```

Alternatively, as in this example, you can use a conditional expression to achieve the same result.

```
y = (x > 0) ? 1 : -1;
```

Conditional expressions are in a completely different style, with no explicit `if` in the statement. The syntax is shown below:

```
booleanExpression ? expression1 : expression2;
```

The result of this conditional expression is `expression1` if `booleanExpression` is true, otherwise the result is `expression2`.

Suppose you want to assign the larger number between variable `num1` and `num2` to `max`. You can simply write a statement using the conditional expression:

```
max = (num1 > num2) ? num1 : num2;
```

For another example, the following statement displays a message "num is even" if num is even, and otherwise displays "num is odd."

```
System.out.println((num % 2 == 0) ? "num is even" : "num is odd");
```

NOTE

The symbols ? and : appear together in a conditional expression. They form a conditional operator. This operator is called a *ternary operator* because it uses three operands. This is the only ternary operator in Java.

3.3   Loop Statements

Loops are structures that control repeated executions of a block of statements. The part of the loop that contains the statements to be repeated is called the *loop body*. A one-time execution of a loop body is referred to as an *iteration of the loop*. Each loop contains a `loop-continuation-condition`, a Boolean expression that controls the execution of the body. After each iteration, the `loop-continuation-condition` is reevaluated. If the condition is `true`, the execution of the loop body is repeated. If the condition is `false`, the loop terminates.

The concept of looping is fundamental to programming. Java provides three types of loop statements: the `while` loop, the `do-while` loop, and the `for` loop.

3.3.1   The *while* Loop

The syntax for the `while` loop is as follows:

```
while (loop-continuation-condition) {
   // Loop body;
}
```

The braces enclosing a `while` loop or any other loop can be omitted only if the loop body contains one or no statement. The `while` loop flow chart is shown in Figure 3.5.

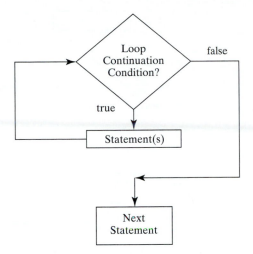

Figure 3.5   *The* while *loop repeatedly executes the statements in the loop body when the* loop-con-tinuation-condition *evaluates as* true.

The loop-continuation-condition, a Boolean expression, must appear inside the parentheses. It is always evaluated before the loop body is executed. If its evaluation is true, the loop body is executed; if its evaluation is false, the entire loop terminates and the program control turns to the statement that follows the while loop. For example, the following while loop prints Welcome to Java! a hundred times.

```
int i = 0;
while (i < 100) {
  System.out.println("Welcome to Java!");
  i++;
}
```

The flow chart of the preceding statement is shown in Figure 3.6.

The variable i is initially 0. The loop checks whether (i < 100) is true. If so, it executes the loop body to print the message Welcome to Java! and increments i by 1. It repeatedly executes the loop body until (i < 100) becomes false. When (i < 100) is false, the loop terminates and the next statement after the loop statement is executed.

CAUTION
Make sure that the loop-continuation-condition eventually becomes false so that the program will terminate. A common programming error involves infinite loops. That is, the program cannot terminate because of a mistake on the loop continuation condition. For instance, if you forgot to increase i (i++) in the code, the program would not stop. To terminate the program, press CTRL+C.

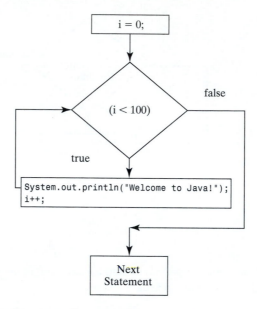

Figure 3.6   *The* while *loop repeatedly executes the statements in the loop body for a total of a hundred times.*

Example 3.2 Using while **Loops**

Problem

Write a program that reads and calculates an unspecified number of integers. The input 0 signifies the end of the input.

Solution

The following code gives the solution to the problem. The program's sample run is shown in Figure 3.7.

```
1    // TestWhile.java: Test the while loop
2    import javax.swing.JOptionPane;
3
4    public class TestWhile {
5      /** Main method */
6      public static void main(String[] args) {
7        int data;
8        int sum = 0;
9
10       // Read an initial data
11       String dataString = JOptionPane.showInputDialog(null,
12         "Enter an int value, \nthe program exits if the input is 0",
13         "Example 3.2 Input", JOptionPane.QUESTION_MESSAGE);
14
15       data = Integer.parseInt(dataString);
16
17       // Keep reading data until the input is 0
18       while (data != 0) {
19         sum += data;
20
```

```
21              // Read the next data
22              dataString = JOptionPane.showInputDialog(null,
23                "Enter an int value, \nthe program exits if the input is 0",
24                "Example 3.2 Input", JOptionPane.QUESTION_MESSAGE);
25
26              data = Integer.parseInt(dataString);
27          }
28
29          JOptionPane.showMessageDialog(null, "The sum is " + sum,
30            "Example 3.2 Output", JOptionPane.INFORMATION_MESSAGE);
31
32          System.exit(0);
33      }
34  }
```

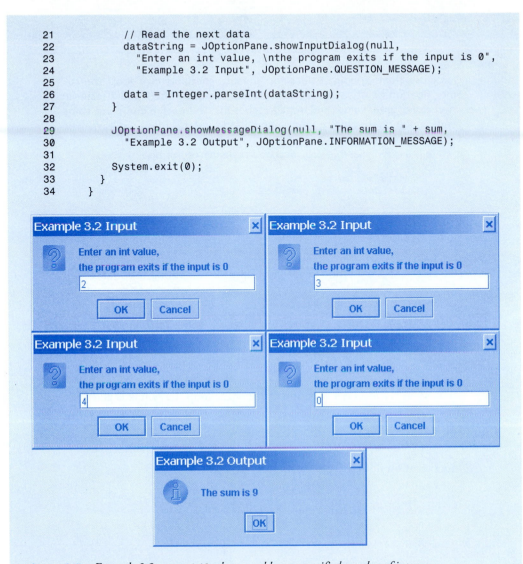

Figure 3.7   *Example 3.2 uses a* while *loop to add an unspecified number of integers.*

Review

If data is not 0, it is added to the sum (Line 19) and the next input data are read (Lines 21–26). If data is 0, the loop body is not executed and the while loop terminates.

Note that if the first input read is 0, the loop body never executes, and the resulting sum is 0.

NOTE

The program uses the input value 0 as the end of the input. A special input value, such as 0 in this example, is also known as a *sentinel value* that signifies the end of the input.

---

continues

Example 3.2 continued

■ CAUTION
Don't use floating-point values for equality checking in a loop control. Since floating-point values are approximations, using them could result in imprecise counter values and inaccurate results. This example uses `int` value for `data`. If a floating-point type value is used for `data`, `(data != 0)` may be true even though `data` is 0.

Here is a good example provided by a reviewer of this book:

```
// data should be zero
double data = Math.pow(Math.sqrt(2), 2) - 2;

if (data == 0)
  System.out.println("data is zero");
else
  System.out.println("data is not zero");
```

Like `pow`, `sqrt` is a method in the `Math` class for computing the square root of a number. The variable `data` in the above code should be zero, but it is not because of rounding-off errors.

3.3.2   The *do-while* Loop

The `do-while` loop is a variation of the `while` loop. Its syntax is given below:

```
do {
  // Loop body;
} while (loop-continuation-condition);
```

Its execution flow chart is shown in Figure 3.8.

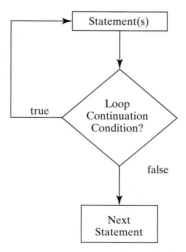

Figure 3.8   *The* `do-while` *loop executes the loop body first, and then checks the* `loop-continua-tion-condition` *to determine whether to continue or terminate the loop.*

The loop body is executed first. Then the `loop-continuation-condition` is evaluated. If the evaluation is `true`, the loop body is executed again; if it is `false`, the do-while loop terminates. The major difference between a `while` loop and a `do-while` loop is the order in which the `loop-continuation-condition` is evaluated and the loop body executed. The `while` loop and the `do-while` loop have equal expressive power. Sometimes it is more convenient to choose one over the other. For example, you can rewrite Example 3.2 as follows:

```java
// TestDo.java: Test the do-while loop
import javax.swing.JOptionPane;

public class TestDo {
  /** Main method */
  public static void main(String[] args) {
    int data;
    int sum = 0;

    // Keep reading data until the input is 0
    do {
      // Read the next data
      String dataString = JOptionPane.showInputDialog(null,
        "Enter an int value, \nthe program exits if the input is 0",
        "TestDo", JOptionPane.QUESTION_MESSAGE);

      data = Integer.parseInt(dataString);

      sum += data;
    } while (data != 0);

    JOptionPane.showMessageDialog(null, "The sum is " + sum,
      "TestDo", JOptionPane.INFORMATION_MESSAGE);

    System.exit(0);
  }
}
```

TIP

I recommend the `do-while` loop if you have statements inside the loop that must be executed at least once, as in the case of the `do-while` loop in the preceding `TestDo` program. These statements must appear before the loop as well as inside the loop if you are using a `while` loop.

3.3.3   The *for* Loop

Often you write the loop in the following common form:

```java
i = initialValue;  // Initialize loop control variable
while (i < endValue) {
  // Loop body
  ...
  i++; // Adjust loop control variable
}
```

A `for` loop can be used to simplify the above loop:

```java
for (i = initialValue; i < endValue; i++) {
  // Loop body
  ...
}
```

In general, the syntax of a `for` loop is as shown below:

```
for (initial-action; loop-continuation-condition;
    action-after-each-iteration) {
  // Loop body;
}
```

The flow chart of the `for` loop is shown in Figure 3.9.

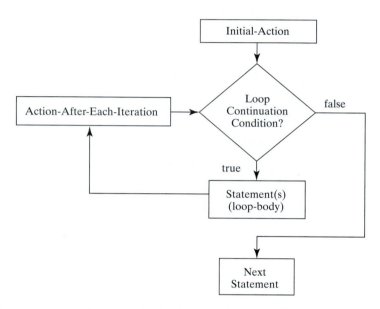

Figure 3.9 *A* `for` *loop performs an initial action once, then repeatedly executes the statements in the loop body, and performs an action after an iteration when the* `loop-continuation-condition` *evaluates as* `true`.

The `for` loop statement starts with the keyword `for`, followed by a pair of parentheses enclosing `initial-action`, `loop-continuation-condition`, and `action-after-each-iteration`, and the loop body, enclosed inside braces. `initial-action`, `loop-continuation-condition`, and `action-after-each-iteration` are separated by semicolons.

A `for` loop generally uses a variable to control how many times the loop body is executed and when the loop terminates. This variable is referred to as a *control variable*. The `initial-action` often initializes a control variable, the `action-after-each-iteration` usually increments or decrements the control variable, and the `loop-continuation-condition` tests whether the control variable has reached a termination value. For example, the following `for` loop prints `Welcome to Java!` a hundred times:

```
int i;
for (i = 0; i < 100; i++) {
  System.out.println("Welcome to Java!");
}
```

The flow chart of the statement is shown in Figure 3.10.

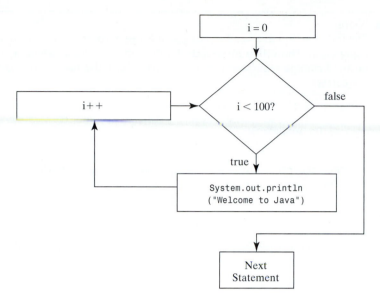

Figure 3.10   *The* for *loop initializes* i *to* 0*, then repeatedly executes the* println *statement and evaluates* i++ *if* i *is less than* 100*.*

The initial-action, i = 0, initializes the control variable, i.

The loop-continuation-condition, i < 100, is a Boolean expression. The expression is evaluated at the beginning of each iteration. If this condition is true, execute the loop body. If it is false, the loop terminates and the program control turns to the line following the loop.

The action-after-each-iteration, i++, is a statement that adjusts the control variable. This statement is executed after each iteration. It increments the control variable. Eventually, the value of the control variable forces the loop-continuation-condition to become false.

The loop control variable can be declared and initialized in the for loop. Here is an example:

```
for (int i = 0; i < 100; i++) {
   System.out.println("Welcome to Java!");
}
```

If there is only one statement in the loop body, as in this example, the braces can be omitted.

TIP

The control variable must always be declared inside the control structure of the loop or before the loop. If the loop control variable is used only in the loop, and not elsewhere, it is good programming practice to declare it in the initial-action of the for loop. If the variable is declared inside the loop control structure, it cannot be referenced outside the loop. For example, you cannot reference i outside the for loop in the preceding code, because it is declared inside the for loop.

NOTE

The initial-action in a `for` loop can be a list of zero or more comma-separated expressions. The action-after-each-iteration in a `for` loop can be a list of zero or more comma-separated statements. Therefore, the following two `for` loops are correct.

```
for (int i = 1; i < 100; System.out.println(i++));
for (int i = 0, j = 0; (i + j < 10); i++, j++) {
  // Do something
}
```

If the `loop-continuation-condition` in a `for` loop is omitted, it is implicitly true. Thus the statement given below, which is an infinite loop, is correct.

```
for ( ; ; ) {
}
```

Nevertheless, I recommend that you use the following equivalent loop to avoid confusion:

```
while (true) {
}
```

Example 3.3 Using `for` Loops

Problem

Write a program that computes the summation of a series that starts with 0.01 and ends with 1.0. The numbers in the series will increment by 0.01, as follows: 0.01 + 0.02 + 0.03 and so on.

Solution

The following code gives the solution to the problem. The output of this program appears in Figure 3.11.

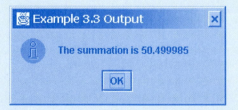

Figure 3.11 *Example 3.3 uses a `for` loop to sum a series from 0.01 to 1 in increments of 0.01.*

```
1    // TestSum.java: Compute sum = 0.01 + 0.02 + ... + 1;
2    import javax.swing.JOptionPane;
3
4    public class TestSum {
5      /** Main method */
6      public static void main(String[] args) {
7        // Initialize sum
8        float sum = 0;
```

```
 9          // Keep adding 0.01 to sum
10          for (float i = 0.01f; i <= 1.0f; i = i + 0.01f)
11            sum += i;
12
13          // Display result
14          JOptionPane.showMessageDialog(null, "The summation is " + sum,
15            "Example 3.3 Output", JOptionPane.INFORMATION_MESSAGE);
16
17          System.exit(0);
18      }
19   }
```

Review

The `for` loop (Lines 10–11) repeatedly adds the control variable `i` to the sum. This variable, which begins with 0.01, is incremented by 0.01 after each iteration. The loop terminates when `i` exceeds 1.0.

The `for` loop initial action can be any statement, but often it is used to initialize a control variable. From this example, you can see that a control variable can be a `float` type. In fact, it can be any data type.

You may have noticed that the answer is not precise. This is because computers use a fixed number of bits to represent floating-point numbers, and thus cannot represent some floating-point numbers exactly. If you change `float` in the program to `double`, you will see a slight improvement in precision because a double variable takes sixty-four bits, whereas a float variable takes thirty-two bits.

CAUTION

Always use semicolons rather than commas to separate the control elements in the `for` loop header. Using commas in the `for` loop header is a common mistake.

Do not change the value of the control variable inside the `for` loop body, even though it is perfectly legal to do so. Changing the value makes the program difficult to understand and could lead to subtle errors.

Example 3.4 Using Nested `for` Loops

Problem

Write a program that uses nested `for` loops to print a multiplication table. Nested loops consists of an outer loop and one or more inner loops. Each time the outer loop is repeated, the inner loops are reentered, their loop control parameters are reevaluated, and all required iterations are performed.

Solution

The following code gives the solution to the problem. The output of the program is shown in Figure 3.12.

continues

Example 3.4 continued

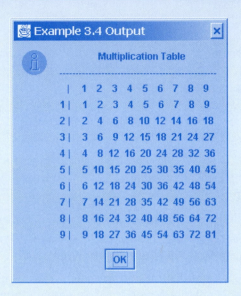

Figure 3.12   *Example 3.4 uses nested* for *loops to print a multiplication table.*

```
1    // TestMulTable.java: Display a multiplication table
2    import javax.swing.JOptionPane;
3
4    public class TestMulTable {
5      /** Main method */
6      public static void main(String[] args) {
7        // Display the table heading
8        String output = "                  Multiplication Table\n";
9        output += "—————————————————————————————-\n";
10
11       // Display the number title
12       output += "    ¦ ";
13       for (int j = 1; j <= 9; j++)
14         output += "    " + j;
15
16       output += "\n";
17
18       // Print table body
19       for (int i = 1; i <= 9; i++) {
20         output += i + " ¦ ";
21         for (int j = 1; j <= 9; j++) {
22           // Display the product and align properly
23           if (i * j < 10)
24             output += "    " + i * j;
25           else
26             output += "   " + i * j;
27         }
28         output += "\n";
29       }
30
31       // Display result
32       JOptionPane.showMessageDialog(null, output,
33         "Example 3.4 Output", JOptionPane.INFORMATION_MESSAGE);
34
35       System.exit(0);
36     }
37   }
```

Review

The program displays a title (Line 8) on the first line and dashes (-) (Line 9) on the second line in the output. The first `for` loop (Lines 13–14) displays the numbers 1 through 9 on the third line.

The next loop (Lines 19–29) is a nested `for` loop with the control variable `i` in the outer loop and `j` in the inner loop. For each `i`, the product `i * j` is displayed on a line in the inner loop, with `j` being 1, 2, 3, . . ., 9. The `if` statement in the inner loop (Lines 23–26) is used so that the product will be aligned properly. If the product is a single digit, it is displayed with an extra space before it.

3.4   Which Loop to Use?

The three forms of loop statements, `while`, `do-while`, and `for`, are expressively equivalent; that is, you can write a loop in any of these three forms. For example, a `while` loop

```
while (loop-continuation-condition) {
  // Loop body
}
```

can always be converted into the following `for` loop:

```
for ( ; loop-continuation-condition; ) {
  // Loop body
}
```

A `for` loop

```
for (initial-action; loop-continuation-condition;
     action-after-each-iteration) {
  // Loop body;
}
```

can generally be converted into the following `while` loop except in certain special cases (see Review Question 3.20 for one of them):

```
initial-action;
while (loop-continuation-condition) {
  // Loop body;
  action-after-each-iteration;
}
```

I recommend that you use the loop statement that is most intuitive and comfortable for you. In general, a `for` loop may be used if the number of repetitions is known, as, for example, when you need to print a message a hundred times. A `while` loop may be used if the number of repetitions is not known, as in the case of reading the numbers until the input is 0. A `do-while` loop can be used to replace a `while` loop if the loop body has to be executed before the continuation condition is tested.

CAUTION

Adding a semicolon at the end of the `for` clause before the loop body is a common mistake, as shown below:

```
for (int i = 0; i < 10; i++);  ◄─────── Logic error
{
    System.out.println("i is " + i);
}
```

Similarly, the following loop is also wrong:

```
int i = 0;
while (i < 10);  ◄─────── Logic error
{
    System.out.println("i is " + i);
    i++;
}
```

In both cases, the semicolon signifies the end of the loop prematurely. These errors often occur when you use the next-line block style.

In the case of the `do-while` loop, the semicolon is needed to end the loop.

```
int i = 0;
do {
    System.out.println("i is " + i);
    i++;
} while (i < 10);  ◄─────── Correct
```

3.5 Using the Keywords *break* and *continue*

Two statements, `break` and `continue`, can be used in loop statements to provide the loop with additional control.

- **break** immediately ends the innermost loop that contains it. It is generally used with an `if` statement.

- **continue** only ends the current iteration. Program control goes to the end of the loop body. This keyword is generally used with an `if` statement.

You have already used the keyword `break` in a `switch` statement. You can also use `break` and `continue` in any of the three kinds of loop statements.

Figures 3.13 and 3.14 illustrate the functions of `break` and `continue` in a loop statement.

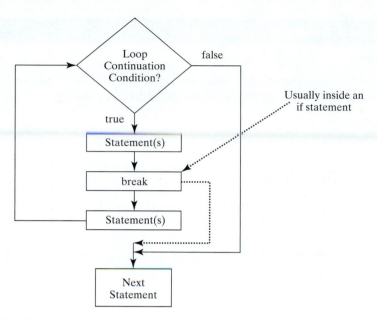

Figure 3.13   *The* break *statement forces its containing loop to exit.*

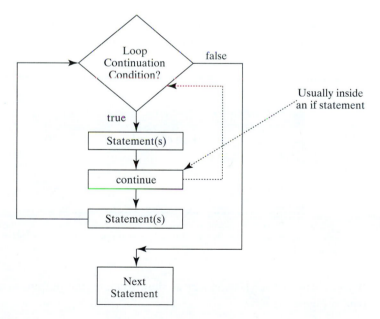

Figure 3.14   *The* continue *statement forces the current iteration of the loop to end.*

Example 3.5 Testing a break Statement

Problem

Write a program that demonstrates using the break keyword in a loop. You will see how a break statement affects the results of a program.

Solution

The following code gives the solution to the problem.

```
1    // TestBreak.java: Test the break keyword in the loop
2    public class TestBreak {
3      /** Main method */
4      public static void main(String[] args) {
5        int sum = 0;
6        int item = 0;
7
8        while (item < 5) {
9          item ++;
10         sum += item;
11         if (sum >= 6) break;
12       }
13
14       System.out.println("The sum is " + sum);
15     }
16   }
```

Review

Without the if statement (Line 11), this program calculates the sum of the numbers from 1 to 5. But with the if statement, the loop terminates when the sum becomes greater than or equal to 6. The output of the program is shown in Figure 3.15.

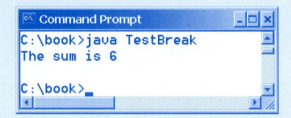

Figure 3.15   *The* break *statement in the* TestBreak *program forces the* while *loop to exit when* sum *is greater than 6.*

If you changed the if statement as shown below, the output would resemble that in Figure 3.16.

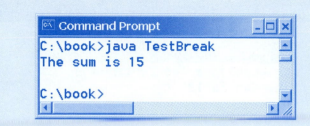

Figure 3.16 *The* break *statement is not executed in the modified* TestBreak *program because* sum == 5 *cannot be* true.

```
if (sum == 5) break;
```

In this case, the if condition will never be true. Therefore, the break statement will never be executed.

Example 3.6 Using a continue Statement

Problem

Write a program that demonstrates using the continue keyword in a loop. You will see the effect of a continue statement on a program.

Solution

The following code gives the solution to the problem.

```
1    // TestContinue.java: Test the continue keyword
2    public class TestContinue {
3      /** Main method */
4      public static void main(String[] args) {
5        int sum = 0;
6        int item = 0;
7
8        while (item < 5) {
9          item++;
10         if (item == 2) continue;
11         sum += item;
12       }
13
14       System.out.println("The sum is " + sum);
15     }
16   }
```

Review

With the if statement in the program (Line 10), the continue statement is executed when item becomes 2. The continue statement ends the current iteration so that the rest of the statement in the loop body is not executed; therefore, item is not added to sum when it is 2. The output of the program is shown in Figure 3.17.

continues

Example 3.6 continued

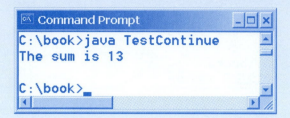

Figure 3.17   *The* `continue` *statement in the* `TestContinue` *program forces the current iteration to end when* `item` *equals 2.*

Without the `if` statement in the program, the output would look like Figure 3.18.

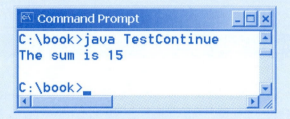

Figure 3.18   *Since the modified* `TestContinue` *program has no* `continue` *statement, every item is added to* `sum`*.*

Without the `if` statement, all of the items are added to `sum`, including when `item` is 2. Therefore, the result is 15, which is two more than it was with the `if` statement.

NOTE

The `continue` statement is always inside a loop. In the `while` and `do-while` loops, the `loop-continuation-condition` is evaluated immediately after the `continue` statement. In the `for` loop, the `action-after-each-iteration` is performed, then the `loop-continuation-condition` is evaluated, immediately after the `continue` statement. See Review Question 3.20.

TIP

You can always write a program without using `break` or `continue` in a loop. See Review Question 3.21. In general, it is appropriate to use `break` and `continue` if their use simplifies coding and makes programs easier to read.

3.5.1   Statement Labels and Breaking with Labels

Every statement in Java can have an optional label as an identifier. Labels are often used with break and continue statements. You can use a break statement with a label to break out of the labeled statement, and a continue statement with a label to break out of the current iteration of the labeled loop statement.

The break statement given below, for example, breaks out of the outer loop and transfers control to the statement immediately following the outer loop.

```
outer:
  for (int i = 1; i < 10; i++) {
  inner:
    for (int j = 1; j < 10; j++) {
      if (i * j > 50)
        break outer;

      System.out.println(i * j);
    }
  }
```

If you replace break outer with break in the preceding statement, the break statement would break out of the inner loop and continue to stay inside the outer loop.

The following continue statement breaks out of the inner loop and starts a new iteration of the outer loop if i < 10 is true after i is incremented by 1.

```
outer:
  for (int i = 1; i < 10; i++) {
  inner:
    for (int j = 1; j < 10; j++) {
      if (i * j > 50)
        continue outer;

      System.out.println(i * j);
    }
  }
```

If you replace continue outer with continue in the preceding statement, the continue statement would break out of the current iteration of the inner loop and continue the next iteration of the inner loop if j < 10 is true after j is incremented by 1.

NOTE

Some programming languages have a goto statement, but labeled break statements and labeled continue statements in Java are completely different from goto statements. The goto label statement would transfer the control to where the label is in the program and execute the labeled statement.

3.6   Case Studies

Control statements are fundamental in programming. The ability to write control statements is essential in learning Java programming. This section presents three additional examples of the use of selection statements and loops to solve problems.

Example 3.7 Finding the Sales Amount

Problem

You have just started a sales job in a department store. Your pay consists of a base salary and a commission. The base salary is $5,000. The scheme shown below is used to determine the commission rate.

Sales Amount	Commission Rate
$0.01–$5,000	8 percent
$5,000.01–$10,000	10 percent
$10,000.01 and above	12 percent

Your goal is to earn $30,000 in a year. Write a program that will find out the minimum amount of sales you have to generate in order to make $30,000.

Solution

Since your base salary is $5,000, you have to make $25,000 in commissions to earn $30,000 in a year. What is the sales amount for a $25,000 commission? If you know the sales amount, the commission can be computed as follows:

```
if (salesAmount >= 10000.01)
  commission =
    5000 * 0.08 + 5000 * 0.1 + (salesAmount - 10000) * 0.12;
else if (salesAmount >= 5000.01)
  commission = 5000 * 0.08 + (salesAmount - 5000) * 0.10;
else
  commission = salesAmount * 0.08;
```

This suggests that you can try to find the salesAmount to match a given commission through incremental approximation. For salesAmount of $0.01 (one cent), find commission. If commission is less than $25,000, increment salesAmount by 0.01 and find commission again. If commission is less than $25,000, repeat the process until the commission is greater than $25,000. This is a tedious job for humans, but it is exactly what a computer is good for. You can write a loop and let a computer execute it painlessly.

Here is the algorithm for the problem:

```
Set COMMISSION_SOUGHT as a constant;
Set an initial salesAmount;

do {
  Increase salesAmount by 1 cent;
  Compute the commission from the current salesAmount;
} while (commission < COMMISSION_SOUGHT);
```

The complete program is given below, and a sample run of the program is shown in Figure 3.19.

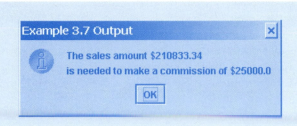

Figure 3.19 *The program finds the sales amount for the given commission.*

```java
1    // FindSalesAmount.java: Find the sales amount to get the desired
2    // commission
3    import javax.swing.JOptionPane;
4
5    public class FindSalesAmount {
6      /** Main method */
7      public static void main(String[] args) {
8        // The commission sought
9        final double COMMISSION_SOUGHT = 25000;
10       final double INITIAL_SALES_AMOUNT = 0.01;
11       double commission = 0;
12       double salesAmount = INITIAL_SALES_AMOUNT;
13
14       do {
15         // Increase salesAmount by 1 cent
16         salesAmount += 0.01;
17
18         // Compute the commission from the current salesAmount;
19         if (salesAmount >= 10000.01)
20           commission =
21             5000 * 0.08 + 5000 * 0.1 + (salesAmount - 10000) * 0.12;
22         else if (salesAmount >= 5000.01)
23           commission = 5000 * 0.08 + (salesAmount - 5000) * 0.10;
24         else
25           commission = salesAmount * 0.08;
26       } while (commission < COMMISSION_SOUGHT);
27
28       // Display the sales amount
29       String output =
30         "The sales amount $" + (int)(salesAmount * 100) / 100.0 +
31         "\nis needed to make a commission of $" + COMMISSION_SOUGHT;
32       JOptionPane.showMessageDialog(null, output,
33         "Example 3.7 Output", JOptionPane.INFORMATION_MESSAGE);
34
35       System.exit(0);
36     }
37   }
```

Review

The do-while loop (Lines 14–26) is used to repeatedly compute commission for an incremental salesAmount. The loop terminates when commission is greater than or equal to a constant COMMISSION_SOUGHT.

In Exercise 3.11, you will rewrite this program to let the user enter COMMISSION_SOUGHT dynamically from an input dialog.

You can improve the performance of this program by estimating a higher INITIAL_SALES_AMOUNT (e.g., 25000).

continues

Example 3.7 continued

You can further improve the performance of this program by using the *binary search* approach. The binary search approach is introduced in Chapter 5, "Arrays." A rewrite of this program using a binary search is proposed in Exercise 5.12.

Tip

This example uses constants `COMMISSION_SOUGHT` and `INITIAL_SALES_AMOUNT`. Using constants makes programs easy to read and maintain.

Example 3.8 Displaying a Pyramid of Numbers

Problem

Write a program that uses nested loops to print the following output:

```
        1
       212
      32123
     4321234
    543212345
```

Line 3 ——————→

Solution

Your program prints five lines. Each line has three parts. The first part comprises the spaces before the numbers; the second part, the leading numbers, such as 3 2 1 on Line 3; and the last part, the ending numbers, such as 2 3 on Line 3.

You can use an outer loop to control the lines. At the nᵗʰ row, there are 5 - n leading spaces, the leading numbers are n, n-1, . . ., 1, and the ending numbers are 2, . . ., n. You can use three separate inner loops to print each part.

Here is the algorithm for the problem:

```
Set the number of lines to be printed as a constant NUM_OF_LINES;

for (int row = 1; row <= NUM_OF_LINES; row++) {
  Print leading spaces;
  Print leading numbers;
  Print ending numbers;
  Start a new line;
}
```

The complete program is given below, and a sample run of the program is shown in Figure 3.20.

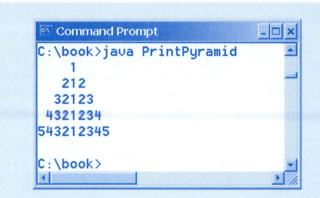

Figure 3.20   *The program uses nested loops to print numbers in a triangular pattern.*

```
1      // PrintPyramid.java: Print a pyramid of numbers
2      public class PrintPyramid {
3        /** Main method */
4        public static void main(String[] args) {
5          final int NUM_OF_LINES = 5;
6
7          for (int row = 1; row <= NUM_OF_LINES; row++) {
8            // Print leading spaces
9            for (int column = 1; column <= NUM_OF_LINES - row; column++)
10             System.out.print(" ");
11
12           // Print leading numbers
13           for (int num = row; num >= 1; num--)
14             System.out.print(num);
15
16           // Print ending numbers
17           for (int num = 2; num <= row; num++)
18             System.out.print(num);
19
20           // Start a new line
21           System.out.println();
22         }
23       }
24     }
```

Review

The program uses the print method (Lines 10, 14, and 18) to display a string to the console. This method is identical to the println method except that println moves the cursor to the next line after displaying the string, but print does not advance the cursor to the next line when completed.

Printing patterns like this one and the ones in Exercises 3.7 and 3.8 is my favorite exercise for practicing loop control statements. The key is to understand the pattern and to describe it using loop control variables.

The last line in the outer loop (Line 21), System.out.println(), does not have any argument in the method. This call moves the cursor to the next line.

Example 3.9 Displaying Prime Numbers

Problem

Write a program that displays the first fifty prime numbers in five lines, each of which contains ten numbers. An integer greater than 1 is *prime* if its only positive divisor is 1 or itself. For example, 2, 3, 5, and 7 are prime numbers, but 4, 6, 8, and 9 are not.

Solution

The problem can be broken into the following tasks:

- For number = 2, 3, 4, 5, 6, . . ., test whether the number is prime.

- Determine whether a given number is prime.

- Count the prime numbers.

- Print each prime number, and print ten numbers per line.

Obviously, you need to write a loop and repeatedly test whether a new number is prime. If the number is prime, increase the count by 1. The count is 1 initially. When the count exceeds 50, the loop terminates.

Here is the algorithm for the problem:

```
Set the number of prime numbers to be printed as
  a constant NUM_OF_PRIMES;
Use count to track the number of prime numbers and
  set an initial count to 1;
Set an initial number to 2;

while (count <= NUM_OF_PRIMES) {
  Test if number is prime;

  if number is prime {
    Print the prime number and increase the count;
  }

  Increment number by 1;
}
```

To test whether a number is prime, check if the number is divisible by 2, 3, 4, up to number/2. If a divisor is found, the number is not a prime. The algorithm can be described as follows:

```
Use a boolean variable isPrime to denote whether
  the number is prime; Set isPrime to true initially;

for (int divisor = 2; divisor <= number / 2; divisor++) {
  if (number % divisor == 0) {
    Set isPrime to false
    Exit the loop;
  }
}
```

The program is given as shown below. Figure 3.21 contains a sample run of the program.

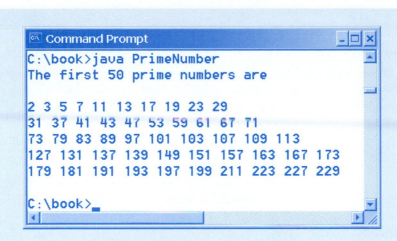

```
Command Prompt                                    _ □ x
C:\book>java PrimeNumber
The first 50 prime numbers are

2 3 5 7 11 13 17 19 23 29
31 37 41 43 47 53 59 61 67 71
73 79 83 89 97 101 103 107 109 113
127 131 137 139 149 151 157 163 167 173
179 181 191 193 197 199 211 223 227 229

C:\book>_
```

Figure 3.21 *The program displays the first fifty prime numbers.*

```
1    // PrimeNumber.java: Print first 50 prime numbers
2    public class PrimeNumber {
3      /** Main method */
4      public static void main(String[] args) {
5        final int NUM_OF_PRIMES = 50;
6        int count = 1; // Count the number of prime numbers
7        int number = 2; // A number to be tested for primeness
8        boolean isPrime = true;  // Is the current number prime?
9
10       System.out.println("The first 50 prime numbers are \n");
11
12       // Repeatedly find prime numbers
13       while (count <= NUM_OF_PRIMES) {
14         // Assume the number is prime
15         isPrime = true;
16
17         // Test if number is prime
18         for (int divisor = 2; divisor <= number / 2; divisor++) {
19           //If true, the number is not prime
20           if (number % divisor == 0) {
21             // Set isPrime to false, if the number is not prime
22             isPrime = false;
23             break;  // Exit the for loop
24           }
25         }
26
27         // Print the prime number and increase the count
28         if (isPrime) {
29           if (count % 10 == 0) {
30             // Print the number and advance to the new line
31             System.out.println(number);
32           }
33           else
34             System.out.print(number + " ");
35
36           count++;  // Increase the count
37         }
38
39         // Check if the next number is prime
40         number++;
41       }
42     }
43   }
```

continues

Example 3.9 continued

Review

This is a complex example for novice programmers. The key to developing a programmatic solution to this problem, and to many other problems, is to break it into subproblems and develop solutions for each of them. Do not attempt to develop a complete solution in the first trial. Instead, begin by writing the code to determine whether a given number is prime, then expand the program to test whether other numbers are prime in a loop.

To determine whether a number is prime, check whether it is divisible by a number between 2 and number/2 inclusive. If so, it is not a prime number; otherwise, it is a prime number. For a prime number, display it. If the count is divisible by 10, advance to a new line. The program ends when the count becomes 51.

▮▮ NOTE

The program uses the `break` statement in Line 23 to exit the `for` loop as soon as the number is found to be a nonprime. You can rewrite the loop without using the `break` statement. However, using the `break` statement here makes this program simpler and easier to read.

Chapter Summary

Program control specifies the order in which statements are executed in a program. In this chapter, you learned about two types of control statements: selection control and loop control.

Selection statements are used for building selection steps into programs. You learned several forms of selection statements: `if` statements, `if . . . else` statements, nested `if` statements, `switch` statements, and conditional expressions.

The various `if` statements all make control decisions based on a Boolean expression. Based on the `true` or `false` evaluation of that expression, these statements take one or two possible courses. The `switch` statement makes control decisions based on a switch variable of type `char`, `byte`, `short`, `int`, or `boolean`.

You learned three types of repetition statements: the `while` loop, the `do-while` loop, and the `for` loop. In designing loops, you need to consider both the loop control structure and the loop body.

The `while` loop checks the `loop-continuation-condition` first. If the condition is `true`, the loop body is executed; if it is `false`, the loop terminates. The `do-while` loop is similar to the `while` loop, except that the `do-while` loop executes the loop body first and then checks the `loop-continuation-condition` to decide whether to continue or to terminate.

Since the `while` loop and the `do-while` loop contain the `loop-continuation-condition`, which is dependent on the loop body, the number of repetitions is determined by the loop body. The `while` loop and the `do-while` loop are often used when the number of repetitions is unspecified.

The `for` loop is generally used to execute a loop body for a predictable number of times; this number is not determined by the loop body. The loop control has three parts. The first part is an initial action that often initializes a control variable. The second part, the `loop-continuation-condition`, determines whether the loop body is to be executed. The third part is executed after each iteration and is often used to adjust the control variable. Usually, the loop control variables are initialized and changed in the control structure.

You learned the `break` and `continue` keywords. The `break` keyword immediately ends the innermost loop, which contains the break. The `continue` keyword only ends the current iteration.

Review Questions

3.1 Show the output, if any, of the following code:

```
x = 2;
y = 3;

if (x > 2)
  if (y > 2) {
    int z = x + y;
    System.out.println("z is " + z);
  }
else
  System.out.println("x is " + x);
```

3.2 Show the output, if any, of the following code:

```
x = 3;
y = 2;

if (x > 2) {
  if (y > 2) {
    int z = x + y;
    System.out.println("z is " + z);
  }
}
else
  System.out.println("x is " + x);
```

3.3 Which of the following statements are equivalent?

a.

```
if (i > 0) if (j > 0) x = 0; else if (k > 0) y = 0; else z = 0;
```

b.

```
if (i > 0) {
  if (j > 0)
    x = 0;
  else if (k > 0)
    y = 0;
}
else
  z = 0;
```

c.

```
if (i > 0)
  if (j > 0)
    x = 0;
  else if (k > 0)
    y = 0;
  else
    z = 0;
```

d.

```
if (i > 0)
  if (j > 0)
    x = 0;
  else if (k > 0)
    y = 0;
else
  z = 0;
```

3.4 Write a statement to determine whether an integer i is even or odd.

3.5 What data types are required for a switch variable? If the keyword break is not used after a case is processed, what is the next statement to be executed? Can you convert a switch statement to an equivalent if statement, or vice versa? What are the advantages of using a switch statement?

3.6 What is y after the following switch statement is executed?

```
x = 3;
switch (x + 3) {
  case 6:   y = 1;
  default: y += 1;
}
```

3.7 Use a switch statement to rewrite the following if statement:

```
if (a == 1)
  x += 5;
else if (a == 2)
  x += 10;
else if (a == 3)
  x += 16;
else if (a == 4)
  x += 34;
```

3.8 What is y after the following statement is executed?

```
x = 0;
y = (x > 0) ? 1 : -1;
```

3.9 How many times is the following loop body repeated? What is the printout of the loop?

```
int i = 1;
while (i < 10)
  if ((i++) % 2 == 0)
    System.out.println(i);
```

3.10 What are the differences between a while loop and a do-while loop?

3.11 Do the following two statements result in the same value in sum?

```
for (int i = 0; i < 10; ++i) {
  sum += i;
}

for (int i = 0; i < 10; i++) {
  sum += i;
}
```

3.12 What are the three parts of a `for` loop control? Write a `for` loop that will print the numbers from 1 to 100.

3.13 What does the following statement do?

```
for ( ; ; ) {
  do something;
}
```

3.14 If a variable is declared in the `for` loop control, can it be used after the loop exits?

3.15 Can you convert a `for` loop to a `while` loop? List the advantages of using `for` loops.

3.16 Convert the following `for` loop statement to a `while` loop and to a `do-while` loop:

```
long sum = 0;
for (int i = 0; i <= 1000; i++)
  sum = sum + i;
```

3.17 What is the keyword `break` for? Will the following program terminate? If so, give the output.

```
int balance = 1000;
while (true) {
  if (balance < 9)
    break;
  balance = balance - 9;
}

System.out.println("Balance is " + balance);
```

3.18 What is the keyword `continue` for? Will the following program terminate? If so, give the output.

```
int balance = 1000;
while (true) {
  if (balance < 9)
    continue;
  balance = balance - 9;
}

System.out.println("Balance is " + balance);
```

3.19 Can you always convert a `while` loop into a `for` loop? Convert the following `while` loop into a `for` loop.

```
int i = 1;
int sum = 0;
while (sum < 10000) {
  sum = sum + i;
  i++;
}
```

3.20 The following `for` loop on the left is converted into the `while` loop on the right. What is wrong? Correct it.

```
for (int i = 0; i < 4; i++) {
  if (i % 3 == 0) continue;
    sum += i;
}
```

```
int i = 0;

while (i < 4) {
  if (i % 3 == 0) continue;
    sum += i;
    i++;
}
```

3.21 Rewrite the programs `TestBreak` and `TestContinue` without using `break` and `continue` (see Examples 3.5 and 3.6).

3.22 After the `break  outer` statement is executed in the following loop, which statement is executed?

```
outer:
  for (int i = 1; i < 10; i++) {
  inner:
    for (int j = 1; j < 10; j++) {
      if (i * j > 50)
        break outer;

      System.out.println(i * j);
    }
  }
next:
```

a. The statement labeled inner.
b. The statement labeled outer.
c. The statement labeled next.
d. None of the above.

3.23 After the `continue  outer` statement is executed in the following loop, which statement is executed?

```
outer:
  for (int i = 1; i < 10; i++) {
  inner:
    for (int j = 1; j < 10; j++) {
      if (i * j > 50)
        continue outer;

      System.out.println(i * j);
    }
  }
next:
```

a. The control is in the outer loop, and the next iteration of the outer loop is executed.
b. The control is in the inner loop, and the next iteration of the inner is loop executed.
c. The statement labeled next.
d. None of the above.

3.24 Identify and fix the errors in the following code:

```java
public class Test {
  public void main(String[] args) {
    for (int i = 0; i < 10; i++);
      sum += i;
    if (i < j);
      System.out.println(i)
    else
      System.out.println(j);

    while (j < 10);
    {
      j++;
    };

    do {
      j++;
    } while (j < 10)
  }
}
```

3.25 What is wrong with the following program?

```java
public class ShowErrors {
  public static void main(String[] args) {
    int i;
    int j = 5;

    if (j > 3)
      System.out.println(i + 4);
  }
}
```

3.26 What is wrong with the following program?

```java
public class ShowErrors {
  public static void main(String[] args) {
    for (int i = 0; i < 10; i++);
      System.out.println(i + 4);
  }
}
```

3.27 Show the output of the following programs:

a.

```java
public class Test {
  /** Main method */
  public static void main(String[] args) {
    int i = 0;
    while (i < 5) {
      for (int j = i; j > 1; j--)
        System.out.print(j + " ");
      System.out.println("****");
      i++;
    }
  }
}
```

b.

```java
public class Test {
  public static void main(String[] args) {
    int i = 5;

    while (i >= 1) {
      int num = 1;
      for (int j = 1; j <= i; j++) {
        System.out.print(num + "xxx");
        num *= 2;
      }

      System.out.println();
      i--;
    }
  }
}
```

c.

```java
public class Test {
  public static void main(String[] args) {
    int i = 1;

    do {
      int num = 1;

      for (int j = 1; j <= i; j++) {
        System.out.print(num + "G");
        num += 2;
      }

      System.out.println();
      i++;
    } while (i <= 5);
  }
}
```

3.28 Reformat the following programs according to the programming style and documentation guidelines proposed in Section 2.15. Use the next-line brace style.

a.

```java
public class Test {
  public static void main(String[] args) {
    int i = 0;
    if (i>0)
    i++;
    else
    i--;

    char grade;

    if (i >= 90)
     grade = 'A';
    else
      if (i >= 80)
        grade = 'B';

  }
}
```

b.

```
public class Test {
  public static void main(String[] args) {
  for (int i = 0; i<10; i++)
    if (i>0)
      i++;
    else
      i--;
  }
}
```

Programming Exercises

3.1 Modify Example 2.4, "Computing Changes." Display the non-zero denominations only. Display singular words for single units like 1 dollar and 1 penny, and display plural words for more than one unit like 2 dollars and 3 pennies. (Use 23.67 to test your program.)

3.2 Write a program that will sort three integers. The integers are entered from the input dialogs and stored in variables num1, num2, and num3, respectively. The program sorts the numbers so that num1 <= num2 <= num3.

3.3 Write a program that will compute sales commissions using the same scheme as in Example 3.7. Your program reads the sales amount from an input dialog and displays the result on the console.

3.4 Write a program that will read an unspecified number of integers and determine how many positive and negative values have been read. Your program ends when the input is 0.

3.5 Write a program that will read integers and find the total and average of the input values, not counting zeros. Your program ends with the input 0. Display the average as a floating-point number. (For example, if you entered 1, 2, and 0, the average should be 1.5.)

3.6 Use a while loop to find the smallest integer n such that n^2 is greater than 12000.

3.7 Use nested loops that will print the following patterns in separate programs:

```
    Pattern I      Pattern II      Pattern III      Pattern IV

    1              1 2 3 4 5 6                1      1 2 3 4 5 6
    1 2            1 2 3 4 5               2 1        1 2 3 4 5
    1 2 3          1 2 3 4              3 2 1          1 2 3 4
    1 2 3 4        1 2 3             4 3 2 1             1 2 3
    1 2 3 4 5      1 2             5 4 3 2 1               1 2
    1 2 3 4 5 6    1            6 5 4 3 2 1                  1
```

3.8 Write a nested `for` loop that will print the following output:

```
                        1
                  1     2     1
            1     2     4     2     1
      1     2     4     8     4     2     1
   1  2     4     8    16     8     4     2     1
1  2  4     8    16    32    16     8     4     2     1
1  2  4     8    16    32    64    32    16     8     4     2     1
1  2  4     8    16    32    64   128    64    32    16     8     4     2     1
```

■ HINT

Here is the pseudocode solution:

```
for the row from 0 to 7 {
  Pad leading blanks in a row using a loop like this:
  for the column from 1 to 7-row
    System.out.print("    ");

  Print left half of the row for numbers 1, 2, 4, up to
  2^row using a look like this:
  for the column from 0 to row
    System.out.print("    " + (int)Math.pow(2, column));

  Print the right half of the row for numbers
  2^row-1, 2^row-2, ..., 1 using a loop like this:
  for (int column = row - 1; column >= 0; col--)
    System.out.print("    " + (int)Math.pow(2, column));

  Start a new line
  System.out.println();
}
```

You need to figure out how many spaces to print before the number. The number of spaces to print before a number is dependent on the number. If a number is a single digit, print four spaces. If a number has two digits, print three spaces. If a number has three digits, print two spaces.

The `Math.pow()` method was introduced in Example 2.3. Can you write this program without using it?

3.9 Modify Example 3.9 to print all the prime numbers between 2 and 10,000. Display eight prime numbers per line.

3.10 Write a program that reads an integer and displays all its smallest factors. For example, if the input integer is 120, the output should be as follows: 2, 2, 2, 3, 5.

3.11 Rewrite Example 3.7 as follows:

■ Use a `for` loop instead of a `while` loop.

■ Let the user enter `COMMISSION_SOUGHT` from the keyboard instead of fixing it as a constant.

3.12 You can approximate π by using the following series:

```
p = 4*(1-1/3+1/5-1/7+1/9-1/11+1/13+...)
```

Write a program that will find out how many terms of this series you need to use before you first get 3.14159.

3.13 A *cancellation error* occurs when you are manipulating a very large number with a very small number. The large number may cancel out the smaller number. For example, the result of 100000000.0 + 0.000000001 is equal to 100000000.0. To avoid cancellation errors and obtain more accurate results, carefully select the order of computation. For example, in computing the following series, you will obtain more accurate results by computing from right to left:

$$1 + 1/2 + 1/3 + \ldots + 1/n$$

Write a program that compares the results of the summation of the preceding series, computing from left to right and from right to left with n = 50000.

3.14 Write a program that lets the user enter the loan amount and loan period in number of years and displays the monthly and total payments for each interest rate starting from 5% to 8%, with an increment of 1/8. Suppose you enter the loan amount 10000 for five years, display a table as follows:

```
Loan Amount: 10000
Number of Years: 5
Interest Rate        Monthly Payment        Total Payment
5%                   188.71                 11322.74
5.125%               189.28                 11357.13
5.25%                189.85                 11391.59
...
7.75%                201.56                 12094.17
7.85%                202.16                 12129.97
8.0%                 202.76                 12165.83
```

3.15 The monthly payment for a given loan pays the principal and the interest. The monthly interest is computed by multiplying the monthly interest rate and the balance (the remaining principal). The principal paid for the month is therefore the monthly payment minus the monthly interest. Write a program that lets the user enter the loan amount, number of years, and interest rate, and displays the amortization schedule for the loan. Suppose you enter the loan amount 10000 for one year with an interest rate of 7%, display a table as follows:

```
Loan Amount: 10000
Number of Years: 1
Interest Rate: 7%

Monthly Payment: 865.26
Total Payment: 10383.21

Payment#        Interest        Principal        Balance
1               58.33           806.93           9193.07
2               53.62           811.64           8381.43
3               48.89           816.37           7565.06
...
10              14.96           850.3            1715.53
11              10.0            855.26           860.27
12              5.01            860.25           0.01
```

NOTE

The balance after the last payment may not be zero. If so, the last payment should be the normal monthly payment plus the final balance.

HINT

Write a loop to print the table. Since monthly payment is the same for each month, it should be computed before the loop. The balance is initially the loan amount. For each iteration in the loop, compute the interest and principal, and update the balance. The loop may look like this:

```
for (i = 1; i <= numOfYears * 12; i++) {
   interest = (int)(monthlyInterestRate * balance * 100) / 100.0;
   principal = (int)((monthlyPayment - interest) * 100) / 100.0;
   balance = (int)((balance - principal) * 100) / 100.0;
   System.out.println(i + "\t\t" + interest
     + "\t\t" + principal + "\t\t" + balance);
}
```

METHODS

Objectives

- To learn the benefits of methods.
- To create and invoke methods.
- To understand the role of arguments in a method.
- To learn to pass parameters to a method.
- To use method overloading and know ambiguous overloading.
- To understand the scope of local variables.
- To learn the concept of method abstraction.
- To become familiar with the Math class.
- To use the divide-and-conquer approach in developing programs.
- To become familiar with recursion. (Optional)

4.1   Introduction

In the preceding chapters, you learned about such methods as `System.out.println`, `JOptionPane.showMessageDialog`, `JOptionPane.showInputDialog`, `Integer.parseInt`, `Double.parseDouble`, and `Math.pow`. A method is a collection of statements that are grouped together to perform an operation. When you call the `System.out.println` method, for example, the system actually executes several statements in order to display a message on the console.

This chapter introduces several topics that involve, or are related to, methods. You will learn how to create your own methods with or without return values, invoke a method with or without parameters, overload methods using the same names, write a recursive method that invokes itself, and apply method abstraction in the program design.

4.2   Creating a Method

In general, a method has the following structure:

```
modifier returnValueType methodName(list of parameters) {
   // Method body;
}
```

Let's take a look at a method created to find which of two integers is bigger. This method, named `max`, has two `int` parameters, `num1` and `num2`, the larger of which is returned by the method. Figure 4.1 illustrates the components of this method.

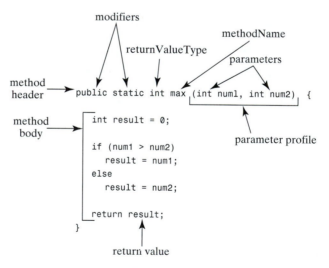

Figure 4.1   *A method declaration consists of a method header and a method body.*

The method header specifies the *modifiers, return value type, method name,* and *parameters* of the method. The modifier, which is optional, tells the compiler how to call the method. The static modifier is used for all the methods in this chapter. The reason for using it will be discussed in Chapter 6, "Objects and Classes."

A method may return a value. The `returnValueType` is the data type of the value the method returns. If the method does not return a value, the `returnValueType` is the keyword `void`. For example, the `returnValueType` in the `main` method is `void`. All methods except constructors require `returnValueType`. Constructors are introduced in Chapter 6.

The *parameter profile* refers to the type, order, and number of the parameters of a method. The method name and the parameter profiles together constitute the *method signature*. Parameters are optional; that is, a method may contain no parameters.

The parameters defined in the method header are known as *formal parameters*. When a method is invoked, its formal parameters are replaced by variables or data, which are referred to as *actual parameters*.

The method body contains a collection of statements that define what the method does. The method body of the `max` method uses an `if` statement to determine which number is larger and return the value of that number. A return statement using the keyword `return` is *required* for a nonvoid method to return a result. The method terminates when a return statement is executed.

NOTE

In certain other languages, methods are referred to as *procedures* and *functions*. A method with a nonvoid return value type is called a *function*; a method with a `void` return value type is called a *procedure*.

NOTE

A return statement can also be used in a void method for terminating the method and returning to the method's caller. This is useful for circumventing the normal flow of control in a method. See Review Question 4.3.

CAUTION

You need to declare a separate data type for each parameter. For instance, `int num1, num2` should be replaced by `int num1, int num2`.

4.3   Calling a Method

In creating a method, you give a definition of what the method is to do. To use a method, you have to *call* or *invoke* it. There are two ways to call a method; the choice is based on whether the method returns a value or not.

If the method returns a value, a call to the method is usually treated as a value. For example,

```
int larger = max(3, 4);
```

calls max(3, 4) and assigns the result of the method to the variable larger. Another example of a call that is treated as a value is

```
System.out.println(max(3, 4));
```

which prints the return value of the method call max(3, 4).

If the method returns void, a call to the method must be a statement. For example, the method println returns void. The following call is a statement:

```
System.out.println("Welcome to Java!");
```

NOTE

A method with a nonvoid return value type can also be invoked as a statement in Java. In this case, the caller simply ignores the return value. In the majority of cases, a call to a method with return value is treated as a value. In some cases, however, the caller is not interested in the return value. For example, many methods in database applications return a Boolean value to indicate whether the operation is successful. You can choose to ignore the return value if you know the operation will always succeed. I recommend, though, that you always treat a call to a method with return value as a value in order to avoid programming errors.

When a program calls a method, program control is transferred to the called method. A called method returns control to the caller when its return statement is executed or when its method-ending closing brace is reached.

The example shown below gives the complete program that is used to test the max method.

Example 4.1 Testing the max Method

Problem

Write a program that demonstrates how to create and invoke the max method.

Solution

The following code gives the solution to the problem. The output of the program is shown in Figure 4.2.

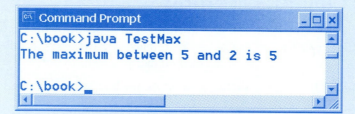

Figure 4.2   *The program invokes* max(i, j) *in order to get the maximum value between* i *and* j.

```
1    // TestMax.java: demonstrate using the max method
2    public class TestMax {
3      /** Main method */
4      public static void main(String[] args) {
5        int i = 5;
6        int j = 2;
7        int k = max(i, j);
8        System.out.println("The maximum between " + i +
9          " and " + j + " is " + k);
10     }
11
12     /** Return the max between two numbers */
13     public static int max(int num1, int num2) {
14       int result;
15
16       if (num1 > num2)
17         result = num1;
18       else
19         result = num2;
20
21       return result;
22     }
23   }
```

Review

This program contains the main method and the max method. The main method is just like any other method except that it is invoked by the Java interpreter.

The main method's header is always the same, like the one in this example, with the modifiers public and static, return value type void, method name main, and a parameter of the String[] type. String[] indicates that the parameter is an array of String, a subject addressed in Chapter 5, "Arrays."

The statements in main may invoke other methods that are defined in the class that contains the main method or in other classes. In this example, the main method invokes max(i, j), which is defined in the same class with the main method.

When the max method is invoked (Line 7), variable i's value 5 is passed to num1, and variable j's value 2 is passed to num2 in the max method. The flow of control transfers to the max method. The max method is executed. When the return statement in the max method is executed, the max method returns the control to its caller (in this case the caller is the main method). This process is illustrated in Figure 4.3.

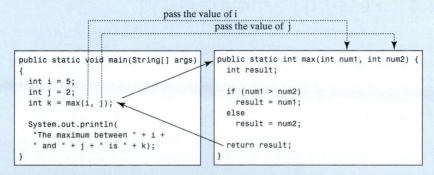

Figure 4.3   *When the* max *method is invoked, the flow of control transfers to the* max *method. Once the* max *method is finished, it returns the control back to the caller.*

continues

Example 4.1 continued

The variables defined in the `main` method are `i`, `j`, and `k`. The variables defined in the `max` method are `num1`, `num2`, and `result`. The variables `num1` and `num2` are defined in the method signature and are parameters of the method. Their values are passed through method invocation. Figure 4.4 illustrates the variables in the methods.

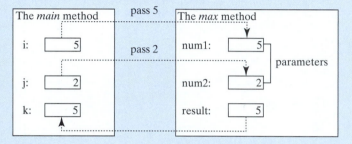

Figure 4.4 *When the* `max` *method is invoked, the flow of control transfers to the* `max` *method. Once the* `max` *method is finished, it returns the control back to the caller.*

■ **CAUTION**

A `return` statement is required for a nonvoid method. The method shown below is logically correct, but it has a compilation error because the Java compiler thinks it possible that this method does not return any value.

```
public static int xMethod(int n) {
   if (n > 0) return 1;
   else if (n == 0) return 0;
   else if (n < 0) return -1;
}
```

To fix this problem, delete `if (n < 0)` in the code, so that the compiler will see a `return` statement to be reached regardless of how the `if` statement is evaluated.

4.4 Passing Parameters

The power of a method is its ability to work with parameters. You can use `println` to print any message and `max` to find the maximum between any two `int` values. When calling a method, you need to provide actual parameters, which must be given in the same order as their respective formal parameters in the method specification. This is known as *parameter order association*. For example, the following method prints a message n times:

```
public static void nPrintln(String message, int n) {
   for (int i = 0; i < n;  i++)
      System.out.println(message);
}
```

You can use nPrintln("Hello", 3) to print "Hello" three times. The nPrintln("Hello", 3) statement passes the actual string parameter, "Hello", to the formal parameter, message; passes 3 to n; and prints "Hello" three times. However, the statement nPrintln(3, "Hello") would be wrong. The data type of 3 does not match the data type for the first formal parameter, message, nor does the second parameter, "Hello", match the second formal parameter, n.

CAUTION

The actual parameters must match the formal parameters in *order*, *number*, and *compatible type*, as defined in the method signature. Compatible type means that you can pass an actual parameter to a formal parameter without explicit casting.

4.4.1   Pass by Value

When you invoke a method with parameters, a copy of the value of the actual parameter is passed to the method. This is referred to as *pass by value*. The actual variable outside the method is not affected, regardless of the changes made to the formal parameter inside the method. Let's examine an interesting scenario in the following example, in which the formal parameters are changed in the method but the actual parameters are not affected.

The program given below shows the effect of pass by value.

Example 4.2 Testing Pass by Value

Problem

Write a program that demonstrates the effect of passing by value.

Solution

The following code creates a method for swapping two variables. The swap method is invoked by passing two actual parameters. Interestingly, the actual parameters are not changed after the method is invoked. The output of the program is shown in Figure 4.5.

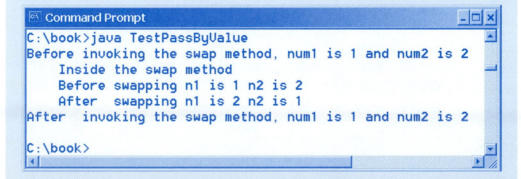

Figure 4.5   *The contents of the actual parameters are not swapped after the* swap *method is invoked.*

continues

Example 4.2 continued

```
1    // TestPassByValue.java: Demonstrate passing values to methods
2    public class TestPassByValue {
3      /** Main method */
4      public static void main(String[] args) {
5        // Declare and initialize variables
6        int num1 = 1;
7        int num2 = 2;
8
9        System.out.println("Before invoking the swap method, num1 is " +
10         num1 + " and num2 is " + num2);
11
12       // Invoke the swap method to attempt to swap two variables
13       swap(num1, num2);
14       System.out.println("After  invoking the swap method, num1 is " +
15         num1 + " and num2 is " + num2);
16     }
17
18     /** Swap two variables */
19     public static void swap(int n1, int n2) {
20       System.out.println("    Inside the swap method");
21       System.out.println("    Before swapping n1 is " + n1
22         + " n2 is " + n2);
23
24       // Swapping n1 with n2
25       int temp = n1;
26       n1 = n2;
27       n2 = temp;
28
29       System.out.println("    After  swapping n1 is " + n1
30         + " n2 is " + n2);
31     }
32   }
```

Review

Before the swap method is invoked (Line 13), num1 is 1 and num2 is 2. After the swap method is invoked, num1 continues to be 1 and num2 continues to be 2. Their values are not swapped when the swap method is invoked. As shown in Figure 4.6, the values of the actual parameters num1 and num2 are passed to n1 and n2, but n1 and n2 have their own memory locations independent of num1 and num2. Therefore, changes in n1 and n2 do not affect the contents of num1 and num2.

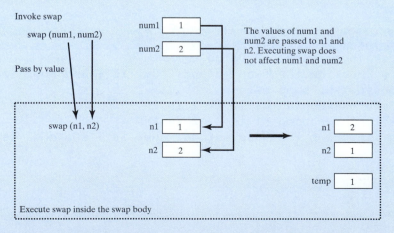

Figure 4.6   *The values of the variables are passed to the parameters of the method.*

Another twist is to change the formal parameter name n1 in swap to num1. What effect does this have? No change occurs because it makes no difference whether the formal parameter and the actual parameter have the same name. The formal parameter is a local variable in the method with its own memory space. The local variable is allocated when the method is invoked, and it disappears when the method is returned to its caller.

4.5   Overloading Methods

The max method that was used earlier works only with the int data type. But what if you need to find which of two floating-point numbers has the maximum value? The solution is to create another method with the same name but different parameters, as shown in the following code:

```
public static double max(double num1, double num2) {
  if (num1 > num2)
    return num1;
  else
    return num2;
}
```

If you call max with int parameters, the max method that expects int parameters will be invoked; if you call max with double parameters, the max method that expects double parameters will be invoked. This is referred to as *method overloading*; that is, two methods have the same name but different parameter profiles. The Java compiler determines which method is used based on the method signature.

Example 4.3 Overloading the max Method

Problem

Write a program that creates three methods. The first finds the maximum integer, the second finds the maximum double, and the third finds the maximum among three double values. All three methods are named max.

Solution

The following code gives the solution to the problem. The output of the program is shown in Figure 4.7.

```
1   // TestMethodOverloading.java: Demonstrate method overloading
2   public class TestMethodOverloading {
3     /** Main method */
4     public static void main(String[] args) {
5       // Invoke the max method with int parameters
6       System.out.println("The maximum between 3 and 4 is "
7         + max(3, 4));
8
9       // Invoke the max method with the double parameters
10      System.out.println("The maximum between 3.0 and 5.4 is "
11        + max(3.0, 5.4));
12
13      // Invoke the max method with three double parameters
```

continues

125

Example 4.3 continued

```
14          System.out.println("The maximum between 3.0, 5.4, and 10.14 is "
15            + max(3.0, 5.4, 10.14));
16      }
17
18      /** Return the max between two int values */
19      public static int max(int num1, int num2) {
20        if (num1 > num2)
21          return num1;
22        else
23          return num2;
24      }
25
26      /** Find the max between two double values */
27      public static double max(double num1, double num2) {
28        if (num1 > num2)
29          return num1;
30        else
31          return num2;
32      }
33
34      /** Find the max among three double values */
35      public static double max(double num1, double num2, double num3) {
36        return max(max(num1, num2), num3);
37      }
38    }
```

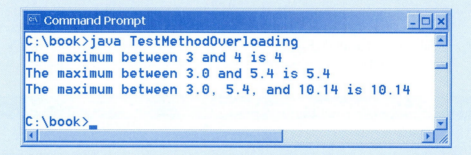

Figure 4.7 *The program invokes three different* max *methods that all have the same name:* max(3, 4), max(3.0, 5.4), *and* max(3.0, 5.4, 10.14).

Review

When calling max(3, 4) (Line 7), the max method for finding maximum integers is invoked. When calling max(3.0, 5.4) (Line 11), the max method for finding maximum doubles is invoked. When calling max(3.0, 5.4, 10.14) (Line 15), the max method for finding the maximum of three double values is invoked.

Can you invoke the max method with an int value and a double value, such as max(2, 2.5)? If so, which of the max methods is invoked? The answer to the first question is yes. The answer to the second is that the max method for finding the maximum of two double values is invoked. The actual parameter 2 is automatically converted into a double value and passed to this method.

You may be wondering why the method max(double, double) is not invoked for the call max(3, 4). Both max(double, double) and max(int, int) are possi-

126

ble matches for max(3, 4). The Java compiler finds the most specific method for a method invocation. Since the method max(int, int) is more specific than max(double, double), max(int, int) is used to invoke max(3, 4).

TIP

Overloading methods can make programs clearer and more readable. Methods that perform closely related tasks should be given the same name.

NOTE

The overloaded methods must have different parameter profiles. You cannot overload methods based on different modifiers or return types.

4.5.1   Ambiguous Invocation

Sometimes there are two or more possible matches for an invocation of a method, but the compiler cannot determine the most specific match. This is referred to as *ambiguous invocation*. Ambiguous invocation is a compilation error. Consider the following code:

```java
public class AmbiguousOverloading {
  public static void main(String[] args) {
    System.out.println(max(1, 2));
  }

  public static double max(int num1, double num2) {
    if (num1 > num2)
      return num1;
    else
      return num2;
  }

  public static double max(double num1, int num2) {
    if (num1 > num2)
      return num1;
    else
      return num2;
  }
}
```

Both max(int, double) and max(double, int) are possible candidates to match max(1, 2). Since neither of them is more specific than the other, the invocation is ambiguous.

4.6   The Scope of Local Variables

The *scope of a variable* is the part of the program where the variable can be referenced. A variable defined inside a method is referred to as a *local variable*. In Chapter 6, "Objects and Classes," you will learn about instance variables and static variables.

The scope of a local variable starts from its declaration and continues to the end of the block that contains the variable. A local variable must be declared before it can be used.

You can declare a local variable with the same name multiple times in different non-nesting blocks in a method, but you cannot declare a local variable twice in nested blocks. Thus, the following code is correct.

```
public static void correctMethod() {
  int x = 1;
  int y = 1;

  // i is declared
  for (int i = 1; i < 10; i++) {
    x += i;
  }

  // i is declared again
  for (int i = 1; i < 10; i++) {
    y += i;
  }
}
```

However, the next code would cause a compilation error because x is declared in the for loop body block, which is nested inside the method body block where another x is declared.

```
public static void incorrectMethod() {
  int x = 1;
  int y = 1;

  for (int i = 1; i < 10; i++) {
    int x = 0;
    x += i;
  }
}
```

If a variable is declared as a method parameter, it cannot be redeclared inside the method. The scope of a method parameter covers the entire method.

A variable declared in the initial action part of a for loop header has its scope in the entire loop. But a variable declared inside a for loop body has its scope limited in the loop body from its declaration and to the end of the block that contains the variable.

TIP

Do not declare a variable inside a block and then use it outside the block. Here is an example of a common mistake:

```
for (int i = 0; i < 10; i++) {
}

int j = i;
```

The last statement would cause an error because variable i is not defined outside of the for loop.

4.7 Method Abstraction

The key to developing software is to apply the concept of abstraction. You will learn many levels of abstraction from this book. *Method abstraction* is defined as separating the use of a method from its implementation. The client can use a method without knowing how it is implemented. The details of the implementation are encapsulated in the method and hidden from the client who invokes the method. This is known as *information hiding* or *encapsulation*. If you decide to change the implementation, the client program will not be affected provided that you do not change the method signature. The implementation of the method is hidden in a black box from the client, as shown in Figure 4.8.

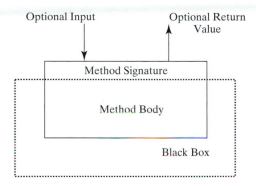

Figure 4.8   *The method body can be thought of as a black box that contains the detailed implementation for the method.*

You have already used the `System.out.print` method to display a string, the `JOptionPane.showInputDialog` method to read a string from a dialog box, and the `max` method to find the maximum number. You know how to write the code to invoke these methods in your program, but as a user of these methods, you are not required to know how they are implemented.

4.8   The *Math* Class

The `Math` class contains the methods needed to perform basic mathematical functions. You have already used the `pow(a, b)` method to compute a^b in Example 2.3, "Computing Mortgages." This section introduces other useful methods in the `Math` class. They can be categorized as *trigonometric methods, exponent methods,* and *service methods*. Besides methods, the `Math` class provides two useful `double` constants, `PI` and `E` (the base of natural logarithms). You can use these constants as `Math.PI` and `Math.E` in any program.

4.8.1   Trigonometric Methods

The `Math` class contains the following trigonometric methods:

```
public static double sin(double radians)
public static double cos(double radians)
public static double tan(double radians)
public static double asin(double radians)
public static double acos(double radians)
public static double atan(double radians)
```

Each method has a single `double` parameter, and its return type is `double`. The parameter represents an angle in radians. One degree is equal to $\pi/180$ in radians. For example, `Math.sin(Math.PI)` returns the trigonometric sine of π. Since

JDK 1.2, the Math class has also provided the method toRadians(double angdeg) for converting an angle in degrees to radians, and the method toDegrees(double angrad) for converting an angle in radians to degrees.

4.8.2   Exponent Methods

There are four methods related to exponents in the Math class:

```
/** Return e raised to the power of a (eᵃ) */
public static double exp(double a)

/** Return the natural logarithm of a (ln(a) = log_e(a)) */
public static double log(double a)

/** Return a raised to the power of b (aᵇ) */
public static double pow(double a, double b)

/** Return the square root of a (√a) */
public static double sqrt(double a)
```

4.8.3   The Rounding Methods

The Math class contains five rounding methods:

```
/** x rounded up to its nearest integer. This integer is
  * returned as a double value. */
public static double ceil(double x)

/** x is rounded down to its nearest integer. This integer is
  * returned as a double value. */
public static double floor(double x)

/** x is rounded to its nearest integer. If x is equally close
  * to two integers, the even one is returned as a double. */
public static double rint(double x)

/** Return (int)Math.floor(x + 0.5). */
public static int round(float x)

/** Return (long)Math.floor(x + 0.5). */
public static long round(double x)
```

For example,

```
Math.ceil(2.1) returns 3.0
Math.ceil(2.0) returns 2.0
Math.ceil(-2.0) returns -2.0
Math.ceil(-2.1) returns -2.0
Math.floor(2.1) returns 2.0
Math.floor(2.0) returns 2.0
Math.floor(-2.0) returns -2.0
Math.floor(-2.1) returns -3.0
Math.rint(2.1) returns 2.0
Math.rint(2.0) returns 2.0
Math.rint(-2.0) returns -2.0
Math.rint(-2.1) returns -2.0
Math.rint(2.5) returns 2.0
Math.rint(-2.5) returns -2.0
Math.round(2.6f) returns 3
Math.round(2.0) returns 2
Math.round(-2.0f) returns -2
Math.round(-2.6) returns -3
```

4.8.4   The *min, max, abs,* and *random* Methods

The min and max methods are overloaded to return the minimum and maximum numbers between two numbers (int, long, float, or double). For example, max(3.4, 5.0) returns 5.0, and min(3, 2) returns 2.

The abs method is overloaded to return the absolute value of the number (int, long, float, and double). For example, abs(-3.03) returns 3.03.

The Math class also has a powerful method, random, which generates a random double floating-point number greater than or equal to 0.0 and less than 1.0 (0 <= Math.random() < 1.0).

TIP

You can view the complete documentation for the Math class online from http://java.sun.com/j2se/1.4/docs/api/index.html, as shown in Figure 4.9. You can also download j2sdk-1_4_0-doc.zip from http://java.sun.com/j2se/1.4/docs/index.html and install it on your PC so that you can browse the documents locally. Please see Installing JDK from the Companion CD-ROM at www.prenhall.com/liang/intro4e.html.

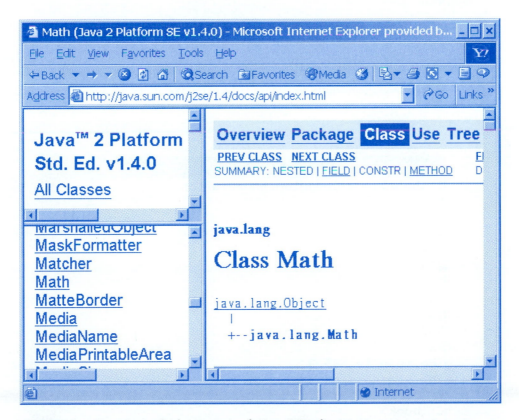

Figure 4.9   *You can view the documentation for Java API online at* http://java.sun.com/j2se/1.4/docs/api/index.html.

> ■ **NOTE**
> Not all classes need a `main` method. The `Math` class and `JOptionPane` class do not have `main` methods. These classes contain methods for other classes to use.

Example 4.4 Computing Mean and Standard Deviations

Problem

In this example, you will write a program that generates ten random numbers between 0 and 1000 (excluding 1000), and computes the mean and standard deviations of these numbers using the following formula:

$$mean = \frac{\sum_{i=1}^{n} x_i}{n} = \frac{x_1 + x_2 + \dots + x_n}{n} \qquad deviation = \sqrt{\frac{\sum_{i=1}^{n} x_i^2 - \frac{\left(\sum_{i=1}^{n} x_i\right)^2}{n}}{n-1}}$$

Solution

The mean is simply the average of the numbers. The standard deviation is a statistic that tells you how tightly all the various data are clustered around the mean in a set of data. When you wrote the program to compute mortgage payments using the formula in Example 2.3, "Computing Mortgages," you did not know how the formula was derived. Likewise, you don't need to know how the formula for deviation is derived. A sample run of the following program is shown in Figure 4.10.

Figure 4.10   *The program finds the mean and standard deviations of ten random integers.*

```
1    // ComputeMeanDeviation.java: Demonstrate using the math methods
2    public class ComputeMeanDeviation {
3      /** Main method */
4      public static void main(String[] args) {
5        final int COUNT = 10; // Total numbers
6        int number = 0; // Store a random number
7        double sum = 0; // Store the sum of the numbers
8        double squareSum = 0; // Store the sum of the squares
9
10       // Create numbers, find its sum, and its square sum
11       for (int i = 0; i < COUNT; i++) {
12         // Generate a new random number
13         number = (int)Math.round(Math.random() * 1000);
14         System.out.println(number);
15
16         // Add the number to sum
17         sum += number;
18
19         // Add the square of the number to squareSum
20         squareSum += Math.pow(number, 2); // Same as number*number;
21       }
22
23       // Find mean
24       double mean = sum / COUNT;
25
26       // Find standard deviation
27       double deviation =
28         Math.sqrt((squareSum - sum * sum / COUNT) / (COUNT - 1));
29
30       // Display result
31       System.out.println("The mean is " + mean);
32       System.out.println("The standard deviation is " + deviation);
33     }
34   }
```

On line 7, the comment includes $\left(\sum\limits_{i=1}^{n}\right)$ and on line 8 the comment includes $\left(\sum\limits_{i=1}^{n} x_i^2\right)$.

Review

The program demonstrates the use of the math methods random, round, pow, and sqrt. The random method (Line 13) generates a double value that is greater than or equal to 0 and less than 1.0. After the generated number is multiplied by 1000, the random number is greater than or equal to 0 and less than 1000.0. The round method converts the double number into a long value, which is cast into an int variable number.

Invoking pow(number, 2) (Line 20) returns the square of number. The sqrt method (Line 28) is used to get the square root of a double value.

Run the program with COUNT set to 100, 1000, and 10000, and observe the mean and deviation. As COUNT increases, the mean will become closer to 500 and the deviation closer to 288. Comment the println statement on Line 14 when you run the program so you will not be distracted by a large output of numbers.

The formula for computing standard deviation used in the example is equivalent to the following formula:

$$deviation = \sqrt{\frac{\sum\limits_{i=1}^{n} (x_i - mean)^2}{n - 1}}$$

To use this formula, you have to store the individual numbers using an array so that they can be used after the mean is obtained. See Example 5.4 for writing a program to compute the standard deviation using this formula.

Example 4.5 Obtaining Random Characters

Problem

Write the methods for generating random characters. The program uses these methods to generate 175 random characters between '!' and '~' (inclusive) and displays 25 characters per line.

Solution

To find out what characters are between '!' and '~', see Appendix B, "The ASCII Character Set." The ASCII code for '!' is 33 and for '~' is 126. To generate a random character between '!' and '~', you may generate a Unicode whose integer value is randomly chosen between 33 to 126, using the following expression:

```
value = (int)(33 + (126 - 33 + 1) * Math.random(x));
```

Since 0 <= (126 - 33 + 1) * Math.random(x) < 94, 33 <= 33 + (126 - 33 + 1) * Math.random(x) < 127. Therefore, 33 <= value <= 126. Thus (char)value is a character between '!' and '~' inclusively.

A sample run of the program is shown in Figure 4.11.

Figure 4.11 *The program displays 175 random characters from '!' to '~'.*

```
1    // RandomCharacter.java: Generate random characters
2    public class RandomCharacter {
3      /** Main method */
4      public static void main(String args[]) {
5        final int NUM_OF_CHARS = 175;
6        final int CHARS_PER_LINE = 25;
7
8        // Print random characters between '!' and '~', 25 chars per line
9        for (int i = 0; i < NUM_OF_CHARS; i++) {
10         if ((i + 1) % CHARS_PER_LINE == 0)
11           System.out.println(getRandomChar('!', '~'));
12         else
13           System.out.print(getRandomChar('!', '~') + " ");
14       }
15     }
16
```

```
17        /** Generate a random character between fromChar and toChar */
18        public static char getRandomChar(char fromChar, char toChar) {
19          // Get the Unicode of the character
20          int unicode = fromChar +
21            (int)((toChar - fromChar + 1) * Math.random());
22
23          // Return the character
24          return (char)unicode;
25        }
26
27        /** Generate a random character */
28        public static char getRandomChar() {
29          return getRandomChar('\u0000', '\uFFFF');
30        }
31      }
```

Review

The `RandomCharacter` class contains two overloaded `getRandomChar` methods (Lines 18, 28). The `getRandomChar(char fromChar, char toChar)` method (Lines 18–25) returns a random character between `fromChar` and `toChar`. The `getRandomChar()` method (Lines 28–30) returns a random character. The latter method is implemented by invoking the former method with the arguments `'\u0000'` and `'\uFFFF'`. The Unicodes of the characters are between `'\u0000'` and `'\uFFFF'`, inclusively.

The Unicode of a random character is created in Lines 20–21. When a character is involved in numeric computation, its integer equivalent is used in the operand. The expression `toChar - fromChar + 1` yields the number of characters between `fromChar` and `toChar`. So, `(toChar - fromChar + 1) * Math.random()` yields a random `double` number that is greater than or equal to 0 and less than `toChar - fromChar + 1`. Thus, `(int)((toChar - fromChar + 1) * Math.random())` yields an integer between 0 and `toChar - fromChar`. When this number is added to `fromChar`, the Unicode of the character `fromChar` is used. The result of the addition represents the Unicode of a character between `fromChar` and `toChar`. Finally, `(char)` casts the int value into a character that is returned from the method.

The `for` loop in the `main` method (Lines 9–14) generates 175 characters between '!' and '~', and displays them 25 characters per line.

4.9   Case Studies

The concept of method abstraction can be applied to the process of developing programs. When writing a large program, you can use the "divide and conquer" strategy to decompose it into subproblems. The subproblems can be further decomposed into smaller, more manageable problems.

The following example demonstrates the divide-and-conquer approach to the development of programs.

Example 4.6 Displaying Calendars

Problem

Write a program that displays the calendar for a given month of the year. The program prompts the user to enter the year and the month, and then displays the entire calendar for the month, as shown in Figure 4.12.

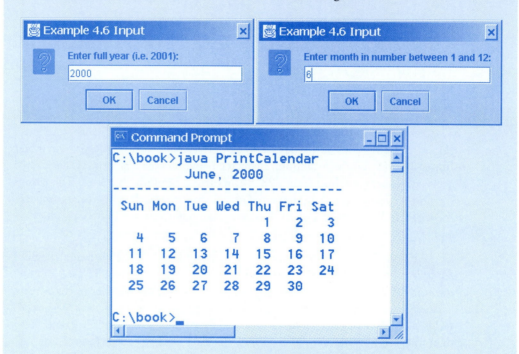

Figure 4.12 *After prompting the user to enter the year and the month, the program displays the calendar for that month.*

Solution

How would you get started on such a program? Would you immediately start coding? Beginning programmers often start by trying to work out the solution to every detail. Although details are important in the final program, concern for detail in the early stages may block the problem-solving process. To make problem-solving flow as smoothly as possible, this example begins by using method abstraction to isolate details from design and only later implements the details.

For this example, the problem is first broken into two subproblems: get input from the user, and print the monthly calendar. At this stage, the creator of the program should be concerned with what the subproblems will achieve, not with how to get input and print the calendar for the month. You can draw a structure chart to help visualize the decomposition of the problem (see Figure 4.13).

Use the `JOptionPane.showInputDialog` method to display input dialog boxes that prompt the user to enter the year and the month.

In order to print the calendar for a month, you need to know which day of the week is the first day of the month and how many days the month has. With this

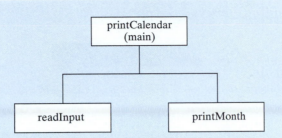

Figure 4.13   *The structure chart shows that the* printCalendar *problem is divided into two sub-problems:* readInput *and* printMonth.

information, you can print the title and body of the calendar. Therefore, the print-month problem would be further decomposed into four subproblems: get the start day, get the number of days in the month, print title, and print month body.

How would you get the start day for the first date in a month? There are several ways to find the start day. The simplest approach is to use the Date and Calendar classes in Chapter 14, "Internationalization." For now, an alternative approach is used. Assume that you know that the start day (startDay1800 = 3) for Jan 1, 1800 was Wednesday. You could compute the total number of days (totalNumOfDays) between Jan 1, 1800 and the first date of the calendar month. The start day for the calendar month is (totalNumOfDays + startDay1800) % 7.

To compute the total days (totalNumOfDays) between Jan 1, 1800 and the first date of the calendar month, you could find the total number of days between the year 1800 and the calendar year and then figure out the total number of days prior to the calendar month in the calendar year. The sum of these two totals is totalNumOfDays.

You would also need to know the number of days in a month and in a year. Remember the following:

■ January, March, May, July, August, October, and December have 31 days.

■ April, June, September, and November have 30 days.

■ February has 28 days during a regular year and 29 days during a leap year. A regular year, therefore, has 365 days, whereas a leap year has 366 days.

Use the following condition to determine whether a year is a leap year:

```
if ((year % 400 == 0) || ((year % 4 == 0) && (year % 100 != 0)))
   return true;
else
   return false;
```

To print a title, use println() to display three lines, as shown in Figure 4.14.

continues

Example 4.6 continued

Figure 4.14   *The calendar title consists of three lines: month and year, a dash line, and the names of the seven days of the week.*

To print a body, first pad some space before the start day and then print the lines for every week, as shown for June 2000 (see Figure 4.12).

In general, a subproblem corresponds to a method in the implementation, although some are so simple that this is unnecessary. You would need to decide which modules to implement as methods and which to combine in other methods. Decisions of this kind should be based on whether the overall program will be easier to read as a result of your choice. In this example, the subproblem `readInput` was implemented in the `main` method (see Figure 4.15).

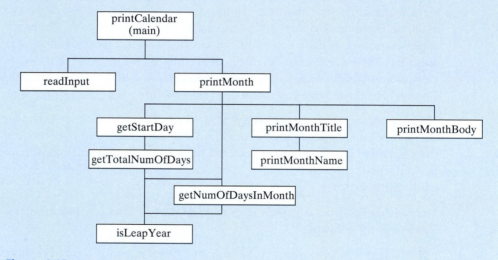

Figure 4.15   *The structure chart shows the hierarchical relationship of the subproblems in the program.*

When implementing the program, use a "top-down" approach. In other words, implement one method in the structure chart at a time—from the top to the bottom. Stubs can be used for the methods waiting to be implemented. A *stub* is a simple but incomplete version of a method. The use of stubs enables you to test invoking the method from a caller. Implement the `main` method first and then use a stub for the `printMonth` method. For example, let `printMonth` display the year and the month in the stub. Thus, your program may begin like this:

```
// PrintCalendar.java: Print a calendar for a given month in a year
public class PrintCalendar {
  /** Main method */
  public static void main(String[] args) {
    // Prompt the user to enter year
    String yearString = JOptionPane.showInputDialog(null,
```

```
            "Enter full year (i.e. 2001):",
            "Example 4.6 Input", JOptionPane.QUESTION_MESSAGE);

        // Convert string into integer
        int year = Integer.parseInt(yearString);

        // Prompt the user to enter month
        String monthString = JOptionPane.showInputDialog(null,
          "Enter month in number between 1 and 12:",
          "Example 4.6 Input", JOptionPane.QUESTION_MESSAGE);

        // Convert string into integer
        int month = Integer.parseInt(monthString);

        // Print calendar for the month of the year
        printMonth(year, month);

        System.exit(0);
      }

      /** A stub for printMonth may look like this */
      public static void printMonth(int year, int month) {
        System.out.print(month + ", " + year);
      }
    }
```

Compile and test the program, and fix any errors. You can now implement the `printMonth` method. For methods invoked from the `printMonth` method, you can again use stubs. This top-down incremental implementation approach helps to isolate programming errors and makes debugging easy.

The complete program is given as follows:

```
1   // PrintCalendar.java: Print a calendar for a given month in a year
2   import javax.swing.JOptionPane;
3
4   public class PrintCalendar {
5     /** Main method */
6     public static void main(String[] args) {
7       // Prompt the user to enter year
8       String yearString = JOptionPane.showInputDialog(null,
9         "Enter full year (i.e. 2001):",
10        "Example 4.6 Input", JOptionPane.QUESTION_MESSAGE);
11
12      // Convert string into integer
13      int year = Integer.parseInt(yearString);
14
15      // Prompt the user to enter month
16      String monthString = JOptionPane.showInputDialog(null,
17        "Enter month in number between 1 and 12:",
18        "Example 4.6 Input", JOptionPane.QUESTION_MESSAGE);
19
20      // Convert string into integer
21      int month = Integer.parseInt(monthString);
22
23      // Print calendar for the month of the year
24      printMonth(year, month);
25
26      System.exit(0);
27    }
28
29    /** Print the calendar for a month in a year */
30    static void printMonth(int year, int month) {
31      // Get start day of the week for the first date in the month
32      int startDay = getStartDay(year, month);
33
```

continues

Example 4.6 continued

```
34        // Get number of days in the month
35        int numOfDaysInMonth = getNumOfDaysInMonth(year, month);
36
37        // Print headings
38        printMonthTitle(year, month);
39
40        // Print body
41        printMonthBody(startDay, numOfDaysInMonth);
42      }
43
44    /** Get the start day of the first day in a month */
45    static int getStartDay(int year, int month) {
46        // Get total number of days since 1/1/1800
47        int startDay1800 = 3;
48        long totalNumOfDays = getTotalNumOfDays(year, month);
49
50        // Return the start day
51        return (int)((totalNumOfDays + startDay1800) % 7);
52      }
53
54    /** Get the total number of days since Jan 1, 1800 */
55    static long getTotalNumOfDays(int year, int month) {
56        long total = 0;
57
58        // Get the total days from 1800 to year -1
59        for (int i = 1800; i < year; i++)
60          if (isLeapYear(i))
61            total = total + 366;
62          else
63            total = total + 365;
64
65        // Add days from Jan to the month prior to the calendar month
66        for (int i = 1; i < month; i++)
67          total = total + getNumOfDaysInMonth(year, i);
68        return total;
69      }
70
71    /** Get the number of days in a month */
72    static int getNumOfDaysInMonth(int year, int month) {
73        if (month == 1 || month==3 || month == 5 || month == 7 ||
74          month == 8 || month == 10 || month == 12)
75          return 31;
76
77        if (month == 4 || month == 6 || month == 9 || month == 11)
78          return 30;
79
80        if (month == 2)
81          if (isLeapYear(year))
82            return 29;
83          else
84            return 28;
85
86      return 0; // If month is incorrect.
87      }
88
89    /** Determine if it is a leap year */
90    static boolean isLeapYear(int year) {
91      if ((year % 400 == 0) || ((year % 4 == 0) && (year % 100 != 0)))
92        return true;
93
94      return false;
95      }
96
97    /** Print month body */
98    static void printMonthBody(int startDay, int numOfDaysInMonth) {
99        // Pad space before the first day of the month
100       int i = 0;
```

```
101        for (i = 0; i < startDay; i++)
102          System.out.print("    ");
103
104        for (i = 1; i <= numOfDaysInMonth; i++) {
105          if (i < 10)
106            System.out.print("   " + i);
107          else
108            System.out.print("  " + i);
109
110          if ((i + startDay) % 7 == 0)
111            System.out.println();
112        }
113
114        System.out.println();
115      }
116
117      /** Print the month title, i.e. May, 1999 */
118      static void printMonthTitle(int year, int month) {
119        System.out.println("          " + getMonthName(month)
120          + ", " + year);
121        System.out.println("———————————————·");
122        System.out.println(" Sun Mon Tue Wed Thu Fri Sat");
123      }
124
125      /** Get the English name for the month */
126      static String getMonthName(int month) {
127        String monthName = null;
128        switch (month) {
129          case 1: monthName = "January"; break;
130          case 2: monthName = "February"; break;
131          case 3: monthName = "March"; break;
132          case 4: monthName = "April"; break;
133          case 5: monthName = "May"; break;
134          case 6: monthName = "June"; break;
135          case 7: monthName = "July"; break;
136          case 8: monthName = "August"; break;
137          case 9: monthName = "September"; break;
138          case 10: monthName = "October"; break;
139          case 11: monthName = "November"; break;
140          case 12: monthName = "December";
116        }
141
142        return monthName;
143      }
144    }
```

Review

The program does not validate user input. For instance, if the user enters a month not in the range between 1 and 12, or a year before 1800, the program would display an erroneous calendar. To avoid this error, add an `if` statement to check the input before printing the calendar.

This program prints calendars for a month but could easily be modified to print calendars for a whole year. Although it can only print months after January 1800, it could also be modified to trace the day of a month before 1800.

The calendar is displayed in the command window. You can modify the program to display the calendar in a message dialog box. See Exercise 6.5.

See Chapter 14, "Internationalization," to find out how to use the `Date` and `Calendar` classes to simplify the program.

continues

Example 4.6 continued

■ NOTE
Method abstraction modularizes programs in a neat, hierarchical manner. Programs written as collections of concise methods are easier to write, debug, maintain, and modify than would otherwise be the case. This writing style also promotes method reusability.

■ TIP
When implementing a large program, use the top-down coding approach. Start with the `main` method, and code and test one method at a time. Do not write the entire program at once. This approach seems to take more time for coding (because you are repeatedly compiling and running the program), but it actually saves time and makes debugging easier.

4.10   Recursion (Optional)

You have seen a method calling another method; that is, a statement contained in a method body calling another method. Can a method call itself? And what happens if it does? This section examines these questions and uses three classic examples to demonstrate recursive programming.

4.10.1   Computing Factorials

Recursion, a powerful mathematical concept, is the process of a function calling itself, directly or indirectly. Many mathematical functions are defined using recursion. The factorial of a number n can be recursively defined as follows:

```
0! = 1;
n! = n × (n - 1)!; n > 0
```

How do you find n! for a given n? It is easy to find 1! because you know 0! and 1! is 1 × 0!. Assuming that you know (n-1)!, n! can be obtained immediately using n × (n-1)!. Thus, the problem of computing n! is reduced to computing (n-1)!. When computing (n-1)!, you can apply the same idea recursively until n is reduced to 0.

Let `factorial(n)` be the method for computing n!. If you call the method with n=0, it immediately returns the result. The method knows how to solve the simplest case, which is referred to as the *base case* or the *stopping condition*. If you call the method with n>0, it reduces the problem into a subproblem for computing the factorial of n-1. The subproblem is essentially the same as the original problem, but is slightly simpler or smaller than the original. Because the subproblem has the same property as the original, you can call the method with a different actual parameter, which is referred to as a *recursive call*.

The recursive algorithm for computing `factorial(n)` can be simply described as follows:

```
if (n == 0)
  return 1;
else
  return n * factorial(n - 1);
```

A recursive call can result in many more recursive calls because the method is dividing a subproblem into new subproblems. For a recursive method to terminate, the problem must eventually be reduced to a stopping case. When it reaches a stopping case, the method returns a result to its caller. The caller then performs a computation and returns the result to its own caller. This process continues until the result is passed back to the original caller. The original problem can now be solved by multiplying n with the result of factorial(n-1).

Example 4.7 Computing Factorials

Problem

Write a recursive method for computing a factorial factorial(n), given n. The test program prompts the user to enter n.

Solution

The following code gives the solution to the problem. A sample run of the program is shown in Figure 4.16.

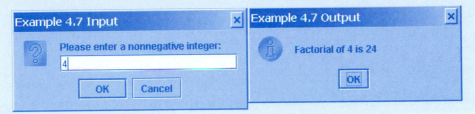

Figure 4.16 *The program prompts the user to enter a non-negative integer and then displays the factorial for the number.*

```
1   // ComputeFactorial.java: Compute factorial of an integer
2   import javax.swing.JOptionPane;
3
4   public class ComputeFactorial {
5     /** Main method */
6     public static void main(String[] args) {
7       // Prompt the user to enter an integer
8       String intString = JOptionPane.showInputDialog(null,
9         "Please enter a nonnegative integer:",
10        "Example 4.7 Input", JOptionPane.QUESTION_MESSAGE);
11
12      // Convert string into integer
13      int n = Integer.parseInt(intString);
14
15      // Display factorial
16      JOptionPane.showMessageDialog(null,
17        "Factorial of " + n + " is " + factorial(n),
18        "Example 4.7 Output", JOptionPane.INFORMATION_MESSAGE);
19    }
20
21    /** Return the Fibonacci number for a specified index */
22    static long factorial(int n) {
23      if (n == 0) // Stopping condition
24        return 1;
25      else
26        return n * factorial(n - 1); // Call factorial recursively
27    }
28  }
```

continues

143

Example 4.7 continued

Review

The `factorial` method (Lines 22–27) is essentially a direct translation of the recursive mathematical definition for the factorial into Java code. The call to `factorial` is recursive because it calls itself. The parameter passed to `factorial` is decremented until it reaches the base case of 0.

Figure 4.17 illustrates the execution of the recursive calls, starting with n=4.

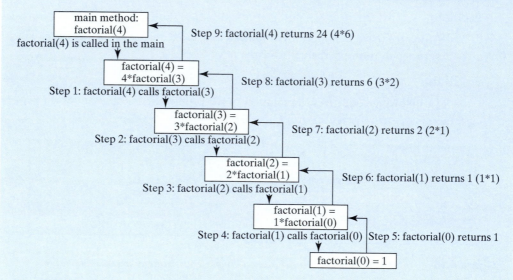

Figure 4.17 *Invoking* `factorial(4)` *spawns recursive calls to* `factorial`.

Each time a method is invoked, the system stores parameters, local variables, and system registers in a space known as a *stack*. When a method calls another method, the caller's stack space is kept intact, and new space is created to handle the new method call. When a method finishes its work and returns to its caller, its associated space is released. The use of stack space for recursive calls is shown in Figure 4.18.

■ **NOTE**

All recursive methods have the following characteristics:

- ■ One or more base cases (the simplest case) are used to stop recursion.
- ■ Every recursive call reduces the original problem, bringing it increasingly closer to a base case until it becomes that case.

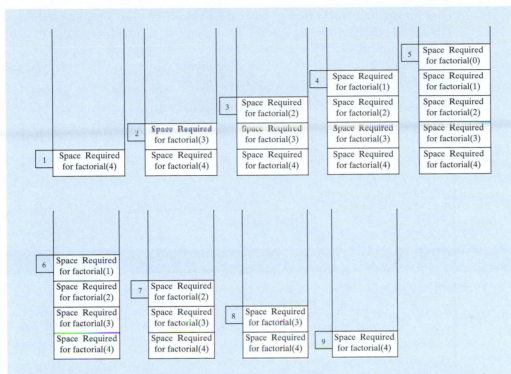

Figure 4.18 *When* `factorial(4)` *is being executed, the* `factorial` *method is called recursively, causing memory space to dynamically change.*

CAUTION

Infinite recursion can occur if recursion does not reduce the problem in a manner that allows it to eventually converge into the base case.

4.10.2   Computing Fibonacci Numbers

The preceding example could be easily rewritten without using recursion. In some cases, however, using recursion enables you to give a natural, straightforward, simple solution to a program that would otherwise be difficult to solve. Consider the well-known Fibonacci series problem. The Fibonacci series

0, 1, 1, 2, 3, 5, 8, 13, 21, 34, . . .,

begins with 0, and 1, and each subsequent number is the sum of the preceding two numbers in the series. The series can be recursively defined as follows:

```
fib(0) = 0;
fib(1) = 1;
fib(n) = fib(n - 2) + fib(n - 1); n >= 2
```

The Fibonacci series was named for Leonardo Fibonacci, a medieval mathematician, who originated it to model the growth of the rabbit population. It can be applied in numeric optimization and in various other areas.

How do you find `fib(n)` for a given n? It is easy to find `fib(2)` because you know `fib(0)` and `fib(1)`. Assuming that you know `fib(n-2)` and `fib(n-1)`, `fib(n)` can be obtained immediately. Thus, the problem of computing `fib(n)` is reduced to computing `fib(n-2)` and `fib(n-1)`. When computing `fib(n-2)` and `fib(n-1)`, you can apply the idea recursively until n is reduced to 0 or 1.

The base case is n=0 or n=1. If you call the method with n=0 or n=1, it immediately returns the result. If you call the method with n>=2, it divides the problem into two subproblems for computing `fib(n-1)` and `fib(n-2)` using recursive calls. The recursive algorithm for computing `fib(n)` can be simply described as follows:

```
if ((n == 0) || (n == 1))
  return n;
else
  return fib(n - 1) + fib(n - 2);
```

Example 4.8 Computing Fibonacci Numbers

Problem

Write a recursive method for computing a Fibonacci number `fib(n)`, given index n. The test program prompts the user to enter index n, then calls the method and displays the result.

Solution

The following code gives the solution to the problem. A sample run of the program is shown in Figure 4.19.

Figure 4.19   *The program prompts the user to enter an index for the Fibonacci number and then displays the number at the index.*

```
1    // ComputeFibonacci.java: Find a Fibonacci number for a given index
2    import javax.swing.JOptionPane;
3
4    public class ComputeFibonacci {
5      /** Main method */
6      public static void main(String args[]) {
7        // Read the index
8        String intString = JOptionPane.showInputDialog(null,
9          "Enter an index for the Fibonacci number:",
10         "Example 4.8 Input", JOptionPane.QUESTION_MESSAGE);
11
12       // Convert string into integer
13       int n = Integer.parseInt(intString);
14
15       // Find and display the Fibonacci number
16       JOptionPane.showMessageDialog(null,
17         "Fibonacci number at index " + n + " is " + fib(n),
```

```
18                  "Example 4.8 Output", JOptionPane.INFORMATION_MESSAGE);
19
20          System.exit(0);
21       }
22
23       /** The method for finding the Fibonacci number */
24       public static long fib(long n) {
25         if ((n == 0) || (n == 1))  // Stopping condition
26           return n;
27         else  // Reduction and recursive calls
28           return fib(n - 1) + fib(n - 2);
29       }
30    }
```

Review

The implementation of the method is very simple and straightforward. The solution is slightly more difficult if you do not use recursion. For a hint on computing Fibonacci numbers using iterations, see Exercise 4.9.

The program does not show the considerable amount of work done behind the scenes by the computer. Figure 4.20, however, shows successive recursive calls for evaluating fib(4). The original method, fib(4), makes two recursive calls, fib(3) and fib(2), and then returns fib(3) + fib(2). But in what order are these methods called? In Java, operands are evaluated from left to right. The upper-left-corner labels in Figure 4.20 show the order in which methods are called.

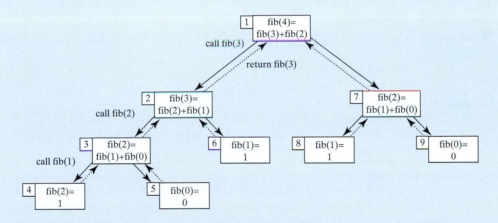

Figure 4.20 *Invoking* fib(4) *spawns recursive calls to* fib.

As shown in Figure 4.20, there are many duplicated recursive calls. For instance, fib(2) is called twice, fib(1) is called three times, and fib(0) is called twice. In general, computing fib(n) requires twice as many recursive calls as are needed for computing fib(n - 1). As you try larger index values, the number of calls substantially increases.

Besides the large number of recursive calls, the computer requires more time and space to run recursive methods. For more discussion, see Section 4.10.4, "Recursion versus Iteration."

4.10.3   The Tower of Hanoi Problem

You have seen a recursive method with a return value. Here is an example of a recursive method with a return type of void.

The problem involves moving a specified number of disks of a distinct size from one tower to another while observing the following rules:

- There are *n* disks labeled 1, 2, 3, . . ., *n*, and three towers labeled A, B, and C.

- No disk can be on top of a smaller disk at any time.

- All the disks are initially placed on tower A.

- Only one disk can be moved at a time, and it must be the top disk on the tower.

The objective of the problem is to move all the disks from A to B with the assistance of C. For example, if you have three disks, as shown in Figure 4.21, the following steps will move all of the disks from A to B:

1. Move disk 1 from A to B.

2. Move disk 2 from A to C.

3. Move disk 1 from B to C.

4. Move disk 3 from A to B.

5. Move disk 1 from C to A.

6. Move disk 2 from C to B.

7. Move disk 1 from A to B.

NOTE

The Towers of Hanoi is a classic computer science problem. There are many Websites devoted to this problem. The Website www.cut-the-knot.com/recurrence/hanoi.html is worth seeing.

In the case of three disks, you can find the solution manually. However, the problem is quite complex for a larger number of disks—even for four. Fortunately, the problem has an inherently recursive nature, which leads to a straightforward recursive solution.

The base case for the problem is n == 1. If n == 1, you could simply move the disk from A to B. When n > 1, you could split the original problem into three subproblems and solve them sequentially.

1. Move the first n - 1 disks from A to C with the assistance of tower B.

2. Move disk n from A to B.

3. Move n - 1 disks from C to B with the assistance of tower A.

148

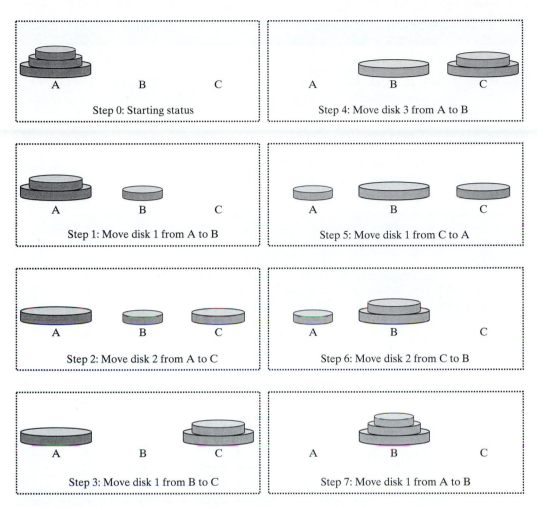

Figure 4.21   *The goal of the Towers of Hanoi problem is to move disks from tower A to tower B without breaking the rules.*

The following method moves *n* disks from the `fromTower` to the `toTower` with the assistance of the `auxTower`:

```
void moveDisks(int n, char fromTower, char toTower, char auxTower)
```

The algorithm for the method can be described as follows:

```
if (n == 1) // Stopping condition
  Move disk 1 from the fromTower to the toTower;
else {
  moveDisks(n - 1, fromTower, auxTower, toTower);
  Move disk n from the fromTower to the toTower;
  moveDisks(n - 1, auxTower, toTower, fromTower);
}
```

Example 4.9 Solving the Towers of Hanoi Problem

Problem

Write a program that finds a solution for the Towers of Hanoi problem. The program prompts the user to enter the number of disks and invokes the recursive method `moveDisks` to display the solution for moving the disks.

Solution

The following code gives the solution to the problem. The sample run of the following program appears in Figure 4.22.

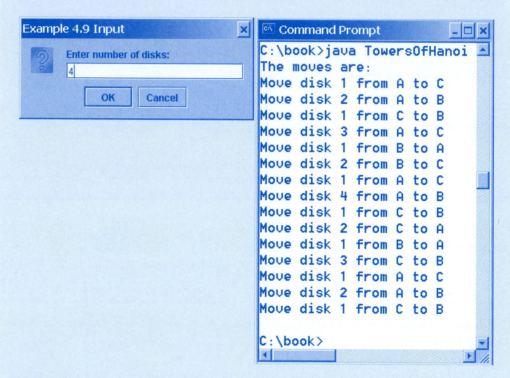

Figure 4.22 *The program prompts the user to enter the number of disks and then displays the steps that must be followed to solve the Towers of Hanoi problem.*

```
1    // TowersOfHanoi.java: Find solutions for the Towers of Hanoi problem
2    import javax.swing.JOptionPane;
3
4    public class TowersOfHanoi {
5      /** Main method */
6      public static void main(String[] args) {
7        // Read number of disks, n
8        String intString = JOptionPane.showInputDialog(null,
9          "Enter number of disks:",
10         "Example 4.9 Input", JOptionPane.QUESTION_MESSAGE);
11
12       // Convert string into integer
13       int n = Integer.parseInt(intString);
14
```

```
15        // Find the solution recursively
16        System.out.println("The moves are:");
17        moveDisks(n, 'A', 'B', 'C');
18
19        System.exit(0);
20      }
21
22      /** The method for finding the solution to move n disks
23          from fromTower to toTower with auxTower */
24      public static void moveDisks(int n, char fromTower,
25        char toTower, char auxTower) {
26        if (n == 1) // Stopping condition
27          System.out.println("Move disk " + n + " from " +
28            fromTower + " to " + toTower);
29        else {
30          moveDisks(n - 1, fromTower, auxTower, toTower);
31          System.out.println("Move disk " + n + " from " +
32            fromTower + " to " + toTower);
33          moveDisks(n - 1, auxTower, toTower, fromTower);
34        }
35      }
36    }
```

Review

This problem is inherently recursive. Using recursion makes it possible to find a natural, simple solution. It would be difficult to solve the problem without using recursion.

Consider tracing the program for n=3. The successive recursive calls are shown in Figure 4.23. As you can see, writing the program is easier than tracing the recursive calls. The system uses stacks to trace the calls behind the scenes. To some extent, recursion provides a level of abstraction that hides iterations and other details from the user.

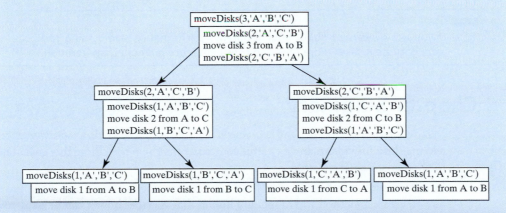

Figure 4.23 *Invoking* moveDisks(3, 'A', 'B', 'C') *spawns calls to* moveDisks *recursively.*

The fib method in the preceding example returns a value to its caller, but the moveDisks method in this example does not return a value to its caller.

4.10.4   Recursion versus Iteration

Recursion is an alternative form of program control. It is essentially repetition without a loop control. When you use loops, you specify a loop body. The repetition of the loop body is controlled by the loop-control structure. In recursion, the method itself is called repeatedly. A selection statement must be used to control whether to call the method recursively or not.

Recursion bears substantial overhead. Each time the program calls a method, the system must assign space for all of the method's local variables and parameters. This can consume considerable memory and requires extra time to manage the additional space.

Any problem that can be solved recursively can be solved nonrecursively with iterations. Recursion has many negative aspects: it uses up too much time and too much memory. Why, then, should you use it? In some cases, using recursion enables you to specify a clear, simple solution that would otherwise be difficult to obtain.

The decision whether to use recursion or iteration should be based on the nature of the problem you are trying to solve and your understanding of the problem. The rule of thumb is to use recursion or iteration to develop an intuitive solution that naturally mirrors the problem. If an iterative solution is obvious, use it. It will generally be more efficient than the recursive option.

NOTE
Your recursive program could run out of memory, causing a runtime error. In Chapter 13, "Exception Handling," you will learn how to handle errors so that the program terminates gracefully when there is a stack overflow.

TIP
If you are concerned about your program's performance, avoid using recursion, because it takes more time and consumes more memory than iteration.

Chapter Summary

Making programs modular and reusable is one of the central goals in software engineering. Java provides many powerful constructs that help to achieve this goal. The method is one such construct.

In this chapter, you have learned how to write reusable methods. You now know how to create a method with a method header that specifies how it can be used and a method body that implements it.

You have also learned how to call a method by passing actual parameters that replace the formal parameters in the method specification. The arguments that are passed to a method should have the same number, type, and order as the parameters in the method definition. Outside of the method, the actual values of the primitive parameters are not affected by the method call.

In addition, you have learned that a method can be overloaded. For example, two methods can have the same name as long as their method parameter profiles differ.

The scope of a variable is the portion of the program where the variable can be accessed. The scope of a local variable is limited locally to a method. The scope of a local variable starts from its declaration and continues to the end of the block that contains the variable. A local variable must be declared before it can be used, and it must be initialized before it is referenced.

You have learned the Math class. The Math class contains methods that perform trigonometric functions (sin, cos, tan, acos, asin, atan), exponent functions (exp, log, pow, sqrt), and some service functions (min, max, abs, round, random). All of these methods operate on double values; min, max, and abs can also operate on int, long, float, and double.

You are now familiar with the divide-and-conquer strategy. The best way to develop and maintain a large program is to divide it into several subproblems that are individually more manageable than the original problem.

Finally, you have learned the techniques needed to write recursive methods. Recursion is an alternative form of program control. It can be used to specify simple, clear solutions for inherently recursive problems that would otherwise be difficult to solve.

Review Questions

4.1 What is the purpose of using a method? How do you declare a method? How do you invoke a method?

4.2 What is the return type of a main method?

4.3 What would be wrong with not writing a return statement in a nonvoid method? Can you have a return statement in a void method, such as the following?

```
public static void main(String[] args) {
  int i;
  while (true) {
    // Prompt the user to enter an integer
    String intString = JOptionPane.showInputDialog(null,
      "Enter an integer:",
      "Test", JOptionPane.QUESTION_MESSAGE);

    // Convert a string into int
    int i = Integer.parseInt(intString);
    if (i == 0)
      return;

    System.out.println("i = " + i);
  }
}
```

4.4 What is method overloading? Is it possible to define two methods that have the same name but different parameter types? Is it possible to define two methods in a class that have identical method names and parameter profiles with different return value types or different modifiers?

4.5 How do you pass actual parameters to a method? Can the actual parameter have the same name as its formal parameter?

4.6 What is pass by value? Show the result of the following method call:

```java
public class Test {
  public static void main(String[] args) {
    int max = 0;
    max(1, 2, max);
    System.out.println(max);
  }

  public static void max(int value1, int value2, int max) {
    if (value1 > value2)
      max = value1;
    else
      max = value2;
  }
}
```

4.7 Show the output of the following programs:

a.

```java
public class Test {
  public static void main(String[] args) {
    // Initialize times
    int times = 3;
    System.out.println("Before the call, variable times is "
      + times);

    // Invoke nPrintln and display times afterwards
    nPrintln("Welcome to Java!", times);
    System.out.println("After the call, variable times is "
      + times);
  }

  // Print the message n times
  static void nPrintln(String message, int n) {
    while (n > 0) {
      System.out.println("n = " + n);
      System.out.println(message);
      n--;
    }
  }
}
```

b.

```java
public class Test {
  public static void main(String[] args) {
    int i = 1;
    while (i <= 6) {
      xMethod(i, 2);
      i++;
    }
  }

  public static void xMethod(int i, int num) {
    for (int j = 1; j <= i; j++) {
      System.out.print(num + " ");
      num *= 2;
    }

    System.out.println();
  }
}
```

c.

```java
public class Test {
  public static void main(String[] args) {
    int i = 0;
    while (i <= 4) {
      xMethod(i);
      i++;
    }

    System.out.println("i is " + i);
  }
  public static void xMethod(int i) {
    do {
      if (i % 3 != 0)
        System.out.print(i + " ");
      i--;
    }
    while (i >= 1);

    System.out.println();
  }
}
```

4.8 A call to a method with a `void` return type is always a statement itself, but a call to a method with a nonvoid return type is always a component of an expression. Is this statement true or false?

4.9 Does the `return` statement in the following method cause syntax errors?

```java
public static void main(String[] args) {
  int max = 0;

  if (max != 0)
    System.out.println(max);
  else
    return;
}
```

4.10 In some other languages, you can define methods inside a method. Can you define a method inside a method in Java?

4.11 For each of the following, decide whether a `void` method or a nonvoid method is the most appropriate implementation:

- Computing a sales commission, given the sales amount and the commission rate.

- Printing a calendar for a month.

- Computing a square root.

- Testing whether a number is even, and returning true if it is.

- Printing a message a specified number of times.

- Computing the monthly payment, given the loan amount, number of years, and annual interest rate.

- Finding the corresponding uppercase letter, given a lowercase letter.

4.12 Which of the following is a possible output from invoking `Math.random()`?

    a. 323.4

    b. 0.5

    c. 34

    d. 1.0

    e. b and d.

4.13 Evaluate the following method calls:

```
Math.sqrt(4)
Math.sin(2 * Math.PI)
Math.cos(2 * Math.PI)
Math.pow(2, 2)
Math.log(Math.E)
Math.exp(1)
Math.max(2, Math.min(3, 4))
Math.rint(-2.5)
Math.ceil(-2.5)
Math.floor(-2.5)
Math.round(-2.5f)
Math.round(-2.5)
Math.rint(2.5)
Math.ceil(2.5)
Math.floor(2.5)
Math.round(2.5f)
Math.round(2.5)
Math.round(Math.abs(-2.5))
```

4.14 What is a recursive method?

4.15 Describe the characteristics of recursive methods.

4.16 Show the output of the following program:

```java
public class Test {
  public static void main(String[] args) {
    int sum = xMethod(5);
    System.out.println("Sum is " + sum);
  }

  public static int xMethod(int n) {
    if (n == 1)
      return 1;
    else
      return n + xMethod(n - 1);
  }
}
```

4.17 Identify and correct the errors in the following program:

```java
public class Test {
  public static method1(int n, m) {
    n += m;
    xMethod(3.4);
  }

  public static int xMethod(int n);
  {
    if (n > 0) return 1;
    else if (n == 0) return 0;
    else if (n < 0) return -1;
  }
}
```

4.18 Identify and correct the errors in the following program:

```java
public class Test {
  public static void main(String[] args) {
    nPrintln("Welcome to Java!", 5);
  }

  public static void nPrintln(String message, int n) {
    int n = 1;
    for (int i = 0; i < n; i++)
      System.out.println(message);
  }
}
```

4.19 Reformat the following program according to the programming style and documentation guidelines proposed in Section 2.15, "Programming Style and Documentation." Use the next-line brace style.

```java
public class Test {
  public static double xMethod(double i,double j)
  {
  while (i<j) {
    j--;
  }

  return j;
  }
}
```

Programming Exercises

4.1 Write a method that converts an uppercase letter to a lowercase letter. Use the following method declaration:

```java
public static char upperCaseToLowerCase(char ch)
```

For example, upperCaseToLowerCase('B') returns b.

HINT

See Exercise 2.10.

4.2 Write a method that computes the sum of the digits in an integer. Use the following method declaration:

```java
public static int sumDigits(long n)
```

For example, sumDigits(234) returns $2 + 3 + 4 = 9$.

HINT

Use the % operator to extract digits, and use the / operator to remove the extracted digit. For instance, 234 % 10 = 4 and 234 / 10 = 23. Use a loop to repeatedly extract and remove the digit until all the digits are extracted.

4.3 Write a method that computes future investment value at a given interest rate for a specified number of years. The future investment is determined using the formula in Exercise 2.9.

Use the following method declaration:

```
public static double futureInvestmentValue(
    double investmentAmount, double monthlyInterestRate, int years)
```

For example, `futureInvestmentValue(10000, 0.05/12, 5)` returns 12833.59.

Write a test program that prompts the user to enter the investment amount and the interest rate, and print a table that displays future value for the years from 1 to 30, as shown below:

```
Enter the amount invested: 1000
Enter annual interest rate: 9%
Years              Future Value
1                  1093.8
2                  1196.41
...
29                 13467.25
30                 14730.57
```

4.4 Write a method that converts Celsius to Fahrenheit using the following declaration:

```
public static double celsToFahr(double cels)
```

The formula for the conversion is as follows:

```
Fahrenheit = (9.0 / 5) * celsius + 32
```

Write a program that uses a for loop and calls the `celsToFahr` method in order to produce the following output:

```
Cels. Temp.        Fahr. Temp.
40.00              104.00
39.00              102.20
38.00              100.40
37.00              98.60
36.00              96.80
35.00              95.00
34.00              93.20
33.00              91.40
32.00              89.60
31.00              87.80
```

4.5 Write a program that prints the following table using the `sqrt` method in the Math class.

```
Number        SquareRoot
0             0.0000
2             1.4142
4             2.0000
6             2.4495
8             2.8284
10            3.1623
12            3.4641
14            3.7417
16            4.0000
18            4.2426
20            4.4721
```

4.6 Print the following table to display the sin value and cos value of degrees from 0 to 360 with increments of 10 degrees. Round the value to keep four digits after the decimal point.

```
Degree      Sin          Cos

0           0.0          1.0
10          0.1736       0.9848
...
350         -0.1736      0.9848
360         0.0          1.0
```

4.7 You used the `sqrt` method in the `Math` class in Example 4.4. In this exercise, write your own method to compute square roots. The square root of a number, `num`, can be approximated by repeatedly performing a calculation using the following formula:

```
nextGuess = (lastGuess + (num / lastGuess)) / 2
```

When `nextGuess` and `lastGuess` are almost identical, `nextGuess` is the approximated square root.

The initial guess will be the starting value of `lastGuess`. If the difference between `nextGuess` and `lastGuess` is less than a very small number, such as 0.0001, you can claim that `nextGuess` is the approximated square root of `num`.

4.8 Rewrite Example 4.7 using iterations.

4.9 Write a nonrecursive method that computes Fibonacci numbers.

HINT

To compute `fib(n)` without recursion, you need to obtain `fib(n-2)` and `fib(n-1)` first. Let `f0` and `f1` denote the two previous Fibonacci numbers. The current Fibonacci number would then be `f0 + f1`. The algorithm can be described as follows:

```
f0 = 0; // For fib(0)
f1 = 1; // For fib(1)

for (int i = 1; i <= n; i++) {
  currentFib = f0 + f1;
  f0 = f1;
  f1 = currentFib;
}

// After the loop, currentFib is fib(n)
```

4.10 Modify Example 4.9 so that the program finds the number of moves needed to move *n* disks from tower A to tower B.

4.11 Write a recursive method and a nonrecursive method for the greatest common divisor (GCD). Given two positive integers, the GCD is the largest integer that divides them both. `GCD(m, n)` can be defined as follows:

- If n is less than or equal to m, and n divides m, `GCD(m, n)` is n.

- Otherwise, `GCD(m, n)` is `GCD(n, m % n)`.

4.12 Write a method that displays a specified number of digits after the decimal point. The signature of the method is as follows:

```
public static double format(double number, int numOfDigits)
```

For example, format(10.3422345, 2) returns 10.34, and format(-0.343434, 3) returns −0.343. Use the following main method to test it:

```
public static void main(String[] args) {
  System.out.println(format(10.3422345, 2));
  System.out.println(format(-0.343434, 3));
}
```

4.13 Write a program that meets the following requirements:

■ Declare a method to determine whether an integer is a prime number. Use the following method declaration:

```
public static boolean isPrime(int num)
```

■ An integer greater than 1 is a *prime number* if its only divisor is 1 or itself. For example, isPrime(11) returns true, and isPrime(9) returns false.

■ Use the isPrime method to find the first thousand prime numbers and display every ten prime numbers in a row, as follows:

2   3   5   7   11   13   17   19   23   29

31   37   41   43   47   53   59   61   67   71

73   79   83   89   97   ...

...

4.14 Rewrite Exercise 4.2 using recursion.

CHAPTER 5

ARRAYS

Objectives

- To understand the concept of arrays.
- To learn the steps involved in using arrays: declaring array reference variables, creating arrays, initializing arrays, and processing arrays.
- To learn how to pass arrays to methods.
- To know how to copy arrays.
- To learn how to use multidimensional arrays.
- To become familiar with search and sorting algorithms.

5.1   Introduction

In earlier chapters, you studied examples in which values were overwritten during the execution of a program. In those examples, such as Example 3.2, "Using `while` loops," you did not need to worry about storing former values. Sometimes, however, you will have to store a large number of values in memory during the execution of a program. Suppose, for instance, that you want to sort a group of numbers. The numbers must all be stored in memory because later you will have to compare each of them with all of the others.

In order to store the numbers, you must declare variables in the program. From the standpoint of practicality, it is impossible to declare variables for each number. You need an efficient, organized approach. Java and all other high-level languages provide a data structure, the *array*, which stores a collection of data of the same type.

5.2   Declaring Array Variables and Creating Arrays

To use an array in a program, you must declare a variable to reference the array and specify the type of array the variable can reference. Here is the syntax for declaring an array variable:

```
dataType[] arrayName;
```

or

```
dataType arrayName[];
```

The following code snippets are examples of this syntax:

```
double[] myList;
```

or

```
double myList[];
```

NOTE

The style `dataType[] arrayName` is preferred. The style `dataType arrayName[]` comes from the C language and was adopted in Java to accommodate C programmers.

Unlike declarations for primitive data type variables, the declaration of an array variable does not allocate any space in memory for the array. An array variable is not a primitive data type variable. An array variable contains a reference to an array. If a variable does not reference to an array, the value of the variable is `null`. You cannot assign elements to an array unless it has already been created. After an array variable is declared, you can create an array by using the `new` operator with the following syntax:

```
arrayName = new dataType[arraySize];
```

This statement does two things: (1) it creates an array using `new dataType[array-Size]`; (2) it assigns the reference of the newly created array to the variable `arrayName`.

Declaring an array variable, creating an array, and assigning the reference of the array to the variable can be combined in one statement, as follows:

```
dataType[] arrayName = new dataType[arraySize];
```

or

```
dataType arrayName[] = new dataType[arraySize];
```

Here is an example of such a statement:

```
double[] myList = new double[10];
```

This statement declares an array variable, `myList`, creates an array of ten elements of `double` type, and assigns its reference to `myList`, as shown in Figure 5.1. When space for an array is allocated, the array size must be given, to specify the number of elements that can be stored in it. The size of an array cannot be changed after the array is created. Size can be obtained using `array.length`. For example, `myList.length` is 10.

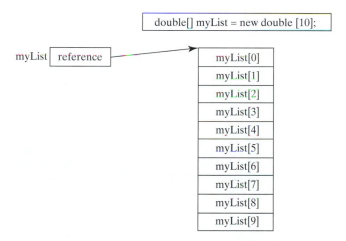

Figure 5.1   *The array* `myList` *has ten elements of* `double` *type and* `int` *indices from 0 to 9.*

NOTE

An array variable that appears to hold an array actually contains a reference to that array. Strictly speaking, an array variable and an array are different, but most of the time the distinction between them can be ignored. Thus it is all right to say, for simplicity, that `myList` is an array, instead of stating, at greater length, that `myList` is a variable that contains a reference to an array of ten double elements. When the distinction makes a subtle difference, the longer phrase should be used.

5.3   Initializing and Processing Arrays

When an array is created, its elements are assigned the default value of `0` for the numeric primitive data types, `'\u0000'` for `char` types, and `false` for `boolean` types. The size of an array is denoted by `array.length`.

The array elements are accessed through the index. The array indices are from `0` to `array.length-1`. In the example in Figure 5.1, `myList` holds ten `double` values and the indices are from `0` to `9`.

Each element in the array is represented using the following syntax:

```
arrayName[index];
```

For example, `myList[9]` represents the last element in the array `myList`.

NOTE

In Java, an array index must be an integer or an integer expression. In many other languages, such as Ada and Pascal, the index can be either an integer or another type of value.

CAUTION

Some languages use parentheses to reference an array element, as in `myList(9)`. But Java uses brackets, as in `myList[9]`.

After an array is created, you can enter values into the array elements. See, for example, the following loop:

```
for (int i = 0; i < myList.length; i++)
  myList[i] = i;
```

In this example, `myList.length` returns the array size (10) for `myList`.

Java has a shorthand notation that combines declaring an array, creating an array, and initializing it at the same time. Here is an example of its syntax at work:

```
double[] myList = {1.9, 2.9, 3.4, 3.5};
```

This statement declares and creates the array `myList`, which consists of four elements. Therefore, `myList.length` is 4 and `myList[0]` is 1.9. Note that the `new` operator was not used in the syntax. This shorthand notation is equivalent to the following statements:

```
double[] myList = new double[4];
myList[0] = 1.9;
myList[1] = 2.9;
myList[2] = 3.4;
myList[3] = 3.5;
```

■ CAUTION

Using the shorthand notation, you have to declare, create, and initialize the array all in one statement. Splitting it would cause a syntax error. Thus the next statement is wrong:

```
double[] myList;
myList = {1.9, 2.9, 3.4, 3.5};
```

■ NOTE

You can also create and initialize an array using the following syntax:

```
new dataType[]{literal0, literal1, . . ., literalk};
```

Using this syntax, you can create an array with initial values and assign its reference to an array variable. For example, these statements are correct.

```
double[] myList = {1, 2, 3};
// Sometimes later  . . .
myList = new double[]{1.9, 2.9, 3.4, 3.5};
```

When processing array elements, you will often use a for loop. Here are the reasons why:

■ All of the elements in an array are of the same type. They are evenly processed in the same fashion by repeatedly using a loop.

■ Since the size of the array is known, it is natural to use a for loop.

Example 5.1 Testing Arrays

Problem

Write a program that reads six integers, finds the largest of them, and counts its occurrences. Suppose that you entered the numbers shown in Figure 5.2; the program finds that the largest is 5 and the occurrence count is 4.

Solution

Your program should read the number and store them in an array, then find the largest number in the array, and finally count the occurrence of the largest number in the array. The source code for the program is shown below:

```
1    // TestArray.java: Count the occurrences of the largest number
2    import javax.swing.JOptionPane;
3
4    public class TestArray {
5      /** Main method */
6      public static void main(String[] args) {
7        int[] numbers = new int[6];
8
9        // Read all numbers
10       for (int i = 0; i < numbers.length; i++) {
11         String numString = JOptionPane.showInputDialog(null,
12           "Enter a number:",
13           "Example 5.1 Input", JOptionPane.QUESTION_MESSAGE);
14
```

continues

Example 5.1 continued

```
15          // Convert string into integer
16          numbers[i] = Integer.parseInt(numString);
17        }
18
19        // Find the largest
20        int max = numbers[0];
21        for (int i = 1; i < numbers.length; i++) {
22          if (max < numbers[i])
23            max = numbers[i];
24        }
25
26        // Find the occurrence of the largest number
27        int count = 0;
28        for (int i = 0; i < numbers.length; i++) {
29          if (numbers[i] == max) count++;
30        }
31
32        // Prepare the result
33        String output = "The array is ";
34        for (int i = 0; i < numbers.length; i++) {
35          output += numbers[i] + " ";
36        }
37
38        output += "\nThe largest number is " + max;
39        output += "\nThe occurrence count of the largest number "
40          + "is " + count;
41
42        // Display the result
43        JOptionPane.showMessageDialog(null, output,
44          "Example 5.1 Output", JOptionPane.INFORMATION_MESSAGE);
45
46        System.exit(0);
47      }
48    }
```

Review

The program declares and creates an array of six integers (Line 7). It finds the largest number in the array (Lines 20–24), counts its occurrences (Lines 27–30), and displays the result (Lines 32–44). To display the array, you need to display each element in the array using a loop.

Without using the numbers array, you would have to declare a variable for each number entered, because all the numbers are compared to the largest number to count its occurrences after it is found.

CAUTION

Accessing an array out of bounds is a common programming error. To avoid it, make sure that you do not use an index beyond array.length - 1.

Programmers often mistakenly reference the first element in an array with index 1, so that the index of the tenth element becomes 10. This is called the *off-by-one error*.

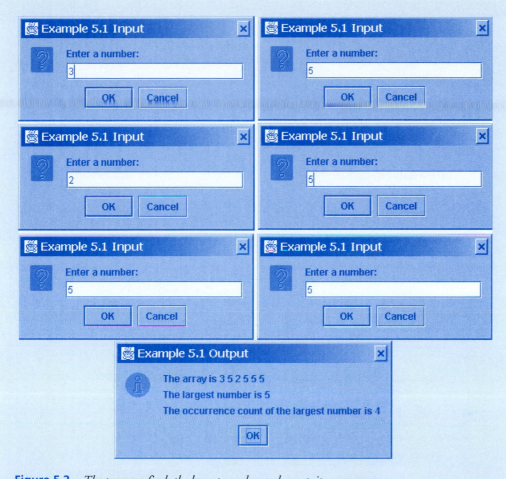

Figure 5.2   *The program finds the largest number and counts its occurrences.*

Example 5.2 Assigning Grades

Problem

Write a program that reads student scores, gets the best score, and then assigns grades based on the following scheme:

Grade is A if score is >= best − 10;

Grade is B if score is >= best − 20;

Grade is C if score is >= best − 30;

Grade is D if score is >= best − 40;

Grade is F otherwise.

continues

Example 5.2 Assigning Grades

The program prompts the user to enter the total number of students, then prompts the user to enter all of the scores, and concludes by displaying the grades.

Solution

The program reads the scores, then finds the best score, and finally assigns the grades to the students based on the preceding scheme. The following code gives the solution to the problem. The output of a sample run of the program is shown in Figure 5.3.

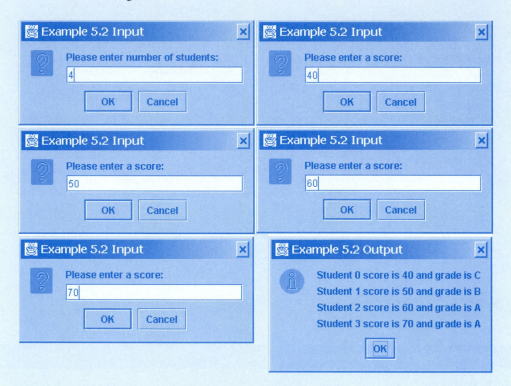

Figure 5.3   *The program receives the number of students and their scores, and then assigns grades.*

```
1      // AssignGrade.java: Assign grade
2      import javax.swing.JOptionPane;
3
4      public class AssignGrade {
5        /** Main method */
6        public static void main(String[] args) {
7          int numOfStudents = 0; // The number of students
8          int[] scores; // Array scores
9          int best = 0; // The best score
10         char grade; // The grade
11
12         // Get number of students
13         String numOfStudentsString = JOptionPane.showInputDialog(null,
14           "Please enter number of students:",
15           "Example 5.2 Input", JOptionPane.QUESTION_MESSAGE);
16
```

```
17           // Convert string into integer
18           numOfStudents = Integer.parseInt(numOfStudentsString);
19
20           // Create array scores
21           scores = new int[numOfStudents];
22
23           // Read scores and find the best score
24           for (int i = 0; i < scores.length; i++) {
25             String scoreString = JOptionPane.showInputDialog(null,
26               "Please enter a score:",
27               "Example 5.2 Input", JOptionPane.QUESTION_MESSAGE);
28
29             // Convert string into integer
30             scores[i] = Integer.parseInt(scoreString);
31             if (scores[i] > best)
32               best = scores[i];
33           }
34
35           // Declare and initialize output string
36           String output = "";
37
38           // Assign and display grades
39           for (int i = 0; i < scores.length; i++) {
40             if (scores[i] >= best - 10)
41               grade = 'A';
42             else if (scores[i] >= best - 20)
43               grade = 'B';
44             else if (scores[i] >= best - 30)
45               grade = 'C';
46             else if (scores[i] >= best - 40)
47               grade = 'D';
48             else
49               grade = 'F';
50
51             output += "Student " + i + " score is " +
52               scores[i] + " and grade is " + grade + "\n";
53           }
54
55           // Display the result
56           JOptionPane.showMessageDialog(null, output,
57             "Example 5.2 Output", JOptionPane.INFORMATION_MESSAGE);
58
59           System.exit(0);
60       }
61     }
```

Review

The program declares scores as an array of int type in order to store the students' scores (Line 8). The size of the array is undetermined when the array is declared. After the user enters the number of students into numOfStudents in Lines 12–18, an array with the size numOfStudents is created in Line 21. The size of the array is set at runtime; it cannot be changed once the array is created.

The array is not needed to find the best score, but it is needed to keep all of the scores so that grades can be assigned later on, and it is needed when scores are printed along with the students' grades.

5.4 Passing Arrays to Methods

Just as you can pass the parameters of primitive types to methods, you can also pass the parameters of array types to methods. The next example passes the array `list` as an argument to the method `printArray`:

```
public class TestPassingArray {
  public static void main(String[] args) {
    int[] list = {1, 3, 5, 7, 9, 11, 13};
    printArray(list);
  }

  public static void printArray(int[] array) {
    for (int i = 0; i < array.length; i++) {
      System.out.println(array[i]);
    }
  }
}
```

Java uses *pass by value* to pass parameters to a method. There are important differences between passing the values of variables of primitive data types and passing arrays.

■ For a parameter of a primitive type value, the actual value is passed. Changing the value of the local parameter inside the method does not affect the value of the variable outside the method.

■ For a parameter of an array type, the value of the parameter contains a reference to an array; this reference is passed to the method. Any changes to the array that occur inside the method body will affect the original array that was passed as the argument.

The difference is illustrated in the following example.

Example 5.3   Passing Arrays as Arguments

Problem

Write two methods for swapping elements in an array. The first method, named `swap`, attempts to swap two `int` arguments. The second method, named `swapFirstTwoInArray`, attempts to swap the first two elements in the array argument.

Solution

The program is given below. Figure 5.4 shows a sample run of the program.

```
1    // TestPassArray.java: Demonstrate passing arrays to methods
2    public class TestPassArray {
3      /** Main method */
4      public static void main(String[] args) {
5        int[] a = {1, 2};
6
7        // Swap elements using the swap method
8        System.out.println("Before invoking swap");
9        System.out.println("array is {" + a[0] + ", " + a[1] + "}");
10       swap(a[0], a[1]);
```

```
11        System.out.println("After invoking swap");
12        System.out.println("array is {" + a[0] + ", " + a[1] + "}");
13
14        // Swap elements using the swapFirstTwoInArray method
15        System.out.println("Before invoking swapFirstTwoInArray");
16        System.out.println("array is {" + a[0] + ", " + a[1] + "}");
17        swapFirstTwoInArray(a);
18        System.out.println("After invoking swapFirstTwoInArray");
19        System.out.println("array is {" + a[0] + ", " + a[1] + "}");
20      }
21
22      /** Swap the first two elements in the array */
23      public static void swapFirstTwoInArray(int[] array) {
24        int temp = array[0];
25        array[0] = array[1];
26        array[1] = temp;
27      }
28
29      public static void swap(int n1, int n2) {
30        int temp = n1;
31        n1 = n2;
32        n2 = temp;
33      }
34    }
```

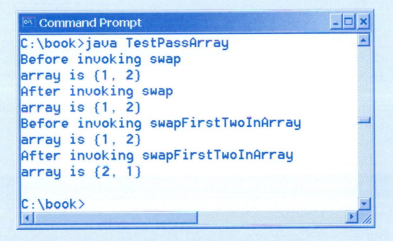

```
Command Prompt                              _ □ ×

C:\book>java TestPassArray
Before invoking swap
array is {1, 2}
After invoking swap
array is {1, 2}
Before invoking swapFirstTwoInArray
array is {1, 2}
After invoking swapFirstTwoInArray
array is {2, 1}

C:\book>
```

Figure 5.4   *The program attempts to swap two elements using the* swap *method and the* swap-FirstTwoInArray *method.*

Review

As shown in Figure 5.4, the first method does not work. The two elements are not swapped using the swap method. The second method works. The two elements are actually swapped using the swapFirstTwoInArray method. Since the arguments in the first method are primitive type, the values of a[0] and a[1] are passed to n1 and n2 inside the method when invoking swap(a[0], a[1]). The memory locations for n1 and n2 are independent of the ones for a[0] and a[1]. The contents of the array are not affected by this call. This is pictured in Figure 5.5.

continues

Example 5.3   continued

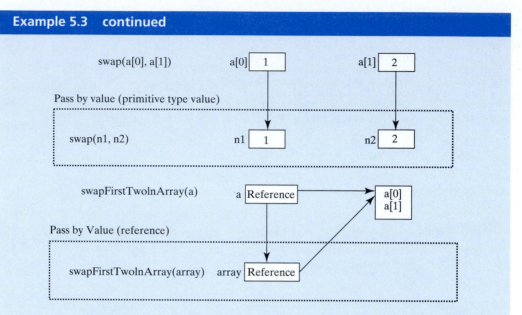

Figure 5.5   *When passing an array to a method, the reference of the array is passed to the method.*

The argument in the second method is an array. As shown in Figure 5.5, the reference of the array is passed to the method. Thus the variables a (outside the method) and array (inside the method) both refer to the same array in the same memory location. Therefore, swapping array[0] with array[1] inside the method swapFirstTwoInArray is the same as swapping a[0] with a[1] outside of the method.

Example 5.4 Computing Deviation Using Arrays

Problem

Example 4.4, "Computing Mean and Standard Deviation," computes the mean and standard deviation of numbers. This example uses a different but equivalent formula to compute the mean and standard deviation of n numbers.

$$deviation = \sqrt{\frac{\sum_{i=1}^{n}(x_i - mean)^2}{n-1}} \qquad mean = \frac{\sum_{i=1}^{n}x_i}{n} = \frac{x_1 + x_2 + \cdots + x_n}{n}$$

To compute deviation with this formula, you have to store the individual numbers using an array, so that they can be used after the mean is obtained. This example presents the methods for finding the mean and standard deviation for an array of numbers.

Solution

The program is given below. Figure 5.6 shows a sample run of the program.

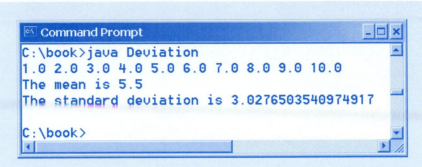

Figure 5.6   *The program obtains mean and standard deviation for an array of numbers {1, 2, 3, 4, 5, 6, 7, 8, 9, 10}.*

```
1    // Deviation.java: Compute deviation
2    public class Deviation {
3      /** Main method */
4      public static void main(String[] args) {
5        // Declare and create an array for 10 numbers
6        double[] numbers = {1, 2, 3, 4, 5, 6, 7, 8, 9, 10};
7
8        // Print numbers
9        printArray(numbers);
10
11       // Display mean and deviation
12       System.out.println("The mean is " + mean(numbers));
13       System.out.println("The standard deviation is " +
14         deviation(numbers));
15     }
16
17     /** Method for computing deviation of double values*/
18     public static double deviation(double[] x) {
19       double mean = mean(x);
20       double squareSum = 0;
21
22       for (int i = 0; i < x.length; i++) {
23         squareSum += Math.pow(x[i] - mean, 2);
24       }
25
26       return Math.sqrt((squareSum) / (x.length - 1));
27     }
28
29     /** Method for computing deviation of int values*/
30     public static double deviation(int[] x) {
31       double mean = mean(x);
32       double squareSum = 0;
33
34       for (int i = 0; i < x.length; i++) {
35         squareSum += Math.pow(x[i] - mean, 2);
36       }
37
38       return Math.sqrt((squareSum) / (x.length - 1));
39     }
40
41     /** Method for computing mean of an array of double values*/
42     public static double mean(double[] x) {
43       double sum = 0;
```

continues

173

Example 5.4 continued

```
44
45              for (int i = 0; i < x.length; i++)
46                sum += x[i];
47
48              return sum / x.length;
49          }
50
51          /** Method for computing mean of an array of int values*/
52          public static double mean(int[] x) {
53            int sum = 0;
54            for (int i = 0; i < x.length; i++)
55              sum += x[i];
56
57            return sum / x.length;
58          }
59
60          /** Method for printing array */
61          public static void printArray(double[] x) {
62            for (int i = 0; i < x.length; i++)
63              System.out.print(x[i] + " ");
64            System.out.println();
65          }
66      }
```

Review

The `numbers` array is declared as an array of `double` type to store ten numbers (Line 6). This variable is passed to the `printArray` method, which prints the numbers (Line 9). This is then passed to the `mean` method, which computes the mean of the numbers (Line 12). Finally, this variable is passed to the `deviation` method, which computes the deviation of the numbers (Line 14).

When passing an array to a method in Java, you don't need to pass the size of the array. The size of the array is obtained using `array.length`. In other languages, such as Pascal and Ada, you have to pass the size.

There are two overloaded `deviation` methods: one for an array of `double` values in Lines 18–27 and the other for an array of `int` values in Lines 30–39. Similarly, there are two overloaded `mean` methods. So you can use methods for either array of `double` values and `int` values.

Example 5.5 Counting the Occurrences of Each Letter

Problem

Write a program that does the following:

1. Generate a hundred lowercase letters randomly and assign them to an array of characters.

2. Count the occurrences of each letter in the array.

3. Find the mean and standard deviation of the counts.

Solution

You can obtain a random letter by using the getRandomChar(toChar, fromChar) method in the RandomCharacter class in Example 4.5, "Obtaining Random Characters," and find mean and deviation using the mean and deviation methods in the Deviation class in the preceding example. The program is given below. Figure 5.7 shows a sample run of the program.

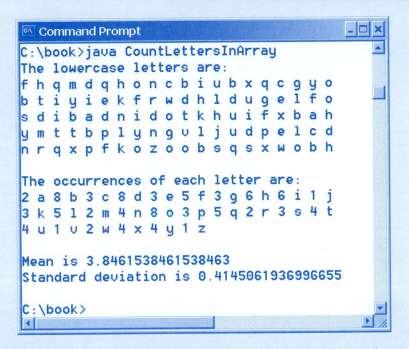

```
C:\book>java CountLettersInArray
The lowercase letters are:
f h q m d q h o n c b i u b x q c g y o
b t i y i e k f r w d h l d u g e l f o
s d i b a d n i d o t k h u i f x b a h
y m t t b p l y n g v l j u d p e l c d
n r q x p f k o z o o b s q s x w o b h

The occurrences of each letter are:
2 a 8 b 3 c 8 d 3 e 5 f 3 g 6 h 6 i 1 j
3 k 5 l 2 m 4 n 8 o 3 p 5 q 2 r 3 s 4 t
4 u 1 v 2 w 4 x 4 y 1 z

Mean is 3.8461538461538463
Standard deviation is 0.4145061936996655

C:\book>
```

Figure 5.7   *The program generates a hundred lowercase letters randomly and counts the occurrences of each letter.*

```
1    // CountLettersInArray.java: Count occurrences of each letter in
2    // in the array
3    public class CountLettersInArray {
4      /** Main method */
5      public static void main(String args[]) {
6        // Declare and create an array
7        char[] chars = createArray();
8
9        // Display the array
10       System.out.println("The lowercase letters are:");
11       displayArray(chars);
12
13       // Count the occurrences of each letter
14       int[] counts = countLetters(chars);
15
16       // Display counts
17       System.out.println();
18       System.out.println("The occurrences of each letter are:");
19       displayCounts(counts);
20
```

continues

Example 5.5 continued

```
21        // Display mean and standard deviation of the counts
22        System.out.println("\n\nMean is " + Deviation.mean(counts));
23        System.out.println("Standard deviation is " +
24          Deviation.deviation(counts));
25      }
26
27      /** Create an array of characters */
28      public static char[] createArray() {
29        // Declare an array of characters and create it
30        char[] chars = new char[100];
31
32        // Create lowercase letters randomly and assign
33        // them to the array
34        for (int i = 0; i < chars.length; i++)
35          chars[i] = RandomCharacter.getRandomChar('a', 'z');
36
37        // Return the array
38        return chars;
39      }
40
41      /** Display the array of characters */
42      public static void displayArray(char[] chars) {
43        // Display the characters in the array 20 on each line
44        for (int i = 0; i < chars.length; i++) {
45          if ((i + 1) % 20 == 0)
46            System.out.println(chars[i] + " ");
47          else
48            System.out.print(chars[i] + " ");
49        }
50      }
51
52      /** Count the occurrences of each letter */
53      public static int[] countLetters(char[] chars) {
54        // Declare and create an array of 26 int
55        int[] counts = new int[26];
56
57        // For each lowercase letter in the array, count it
58        for (int i = 0; i < chars.length; i++)
59          counts[chars[i] - 'a']++;
60
61        return counts;
62      }
63
64      /** Display counts */
65      public static void displayCounts(int[] counts) {
66        for (int i = 0; i < counts.length; i++) {
67          if ((i + 1) % 10 == 0)
68            System.out.println(counts[i] + " " + (char)(i + 'a'));
69          else
70            System.out.print(counts[i] + " " + (char)(i + 'a') + " ");
71        }
72      }
73    }
```

Review

The createArray method (Lines 28–39) generates an array of one hundred random lowercase letters. Line 7 invokes the method and assigns the array to chars. What would be wrong if you rewrote the code as follows?

```
char[] chars = new char[100];
chars = createArray();
```

You would be creating two arrays. The first line would create an array by using `new char[100]`. The second line would create an array by invoking `createArray()` and assigns the reference of the array to `chars`. The array created in the first line would be garbage because it is no longer referenced. Java automatically collects garbage behind the scenes. Your program would compile and run correctly, but it would create an array unnecessarily.

The `getRandomChar('a', 'z')` method (Line 35) generates a random lowercase letter. This method is defined in the `RandomCharacter` class in Example 4.5 in Chapter 4, "Methods."

The `countLetters` method (Lines 53–62) returns an array of twenty-six int values, each of which stores the number of occurrences of a letter. `counts[0]` stores the number of occurrences for `'a'`. In Line 59, `chars[i] - 'a'` yields the difference between the Unicode of `chars[i]` and the Unicode of `'a'`. `counts[chars[i] - 'a']` stores the number of occurrences for the character in `chars[i]`.

The statements in Lines 22–24 invoke the `mean` and `deviation` methods in the `Deviation` class in Example 5.4 to obtain the mean and deviation of the counts.

5.5   Copying Arrays

Often, in a program, you need to duplicate an array or a part of an array. In such cases you could attempt to use the assignment statement (=), as follows:

```
newList = list;
```

It seems to work fine. But if you ran the following program, you would discover that it does not work. The following example explains why.

Example 5.6 Copying Arrays

Problem

Write a program that creates two arrays and attempts to copy one to the other, using an assignment statement. The output of the program, shown in Figure 5.8, demonstrates that the two array variables reference the same array after the attempted copy.

Solution

The source code for the problem is given as follows.

```
1    // TestCopyArray.java: Demonstrate copying arrays
2    public class TestCopyArray {
3      /** Main method */
4      public static void main(String[] args) {
```

continues

Example 5.6 continued

```
5        // Create an array and assign values
6        int[] list1 = {0, 1, 2, 3, 4 ,5};
7
8        // Create an array with default values
9        int[] list2 = new int[list1.length];
10
11       // Assign array list1 to array list2
12       list2 = list1;
13
14       // Display list1 and list2
15       System.out.println("Before modifying list1");
16       printList("list1 is ", list1);
17       printList("list2 is ", list2);
18
19       // Modify list1
20       for (int i = 0; i < list1.length; i++)
21         list1[i] = 0;
22
23       // Display list1 and list2 after modifying list1
24       System.out.println("\nAfter modifying list1");
25       printList("list1 is ", list1);
26       printList("list2 is ", list2);
27     }
28
29     /** The method for printing a list */
30     public static void printList(String s, int[] list) {
31       System.out.print(s + " ");
32       for (int i = 0; i < list.length; i++)
33         System.out.print(list[i] + " ");
34
35       System.out.println();
36     }
37   }
```

Figure 5.8 *Copying reference array variables makes two variables refer to the same array.*

Review

The program creates two arrays, list1 and list2 (Lines 5-9), assigns list1 to list2 (Line 12), and displays both list1 and list2 (Lines 16–17). The program then changes the value in list1 (Lines 19-21) and redisplays list1 and list2 (Lines 23-26). As shown in Figure 5.8, the contents of list2 were also changed. This occurs because the assignment statement list2 = list1 actually copies the reference of list1 to list2, and makes list2 point to list1's memory location, as shown in Figure 5.9. The array referenced by the previous list2 is no longer referenced; it becomes garbage, which will be automatically collected by the Java Virtual Machine.

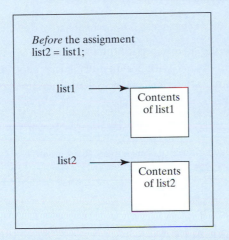
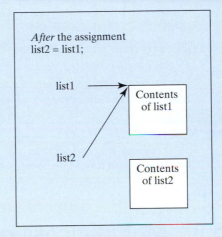

Figure 5.9 *Before the assignment statement,* list1 *and* list2 *point to separate memory locations. After the assignment, the reference of the* list1 *array is passed to* list2.

In Java, you can use assignment statements to copy primitive data type variables, but not arrays. Assigning one array variable to another array variable actually copies one reference to another and makes both variables point to the same memory location.

There are three ways to copy arrays:

- Use a loop to copy individual elements.

- Use the static arraycopy method in the System class.

- Use the clone method to copy arrays; this will be introduced in Chapter 8, "Class Inheritance and Interfaces."

You can write a loop to copy every element, from the source array to the corresponding element in the target array. The following code, for instance, copies the sourceArray to the targetArray using a for loop.

```
for (int i = 0; i < sourceArray.length; i++)
  targetArray[i] = sourceArray[i];
```

Another approach is to use the arraycopy method in the java.lang.System class to copy arrays instead of using a loop. The syntax for arraycopy is as follows:

```
arraycopy(sourceArray, src_pos, targetArray, tar_pos, length);
```

continues

Example 5.6 continued

The parameters `src_pos` and `tar_pos` indicate the starting positions in `sourceArray` and `targetArray`, respectively. The number of elements copied from `sourceArray` to `targetArray` is indicated by `length`. For example, you can rewrite the loop using the following statement:

```java
int[] sourceArray = {2, 3, 1, 5, 10};
int[] targetArray = new int[sourceArray.length];
System.arraycopy(sourceArray, 0, targetArray, 0, sourceArray.length);
```

The `arraycopy` method does not allocate memory space for the target array. The target array must have already been created with its memory space allocated. After the copying takes place, `targetArray` and `sourceArray` have the same content, but independent memory locations.

NOTE

The `arraycopy` method violates the Java naming convention. By convention, this method should be named `arrayCopy`.

5.6 Multidimensional Arrays

Thus far, you have used one-dimensional arrays to model linear collections of elements. To represent a matrix or a table, it is necessary to use a two-dimensional array. Occasionally, you will need to represent *n*-dimensional data structures. In Java, you can create *n*-dimensional arrays for any integer *n*, as long as your computer has sufficient memory to store the array.

5.6.1 Declaring Variables of Multidimensional Arrays and Creating Multidimensional Arrays

In Java, a two-dimensional array is declared as an array of arrays. Here is the syntax for declaring a two-dimensional array:

```java
dataType[][] arrayVariable;
```

or

```java
dataType arrayVariable[][];
```

As an example, here is how you would declare a two-dimensional array variable `matrix` of `int` values:

```java
int[][] matrix;
```

or

```java
int matrix[][];
```

You can create a two-dimensional array of 5 by 5 int values and assign it to matrix using this syntax:

```
matrix = new int[5][5];
```

Two subscripts are used in a two-dimensional array, one for the row, and the other for the column. As in a one-dimensional array, the index for each subscript is of the int type and starts from 0, as shown in Figure 5.10.

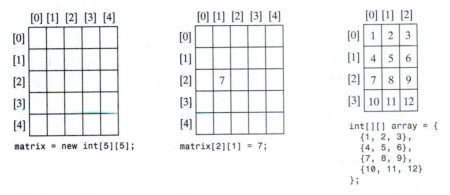

Figure 5.10 *The index of each subscript of a multidimensional array is an* int *value starting from 0.*

To assign the value 7 to a specific element at row 2 and column 0, you can use the following:

```
matrix[2][0] = 7;
```

CAUTION

It is a common mistake to use matrix[2, 0] to access the element at row 2 and column 0. In Java, each subscript must be enclosed in a pair of square brackets.

You can also use a shorthand notation to declare, create, and initialize a two-dimensional array. For example,

```
int[][] array = {
  {1, 2, 3},
  {4, 5, 6},
  {7, 8, 9},
  {10, 11, 12}
};
```

This is equivalent to the following statements:

```
int[][] array = new int[4][3];
array[0][0] = 1; array[0][1] = 2; array[0][2] = 3;
array[1][0] = 4; array[1][1] = 5; array[1][2] = 6;
array[2][0] = 7; array[2][1] = 8; array[2][2] = 9;
array[3][0] = 10; array[3][1] = 11; array[3][2] = 12;
```

The way to declare two-dimensional array variables and create two-dimensional arrays can be generalized to declare *n*-dimensional array variables and create *n*-dimensional arrays for *n* >= 3. For example, the following syntax declares a three-dimensional array variable scores, creates an array, and assigns its reference to scores.

```
double[][][] scores = new double[10][5][2];
```

5.6.2   Obtaining the Lengths of Multidimensional Arrays

A two-dimensional array consists of an array of elements, each of which is a one-dimensional array. A three-dimensional array consists of an array of two-dimensional arrays, each of which is an array of one-dimensional arrays. The length of an array x is the number of elements in the array, which can be obtained using x.length. x[0], x[1], ..., and x[x.length-1] are arrays. Their lengths can be obtained using x[0].length, x[1].length, ..., and x[x.length-1].length. For example, scores.length is 10, scores[0].length is 5 and scores[9].length is 5, scores[0][0].length is 2, and scores[9][4].length is 2 for the scores in the preceding section.

5.6.3   Ragged Arrays

Each row in a two-dimensional array is itself an array. Thus the rows can have different lengths. An array of this kind is known as a *ragged array*. Here is an example of creating a ragged array:

```
int[][] triangleArray = {
  {1, 2, 3, 4, 5},
  {2, 3, 4, 5},
  {3, 4, 5},
  {4, 5},
  {5}
};
```

So, triangleArray[0].length is 5, triangleArray[1].length is 4, triangleArray[2].length is 3, triangleArray[3].length is 2, and triangleArray[4].length is 1.

If you don't know the values in a ragged array in advance, you can create a ragged array using the syntax that follows:

```
int[][] triangleArray = new int[5][];
triangleArray[0] = new int[5];
triangleArray[1] = new int[4];
triangleArray[2] = new int[3];
triangleArray[3] = new int[2];
triangleArray[4] = new int[1];
```

You can now assign random values to the array using the following loop:

```
for (int row = 0; row < triangleArray.length; row++)
  for (int column = 0; column < triangleArray[row].length; column++)
    triangleArray[row][column] = (int)(Math.random() * 1000);
```

■ NOTE

The syntax new int[5][] for creating an array requires the first index to be specified. The syntax new int[][] would be wrong.

Example 5.7 Adding and Multiplying Two Matrices

Problem

Write a program that uses two-dimensional arrays to represent two matrices. The program then adds and multiplies the two matrices.

Solution

In order to be added, two matrices must have the same dimensions and the same or compatible types of elements. As shown below, two matrices are added by adding the two elements of the arrays with the same index

$$
\begin{pmatrix}
a_{11} & a_{12} & a_{13} & a_{14} & a_{15} \\
a_{21} & a_{22} & a_{23} & a_{24} & a_{25} \\
a_{31} & a_{32} & a_{33} & a_{34} & a_{35} \\
a_{41} & a_{42} & a_{43} & a_{44} & a_{45} \\
a_{51} & a_{52} & a_{53} & a_{54} & a_{55}
\end{pmatrix}
+
\begin{pmatrix}
b_{11} & b_{12} & b_{13} & b_{14} & b_{15} \\
b_{21} & b_{22} & b_{23} & b_{24} & b_{25} \\
b_{31} & b_{32} & b_{33} & b_{34} & b_{35} \\
b_{41} & b_{42} & b_{43} & b_{44} & b_{45} \\
b_{51} & b_{52} & b_{53} & b_{54} & b_{55}
\end{pmatrix}
=
$$

$$
\begin{pmatrix}
a_{11}+b_{11} & a_{12}+b_{12} & a_{13}+b_{13} & a_{14}+b_{14} & a_{15}+b_{15} \\
a_{21}+b_{21} & a_{22}+b_{22} & a_{23}+b_{23} & a_{24}+b_{24} & a_{25}+b_{25} \\
a_{31}+b_{31} & a_{32}+b_{32} & a_{33}+b_{33} & a_{34}+b_{34} & a_{35}+b_{35} \\
a_{41}+b_{41} & a_{42}+b_{42} & a_{43}+b_{43} & a_{44}+b_{44} & a_{45}+b_{45} \\
a_{51}+b_{51} & a_{52}+b_{52} & a_{53}+a_{53} & b_{54}+b_{54} & a_{55}+b_{55}
\end{pmatrix}
$$

To multiply matrix a by matrix b, the number of columns in a must be the same as the number of rows in b, and the two matrices must have elements of the same or compatible types. Let c be the result of the multiplication, and a, b, and c are denoted as follows :

$$
\begin{pmatrix}
a_{11} & a_{12} & a_{13} & a_{14} & a_{15} \\
a_{21} & a_{22} & a_{23} & a_{24} & a_{25} \\
a_{31} & a_{32} & a_{33} & a_{34} & a_{35} \\
a_{41} & a_{42} & a_{43} & a_{44} & a_{45} \\
a_{51} & a_{52} & a_{53} & a_{54} & a_{55}
\end{pmatrix}
\times
\begin{pmatrix}
b_{11} & b_{12} & b_{13} & b_{14} & b_{15} \\
b_{21} & b_{22} & b_{23} & b_{24} & b_{25} \\
b_{31} & b_{32} & b_{33} & b_{34} & b_{35} \\
b_{41} & b_{42} & b_{43} & b_{44} & b_{45} \\
b_{51} & b_{52} & b_{53} & b_{54} & b_{55}
\end{pmatrix}
=
\begin{pmatrix}
c_{11} & c_{12} & c_{13} & c_{14} & c_{15} \\
c_{21} & c_{22} & c_{23} & c_{24} & c_{25} \\
c_{31} & c_{32} & c_{33} & c_{34} & c_{35} \\
c_{41} & c_{42} & c_{43} & c_{44} & c_{45} \\
c_{51} & c_{52} & c_{53} & c_{54} & c_{55}
\end{pmatrix}
$$

Where $c_{ij} = a_{i1} \times b_{1j} + a_{i2} \times b_{2j} + a_{i3} \times b_{3j} + a_{i4} \times b_{4j} + a_{i5} \times b_{5j}$

Assume that both arrays are 5 by 5 with int type elements. The program is given below. The output of the program is shown in Figure 5.11.

```
1    // TestMatrixOperation.java: Add and multiply two matrices
2    public class TestMatrixOperation {
3      /** Main method */
4      public static void main(String[] args) {
5        // Create two matrices as two dimensional arrays
6        int[][] matrix1 = new int[5][5];
7        int[][] matrix2 = new int[5][5];
8
9        // Assign random values to matrix1 and matrix2
10       for (int i = 0; i < matrix1.length; i++)
```

continues

Example 5.7 continued

```
11          for (int j = 0; j < matrix1[i].length; j++) {
12            matrix1[i][j] = (int)(Math.random() * 10);
13            matrix2[i][j] = (int)(Math.random() * 10);
14          }
15
16        // Add two matrices and print the result
17        int[][] resultMatrix = addMatrix(matrix1, matrix2);
18        System.out.println("The addition of the matrices is ");
19        printResult(matrix1, matrix2, resultMatrix, '+');
20
21        // Multiply two matrices and print the result
22        resultMatrix = multiplyMatrix(matrix1, matrix2);
23        System.out.println("\nThe multiplication of the matrices is ");
24        printResult(matrix1, matrix2, resultMatrix, '*');
25      }
26
27      /** The method for adding two matrices */
29      public static int[][] addMatrix(int[][] m1, int[][] m2) {
29        int[][] result = new int[m1.length][m1[0].length];
30        for (int i = 0; i < result.length; i++)
31          for (int j = 0; j < result[0].length; j++)
32            result[i][j] = m1[i][j] + m2[i][j];
33
34        return result;
35      }
36
37      /** The method for multiplying two matrices */
38      public static int[][] multiplyMatrix(int[][] m1, int[][] m2) {
39        int[][] result = new int[m1.length][m2[0].length];
40        for (int i = 0; i < m1.length; i++)
41          for (int j = 0; j < result.length; j++)
42            for (int k = 0; k < result[0].length; k++)
43              result[i][j] += m1[i][k] * m2[k][j];
44
45        return result;
46      }
47
48      /** Print result */
49      public static void printResult(
50        int[][] m1, int[][] m2, int[][] m3, char op) {
51        for (int i = 0; i < m1.length; i++) {
52          for (int j = 0; j < m1[0].length; j++)
53            System.out.print(" " + m1[i][j]);
54
55          if (i == m1.length / 2)
56            System.out.print( "  " + op + "  " );
57          else
58            System.out.print( "     " );
59
60          for (int j = 0; j < m2[0].length; j++)
61            System.out.print(" " + m2[i][j]);
62
63          if (i == m1.length / 2)
64            System.out.print( "  =  " );
65          else
66            System.out.print( "     " );
67
68          for (int j = 0; j < m3[0].length; j++)
69            System.out.print(" " + m3[i][j]);
70
71          System.out.println();
72        }
73      }
74    }
```

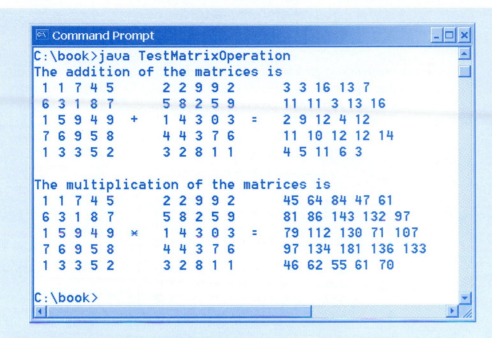

Figure 5.11 *The program adds and multiplies two matrices that are represented in two-dimensional arrays.*

Review

The statement `int[][] matrix1 = new int[5][5]` declares and creates a 5 by 5 matrix (Line 6).

Nested `for` loops are often used to process multidimensional array elements. The matrices `matrix1` and `matrix2` are initialized by using a nested `for` loop with random values (Lines 10–14).

The `addMatrix(int[][] m1, int[][] m2)` method adds `m1` and `m2` and returns the result matrix (Line 17). The return value type of this method is an array type `int[][]`.

The `multiplyMatrix(int[][] m1, int[][] m2)` method multiplies `m1` and `m2` and returns the result matrix (Line 22).

The `printResult(int[][] m1, int m2[][], int[][] m3, char op)` method (Lines 49–73) displays the contents of `m1`, `m2`, and `m3` in the format `m1 op m2 = m3`.

Example 5.8   Grading a Multiple-Choice Test

Problem

Write a program that grades multiple-choice tests. Suppose there are eight students and ten questions, and the answers are stored in a two-dimensional array. Each row records a student's answers to the questions. For example, the following array stores the test.

Students' Answers to the Questions:

```
             0 1 2 3 4 5 6 7 8 9
Student 0    A B A C C D E E A D
Student 1    D B A B C A E E A D
Student 2    E D D A C B E E A D
Student 3    C B A E D C E E A D
Student 4    A B D C C D E E A D
Student 5    B B E C C D E E A D
Student 6    B B A C C D E E A D
Student 7    E B E C C D E E A D
```

The key is stored a one-dimensional array, as follows:

Key to the Questions:

```
          0  1  2  3  4  5  6  7  8  9
Key       D  B  D  C  C  D  A  E  A  D
```

Your program grades the test and displays the result, as shown in Figure 5.12.

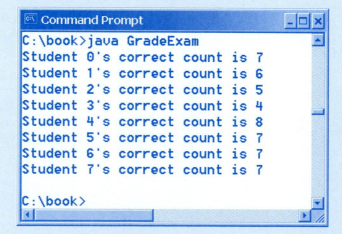

```
C:\book>java GradeExam
Student 0's correct count is 7
Student 1's correct count is 6
Student 2's correct count is 5
Student 3's correct count is 4
Student 4's correct count is 8
Student 5's correct count is 7
Student 6's correct count is 7
Student 7's correct count is 7

C:\book>
```

Figure 5.12   *The program grades students' answers to the multiple-choice questions.*

Solution

The following code gives the solution to the problem.

```java
1    // GradeExam.java: Grade answers to multiple choice questions
2    public class GradeExam {
3      /** Main method */
4      public static void main(String args[]) {
5        // Students' answers to the questions
6        char[][] answers = {
7          {'A', 'B', 'A', 'C', 'C', 'D', 'E', 'E', 'A', 'D'},
8          {'D', 'B', 'A', 'B', 'C', 'A', 'E', 'E', 'A', 'D'},
9          {'E', 'D', 'D', 'A', 'C', 'B', 'E', 'E', 'A', 'D'},
10         {'C', 'B', 'A', 'E', 'D', 'C', 'E', 'E', 'A', 'D'},
11         {'A', 'B', 'D', 'C', 'C', 'D', 'E', 'E', 'A', 'D'},
12         {'B', 'B', 'E', 'C', 'C', 'D', 'E', 'E', 'A', 'D'},
13         {'B', 'B', 'A', 'C', 'C', 'D', 'E', 'E', 'A', 'D'},
14         {'E', 'B', 'E', 'C', 'C', 'D', 'E', 'E', 'A', 'D'}};
15
16       // Key to the questions
17       char[] keys = {'D', 'B', 'D', 'C', 'C', 'D', 'A', 'E', 'A', 'D'};
18
19       // Grade all answers
20       for (int i = 0; i < answers.length; i++) {
21         // Grade one student
22         int correctCount = 0;
23
24         for (int j = 0; j < answers[i].length; j++) {
25           if (answers[i][j] == keys[j])
26             correctCount++;
27         }
28
29         System.out.println("Student " + i + "'s correct count is " +
30           correctCount);
31       }
32     }
33   }
```

Review

The statement in Lines 6–14 declares, creates, and initializes a two-dimensional array of characters and assigns the reference to answers of the char[][] type.

The statement in Line 17 declares, creates, and initializes an array of int values and assigns the reference to keys of the char[][] type.

Each row in the array answers stores a student's answer, which is graded by comparing it with the key in the array keys. The result is displayed immediately after a student's answer is graded. In Exercise 5.7, you will modify the program to display the mean and standard deviation of the number of correct answers, and the students in increasing order of the number of correct answers.

Example 5.9 Calculating Total Scores

Problem

Write a program that calculates the total score for the students in a class. Suppose the scores are stored in a three-dimensional array named scores. The first index in scores refers to a student, the second refers to an exam, and the third refers to a part of the exam. Suppose there are seven students, five exams, and each exam has two parts: a multiple-choice part and a programming part. scores[i][j][0] represents the score on the multiple-choice part for the i's student on the j's exam. Your program displays the total score for each student, as shown in Figure 5.13.

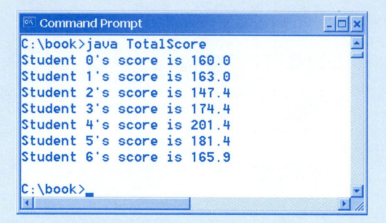

Figure 5.13   *The program displays the total score for each student.*

Solution

The program compares each student's answer with the key, counts the number of correct answers, and displays it. The source code for the program is shown below:

```
1    // TotalScore.java: Find the total score for each student
2    public class TotalScore {
3      /** Main method */
4      public static void main(String args[]) {
5        double[][][] scores = {
6          {{7.5, 20.5}, {12, 22.5}, {12, 33.5}, {13, 21.5}, {15, 2.5}},
7          {{4.5, 21.5}, {12, 22.5}, {12, 34.5}, {12, 20.5}, {14, 9.5}},
8          {{5.5, 30.5}, {9.4, 2.5}, {13, 33.5}, {11, 23.5}, {16, 2.5}},
9          {{6.5, 23.5}, {9.4, 32.5}, {13, 34.5}, {11, 20.5}, {16, 7.5}},
10         {{8.5, 25.5}, {9.4, 52.5}, {13, 36.5}, {13, 24.5}, {16, 2.5}},
11         {{9.5, 20.5}, {9.4, 42.5}, {13, 31.5}, {12, 20.5}, {16, 6.5}},
12         {{1.5, 29.5}, {6.4, 22.5}, {14, 30.5}, {10, 30.5}, {16, 5.}}};
13
14         // Calculate and display total score for each student
15         for (int i = 0; i < scores.length; i++) {
16           double totalScore = 0;
17           for (int j = 0; j < scores[i].length; j++)
18             for (int k = 0; k < scores[i][j].length; k++)
19               totalScore += scores[i][j][k];
20
```

```
21          System.out.println("Student " + i + "'s score is " +
22             totalScore);
23        }
24      }
25    }
```

Review

The statement in Lines 5–12 declares, creates, and initializes a three-dimensional array of `double` values and assigns the reference to `scores` of the `double[][][]` type.

The scores for each student are added in Lines 17–19, and the result is displayed in Lines 21–22. The `for` loop in Line 15 process the scores for all the students.

5.7 Searching Arrays

Searching is the process of looking for a specific element in an array; for example, discovering whether a certain score is included in a list of scores. Searching is a common task in computer programming. There are many algorithms and data structures devoted to searching. In this section, two commonly used approaches are discussed, *linear search* and *binary search*.

5.7.1 The Linear Search Approach

The linear search approach compares the key element `key` with each element in the array `list[]`. The method continues to do so until the key matches an element in the list or the list is exhausted without a match being found. If a match is made, the linear search returns the index of the element in the array that matches the key. If no match is found, the search returns `-1`. The algorithm can be simply described as follows:

```
for (int i = 0; i < list.length; i++) {
  if (key == list[i])
    return i;
}
return -1;
```

The example given below demonstrates a linear search.

Example 5.10 Testing Linear Search

Problem

Write a program that implements and tests the linear search method. The program creates an array of ten random elements of `int` type and then displays it. The program prompts the user to enter a key for testing linear search.

Solution

The following code gives the solution to the problem. The output of a sample run of the program is shown in Figure 5.14.

continues

189

Example 5.10 continued

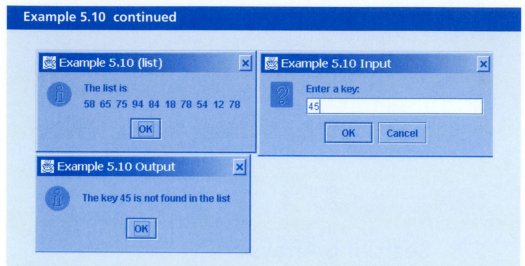

Figure 5.14   *The program uses linear search to find a key in a list of* int *elements.*

```
1    // LinearSearch.java: Search for a number in a list
2    import javax.swing.JOptionPane;
3
4    public class LinearSearch {
5      /** Main method */
6      public static void main(String[] args) {
7        int[] list = new int[10];
8
9        // Declare and initialized output string
10       String output = "";
11
12       // Create the list randomly and display it
13       output += "The list is\n";
14       for (int i =0; i < list.length; i++) {
15         list[i] = (int)(Math.random() * 100);
16         output += list[i] + "   ";
17       }
18
19       // Display the list
20       JOptionPane.showMessageDialog(null, output,
21         "Example 5.10 (list)", JOptionPane.INFORMATION_MESSAGE);
22
23       // Prompt the user to enter a key
24       String keyString = JOptionPane.showInputDialog(null,
25         "Enter a key:",
26         "Example 5.10 Input", JOptionPane.QUESTION_MESSAGE);
27
28       // Convert string into integer
29       int key = Integer.parseInt(keyString);
30
31       // Empty the output string
32       output = "";
33
34       // Search for key
35       int index = linearSearch(key, list);
36       if (index != -1)
37         output = "The key is found in index " + index;
38       else
39         output = "The key " + key + " is not found in the list";
40
```

```
41         // Display the result
42         JOptionPane.showMessageDialog(null, output,
43           "Example 5.10 Output", JOptionPane.INFORMATION_MESSAGE);
44
45         System.exit(0);
46       }
47
48       /** The method for finding a key in the list */
49       public static int linearSearch(int key, int[] list) {
50         for (int i = 0; i < list.length; i++)
51           if (key == list[i])
52             return i;
53         return -1;
54       }
55     }
```

Review

A sample array for testing purposes is created by using a random number generator. `Math.random()` (Line 15) generates a random `double` value greater than or equal to 0.0 and less than 1.0. Therefore, `(int)(Math.random() * 100)` is a random integer value greater than or equal to 0 and less than 100.

If there is a match, the algorithm returns the index of the first element in the array that matches the key. If there is no match, the algorithm returns -1.

The linear search method compares the key with each element in the array. The elements in the array can be in any order. On average, the algorithm will have to compare half of the elements in an array. Since the execution time of a linear search increases linearly as the number of array elements increases, linear search is inefficient for a large array.

5.7.2   The Binary Search Approach (Optional)

Binary search is the other common search approach. For binary search to work, the elements in the array must already be ordered. Without loss of generality, assume that the array is in ascending order. The binary search first compares the key with the element in the middle of the array. Consider the following three cases:

- If the key is less than the middle element, you only need to search the key in the first half of the array.

- If the key is equal to the middle element, the search ends with a match.

- If the key is greater than the middle element, you only need to search the key in the second half of the array.

Figure 5.15 shows how to find key 11 in the list {2, 4, 7, 10, 11, 45, 50, 59, 60, 66, 69, 70, 79} using binary search.

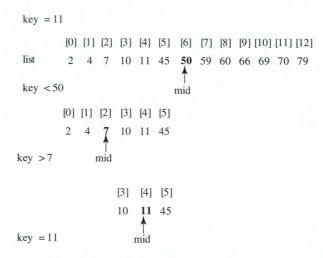

Figure 5.15   *The binary search eliminates half of list from further consideration after each comparison.*

Clearly, the binary search method eliminates half of the array after each comparison. Suppose that the array has *n* elements. For convenience, let n be a power of 2. After the first comparison, there are n/2 elements left for further search; after the second comparison, there are (n/2)/2 elements left for further search. After the kth comparison, there are $n/2^k$ elements left for further search. When k = $\log_2 n$, only one element is left in the array, and you only need one more comparison. Therefore, in the worst case, you need $\log_2 n+1$ comparisons to find an element in the sorted array when using the binary search approach. For a list of 1,024 (2^{10}) elements, binary search requires only eleven comparisons in the worst case, whereas a linear search would take 1024 comparisons in the worst case.

The portion of the array being searched shrinks after each comparison. Let low and high denote, respectively, the first index and last index of the array that is currently being searched. Initially, low is 0 and high is list.length-1. Let binarySearch(int key, int[] list, int low, int high) denote the method that finds the key in the list that has the specified low index and high index. The algorithm can be described recursively as follows:

```
public static int binarySearch
  (int key, int[] list, int low, int high) {
  if (low > high)
    the list has been searched without a match, return -1;
  // Find mid, the index of the middle element in list[low..high]
  int mid = (low + high) / 2;
  if (key < list[mid])
    // Search in list[low..mid-1] recursively.
    return binarySearch(key, list, low, mid-1);
  else if (key == list[mid])
    // A match is found
    return mid;
  else
    // Search in list[mid+1..high] recursively.
    return binarySearch(key, list, mid + 1, high);
}
```

The next example demonstrates the binary search approach.

Example 5.11 Testing Binary Search

Problem

Write a program that implements and tests the binary search method. The program first creates an array of ten elements of int type. It displays this array and then prompts the user to enter a key for testing binary search.

Solution

The following code gives the solution to the problem. The output of a sample run of the program is shown in Figure 5.16.

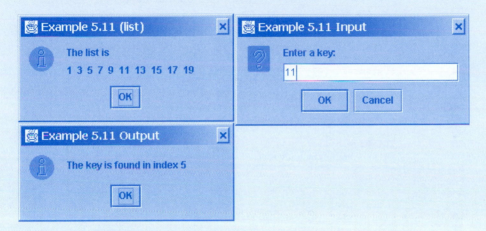

Figure 5.16   *The program uses binary search to find a key in a list of int elements.*

```
1   // BinarySearch.java: Search a key in a sorted list
2   import javax.swing.JOptionPane;
3
4   public class BinarySearch {
5     /** Main method */
6     public static void main(String[] args) {
7       int[] list = new int[10];
8
9       // Declare and initialized output string
10      String output = "The list is\n";
11
12      // Create a sorted list
13      for (int i = 0; i < list.length; i++) {
14        list[i] = 2 * i + 1;
15        output += list[i] + "  ";
16      }
17
18      // Display the list
19      JOptionPane.showMessageDialog(null, output,
20        "Example 5.11 (list)", JOptionPane.INFORMATION_MESSAGE);
21
22      // Prompt the user to enter a key
23      String keyString = JOptionPane.showInputDialog(null,
24        "Enter a key:",
25        "Example 5.11 Input", JOptionPane.QUESTION_MESSAGE);
26
```

continues

Example 5.11 continued

```
26        // Convert string into integer
27        int key = Integer.parseInt(keyString);
28
30        // Empty the output string
31        output = "";
32
33        // Search for key
34        int index = binarySearch(key, list);
35        if (index != -1)
36          output += "The key is found in index " + index;
37        else
38          output += "The key is not found in the list";
39
40        // Display the result
41        JOptionPane.showMessageDialog(null, output,
42          "Example 5.11 Output", JOptionPane.INFORMATION_MESSAGE);
43
44        System.exit(0);
45      }
46
47    /** Use binary search to find the key in the list */
48    public static int binarySearch(int key, int[] list) {
49      int low = 0;
50      int high = list.length - 1;
51      return binarySearch(key, list, low, high);
52    }
53
54    /** Use binary search to find the key in the list between
55        list[low] list[high] */
56    public static int binarySearch(int key, int[] list,
57      int low, int high) {
58      if (low > high)  // The list has been exhausted without a match
59        return -1;
60
61      int mid = (low + high) / 2;
62      if (key < list[mid])
63        return binarySearch(key, list, low, mid-1);
64      else if (key == list[mid])
65        return mid;
66      else
67        return binarySearch(key, list, mid+1, high);
68      }
69    }
```

Review

There are two overloaded methods named binarySearch in the program: binarySearch(int key, int[] list) (Lines 48–52) and binarySearch(int key, int[] list, int low, int high) (Lines 56–68). The first method finds a key in the whole list. The second method finds a key in the list with index from low to high.

The first binarySearch method passes the initial array with low = 0 and high = list.length-1 to the second binarySearch method (Line 51). The second method is invoked recursively to find the key in an ever-shrinking subarray. It is a common design technique in recursive programming to choose a second method that can be called recursively.

There are two reasons why this is a good example of using recursion. First, using recursion enables you to specify a clear, simple solution for the binary search problem. Second, the number of recursive calls is less than the size of the list. So the solution is reasonably efficient. In Exercise 5.11, you will use iterations to rewrite this program.

NOTE

Linear search is useful for finding an element in a small array or an un-sorted array, but it is inefficient for large arrays. Binary search is more efficient, but requires that the array be sorted. The following section introduces sorting arrays.

5.8   Sorting Arrays

Sorting, like searching, is a common task in computer programming. It would be used, for instance, if you wanted to display the grades from Example 5.2 in alphabetical order. Once an array is sorted, you can use binary search to quickly find elements in the array. Many different algorithms are used for sorting. In this section, a simple, intuitive sorting algorithm, *selection sort,* is introduced.

Suppose that you want to sort a list in ascending order. Selection sort finds the largest number in the list and places it last. It then finds the largest number remaining and places it next to last, and so on until the list contains only a single number.

Consider the following list:

2 **9** 5 4 8 1 **6**

If you selected 9 (the largest number) and swapped it with 6 (the last in the list), the new list would be:

2 **6** 5 4 8 1 <u>9</u>

The number 9 would now be in the correct position and thus no longer need to be considered. (Underlining indicates that a number has already been sorted.) The list is now:

2 6 5 4 **8** 1 <u>9</u>

If you applied selection sort to the remaining numbers, you would select 8 and swap it with 1. The new list would be:

2 6 5 4 1 <u>8 9</u>

Since the number 8 has been placed in the correct position, it would no longer need to be considered. If you continued the same process, eventually the entire list would be sorted.

The algorithm can be described as follows:

```
for (int i = list.length - 1; i >= 1; i--) {
  select the largest element in list[1..i];
  swap the largest with list[i], if necessary;
  // list[i] is in place. The next iteration apply on list[1..i-1]
}
```

The code is given in the next example.

Example 5.12 Using Arrays in Sorting

Problem

Implement the selectionSort method that sorts a list of double floating-point numbers.

Solution

The following code gives the solution to the problem. The output of the program is shown in Figure 5.17.

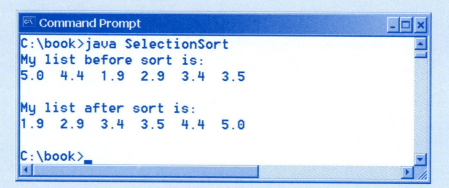

Figure 5.17   *The program invokes* selectionSort *in order to sort a list of* double *values.*

```
1    // SelectionSort.java: Sort numbers using selection sort
2    public class SelectionSort {
3      /** Main method */
4      public static void main(String[] args) {
5        // Initialize the list
6        double[] myList = {5.0, 4.4, 1.9, 2.9, 3.4, 3.5};
7
8        // Print the original list
9        System.out.println("My list before sort is: ");
10       printList(myList);
11
12       // Sort the list
13       selectionSort(myList);
14
15       // Print the sorted list
16       System.out.println();
17       System.out.println("My list after sort is: ");
18       printList(myList);
19     }
20
```

```
21        /** The method for printing numbers */
22        static void printList(double[] list) {
23          for (int i = 0; i < list.length; i++)
24            System.out.print(list[i] + "  ");
25          System.out.println();
26        }
27
28        /** The method for sorting the numbers */
29        static void selectionSort(double[] list) {
30          for (int i = list.length - 1; i >= 1; i--) {
31            // Find the maximum in the list[0..i]
32            double currentMax = list[0];
33            int currentMaxIndex = 0;
34
35            for (int j = 1; j <= i; j++) {
36              if (currentMax < list[j]) {
37                currentMax = list[j];
38                currentMaxIndex = j;
39              }
40            }
41
42            // Swap list[i] with list[currentMaxIndex] if necessary;
43            if (currentMaxIndex != i) {
44              list[currentMaxIndex] = list[i];
45              list[i] = currentMax;
46            }
47          }
48        }
49      }
```

Review

An array `myList` of length 6 was created in Line 6. Its initial values are listed in the following single statement:

```
double[] myList = {5.0, 4.4, 1.9, 2.9, 3.4, 3.5};
```

The `selectionSort(double[] list)` method sorts any array of double elements. The method is implemented with a nested `for` loop. The outer loop (with the loop control variable `i`) (Line 30) is iterated in order to find the largest element in the list, which ranges from `list[0]` to `list[i]`, and exchange it with the current last element, `list[i]`.

The variable `i` is initially `list.length-1`. After each iteration of the outer loop, `list[i]` is in the right place. Eventually, all the elements are put in the right place; therefore, the whole list is sorted.

■ NOTE

Most students will not be able to derive the algorithm on their first attempt. I suggest that you write the code for the first iteration to find the largest element in the list and swap it with the last element, and then observe what would be different for the second iteration, the third, and so on. From the observation, you can write the outer loop and derive the algorithm.

Chapter Summary

In this chapter, you learned about the use of arrays to store a collection of data of the same type. You learned how to declare and create arrays and how to access individual elements in an array. Java stores lists of values in arrays, which are contiguous groups of adjacent memory locations. To refer to a particular location or element of an array, you specify the name of the array and then give the index, which is placed in brackets. An index must be an integer or an integer expression.

After an array is created, its size becomes permanent and can be obtained using `arrayReferenceVariable.length`. Since the index of an array always begins with 0, the last index is always `arrayReferenceVariable.length-1`. An out-of-bounds error will occur if you attempt to reference elements beyond the bounds of an array.

The `for` loop is often used to process all of the elements in an array. You can use `for` loops to initialize arrays, display arrays, and control and manipulate array elements.

Arrays can be passed to a method as actual parameters. When you pass an array, you are actually passing the reference of the array; that is, the called method can modify the elements in the caller's original arrays.

You also learned how to search a key in an array using the linear search and binary search approaches, and how to sort an array using the selection sort method.

You can use arrays of arrays to form multidimensional arrays. You learned a convenient syntax that can declare multidimensional arrays, and you saw examples of the use of a multidimensional array.

Review Questions

5.1 How do you declare and create an array?

5.2 How do you access elements of an array?

5.3 Is memory allocated when an array is declared? When is the memory allocated for an array?

5.4 Indicate true or false for the following statements:

- Every element in an array has the same type.

- The array size is fixed after it is declared.

- The array size is fixed after it is created.

- The elements in the array must be of primitive data type.

5.5 Which of the following statements are valid array declarations?

```
int i = new int(30);
double d[] = new double[30];
char[] r = new char(1..30);
int i[] = (3, 4, 3, 2);
float f[] = {2.3, 4.5, 5.6};
char[] c = new char();
int[][] r = new int[2];
```

5.6   What is the array index type? What is the lowest index?

5.7   What is the representation of the third element in an array named a?

5.8   What happens when your program attempts to access an array element with an invalid index?

5.9   Identify and fix the errors in the following code:

```java
public class Test {
  public static void main(String[] args) {
    double[] r;

    for (int i = 0; i < r.length(); i++);
      r(i) = Math.random * 100;
  }
}
```

5.10 Use the arraycopy() method to copy the following array to a target array t:

```java
int[] source = {3, 4, 5};
```

5.11 Declare and create a 4 × 5 int matrix.

5.12 Once an array is created, its size cannot be changed. Does the following code resize the array?

```java
int[] myList;
myList = new int[10];
// Sometime later . . .
myList = new int[20];
```

5.13 Can the rows in a two-dimensional array have different lengths?

5.14 What is the output of the following code?

```java
int[][] array = new int[5][6];
int[] x = {1, 2};
array[0] = x;
System.out.println("array[0][1] is " + array[0][1]);
```

Programming Exercises

5.1   Write a program that will read ten integers and display them in reverse order.

5.2   Write a method that finds the average in an array of floating-point values. Use {15, 20.3, 4.5, 5.5, 10.3, 450, 20.4, -22.3} to test the method.

5.3   Write a method that finds the smallest element in an array of integers. Use {1, 2, 4, 5, 10, 100, 2, -22} to test the method.

5.4   Write a method that returns a new array that is a reversal of the original array. Use {5.0, 4.4, 1.9, 2.9, 3.4, 3.5} to test the method.

5.5   Write a method that sums all the integers in the major diagonal in a matrix of integers. Use {{1, 2, 4, 5}, {6, 7, 8, 9}, {10, 11, 12, 13}, {14, 15, 16, 17}} to test the method.

5.6 Write a method that sums all the integers in a matrix of integers. Use {{1, 2, 4, 5}, {6, 7, 8, 9}, {10, 11, 12, 13}, {14, 15, 16, 17}} to test the method.

5.7 Rewrite Example 5.8 to display the mean and standard deviation of the number of correct answers. Display the students in increasing order of the number of correct answers.

5.8 Write a program that computes weekly hours for each employee. Suppose the weekly hours for all employees are stored in a two-dimensional array. Each row records an employee's seven-day work hours with seven columns. For example, the following array stores the work hours for eight employees. Display employees and the total hours of each employee in decreasing order of the total hours.

	Su	M	T	W	R	F	Sa
Employee 0	2	4	3	4	5	8	8
Employee 1	7	3	4	3	3	4	4
Employee 2	3	3	4	3	3	2	2
Employee 3	9	3	4	7	3	4	1
Employee 4	3	5	4	3	6	3	8
Employee 5	3	4	4	6	3	4	4
Employee 6	3	7	4	8	3	8	4
Employee 7	6	3	5	9	2	7	9

5.9 Use recursion to rewrite the selection sort used in Example 5.12.

5.10 In Example 5.12, you used selection sort to sort an array. The selection sort method repeatedly finds the largest number in the current array and swaps it with the last number in the array. Rewrite this example by finding the smallest number and swapping it with the first number in the array.

5.11 Use iterations to rewrite the binary search used in Example 5.11.

HINT

You can use a loop to find the key in the list, as follows:

```
public static int binarySearch(int key, int[] list) {
  int low = 0;
  int high = list.length - 1;
  while (high >= low) {
    int mid = (low + high) / 2;
    if (key < list[mid])
      high = mid - 1;
    else if (key == list[mid])
      return mid;
    else
      low = mid + 1;
  }
  return -1;
}
```

5.12 Rewrite Example 3.7, "Finding the Sales Amount," using the binary search approach. Since the sales amount is between 1 and `COMMISSION_SOUGHT`/`0.08`, you can use a binary search to improve Example 3.7.

5.13 Write a sort method that uses the bubble-sort algorithm. The bubble-sort algorithm makes several passes through the array. On each pass, successive neighboring pairs are compared. If a pair is in decreasing order, its values are swapped; otherwise, the values remain unchanged. The technique is called a *bubble sort* or *sinking sort* because the smaller values gradually "bubble" their way to the top and the larger values sink to the bottom.

The algorithm can be described as follows:

```
boolean changed = true;
do {
  changed = false;
  for (int j = 0; j < list.length - 1; j++)
    if (list[j] > list[j + 1]) {
      swap list[j] with list[j + 1];
      changed = true;
    }
}
while (changed);
```

Clearly, the list is in increasing order when the loop terminates. It is easy to show that the do loop executes at most `list.length` - 1 times.

Use {5.0, 4.4, 1.9, 2.9, 3.4, 3.5} to test the method.

PART II

OBJECT-ORIENTED PROGRAMMING

In Part I, "Fundamentals of Programming," you learned how to write simple Java applications using primitive data types, control statements, methods, and arrays, all of which are features commonly available in procedural programming languages. Java, however, is an object-oriented programming language that uses abstraction, encapsulation, inheritance, and polymorphism to provide great flexibility, modularity, and reusability for developing software. In this part of the book you will learn how to define, extend, and work with classes and their objects.

CHAPTER 6

OBJECTS AND CLASSES

Objectives

- To understand objects and classes and the relationship between them.
- To learn how to define a class and how to create an object of a class.
- To understand the roles of constructors.
- To understand object references and learn how to pass object references to methods.
- To understand instance variables and methods.
- To understand static variables, constants, and methods.
- To use objects as array elements.
- To use UML graphical notations to describe classes and objects.
- To understand the scope of variables in the context of a class.
- To become familiar with the organization of the Java API.

6.1   Introduction

Programming in procedural languages like C, Pascal, BASIC, Ada, and COBOL involves choosing data structures, designing algorithms, and translating algorithms into code. An object-oriented language like Java combines the power of procedural languages with an added dimension that provides more flexibility, modularity, clarity, and reusability through class encapsulation, class inheritance, and dynamic binding.

In procedural programming, data and operations on the data are separate, and this methodology requires sending data to procedures and functions. Object-oriented programming places data and the operations that pertain to them within a single entity called an *object*; this approach solves many of the problems inherent in procedural programming. The object-oriented programming approach organizes programs in a way that mirrors the real world, in which all objects are associated with both attributes and activities. Programming in Java involves thinking in terms of objects; a Java program can be viewed as a collection of cooperating objects.

This chapter introduces the fundamentals of object-oriented programming: declaring classes, creating objects, manipulating objects, and making objects work together.

6.2 Defining Classes for Objects

Object-oriented programming (OOP) involves programming using objects. An *object* represents an entity in the real world that can be distinctly identified. For example, a student, a desk, a circle, a button, and even a mortgage loan can all be viewed as objects. An object has a unique identity, state, and behaviors. The *state* of an object consists of a set of fields with their current values. The *behavior* of an object is defined by a set of methods. Figure 6.1 shows a diagram of an object with its data fields and methods.

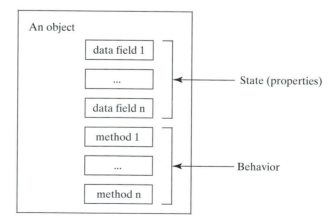

Figure 6.1   *An object has both a state and behavior. The state defines the object, and the behavior defines what the object does.*

A `Circle` object, for example, has a data field, `radius`, which is the property that characterizes a circle. One behavior of a circle is that its area can be computed. A `Circle` object is shown in Figure 6.2.

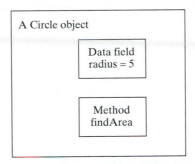

Figure 6.2   *A* `Circle` *object contains the* `radius` *data field and the* `findArea` *method.*

Classes are constructs that define objects of the same type. In a Java class, data are used to describe properties, and methods are used to define behaviors. The class for an object comprises a collection of data and method definitions. Here is an example of the class for a circle:

```
class Circle {
  /** The radius of this circle */
  double radius = 1.0;                  ← Data field

  /** Return the area of this circle */
  double findArea() {                   ← Method
    return radius * radius * 3.14159;
  }
}
```

This class is different from all of the other classes you have seen thus far. The `Circle` class does not have a `main` method and therefore cannot be run; it is merely a definition used to declare and create `Circle` objects. For convenience, the class that contains the `main` method will be referred to as the *main class* in this book.

A class is a blueprint that defines what an object's data and methods will be. An object is an instance of a class. You can create many instances of a class (see Figure 6.3). Creating an instance is referred to as *instantiation*. The terms *object* and *instance* are often interchangeable. The relationship between classes and objects is analogous to the relationship between apple pie recipes and apple pies. You can make as many apple pies as you want from a single recipe.

▬ **NOTE**
Figure 6.3 uses the graphical notations adopted in the Unified Modeling Language (UML) to illustrate classes and objects. UML has become the standard for object-oriented modeling. For more information on UML, see `www.rational.com/uml/`. For a summary of the graphical notations used in this book, see Appendix G, "UML Graphical Notations."

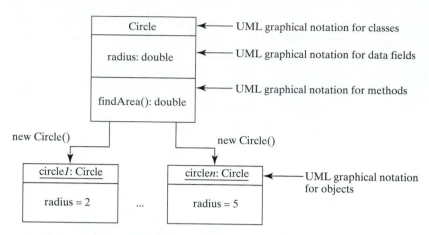

Figure 6.3 *A class can have many different objects.*

6.3 Creating Objects and Object Reference Variables

Objects are created using the new operator, as follows:

```
new ClassName();
```

For example, new Circle() creates an object of the Circle class. Newly created objects are allocated in the memory. Objects are accessed via object *reference variables*, which contain references to the objects. Such variables are declared using the following syntax:

```
ClassName objectReference;
```

The types of reference variables are known as *reference types*. The following statement declares the variable myCircle to be of the Circle type:

```
Circle myCircle;
```

The variable myCircle can reference a Circle object. The next statement creates an object and assigns its reference to myCircle.

```
myCircle = new Circle();
```

Using the syntax shown below, you can write one statement that combines the declaration of an object reference variable, the creation of an object, and the assigning of an object reference to the variable.

```
ClassName objectReference = new ClassName();
```

Here is an example:

```
Circle myCircle = new Circle();
```

The variable myCircle holds a reference to a Circle object.

■■ NOTE

NOTE

An object reference variable that appears to hold an object actually contains a reference to that object. Strictly speaking, an object reference variable and an object are different, but most of the time the distinction between them can be ignored. So it is fine, for simplicity, to say that myCircle is a Circle object rather than a more long-winded phrase stating that myCircle is a variable that contains a reference to a Circle object. When the distinction makes a subtle difference, the long phrase should be used.

NOTE

Arrays are treated as objects in Java. Arrays are created using the new operator. An array variable is actually a variable that contains a reference to an array.

6.3.1 Differences between Variables of Primitive Types and Reference Types

Every variable represents a memory location that holds a value. For a variable of a primitive type, the value is of the primitive type. For a variable of a reference type, the value is a reference to where an object is located. For example, as shown in Figure 6.4, the value of int variable i is int value 1, and the value of Circle object c holds a reference to where the contents of the Circle object are stored in the memory.

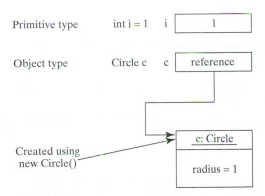

Figure 6.4   *A variable of a primitive type holds a value of the primitive type, and a variable of a reference type holds a reference to where an object is stored in the memory.*

When a variable of a reference type is declared, the variable holds a special Java value, null, which means that the variable does not reference any object. Once an object is created, its reference can be assigned to a variable. For example, the statement

```
c = new Circle();
```

creates a Circle object by allocating the memory space for it, and assigns its memory reference to the variable c.

When you assign one variable to another, the other variable is set to the same value. For a variable of a primitive type, the real value of one variable is assigned to the other variable. For a variable of a reference type, the reference of one variable is assigned to the other variable. As shown in Figure 6.5, the assignment statement `i = j` copies the contents of `j` into `i` for primitive variables, and the assignment statement `c1 = c2` copies the reference of `c2` into `c1` for object variables. After the assignment, variables `c1` and `c2` refer to the same object.

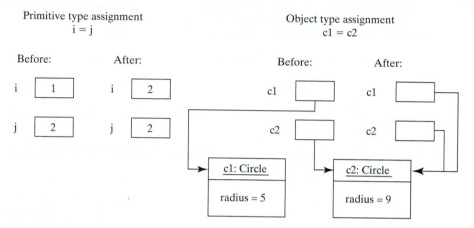

Figure 6.5   *Copying an object variable to another variable does not make a copy of the object; it merely assigns the reference of the object to the other variable.*

6.3.2   Garbage Collection

As shown in Figure 6.5, after the assignment statement `c1 = c2`, `c1` points to the same object referenced by `c2`. The object previously referenced by `c1` is no longer useful and therefore is now known as *garbage*. Garbage occupies memory space. The Java runtime system detects garbage and automatically reclaims the space it occupies. This process is called *garbage collection*.

TIP

If you know that an object is no longer needed, you can explicitly assign `null` to a reference variable for the object. The Java Virtual Machine will automatically collect the space if the object is not referenced.

6.3.3 Accessing an Object's Data and Methods

After an object is created, its data can be accessed and its methods invoked using the following dot notation:

- `objectReference.data` references an object's data.

- `objectReference.method(arguments)` invokes an object's method.

For example, `myCircle.radius` references the radius of `myCircle`, and `myCircle.findArea()` invokes the `findArea` method of `myCircle`. Methods are invoked as operations on objects.

The data field `radius` is referred to as an *instance variable* because it is dependent on a specific instance. For the same reason, the method `findArea` is referred to as an *instance method*, because you can only invoke it on a specific instance.

▬▬ NOTE

Most of the time, you create an object and assign it to a variable. Later you can use the variable to reference the object. Occasionally, an object does not need to be referenced later. In this case, you can create an object without explicitly assigning it to a variable, as shown below:

```
new Circle();
```

Or

```
System.out.println("Area is " + new Circle().findArea());
```

The former statement creates a `Circle` object. The latter statement creates a `Circle` object and invokes its `findArea` method to return its area. An object created in this way is known as an *anonymous object*.

Example 6.1 Declaring Classes and Creating Objects

Problem

Write a program that creates a `Circle` object from the `Circle` class and uses the data and method in the object.

Solution

The following code gives the solution to the problem. The output of the program is shown in Figure 6.6.

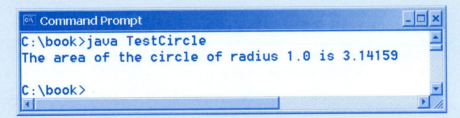

Figure 6.6 *This program creates a* `Circle` *object and displays its* radius *and* area.

```
1    // TestCircle.java: Demonstrate creating and using an object
2    public class TestCircle {
3      /** Main method */
4      public static void main(String[] args) {
5        Circle myCircle = new Circle();  // Create a Circle object
6        System.out.println("The area of the circle of radius "
7          + myCircle.radius + " is " + myCircle.findArea());
8      }
9    }
10
11   // Define the Circle class
12   class Circle {
13     double radius = 1.0;
14
```

continues

Example 6.1 continued

```
15       /** Return the area of this circle */
16       double findArea() {
17         return radius * radius * 3.14159;
18       }
19     }
```

Review

The program contains two classes. The first class, TestCircle (Line 2), is the main class. Its sole purpose is to test the second class, Circle (Line 12). Every time you run the program, the Java runtime system invokes the main method in the main class.

You can put the two classes into one file, but only one class in the file can be a public class. Furthermore, the public class must have the same name as the file name. Therefore, the file name is TestCircle.java if the TestCircle and Circle classes are both in the same file.

The main class contains the main method (Line 4) that creates an object of the Circle class and prints its radius and area. The Circle class contains the findArea method and the radius data field.

To write the findArea method in a procedural programming language like Pascal, you would pass radius as an argument to the method. But in the object-oriented programming, radius and findArea are defined in the same class. The radius is a data member in the Circle class, which is accessible by the findArea method. In procedural programming languages, data and methods are separated, but in an object-oriented programming language, data and methods are defined together in a class.

The findArea method is an instance method that is always invoked by an instance in which the radius is specified.

There are many ways to write Java programs. For instance, you can combine the two classes in the example into one, as shown below:

```
public class Circle {
  double radius = 1.0;
  /** Return the area of this circle */
  double findArea() {
    return radius * radius * 3.14159;
  }

  public static void main(String[] args) {
    // Create a Circle object
    Circle myCircle = new Circle();
    System.out.println("The area of the circle of radius "
      + myCircle.radius + " is " + myCircle.findArea());
  }
}
```

Since the combined class has a main method, it can be executed by the Java interpreter. The main method creates myCircle as a Circle object and then displays radius and finds area in myCircle. This demonstrates that you can test a class by simply adding a main method in the same class.

■ **CAUTION**

You must always create an object before referencing it through a reference variable. Referencing an object that has not been created would cause a runtime `NullPointerException`. Exception handling will be introduced in Chapter 13, "Exception Handling."

■ **NOTE**

The default value of a data field is `null` for a reference type, `0` for a numeric type, `false` for a `boolean` type, and `'\u0000'` for a `char` type. For example, if `radius` is not initialized in the `Circle` class, Java assigns a default value of `0` to it. However, Java assigns no default value to a local variable inside a method. The following code is erroneous because `x` is not initialized:

```java
class Test {
  public static void main(String[] args) {
    int x; // x has no default value
    System.out.println("x is " + x);
  }
}
```

The preceding example declared the `Circle` class and created objects from the class. Often you will use the classes in the Java library to develop programs. When you develop programs to create graphical user interfaces, you will use Java classes to create frames, buttons, radio buttons, combo boxes, lists, and so on. Here is an example that creates frames.

Example 6.2 Using Classes From the Java Library

Problem

Write a program that demonstrates using classes from the Java library. You will use the `JFrame` class in the `javax.swing` package to create two frames; you will use the methods in the `JFrame` class to set the title, size and location of the frames and to display the frames.

Solution

The following code demonstrates how to use the `JFrame` class. The output of the program is shown in Figure 6.7.

Figure 6.7 *The program creates two windows using the `JFrame` class.*

continues

213

Example 6.2 continued

```
1    import javax.swing.JFrame;
2
3    class TestFrame {
4      public static void main(String[] args) {
5        JFrame frame1 = new JFrame();
6        frame1.setTitle("Window 1");
7        frame1.setSize(300, 300);
8
9        frame1.setLocation(200, 100);
10       frame1.setVisible(true);
11       JFrame frame2 = new JFrame();
12       frame2.setTitle("Window 2");
13       frame2.setSize(300, 300);
14       frame2.setLocation(300, 300);
15       frame2.setVisible(true);
16     }
17   }
```

Review

This program creates two objects of the JFrame class and then uses the methods setTitle, setSize, setLocation, and setVisible to set the properties of the objects. The setTitle method sets a title for the window. The setSize method sets the window's width and height. The setLocation method specifies the location of the window's upper-left corner. The setVisible method displays the window. You can add graphical user interface components, such as buttons, labels, text fields, combo boxes, lists, and menus, to the window. The components are defined using classes. GUI programming will be introduced in Part III, "GUI Programming."

6.4   Constructors

One problem with the Circle class discussed above is that all of the objects created from it have the same radius (1.0). Wouldn't it be more useful to create circles with radii of various lengths? Java enables you to define a special method in the class, known as the *constructor*, which can be used to initialize an object's data. You can use a constructor to assign an initial radius when you create an object.

The constructor has exactly the same name as the defining class. Like methods, constructors can be overloaded, making it easier to construct objects with different initial data values. Let's see what happens when the following constructors are added to the Circle class:

```
/** Construct a circle with the specified radius */
Circle(double r) {
  radius = r;
}
```

```
/** Construct a circle with the default radius */
Circle() {
  radius = 1.0;
}
```

When creating a new `Circle` object that has a radius of 5.0, you can use the following, which assigns 5.0 to `myCircle.radius`:

```
myCircle = new Circle(5.0);
```

If you create a circle using the next statement, the second constructor is used, which assigns the default radius 1.0 to `myCircle.radius`:

```
myCircle = new Circle();
```

A constructor with no parameters is referred to as a *default constructor*. The second constructor is a default constructor. Now you know why the syntax `ClassName()` is used to create the object. This syntax invokes a constructor. A constructor, like a method, can perform any action, but constructors are designed to perform initializing actions, such as initializing the data fields of objects. If a class does not explicitly define any constructors, a default constructor is defined implicitly.

A class usually provides many constructors with which users can initialize objects. For example, the `JFrame` class has a default constructor and another one to initialize the title. You can use the following statement to create a frame entitled "Window 1".

```
JFrame frame1 = new JFrame("Window 1");
```

NOTE

Constructors are a special kind of method, with three differences:

- Constructors must have the same name as the class itself.
- Constructors do not have a return type—not even `void`.
- Constructors are invoked using the `new` operator when an object is created. Constructors play the role of initializing objects.

CAUTION

It is a common mistake to put the `void` keyword in front of a constructor. For example,

```
public void Circle() {
}
```

In this case, `Circle()` is method, not a constructor.

Example 6.3 Using Constructors

Problem

Declare a new circle class named `CircleWithConstructors` with two constructors. Write a program that uses constructors in the `CircleWithConstructors` class to create two objects of different radii.

Solution

The following code gives the solution to the problem. The output of the program is shown in Figure 6.8.

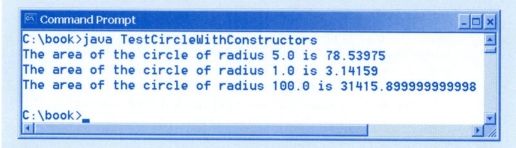

```
C:\book>java TestCircleWithConstructors
The area of the circle of radius 5.0 is 78.53975
The area of the circle of radius 1.0 is 3.14159
The area of the circle of radius 100.0 is 31415.899999999998

C:\book>
```

Figure 6.8   *The program constructs two circles with radii of 5 and 1, and displays their radii and areas.*

```
1    // TestCircleWithConstructors.java: Demonstrate constructors
2    public class TestCircleWithConstructors {
3      /** Main method */
4      public static void main(String[] args) {
5        // Create a Circle with radius 5.0
6        CircleWithConstructors myCircle =
7          new CircleWithConstructors(5.0);
8        System.out.println("The area of the circle of radius "
9          + myCircle.radius + " is " + myCircle.findArea());
10
11       // Create a Circle with default radius
12       CircleWithConstructors yourCircle = new CircleWithConstructors();
13       System.out.println("The area of the circle of radius "
14         + yourCircle.radius + " is " + yourCircle.findArea());
15
16       // Modify circle radius
17       yourCircle.radius = 100;
18       System.out.println("The area of the circle of radius "
19         + yourCircle.radius + " is " + yourCircle.findArea());
20     }
21   }
22
23   // Define the Circle class with two constructors
24   class CircleWithConstructors {
25   double radius;
26
27     /** Default constructor */
28     CircleWithConstructors() {
29       radius = 1.0;
30     }
31
```

```
32        /** Construct a circle with a specified radius */
33        CircleWithConstructors(double r) {
34          radius = r;
35        }
36
37        /** Return the area of this circle */
38        double findArea() {
39          return radius * radius * 3.14159;
40        }
41      }
```

Review

The new circle class is named `CircleWithConstructors`. This new class has two constructors. You can specify a radius or use the default radius to create a circle object. In this example, two objects were created. The constructor `CircleWith-Constructors(5.0)` was used to create `myCircle` with a radius of 5.0 (Line 7), and the constructor `CircleWithConstructors()` was used to create `yourCircle` with a default radius of 1.0 (Line 12).

These two objects (referenced by `myCircle` and `yourCircle`) have different data but share the same methods. Therefore, you can compute their respective areas by using the `findArea()` method.

NOTE

If a class does not explicitly define any constructors, a default constructor is defined implicitly. If a class does explicitly define constructors, a default constructor does not exist unless it is defined explicitly. Therefore, you cannot use the default constructor to create an object using new `Class-Name()` if its default constructor is not available. See Review Questions 6.11 and 6.12.

6.5 Visibility Modifiers and Accessor Methods

Example 6.3 works fine, but it is not a good practice to let the client modify fields directly through the object reference. Doing so often causes programming errors that are difficult to debug. To prevent direct modifications of properties through the object reference, you can declare the field private, using the `private` modifier. Java provides several modifiers that control access to data, methods, and classes. This section introduces the `public`, `private`, and default modifiers.

- `public` defines classes, methods, and data in such a way that all programs can access them.

- `private` defines methods and data in such a way that they can be accessed by the declaring class but not by any other class.

> **NOTE**
>
> The modifier `private` applies solely to data or methods, not to classes (except inner classes). Inner classes will be introduced in Chapter 8, "Class Inheritance and Interfaces." If `public` or `private` is not used, then by default the classes, methods, and data are accessible by any class in the same package. Packages are introduced in Appendix H, "Packages." Java has another visibility modifier called `protected`, which will be introduced in Chapter 8. The various Java modifiers are summarized in the table in Appendix D, "Java Modifiers."
>
> Visibility modifiers are used for the members of the class, not local variables inside the methods. Using a visibility modifier inside a method body would cause a compilation error.

> **NOTE**
>
> In most cases, the constructor should be public. However, if you want to prohibit the user from creating an instance of a class, you can use a private constructor. For example, there is no reason to create an instance from the `Math` class because all of the data and methods are static. One solution is to define a dummy private constructor in the class. The `Math` class cannot be instantiated because it has a private constructor, as follows:
>
> ```
> private Math() {
> }
> ```
>
> The `Math` class that comes with the Java system was introduced in Section 4.8, "The `Math` Class," in Chapter 4, "Methods."

A private data field cannot be accessed by an object through a direct reference outside the class that defines the private field. But often a client needs to retrieve and modify a data field. To make a private data field accessible, you can provide a *get* method and a *set* (or *mutator*) method. Because these methods regulate access to internal data fields, they are referred to colloquially as *accessor methods*. The data fields are called *properties* of the object.

> **NOTE**
>
> Colloquially, a get method is referred to as a *getter*, and a set method is referred to as a *setter*.

A get method has the following signature:

```
public returnType getPropertyName()
```

If the `returnType` is `boolean`, the get method should be defined as follows by convention:

```
public boolean isPropertyName()
```

A set method has the following signature:

```
public void setPropertyName(dataType propertyValue)
```

The example given below demonstrates the use of the `private` modifier and accessor methods.

Example 6.4 Using the `private` Modifier and Accessor Methods

Problem

Declare a new circle class, in which private data are used for the radius, and the accessor methods `getRadius` and `setRadius` are provided for the client to retrieve and modify the radius. The program creates an instance of the `CircleWith-Accessors` class and modifies the radius using the `setRadius` method.

Solution

The following code gives the solution to the problem. The output of a sample run is shown in Figure 6.9.

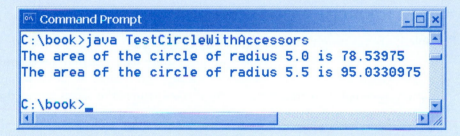

```
C:\book>java TestCircleWithAccessors
The area of the circle of radius 5.0 is 78.53975
The area of the circle of radius 5.5 is 95.0330975

C:\book>
```

Figure 6.9 *This program creates a* `CircleWithAccessors` *object and uses the get method to read its radius, and the set method to modify its radius.*

```
1    // TestCircleWithAccessors.java: Demonstrate private modifier
2    public class TestCircleWithAccessors {
3      /** Main method */
4      public static void main(String[] args) {
5        // Create a Circle with radius 5.0
6        CircleWithAccessors myCircle = new CircleWithAccessors(5.0);
7        System.out.println("The area of the circle of radius "
8          + myCircle.getRadius() + " is " + myCircle.findArea());
9
10       // Increase myCircle's radius by 10%
11       myCircle.setRadius(myCircle.getRadius() * 1.1);
12       System.out.println("The area of the circle of radius "
13         + myCircle.getRadius() + " is " + myCircle.findArea());
14     }
15   }
```

```
1    // CircleWithAccessors.java: The circle class with accessor methods
2    public class CircleWithAccessors {
3      /** The radius of the circle */
4      private double radius;
5
6      /** Default constructor */
7      public CircleWithAccessors() {
8        radius = 1.0;
9      }
10
11     /** Construct a circle with a specified radius */
12     public CircleWithAccessors(double r) {
13       radius = r;
14     }
15
```

continues

Example 6.4 continued

```
16       /** Return radius */
17       public double getRadius() {
18         return radius;
19       }
20
21       /** Set a new radius */
22       public void setRadius(double newRadius) {
23         radius = newRadius;
24       }
25
26       /** Return the area of this circle */
27       public double findArea() {
28         return radius * radius * 3.14159;
29       }
30     }
```

Review

The data field `radius` is declared private. Private data can only be accessed within their defining class. You cannot use `myCircle.radius` in the client program. A compilation error would occur if you attempted to access private data from a client.

To access radius, you have to use the `getRadius` method to retrieve the radius and the `setRadius` method to modify the radius.

Suppose you combined `TestCircleWithAccessors` and `CircleWithAccessors` into one class by moving the main method in `TestCircleWithAccessors` into `CircleWithAccessors`. Could you use `myCircle.radius` in the main method? See Review Question 6.16 for the answer.

■ **NOTE**

`TestCircleWithAccessors` and `CircleWithAccessors` are stored in two separate files. If classes in different files are listed one after the other, the book separates them using a separator line.

6.6   Passing Objects to Methods

So far, you have learned to pass parameters of primitive types and arrays to methods, and you can also pass objects to methods. Like passing an array, passing an object is actually passing the reference of the object. The following code passes the `myCircle` object as an argument to the method `printCircle`:

```
class TestPassingObject {
  public static void main(String[] args) {
    CircleWithAccessors myCircle = new CircleWithAccessors(5.0);
    printCircle(myCircle);
  }
```

```
      public static void printCircle(CircleWithAccessors c) {
        System.out.println("The area of the circle of radius "
          + c.getRadius() + " is " + c.findArea());
      }
    }
```

Java uses exactly one mode of passing parameters: pass by value. In the preceding code, the value of `myCircle` is passed to the `printCircle` method. This value is a reference to a circle object.

Example 6.5 Passing Objects as Arguments

Problem

Write a program that passes a circle object and an integer value to the method `printAreas`, which prints a table of areas for radii 1, 2, 3, 4, and 5.

Solution

The following code gives the solution to the problem. The output of the program is shown in Figure 6.10.

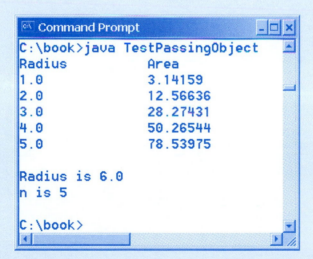

Figure 6.10 *The program passes a circle object* myCircle *and an integer value* n *as parameters to the* printAreas *method, which displays a table of the areas for radii 1, 2, 3, 4, and 5.*

```
1     // TestPassingObject.java: Demonstrate passing objects to methods
2     public class TestPassingObject {
3       /** Main method */
4       public static void main(String[] args) {
5         // Create a Circle object with default radius 1
6         CircleWithAccessors myCircle = new CircleWithAccessors();
7
8         // Print areas for radius 1, 2, 3, 4, and 5.
9         int n = 5;
10        printAreas(myCircle, n);
11
```

continues

Example 6.5 continued

```
12          // See myCircle.radius and times
13          System.out.println("\n" + "Radius is " + myCircle.getRadius());
14          System.out.println("n is " + n);
15       }
16
17       /** Print a table of areas for radius */
18       public static void printAreas(CircleWithAccessors c, int times) {
19          System.out.println("Radius \t\tArea");
20          while (times >= 1) {
21             System.out.println(c.getRadius() + "\t\t" + c.findArea());
22             c.setRadius(c.getRadius() + 1);
23             times--;
24          }
25       }
26    }
```

Review

The `main` method invokes the `printAreas` method (Line 10) by passing an object `myCircle` and an integer `n` to the `printAreas` method, as shown in Figure 6.11.

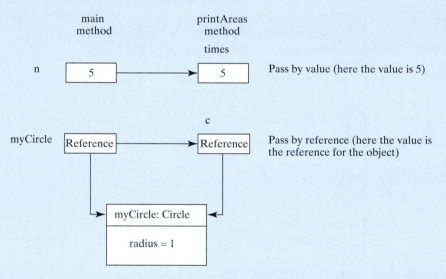

Figure 6.11   *The value of* n *is passed to* times, *and the reference of* myCircle *is passed to* c *in the* printAreas *method.*

When passing a parameter of a primitive data type, the value of the actual parameter is passed. In this case, the value of n (5) is passed to `times`. Inside the `printAreas` method, the content of `times` is changed; this does not affect the content of n. When passing a parameter of a reference type, the reference of the object is passed. In this case, c contains a reference for the object that is also referenced via `myCircle`. Therefore, changing the properties of the object through c inside the `printAreas` method has the same effect as doing so outside the method through the variable `myCircle`.

6.7 Static Variables, Constants, and Methods

The variable radius in the circle classes in the preceding examples is known as an *instance variable*. An instance variable is tied to a specific instance of the class; it is not shared among objects of the same class. For example, suppose that you create the following objects:

```
Circle circle1 = new Circle();
Circle circle2 = new Circle(5);
```

The radius in circle1 is independent of the radius in circle2, and is stored in a different memory location. Changes made to circle1's radius do not affect circle2's radius, and vice versa.

If you want all the instances of a class to share data, use *static variables*, also known as *class variables*. Static variables store values for the variables in a common memory location. Because of this common location, all objects of the same class are affected if one object changes the value of a static variable.

To declare a static variable, put the modifier static in the variable declaration. Suppose that you want to track the number of objects of the CircleWithStaticVariable class, you can define the static variable as follows:

```
static int numOfObjects;
```

Figure 6.12 pictures the instance variables and static variables.

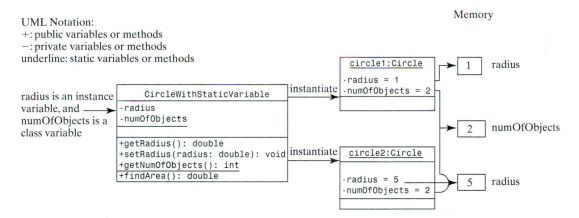

Figure 6.12 *The instance variables, which belong to the instances, have memory storage independent of one other. The static variables are shared by all the instances of the same class.*

To declare a class constant, add the final keyword in the preceding declaration. For example, the constant PI in the Math class is defined as:

```
public final static double PI = 3.14159265358979323846;
```

Instance methods belong to instances and can only be applied after the instances are created. They are called by the following:

```
objectName.methodName();
```

The methods defined in the previous circle classes are instance methods. Java supports static methods as well as static variables. *Static methods*, also known as *class methods*, can be called without creating an instance of the class. To define a static method, put the modifier static in the method declaration:

```
static returnValueType staticMethod();
```

Examples of static methods are showMessageDialog and showInputDialog in the JOptionPane class, and all the methods in the Math class. In fact, so are all the methods used in Part I of this book, including the main method.

Static methods are called by one of the following syntaxes:

```
ClassName.methodName();
objectName.methodName();
```

For example, JOptionPane.showInputDialog is invoked to receive input from the user. JOptionPane is a class, not an object.

NOTE

Static variables can be accessed from instance or static methods in the class. Instance variables can be accessed from instance methods in a class, but not from static methods in the class, since static methods are invoked regardless of specific instances. Thus the code given below would be wrong.

```
class Foo {
  int i = 5;

  static void p() {
    int j = i; // Wrong because p() is static and i is non-static
  }
}
```

TIP

A method that does not use instance variables can be defined as a static method. It can be invoked without creating an object of the class.
   Variables that describe common properties of objects should be declared as static variables.
   You should define a constant as static data that can be shared by all class objects.

The next example demonstrates how to use instance and static variables and methods, and illustrates the effects of using them.

Example 6.6 Using Instance and Static Variables and Methods

Problem

Modify the circle class by adding a static variable numOfObjects to track the number of circle objects created. The new circle class can be shown using the graphical notations in Figure 6.13.

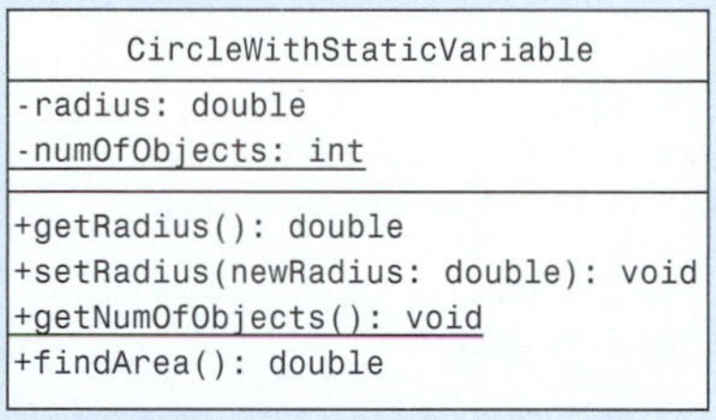

```
         CircleWithStaticVariable
-radius: double
-numOfObjects: int

+getRadius(): double
+setRadius(newRadius: double): void
+getNumOfObjects(): void
+findArea(): double
```

Figure 6.13   *The* CircleWithStaticVariable *class defines the instance variable* radius, *the static variable* numOfObjects, *the instance methods* getRadius, setRadius, *and* findArea, *and the static method* getNumOfObjects.

The main method creates two circles, circle1 and circle2, and modifies the instance and static variables. You will see the effect of using instance and static variables after changing the data in the circles.

Solution

The following code gives the solution to the problem. The output of the program is shown in Figure 6.14.

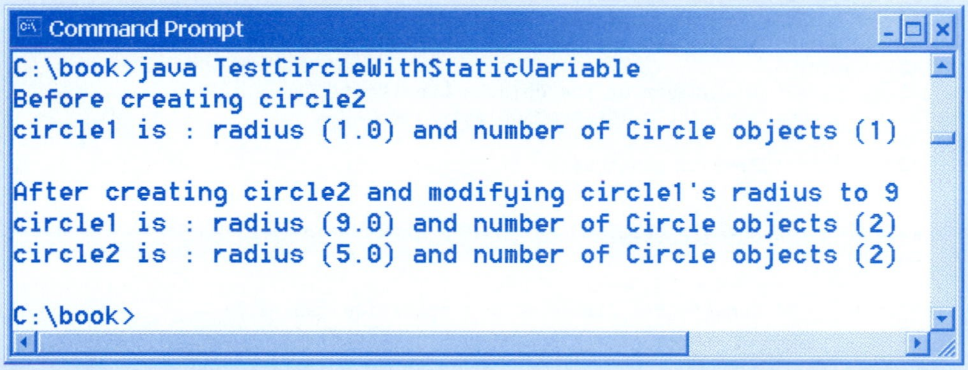

```
Command Prompt

C:\book>java TestCircleWithStaticVariable
Before creating circle2
circle1 is : radius (1.0) and number of Circle objects (1)

After creating circle2 and modifying circle1's radius to 9
circle1 is : radius (9.0) and number of Circle objects (2)
circle2 is : radius (5.0) and number of Circle objects (2)

C:\book>
```

Figure 6.14   *The program uses the instance variable* radius *as well as the static variable* numOfObjects. *All of the objects share the same* numOfObjects.

```
1    // TestCircleWithStaticVariable.java: Demonstrate using instance and
2    // static variables
3    public class TestCircleWithStaticVariable {
4      /** Main method */
5      public static void main(String[] args) {
```

continues

Example 6.6 Using Instance and Static Variables and Methods

```
 6          // Create circle1
 7          CircleWithStaticVariable circle1 =
 8            new CircleWithStaticVariable();
 9
10          // Display circle1 BEFORE circle2 is created
11          System.out.println("Before creating circle2");
12          System.out.print("circle1 is : ");
13          printCircle(circle1);
14
15          // Create circle2
16          CircleWithStaticVariable circle2 =
17            new CircleWithStaticVariable(5);
18
19          // Change the radius in circle1
20          circle1.setRadius(9);
21
22          // Display circle1 and circle2 AFTER circle2 was created
23          System.out.println("\nAfter creating circle2 and modifying " +
24            "circle1's radius to 9");
25          System.out.print("circle1 is : ");
26          printCircle(circle1);
27          System.out.print("circle2 is : ");
28          printCircle(circle2);
29        }
30
31      /** Print circle information */
32      public static void printCircle(CircleWithStaticVariable c) {
33        System.out.println("radius (" + c.getRadius() +
34          ") and number of Circle objects (" +
35          c.getNumOfObjects() + ")");
36      }
37    }
38
39    class CircleWithStaticVariable {
40      /** The radius of the circle */
41      private double radius;
42
43      /** The number of the objects created */
44      private static int numOfObjects = 0;
45
46      /** Default constructor */
47      public CircleWithStaticVariable() {
48        radius = 1.0;
49        numOfObjects++;
50      }
51
52      /** Construct a circle with a specified radius */
53      public CircleWithStaticVariable(double r) {
54        radius = r;
55        numOfObjects++;
56      }
57
58      /** Return radius */
59      public double getRadius() {
60        return radius;
61      }
62
63      /** Set a new radius */
64      public void setRadius(double newRadius) {
65        radius = newRadius;
66      }
67
```

```
68        /** Return numOfObjects */
69        public static int getNumOfObjects() {
70          return numOfObjects;
71        }
72
73        /** Return the area of this circle */
74        public double findArea() {
75          return radius * radius * Math.PI;
76        }
77      }
```

Review

The instance variable radius in circle1 is modified to become 9 (Line 20). This change does not affect the instance variable radius in circle2, since these two instance variables are independent. The static variable numOfObjects becomes 1 after circle1 is created (Lines 7–8), and it becomes 2 after circle2 is created (Lines 16–17). This change affects all the instances of the Circle class, since the static variable numOfObjects is shared by all the instances of the Circle class.

Since numOfObjects is private, it cannot be modified. This prevents tampering. For example, the user cannot set numOfObjects to 100. The only way to make it 100 is to create one hundred objects of the CircleWithStaticVariable class.

Note that Math.PI (Line 75) is used to access PI, and that c.numOfObjects in the printCircle method is used to access numOfObjects. Math is the class name, and c is an object of the Circle class. To access a constant like PI, you can use either the ClassName.CONSTANTNAME or the objectName.CONSTANTNAME. To access an instance variable like radius, you need to use objectName.variableName.

TIP

I recommend that you invoke static variables and methods using ClassName.variable and ClassName.method. This improves readability because the user can easily recognize the static variables and methods. In this example you should replace c.getNumOfObjects() with CircleWithStaticVariable.getNumOfObjects().

TIP

How do you decide whether a variable or method should be an instance or a static variable or method? A variable or method that is dependent on a specific instance of the class should be an instance variable or method. A variable or method that is not dependent on a specific instance of the class should be a static variable or method. For instance, every circle has its own radius. Radius is dependent on a specific circle. Therefore, radius is an instance variable of the Circle class. Since the findArea method is dependent on a specific circle, it is an instance method. None of the methods in the Math class, such as random, pow, sin, and cos, are dependent on a specific instance. Therefore, these methods are static methods. The main method is static, and can be invoked directly from a class.

6.8   The Scope of Variables

Chapter 4, "Methods," discussed local variables and their scope rules. Local variables are declared and used inside a method locally. This section discusses the scope rules of all the variables in the context of a class.

The scope of a class's variables (instance and static variables) is the entire class, regardless of where the variables are declared. A class's variables can be declared anywhere in the class. For example, as shown below, you can declare a variable at the end of a class and use it in a method defined earlier in the class.

```
class Circle {
  double findArea() {
    return radius * radius * Math.PI;
  }

  double radius = 1;
}
```

NOTE

The data fields and methods are the members of the class. Since there is no order among them, they can be declared in any order in a class. The exception is when a data field is initialized based on a reference to another data field. In such cases, the other data field must be declared first. For example, in the following class, i must be declared before j because i's value is used to initialize j.

```
public class Foo {
  int i;
  int j = i + 1;
}
```

You can declare a variable only once as a class member (instance variable or static variable), but you can declare the same variable in a method many times in different non-nesting blocks.

If a local variable has the same name as a class's variable, the local variable takes precedence and the class's variable with the same name is hidden. For example, in the following program, x is defined as an instance variable and as a local variable in the method.

```
class Foo {
  int x = 0; // instance variable
  int y = 0;

  Foo() {
  }

  void p() {
    int x = 1; // local variable
    System.out.println("x = " + x);
    System.out.println("y = " + y);
  }
}
```

What is the printout for `f.p()`, where `f` is an instance of `Foo`? The printout for `f.p()` is 1 for `x` and 0 for `y`. Here is why:

- `x` is declared as a data field with the initial value of 0 in the class, but is also defined in the method `p()` with an initial value of 1. The latter `x` is referenced in the `System.out.println` statement.

- `y` is declared outside the method `p()`, but is accessible inside it.

 TIP

As demonstrated in the example, it is easy to make mistakes. To avoid confusion, do not declare the same variable names in a class, except for method parameters.

6.9   The Keyword *this*

Sometimes you need to reference a class's hidden variable in a method. For example, a property name is often used as the parameter name in a set method for the property. In this case, you need to reference the hidden property name in the method in order to set a new value to it. A hidden static variable can be accessed simply by using the `ClassName.StaticVariable` reference. A hidden instance variable can be accessed by using the keyword `this`, as shown in the following code:

```
class Foo {
  int i = 5;

  void setI(int i) {
    this.i = i;
  }
}
```

The line `this.i = i` means "assign argument `i` to the object's data field `i`."

You can also use the keyword `this` in the constructor. For example, you can redefine the `Circle` class as follows:

```
public class Circle {
  private double radius;

  public Circle(double radius) {
    this.radius = radius;
  }

  public Circle() {
    this(1.0);
  }

  public double findArea() {
    return radius * radius * Math.PI;
  }
}
```

The line `this(1.0)` invokes the constructor with a `double` value argument in the class.

TIP

If a class has multiple constructors, I recommend that you implement them using `this(arg-list)` as much as possible. In general, a constructor with no or fewer arguments can invoke the constructor with more arguments using `this(arg-list)`. This often simplifies coding and makes the class easier to read.

NOTE

Java requires that the `this(arg-list)` statement appear first in the constructor before any other statements.

6.10   Array of Objects

In Chapter 5, "Arrays," arrays of primitive type elements were created. You can also create arrays of objects. For example, the following statement declares and creates an array of ten `Circle` objects:

```
Circle[] circleArray = new Circle[10];
```

To initialize the `circleArray`, you can use a `for` loop like this one:

```
for (int i = 0; i < circleArray.length; i++) {
    circleArray[i] = new Circle();
}
```

An array of objects is actually an *array of reference variables*. So invoking `circleArray[1].findArea()` involves two levels of referencing, as shown in Figure 6.15. `circleArray` references the entire array. `circleArray[1]` references a `Circle` object.

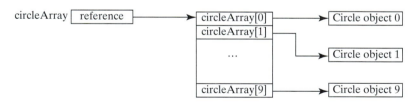

Figure 6.15   *In an array of objects, an element of the array contains a reference to an object.*

NOTE

When an array of objects is created using the `new` operator, each element is a reference variable with a default value of `null`.

The next example demonstrates how to use an array of objects.

Example 6.7 Summarizing the Areas of the Circles

Problem

Write a program that summarizes the areas of an array of circles. The program creates circleArray, an array composed of ten circle objects; it then initializes circle radii with random values, and displays the total area of the circles in the array.

Solution

The following code gives the solution to the problem. The output of a sample run of the program is shown in Figure 6.16.

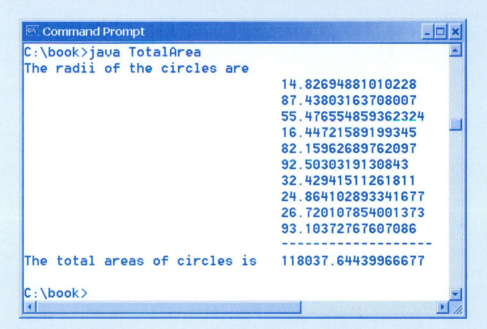

Figure 6.16   *The program creates an array of Circle objects, then displays their total area.*

```
1    // TotalArea.java: Test passing an array of objects to the method
2    public class TotalArea {
3      /** Main method */
4      public static void main(String[] args) {
5        // Declare circleArray
6        CircleWithAccessors[] circleArray;
7
8        // Create circleArray
9        circleArray = createCircleArray();
10
11       // Print circleArray and total areas of the circles
12       printCircleWithAccessorsArray(circleArray);
13     }
14
15     /** Create an array of CircleWithAccessors objects */
16     public static CircleWithAccessors[] createCircleArray() {
17       CircleWithAccessors[] circleArray = new CircleWithAccessors[10];
18
```

continues

231

Example 6.7 Summarizing the Areas of the Circles

```
19          for (int i = 0; i < circleArray.length; i++) {
20            circleArray[i] = new CircleWithAccessors(Math.random() * 100);
21          }
22
23          // Return CircleWithAccessors array
24          return circleArray;
25        }
26
27        /** Print an array of circles and their total area */
28        public static void printCircleWithAccessorsArray
29          (CircleWithAccessors[] circleArray) {
30          System.out.println("The radii of the circles are");
31          for (int i = 0; i < circleArray.length; i++) {
32            System.out.print("\t\t\t\t" +
33              circleArray[i].getRadius() + '\n');
34          }
35
36          System.out.println("\t\t\t\t— — — — — — — — — ·");
37
38          // Compute and display the result
39          System.out.println("The total areas of circles is \t" +
40            sum(circleArray));
41        }
42
43        /** Add circle areas */
44        public static double sum(CircleWithAccessors[] circleArray) {
45          // Initialize sum
46          double sum = 0;
47
48          // Add areas to sum
49          for (int i = 0; i < circleArray.length; i++)
50            sum += circleArray[i].findArea();
51
52          return sum;
53        }
54      }
```

Review

The program uses the createCircleArray method (Line 9) to create an array of ten Circle objects. Several circle classes were introduced in this chapter. This example uses the CircleWithAccessors class introduced in Example 6.4, "Using the private Modifier and Accessor Methods."

The circle radii are randomly generated using the Math.random() method (Line 20). The createCircleObject method returns an array of CircleWithAccessors objects (Line 24). The array is passed to the printCircleArray method, which displays the radii of the total area of the circles.

The sum of the areas of the circle is computed using the sum method (Line 40), which takes the array of Circle objects as the argument and returns a double value for the total area.

6.11   Class Abstraction

In Chapter 4, "Methods," you learned about method abstraction and used it in program development. Java provides many levels of abstraction. *Class abstraction* is the separation of class implementation from the use of a class. The creator of a class provides a description of the class and lets the user know how the class can be used. The collection of methods and fields that are accessible from outside the class, together with the description of how these members are expected to behave, serves as the *class's contract*. The user of the class does not need to know how the class is implemented. The details of implementation are encapsulated and hidden from the user. This is known as *class encapsulation*. For example, you can create a `Circle` object and find the area of the circle without knowing how the area is computed.

There are many real-life examples that illustrate the concept of class abstraction. Consider building a computer system, for instance. Your personal computer is made up of many components, such as a CPU, CD-ROM, floppy disk, motherboard, fan, and so on. Each component can be viewed as an object that has properties and methods. To get the components to work together, all you need to know is how each component is used and how it interacts with the others. You don't need to know how it works internally. The internal implementation is encapsulated and hidden from you. You can build a computer without knowing how a component is implemented.

The computer-system analogy precisely mirrors the object-oriented approach. Each component can be viewed as an object of the class for the component. For example, you might have a class that models all kinds of fans for use on a computer, with properties like fan size and speed, and methods like start, stop, and so on. A specific fan is an instance of this class with specific property values.

Consider paying a mortgage, for another example. A specific mortgage can be viewed as an object of a `Mortgage` class. Interest rate, loan amount, and loan period are its data properties, and computing monthly payment and total payment are its methods. When you buy a house, a mortgage object is created by instantiating the class with your mortgage interest rate, loan amount, and loan period. You can then use the mortgage methods to easily find the monthly payment and total payment of your loan. As a user of the `Mortgage` class, you don't need to know how these methods are implemented.

6.12   Case Studies

This section provides two examples that demonstrate the creation and use of classes.

Example 6.8 Using the Mortgage Class

Problem

Write a mortgage class named Mortgage with the following data fields: annualInterestRate, numOfYears, and loanAmount, and the methods getAnnual-InterestRate, getNumOfYears, getLoanAmount, setAnnualInterestRate, setNum-OfYears, setLoanAmount, monthlyPayment, and totalPayment, as shown in Figure 6.17. The monthlyPayment method returns the monthly payment, and the to-talPayment method returns the total payment.

```
                          Mortgage

-annualInterestRate: double
-numOfYears: int
-loanAmount: double

+Mortgage()
+Mortgage(annualInterestRate: double, numOfYears: int,
 loanAmount: double)
+getAnnualInterestRate(): double
+getNumOfYears(): int
+getLoanAmount(): double
+setAnnualInterestRate(annualInterestRate: double): void
+setNumOfYears(numOfYears: int): void
+setLoanAmount(loanAmount: double): void
+monthlyPayment(): double
+totalPayment(): double
```

Figure 6.17   *The* Mortgage *class models the properties and behaviors of mortgages.*

Solution

The Mortgage class is given below, followed by a test program. Figure 6.18 shows the output of a sample run of the program.

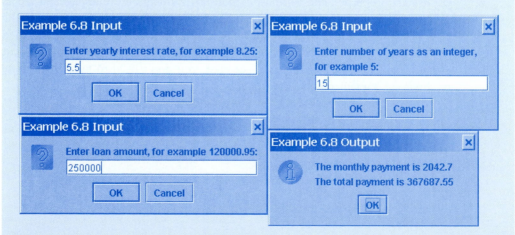

Figure 6.18   *The program creates a* Mortgage *instance with the annual interest rate, number of years, and loan amount, and displays monthly payment and total payment by invoking the methods of the instance.*

```
1    // Mortgage.java: Encapsulate mortgage information
2    public class Mortgage {
3      private double annualInterestRate;
4      private int numOfYears;
5      private double loanAmount;
6
7      /** Default constructor */
8      public Mortgage() {
9        this(7.5, 30, 100000);
10     }
11
12     /** Construct a mortgage with specified annual interest rate,
13         number of years and loan amount
14       */
15     public Mortgage(double annualInterestRate, int numOfYears,
16       double loanAmount) {
17       this.annualInterestRate = annualInterestRate;
18       this.numOfYears = numOfYears;
19       this.loanAmount = loanAmount;
20     }
21
22     /** Return annualInterestRate */
23     public double getAnnualInterestRate() {
24       return annualInterestRate;
25     }
26
27     /** Set a new annualInterestRate */
28     public void setAnnualInterestRate(double annualInterestRate) {
29       this.annualInterestRate = annualInterestRate;
30     }
31
32     /** Return numOfYears */
33     public int getNumOfYears() {
34       return numOfYears;
35     }
36
37     /** Set a new numOfYears */
38     public void setNumOfYears(int numOfYears) {
39       this.numOfYears = numOfYears;
40     }
41
42     /** Return loanAmount */
43     public double getLoanAmount() {
44       return loanAmount;
45     }
46
47     /** Set a newloanAmount */
48     public void setLoanAmount(double loanAmount) {
49       this.loanAmount = loanAmount;
50     }
51
52     /** Find monthly payment */
53     public double monthlyPayment() {
54       double monthlyInterestRate = annualInterestRate / 1200;
55       return loanAmount * monthlyInterestRate / (1 -
56         (Math.pow(1 / (1 + monthlyInterestRate), numOfYears * 12)));
57     }
58
```

continues

Example 6.8 continued

```
59        /** Find total payment */
60        public double totalPayment() {
61          return monthlyPayment() * numOfYears * 12;
62        }
63      }
```

```
1    // TestMortgageClass.java: Demonstrate using the Mortgage class
2    import javax.swing.JOptionPane;
3
4    public class TestMortgageClass {
5      /** Main method */
6      public static void main(String[] args) {
7        // Enter yearly interest rate
8        String annualInterestRateString = JOptionPane.showInputDialog(
9          null, "Enter yearly interest rate, for example 8.25:",
10         "Example 6.8 Input", JOptionPane.QUESTION_MESSAGE);
11
12       // Convert string to double
13       double annualInterestRate =
14         Double.parseDouble(annualInterestRateString);
15
16       // Enter number of years
17       String numOfYearsString = JOptionPane.showInputDialog(null,
18         "Enter number of years as an integer, \nfor example 5:",
19         "Example 6.8 Input", JOptionPane.QUESTION_MESSAGE);
20
21       // Convert string to int
22       int numOfYears = Integer.parseInt(numOfYearsString);
23
24       // Enter loan amount
25       String loanString = JOptionPane.showInputDialog(null,
26         "Enter loan amount, for example 120000.95:",
27         "Example 6.8 Input", JOptionPane.QUESTION_MESSAGE);
28
29       // Convert string to double
30       double loanAmount =  Double.parseDouble(loanString);
31
32       // Create Mortgage object
33       Mortgage mortgage =
34         new Mortgage(annualInterestRate, numOfYears, loanAmount);
35
36       // Format to keep two digits after the decimal point
37       double monthlyPayment =
38         (int)(mortgage.monthlyPayment()*100)/100.0;
39       double totalPayment = (int)(mortgage.totalPayment()*100)/100.0;
40
41       // Display results
42       String output = "The monthly payment is " + monthlyPayment +
43         "\nThe total payment is " + totalPayment;
44       JOptionPane.showMessageDialog(null, output,
45         "Example 6.8 Output", JOptionPane.INFORMATION_MESSAGE);
46
47       System.exit(0);
48     }
49   }
```

Review

The Mortgage class contains a constructor, three get methods, and the methods for finding monthly payment and total payment. You can construct a Mortgage object by using three parameters: annual interest rate, number of years, and loan amount. The three get methods, `getAnnualInterest`, `getNumOfYears`, and `getLoanAmount`, return annual interest rate, payment years, and loan amount, respectively. All the data properties and methods in this class are tied to a specific instance of the `Mortgage` class. Therefore, they are instance variables or methods.

The main class `TestMortgageClass` reads interest rate, payment period (in years), and loan amount; creates a `Mortgage` object; and then obtains the monthly payment (Lines 37–38) and total payment (Line 39) using the instance methods in the `Mortgage` class.

Since the `Mortgage` class will be used later in the book, it must be declared `public` and stored in a separate file.

The data fields in the preceding example are of primitive data types. The following example demonstrates how to use object-type data fields.

Example 6.9 The `Vote` and `Candidate` Classes

Problem

Create two classes, `Vote` and `Candidate`. The `Vote` class has the data field `count` to count votes, and the methods `getCount`, `setCount`, `clear`, `increment`, and `decrement` for reading and handling the votes, as shown in Figure 6.19. The `clear` method sets the count to 0. The `increment` and `decrement` methods increase and decrease the count. The `Candidate` class has the data fields `name` (name of the candidate), `vote` (track the votes received by the candidate), and `numOfCandidates` (track the total number of candidates), and the methods `getName`, `getVote`, and `getNumOfCandidates` for reading the `name`, `vote`, and `numOfCandidates`, as shown in Figure 6.19.

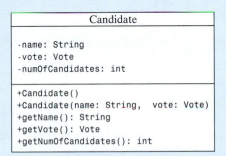

```
                Vote
-------------------------------------
-count: int
-------------------------------------
+Count()
+getCount(): int
+setCount(count: int): void
+clear(): void
+increment(): void
+decrement(): void
```

```
              Candidate
-------------------------------------------
-name: String
-vote: Vote
-numOfCandidates: int
-------------------------------------------
+Candidate()
+Candidate(name: String,  vote: Vote)
+getName(): String
+getVote(): Vote
+getNumOfCandidates(): int
```

Figure 6.19   *The* Vote *class encapsulates the vote counts, and the* Candidate *class encapsulates the candidate.*

continues

Example 6.9 continued

Solution

The `Vote` and `Candidate` classes and a test program are presented below. The test program counts votes for two candidates for student body president. The votes are entered from the input dialog boxes. Number 1 is a vote for Candidate 1, and number 2 is a vote for Candidate 2. Number –1 deducts a vote from Candidate 1, and –2 deducts a vote from Candidate 2. Number 0 signifies the end of the count. Figure 6.20 shows a sample run of the program.

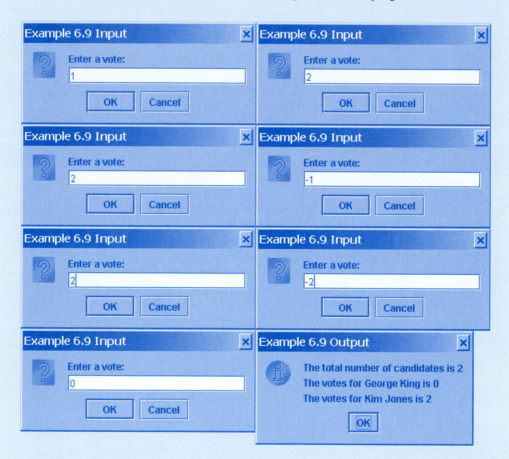

Figure 6.20   *The program creates two instances of the* `Candidate` *class and counts the votes.*

```
1     // TestCandidateVoteClass.java: Count votes
2     import javax.swing.JOptionPane;
3
4     public class TestCandidateVoteClass {
5       /** Main method */
6       public static void main(String[] args) {
7         // Create two candidates
8         Candidate candidate1 = new Candidate("George King");
9         Candidate candidate2 = new Candidate("Kim Jones");
10
```

```
11          // Count votes
12          while (true) {
13            // Prompt the user to enter a vote for a candidate
14            String voteString = JOptionPane.showInputDialog(null,
15              "Enter a vote:",
16              "Example 6.9 Input", JOptionPane.QUESTION_MESSAGE);
17
18            // Convert string into integer
19            int vote = Integer.parseInt(voteString);
20            if (vote == 0) break; // End of the votes
21            else if (vote == 1) candidate1.getVote().increment();
22            else if (vote == 2) candidate2.getVote().increment();
23            else if (vote == -1) candidate1.getVote().decrement();
24            else if (vote == -2) candidate2.getVote().decrement();
25          }
26
27          // Prepare the result
28          String output = "The total number of candidates is " +
29            Candidate.getNumOfCandidates();
30          output += "\nThe votes for " + candidate1.getName() + " is " +
31            candidate1.getVote().getCount();
32          output += "\nThe votes for " + candidate2.getName() + " is " +
33            candidate2.getVote().getCount();
34
35          // Display the result
36          JOptionPane.showMessageDialog(null, output,
37            "Example 6.9 Output", JOptionPane.INFORMATION_MESSAGE);
38
39          System.exit(0);
40        }
41      }
42
43    // Define the Vote class
44    class Vote {
45      /** The count for a Vote object */
46      private int count = 0;
47
48      /** Return the count */
49      public int getCount() {
50        return count;
51      }
52
53      /** Set a new count */
54      public void setCount(int count) {
55        this.count = count;
56      }
57
58      /** Clear this count */
59      public void clear() {
60        count = 0;
61      }
62
63      /** Increment this count */
64      public void increment() {
65        count++;
66      }
67
68      /** Decrement this count */
69      public void decrement() {
70        count--;
71      }
72    }
73
```

continues

Example 6.9 continued

```
74    class Candidate {
75      private String name;
76      private Vote vote;
77      private static int numOfCandidates = 0;
78
79      public Candidate(String name) {
80        this.name = name;
81        vote = new Vote();
82        numOfCandidates++;
83      }
84
85      /** Return the vote of the candidate */
86      public Vote getVote() {
87        return vote;
88      }
89
90      /** Return the name of the candidate */
91      public String getName() {
92        return name;
93      }
94
95      /** Return the number of candidates */
96      public static int getNumOfCandidates() {
97        return numOfCandidates;
98      }
99    }
```

Review

The constructor of the `Candidate` class (Lines 79–83) assigns a name to the candidate, creates an instance of the `Vote` class, and increments `numOfCandidates` by 1. Whenever a `Candidate` object is created, `numOfCandidates` is incremented by 1. Since `numOfCandidates` is a static data field, it tracks the total number of candidates created.

The default value for `count` is 0 (Line 46). When a `Vote` instance is constructed, its initial count value is 0.

The test program creates two `Candidate` instances in Lines 8–9. In Line 21, `candidate1.getVote().increment()` is equivalent to

```
Vote vote = candidate1.getVote();
vote.increment();
```

6.13   Java Application Program Interface

Java comes with a rich set of classes that can be used to build applications. These classes are grouped into packages that provide a convenient way to organize them. You can put the classes you have developed into packages and distribute them to other people. Think of packages as libraries to be shared by many users. Appendix H, "Packages," contains information on creating packages, putting classes into packages, and using packages.

You learned the `Math` class in the `java.lang` package in Chapter 4, "Methods." You will learn more about Java system predefined packages in the coming chapters.

The Java API (*Application Program Interface, Application Programming Interface,* or *Application Programmer interface*) consists of numerous classes and interfaces grouped into fifteen core packages, such as `java.lang`, `java.awt`, `java.event`, `javax.swing`, `java.applet`, `java.util`, `java.io`, and `java.net`. Interfaces are a new construct that will be introduced in Chapter 8, "Class Inheritance and Interfaces."

- `java.lang` contains core Java classes (e.g., `System`, `Math`, `Object`, `String`, `StringBuffer`, `Number`, `Character`, `Boolean`, `Byte`, `Short`, `Integer`, `Long`, `Float`, and `Double`). This package is implicitly imported to every Java program.

- `java.awt` contains classes for drawing geometrical figures, managing component layout, and creating peer-based (so-called heavyweight) components, such as windows, frames, panels, menus, buttons, fonts, lists, and many others.

- `java.awt.event` contains classes for handling events in event-driven graphical user interface programming.

- `javax.swing` contains the lightweight graphical user interface components.

- `java.applet` contains classes for supporting applets.

- `java.io` contains classes for input and output streams and files.

- `java.util` contains many utilities, such as date, calendar, locale, system properties, sets, lists, vectors, hashing, and stacks.

- `java.text` contains classes for formatting information, such as date and time, in a number of formatting styles based on language, country, and culture.

- `java.net` contains classes for supporting network communications.

The most fundamental package supporting basic operations is `java.lang`. Many of the popular classes in `java.lang` are introduced later in the book. See the following chapters for information on these classes:

- Chapter 7, "Strings," introduces the `String` class, `Character` class, and `StringBuffer` class in the `java.lang` package, and the `StringTokenizer` class in the `java.util` package.

- Chapter 8, "Class Inheritance and Interfaces," covers the `Object` class and the interfaces `Comparable` and `Cloneable` in the `java.lang` package.

- Chapter 9, "Object-Oriented Software Development," introduces wrapper classes, such as `Integer` and `Double`, in the `java.lang` package.

- Chapter 10, "Getting Started with GUI Programming," and Chapter 11, "Creating User Interfaces," introduce the classes in the packages `java.awt`, `java.awt.event`, and `javax.swing`, which are used for drawing geometrical figures, event-driven programming, and creating graphical user interfaces.

- Chapter 12, "Applets and Advanced GUI," introduces the `Applet class` in the `java.applet` package, which is used to program Java applets.

- Chapter 13, "Exception Handling," discusses using the `java.lang.Throwable` class and its subclasses for exception handling.

- Chapter 14, "Internationalization," introduces the classes `java.util.Date`, `java.util.TimeZone`, `java.util.Calendar`, and `java.text.DateFormat` for processing and formatting date and time based on locale.

- Chapter 15, "Multithreading," focuses on the `java.lang.Thread` class and the `java.lang.Runnable` interface, which are used for multithreading.

- Chapter 16, "Multimedia," addresses the use of multimedia by several classes in the `java.awt` and `java.applet` packages.

- Chapter 17, "Input and Output," discusses the use of the classes in the `java.io package` by input and output streams.

- Chapter 18, "Networking," discusses the use of the classes in the `java.net` package for network programming.

- Chapter 19, "Java Data Structures," introduces the classes and interfaces in the Java Collections Framework. These classes are in the `java.util` package.

TIP

You can view the Java API documentation online at `http://java.sun.com/j2se/1.4/docs/api/index.html`.

Once you understand the concept of Java programming, the most important lesson in Java is learning how to use the API to develop useful programs. You will learn core Java API and use the classes in the coming chapters.

Chapter Summary

In this chapter, you learned how to program using objects and classes. You learned how to define classes, create objects, and use objects. You also learned about visibility modifiers, instance variables, static variables, instance methods, and static methods.

A class is a template for objects. It defines the generic properties of objects and provides methods for manipulating them.

An object is an instance of a class. It is declared in the same way as a primitive type variable. You use the `new` operator to create an object, and the dot (.) operator to access members of that object.

A constructor is a special method that is called when an object is created. Constructors can be overloaded.

Modifiers specify how the class, method, and data are accessed. You learned about `public`, `private`, and `static` modifiers. A `public` class, method, or data is accessible to all clients. A `private` method or data is only visible inside the class. You should make instance data `private`. You can provide a get method or a set method to enable clients to see or modify the data. A static variable or a static method is defined using the keyword static.

All parameters are passed to methods using pass by value. For a parameter of a primitive type, the actual value is passed; for a parameter of a reference type, the reference for the object is passed.

An instance variable is a variable that belongs to an instance of a class. Its use is associated with individual instances. A static variable is a variable shared by all instances of the same class.

An instance method is a method that belongs to an instance of a class. Its use is associated with individual instances. A static method is a method that can be invoked without using instances.

The scope of instance and static variables is the entire class, regardless of where the variables are declared. The instance and static variables can be declared anywhere in the class.

The this keyword is used to reference the members of the class, including the constructors.

A Java array is an object that can contain primitive type values or object type values. When an array is created, its elements are assigned the default value of 0 for the numeric primitive data types, '\u0000' for char types, false for boolean types, and null for object types.

Review Questions

6.1 Describe the relationship between an object and its defining class. How do you declare a class? How do you declare an object? How do you create an object? How do you declare and create an object in one statement?

6.2 What are the differences between constructors and methods?

6.3 Describe the difference between passing a parameter of a primitive type and passing a parameter of a reference type. Show the output of the following program:

```java
public class Test {
  public static void main(String[] args) {
    Count myCount = new Count();
    int times = 0;

    for (int i = 0; i < 100; i++)
      increment(myCount, times);

    System.out.println("count is " + myCount.count);
    System.out.println("times is " + times);
  }

  public static void increment(Count c, int times) {
    c.count++;
    times++;
  }
```

```
  }

class Count {
  public int count;

  Count(int c) {
    count = c;
  }

  Count() {
    count = 1;
  }
}
```

6.4 Show the output of the following program:

a.

```
public class Test {
  public static void main(String[] args) {
    Circle circle1 = new Circle(1);
    Circle circle2 = new Circle(2);

    // Attempt to swap circle1 with circle2
    System.out.println("Before swap: circle1 = " +
      circle1.radius + " circle2 = " + circle2.radius);
    swap(circle1, circle2);
    System.out.println("After swap: circle1 = " +
      circle1.radius + " circle2 = " + circle2.radius);
  }

  public static void swap(Circle x, Circle y) {
    System.out.println("Before swap: x = " +
      x.radius + " y = " + y.radius);

    Circle temp = x;
    x = y;
    y = temp;

    System.out.println("After swap: x = " +
      x.radius + " y = " + y.radius);
  }
}

class Circle {
  double radius;

  Circle(double r) {
    radius = r;
  }
}
```

b.
```
public class Test {

  public static void main(String[] args) {
    Circle circle1 = new Circle(1.0);
    Circle circle2 = new Circle(2.0);

    // Attempt to swap circle1 with circle2
    System.out.println("Before swap: circle1 = " +
      circle1.radius + " circle2 = " + circle2.radius);
    swap(circle1, circle2);
```

```
        System.out.println("After swap: circle1 = " +
          circle1.radius + " circle2 = " + circle2.radius);
      }

      public static void swap(Circle x, Circle y) {
        System.out.println("Before swap: x = " +
          x.radius + " y = " + y.radius);

        double temp = x.radius;
        x.radius = y.radius;
        y.radius = temp;

        System.out.println("After swap: x = " +
          x.radius + " y = " + y.radius);
      }
    }

    class Circle {
      double radius;

      Circle(double r) {
        radius = r;
      }
    }
```

6.5 Suppose that the class Foo is defined as follows:

```
    public class Foo {
      int i;
      static String s;

      void imethod() {
      }

      static void smethod() {
      }
    }
```

Let f be an instance of Foo. Which of the following statements are correct?

```
    System.out.println(f.i);
    System.out.println(f.s);
    f.imethod();
    f.smethod();
    System.out.println(Foo.i);
    System.out.println(Foo.s);
    Foo.imethod();
    Foo.smethod();
```

6.6 What is the output of the following program?

```
    public class Foo {
      static int i = 0;
      static int j = 0;

      public static void main(String[] args) {
        int i = 2;
        int k = 3;

        {
          int j = 3;
          System.out.println("i + j is " + i+j);
        }
```

```
      k = i + j;
      System.out.println("k is "+k);
      System.out.println("j is "+j);
    }
  }
```

6.7 What is wrong with the following program?

```
public class ShowErrors {
  public static void main(String[] args) {
    ShowErrors t = new ShowErrors(5);
  }
}
```

6.8 What is wrong with the following program?

```
public class ShowErrors {
  public static void main(String[] args) {
    ShowErrors t = new ShowErrors();
    t.x();
  }
}
```

6.9 List the modifiers that you learned in this chapter and describe their purposes.

6.10 Describe the role of the `this` keyword.

6.11 Analyze the following code:

```
class Test {
  public static void main(String[] args) {
    A a = new A();
    a.print();
  }
}

class A {
  String s;

  A(String s) {
    this.s = s;
  }

  public void print() {
    System.out.print(s);
  }
}
```

a. The program does not compile because `Test` does not have a constructor `Test()`.

b. The program does not compile because new `A()` is used in class `Test`, but class `A` does not have a default constructor.

c. The program does not compile because class `A` does not have a default constructor, and a default constructor must be defined explicitly for every class.

d. The program compiles, but it has a runtime error because of the conflict on the method name print.

e. None of the above.

246

6.12 What is wrong in the following code?

```
class Test {
  public static void main(String[] args) {
    C c = new C(5.0);
    System.out.println(c.value);
  }
}

class C {
  int value = 2;
}
```

a. The program has a compilation error because class C does not have a default constructor.

b. The program has a compilation error because class C does not have a constructor with a double argument.

c. The program compiles fine, but it does not run because class C is not public.

d. a and b.

6.13 What is wrong in the following code?

```
public class Foo {
  public void method1() {
    Circle c;
    System.out.println("What is radius " + c.getRadius());
    c = new Circle();
  }
}
```

a. The program has a compilation error because class Foo does not have a main method.

b. The program has a compilation error because class Foo does not have a default constructor.

c. The program has a compilation error in the println statement because c has not been assigned an inintial value.

d. The program compiles fine, but it has a runtime error because variable c is null when the println statement is executed.

6.14 What is wrong in the following code?

```
public class Foo {
  public static void main(String[] args) {
    method1();
  }

  public void method1() {
    method2();
  }

  public void method2() {
    System.out.println("What is radius " + c.getRadius());
  }

  Circle c = new Circle();;
}
```

a. method2 should be declared before method1, since method2 is invoked from method1.

b. c should be declared before method2, since c is used in method2.

c. The program has a compilation error in the println statement where c has not been defined.

d. The program compiles fine, but it has a runtime error because variable c is null when the println statement is executed.

e. The program compiles and runs fine.

6.15 Analyze the following code and choose the best answer:

```
public class Foo {
  private int x;

  public static void main(String[] args) {
    Foo foo = new Foo();
    System.out.println(foo.x);
  }
}
```

a. Since x is private, it cannot be accessed from an object foo.

b. Since x is defined in the class Foo, it can be accessed by any method inside the class without using an object. You can write the code to access x without creating an object such as foo in this code.

c. Since x is an instance variable, it cannot be directly used inside a main method. However, it can be accessed through an object such as foo in this code.

d. You cannot create a self-referenced object; that is, foo is created inside the class Foo.

6.16 In the following class, radius is private in the Circle class, and myCircle is an object of the Circle class. Can the following code compile and run? Explain why.

```
public class Circle {
  private double radius = 1.0;

  /** Find the area of this circle */
  double findArea() {
    return radius * radius * 3.14159;
  }

  public static void main(String[] args) {
    Circle myCircle = new Circle();
    System.out.println("Radius is " + myCircle.radius);
  }
}
```

6.17 Is an array an object or a primitive type value? Can an array contain elements of a primitive type as well as an object type? Describe the default value for the elements of an array.

6.18 Show the printout of the following code:

a.

```
public class Test {
  public static void main(String[] args) {
    int[] a = {1, 2};
    swap(a[0], a[1]);
    System.out.println("a[0] = " + a[0] + " a[1] = " + a[1]);
  }

  public static void swap(int n1, int n2) {
    int temp = n1;
    n1 = n2;
    n2 = temp;
  }
}
```

b.

```
public class Test {
  public static void main(String[] args) {
    int[] a = {1, 2};
    swap(a);
    System.out.println("a[0] = " + a[0] + " a[1] = " + a[1]);
  }

  public static void swap(int[] a) {
    int temp = a[0];
    a[0] = a[1];
    a[1] = temp;
  }
}
```

c.

```
public class Test {
  public static void main(String[] args) {
    T t = new T();
    swap(t);
    System.out.println("e1 = " + t.e1 + " e2 = " + t.e2);
  }

  public static void swap(T t) {
    int temp = t.e1;
    t.e1 = t.e2;
    t.e2 = temp;
  }
}

class T {
  int e1 = 1;
  int e2 = 2;
}
```

d.

```
public class Test {
  public static void main(String[] args) {
    T t1 = new T();
    T t2 = new T();
    System.out.println("t1's i=" + t1.i + " and j=" + t1.j);
    System.out.println("t2's i=" + t2.i + " and j=" + t2.j);
  }
```

```
  }
  class T {
    static int i = 0;
    int j = 0;

    T() {
      i++;
      j = 1;
    }
  }
```

Programming Exercises

6.1 Write a class named `Rectangle` to represent rectangles. The data fields are `width`, `height`, and `color`. Use `double` for `width` and `height`, and `String` for color. Suppose that all the rectangles are the same color. Use a static variable for color. You need to provide the accessor methods for the properties and a method `findArea()` for computing the area of the rectangle.

The outline of the class is given as follows:

```java
public class Rectangle {
  private double width = 1;
  private double height = 1;
  private static String color = "white";

  public Rectangle() {
  }

  public Rectangle(double width, double height, String color) {
  }

  public double getWidth() {
  }

  public void setWidth(double width) {
  }

  public double getHeight() {
  }

  public void setHeight(double height) {
  }

  public static String getColor() {
  }

  public static void setColor(String color) {
  }

  public double findArea() {
  }
}
```

Write a client program to test the class `Rectangle`. In the client program, create two `Rectangle` objects. Assign any width and height to each of the two objects. Assign the first object the color red, and the second, yellow. Display the properties of both objects and find their areas.

6.2 Write a class named `Fan` to model fans. The properties are `speed`, `on`, `radius`, and color. You need to provide the accessor methods for the properties, and the `toString` method for returning a string consisting of all the string values of all the properties in this class. Suppose the fan has three fixed speeds. Use constants 1, 2, and 3 to denote slow, medium, and fast speed.

The outline of the class is given as follows:

```
public class Fan {
  public static int SLOW = 1;
  public static int MEDIUM = 2;
  public static int FAST = 3;

  private int speed = SLOW;
  private boolean on = false;
  private double radius = 5;
  private String color = "white";

  public Fan() {
  }

  public int getSpeed() {
  }

  public void setSpeed(int speed) {
  }

  public boolean isOn() {
  }

  public void setOn(boolean trueOrFalse) {
  }

  public double getRadius() {
  }

  public void setRadius(double radius) {
  }

  public String getColor() {
  }

  public void setColor(String color) {
  }
}
```

Write a client program to test the `Fan` class. In the client program, create a `Fan` object. Assign maximum speed, radius 10, color yellow, and turn it on. Display the object by invoking its `toString` method.

6.3 Write a class named `Account` to model accounts. The properties and methods of the class are shown in Figure 6.21. Interest is compounded monthly.

Write a client program to test the `Account` class. In the client program, create an `Account` object with an account ID of 1122, a balance of 20,000, and an annual interest rate of 4.5%. Use the `withdraw` method to withdraw $2500, use the `deposit` method to deposit $3000, and print the balance and the monthly interest.

```
                          Account
-id: int
-balance: double
-annualInterestRate: double

+Account()
+Account(id: int, balance: double, annualInterestRate: double)
+getID(): int
+getBalance(): double
+getAnnualInterestRate(): double
+setID(id: int): void
+setBalance(balance: double): void
+setAnnualInterestRate(annualInterestRate: double): void
+getMonthlyInterest(): double
+withdraw(amount: double): void
+deposit(amount: double): void
```

Figure 6.21 *The Account class contains the properties id, balance, annual interest rate, accessor methods, and the methods for computing interest, withdrawing money, and depositing money.*

6.4 Write a class named `Stock` to model a stock. The properties and methods of the class are shown in Figure 6.22. The method `changePercent` computes the percentage of the change between the current price and the previous closing price.

```
                          Stock
-symbol: String
-name: String
-previousClosingPrice: double
-currentPrice: double

+Stock()
+Stock(symbol: String, name: String)
+getSymbol():String
+getName():String
+getPreviousClosingPrice(): double
+getCurrentPrice(): double
+setSymbol(symbol: String): void
+setName(name: String): void
+setPreviousClosingPrice(price: double): void
+setCurrentPrice(price: double): void
+changePercent(newPercent: double): double
```

Figure 6.22 *The Stock class contains the properties symbol, name, previous closing price, and current price, accessor methods, and the methods for computing price changes.*

Write a client program to test the `Stock` class. In the client program, create a `Stock` object with the stock symbol SUNW, the name Sun Microsystems Inc, and the previous closing price of 100. Set a new current price randomly and display the price-change percentage.

6.5 Rewrite Example 4.6, "Displaying Calendars," to display calendars in a message dialog box. You can define a static `String` variable output for storing the output and display it in a message dialog box.

STRINGS

Objectives

- To learn how to process strings using the `String` class, the `StringBuffer` class, and the `StringTokenizer` class.
- To use the `String` class to process fixed strings.
- To learn to use the `Character` class.
- To use the `StringBuffer` class to process flexible strings.
- To use the `StringTokenizer` class to extract tokens from a string.
- To know how to use command-line arguments.

7.1   Introduction

Strings are used often in programming. A *string* is sequence of characters. In many languages, strings are treated as arrays of characters, but in Java a string is an object. Java provides the `String` class, the `StringBuffer` class, and the `StringTokenizer` class for storing and processing strings.

In most cases, you use the `String` class to create strings. The `String` class is efficient for storing and processing strings, but strings created with the `String` class cannot be modified. The `StringBuffer` class enables you to create flexible strings that can be modified. `StringTokenizer` is a utility class that can be used to extract tokens from a string.

7.2   The *String* Class

The `java.lang.String` class models a sequence of characters as a string. You have already used string literals, such as the parameter in the `println(String s)` method. The Java compiler converts the string literal into a string object and passes it to `println`.

The `String` class has eleven constructors and more than forty methods for examining individual characters in a sequence, comparing strings, searching substrings, extracting substrings, and creating a copy of a string with all the characters translated to uppercase or lowercase. The most frequently used methods are listed in Figure 7.1.

7.2.1   Constructing a String

You can create a string from a string value or from an array of characters. To create a string from a string literal, use a syntax like this one:

```
String newString = new String(stringLiteral);
```

The argument `stringLiteral` is a sequence of characters enclosed inside double quotes. The following statement creates a `String` object `message` for the string literal `"Welcome to Java!"`:

```
String message = new String("Welcome to Java!");
```

Since strings are used frequently, Java provides a shorthand notation for creating a string:

```
String message = "Welcome to Java!";
```

NOTE

A `String` object is immutable, its contents cannot be changed. To improve efficiency and save memory, Java Virtual Machine stores two `String` objects in the same object if the two `String` objects were created with the same string literal using the shorthand notation. Therefore, the shorthand notation is preferred in creating strings.

```
                                String
+String()
+String(value: String)
+String(value: char[])
+charAt(index: int): char
+compareTo(anotherString: String): int
+compareToIgnoreCase(anotherString: String): int
+concat(anotherString: String): String
+endsWith(suffix: String): boolean
+equals(anotherString: String): boolean
+equalsIgnoreCase(anotherString: String): boolean
+indexOf(ch: int): int
+indexOf(ch: int, fromIndex: int): int
+indexOf(str: String): int
+indexOf(str: String, fromIndex: int): int
+intern(): String
+regionMatches(toffset: int, other: String, offset: int, len: int): boolean
+length(): int
+replace(oldChar: char, newChar: char): String
+startsWith(prefix: String): boolean
+subString(beginIndex: int): String
+subString(beginIndex: int, endIndex: int): String
+toCharArray(): char[]
+toLowerCase(): String
+toString(): String
+toUpperCase(): String
+trim(): String
+copyValueOf(data: char[]): String
+valueOf(c: char): String
+valueOf(data: char[]): String
+valueOf(d: double): String
+valueOf(f: float): String
+valueOf(i: int): String
+valueOf(l: long): String
```

Figure 7.1   *The* String *class provides the methods for processing a string.*

NOTE

A string that is created using the shorthand notation is known as a *canonical string*. You can use a String object's intern method to return a canonical string, which is the same string that is created using the shorthand notation.

For example, the following statements

```
String s = "Welcome to Java!";
String s1 = new String("Welcome to Java!");
String s2 = s1.intern(); // Return a canonical string
System.out.println("s1 == s is " + (s1 == s));
System.out.println("s2 == s is " + (s2 == s));
System.out.println("s1 == s2 is " + (s1 == s2));
```

display

```
s1 == s is false
s2 == s is true
s1 == s2 false
```

In the preceding statements, s and s1 are two different strings. Since s was created using the shorthand notation, it is a canonical string. s1.intern() returns a canonical string that is the same as s. Therefore, s1 == s2 is true.

NOTE

For two strings x and y, x.equals(y) if and only if x.intern() == y.intern().

You can also create a string from an array of characters. For example, the following statements create the string "Good Day."

```
char[] charArray = {'G', 'o', 'o', 'd', ' ', 'D', 'a', 'y'};
String message = new String(charArray);
```

NOTE

A String variable holds a reference to a String object that stores a string value. Strictly speaking, the terms *String variable*, *String object*, and *string value* are different, but the distinctions among them can be ignored most of the time. For simplicity, the term *string* will often be used to refer to String variable, String object, and string value.

7.2.2   String Length and Retrieving Individual Characters

You can get the length of a string by invoking its length() method. For example, message.length() returns the length of the string message.

The s.charAt(index) method can be used to retrieve a specific character in a string s, where the index is between 0 and s.length()-1. For example, message.charAt(0) returns the character W, as shown in Figure 7.2.

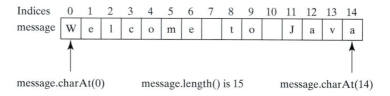

Figure 7.2   *A* String *object is represented using an array internally.*

NOTE

When you use a string, you often know its literal value. For convenience, Java allows you to use the string literal directly to refer to the strings without creating new variables. Thus, "Welcome to Java!".charAt(0) is correct and returns W.

NOTE

A string value is represented using a private array variable internally. The array cannot be accessed outside of the String class. The String class provides many public methods, such as length() and charAt(index), to retrieve the array information. This is a good example of encapsulation: the detailed data structure of the class is hidden from the user through the private modifier, and thus the user cannot directly manipulate the internal data structure. If the array were not private, the user would be able to change the string content by modifying the array. This would violate the tenet that the String class is immutable.

CAUTION

Accessing characters in a string s out of bounds is a common programming error. To avoid it, make sure that you do not use an index beyond s.length() - 1. For example, s.charAt(s.length()) would cause a runtime error.

CAUTION

length is a method in the String class, but length is a property in an array object. So you have to use s.length() to get the number of characters in string s, and use a.length to get the number of elements in array a.

7.2.3   String Concatenation

You can use the concat method to concatenate two strings. The statement shown below, for example, concatenates strings s1 and s2 into s3:

```
String s3 = s1.concat(s2);
```

Since string concatenation is heavily used in programming, Java provides a convenient way to concatenate strings. You can use the plus (+) sign to concatenate two or more strings. The following code combines the strings message, " and ", and "HTML!" into one string:

```
String myString = message + " and " + "HTML!";
```

Recall that you used the + sign to concatenate a number with a string in the println method. A number is converted into a string and then concatenated.

7.2.4   Extracting Substrings

String is an immutable class. After a string is created, its value cannot be modified. For example, you cannot change "Java" in message to "HTML". So what can you do if you need to change the message string? You assign a completely new string to message. The following code illustrates this:

```
message = "Welcome to HTML!";
```

As an alternative, you can use the substring method. You extract a substring from a string by using the substring method in the String class. The substring method has two versions:

■ `public String substring(int beginIndex, int endIndex)`

Returns a new string that is a substring of the string. The substring begins at the specified beginIndex and extends to the character at index endIndex - 1, as shown in Figure 7.3. Thus the length of the substring is endIndex-beginIndex.

■ `public String substring(int beginIndex)`

Returns a new string that is a substring of the string. The substring begins with the character at the specified index and extends to the end of the string, as shown in Figure 7.3.

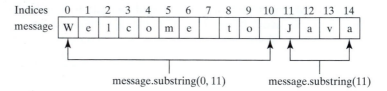

Figure 7.3 *The* `substring` *method extracts a substring from a string.*

For example,

```
String message = "Welcome to Java".substring(0, 11) + "HTML!";
```

The string `message` now becomes `"Welcome to HTML!"`.

7.2.5 String Comparisons

Often, in a program, you need to compare the contents of two strings. You might attempt to use the `==` operator, as follows:

```
if (string1 == string2)
  System.out.println("string1 and string2 are the same object");
else
  System.out.println("string1 and string2 are different objects");
```

However, the `==` operator only checks whether `string1` and `string2` refer to the same object; it does not tell you whether `string1` and `string2` contain the same contents when they are different objects. Therefore, you cannot use the `==` operator to find out whether two string variables have the same contents. Instead, you should use the `equals()` method for an equality comparison of the contents of objects. The code given below, for instance, can be used to compare two strings.

```
if (string1.equals(string2))
  System.out.println("string1 and string2 have the same contents");
else
  System.out.println("string1 and string2 are not equal");
```

■ **NOTE**

Two `String` references are the same if they are created with the same literal value using the shorthand notation. But strings with the same contents do not always share the same object. For example, the following two variables, `s1` and `s2`, are different even though their contents are identical.

```
String s0 = " Java!";
String s1 = "Welcome to" + s0;
String s2 = "Welcome to Java!";

System.out.println("s1 == s2 is " + (s1 == s2));
System.out.println("s1.equals(s2) is " + (s1.equals(s2)));
```

In this case, s1 == s2 is false, but s1.equals(s2) is true. For safety and clarity, you should always use the equals method to test whether two strings have the same contents, and the == operator to test whether the two strings have the same references (i.e., point to the same memory location).

The compareTo method can also be used to compare two strings. For example, see the following code:

```
s1.compareTo(s2)
```

The method returns the value 0 if s1 is equal to s2, a value less than 0 if s1 is lexicographically less than s2, and a value greater than 0 if s1 is lexicographically greater than s2.

The actual value returned from the compareTo method depends on the offset of the first two distinct characters in s1 and s2 from left to right. For example, suppose s1 is "abc" and s2 is "abe", and s1.compareTo(s2) returns -2. The first two characters (a vs. a) from s1 and s2 are compared. Because they are equal, the second two characters (b vs. b) are compared. Because they are also equal, the third two characters (c vs. e) are compared. Since the character c is 2 less than e, the comparison returns -2.

CAUTION
Syntax errors will occur if you compare strings by using comparison operators, such as >, >=, <, or <=. Instead, you have to use s1.compareTo(s2).

NOTE
The equals method returns true if two strings are equal, and false if they are not equal. The compareTo method returns 0, a positive integer, or a negative integer, depending on whether one string is equal to, greater than, or less than the other string.

The String class also provides equalsIgnoreCase and regionMatches methods for comparing strings. The equalsIgnoreCase method ignores the case of the letters when determining whether two strings are equal. The regionMatches method compares portions of two strings for equality. You can also use str.startsWith(prefix) to check whether string str starts with a specified prefix, and str.endsWith-(suffix) to check whether string str ends with a specified suffix. For more information, please refer to the Java 2 API documentation.

7.2.6 String Conversions

The contents of a string cannot be changed once the string is created. But you can convert a string to a new string using the toLowerCase, toUpperCase, trim, and replace methods. The toLowerCase and toUpperCase methods return a new string by converting all the characters in the string to lowercase or uppercase. The trim method returns a new string by eliminating blank characters from both ends of the string. The replace(oldChar, newChar) method can be used to replace a character in the string with a new character.

7.2.7   Finding a Character or a Substring in a String

You can use the indexOf method to find a character or a substring in a string. Four overloaded indexOf methods are defined in the String class.

- `public int indexOf(int ch)`

  Returns the index of the first character in the string that matches the specified character ch. Returns −1 if the specified character is not in the string.

- `public int indexOf(int ch, int fromIndex)`

  Returns the index of the first character in the string starting from the specified fromIndex that matches the specified character ch. Returns −1 if the specified character is not in the string.

- `public int indexOf(String str)`

  Returns the index of the first character of the substring in the string that matches the specified string str. Returns −1 if the character is not in the string.

- `public int indexOf(String str, int fromIndex)`

  Returns the index of the first character of the substring in the string starting from the specified fromIndex that matches the specified string str. Returns −1 if the character is not in the string.

For example,

```
"Welcome to Java!".indexOf('W')) returns 0.
"Welcome to Java!".indexOf('x')) returns −1.
"Welcome to Java!".indexOf('o', 5)) returns 9.
"Welcome to Java!".indexOf("come")) returns 3.
"Welcome to Java!".indexOf("Java", 5)) returns 11.
"Welcome to Java!".indexOf("java", 5)) returns −1.
```

7.2.8   Conversion between Strings and Arrays

Strings are not arrays, but a string can be converted into an array and vice versa. To convert a string to an array of characters, use the toCharArray method. For example, the following statement converts the string "Java" to an array.

```
char[] charArray = "Java".toCharArray();
```

So charArray[0] is 'J', charArray[1] is 'a', charArray[2] is 'v', and charArray[3] is 'a',

To convert an array of characters into a string, use the String(char[]) constructor or the valueOf(char[]) method. For example, the following statement constructs a string from an array using the String constructor.

```
String str = new String(new char[]{'J', 'a', 'v', 'a'});
```

The following statement constructs a string from an array using the valueOf method.

```
String str = String.valueOf(new char[]{'J', 'a', 'v', 'a'});
```

7.2.9   Converting Characters and Numeric Values to Strings

The `valueOf` method can be used to convert an array of characters into a string. There are several overloaded versions of the `valueOf` method that can be used to convert a character and numeric values to strings, with different argument types, `char`, `double`, `long`, `int`, and `float`. For example, to convert a double value to a string, use `String.valueOf(5.44)`. The return value is a string consisting of the characters '5', '.', '4', and '4'.

■ NOTE

To convert a numeric string to a number, you have used `Double.parse-Double(str)` or `Integer.parseInt(str)` to convert a string to a `double` value or an `int` value.

Example 7.1 Checking Palindromes

Problem

Write a program that checks whether a string is a palindrome: that is, whether it reads the same forward and backward. The words "mom," "dad," and "noon," for instance, are all palindromes.

Solution

Here is the algorithm to determine whether a string s is a palindrome. Use a loop to check whether the first character in the string is the same as the last character. If so, check whether the second character is the same as the second-last character. This process continues until a mismatch is found or all the characters in the string are checked, except for the middle character if the string has an odd number of characters.

The program prompts the user to enter a string and reports whether the string is a palindrome. The output of a sample run of the program is shown in Figure 7.4.

```
1    // CheckPalindrome.java: Check whether a string is a palindrome
2    import javax.swing.JOptionPane;
3
4    public class CheckPalindrome {
5      /** Main method */
6      public static void main(String[] args) {
7        // Prompt the user to enter a string
8        String s = JOptionPane.showInputDialog(null,
9          "Enter a string:", "Example 7.1 Input",
10         JOptionPane.QUESTION_MESSAGE);
11
12       // Declare and initialize output string
13       String output = "";
14
15       if (isPalindrome(s))
16         output += s + " is a palindrome";
```

continues

Example 7.1 continued

```
17          else
18            output += s + " is not a palindrome";
19
20          // Display the result
21          JOptionPane.showMessageDialog(null, output,
22            "Example 7.1 Output", JOptionPane.INFORMATION_MESSAGE);
23
24          System.exit(0);
25        }
26
27        /** Check if a string is a palindrome */
28        public static boolean isPalindrome(String s) {
29          // The index of the first character in the string
30          int low = 0;
31
32          // The index of the last character in the string
33          int high = s.length() - 1;
34
35          while (low < high) {
36            if (s.charAt(low) != s.charAt(high))
37              return false; // Not a palindrome
38
39            low++;
40            high--;
41          }
42
43          return true; // The string is a palindrome
44        }
45      }
```

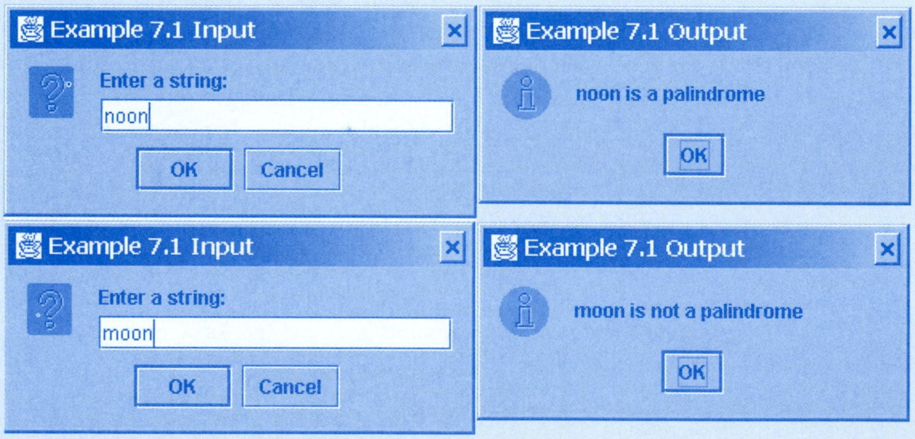

Example 7.1 Input
Enter a string:
noon
OK   Cancel

Example 7.1 Output
noon is a palindrome
OK

Example 7.1 Input
Enter a string:
moon
OK   Cancel

Example 7.1 Output
moon is not a palindrome
OK

Figure 7.4   *The program checks whether a string is a palindrome.*

Review

The isPalindrome method uses a while loop (Lines 35–41) to compare characters and determine whether a string is a palindrome.

Alternatively, you can create a new string that is a reversal of the original string. If both strings have the same contents, the original string is a palindrome. The

String class does not have a method for reversing a string. You can create a method of your own to return a reversed string (see Exercise 7.1) or you can use the reverse method provided in the StringBuffer class. Exapmle 7.3 uses StringBuffer and the reverse method to determine whether a string is a palindrome.

7.3   The *Character* Class

Java provides a wrapper class for every primitive data type. These classes are Character, Boolean, Byte, Short, Integer, Long, Float, and Double for char, boolean, byte, short, int, long, float, and double. All these classes are in the java.lang package. They enable the primitive data values to be treated as objects. They also contain useful methods for processing primitive values. This section introduces the Character class. The other wrapper classes will be introduced in Chapter 9, "Object-Oriented Software Development."

The Character class has a constructor and more than thirty methods for manipulating a character. The most frequently used methods are shown in Figure 7.5.

```
                       Character
+Character(value: char)
+charValue(): char
+compareTo(anotherCharacter: Character): int
+equals(anotherCharacter: Character): boolean
+isDigit(ch: char): boolean
+isLetter(ch: char): boolean
+isLetterOrDigit(ch: char): boolean
+isLowerCase(ch: char): boolean
+isUpperCase(ch: char): boolean
+toLowerCase(ch: char): char
+toUpperCase(ch: char): char
```

Figure 7.5   *The* Character *class provides the methods for manipulating a character.*

You can create a Character object from a char value. For example, the following statement creates a Character object for the character 'a'.

```
Character character = new Character('a');
```

The charValue method returns the character value wrapped in the Character object. The compareTo method compares this character with another character and returns an integer that is the difference between the Unicodes of this character and the other character. The equals method returns true if and only if the two characters are the same. For example, suppose charObject is new Character('b').

```
charObject.compareTo(new Character('a')) returns 1
charObject.compareTo(new Character('b')) returns 0
charObject.compare To(new Character('c')) returns -1
charObject.compareTo(new Character('d') returns -2
charObject.equals(new Character('b')) returns true
charObject.equals(new Character('d')) returns false
```

Most of the methods in the Character class are static methods. The isDigit(char ch) method returns true if the character is a digit. The isLetter(char ch) method returns true if the character is a letter. The isLetterOrDigit(char ch) method is true if the character is a letter or a digit. The isLowerCase(char ch) method is true if the character is a lowercase letter. The isUpperCase(char ch) method is true if the character is an uppercase letter. The toLowerCase(char ch) method returns the lowercase letter for the character, and the toUpperCase(char ch) method returns the uppercase letter for the character.

Example 7.2 Counting Each Letter in a String

Problem

Write a program that counts the number of occurrences of each letter in a string. Assume that the letters are not case-sensitive.

Solution

Here are the steps to solve this problem:

1. Convert all uppercase letters to lowercase in a string using the toLowerCase method in the String class.

2. Create an array of twenty-six int values, each of which counts the occurrences of a letter. For each character in the string, check whether it is a lowercase letter. If so, increment the corresponding count in the array.

The program is shown below, and the output of a sample run is shown in Figure 7.6.

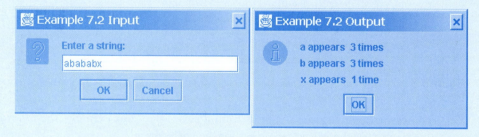

Figure 7.6   *The program counts the number of occurrences for each letter in the string.*

```
1     // CountEachLetter.java: Count letters in the string
2     import javax.swing.JOptionPane;
3
4     public class CountEachLetter {
5       /** Main method */
6       public static void main(String[] args) {
7         // Prompt the user to enter a string
8         String s = JOptionPane.showInputDialog(null,
9           "Enter a string:", "Example 7.2 Input",
10          JOptionPane.QUESTION_MESSAGE);
11
```

```
12        // Invoke the countLetters method to count each letter
13        int[] count = countLetters(s.toLowerCase());
14
15        // Declare and initialize output string
16        String output = "";
17
18        // Display results
19        for (int i = 0; i < count.length; i++) {
20          if (count[i] != 0)
21            output += (char)('a' + i) + " appears   " +
22              count[i] + ((count[i] == 1) ? " time\n" : " times\n");
23        }
24
25        // Display the result
26        JOptionPane.showMessageDialog(null, output,
27          "Example 7.2 Output", JOptionPane.INFORMATION_MESSAGE);
28
29        System.exit(0);
30      }
31
32      // Count each letter in the string
33      public static int[] countLetters(String s) {
34        int[] count = new int[26];
35
36        for (int i = 0; i < s.length(); i++) {
37          if (Character.isLetter(s.charAt(i)))
38            count[(int)(s.charAt(i) - 'a')]++;
39        }
40
41        return count;
42      }
43    }
```

Review

The countLetters method (Lines 32–42) returns an array of twenty-six elements. Each element counts the number of occurrences of a letter. In this method count[0] counts the number of a's, count[1] counts the number of b's, and so on. The method processes each character in the string. If the character is a letter, its corresponding count is increased by one.

The main method reads a string and counts the number of occurrences of each letter in the string by invoking the countLetters method. Since the case of the letters is ignored, the program uses the toLowerCase method to convert a string into all lowercase and pass the new string to the countLetters method.

7.4   The *StringBuffer* Class

The StringBuffer class is an alternative to the String class. In general, a string buffer can be used wherever a string is used. StringBuffer is more flexible than String. You can add, insert, or append new contents into a string buffer, whereas the value of a string is fixed once the string is created.

The `StringBuffer` class has three constructors and more than thirty methods for managing the buffer and modifying strings in the buffer. The most frequently used methods are listed in Figure 7.7.

```
                               StringBuffer
+append(data: char[]): StringBuffer
+append(data: char[], offset: int, len: int): StringBuffer
+append(v: aPrimitiveType): StringBuffer
+append(str: String): StringBuffer
+capacity(): int
+charAt(index: int): char
+delete(startIndex: int, endIndex: int): StringBuffer
+deleteCharAt(int index): StringBuffer
+insert(index: int, data: char[], offset: int, len: int): StringBuffer
+insert(offset: int, data: char[]): StringBuffer
+insert(offset: int, b: aPrimitiveType): StringBuffer
+insert(offset: int, str: String): StringBuffer
+length(): int
+replace(int startIndex, int endIndex, String str): StringBuffer
+reverse(): StringBuffer
+setCharAt(index: int, ch: char): void
+setLength(newLength: int): void
+substring(start: int): StringBuffer
+substring(start: int, end: int): StringBuffer
```

Figure 7.7   *The* `StringBuffer` *class provides the methods for processing a string buffer.*

7.4.1   Constructing a String Buffer

The `StringBuffer` class provides three constructors:

■   `public StringBuffer()`

Constructs a string buffer with no characters in it and an initial capacity of sixteen characters.

■   `public StringBuffer(int length)`

Constructs a string buffer with no characters in it and an initial capacity specified by the length argument.

■   `public StringBuffer(String string)`

Constructs a string buffer for the string argument. The initial capacity of the string buffer is sixteen plus the length of the string argument.

7.4.2   Modifying Strings in the Buffer

You can append new contents at the end of a string buffer, insert new contents at a specified position in a string buffer, and delete or replace characters in a string buffer.

The `StringBuffer` class provides several overloaded methods to append `boolean`, `char`, `char array`, `double`, `float`, `int`, `long`, and `String` into a string buffer. For example, the following code appends strings and characters into strBuf to form a new string, "Welcome to Java".

```
StringBuffer strBuf = new StringBuffer();
strBuf.append("Welcome");
strBuf.append(' ');
strBuf.append("to");
strBuf.append(' ');
strBuf.append("Java");
```

The StringBuffer class also contains overloaded methods to insert boolean, char, char array, double, float, int, long, and String into a string buffer. Consider the following code:

```
strBuf.insert(11, "HTML and ");
```

Suppose strBuf contains "Welcome to Java" before the insert() method is applied. This code inserts "HTML and " at position 11 in strBuf (just before J). The new strBuf is "Welcome to HTML and Java".

You can also delete characters from a string in the buffer using the two delete methods, reverse the string using the reverse method, replace characters using the replace method, or set a new character in a string using the setCharAt method.

NOTE
All these modification methods do two things: (1) change the contents of the string buffer, (2) return the reference of the string buffer. A method with non-void return value type can also be invoked as a statement in Java, if you are not interested in the return value of the method. In this case, the return value is simply ignored.

NOTE
Every string buffer has a capacity. Internally, characters in a string buffer are stored in an array of characters. If its capacity is exceeded, the buffer is automatically made larger to accommodate the additional characters using a new array.

TIP
If a string does not require any change, use String rather than StringBuffer. Java can perform some optimizations for String, such as sharing canonical strings.

7.4.3 The *toString, capacity, length, setLength,* and *charAt* Methods

The StringBuffer class provides many other methods for manipulating string buffers.

The toString() method returns the string from the string buffer.

The `capacity()` method returns the current capacity of the string buffer. The capacity is the number of new characters it is able to store.

The `length()` method returns the number of characters actually stored in the string buffer.

The `setLength(newLength)` method sets the length of the string buffer. If the `newLength` argument is less than the current length of the string buffer, the string buffer is truncated to contain exactly the number of characters given by the `newLength` argument. If the `newLength` argument is greater than or equal to the current length, sufficient null characters (`'\u0000'`) are appended to the string buffer so that `length` becomes the `newLength` argument. The `newLength` argument must be greater than or equal to 0.

The `charAt` method returns the character at a specific index in the string buffer. The first character of a string buffer is at index 0, the next at index 1, and so on. The `index` argument must be greater than or equal to 0, and less than the length of the string buffer.

> **NOTE**
>
> Many of the methods in the `StringBuffer` class are synchronized to ensure that the contents of `StringBuffer` are not corrupted when running with multiple threads. (Synchronization will be introduced in Chapter 15, "Multithreading.")

Example 7.3 Ignoring Non-alphanumeric Characters When Checking Palindromes

Problem

Example 7.1 considered all the characters in a string to check whether it was a palindrome. Write a new program that ignores non-alphanumeric characters in checking whether a string is a palindrome.

Solution

Here are the steps to solve the problem:

1. Filter the string by removing the non-alphanumeric characters. This can be done by creating an empty string buffer, adding each alphanumeric character in the string to a string buffer, and returning the string from the string buffer. You can use the `isLetterOrDigit(ch)` method in the `Character` class to check whether character `ch` is a letter or a digit.

2. Obtain a new string that is the reversal of the filtered string. Compare the reversed string with the filtered string using the `equals` method.

The program is shown below, and the output of a sample run is shown in Figure 7.8.

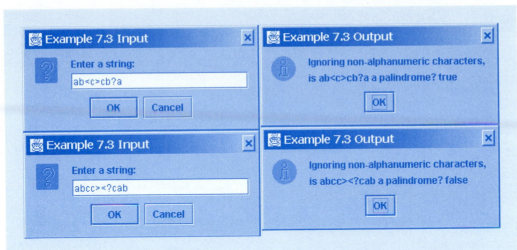

Figure 7.8 *The program checks whether a string is a palindrome, ignoring non-alphanumeric characters.*

```
1    // PalindromeIgnoreNonAlphanumeric.java
2    import javax.swing.JOptionPane;
3
4    public class PalindromeIgnoreNonAlphanumeric {
5      /** Main method */
6      public static void main(String[] args) {
7        // Prompt the user to enter a string
8        String s = JOptionPane.showInputDialog(null,
9          "Enter a string:", "Example 7.3 Input",
10         JOptionPane.QUESTION_MESSAGE);
11
12       // Declare and initialize output string
13       String output = "Ignoring non-alphanumeric characters, \nis "
14         + s + " a palindrome? " + isPalindrome(s);
15
16       // Display the result
17       JOptionPane.showMessageDialog(null, output,
18         "Example 7.3 Output", JOptionPane.INFORMATION_MESSAGE);
19
20       System.exit(0);
21     }
22
23     /** Return true if a string is a palindrome */
24     public static boolean isPalindrome(String s) {
25       // Create a new string by eliminating non-alphanumeric chars
26       String s1 = filter(s);
27
28       // Create a new string that is the reversal of s1
29       String s2 = reverse(s1);
30
31       // Compare if the reversal is the same as the original string
32       return s2.equals(s1);
33     }
34
35     /** Create a new string by eliminating non-alphanumeric chars */
36     public static String filter(String s) {
37       // Create a string buffer
38       StringBuffer strBuf = new StringBuffer();
39
```

continues

Example 7.3 continued

```
40          // Examine each char in the string to skip alphanumeric char
41          for (int i = 0; i < s.length(); i++) {
42            if (Character.isLetterOrDigit(s.charAt(i))) {
43              strBuf.append(s.charAt(i));
44            }
45          }
46
47          // Return a new filtered string
48          return strBuf.toString();
49        }
50
51        /** Create a new string by reversing a specified string */
52        public static String reverse(String s) {
53          StringBuffer s1 = new StringBuffer(s);
54          s1.reverse(); // Use the reverse method for StringBuffer object
55          return s1.toString();
56        }
57      }
```

Review

The `filter(String s)` method (Lines 36–49) examines each character in string s and copies it to a string buffer if the character is a letter or a numeric character. The `filter` method returns the string in the buffer. The `reverse(String s)` method (Lines 52–56) creates a new string that reverses the specified string s. The `filter` and `reverse` methods both return a new string. The original string is not changed.

The program in Example 7.1 checks whether a string is a palindrome by comparing pairs of characters from both ends of the string. This example uses the `reverse` method in the `StringBuffer` class to reverse the string, then compares whether the two strings are equal to determine whether the original string is a palindrome.

7.5   The *StringTokenizer* Class

Another useful class related to processing strings is the `java.util.StringTokenizer` class. This class is used to break a string into pieces so that information contained in it can be retrieved and processed. For example, to get all of the words in a string like `"I am learning Java now"`, you create an instance of the `StringTokenizer` class for the string and then retrieve individual words in the string by using the methods in the `StringTokenizer` class. The methods in the `StringTokenizer` class are shown in Figure 7.9.

StringTokenizer
+countTokens(): int
+hasMoreTokens(): boolean
+nextToken(): String
+nextToken(delim: String): String

Figure 7.9   *The* `StringTokenizer` *class provides the methods for processing tokens in a string.*

How does the `StringTokenizer` class recognize individual words? You can specify a set of characters as delimiters when constructing a `StringTokenizer` object. The delimiters break a string into pieces known as *tokens*.

Listed below are the constructors for `StringTokenizer`.

■ `public StringTokenizer(String s, String delim, boolean returnTokens)`

Constructs a `StringTokenizer` for string s with specified delimiters. If `returnTokens` is `true`, the delimiter is returned as a token.

■ `public StringTokenizer(String s, String delim)`

Constructs a `StringTokenizer` for string s with specified delimiters `delim`, and the delimiter is not a token.

■ `public StringTokenizer(String s)`

Constructs a `StringTokenizer` for string s with default delimiters `" \t\n\r"` (a space, tab, new line, and carriage return), and the delimiter is not a token.

The following instance methods in the `StringTokenizer` class can be used to process tokens. The `hasMoreTokens()` method returns `true` if there is a token left in the string. The `nextToken()` method returns the next token in the string. The `nextToken(String delim)` method returns the next token in the string after resetting the delimiter to `delim`. The `countTokens()` method returns the number of tokens remaining in the string tokenizer.

Example 7.4 Testing `StringTokenizer`

Problem

Write a program that uses a string tokenizer to retrieve words from the string `"I am learning Java. Show me how to use StringTokenizer."` and display them on the console.

Solution

The program creates an instance of `StringTokenizer` for the string "I am learning Java. Show me how to use StringTokenizer." It then uses a loop to repeatedly extract tokens until all tokens are extracted. The source code is shown below, and the output of a sample run is shown in Figure 7.10.

```
1    // TestStringTokenizer.java: Demonstrate StringTokenizer
2    import java.util.StringTokenizer;
3
4    public class TestStringTokenizer {
5      /** Main method */
6      public static void main(String[] args) {
7        // Create a string and string tokenizer
8        String s =
9          "I am learning Java. Show me how to use StringTokenizer.";
10       StringTokenizer st = new StringTokenizer(s);
11
12       // Retrieve and display tokens
13       System.out.println("The total number of words is " +
14         st.countTokens());
15
```

continues

271

Example 7.4 continued

```
16          while (st.hasMoreTokens())
17            System.out.println(st.nextToken());
18        }
19      }
```

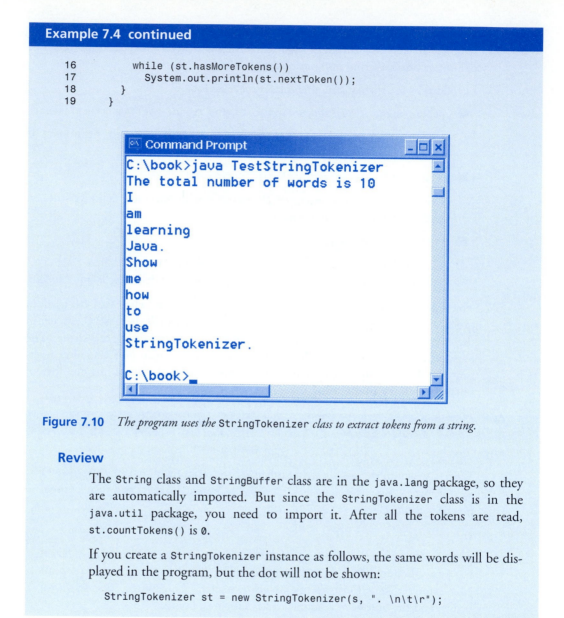

Figure 7.10   *The program uses the* StringTokenizer *class to extract tokens from a string.*

Review

The String class and StringBuffer class are in the java.lang package, so they are automatically imported. But since the StringTokenizer class is in the java.util package, you need to import it. After all the tokens are read, st.countTokens() is 0.

If you create a StringTokenizer instance as follows, the same words will be displayed in the program, but the dot will not be shown:

```
StringTokenizer st = new StringTokenizer(s, ". \n\t\r");
```

7.6   Command-Line Arguments

Perhaps you have already noticed the unusual declarations for the main method, which has parameter args of String[] type. It is clear that args is an array of strings. The main method is just like a regular method with parameters. You can call a regular method by passing actual parameters. Can you pass parameters to main? This section will discuss how to pass and process arguments from the command line.

7.6.1   Passing Arguments to Java Programs

You can pass arguments to a Java program from the command line when you run the program. The following command line, for example, starts the program `TestMain` with three arguments: arg0, arg1, and arg2:

```
java TestMain arg0 arg1 arg2
```

These arguments are strings, but they don't have to appear in double quotes on the command line. The arguments are separated by a space. If an argument itself contains a space, you must use double quotes to group all of the items in the argument. Consider the following command line:

```
java TestMain "First num" alpha 53
```

It starts the program with three arguments: `"First num"` and `alpha`, which are strings, and `53`, a numeric string. Note that `53` is actually treated as a string. You can use `"53"` instead of `53` in the command line.

When the `main` method is invoked, the Java interpreter creates an array to hold the command-line arguments and pass the array reference to args. For example, if you invoke a program with n arguments, the Java interpreter creates an array like this:

```
args = new String[n];
```

the Java interpreter then passes args to invoke the `main` method.

NOTE

If you run the program with no arguments, the array is created with `new String[0]`. In this case, the array is empty with length 0. args references to this empty array. Therefore, args is not `null`, but `args.length` is 0.

7.6.2   Processing Command-Line Parameters

The arguments passed to the main program are stored in args, which is an array of strings. The first parameter is represented by `args[0]`, and `args.length` is the number of arguments passed.

Example 7.5 Using Command-Line Parameters

Problem

Write a program that performs binary operations on integers. The program receives three arguments: an operator and two integers. To add two integers, use this command:

```
java Calculator + 2 3
```

The program will display the following output:

```
2 + 3 = 5
```

continues

273

Example 7.5 continued

Solution

Here are the steps for the program:

1. Use `args.length` to determine whether three arguments have been provided in the command line. If not, terminate the program using `System.exit(0)`.

2. Perform a binary arithmetic operation on the operands `args[1]` and `args[2]` using the operator specified in `args[0]`.

The output of sample runs of the program is shown in Figure 7.11.

```
C:\book>java Calculator
Usage: java Calculator operator operand1 operand2

C:\book>java Calculator + 63 40
63 + 40 = 103

C:\book>java Calculator - 63 40
63 - 40 = 23

C:\book>java Calculator "*" 63 40
63 * 40 = 2520

C:\book>java Calculator / 63 40
63 / 40 = 1

C:\book>
```

Figure 7.11   *The program takes three arguments (an operator and two operands) from the command line and displays the expression and the result of the arithmetic operation.*

```
1   // Calculator.java: Pass parameters from the command line
2   public class Calculator {
3     /** Main method */
4     public static void main(String[] args) {
5       // Check command-line arguments
6       if (args.length != 3) {
7         System.out.println(
8           "Usage: java Calculator operator operand1 operand2");
9         System.exit(0);
10      }
11
12      // The result of the operation
13      int result = 0;
14
```

```
15          // Determine the operator
16          switch (args[0].charAt(0)) {
17            case '+': result = Integer.parseInt(args[1]) +
18                               Integer.parseInt(args[2]);
19                   break;
20            case '-': result = Integer.parseInt(args[1]) -
21                               Integer.parseInt(args[2]);
22                   break;
23            case '*': result = Integer.parseInt(args[1]) *
24                               Integer.parseInt(args[2]);
25                   break;
26            case '/': result = Integer.parseInt(args[1]) /
27                               Integer.parseInt(args[2]);
28          }
29
30          // Display result
31          System.out.println(args[1] + ' ' + args[0] + ' ' + args[2]
32            + " = " + result);
33        }
34      }
```

Review

`Integer.parseInt(args[1])` (Line 17) converts a digital string into an integer. The string must consist of digits. If not, the program will terminate abnormally.

In the sample run, `"*"` had to be used instead of * for the command

```
java Calculator "*" 4 5
```

In JDK 1.1 and above, the * symbol refers to all the files in the current directory when it is used on a command line. Therefore, in order to specify the multiplication operator, the * must be enclosed in quote marks in the command line. The following program displays all the files in the current directory when issuing the command `java Test *`:

```
public class Test {
  public static void main(String[] args) {
    for (int i = 0; i < args.length; i++)
      System.out.println(args[i]);
  }
}
```

Chapter Summary

In this chapter, you learned how to use the `String`, `StringBuffer`, and `StringTokenizer` classes to create objects for processing strings. You also learned how to pass arguments from the command line and process them in the `main` method.

Strings are objects encapsulated in the `String` class. You learned how to create and initialize a string, compare strings, concatenate strings, use substrings, and access individual characters in strings.

The `Character` class is a wrapper class for a single character. The `Character` class provides useful static methods to determine whether a character is a letter, a digit, uppercase, or lowercase.

The `StringBuffer` class can be used to replace the `String` class. The `String` object is immutable, but you can add, insert, or append new contents into a `StringBuffer` object. Use `String` if the string contents do not require any change, and use `StringBuffer` if they change.

The `StringTokenizer` class is used to retrieve and process tokens in a string. You learned the role of delimiters, how to create a `StringTokenizer` from a string, and how to use the `countTokens`, `hasMoreTokens`, and `nextToken` methods to process a string tokenizer.

Review Questions

7.1 Suppose that s1, s2, and s3 are three strings, given as follows:

```
String s1 = "Welcome to Java!";
String s2 = s1;
String s3 = new String("Welcome to Java!");
String s4 = s3.intern();
```

What are the results of the following expressions?

```
s1 == s2
s2 == s3
s1.equals(s2)
s2.equals(s3)
s1.compareTo(s2)
s2.compareTo(s3)
s1 == s4
s1.charAt(0)
s1.indexOf('j')
s1.indexOf("to")
s1.length()
s1.substring(5)
s1.substring(5, 11)
s1.toLowerCase()
```

7.2 Suppose that s1 and s2 are two strings. Which of the following statements or expressions are incorrect?

```
String s = new String("new string");
String s3 = s1 + s2;
String s3 = s1 - s2;
s1 == s2;
s1 >= s2;
s1.compareTo(s2);
int i = s1.length();
char c = s1(0);
char c = s1.charAt(s1.length());
```

7.3 How do you compare whether two strings are equal without considering cases?

7.4 How do you convert all the letters in a string to uppercase? How do you convert all the letters in a string to lowercase?

7.5 Suppose string s is created using new String(); what is s.length()?

7.6 How do you convert a char, an array of characters, or a number to a string?

7.7 How do you determine whether a character is a lowercase letter?

7.8 How do you determine whether a character is alphanumeric?

7.9 How do you create a string buffer for a string? How do you get the string from a string buffer?

7.10 Write three statements to reverse a string s using the reverse method in the StringBuffer class.

7.11 Write three statements to delete a substring from a string s of twenty characters, starting at index 4 and ending with index 10. Use the delete method in the StringBuffer class.

7.12 What is the internal structure of a string and a string buffer?

7.13 Declare a StringTokenizer for a string s with slash (/) and backslash (\) as delimiters.

7.14 What is the output of the following program?

```
import java.util.StringTokenizer;

class TestStringTokenizer {
  public static void main(String[] args) {
    //create a string and string tokenizer
    String s = "I/am\learning Java.";

    StringTokenizer st = new StringTokenizer(s, "/\.");
    //retrieve and display tokens
    while (st.hasMoreTokens())
      System.out.print(st.nextToken() + " ");
  }
}
```

Programming Exercises

7.1 Rewrite Example 7.1, "Checking Palindromes," which checks whether a string is a palindrome. Create your own reverse method. Do not use the reverse method in the StringBuffer class.

7.2 Rewrite Example 7.1, "Checking Palindromes." Ignore cases.

7.3 Rewrite Example 7.1, "Checking Palindromes," by passing the string as a command-line argument.

7.4 You can check whether a string is a substring of another string by using the indexOf method in the String class. Write your own method for this function. Write a program that prompts the user to enter two strings, and check whether the first string is a substring of the second.

7.5 Write a method with the following signature that replaces all oldStr with newStr in the string s, and returns a new string.

```
public static String replace(String oldStr, String newStr,
    String s)
```

7.6 Write a program that passes an unspecified number of integers as command-line arguments and displays their total, as shown in Figure 7.12.

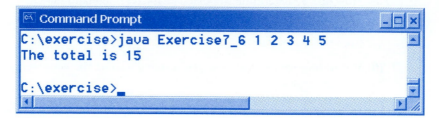

Figure 7.12   *The program adds all numbers passed from the command line.*

7.7 Write a program that passes a string as a command-line argument and displays the number of uppercase letters in the string.

7.8 Rewrite Example 2.3, "Computing Change," to receive the input as a string, and extract the dollars and cents using the `StringTokenizer` class.

7.9 Write a method that returns a sorted string using the following signature:

```
public static String sort(String s)
```

For example, `sort("acb")` returns `abc`.

7.10 Write a method that counts the number of letters in the string using the following signature:

```
public static int countLetters(String s)
```

7.11 Write a method that checks whether two strings are anagrams. Two strings are anagrams if they contain the same characters in any order. For example, "silent" and "listen" are anagrams. The signature of the method is as follows:

```
public static boolean isAnagram(String s1, String s2)
```

CLASS INHERITANCE AND INTERFACES

Objectives

- To understand the concept of class inheritance and the relationship between superclasses and subclasses.
- To create new classes from existing classes.
- To know how to use the keyword `super`.
- To learn how to use three modifiers: `protected`, `final`, and `abstract`.
- To know how to create and use abstract classes.
- To understand polymorphism and object casting.
- To use interfaces to model weak inheritance relationships.
- To become familiar with inner classes.

8.1   Introduction

Object-oriented programming allows you to derive new classes from existing classes. This is called *inheritance*. Inheritance is an important and powerful concept in Java. In fact, every class you define in Java is inherited from an existing class, either explicitly or implicitly. The classes you created in the preceding chapters were all derived implicitly from the `Object` class.

This chapter introduces the concept of inheritance. Specifically, it discusses superclasses and subclasses, the use of the keyword `super`, the modifiers `protected`, `final`, and `abstract`, polymorphism, casting objects, the interface, and inner classes.

8.2   Superclasses and Subclasses

In Java terminology, a class `C1` derived from another class `C2` is called a *subclass*, and `C2` is called a *superclass*. Sometimes a superclass is referred to as a *parent class* or a *base class*, and a subclass is referred to as a *child class*, an *extended class*, or a *derived class*. A subclass inherits functionality from its superclass, and also creates new data and new methods. Subclasses usually have more functionality than their superclasses.

NOTE

Contrary to the conventional interpretation, a subclass is not a subset of its superclass. In fact, a subclass is usually extended to contain more functions and more detailed information than its superclass.

Example 8.1 Demonstrating Inheritance

Problem

To demonstrate inheritance, write a program that creates a new class for `Cylinder` extended from `Circle`. The `Cylinder` class inherits all the data and methods from the `Circle` class. In addition, it has a new data field, `length`, and a new method, `findVolume`.

Solution

The relationship of these two classes is shown in Figure 8.1. An arrow pointing to the superclass is used to denote the inheritance relationship between the two classes involved.

The class for cylinder in this example is named `Cylinder1` to avoid a naming conflict with an improved version of a cylinder class introduced later in this chapter. A better way to avoid class-naming conflicts is to use packages. For more information, please see Appendix H, "Java Packages." Several circle classes are defined in Chapter 6, "Objects and Classes." The `CircleWithAccessor` class is used in this example. The `Cylinder` class can be declared as follows:

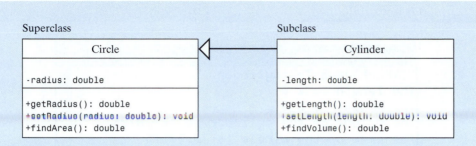

Superclass   Subclass

Circle
-radius: double
+getRadius(): double +setRadius(radius: double): void +findArea(): double

Cylinder
-length: double
+getLength(): double +setLength(length: double): void +findVolume(): double

Figure 8.1 *The* `Cylinder` *class inherits data and methods from the* `Circle` *class and extends the* `Circle` *class with its own data and methods.*

```
1   // Cylinder1.java: Class definition for describing Cylinder
2   public class Cylinder1 extends CircleWithAccessors {
3     private double length;
4
5     /** Default constructor */
6     public Cylinder1() {
7       super(); // Invoke the default superclass constructor
8       length = 1.0;
9     }
10
11    /** Construct a cylinder with specified radius and length */
12    public Cylinder1(double radius, double length) {
13      super(radius); // Invoke superclass constructor Circle(r)
14      this.length = length;
15    }
16
17    /** Return length */
18    public double getLength() {
19      return length;
20    }
21
22    /** Return the volume of this cylinder */
23    public double findVolume() {
24      return findArea() * length;
25    }
26  }
```

The test program creates a cylinder object and explores the relationship between the `Cylinder1` class and the `CircleWithAccessors` class by accessing the data and methods (`radius`, `findArea()`) defined in the `CircleWithAccessors` class and the data and methods (`length`, `findVolume()`) defined in the `Cylinder1` class. The output of the program is shown in Figure 8.2.

```
1   // TestCylinder.java: Use inheritance.
2   public class TestCylinder {
3     public static void main(String[] args) {
4       // Create a Cylinder object and display its properties
5       Cylinder1 myCylinder = new Cylinder1(5.0, 2.0);
6       System.out.println("The length is " + myCylinder.getLength());
7       System.out.println("The radius is " + myCylinder.getRadius());
8       System.out.println("The volume of the cylinder is " +
9         myCylinder.findVolume());
10      System.out.println("The area of the circle is " +
11        myCylinder.findArea());
12    }
13  }
```

continues

Example 8.1 continued

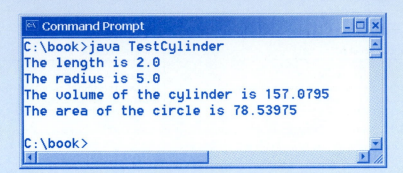

Figure 8.2   *The program creates a cylinder object and accesses the data and methods defined in the* CircleWithAccessors *class and the* Cylinder1 *class.*

Review

The reserved word extends (Line 2) tells the compiler that the Cylinder1 class is derived from the CircleWithAccessors class, thus inheriting data and methods from CircleWithAccessors.

The Cylinder1 class extends the functionality of the CircleWithAccessor class. and inherits all the data and methods in CircleWithAccessors. Therefore, it can access the getRadius and findArea methods defined in the CircleWithAccessor class.

The keyword super is used in the constructors (Lines 7 and 13). This keyword is discussed in the next section.

> **Note**
> If an object is an instance of class A, and class A is a subclass of class B, then the object is also an instance of class B.

8.3   Using the Keyword *super*

In Chapter 6, "Objects and Classes," you learned to use the this keyword. The this keyword refers to the class itself. The keyword super refers to the superclass of the class in which super appears. It can be used in two ways:

- To call a superclass constructor.
- To call a superclass method.

8.3.1   Calling Superclass Constructors

The syntax to call a superclass constructor is:

```
super(), or super(parameters);
```

The statement super() invokes the default constructor of its superclass, and the statement super(parameters) invokes the superclass constructor that matches the parameters. The statement super() or super(parameters) must appear in the first line of the subclass constructor and is the only way to invoke a superclass constructor. *Invoking* super() *can always be omitted, because a subclass's constructor will always invoke* super() *if* super() *or* super(parameters) *is not invoked explicitly in the constructor.*

▬ CAUTION

You must use the keyword super to call the superclass constructor and the call must be the first statement in the constructor. Invoking a superclass constructor's name in a subclass causes a syntax error.

▬ NOTE

A constructor is used to construct an instance of a class. Unlike properties and methods, the constructors of a superclass are not inherited in the subclass. They can only be invoked from the constructors of the subclasses, using the keyword super. *If the keyword super is not explicitly used, the default constructor of the superclass is automatically invoked.* Consider the following code:

```
1    public class C1 extends C2 {
2      public static void main(String[] args) {
3        new C1();
4      }
5
6      public C1() {
7        System.out.println("C1's default constructor is invoked");
8      }
9    }
10
11   class C2 extends C3 {
12     public C2() {
13       System.out.println("C2's default constructor is invoked");
14     }
15   }
16
17   class C3 {
18     public C3() {
19       System.out.println("C3's default constructor is invoked");
20     }
21   }
```

In Line 3, new C1() invokes C1's default constructor. Since C1 is a subclass of C2, C2's default constructor is invoked before any statements in C1's constructor are executed. Since C2 is a subclass of C3, C3's default constructor is invoked before any statements in C2's constructor are executed. Therefore, the output of invoking C1's constructor is:

```
C3's default constructor is invoked
C2's default constructor is invoked
C1's default constructor is invoked
```

NOTE

If a superclass defines constructors other than a default constructor, the subclass cannot use the default constructor of the superclass, because in this case the superclass does not have a default constructor. Consider the following code:

```
1      public class A extends B {
2      }
3
4      class B {
5        public B(String name) {
6          System.out.println("B's constructor is invoked");
7        }
8      }
```

Since no constructor is explicitly defined in A, A's default constructor exists. Since A is a subclass of B, A's default constructor automatically invokes B's default constructor. However, B does not have a default constructor since B has an explicit nondefault constructor defined. Therefore, the program cannot be compiled.

8.3.2   Calling Superclass Methods

The keyword super also can be used to reference a method other than the constructor in the superclass. The syntax is like this:

```
super.method(parameters);
```

You could rewrite the findVolume() method in the Cylinder class as follows:

```
double findVolume() {
  return super.findArea() * length;
}
```

It is not necessary to put super before findArea() in this case, however, because findArea is a method in the Circle class and is inherited by the Cylinder class. Nevertheless, in some cases, like the one in Example 8.2, the keyword super is needed.

8.4   Overriding Methods

A subclass inherits methods from a superclass. Sometimes it is necessary for the subclass to modify the methods defined in the superclass. This is referred to as *method overriding*. The following example demonstrates method overriding.

Example 8.2 Overriding the Methods in a Superclass

Problem

Modify the `Cylinder1` class defined in Example 8.1 to override the `findArea` method in the `CircleWithAccessor` class. The `findArea` method in the `Circle-WithAccessor` class computes the area of a circle, while the `findArea` method in the new cylinder class computes the surface area of a cylinder.

Solution

The following code gives the solution to the problem. The output of the program is shown in Figure 8.3.

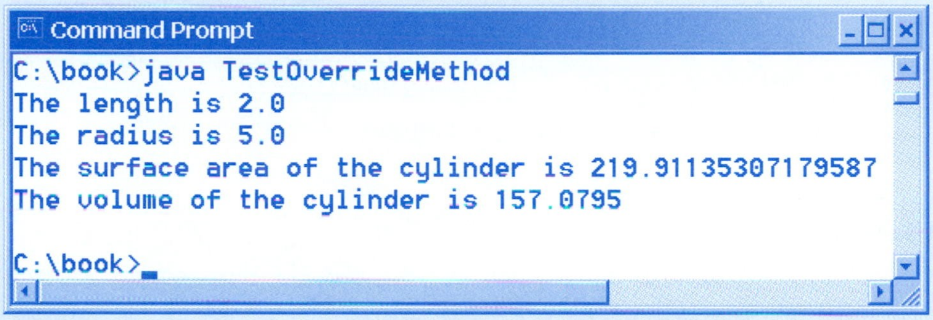

```
Command Prompt                                          _ □ ✕

C:\book>java TestOverrideMethod
The length is 2.0
The radius is 5.0
The surface area of the cylinder is 219.91135307179587
The volume of the cylinder is 157.0795


C:\book>_
```

Figure 8.3   *The new class for cylinder overrides the* findArea *method defined in the* Circle *class.*

```
1   // TestOverrideMethod.java: Test the Cylinder class that overrides
2   // its superclass's methods. The source code of
3   public class TestOverrideMethod {
4     public static void main(String[] args) {
5       Cylinder2 myCylinder = new Cylinder2(5.0, 2.0);
6       System.out.println("The length is " + myCylinder.getLength());
7       System.out.println("The radius is " + myCylinder.getRadius());
8       System.out.println("The surface area of the cylinder is " +
9         myCylinder.findArea());
10      System.out.println("The volume of the cylinder is " +
11        myCylinder.findVolume());
12    }
13  }
```

```
1   // Cylinder2.java: New cylinder class that overrides the findArea()
2   // method defined in the circle class. The source code of
3   public class Cylinder2 extends CircleWithAccessors {
4     /** length of this cylinder */
5     private double length;
6
7     /** Default constructor */
8     public Cylinder2() {
9       super(); // Can be omitted
10      length = 1.0;
11    }
12
13    /** Construct a cylinder with specified radius and length */
```

continues

Example 8.2 continued

```
14        public Cylinder2(double radius, double length) {
15          super(radius);
16          this.length = length;
17        }
18
19        /** Return length */
20        public double getLength() {
21          return length;
22        }
23
24        /** Return the surface area of this cylinder. The formula is
25         * 2*circle area + cylinder body area
26         */
27        public double findArea() {
28          return 2 * super.findArea() + 2 * getRadius() * Math.PI * length;
29        }
30
31        /** Return the volume of this cylinder */
32        public double findVolume() {
33          return super.findArea() * length;
34        }
35    }
```

Review

To avoid naming conflict, the cylinder class in this example is named `Cylinder2`.

The example demonstrates that you can modify a method from the superclass (`CircleWithAccessors`) and can use super to invoke a method in the superclass. The `findArea` method is defined in the `CircleWithAccessors` class and modified in the `Cylinder2` class. Both methods can be used in the `Cylinder2` class. To invoke the `findArea` method defined in the `CircleWithAccessors` class, use `super.findArea()`.

In Line 9 in the `Cylinder2` class, `super()` is used to invoke its superclass's default constructor. This line can be omitted, since `super()` is invoked by default if no superclass constructor is invoked explicitly.

A subclass of the `Cylinder2` class can no longer access the `findArea` method defined in the `CircleWithAccessors` class because the `findArea` method is redefined in the `Cylinder2` class.

■ NOTE

To override a method, the method must be defined in the subclass using the same signature as in its superclass.

■ NOTE

An instance method can be overridden only if it is accessible. Thus a private method cannot be overridden, because it is not accessible outside its own class. If a method defined in a subclass is private in its superclass, the two methods are completely unrelated.

NOTE

Like an instance method, a static method can be inherited. However, a static method cannot be overridden. If a static method defined in the superclass is redefined in a subclass, the method defined in the superclass is hidden. Hiding static methods will be further discussed in Section 8.10, "Hiding Fields and Static Methods."

8.5   The *Object* Class

Every class in Java is descended from the `java.lang.Object` class. If no inheritance is specified when a class is defined, the superclass of the class is `Object`. Classes like `String`, `StringBuffer`, `StringTokenizer`, `Mortgage`, and `CircleWithAccessors` are implicitly the child classes of `Object` (as are all the main classes you have seen in this book so far). It is important to be familiar with the methods provided by the `Object` class so that you can use them in your classes. Three useful instance methods in the `Object` class are:

- `public boolean equals(Object object)`

- `public String toString()`

- `public Object clone()`

8.5.1   The *equals* Method

The `equals` method tests whether two objects are equal. The syntax for invoking it is:

```
object1.equals(object2);
```

The default implementation of the `equals` method in the `Object` class is:

```
public boolean equals(Object obj) {
  return (this == obj);
}
```

Thus, using the `equals` method is equivalent to the `==` operator in the `Object` class, but it is really intended for the subclasses of the `Object` class to modify the `equals` method to test whether two distinct objects have the same content.

You have already used the `equals` method to compare two strings in Section 7.2, "The `String` Class," in Chapter 7, "Strings." The `equals` method in the `String` class is inherited from the `Object` class and is modified in the `String` class to test whether two strings are identical in content.

NOTE

The `==` comparison operator is used for comparing two primitive data type values or for determining whether two objects have the same references. The `equals` method is intended to test whether two objects have the same contents, provided that the method is modified in the defining class of the objects. The `==` operator is stronger than the `equals` method, in that the `==` operator checks whether the two reference variables refer to the same object.

8.5.2   The *toString* Method

Invoking `object.toString()` returns a string that represents this object. By default, it returns a string consisting of a class name of which the object is an instance, an at sign (@), and a number representing the object. For example, consider the following code:

```
Cylinder myCylinder = new Cylinder(5.0, 2.0);
System.out.println(myCylinder.toString());
```

The code displays something like `Cylinder@15037e5`. This message is not very helpful or informative. Usually you should override the `toString` method so that it returns a digestible string representation of the object. For example, you can override the `toString` method in the `Cylinder` class:

```
public String toString() {
   return "Cylinder length = " + length;
}
```

Then `System.out.println(myCylinder.toString())` displays something like the following:

```
Cylinder length = 2.0
```

> **NOTE**
>
> Alternatively, you could write `System.out.println(myCylinder)` instead of `System.out.println(myCylinder.toString())`. The Java compiler automatically translates `myCylinder` into a string by invoking its `toString` method when it is used in the `print` method.

8.5.3   The *clone* Method

Sometimes you need to make a copy of an object. Mistakenly, you might use the assignment statement, as follows:

```
newObject = someObject;
```

This statement does not create a duplicate object. It simply assigns the reference of `someObject` to `newObject`. To create a new object with separate memory space, you need to use the `clone()` method:

```
newObject = someObject.clone();
```

This statement copies `someObject` to a new memory location and assigns the reference of the new object to `newObject`.

> **NOTE**
>
> Not all objects can be cloned. For an object to be cloneable, its class must implement the `java.lang.Cloneable` interface. Interfaces are introduced in Section 8.11, "Interfaces."

NOTE

The `Object` class also contains the `wait` and `notify` methods to control threads, which are covered in Chapter 15, "Multithreading."

TIP

An array is treated as an object in Java and is an instance of the `Object` class. The `clone` method can also be used to copy arrays. The following statement uses the `clone` method to copy the `sourceArray` to the `targetArray`.

```
int[] targetArray = (int[])sourceArray.clone();
```

8.6   The *protected* and *final* Modifiers

You have already used the modifiers `static`, `private`, and `public`. Three new modifiers will now be introduced: `protected`, `final`, and `abstract`. The `protected` and `final` modifiers are introduced in this section, and the `abstract` modifier is introduced in the next section. All three of these modifiers are used with respect to class inheritance.

8.6.1   The *protected* Modifier

The `protected` modifier can be applied to data and methods in a class. A protected datum or a protected method in a public class can be accessed *by any class in the same package or its subclasses*, even if the subclasses are in different packages.

Suppose that class `C1` contains a protected datum named `x` in package `p1`, as shown in Figure 8.4. Consider the following scenarios:

1. If class `C2` in package `p2` is a subclass of `C1`, then `x` is accessible in `C2` because it can be accessed by any subclass of `C1`.

2. If class `C3` in package `p1` contains an instance of `C1` named `c1`, then `x` is visible in `c1` because `C3` and `C1` are in the same package.

3. If class `C4` in package `p2` contains an instance of `C1` named `c1`, then `x` is not visible in `c1` because `C4` and `C1` are in different packages.

8.6.2   Using the Visibility Modifiers

The modifiers `private`, `protected`, and `public` are known as *visibility* or *accessibility modifiers* because they specify how class and class members are accessed. The visibility of these modifiers increases in this order:

`private`, none (if no modifier is used), `protected`, and `public`.

Use the `private` modifier to hide the members of the class completely so that they cannot be accessed directly from outside the class. Use no modifiers to allow the members of the class to be accessed directly from any class within the same package, but not from other packages. This is also known as *package-private*. Use the

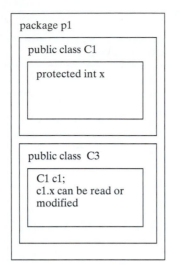
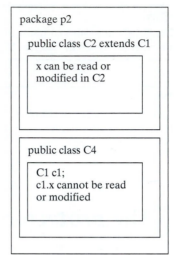

Figure 8.4 *The* `protected` *modifier can be used to prevent a non-subclass in a different package from accessing the class's data and methods.*

`protected` modifier to enable the members of the class to be accessed by the subclasses or classes in the same package. Use the `public` modifier to enable the members of the class to be accessed by any class.

Your class can be used in two ways: for creating instances of the class, and for creating subclasses by extending the class. Make members `private` if they are not intended for use from outside the class. Make the members `public` if they are intended for the users of the class. Make the fields or methods `protected` if they are intended for the extenders of the class but not the users of the class.

The `private` and `protected` modifiers can only be used for members of the class. The `public` modifier can be used on members of the class as well as on the class. A class that is not `public` can only be used by other classes within the same package.

NOTE

In UML, the symbols -, #, and +, respectively, are used to denote `private`, `protected`, and `public` modifiers.

NOTE

A subclass may override a protected method in its superclass and change its visibility to public. However, a subclass cannot weaken the accessibility of a method defined in the superclass. For example, if a method is defined as public in the superclass, it must be defined as public in the subclass.

8.6.3 The *final* Modifier

You have already seen the `final` modifier used in declaring constants. You may occasionally want to prevent classes from being extended. In such cases, use the `final` modifier to indicate that a class is final and cannot be a parent class. The `Math` class, introduced in Chapter 4, "Methods," is a final class. The `String` and `StringBuffer` classes, introduced in Chapter 7, "Strings," are also final classes.

You also can define a method to be final; a final method cannot be modified by its subclasses.

Note

The modifiers are used on classes and class members (data and methods), except that the `final` modifier can also be used on local variables in a method. A final local variable is a constant inside a method.

8.7   Abstract Classes

In the inheritance hierarchy, classes become more specific and concrete *with each new subclass*. If you move from a subclass back up to a superclass, the classes become more general and less specific. Class design should ensure that a superclass contains common features of its subclasses. Sometimes a superclass is so abstract that it cannot have any specific instances. Such a class is referred to as an *abstract class*.

Consider geometric objects. Suppose you want to design the classes to model geometric objects like circles, cylinders, and rectangles. Geometric objects have many common properties and behaviors. They can be drawn in a certain color, filled or unfilled. Color and filled are examples of common properties. Common behaviors include the fact that the areas and perimeters of geometric objects can be computed. Thus a general class `GeometricObject` can be used to model all geometric objects. This class contains the properties `color` and `filled`, and the methods `findArea` and `findPerimeter`. Since a circle is a special type of geometric object, it shares common properties and methods with other geometric objects. Further, since a cylinder is a special type of circle, it shares common properties and behaviors with a circle. Thus it makes sense to define the `Circle` class that extends the `GeometricObject` class and the `Cylinder` class that extends the `Circle` class. Figure 8.5 illustrates the relationship of the classes for geometric objects.

The methods `findArea` and `findPerimeter` cannot be implemented in the `GeometricObject` class because their implementation is dependent on the specific type of geometric object. Such methods are referred to as *abstract methods*. In UML graphic notation, the names of abstract classes and their abstract methods are italicized. The `GeometricObject` class can be defined as follows:

```
// GeometricObject.java: The abstract GeometricObject class
public abstract class GeometricObject {
   private String color = "white";
   private boolean filled;

   /** Default construct */
   protected GeometricObject() {
   }
```

UML Notation:
The abstract class name and the
abstract method names are italicized.

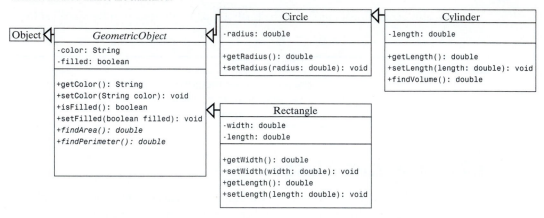

Figure 8.5   *The* `GeometricObject` *class models the common features of geometric objects.*

```
/** Construct a geometric object */
protected GeometricObject(String color, boolean filled) {
  this.color = color;
  this.filled = filled;
}

/** Return color */
public String getColor() {
  return color;
}

/** Set a new color */
public void setColor(String color) {
  this.color = color;
}

/** Return filled. Since filled is boolean,
   so, the get method name is isFilled */
public boolean isFilled() {
  return filled;
}

/** Set a new filled */
public void setFilled(boolean filled) {
  this.filled = filled;
}

/** Abstract method findArea */
public abstract double findArea();

/** Abstract method findPerimeter */
public abstract double findPerimeter();
}
```

Abstract classes are like regular classes with data and methods, but you cannot create instances of abstract classes using the new operator. An abstract method is a
method signature without implementation. Its implementation is provided by the
subclasses. A class that contains abstract methods must be declared abstract.

The `GeometricObject` abstract class provides the common features (data and methods) for geometric objects. Because you don't know how to compute areas and perimeters of geometric objects, `findArea` and `findPerimeter` are defined as abstract methods. These methods are implemented in the subclasses. Here is the implementation of the classes `Circle`, `Rectangle`, and `Cylinder`:

```java
// Circle.java: The circle class that extends GeometricObject
public class Circle extends GeometricObject {
  private double radius;

  /** Default constructor */
  public Circle() {
    this(1.0);
  }

  /** Construct circle with a specified radius */
  public Circle(double radius) {
    this(radius, "white", false);
  }

  /** Construct a circle with specified radius, filled, and color */
  public Circle(double radius, String color, boolean filled) {
    super(color, filled);
    this.radius = radius;
  }

  /** Return radius */
  public double getRadius() {
    return radius;
  }

  /** Set a new radius */
  public void setRadius(double radius) {
    this.radius = radius;
  }

  /** Implement the findArea method defined in GeometricObject */
  public double findArea() {
    return radius * radius * Math.PI;
  }

  /** Implement the findPerimeter method defined in GeometricObject*/
  public double findPerimeter() {
    return 2 * radius * Math.PI;
  }

  /** Override the toString() method defined in the Object class */
  public String toString() {
    return "[Circle] radius = " + radius;
  }
}
```

```java
// Rectangle.java: The Rectangle class that extends GeometricObject
public class Rectangle extends GeometricObject {
  private double width;
  private double height;
```

```java
  /** Default constructor */
  public Rectangle() {
    this(1.0, 1.0);
  }

  /** Construct a rectangle with width and height */
  public Rectangle(double width, double height) {
    this(width, height, "white", false);
  }

  /** Construct a rectangle with specified width, height,
      filled, and color */
  public Rectangle(double width, double height,
    String color, boolean filled) {
    super(color, filled);
    this.width = width;
    this.height = height;
  }

  /** Return width */
  public double getWidth() {
    return width;
  }

  /** Set a new width */
  public void setWidth(double width) {
    this.width = width;
  }

  /** Return height */
  public double getHeight() {
    return height;
  }

  /** Set a new height */
  public void setHeight(double height) {
    this.height = height;
  }

  /** Implement the findArea method in GeometricObject */
  public double findArea() {
    return width*height;
  }

  /** Implement the findPerimeter method in GeometricObject */
  public double findPerimeter() {
    return 2*(width + height);
  }

  /** Override the toString method defined in the Object class */
  public String toString() {
    return "[Rectangle] width = " + width +
      " and height = " + height;
  }
}
```

```java
// Cylinder.java: The new cylinder class that extends the circle
// class. The source code of
// this file is in \book\Cylinder.java
```

```java
public class Cylinder extends Circle {
  private double length;

  /** Default constructor */
  public Cylinder() {
    this(1.0, 1.0);
  }

  /** Construct a cylinder with specified radius, and length */
  public Cylinder(double radius, double length) {
    this(radius, "white", false, length);
  }

  /** Construct a cylinder with specified radius, filled, color, and
     length
   */
  public Cylinder(double radius,
    String color, boolean filled, double length) {
    super(radius, color, filled);
    this.length = length;
  }

  /** Return length */
  public double getLength() {
    return length;
  }

  /** Set a new length */
  public void setLength(double length) {
    this.length = length;
  }

  /** Return the surface area of this cylinder */
  public double findArea() {
    return 2 * super.findArea() + 2 * getRadius() * Math.PI * length;
  }

  /** Return the volume of this cylinder */
  public double findVolume() {
    return super.findArea() * length;
  }

  /** Override the toString method defined in the Object class */
  public String toString() {
    return "[Cylinder] radius = " + getRadius() + " and length "
      + length;
  }
}
```

The data field radius is protected, so it can be referenced by any subclass of Circle. The method toString is defined in the Object class and modified in the Circle, Rectangle, and Cylinder classes. The abstract methods findArea and find-Perimeter defined in the GeometricObject class are implemented in the Circle and Rectangle classes.

NOTE

An abstract method cannot be contained in a nonabstract class. If a subclass of an abstract superclass does not implement all the abstract methods, the subclass must be declared abstract. In other words, in a nonabstract subclass extended from an abstract class, all the abstract methods must be implemented, even if they are not used in the subclass.

NOTE

An abstract class cannot be instantiated using the new operator, but you can still define its constructors, which are invoked in the constructors of its subclasses. For instance, the constructors of GeometricObject are invoked in the Circle class and the Rectangle class.

NOTE

A class that contains abstract methods must be abstract. However, it is possible to declare an abstract class that contains no abstract methods. In this case, you cannot create instances of the class using the new operator. This class is used as a base class for defining a new subclass.

NOTE

A subclass can be abstract even if its superclass is concrete. For example, the Object class is concrete, but its subclasses, such as GeometricObject, may be abstract.

NOTE

A subclass can override a method from its superclass to declare it abstract. This is rare, but useful when the implementation of the method in the superclass becomes invalid in the subclass. In this case, the subclass must be declared abstract.

NOTE

You cannot create an instance from an abstract class using the new operator, but an abstract class can be used as a data type. Therefore, the following statement, which creates an array whose elements are of GeometricObject type, is correct.

```
GeometricObject[] geo = new GeometricObject[10];
```

NOTE

Cylinder inherits the findPerimeter method from Circle. If you invoke this method on a Cylinder object, the perimeter of a circle is returned. This method is not useful for Cylinder objects. It would be nice to remove or disable it from Cylinder, but there is no good way to get rid of this method in a subclass once it is defined as public in its superclass. If you define the findPerimeter method as abstract in the Cylinder class, then the Cylinder class must be declared abstract.

8.8   Polymorphism, Dynamic Binding, and Generic Programming

You may be wondering whether the abstract methods findArea and findPerimeter should be removed from the GeometricObject class and what are the benefits of retaining them in the GeometricObject class. This section addresses these questions.

An object of a subclass can be used by any code designed to work with an object of its superclass. For example, if a method expects a parameter of the GeometricObject type, you can invoke it with a Circle object. A Circle object can be used as both a Circle object and a GeometricObject object. This feature is known as *polymorphism* (from a Greek word meaning "many forms"). A method may be defined in a superclass but is overridden in a subclass. Which implementation of the method is used on a particular call will be determined dynamically by the Java Virtual Machine at runtime. This capability is known as *dynamic binding*.

Dynamic binding works as follows: Suppose an object o is an instance of classes c_1, $c_2, \ldots, c_{n-1}$, and c_n, where c_1 is a subclass of c_2, c_2 is a subclass of $c_3, \ldots$, and c_{n-1} is a subclass of c_n. That is, c_n is the most general class, and c_1 is the most specific class. In Java, c_n is the Object class. If o invokes a method p, the JVM searches the implementation for the method p in $c_1, c_2, \ldots, c_{n-1}$ and c_n, in this order, until it is found. Once an implementation is found, the search stops and the first-found implementation is invoked.

Polymorphism allows methods to be used generically for a wide range of object arguments. This is known as *generic programming*. If a method's parameter type is a superclass (e.g., GeometricObject), you may pass an object to this method of any of the parameter's subclasses (e.g., Circle or Rectangle). When an object (e.g., a Circle object or a Rectangle object) is used in the method, the particular implementation of the method of the object that is invoked (e.g., findArea) is determined dynamically.

The example below demonstrates polymorphism, dynamic binding, and generic programming.

Example 8.3 Testing Polymorphism

Problem

Write a program that creates two geometric objects, a circle and a rectangle, invokes the equalArea method to check whether the two objects have equal areas, and invokes the displayGeometricObject method to display the objects.

Solution

The following code gives the solution to the problem. A sample run of the program is shown in Figure 8.6.

continues

Example 8.3 Testing Polymorphism

```
Command Prompt                                              _ □ ×

C:\book>java TestPolymorphism
The two objects have the same area? false

[Circle] radius = 5.0
The area is 78.53981633974483
The perimeter is 31.41592653589793

[Rectangle] width = 5.0 and height = 3.0
The area is 15.0
The perimeter is 16.0

C:\book>_
```

Figure 8.6   *The program compares the areas of the objects and displays their properties.*

```java
1    // TestPolymorphism.java: Demonstrate polymorphism
2    public class TestPolymorphism {
3      /** Main method */
4      public static void main(String[] args) {
5        // Declare and initialize two geometric objects
6        GeometricObject geoObject1 = new Circle(5);
7        GeometricObject geoObject2 = new Rectangle(5, 3);
8
9        System.out.println("The two objects have the same area? " +
10         equalArea(geoObject1, geoObject2));
11
12       // Display circle
13       displayGeometricObject(geoObject1);
14
15       // Display rectangle
16       displayGeometricObject(geoObject2);
17     }
18
19     /** A method for comparing the areas of two geometric objects */
20     static boolean equalArea(GeometricObject object1,
21       GeometricObject object2) {
22       return object1.findArea() == object2.findArea();
23     }
24
25     /** A method for displaying a geometric object */
26     static void displayGeometricObject(GeometricObject object) {
27       System.out.println();
28       System.out.println(object.toString());
29       System.out.println("The area is " + object.findArea());
30       System.out.println("The perimeter is " + object.findPerimeter());
31     }
32   }
```

Review

The classes `GeometricObject`, `Circle`, and `Rectangle` were presented in the preceding section. The methods `findArea()` and `findPerimeter()` defined in the `GeometricObject` class are overridden in the `Circle` class and the `Rectangle` class. The statements

```
GeometricObject geoObject1 = new Circle(5);
GeometricObject geoObject2 = new Rectangle(5, 3);
```

create a new circle and rectangle, and assign them to the variables `geoObject1` and `geoObject2`. These two variables are of the `GeometricObject` type. These assignments, known as *implicit casting*, are legal because both circles and rectangles are geometric objects. Casting objects is introduced in the next section.

When invoking `equalArea(geoObject1, geoObject2)` (Line 10), the `findArea` method defined in the `Circle` class is used for `object1.findArea()`, since `geoObject1` is a circle, and the `findArea` method defined in the `Rectangle` class is used for `object2.findArea()`, since `geoObject2` is a rectangle.

Similarly, when invoking `displayGeometricObject(geoObject1)` (Line 13), the methods `findArea`, `findPerimeter`, and `toString` defined in the `Circle` class are used, and when invoking `displayGeometricObject(geoObject2)` (Line 16), the methods `findArea`, `findPerimeter`, and `toString` defined in the `Rectangle` class are used. Which of these methods is invoked is dynamically determined at runtime, depending on the type of object.

NOTE

Matching a method signature and binding a method implementation are two issues. The compiler finds a matching method according to parameter type, number of parameters, and order of the parameters at compilation time. A method may be implemented in several subclasses. The JVM dynamically binds the implementation of the method at runtime.

8.9 Casting Objects and the *instanceof* Operator

You have already used the casting operator to convert variables of one primitive type to another. Casting can also be used to convert an object of one class type to another within an inheritance hierarchy. In the preceding section, the statement

```
GeometricObject geoObject1 = new Circle(5);
```

is known as *implicit casting*; it assigns a circle to a variable of the `GeometricObject` type.

Suppose you want to assign `geoObject1` to a variable of the `Circle` type using the following statement:

```
Circle circle = geoObject1;
```

A compilation error would occur. Why does the statement (`GeometricObject geoObject1 = new Circle(5)`) work and the statement (`Circle circle = geoObject1`) doesn't? This is because a `Circle` object is always an instance of `GeometricObject`, but a `GeometricObject` is not necessarily an instance of `Circle`. Even though you can see geoObject1 is really a `Circle` object, the compiler is not so clever to know it. To tell the compiler that geoObject1 is a `Circle` object, use an explicit casting. The syntax is similar to the one used for casting among primitive data types. Enclose the target object type in parentheses and place it before the object to be cast, as follows:

```
Circle circle = (Circle)geoObject1;
```

It is always possible to cast an instance of a subclass to a variable of a superclass, because an instance of a subclass is always an instance of its superclass. When casting an instance of a superclass to a variable of its subclass, explicit casting must be used to confirm your intention to the compiler with the (`SubclassName`) cast notation. For the casting to be successful, you must make sure that the object to be cast is an instance of the subclass. If the superclass object is not an instance of the subclass, a runtime exception occurs. For example, if an object is not an instance of `Cylinder`, it cannot be cast into a variable of `Cylinder`. It is good practice, therefore, to ensure that the object is an instance of another object before attempting a casting. This can be accomplished by using the `instanceof` operator. Consider the following code:

```
/** Suppose myObject is declared as the Object type */
/** Perform casting if myObject is an instance of Cylinder */
if (myObject instanceof Cylinder) {
  Cylinder myCylinder = (Cylinder)myObject;
  System.out.println("The cylinder volume is " +
    myCylinder.findVolume());
  ...
}
```

You may be wondering why it is necessary to perform casting. The data type of a variable is determined at compilation time. The variable myObject is declared as the `Object` type. Using `myObject.findVolume()` would cause a compilation error since the `Object` class does not have the `findVolume` method. So it is necessary to cast myObject into the `Cylinder` type to invoke the `findVolume` method. So why not declare myObject as the `Cylinder` type in the first place? To enable generic programming, it is a good practice to declare a variable with a superclass type, which can accept a value of any subclass type. This is shown in the following example.

Example 8.4 Casting Objects

Problem

Write a program that creates two geometric objects, a circle and a cylinder, and invokes the `displayGeometricObject` method to display them. The `displayGeometricObject` method displays area and perimeter if the object is a circle, and area and volume if the object is a cylinder.

Solution

The following code gives the solution to the problem. A sample run of the program is shown in Figure 8.7.

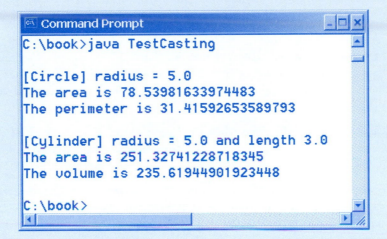

Figure 8.7 *The program creates two objects of* GeometricObject *and casts them to subclasses of* GeometricObject *in order to use the methods defined in the subclasses* Circle *and* Cylinder.

```
1    // TestCasting.java: Demonstrate casting objects
2    public class TestCasting {
3      /** Main method */
4      public static void main(String[] args) {
5        // Declare and initialize two geometric objects
6        GeometricObject geoObject1 = new Circle(5);
7        GeometricObject geoObject2 = new Cylinder(5, 3);
8
9        // Display circle
10       displayGeometricObject(geoObject1);
11
12       // Display cylinder
13       displayGeometricObject(geoObject2);
14     }
15
16     /** A method for displaying a geometric object */
17     static void displayGeometricObject(GeometricObject object) {
18       System.out.println();
19       System.out.println(object.toString());
20
21       if (object instanceof Cylinder) {
22         System.out.println("The area is " +
23           ((Cylinder)object).findArea());
24         System.out.println("The volume is " +
25           ((Cylinder)object).findVolume());
26       }
27       else if (object instanceof Circle) {
28         System.out.println("The area is " + object.findArea());
29         System.out.println("The perimeter is " +
30           object.findPerimeter());
31       }
32     }
33   }
```

continues

Example 8.4 Casting Objects

Review

The program uses implicit casting to assign a Circle object to geoObject1 and a Cylinder object to geoObject2 (Lines 6–7), and then invokes the display-GeometricObject method to display the information on these objects (Lines 9–13).

In the displayGeometricObject method (Lines 17–32), explicit casting is used to cast the object to Cylinder if the object is an instance of Cylinder, and the methods findArea and findVolume are used to display the area and volume of the cylinder.

Casting can only be done when the source object is an instance of the target class. The program uses the instanceof operator to ensure that the source object is an instance of the target class before performing a casting (Lines 21 and 27).

Explicit casting to Cylinder in Line 25 is necessary because the findVolume method is available only in the Cylinder class. However, explicit casting to Circle is not necessary, because the findArea method is defined in the GeometricObject class and overridden in the Circle class. By means of dynamic binding, the findArea method of the Circle is invoked if the geometric object is a circle.

Note that the order in the if statement is significant. If it is reversed (e.g., testing whether the object is an instance of Circle first), then the cylinder will never be cast into Cylinder because Cylinder is an instance of Circle. Try to run the program with the following if statement and observe the effect.

```
if (object instanceof Circle) {
  System.out.println("The area is " + object.findArea());
  System.out.println("The perimeter is " +
    object.findPerimeter());
}
else if (object instanceof Cylinder) {
  System.out.println("The area is " +
    ((Cylinder)object).findArea());
  System.out.println("The volume is " +
    ((Cylinder)object).findVolume());
}
}
```

NOTE

instanceof is a Java keyword. Every letter in a Java keyword is in lowercase.

CAUTION

The object member access operator (.) precedes the casting ((ClassName)object) operator. Use parentheses to ensure that casting is done before the . operator, as in

```
((Cylinder)object).findArea();
```

8.10   Hiding Fields and Static Methods (Optional)

This section is marked optional because hiding fields and static methods are rarely useful, and in my view they should not be used, for the sake of simplicity and clarity. I recommend skipping this section now and consulting it for reference in the future.

You can override an instance method, but you cannot override a field (instance or static) or a static method. If you declare a field or a static method in a subclass with the same name as one in the superclass, the one in the superclass is hidden, but it still exists. The two fields or static methods are independent. You can reference the hidden field or static method using the super keyword in the subclass. The hidden field or method can also be accessed via a reference variable of the superclass's type.

When invoking an instance method from a reference variable, the *actual class of the object* referenced by the variable decides which implementation of the method is used *at runtime*. When accessing a field or a static method, the *declared type* of the reference variable decides which method is used *at compilation time*.

Consider the following example:

```
public class Test {
  public static void main(String[] args) {
    B a = new A();

    // Access s
    System.out.println("a.s is " + a.s);
    System.out.println("((A)a).s is " + ((A)a).s);

    // Invoke static method smile
    System.out.println("a.smile() is " + a.smile());
    System.out.println("((A)a).smile() is " + ((A)a).smile());

    // Invoke overridden method
    System.out.println("a.getS() is " + a.getS());
    System.out.println("((A)a).getS() is " + ((A)a).getS());
  }
}

class B {
  public String s = "In B";

  public static String smile() {
    return "smile from B";
  }

  public String getS() {
    return s;
  }
}

class A extends B {
  public String s = "In A and " + super.s;

  public static String smile() {
    return "smile from A";
  }
```

```
      /**  Override getS in A */
      public String getS() {
        return s;
      }
    }
```

The printout of the program is:

```
a.s is In B
((A)a).s is In A and In B
a.smile() is smile from B
((A)a).smile() is smile from A
a.getS() is In A and In B
((A)a).getS() is In A and In B
```

a.s is "In B" because a's declared type is the class B. To use s in the class A, you need to cast a to A using ((A)a).s. a.smile() invokes the smile method in B because a's declared type is B. ((A)a).smile() invokes the smile method in A because the type for (A)a is A. a.getS() invokes the getS method in A at runtime because a actually references to the object of the class A.

▮ Note

A static method or a static field can always be accessed using its declared class name, regardless of whether it is hidden or not.

8.11   Interfaces

Sometimes it is necessary to derive a subclass from several classes, thus inheriting their data and methods. Java, however, does not allow multiple inheritance. If you use the extends keyword to define a subclass, it allows only one parent class. With interfaces, you can obtain the effect of multiple inheritance.

An interface is a classlike construct that contains only constants and abstract methods. In many ways, an interface is similar to an abstract class, but an abstract class can contain constants and abstract methods as well as variables and concrete methods.

To distinguish an interface from a class, Java uses the following syntax to declare an interface:

```
modifier interface InterfaceName {
  /** Constant declarations */
  /** Method signatures */
}
```

An interface is treated like a special class in Java. Each interface is compiled into a separate bytecode file, just like a regular class. As with an abstract class, you cannot create an instance for the interface using the new operator, but in most cases you can use an interface more or less the same way you use an abstract class. For example, you can use an interface as a data type for a variable, as the result of casting, and so on.

Suppose you want to design a generic method to find the larger of two objects. The objects can be students, circles, or cylinders. Because compare methods are different for different types of objects, you need to define a generic compare method to determine the order of the two objects. Then you can tailor the method to compare students, circles, or cylinders. For example, you can use student ID as the key for comparing students, radius as the key for comparing circles, and volume as the key for comparing cylinders. You can use an interface to define a generic compareTo method, as follows:

```
// Interface for comparing objects, defined in java.lang
package java.lang;

public interface Comparable {
  public int compareTo(Object o);
}
```

The compareTo method determines the order of this object with the specified object o, and returns a negative integer, zero, or a positive integer if this object is less than, equal to, or greater than the specified object o.

NOTE

The Comparable interface has been available since JDK 1.2, and is included in the java.lang package.

A generic max method for finding the maximum between two objects can be declared in a class named Max, as follows:

```
// Max.java: Find a maximum object
public class Max {
  /** Return the maximum between two objects */
  public static Comparable max(Comparable o1, Comparable o2) {
    if (o1.compareTo(o2) > 0)
      return o1;
    else
      return o2;
  }
}
```

The Max class contains the static method named max. To use the max method to find a maximum between two objects, implement the Comparable interface for the class of these objects. Many classes in the Java API implement Comparable. For example, the String class implements Comparable, so you can use the max method to find the larger string. Here is an example:

```
String s1 = "abcdef";
String s2 = "acdef";
String s3 = (String)Max.max(s1, s2);
```

The last statement is equivalent to

```
String s3 = (String)Max.max((Comparable)s1, (Comparable)s2);
```

The String class implements Comparable. Comparable is treated in the same way as a superclass for String. An instance of String is also automatically an instance of Comparable. Therefore, s1 and s2 can be passed to the max method without explicit casting. However, an instance of Comparable is not necessarily an instance of

String. Therefore, to assign the return value from the max method to a String type variable, you need to cast it to String explicitly.

The following example is another demonstration of how the interface is used.

Example 8.5 Using Interfaces

Problem

Write a program that uses the max method to find a maximum circle between two circles and a maximum cylinder between two cylinders.

Solution

The following code gives the solution to the problem. The output of the program is shown in Figure 8.8.

```
Command Prompt                                              _ □ ×

C:\book>java TestInterface
The max circle's radius is 5.0
[Circle] radius = 5.0

cylinder1's volume is 157.07963267948966
cylinder2's volume is 251.32741228718345
The max cylinder's        radius is 4.0
                          length is 5.0
                          volume is 251.32741228718345
[Cylinder] radius = 4.0 and length 5.0

C:\book>
```

Figure 8.8   *The program displays the maximum circle and maximum cylinder.*

```
1    // TestInterface.java: Use the Comparable interface
2    // and the generic max method to find max objects
3    public class TestInterface {
4      /** Main method */
5      public static void main(String[] args) {
6        // Create two comparable circles
7        ComparableCircle circle1 = new ComparableCircle(5);
8        ComparableCircle circle2 = new ComparableCircle(4);
9
10       // Display the max circle
11       Comparable circle = Max.max(circle1, circle2);
12       System.out.println("The max circle's radius is " +
13         ((Circle)circle).getRadius());
14       System.out.println(circle);
15
16       // Create two comparable cylinders
17       ComparableCylinder cylinder1 = new ComparableCylinder(5, 2);
18       ComparableCylinder cylinder2 = new ComparableCylinder(4, 5);
19
```

```
20        // Display the max cylinder
21        Comparable cylinder = Max.max(cylinder1, cylinder2);
22        System.out.println();
23        System.out.println("cylinder1's volume is " +
24          cylinder1.findVolume());
25        System.out.println("cylinder2's volume is " +
26          cylinder2.findVolume());
27        System.out.println("The max cylinder's \tradius is " +
28          ((Cylinder)cylinder).getRadius() + "\n\t\t\tlength is " +
29          ((Cylinder)cylinder).getLength() + "\n\t\t\tvolume is " +
30          ((Cylinder)cylinder).findVolume());
31        System.out.println(cylinder);
32      }
33    }
34
35    // ComparableCircle is a subclass of Circle, which implements the
36    // Comparable interface
37    class ComparableCircle extends Circle implements Comparable {
38      /** Construct a CompareCircle with a specified radius */
39      public ComparableCircle(double r) {
40        super(r);
41      }
42
43      /** Implement the compareTo method defined in Comparable */
44      public int compareTo(Object o) {
45        if (getRadius() > ((Circle)o).getRadius())
46          return 1;
47        else if (getRadius() < ((Circle)o).getRadius())
48          return -1;
49        else
50          return 0;
51      }
52    }
53
54    // ComparableCylinder is a subclass of Cylinder, which implements the
55    // CompareObject interface
56    class ComparableCylinder extends Cylinder implements Comparable {
57      /** Construct a CompareCylinder with radius and length */
58      ComparableCylinder(double radius, double length) {
59        super(radius, length);
60      }
61
62      /** Implement the compareTo method defined in Comparable interface */
63      public int compareTo(Object o) {
64        if (findVolume() > ((Cylinder)o).findVolume())
65          return 1;
66        else if (findVolume() < ((Cylinder)o).findVolume())
67          return -1;
68        else
69          return 0;
70      }
71    }
```

Review

The max method can be used to find a maximum object between two objects of the Comparable type. Any object whose class implements the Comparable interface is an instance of the Comparable type. The example creates the classes ComparableCircle (Lines 37–52) and ComparableCylinder (Lines 56–70) in order to utilize the generic max method. The relationship of the classes and the interface is shown in Figure 8.9.

continues

307

Example 8.5 Using Interfaces

Notation:
The interface name and the method names inside an interface are italicized. The dashed lines and hollow triangles are used to point to the interface.

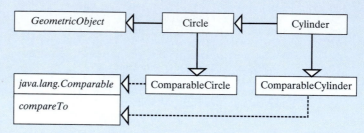

Figure 8.9   *The* `ComparableCircle` *class extends* `Circle` *and implements* `Comparable`; `ComparableCylinder` *extends* `Cylinder` *and implements* `Comparable`.

The common functionality is to compare objects in this example, but the `compareTo` methods are different for different types of objects. Therefore, the interface `Comparable` is used to generalize common functionality and leave the detail for the subclasses to implement.

The keyword `implements` in the `ComparableCircle` class indicates that `ComparableCircle` inherits all the data from the `Comparable` interface and implements the methods in the interface.

The `ComparableCircle` class implements the `compareTo` method for comparing the radii of two circles, and the `ComparableCylinder` class implements the `compareTo` method for comparing the cylinders based on their volumes.

The interface `Comparable` is used as a data type for variables o1 and o2 in the max method, for the variable o. When you invoke `max(circle1, circle2)`, you pass `circle1` and `circle2` to o1 and o2. This is implicit casting. The interface `Comparable` is like a superclass for `Circle`. `circle1` is an instance of `Circle`, as well as an instance of `Comparable`. Invoking `max(circle1, circle2)` returns an object of the `Comparable` type, and this object's reference is assigned to the variable o. To invoke the `getRadius` in the `Circle` class, you have to cast the variable o into a `Circle` object, because `getRadius` is not defined in the `Comparable` interface.

The statement `System.out.println(circle)` (Line 14) displays `circle.toString()`. Since the `toString` method is defined in the `Object` class, it can be accessed by objects of the `Circle` type. By means of polymorphism, the `toString` method for the `Circle` class is used, because `circle` is an instance of `Circle`.

An interface provides another form of generic programming. It would be difficult to use a generic max method to find the maximum of the objects without using an interface in this example, because multiple inheritance would be necessary to inherit `Comparable` and another class, such as `Circle` or `Cylinder`, at the same time.

The `Object` class contains the `equals` method, which is intended for the subclasses of the `Object` class to override in order to compare whether the contents of the objects are the same. Suppose that the `Object` class contains the `compareTo` method, as defined in the `Comparable` interface; the new max method can be used to compare a list of *any* objects. Whether a `compareTo` method should be included in the `Object` class is debatable. Since the `compareTo` method is not defined in the `Object` class, the `Comparable` interface is created in Java 2 to enable objects to be compared if they are instances of the `Comparable` interface.

8.11.1   Interfaces vs. Abstract Classes

An interface can be used just like an abstract class, but defining an interface is different from defining an abstract class.

■ In an interface, the data must be constants; an abstract class can have data fields.

■ Each method in an interface has only a signature without implementation; an abstract class can have concrete methods.

■ Since all the methods defined in an interface are abstract methods, Java does not require that you put the abstract modifier in the method signature in an interface, but you must put the abstract modifier before an abstract method in an abstract class.

Java allows only single inheritance for class extension, but multiple extension for interfaces. For example,

```
public class NewClass extends BaseClass
  implements Interface1, . . ., InterfaceN {
  …
}
```

An interface can inherit other interfaces using the `extends` keyword, as follows:

```
public interface NewInterface extends Interface1, . . ., InterfaceN {
  // constants and abstract methods
}
```

A class implementing `NewInterface` must implement the abstract methods defined in `NewInterface`, `Interface1`, . . ., and `InterfaceN`. An interface can only extend other interfaces, but not classes. A class can extend its superclass and implement multiple interfaces.

All classes share a single root, the `Object` class, but there is no single root for interfaces. As shown in Example 8.5, an interface can be used as an abstract class. If a class extends an interface, this interface is like a superclass for the class. You can use an interface as a data type and cast a variable of an interface type to its subclass, and vice versa. For example, suppose that c is an instance of `Class2` in Figure 8.10. c is also an instance of `Object`, `Class1`, `Interface1`, `Interface1_1`, `Interface1_2`, `Interface2_1`, and `Interface2_2`.

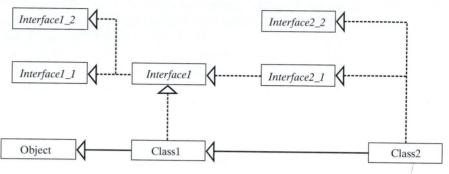

Figure 8.10   *Abstract class Class1 implements Interface1, Interface1 extends Interface1_1 and Interface1_2. Class2 extends Class1 and implements Interface2_1 and Interface2_2.*

Section 9.5.4, "Using Interfaces or Abstract Classes," in Chapter 9, "Object-Oriented Software Development," gives some tips on how to decide whether to use an interface or an abstract class to model common features.

NOTE

Class names are nouns. Interface names may be adjectives or nouns. For example, both `java.lang.Comparable` and `java.awt.event.ActionListener` are interfaces. `Comparable` is an adjective, and `ActionListener` is a noun. `ActionListener` will be introduced in Chapter 10, "Getting Started with GUI Programming."

8.11.2   The *Cloneable* Interface (Optional)

An interface contains constants and abstract methods, but the `Cloneable` interface is a special case. The `Cloneable` interface in the `java.lang` package is defined as follows:

```
package java.lang;

public interface Cloneable {
}
```

This interface is empty. An interface with an empty body is referred to as a *marker interface*. A marker interface does not contain constants or methods, but it has a special meaning in the Java system. The Java system requires a class that implements the `Cloneable` interface to become cloneable. The object of a cloneable class can use the `clone` method defined in the `Object` class to make an identical copy of the object. A class that implements the `Cloneable` interface is marked cloneable.

The following example demonstrates the `Cloneable` interface and the `clone` method, and shows the effect of object cloning.

Example 8.6 Cloning Objects

Problem

Write a program that uses the Cloneable interface to mark classes as cloneable and uses the clone method to copy objects. The program creates two new classes named Name and CloneableCircle. The Name class has the properties firstName, mi, lastName, their associated accessor methods, and the getFullName method for returning the full name. The CloneableCircle class extends Circle and implements the Cloneable interface. The CloneableCircle class has a creator for the circle. The creator's type is Name. The main method in a test class creates a CloneableCircle object and copies it to a new variable.

Solution

The following code gives the solution to the problem. The output of the program is shown in Figure 8.11.

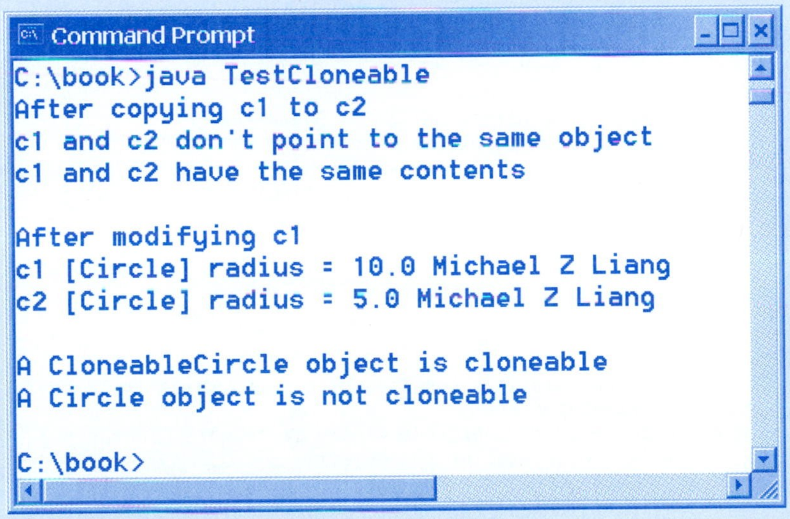

```
C:\book>java TestCloneable
After copying c1 to c2
c1 and c2 don't point to the same object
c1 and c2 have the same contents

After modifying c1
c1 [Circle] radius = 10.0 Michael Z Liang
c2 [Circle] radius = 5.0 Michael Z Liang

A CloneableCircle object is cloneable
A Circle object is not cloneable

C:\book>
```

Figure 8.11 *The* clone *method creates a new copy for the cloneable object.*

```java
1    // TestCloneable.java: Use the TestCloneable interface
2    // to enable cloning
3    public class TestCloneable {
4      /** Main method */
5      public static void main(String[] args) {
6        // Declare and create an instance of CloneableCircle
7        CloneableCircle c1 = new CloneableCircle(5);
8        CloneableCircle c2 = (CloneableCircle)c1.clone();
9        System.out.println("After copying c1 to c2");
10
11       // Check if two variables point to the same object
12       if (c1 == c2)
13         System.out.println("c1 and c2 reference to the same object");
14       else
15         System.out.println("c1 and c2 don't point to the same object");
16
```

continues

311

Example 8.6 continued

```
17        // Check if two objects are of identical contents
18        if (c1.equals(c2))
19          System.out.println("c1 and c2 have the same contents");
20        else
21          System.out.println("c1 and c2 don't have the same contents");
22
23        // Modify c1's radius, name
24        c1.setRadius(10);
25        c1.getCreator().setFirstName("Michael");
26        c1.getCreator().setMi('Z');
27
28        // Display c1 and c2
29        System.out.println("\nAfter modifying c1");
30        System.out.println("c1 " + c1);
31        System.out.println("c2 " + c2);
32
33        System.out.println();
34        if (c1 instanceof Cloneable) {
35          System.out.println("A CloneableCircle object is cloneable");
36        }
37        else {
38          System.out.println(c1 + "is not cloneable");
39        }
40
41        // Check if a Circle object is cloneable
42        Circle c = new Circle();
43        if (c instanceof Cloneable) {
44          System.out.println("A Circle object is cloneable");
45        }
46        else {
47          System.out.println("A Circle object is not cloneable");
48        }
49      }
50    }
51
52    // CloneableCircle is a subclass of Circle, which implements the
53    // Cloneable interface
54    class CloneableCircle extends Circle implements Cloneable {
55      // Store the creator of the object
56      private Name creator = new Name("Yong", 'D', "Liang");
57
58      /** Construct a CloneableCircle with a specified radius */
59      public CloneableCircle(double radius) {
60        super(radius);
61      }
62
63      /** Return creator */
64      public Name getCreator() {
65        return creator;
66      }
67
68      /** Set a new creator */
69      public void setCreator(Name name) {
70        creator = name;
71      }
72
73      /** Override the protected clone method defined in the Object
74         class, and strengthen its accessibility */
75      public Object clone() {
76        try {
77          return super.clone();
78        }
```

```
79              catch (CloneNotSupportedException ex) {
80                return null;
81              }
82          }
83
84          /** Override the toString method defined in the Object class */
85          public String toString() {
86            return super.toString() + " " + creator.getFullName();
87          }
88          /** Override the equals method defined in the Object class */
89          public boolean equals(Cylinder cylinder) {
90            return (this.getRadius() == cylinder.getRadius()) &&
91          }
92
93      }
```

```
1      // Name.java: Encapsulate name information
2      public class Name implements Cloneable {
3        private String firstName;
4        private char mi;
5        private String lastName;
6
7        /** Default constructor */
8        public Name() {
9          this("Jill", 'S', "Barr");
10        }
11
12        /** Construct a name with firstName, mi, and lastName */
13        public Name(String firstName, char mi, String lastName) {
14          this.firstName = firstName;
15          this.mi = mi;
16          this.lastName = lastName;
17        }
18
19        /** Return firstName */
20        public String getFirstName() {
21          return firstName;
22        }
23
24        /** Set a new firstName */
25        public void setFirstName(String firstName) {
26          this.firstName = firstName;
27        }
28
29        /** Return middle name initial */
30        public char getMi() {
31          return mi;
32        }
33
34        /** Set a new middlename initial */
35        public void setMi(char mi) {
36          this.mi = mi;
37        }
38
39        /** Return lastName */
40        public String getLastname() {
41          return lastName;
42        }
43
44        /** Set a new lastName */
45        public void setLastName(String lastName) {
46          this.lastName = lastName;
47        }
48
```

continues

313

Example 8.6 continued

```
49       /** Obtain full name */
50       public String getFullName() {
51         return firstName + ' ' + mi + ' ' + lastName;
52       }
53
54       /** Override the protected clone method defined in the Object
55           class, and strengthen its accessibility */
56       public Object clone() {
57         try {
58           return super.clone();
59         }
60
61         catch (CloneNotSupportedException ex) {
62           return null;
63         }
64       }
65     }
```

Review

The CloneableCircle and Name classes override the clone method (Lines 75–82 in TestCloneable.java and Lines 56–64 in Name.java) defined in the Object class. The clone method in the Object class is defined as follows:

```
protected native Object clone() throws CloneNotSupportedException;
```

The keyword native indicates that this method is not written in Java, but is implemented in the JVM for the native platform. The keyword protected indicates that this method cannot be directly invoked by an object of the class in a different package. For this reason, the Cloneable class must override the method and change the visibility modifier to public so that the method can be used in any package. Since the clone method implemented for the native platform in the Object class performs the task of cloning objects, the clone method in the CloneableCircle and Name classes simply invokes super.clone(). The clone method defined in the Object class may throw CloneNotSupportedException. Thus, super.clone() must be placed in a try/catch block. Exceptions and the try/catch block are introduced in Chapter 13, "Exception Handling."

The main method creates a CloneableCircle object c1 and clones c1 into c2. The clone method in the Object class copies each field from the original object to the target object. If the field is of a primitive type, its value is copied. For example, the value of radius (double type) is copied from c1 to c2. If the field is of an object, the reference of the field is copied. For example, the field creator is of the Name class type, the reference of creator in c1 is copied into c2. As shown in Figure 8.12, the reference of creator in c1 is copied into c2. Therefore, c1.getCreator() == c2.getCreator() is true, although c1 == c2 is false. This is referred to as a *shallow copy* rather than a *deep copy*, meaning that if the field is of an object, the reference of the field is copied rather than its contents.

If you want to perform a deep copy, you can override the clone method with custom cloning operations instead of invoking super.clone(). See Exercise 8.7.

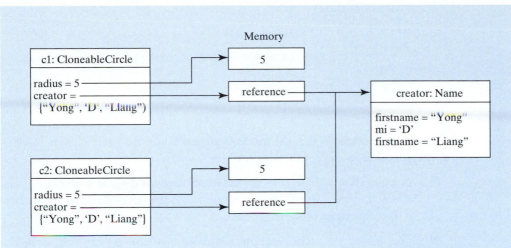

Figure 8.12   *The* clone *method copies the values of primitive type fields and the references of object type fields.*

NOTE

You learned how to use the arraycopy method to copy arrays in Chapter 5, "Arrays." This method provides shallow copies. It works fine for arrays of primitive data type elements, but not for arrays of object type elements. To support a deep copy, you have to deal with how to copy individual object elements in the array.

NOTE

An instance of CloneableCircle is also an instance of Cloneable. This means that you can copy the instance using the clone method. Since the Circle class does not implement the Cloneable interface, an instance of the Circle class is not cloneable. If you attempt to copy an instance of the Circle class, you will get a CloneNotSupportedException. Exceptions will be introduced in Chapter 13, "Exception Handling."

8.12   Inner Classes

An *inner class*, or *nested class*, is a class defined within the scope of another class. Here is an example of an inner class:

```
// ShowInnerClass.java: Demonstrate using inner classes
public class ShowInnerClass {
  private int data;

  /** A method in the outer class */
  public void m() {
    // Do something
    InnerClass instance = new InnerClass();
  }
```

```
// An inner class
class InnerClass {
  /** A method in the inner class */
  public void mi() {
    // Directly reference data and method defined in its outer class
    data++;
    m();
  }
}
}
```

The class `InnerClass` is defined inside `ShowInnerClass`. An inner class is just like any regular class, with the following features:

- An inner class can reference the data and methods defined in the outer class in which it nests, so you do not need to pass the reference of the outer class to the constructor of the inner class.

- Inner classes can make programs simple and concise. As you will see in Example 12.8, "The TicTacToe Game," a program that uses inner classes is shorter and leaner.

- An inner class supports the work of its containing outer class and is compiled into a class named *OutClassName$InnerClassName*.class. For example, the inner class `InnerClass` in `ShowInnerClass` is compiled into *ShowInnerClass$InnerClass*.class.

- An inner class can be declared `public`, `protected`, or `private` subject to the same visibility rules applied to a member of the class.

- An inner class can be declared `static`. A `static` inner class can be accessed using the outer class name. A `static` inner class cannot access nonstatic members of the outer class.

- Objects of an inner class are often created in the outer class. But you can also create an object of an inner class from another class. If the inner class is nonstatic, you must first create an instance of the outer class, then use the following syntax to create an object for the inner class:

  ```
  OuterClass.InnerClass innerObject = outerObject.new InnerClass();
  ```

- If the inner class is static, use the following syntax to create an object for it:

  ```
  OuterClass.InnerClass innerObject = new OuterClass.InnerClass();
  ```

An inner class can be further shortened by using an anonymous inner class. Many Java development tools use anonymous inner classes to generate adapters for handling events. Since anonymous inner classes are used mainly to create event adapters, they will be discussed along with event adapters in Chapter 12, "Applets and Advanced GUI."

8.13   Initialization Blocks (Optional)

Initialization blocks can be used to initialize objects along with the constructors. An initialization block is a block of statements enclosed inside a pair of braces. An initialization block appears within the class declaration, but not inside methods or constructors. It is executed as if it were placed at the beginning of every constructor in the class.

Initialization blocks can simplify the classes if you have multiple constructors sharing a common code and none of the constructors can invoke other constructors. The common code can be placed in an initialization block, as shown in the following example:

```java
public class Book {
  private static int numOfObjects = 0;
  private String title;
  private String isbn;

  public Book(String title) {
    this.title = title;
  }

  public Book(String isbn) {
    this.isbn = isbn;
  }

  {
    numOfObjects++;
  }
}
```

In this example, none of the constructors can invoke any of the others using the syntax this(. . .). When an instance is created using a constructor of the Book class, the initialization block is executed to increase the object count by 1.

NOTE

A class may have multiple initialization blocks. In such cases, the blocks are executed in the order they appear in the class.

8.13.1   Static Initialization Block

A static initialization block is much like a nonstatic initialization block except that it is declared static, can only refer to static members of the class, and is invoked when the class is loaded. The Java runtime system loads a class when it is needed. A superclass is loaded before its subclasses. For an illustration, see the following code:

```java
public class Test {
  public static void main(String[] args) {
    new A();
  }

  {
    System.out.println("Test's non-static initialization " +
      "block is invoked");
  }

  static {
    System.out.println("Test's static initialization block " +
      "is invoked");
  }
```

```java
}
class A extends B {
  A() {
    System.out.println("A's constructor is invoked");
  }

  {
    System.out.println("A's non-static initialization block " +
      "is invoked");
  }

  static {
    System.out.println("A's static initialization block is invoked");
  }
}

class B {
  B() {
    System.out.println("B's constructor is invoked");
  }

  {
    System.out.println("B's non-static initialization block " +
      "is invoked");
  }

  static {
    System.out.println("B's static initialization block is invoked");
  }
}
```

The following is the output of this program:

```
Test's static initialization block is invoked
B's static initialization block is invoked
A's static initialization block is invoked
B's non-static initialization block is invoked
B's constructor is invoked
A's non-static initialization block is invoked
A's constructor is invoked
```

The classes Test, B, and A are loaded in this order, therefore the static blocks of Test, B, and A are invoked in the same order. Since Test's constructor is not invoked, its nonstatic initialization block is not invoked. When invoking new A(), the default constructor of A's superclass is invoked first, therefore, B's nonstatic initialization block is invoked followed by the regular code in B's default constructor. Finally, A's nonstatic initialization block is invoked followed by the regular code in A's constructor.

Chapter Summary

In this chapter, you learned about inheritance, an important and powerful concept in object-oriented programming. The benefits of inheritance are immediately apparent in Java GUI programming, exception handling, internationalization, multithreading, multimedia, I/O, network programming, and every Java program that inherits and extends existing classes.

You learned how to create a subclass from a superclass by adding new fields and methods. You can also override the methods in the superclass. The keywords super and this are used to reference superclasses and subclasses, respectively.

You learned how to use the protected modifier to allow data and methods to be accessed by their subclasses, even if the subclasses are in different packages.

You learned how to use the final modifier to prevent changes to a class, method, or variable. A final class cannot be extended. A final method cannot be overridden. A final variable is a constant.

You learned how to use the abstract modifier to design generic superclasses. An abstract class cannot be instantiated. An abstract method contains only the method description without implementation. Its implementation is provided by subclasses.

You learned the concept of polymorphism and Java's dynamic binding ability to determine at runtime which code to run, given multiple methods with the same name in different classes.

You learned about casting objects among classes in the inheritance hierarchy. You can implicitly cast an object of a subclass to its superclass, since this object is always an instance of the superclass. However, an explicit casting must be used to cast an object of the superclass into a subclass.

You learned how to use interfaces. An interface cannot be instantiated. A subclass can only extend one superclass, but it can implement many interfaces to achieve multiple inheritance.

Review Questions

8.1 What is the printout of running the class C?

```
class A {
  public A() {
    System.out.println(
      "The default constructor of A is invoked");
  }
}

class B extends A {
  public B() {
  }
}

public class C {
  public static void main(String[] args) {
    B b = new B();
  }
}
```

8.2 What problem arises in compiling the following program?

```
class A {
  public A(int x) {
  }
}

class B extends A {
  public B() {
```

```
  }
public class C {
  public static void main(String[] args) {
    B b = new B();
  }
}
```

8.3 Define the following terms: inheritance, superclass, subclass, the keywords `super` and `this`, the modifiers `protected`, `final`, and `abstract`, casting objects, interface.

8.4 Identify the problems in the following classes:

```
public class Circle {
  private double radius;

  public Circle(double radius) {
    radius = radius;
  }

  public double getRadius() {
    return radius;
  }

  public double findArea() {
    return radius * radius * Math.PI;
  }
}

class Cylinder extends Circle {
  private double length;

  Cylinder(double radius, double length) {
    Circle(radius);
    length = length;
  }

  /** Return the surface area for the cylinder */
  public double findArea() {
    return findArea()*length;
  }
}
```

8.5 Indicate true or false for the following statements:

- A protected datum or method can be accessed by any class in the same package.

- A protected datum or method can be accessed by any class in different packages.

- A protected datum or method can be accessed by its subclass in any package.

- A final class can have instances.

- An abstract class can have instances created using the constructor of the abstract class.

- A final class can be extended.

- An abstract class can be extended.

■ A final method can be overridden.

■ You can always successfully cast an instance of a subclass to a superclass.

■ You can always successfully cast an instance of a superclass to a subclass.

■ An interface is compiled into a separate bytecode file.

■ The order in which modifiers appear before a method is important.

■ A subclass of a nonabstract superclass cannot be abstract.

■ A subclass cannot override a concrete method in a superclass to declare it abstract.

8.6 Explain the difference between method overloading and method overriding.

8.7 Does every class have a `toString` method and an `equals` method? Where do they come from? How are they used?

8.8 What modifier should you use on a class so that a class in the same package can access it, but a class in a different package cannot access it?

8.9 What modifier should you use so that a class in a different package cannot access the class, but its subclasses in any package can access it?

8.10 Which of the following class definitions defines a legal abstract class?

a.

```
class A {
  abstract void unfinished() {
  }
}
```

b.

```
class A {
  abstract void unfinished();
}
```

c.

```
abstract class A {
  abstract void unfinished();
}
```

d.

```
public class abstract A {
  abstract void unfinished();
}
```

e.

```
abstract class A {
  protected void unfinished();
}
```

8.11 Given the assumptions

```
Circle circle = new Circle(1);
Cylinder cylinder = new Cylinder(1, 1);
```

are the following Boolean expressions true or false?

```
(circle instanceof Cylinder)
(cylinder instanceof Circle)
```

8.12 Are the following statements correct?

```
Cylinder cylinder = new Cylinder(1,1);
Circle circle = cylinder;
```

8.13 Are the following statements correct?

```
Circle circle = new Circle(1);
Cylinder cylinder = (Cylinder)circle;
```

8.14 Suppose that `Fruit`, `Apple`, `Orange`, `Golden Delicious Apple`, and `Macintosh Apple` are declared, as shown in Figure 8.13.

Assume that the following declaration is given:

```
Fruit fruit = new GoldenDelicious();
Orange orange = new Orange();
```

Answer the following questions:

1. Is `fruit instanceof Orange`?

2. Is `fruit instanceof Apple`?

3. Is `fruit instanceof GoldenDelicious`?

4. Is `fruit instanceof Macintosh`?

5. Is `orange instanceof Orange`?

6. Is `orange instanceof Fruit`?

7. Is `orange instanceof Apple`?

8. Suppose the method `makeApple` is defined in the `Apple` class. Can `fruit` invoke this method? Can `orange` invoke this method?

9. Suppose the method `makeOrangeJuice` is defined in the `Orange` class. Can `orange` invoke this method? Can `fruit` invoke this method?

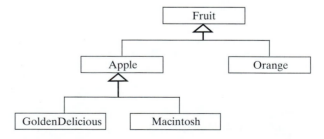

Figure 8.13   `GoldenDelicious` *and* `Macintosh` *are subclasses of* `Apple`, `Apple` *and* `Orange` *are subclasses of* `Fruit`.

8.15 Which of the following is a correct interface?

a.

```
interface A {
  void print() { };
}
```

b.

```
abstract interface A {
  print();
}
```

c.

```
abstract interface A extends I1, I2 {
  abstract void print() { };
}
```

d.

```
interface A {
  void print();
}
```

8.16 What is the output of the following program? This program is the same as the one in Example 8.6 except that one statement is added (see the highlighted line in the code).

```
// TestCloneable.java: Use the TestCloneable interface
// to enable cloning
public class TestCloneable {
  /** Main method */
  public static void main(String[] args) {
    // Declare and create an instance of CloneableCircle
    CloneableCircle c1 = new CloneableCircle(5);
    CloneableCircle c2 = (CloneableCircle)c1.clone();

    System.out.println("After copying c1 to c2");

    // Check if two variables point to the same object
    if (c1 == c2)
      System.out.println("c1 and c2 reference to the same" +
        " object");
    else
      System.out.println("c1 and c2 don't point to the same " +
        " object");

    // Check if two objects are of identical contents
    if (c1.equals(c2))
      System.out.println("c1 and c2 have the same contents");
    else
      System.out.println("c1 and c2 don't have the same " +
        " contents");

    // Modify c1's radius, name
    c1.setRadius(10);
    c1.setCreator(new Name("Bob", "R", "Smith"));
    c1.getCreator().setFirstname("Michael");
    c1.getCreator().setMi("Z");
```

```
      // Display c1 and c2
      System.out.println("\nAfter modifying c1");
      System.out.println("c1 " + c1);
      System.out.println("c2 " + c2);

      System.out.println();
      if (c1 instanceof Cloneable) {
        System.out.println("A CloneableCircle object is " +
          " cloneable");
      }
      else {
        System.out.println("A CloneableCircle object is " +
          " not cloneable");
      }

      // Check if a Circle object is cloneable
      Circle c = new Circle();
      if (c instanceof Cloneable) {
        System.out.println("A Circle object is cloneable");
      }
      else {
        System.out.println("A Circle object is not cloneable");
      }
    }
  }
```

8.17 Analyze the following code:

```
class Test extends A {
  public static void main(String[] args) {
    Test t = new Test();
    t.print();
  }
}

class A {
  String s;

  A(String s) {
    this.s = s;
  }

  public void print() {
    System.out.println(s);
  }
}
```

a. The program does not compile because Test does not have a default constructor Test().

b. The program has an implicit default constructor Test(), but it cannot be compiled because its superclass does not have a default constructor.

c. The program would compile if a default constructor A(){ } is added to class A explicitly.

d. The program compiles, but it has a runtime error due to the conflict on the method name print.

e. b and c.

8.18 Show the output of following program:

```
public class Test {
  public static void main(String[] args) {
    A a = new A(3);
  }
}

class A extends B {
  public A(int t) {
    System.out.println("A's constructor is invoked");
  }
}

class B {
  public B() {
    System.out.println("B's constructor is invoked");
  }
}
```

8.19 Which of the following statements is not true?
- a. A public class can be accessed by a class from a different package.
- b. A private method cannot be accessed by a class in a different package.
- c. A protected method can be accessed by a subclass in a different package.
- d. A method with no visibility modifier can be accessed by a class in a different package.

8.20 When you create an object of a class A, is the constructor in the Object class automatically invoked?

8.21 Can an inner class be used in a class other than the class in which the inner class nests?

8.22 Can the modifiers public, private, protected, and static be used on inner classes?

8.23 Consider redefining the max method in the Max class as follows:

```
public class Max {
  /** Return the maximum between two objects */
  public static Object max(Object o1, Object o2) {
    if (((Comparable)o1).compareTo(o2) > 0)
      return o1;
    else
      return o2;
  }
}
```

What changes do you have to make to enable Example 8.5, "Using Interfaces," to compile and run correctly?

8.24 The findArea and findPerimeter methods may be removed from the GeometricObject class. What are the benefits of defining findArea and findPerimeter as abstract methods in the GeometricObject class?

8.25 You can define the compareTo method in a class without implementing the Comparable interface. What are the benefits of implementing the Comparable interface?

Programming Exercises

8.1 Write a class named `Triangle` that extends `GeometricObject`. The class `Triangle` is defined as follows:

```
public class Triangle extends GeometricObject {
  private double side1, side2, side3;

  /** Construct a triangle with the specified sides */
  public Triangle(double side1, double side2, double side3) {
    // Implement it
  }

  /** Implement the abstract method findArea in
     GeometricObject */
  public double findArea() {
    // Implement it
  }

  /** Implement the abstract method findPerimeter in
     GeometricObject */
  public double findPerimeter() {
    // Implement it
  }
}
```

The formula for computing the area is as follows:

$$s = (side1 + side2 + side3)/2;$$

$$area = \sqrt{s(s - side1)(s - side2)(s - side3)};$$

8.2 Implement a class named `Person` and two subclasses of `Person` named `Student` and `Employee`. Make `Faculty` and `Staff` subclasses of `Employee`. A person has a name, address, phone number, and e-mail address. A student has a class status (freshman, sophomore, junior, or senior). Define the status as a constant. An employee has an office, salary, and date-hired. A faculty member has office hours and a rank. A staff member has a title. Override the `toString` method in each class to display the class name and the person's name.

8.3 In Exercise 6.3, the `Account` class was created to model a bank account. An account has the properties account number, balance, and annual interest rate, and methods to deposit and withdraw. Create two subclasses for checking and saving accounts. A checking account has an overdraft limit, but a savings account cannot go overdrawn.

8.4 Modify the `GeometricObject` class to implement the `Comparable` interface, and define the `max` method in the `GeometricObject` class. Write a test program that uses the `max` method to find a maximum circle between two circles and a maximum cylinder between two cylinders.

8.5 Create a class named `ComparableRectangle` that extends `Rectangle` and implements `Comparable`. Implement the `compareTo` method to compare the rectangles on their areas. Write a test class to find a maximum between two instances of `ComparableRectangle` objects.

8.6 Create an interface named `Eatable`, as follows:

```
public interface Eatable {
  public void howToEat();
}
```

Every class of an eatable object must implement the `Eatable` interface. Create the following two sets of classes:

■ Create a class named `Animal` and its subclasses `Tiger`, `Chicken`, and `Elephant`. Since chicken is eatable, implement the `Eatable` interface for the `Chicken` class.

■ Create a class named `Fruit` and its subclasses `Apple` and `Orange`. Since all fruits are eatable, implement the `Eatable` interface for the `Fruit` class. In the `Fruit` class, give a generic implementation of the `howToEat` method. In the `Apple` class and the `Orange` class, give a specific implementation of the `howToEat` method.

Override the `toString` method in each class to return the name of the class. For example, the `toString` method in the `Animal` class returns `Animal`.

Create a test program that contains a `main` method and a method named `showObject`. The `main` method declares and creates four instances of the `Object` type for a tiger, a chicken, an apple, and an orange. For example, `Object tiger = new Tiger()`. It then invokes the `showObject` method to display the object. The `showObject` method is given as follows:

```
public static void showObject(Object object) {
  System.out.println(object);
  if (object instanceof Eatable) {
    ((Eatable)object).howToEat();
  }
}
```

8.7 Rewrite the `CloneableCircle` class in Example 8.6, "Cloning Objects," to perform a deep copy.

8.8 Rewrite the `Circle` class on Page 293 to extend `GeometricObject` and implement the `Comparable` interface. Override the `equals` method in the `Object` class. Two `Circle` objects are equal if their radii are the same.

8.9 Rewrite the `Rectangle` class on Page 293 to extend `GeometricObject` and implement the `Comparable` interface. Override the `equals` method in the `Object` class. Two `Rectangle` objects are equal if their areas are the same.

OBJECT-ORIENTED
SOFTWARE DEVELOPMENT

Objectives

- To become familiar with the process of program development.

- To be able to analyze relationships among classes: association, aggregation, strong inheritance, and weak inheritance.

- To learn class-design guidelines.

- To use wrapper classes for primitive data values.

- To learn how to create a generic sort method.

- To learn how to design generic classes for matrix operations. (Optional)

- To develop generic linked lists. (Optional)

9.1   Introduction

The preceding chapters introduced objects, classes, class inheritance, and interfaces. You learned the concepts of object-oriented programming. This chapter focuses on the development of software systems using the object-oriented approach, and introduces class modeling using the Unified Modeling Language (UML). You will learn class-design guidelines and the techniques for designing reusable classes through wrapper classes, generic matrix classes, and generic linked list classes.

9.2   The Software Development Process

Developing a software project is an engineering process. Software products, no matter how large or how small, have the same developmental phases: requirements specification, analysis, design, implementation, testing, deployment, and maintenance, as shown in Figure 9.1.

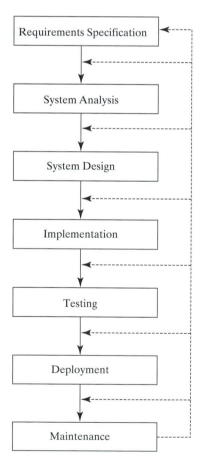

Figure 9.1   *Developing a project involves requirements specification, system analysis, system design, implementation, testing, deployment, and maintenance.*

Requirements specification is a formal process that seeks to understand the problem and document in detail what the software system needs to do. This phase involves close interaction between users and designers. Most of the examples in this book are simple, and their requirements are clearly stated. In the real world, however, problems are not well defined. You need to study a problem carefully to identify its requirements.

System analysis seeks to analyze the business process in terms of data flow, and to identify the system's input and output. Part of the analysis entails modeling the system's behavior. The model is intended to capture the essential elements of the system and to define services to the system.

System design is the process of designing the system's components. This phase involves the use of many levels of abstraction to decompose the problem into manageable components, identify classes and interfaces, and establish relationships among the classes and interfaces.

Implementation is the process of translating the system design into programs. Separate programs are written for each component and put to work together. This phase requires the use of an object-oriented programming language like Java. The implementation involves coding, testing, and debugging.

Testing ensures that the code meets the requirements specification and weeds out bugs. An independent team of software engineers not involved in the design and implementation of the project usually conducts such testing.

Deployment makes the project available for use. For a Java applet, this means installing it on a Web server. For a Java application, install it on the client's computer. A project usually consists of many classes. An effective approach for deployment is to package all the classes into a Java archive file, as will be introduced in Section 12.12, "Packaging and Deploying Java Projects," in Chapter 12, "Applets and Advanced GUI."

Maintenance is concerned with changing and improving the product. A software product must continue to perform and improve in a changing environment. This requires periodic upgrades of the product to fix newly discovered bugs and incorporate changes.

The central task in object-oriented system development is to design classes to model the system. While there are many object-oriented methodologies, UML has become the industry-standard notation for class analysis and design, and itself leads to a methodology. The following sections introduce analyzing, designing, and implementing classes.

9.3   Analyzing Relationships Among Objects

By now you have formed some ideas about objects and classes and their programming features. Object-oriented programming is centered on objects; it is particularly involved with getting objects to work together. The first step in object-oriented program development is to identify the objects and establish relationships among them. Since objects are modeled using classes, a relationship among objects of different classes is also referred to as a relationship among these classes. The relationships can be classified into three types: *association*, *aggregation*, and *inheritance*.

9.3.1   Association

Association represents a general binary relationship that describes an activity between two classes. For example, a student taking a course is an association between the Student class and the Course class, and a faculty member teaching a course is an association between the Faculty class and the Course class. These associations can be represented in UML graphical notations, as shown in Figure 9.2.

Figure 9.2   *A student may take any number of the courses, and a faculty member teaches at most three courses. A course may have from five to sixty students and is taught by only one faculty member.*

An association is illustrated using a solid line between two classes with an optional label that describes the relationship. In Figure 9.2, the labels are *Take* and *Teach*. Each relationship may have an optional small black triangle that indicates the direction of the relationship. In Figure 9.2, the direction indicates that a student takes a course, as opposed to a course taking a student.

Each class involved in the relationship may have a role name that describes the role played by the class in the relationship. In Figure 9.2, *teacher* is the role name for Faculty.

Each class involved in an association may specify a *multiplicity*. A multiplicity could be a number or an interval that specifies how many objects of the class are involved in the relationship. The character * means unlimited number of objects, and the interval 1..u means that the number of objects should be between 1 and u, inclusive. In Figure 9.2, each student may take any number of courses, and each course must have at least five students and at most sixty students. Each course is taught by only one faculty member, and a faculty member may teach from zero to three courses per semester.

Association may exist between objects of the same class. For example, a person may have a supervisor. This is illustrated in Figure 9.3.

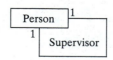

Figure 9.3   *A person may have a supervisor.*

An association is usually represented as a data field in the class. For example, the relationships in Figure 9.2 can be represented in the following classes:

```
public class Student {
  /** Data fields */
  /** Constructors */
  /** Methods */
}
```

```
public class Course {
  private Student
    classList;
  private Faculty faculty;

  /** Data fields */
  /** Constructors */
  /** Methods */
}
```

```
public class Faculty {
  /** Data fields */
  /** Constructors */
  /** Methods */
}
```

Alternatively, it can be represented as follows:

```
public class Student {
  private Course[]
    courseList;

  /** Data fields */
  /** Constructors */
  /** Methods */
}
```

```
public class Course {
  /** Data fields */
  /** Constructors */
  /** Methods */
}
```

```
public class Faculty {
  private Course[]
    courseList;

  /** Data fields */
  /** Constructors */
  /** Methods */
}
```

In the association "a person has a supervisor," a supervisor may be a data field in the Person class, as follows:

```
public class Person {
  private Person supervisor;

  /** Data fields */
  /** Constructors */
  /** Methods */
}
```

9.3.2   Aggregation

Aggregation is a special form of association that represents an ownership relationship between two classes. Aggregation models relationships like has-a, part-of, owns, and employed-by. An object may be owned by several other aggregated objects. If an object is exclusively owned by an aggregated object, the relationship between the object and its aggregated object is referred to as *composition*. For example, a publisher that owns a magazine is a composition between the Publisher class and the Magazine class, whereas a publisher that has consultants is an aggregation between the Publisher class and the Consultant class, since a consultant may work for several publishers. In UML, a filled diamond is attached to the Publisher class of the association to denote the composition relationship, and an empty diamond is attached to the aggregated class of the association to denote the aggregation relationship, as shown in Figure 9.4.

Figure 9.4   *A magazine is owned by a publisher; a consultant may work for several publishers.*

A composing class is usually represented as a data field in the composed class. For example, the relationship "a publisher owns magazines" can be represented in the Magazine class, as follows:

```
public class Magazine {
  private Publisher publisher;

  /** Data fields */
  /** Constructors */
  /** Methods */
}
```

9.3.3   Inheritance

Inheritance models the is-a relationship between two classes. A strong is-a relationship describes a direct inheritance relationship between two classes. A weak is-a relationship describes that a class has certain properties. A strong is-a relationship can be represented using class inheritance. For example, a student is a person, and a faculty member is a person. As shown below, you can define a class for Student that inherits from the Person class, and a class for Faculty that inherits from the Person class.

```
public class Student extends Person {
  /** Data fields */
  /** Constructors */
  /** Methods */
}

public class Faculty extends Person {
  /** Data fields */
  /** Constructors */
  /** Methods */
}
```

A weak is-a relationship can be represented using interfaces. For example, the weak is-a relationship "students are comparable based on their grades" can be represented by implementing the Comparable interface, as follows:

```
public class Student extends Person implements Comparable {
  /** Data fields */
  /** Constructors */
  /** Methods */

  /** Implement the compareTo method */
  public int compareTo(Object object) {
    // ...
  }
}
```

9.4   Class Development

The key to object-oriented programming is to model the application in terms of cooperative objects. Carefully designed classes are critical when a project is being developed. There are many levels of abstraction in system design. You have learned method abstraction and have applied it to the development of large programs. Methods are means to group statements. Classes extend abstraction to a higher level and provide a means of grouping methods. Classes do more than just group methods, however; they also contain data fields. Methods and data fields together describe the properties and behaviors of classes.

The power of classes is further extended by inheritance. Inheritance enables a class to extend the contract and the implementation of an existing class without knowing the details of the existing class. In the development of a Java program, class abstraction is applied to decompose the problem into a set of related classes, and method abstraction is applied to design individual classes.

This section uses two examples to demonstrate identifying classes, analyzing classes, and applying class abstraction in object-oriented program development.

Example 9.1 Borrowing Mortgages

Problem

Develop a system that models borrowing mortgages.

Solution

For simplicity, the example does not attempt to build a complete system for storing, processing, and manipulating mortgages for borrowers; instead it focuses on modeling borrowers and the mortgages for the borrowers. The following steps are usually involved in building an object-oriented system:

1. Identify classes for the system.

2. Describe attributes and methods in each class.

3. Establish relationships among classes.

4. Create classes.

The first step is to identify classes for the system. There are many strategies for identifying classes in a system, one of which is to study how the system works and select a number of use cases, or scenarios. Since a borrower is a person who obtains a mortgage, and a person has a name and an address, you can identify the following classes: Person, Name, Address, Borrower, and Mortgage.

The second step is to describe attributes and methods in each of the classes you have identified. The attributes and methods can be illustrated using UML, as shown in Figure 9.5. The Name class, implemented in Example 8.6, "Cloning

continues

Example 9.1 continued

Objects," has the properties firstName, mi, and lastName, their associated accessor methods, and the getFullName method for returning the full name. The Address class has the properties street, city, state, and zip, their associated accessor methods, and the getAddress method for returning the full address. The Mortgage class, presented in Example 6.8, "Using the Mortgage Class," has the properties annualInterestRate, numOfYears, and loanAmount, and property accessor methods, monthlyPayment, and totalPayment methods. The Person class has the properties name and address, their associated accessor methods, and the toString method for displaying complete information about the person. Borrower is a subclass of Person. Additionally, Borrower has the mortgage property and its associated accessor methods, and the toString method for displaying the person and the person's mortgage.

The third step is to establish relationships among the classes. The relationship is derived clearly from the analysis of the preceding two steps. The first three steps are intertwined. When you identify classes, you also think of the relationship among them. The relationships for the classes in this example are illustrated in Figure 9.5.

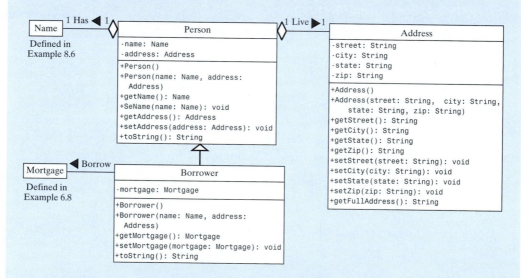

Figure 9.5   *A borrower has a name with an address and borrows a mortgage.*

The fourth step is to write the code for the classes, as follows:

```
1    // Address.java: Encapsulate address information
2    public class Address {
3      private String street;
4      private String city;
5      private String state;
6
```

```
 7       private String zip;
 8
 9       /** Default constructor */
10       public Address() {
11         this("100 Main", "Savannah", "GA", "31411");
12       }
13
14       /** Create address with street, city, state, and zip */
15       public Address(String street, String city,
16         String state, String zip) {
17         this.street = street;
18         this.city = city;
19         this.state = state;
20         this.zip = zip;
21       }
22
23       /** Return street */
24       public String getStreet() {
25         return street;
26       }
27
28       /** Set a new street */
29       public void setStreet(String street) {
30         this.street = street;
31       }
32
33       /** Return city */
34       public String getCity() {
35         return city;
36       }
37
38       /** Set a new city */
39       public void setCity(String city) {
40         this.city = city;
41       }
42
43       /** Return state */
44       public String getState() {
45         return state;
46       }
47
48       /** Set a new state */
49       public void setState(String state) {
50         this.state = state;
51       }
52
53       /** Return zip */
54       public String getZip() {
55         return zip;
56       }
57
58       /** Set a new zip */
59       public void setZip(String zip) {
60         this.zip = zip;
61       }
62
63       /** Get full address */
64       public String getFullAddress() {
65         return street + '\n' + city + ", " + state + ' ' + zip + '\n';
66       }
67     }
```

continues

337

Example 9.1 continued

```
 1    public class Person {
 2      private Name name;
 3
 4      private Address address;
 5
 6      /** Default constructor */
 7      public Person() {
 8        this(new Name("Jill", 'S', "Barr"),
 9          new Address("100 Main", "Savannah", "GA", "31411"));
10      }
11
12      /** Construct a person with specified name and address */
13      public Person(Name name, Address address) {
14        this.name = name;
15        this.address = address;
16      }
17
18      /** Return name */
19      public Name getName() {
20        return name;
21      }
22
23      /** Set a new name */
24      public void setName(Name name) {
25        this.name = name;
26      }
27
28      /** Return address */
29      public Address getAddress() {
30        return address;
31      }
32
33      /** Set a new address */
34      public void setAddress(Address address) {
35        this.address = address;
36      }
37
38      /** Override the toString method */
39      public String toString() {
40        return '\n' + name.getFullName() + '\n' +
41          address.getFullAddress() + '\n';
42      }
43    }
```

```
 1    // Borrower.java: Encapsulate borrower information
 2    public class Borrower extends Person {
 3
 4      private Mortgage mortgage;
 5
 6      /** Default constructor */
 7      public Borrower() {
 8        super();
 9      }
10
11      /** Create a borrower with specified name and address */
12      public Borrower(Name name, Address address) {
13        super(name, address);
14      }
15
16      /** Return mortgage */
17      public Mortgage getMortgage() {
18        return mortgage;
19      }
```

```
20
21        /** Set a new mortgage */
22        public void setMortgage(Mortgage mortgage) {
23          this.mortgage = mortgage;
24        }
25
26        /** String representation for borrower */
27        public String toString() {
28          return super.toString() +
29            "Monthly payment is " + mortgage.monthlyPayment() + '\n' +
30            "Total payment is " + mortgage.totalPayment();
31        }
32      }
```

Immediately below is a test program that uses the classes `Name`, `Address`, `Borrower`, and `Mortgage`. The output of the program is shown in Figure 9.6.

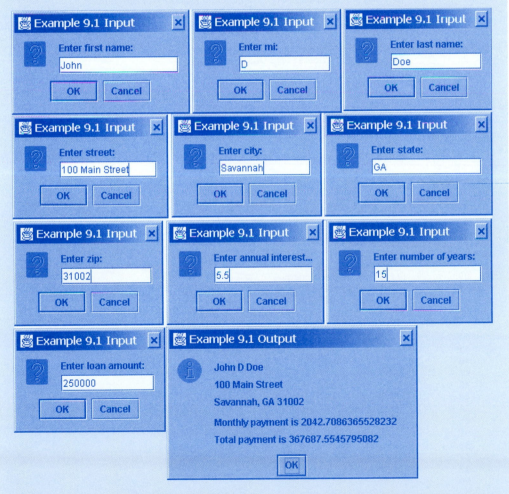

Figure 9.6 *The program obtains name, address, and mortgage, stores the information in a* `Borrower` *object, and displays the information with the mortgage payment.*

continues

339

Example 9.1 continued

```
1    // BorrowMortgage.java: Demonstrate using the classes Borrower
2    // Name, Address, and Mortgage
3    import javax.swing.JOptionPane;
4
5    public class BorrowMortgage {
6      /** Main method */
7      public static void main(String[] args) {
8        // Create one borrower
9        Borrower borrower = new Borrower();
10
11       // Enter the information for the borrower
12
13       // 1. Enter name
14       Name name = new Name();
15       // Prompt the user to enter first name
16       String firstName = JOptionPane.showInputDialog(null,
17         "Enter first name:", "Example 9.1 Input",
18         JOptionPane.QUESTION_MESSAGE);
19
20       // Set first name
21       name.setFirstName(firstName);
22
23       // Prompt the user to enter mi
24       String mi = JOptionPane.showInputDialog(null,
25         "Enter mi:", "Example 9.1 Input",
26         JOptionPane.QUESTION_MESSAGE);
27
28       // Set mi
29       name.setMi(mi.charAt(0));
30
31       // Prompt the user to enter last name
32       String lastName = JOptionPane.showInputDialog(null,
33         "Enter last name:", "Example 9.1 Input",
34         JOptionPane.QUESTION_MESSAGE);
35
36       // Set last name
37       name.setLastName(lastName);
38
39       // 2. Enter address
40       Address address = new Address();
41       // Prompt the user to enter street
42       String street = JOptionPane.showInputDialog(null,
43         "Enter street:", "Example 9.1 Input",
44         JOptionPane.QUESTION_MESSAGE);
45
46       // Set street
47       address.setStreet(street);
48
49       // Prompt the user to enter city
50       String city = JOptionPane.showInputDialog(null,
51         "Enter city:", "Example 9.1 Input",
52         JOptionPane.QUESTION_MESSAGE);
53
54       // Set city
55       address.setCity(city);
56
57       // Prompt the user to enter state
58       String state = JOptionPane.showInputDialog(null,
59         "Enter state:", "Example 9.1 Input",
60         JOptionPane.QUESTION_MESSAGE);
61
```

```
62          // Set state
63          address.setState(state);
64
65          // Prompt the user to enter zip
66          String zip = JOptionPane.showInputDialog(null,
67            "Enter zip:", "Example 9.1 Input",
68            JOptionPane.QUESTION_MESSAGE);
69
70          // Set zip
71          address.setZip(zip);
72
73          // 3. Enter mortgage information
74          Mortgage mortgage = new Mortgage();
75          // Prompt the user to enter annual interest rate
76          String annualInterestRateString = JOptionPane.showInputDialog(
77            null, "Enter annual interest rate (i.e. 7.25):",
78            "Example 9.1 Input", JOptionPane.QUESTION_MESSAGE);
79
80          // Convert string into double
81          double annualInterestRate =
82            Double.parseDouble(annualInterestRateString);
83
84          // Set annual interest rate
85          mortgage.setAnnualInterestRate(annualInterestRate);
86
87          // Prompt the user to enter number of years
88          String numOfYearsString = JOptionPane.showInputDialog(
89            null, "Enter number of years:",
90            "Example 9.1 Input", JOptionPane.QUESTION_MESSAGE);
91
92          // Convert string into integer
93          int numOfYears = Integer.parseInt(numOfYearsString);
94
95          // Set number of years
96          mortgage.setNumOfYears(numOfYears);
97
98          // Prompt the user to enter loan amount
99          String loanAmountString = JOptionPane.showInputDialog(
100           null, "Enter loan amount:",
101           "Example 9.1 Input", JOptionPane.QUESTION_MESSAGE);
102
103         // Convert string into double
104         double loanAmount = Double.parseDouble(loanAmountString);
105
106         // Set loan amount
107         mortgage.setLoanAmount(loanAmount);
108
109         // 4. Set values to the borrower
110         borrower.setName(name);
111         borrower.setAddress(address);
112         borrower.setMortgage(mortgage);
113
114         // Display mortgage information
115         JOptionPane.showMessageDialog(null, borrower.toString(),
116           "Example 9.1 Output", JOptionPane.INFORMATION_MESSAGE);
117
118         System.exit(0);
119       }
120     }
```

continues

341

Example 9.1 continued

Review

Identifying objects is not easy for novice programmers. How do you find the right objects? There is no unique solution even for simple problems. Software development is more an art than a science. The quality of a program ultimately depends on the programmer's intuition, experience, and knowledge.

Once an object is identified, its properties and methods can be defined by analyzing the requirements and scenarios of the system. It is a good practice to provide complete accessor methods. These may not be needed for your current project, but will be useful in other projects, since your classes are designed for reuse in future projects.

Establishing relationships among objects helps you to understand the interactions among objects. An object-oriented system consists of a collection of interrelated, cooperative objects.

Example 9.2 The `Rational` Class

Problem

Develop a class named `Rational` for representing rational numbers.

Solution

A rational number is a number with a numerator and a denominator in the form a/b, where a is the numerator and b is the denominator. For example, 1/3, 3/4, and 10/4.

A rational number cannot have a denominator of 0, but a numerator of 0 is fine. Every integer a is equivalent to a rational number a/1. Rational numbers are used in exact computations involving fractions; for example, 1/3 = 0.33333. . . . This number cannot be precisely represented in floating-point format using data type `double` or `float`. To obtain the exact result, it is necessary to use rational numbers.

There are many equivalent rational numbers; for example, 1/3 = 2/6 = 3/9 = 4/12. For convenience, 1/3 is used in this example to represent all rational numbers that are equivalent to 1/3. The numerator and the denominator of 1/3 have no common divisor except 1, so 1/3 is said to be in lowest terms.

To reduce a rational number to its lowest terms, you need to find the greatest common divisor, or GCD, of the absolute values of its numerator and denominator, then divide both numerator and denominator by this value. Here is Euclid's famous algorithm for finding the GCD of two integers n and d:

```
t1 = Math.abs(n); t2 = Math.abs(d); // Get absolute value of n and d;
r = t1 % t2; // r is the remainder of t1 divided by t2;
while (r != 0) {
  t1 = t2;
  t2 = r;
  r = t1 % t2;
}

// When r is 0, t2 is the greatest common divisor between t1 and t2
return t2;
```

Based upon the foregoing analysis, the following data and methods are needed in the `Rational` class:

- Data field:

    `long numerator`: Represents the numerator of the rational number.

    `long denominator`: Represents the denominator of the rational number.

- Methods:

    `public Rational add(Rational secondRational)`

    Returns the addition of this rational with another.

    public Rational subtract(Rational secondRational)

    Returns the subtraction of this rational with another.

    `public Rational multiply(Rational secondRational)`

    Returns the multiplication of this rational with another.

    `public Rational divide(Rational secondRational)`

    Returns the division of this rational with another.

    `private long gcd(long n, long d)`

    Returns the GCD of two numbers.

Java contains the `Number` class, which is the root class for modeling integer and floating-point numbers. Rational numbers share many common features with integers and floating-point numbers. Thus, the `Rational` class will be defined as a subclass of the `Number` class. The `Number` class contains four abstract methods, `intValue()`, `longValue()`, `floatValue()`, and `doubleValue()`, to convert a number into an `int`, `long`, `float`, or `double` value. The `Rational` class implements all the abstract methods defined in the `Number` class. Additionally, the `Rational` class provides constructors and methods for addition, subtraction, multiplication, and division. Since the rational numbers are comparable, the `Rational` class also implements the `Comparable` interface.

Figure 9.7 is an illustration of the `Rational` class and its relationship to the `Number` class and the `Comparable` interface.

Example 9.2 continued

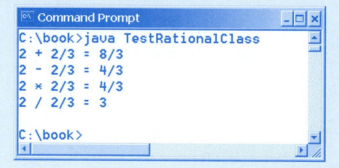

java.lang.Number
+byteValue(): byte
+shortValue(): short
+intValue(): int
+longValue(): long
+floatValue(): float
+doubleValue():double

Rational
-numerator: long
-denominator: long
+Rational()
+Rational(numerator: long, Denomination: long)
+getNumerator(): long
+getDenominator(): long
+add(secondRational: Rational): Rational
+multiply(secondRational: Rational): Rational
+subtract(secondRational: Rational): Rational
+divide(Rational secondRational): Rational
+toString(): String
-gcd(n: long, d: long): long

java.lang.Comparable
+int compareTo(Object)

1 Add, Subtract, Multiply, Divide

Figure 9.7   *The properties and methods of the* Rational *class are illustrated using UML notations.*

The Rational class is presented below, followed by a test program. Figure 9.8 shows a sample run of the program.

```
Command Prompt                                    _ □ ×
C:\book>java TestRationalClass
2 + 2/3 = 8/3
2 - 2/3 = 4/3
2 * 2/3 = 4/3
2 / 2/3 = 3

C:\book>
```

Figure 9.8   *The program creates two instances of the* Rational *class and displays their addition, subtraction, multiplication, and division.*

```
1    // Rational.java: Define a rational number and its associated
2    // operations such as add, subtract, multiply, and divide
3    public class Rational extends Number implements Comparable {
4      // Data fields for numerator and denominator
5      private long numerator = 0;
6      private long denominator = 1;
7
8      /** Default constructor */
9      public Rational() {
10       this(0, 1);
11     }
12
13     /** Construct a rational with specified numerator and denominator */
14     public Rational(long numerator, long denominator) {
15       long gcd = gcd(numerator, denominator);
16       this.numerator = numerator / gcd;
```

```
17         this.denominator = denominator / gcd;
18       }
19
20       /** Find GCD of two numbers */
21       private long gcd(long n, long d) {
22         long t1 = Math.abs(n);
23         long t2 = Math.abs(d);
24         long remainder = t1 % t2;
25
26         while (remainder != 0) {
27           t1 = t2;
28           t2 = remainder;
29           remainder = t1%t2;
30         }
31
32         return t2;
33       }
34
35       /** Return numerator */
36       public long getNumerator() {
37         return numerator;
38       }
39
40       /** Return denominator */
41       public long getDenominator() {
42         return denominator;
43       }
44
45       /** Add a rational number to this rational */
46       public Rational add(Rational secondRational) {
47         long n = numerator * secondRational.getDenominator() +
48           denominator * secondRational.getNumerator();
49         long d = denominator * secondRational.getDenominator();
50         return new Rational(n, d);
51       }
52
53       /** Subtract a rational number from this rational */
54       public Rational subtract(Rational secondRational) {
55         long n = numerator * secondRational.getDenominator()
56           - denominator * secondRational.getNumerator();
57         long d = denominator * secondRational.getDenominator();
58         return new Rational(n, d);
59       }
60
61       /** Multiply a rational number to this rational */
62       public Rational multiply(Rational secondRational) {
63         long n = numerator * secondRational.getNumerator();
64         long d = denominator * secondRational.getDenominator();
65         return new Rational(n, d);
66       }
67
68       /** Divide a rational number from this rational */
69       public Rational divide(Rational secondRational) {
70         long n = numerator * secondRational.getDenominator();
71         long d = denominator * secondRational.numerator;
72         return new Rational(n, d);
73       }
74
75       /** Override the toString() method */
76       public String toString() {
77         if (denominator == 1)
78           return numerator + "";
```

continues

345

Example 9.2 continued

```
 79        else
 80          return numerator + "/" + denominator;
 81      }
 82
 83      /** Override the equals method */
 84      public boolean equals(Object parm1) {
 85        /** @todo: Override this java.lang.Object method */
 86        if ((this.subtract((Rational)(parm1))).getNumerator() == 0)
 87          return true;
 88        else
 89          return false;
 90      }
 91
 92      /** Override the intValue method */
 93      public int intValue() {
 94        /** @todo: implement this java.lang.Number abstract method */
 95        return (int)doubleValue();
 96      }
 97
 98      /** Override the floatValue method */
 99      public float floatValue() {
100        /** @todo: implement this java.lang.Number abstract method */
101        return (float)doubleValue();
102      }
103
104      /** Override the doubleValue method */
105      public double doubleValue() {
106        /** @todo: implement this java.lang.Number abstract method */
107        return numerator * 1.0 / denominator;
108      }
109
110      /** Override the longValue method */
111      public long longValue() {
112        /** @todo: implement this java.lang.Number abstract method */
113        return (long)doubleValue();
114      }
115
116      /** Override the compareTo method */
117      public int compareTo(Object o) {
118        /** @todo: Implement this java.lang.Comparable method */
119        if ((this.subtract((Rational)o)).getNumerator() > 0)
120          return 1;
121        else if ((this.subtract((Rational)o)).getNumerator() < 0)
122          return -1;
123        else
124          return 0;
125      }
126    }
```

```
 1    // TestRationalClass.java: Demonstrate using the Rational class
 2    public class TestRationalClass {
 3      /** Main method */
 4      public static void main(String[] args) {
 5        // Create and initialize two rational numbers r1 and r2.
 6        Rational r1 = new Rational(4, 2);
 7        Rational r2 = new Rational(2, 3);
 8
 9        // Display results
10        System.out.println(r1.toString() + " + " + r2.toString() +
11          " = " + (r1.add(r2)).toString());
12        System.out.println(r1.toString() + " - " + r2.toString() +
13          " = " + (r1.subtract(r2)).toString());
```

```
14          System.out.println(r1.toString() + " * " + r2.toString() +
15            " = " + (r1.multiply(r2)).toString());
16          System.out.println(r1.toString() + " / " + r2.toString() +
17            " = " + (r1.divide(r2)).toString());
18       }
19    }
```

Review

The main method creates two rational numbers, r1 and r2, and displays the results of r1+r2, r1-r2, r1xr2, and r1/r2.

The rational number is encapsulated in a Rational object. Internally, a rational number is represented in its lowest terms; in other words, the greatest common divisor of the numerator and the denominator is 1.

The gcd() method (Lines 21–33 in the Rational class) is private; it is not intended for use by clients. The gcd() method is only for internal use by the Rational class.

The abs(x) method (Lines 22–23 in the Rational class) is defined in the Math class that returns the absolute value of x.

Two Rational objects can interact with each other to perform add, subtract, multiply, and divide operations. To add Rational object r1 to r2, invoke r1.add(r2) (Line 11 in TestRationalClass), which returns a new Rational object.

The methods toString and equals in the Object class are overridden in the Rational class (Lines 75–90). The toString() method returns a string representation of a Rational object in the form numerator/denominator, or simply numerator if denominator is 1. The equals(Object other) method returns true if this rational number is equal to the other rational number.

The abstract methods intValue, longValue, floatValue, and doubleValue in the Number class are implemented in the Rational class (Lines 92–114). These methods return int, long, float, and double value for this rational number.

The compareTo(Object other) method in the Comparable interface is implemented in the Rational class (Lines 115–125) to compare this rational number to the other rational number.

When you divide rational numbers, what happens if the divisor is zero? In this example, the program would terminate with a runtime exception. You need to make sure that this does not occur when you are using the division method. In Chapter 13, "Exception Handling," you will learn how to deal with the zero divisor case for a Rational object.

The numerator and denominator are represented using two variables. It is possible to use an array of two integers to represent the numerator and denominator. See Exercise 9.2. The signatures of the public methods in the Rational class are not changed, although the internal representation of a rational number is changed. This is a good example to illustrate the idea that the data fields of a

continues

347

Example 9.2 continued

class should be kept private so as to encapsulate the implementation of the class from the use of the class.

> **NOTE**
> byteValue and shortValue are not abstract methods in the Number class. They simply return (byte)intValue() and (short)intValue(), respectively.

> **TIP**
> The get methods for the properties numerator and denominator are provided in the Rational class, but the set methods are not provided, so a Rational object cannot be changed. An object that cannot be changed is referred to as *immutable*. The String class is a well-known example of an immutable class. The wrapper classes that will be introduced in Section 9.6, "Processing Primitive Type Values as Objects," are also immutable classes.

9.5 Class Design Guidelines

You have learned how to design classes from the preceding two examples and from many other examples in the preceding chapters. Here are some guidelines.

9.5.1 Designing a Class

A class should describe a single entity or a set of similar operations. You can use a class for students, for example, but you should not combine students and staff in the same class, because students and staff have different operations. Since the Math class provides mathematical operations, it is natural to group the mathematical methods in one class. A single entity with too many responsibilities can be broken into several classes to separate responsibilities. The String class, StringBuffer class, and StringTokenizer class all deal with strings, for example, but have different responsibilities.

Classes are usually designed for use by many different customers. In order to be useful in a wide range of applications, a class should provide a variety of ways for customization through properties and methods.

Classes are designed for reuse. Users can incorporate classes in many different combinations, orders, and environments. Therefore, you should design a class that imposes no restrictions on what or when the user can do with it, design the properties in a way that lets the user set them in any order, with any combination of values, and design methods that function independently of their order of occurrence.

Provide a public default constructor and override the equals method and the toString method defined in the Object class whenever possible.

Follow standard Java programming style and naming conventions. Choose informative names for classes, data fields, and methods. Always place the data declaration before the constructor, and place constructors before methods.

9.5.2   Using the Modifiers *public, protected, private,* and *static*

Each class can present two contracts: one for the users of the class, and one for the extenders of the class. Make the fields private and the accessor methods `public` if they are intended for the users of the class. Make the fields or methods `protected` if they are intended for extenders of the class. The contract for extenders encompasses the contract for users. The extended class may increase the visibility of an instance method from `protected` to `public`, or may change its implementation, but you should never change the implementation in a way that violates the contract.

A class should use the `private` modifier to hide its data from direct access by clients. You can use get methods and set methods to provide users with access to the private data, but only to private data you want them to see or to modify. A class should also hide methods not intended for client use. The `gcd` method in the `Rational` class in Example 9.2, "The `Rational` Class," is private, for example, because it is only for internal use within the class.

A property that is shared by all the instances of a class should be declared as a static property. For example, the variable `numOfObjects` in Example 6.6, "Using Instance and Class Variables and Methods," is shared by all the objects of the `Circle` class, and therefore is declared as a static variable. A method that is not dependent on a specific instance should be declared as a static method. For instance, the `getNumOfObjects` method in Example 6.6 is not tied to a specific instance of the `Circle` class, and therefore is declared as a static method. The class properties and methods are denoted using the `static` modifier.

9.5.3   Using Inheritance or Composition

In general, the difference between inheritance and composition is the difference between an is-a relationship and a has-a relationship. For example, an apple is a fruit; thus, you would use inheritance to model the relationship between the classes `Apple` and `Fruit`. A person has a name; thus, you would use composition to model the relationship between the classes `Person` and `Name`. Sometimes, the choice between inheritance and composition is not obvious. For example, you have used inheritance to model the relationship between the classes `Circle` and `Cylinder`. One could argue that a cylinder consists of circles, and thus that you might use composition to define the `Cylinder` class, as follows:

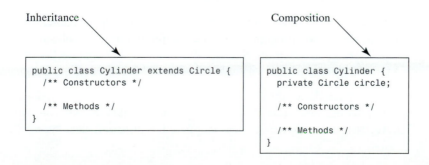

Inheritance

```
public class Cylinder extends Circle {
   /** Constructors */

   /** Methods */
}
```

Composition

```
public class Cylinder {
   private Circle circle;

   /** Constructors */

   /** Methods */
}
```

Both designs are fine. Which one is preferred? If polymorphism is desirable, use the inheritance design. If you don't care about polymorphism, the composition design gives more flexibility because the classes are less dependent when you use composition rather than inheritance.

9.5.4   Using Interfaces or Abstract Classes

Both interfaces and abstract classes can be used to generalize common features. How do you decide whether to use an interface or a class? In general, a *strong is-a relationship* that clearly describes a parent-child relationship should be modeled using classes. For example, since an orange is a fruit, their relationship should be modeled using class inheritance. A *weak is-a relationship*, also known as an *is-kind-of relationship*, indicates that an object possesses a certain property. A weak is-a relationship can be modeled using interfaces. For example, all strings are comparable, so the `String` class implements the `Comparable` interface. A circle or a rectangle is a geometric object, so `Circle` can be designed as a subclass of `GeometricObject`. Circles are different and comparable based on their radii, so `Circle` can implement the `Comparable` interface.

Interfaces are more flexible than abstract classes, because a subclass can extend only one superclass but implement any number of interfaces. However, interfaces cannot contain concrete methods. The virtues of interfaces and abstract classes can be combined by creating an interface with a companion abstract class that implements it. Then you can use the interface or its companion class, whichever is more convenient. For example, the `AbstractSet` class is the companion class for the `Set` interface in the Java Collections Framework, which is introduced in Chapter 19, "Java Data Structures."

9.6   Processing Primitive Type Values as Objects

Primitive data types are not used as objects in Java due to performance considerations. Because of the overhead of processing objects, the language's performance would be adversely affected if primitive data types were treated as objects. However, many Java methods require the use of objects as arguments. Java offers a convenient way to incorporate, or wrap, a primitive data type into an object (e.g., wrapping `int` into the `Integer` class, and wrapping double into the `Double` class). The corresponding class is called a *wrapper class*.

By using wrapper objects instead of a primitive data type variable, you can take advantage of generic programming. Generic programming is illustrated in Example 9.3, "Sorting an Array of Objects," Example 9.4, "Designing Generic Classes for Matrix Operations," and Example 9.5, "Using Linked Lists."

The wrapper classes provide constructors, constants, and conversion methods for manipulating various data types. Java provides `Boolean`, `Character`, `Double`, `Float`, `Byte`, `Short`, `Integer`, and `Long` wrappers for primitive data types. The wrapper

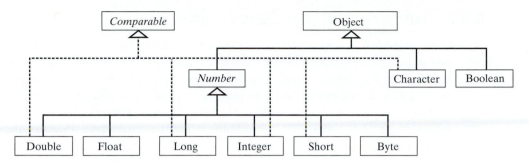

Figure 9.9   *The* Number *class is an abstract superclass for* Double, Float, Long, Integer, Short, *and* Byte.

classes are grouped in the java.lang package. Their inheritance hierarchy is shown in Figure 9.9.

NOTE

The wrapper class name for a primitive type is the same as the primitive data type name with the first letter capitalized. The exceptions are Integer and Character.

The numeric wrapper classes Integer and Double are discussed in the sections that follow. For more detailed information about wrapper classes, refer to the Java API documentation.

9.6.1   Numeric Wrapper Class Constructors

You can construct a numeric wrapper object either from a primitive data type value or from a string representing the numeric value. The constructors for Integer and Double are:

```
public Integer(int value)
public Integer(String s)
public Double(double value)
public Double(String s)
```

For example, you can construct a wrapper object for double value 5.0 using either

```
Double doubleObject = new Double(5.0);
```

or

```
Double doubleObject = new Double("5.0");
```

You can construct a wrapper object for int value 5 using either

```
Integer integerObject = new Integer(5);
```

or

```
Integer integerObject = new Integer("5");
```

9.6.2   Numeric Wrapper Class Constants

Each numerical wrapper class has the constants MAX_VALUE and MIN_VALUE. MAX_VALUE represents the maximum value of the corresponding primitive data type. For Byte, Short, Integer, and Long, MIN_VALUE represents the minimum byte, short, int, and long values. For Float and Double, MIN_VALUE represents the minimum *positive* float and double values. The following statements display the maximum integer (2,147,483,647), the minimum positive float (1.4E-45), and the maximum double floating-point number (1.79769313486231570e+308d).

```
System.out.println("The maximum integer is " + Integer.MAX_VALUE);
System.out.println("The minimum positive float is " +
  Float.MIN_VALUE);
System.out.println(
  "The maximum double precision floating-point number is " +
  Double.MAX_VALUE);
```

9.6.3   Conversion Methods

Each numeric wrapper class implements the abstract methods doubleValue, floatValue, intValue, longValue, and shortValue, which are defined in the Number class. These methods "convert" objects into primitive type values. Each numeric wrapper class also overrides the toString and equals methods defined in the Object class. Since all the numeric wrapper classes implement the Comparable interface, the compareTo method is implemented in these classes.

For example:

```
long l = doubleObject.longValue(); // Note it truncates
```

This converts doubleObject's double value to a long variable l.

```
int i = integerObject.intValue();
```

This assigns the int value of integerObject to i.

```
double d = 5.9;
Double doubleObject = new Double(d);
String s = doubleObject.toString();
```

This converts double d to a string s, which is equivalent to Double.parseDouble(d).

9.6.4   The Static *valueOf* Methods

The numeric wrapper classes have a useful class method, valueOf(String s). This method creates a new object initialized to the value represented by the specified string. For example:

```
Double doubleObject = Double.valueOf("12.4");
Integer integerObject = Integer.valueOf("12");
```

9.6.5   The Methods for Parsing Strings into Numbers

You have used the parseInt method in the Integer class to parse a numeric string into an int value and the parseDouble method in the Double class to parse a numeric string into a double value. Each numeric wrapper class has two overloaded parsing methods to parse a numeric string into an appropriate numeric value. These methods are shown below:

```java
// These two methods are in the Byte class
public static byte parseByte(String s)
public static byte parseByte(String s, int radix)

// These two methods are in the Short class
public static short parseShort(String s)
public static short parseShort(String s, int radix)

// These two methods are in the Integer class
public static int parseInt(String s)
public static int parseInt(String s, int radix)

// These two methods are in the Long class
public static long parseLong(String s)
public static long parseLong(String s, int radix)

// These two methods are in the Float class
public static float parseFloat(String s)
public static float parseFloat(String s, int radix)

// These two methods are in the Double class
public static double parseDouble(String s)
public static double parseDouble(String s, int radix)
```

Example 9.3 Sorting an Array of Objects

Problem

Write a static method for sorting an array of comparable objects. The objects are instances of the Comparable interface, and they are compared using the compareTo method. The method can be used to compare an array of any objects as long as their classes implement the Comparable interface.

Solution

A generic sort method is presented in the following code. To test the method, the program sorts an array of integers, an array of double numbers, an array of rational numbers, and an array of strings. Figure 9.10 shows a sample run of the code.

```java
1    // GenericSort.java: Sort an array of comparable objects
2    public class GenericSort {
3      public static void main(String[] args) {
4        // Declare and create an Integer array
5        Integer[] intArray = {new Integer(2), new Integer(4),
6          new Integer(3)};
7
8        // Declare and create an Double array
9        Double[] doubleArray = {new Double(3.4), new Double(1.3),
10         new Double(-22.1)};
11
```

continues

Example 9.3 Sorting an Array of Objects

```
12          // Declare and create a Rational array
13          Rational[] rationalArray = {new Rational(1, 2),
14            new Rational(2, 3), new Rational(3, 5)};
15
16          // Declare and create a String array
17          String[] stringArray = {"Tom", "John", "Fred"};
18
19          // Sort the arrays
20          sort(intArray);
21          sort(doubleArray);
22          sort(rationalArray);
23          sort(stringArray);
24
25          // Display the sorted arrays
26          System.out.print("Sorted Integer objects: ");
27          printList(intArray);
28          System.out.print("Sorted Double objects: ");
29          printList(doubleArray);
30          System.out.print("Sorted Rational objects: ");
31          printList(rationalArray);
32          System.out.print("Sorted String objects: ");
33          printList(stringArray);
34        }
35
36        /** Sort an array of comparable objects */
37        public static void sort(Object[] list) {
38          Object currentMax;
39          int currentMaxIndex;
40
41          for (int i = list.length - 1; i >= 1; i--) {
42            // Find the maximum in the list[0..i]
43            currentMax = list[i];
44            currentMaxIndex = i;
45
46            for (int j = i - 1; j >= 0; j--) {
47              if (((Comparable)currentMax).compareTo(list[j]) < 0) {
48                currentMax = list[j];
49                currentMaxIndex = j;
50              }
51            }
52
53            // Swap list[i] with list[currentMaxIndex] if necessary;
54            if (currentMaxIndex != i) {
55              list[currentMaxIndex] = list[i];
56              list[i] = currentMax;
57            }
58          }
59        }
60
61        /** Print an array of objects */
62        public static void printList(Object[] list) {
63          for (int i = 0; i < list.length; i++)
64            System.out.print(list[i] + " ");
65          System.out.println();
66        }
67      }
```

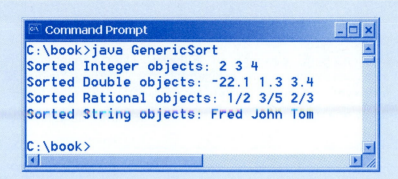

Figure 9.10   *The program uses a generic sort method to sort an array of comparable objects.*

Review

The algorithm for the sort method is the same as in Example 5.12, "Using Arrays in Sorting." The sort method in Example 5.12 sorts an array of double values. The sort method in this example can sort an array of any object type, provided that the objects are also instances of the Comparable interface. This is an example of polymorphism, also known as *generic programming*. Generic programming enables a method to operate on arguments of generic types, making it reusable with multiple types.

The Comparable interface was introduced in Chapter 8, "Class Inheritance and Interfaces." This interface contains the compareTo method, which is used for comparing two objects. Integer, Double, Rational, and String implement Comparable. So the objects of these classes can be compared using the compareTo method. The sort method uses the compareTo method to determine the order of the objects in the array.

> **NOTE**
> The Java Collections Framework contains the Arrays class, which has a static method sort(Object[] a) for sorting an array of objects. The Arrays class will be introduced in Chapter 19.

9.7   Case Studies (Optional)

This section presents a case study on designing classes for matrix operations. The addition and multiplication operations for all matrices are similar except that their element types differ. Therefore, you can design a superclass that describes the common operations shared by matrices of all types regardless of their element types, and you can create subclasses tailored to specific types of matrices. This case study gives implementations for two types: int and Rational. For the int type, the wrapper class Integer should be used to wrap an int value into an object, so that the object is passed in the methods for operations.

Example 9.4 Designing Generic Classes for Matrix Operations

Problem

Develop a generic class for matrix arithmetic. This class implements matrix addition and multiplication common to all types of matrices. You use the `Integer` matrix and the `Rational` matrix to test this generic class.

Figure 9.11 describes these classes and illustrates their relationships.

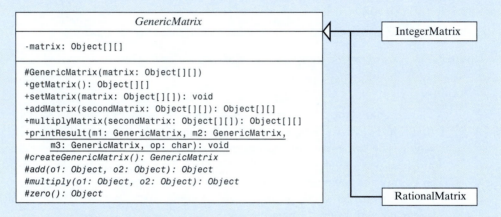

Figure 9.11 *The* `GenericMatrix` *class is an abstract superclass for* `IntegerMatrix` *and* `RationalMatrix`.

The `GenericMatrix` class serves as a wrapper class for a matrix. The class provides matrix operations for matrices of any element type. The data field `matrix` is the internal representation for a generic matrix. The methods `addMatrix` and `multiplyMatrix` add and multiply two matrices of a generic type `Object[][]`. The static method `printResult` displays the matrices, the operations, and their result. The methods `add`, `multiply`, and `zero` are abstract methods, because their implementations are dependent on the specific type of the array elements.

`IntegerMatrix` and `RationalMatrix` are concrete subclasses of `GenericMatrix`. These two classes implement the `add`, `multiply`, and `zero` methods defined in the `GenericMatrix` class.

Solution

Here is the code for the `GenericMatrix`, `IntegerMatrix`, and `RationalMatrix` classes:

```
1    // GenericMatrix.java: Define a matrix and its associated
2    // operations such as add and multiply
3    public abstract class GenericMatrix {
4      // Representation of a matrix using a two-dimensional array
5      private Object[][] matrix;
6
7      /** Construct a matrix */
8      protected GenericMatrix(Object[][] matrix) {
9        this.matrix = matrix;
10     }
11
```

```
12      /** Return matrix */
13      public Object[][] getMatrix() {
14        return matrix;
15      }
16
17      /** Set a new matrix */
18      public void setMatrix(Object[][] matrix) {
19        this.matrix = matrix;
20      }
21
22      public abstract GenericMatrix
23        createGenericMatrix(Object[][] matrix);
24
25      /** Add two matrices */
26      public GenericMatrix addMatrix(
27        GenericMatrix secondGenericMatrix) {
28        // Create a result matrix
29        Object[][] result =
30          new Object[matrix.length][matrix[0].length];
31
32        // Obtain the second matrix
33        Object[][] secondMatrix = secondGenericMatrix.getMatrix();
34
35        // Check bounds of the two matrices
36        if ((matrix.length != secondMatrix.length) ||
37            (matrix[0].length != secondMatrix.length)) {
38          System.out.println(
39            "The matrices do not have the same size");
40          System.exit(0);
41        }
42
43        // Perform addition
44        for (int i = 0; i < result.length; i++)
45          for (int j = 0; j < result[i].length; j++)
46            result[i][j] = add(matrix[i][j], secondMatrix[i][j]);
47
48        return createGenericMatrix(result);
49      }
50
51      /** Multiply two matrices */
52      public GenericMatrix multiplyMatrix(
53        GenericMatrix secondGenericMatrix) {
54        // Obtain the second matrix
55        Object[][] secondMatrix = secondGenericMatrix.getMatrix();
56
57        // Create result matrix
58        Object[][] result -
59          new Object[matrix.length][secondMatrix[0].length];
60
61        // Check bounds
62        if (matrix[0].length != secondMatrix.length) {
63          System.out.println("Bounds error");
64          System.exit(0);
65        }
66
67        // Perform multiplication of two matrices
68        for (int i = 0; i < result.length; i++)
69          for (int j = 0; j < result[0].length; j++) {
70          result[i][j] = zero();
71
```

continues

357

Example 9.4 continued

```
72              for (int k = 0; k < matrix[0].length; k++) {
73                result[i][j] = add(result[i][j],
74                  multiply(this.matrix[i][k], secondMatrix[k][j]));
75              }
76            }
77
78          return createGenericMatrix(result);
79        }
80
81        /** Print matrices, the operator, and their operation result */
82        public static void printResult(
83          GenericMatrix m1, GenericMatrix m2, GenericMatrix m3, char op) {
84          for (int i = 0; i < (m1.getMatrix()).length; i++) {
85            for (int j = 0; j < (m1.getMatrix())[0].length; j++)
86              System.out.print(" " + (m1.getMatrix())[i][j]);
87
88            if (i == (m1.getMatrix()).length / 2)
89              System.out.print( "  " + op + "  " );
90            else
91              System.out.print( "     " );
92
93            for (int j = 0; j < (m2.getMatrix()).length; j++)
94              System.out.print(" " + (m2.getMatrix())[i][j]);
95
96            if (i == (m1.getMatrix()).length / 2)
97              System.out.print( "  =  " );
98            else
99              System.out.print( "     " );
100
101           for (int j = 0; j < (m3.getMatrix()).length; j++)
102             System.out.print(" " + (m3.getMatrix())[i][j]);
103
104           System.out.println();
105         }
106       }
107
108       /** Abstract method for adding two elements of the matrices */
109       protected abstract Object add(Object o1, Object o2);
110
111       /** Abstract method for multiplying two elements of the matrices */
112       protected abstract Object multiply(Object o1, Object o2);
113
114       /** Abstract method for defining zero for the matrix element */
115       protected abstract Object zero();
116     }
```

```
1     // IntegerMatrix.java:
2     // Declare IntegerMatrix derived from GenericMatrix
3     public class IntegerMatrix extends GenericMatrix {
4       /** Construct an IntegerMatrix */
5       public IntegerMatrix(Object[][] m) {
6         super(m);
7       }
8
9       /** Implement the createGenericMatrix method */
10      public GenericMatrix createGenericMatrix(Object[][] matrix) {
11        return new IntegerMatrix(matrix);
12      }
13
```

```
14      /** Implement the add method for adding two matrix elements */
15      protected Object add(Object o1, Object o2) {
16        Integer i1 = (Integer)o1;
17        Integer i2 = (Integer)o2;
18        return new Integer(i1.intValue() + i2.intValue());
19      }
20
21      /** Implement the multiply method for multiplying two
22          matrix elements */
23      protected Object multiply(Object o1, Object o2) {
24        Integer i1 = (Integer)o1;
25        Integer i2 = (Integer)o2;
26        return new Integer(i1.intValue() * i2.intValue());
27      }
28
29      /** Implement the zero method to specify zero for Integer */
30      protected Object zero() {
31        return new Integer(0);
32      }
33    }
```

```
1     /** RationalMatrix.java:
2         Declare RationalMatrix derived from GenericMatrix */
3     public class RationalMatrix extends GenericMatrix {
4       /** Construct a RationalMatrix for a given Rational array */
5       public RationalMatrix(Object[][] m1) {
6         super(m1);
7       }
8
9       /** Implement the createGenericMatrix method */
10      public GenericMatrix createGenericMatrix(Object[][] matrix) {
11        return new RationalMatrix(matrix);
12      }
13
14      /** Implement the add method for adding two rational elements */
15      protected Object add(Object o1, Object o2) {
16        Rational r1 = (Rational)o1;
17        Rational r2 = (Rational)o2;
18        return r1.add(r2);
19      }
20
21      /** Implement the multiply method for multiplying
22          two rational elements */
23      protected Object multiply(Object o1, Object o2) {
24        Rational r1 = (Rational)o1;
25        Rational r2 = (Rational)o2;
26        return r1.multiply(r2);
27      }
28
29      /** Implement the zero method to specify zero for Rational */
30      protected Object zero() {
31        return new Rational(0,1);
32      }
33    }
```

The following is a test program that uses the IntegerMatrix class. A sample run
of the program is shown in Figure 9.12.

continues

Example 9.4 continued

```
Command Prompt                                              _ □ ×

C:\book>java TestIntegerMatrix
m1 + m2 is ...
 0 0 0 0 0        0 1 2 3 4        0 1  2  3  4
 1 1 1 1 1        1 2 3 4 5        2 3  4  5  6
 2 2 2 2 2   +    2 3 4 5 6   =    4 5  6  7  8
 3 3 3 3 3        3 4 5 6 7        6 7  8  9 10
 4 4 4 4 4        4 5 6 7 8        8 9 10 11 12

m1 * m2 is ...
 0 0 0 0 0        0 1 2 3 4         0  0  0   0   0
 1 1 1 1 1        1 2 3 4 5        10 15 20  25  30
 2 2 2 2 2   *    2 3 4 5 6   =    20 30 40  50  60
 3 3 3 3 3        3 4 5 6 7        30 45 60  75  90
 4 4 4 4 4        4 5 6 7 8        40 60 80 100 120

C:\book>
```

Figure 9.12   *The program creates two* Integer *matrices and performs addition and multiplication on them.*

```
1     // TestIntegerMatrix.java: Test matrix operations involving
2     // integer values
3     public class TestIntegerMatrix {
4       public static void main(String[] args) {
5         // Create Integer arrays m1, m2
6         Object[][] m1 = new Integer[5][5];
7         Object[][] m2 = new Integer[5][5];
8
9         // Initialize Integer arrays m1 and m2
10        for (int i = 0; i < m1.length; i++)
11          for (int j = 0; j < m1[0].length; j++) {
12            m1[i][j] = new Integer(i);
13          }
14
15        for (int i = 0; i < m2.length; i++)
16          for (int j = 0; j < m2[0].length; j++) {
17            m2[i][j] = new Integer(i + j);
18          }
19
20        // Create instances of IntegerMatrix
21        IntegerMatrix im1 = new IntegerMatrix(m1);
22        IntegerMatrix im2 = new IntegerMatrix(m2);
23
24        // Perform integer matrix addition, and multiplication
25        IntegerMatrix im3 = (IntegerMatrix)im1.addMatrix(im2);
26        IntegerMatrix im4 = (IntegerMatrix)im1.multiplyMatrix(im2);
27
28        // Display im1, im2, im3, im4
29        System.out.println("m1 + m2 is ...");
30        GenericMatrix.printResult(im1, im2, im3, '+');
31
```

```
32          System.out.println("\nm1 * m2 is ...");
33          GenericMatrix.printResult(im1, im2, im4, '*');
34        }
35      }
```

Next is a test program that uses the `RationalMatrix` class. A sample run of the program is shown in Figure 9.13.

```
C:\book>java TestRationalMatrix
m1 + m2 is ...
 1/3 1/3 1/3 1/3       1/3 1/3 1/3 1/3        2/3 2/3 2/3 2/3
 1/2 1/2 1/2 1/2       1/2 1/2 1/2 1/2        1 1 1 1
 3/5 3/5 3/5 3/5  +    3/5 3/5 3/5 3/5   =    6/5 6/5 6/5 6/5
 2/3 2/3 2/3 2/3       2/3 2/3 2/3 2/3        4/3 4/3 4/3 4/3

m1 * m2 is ...
 1/3 1/3 1/3 1/3       1/3 1/3 1/3 1/3        7/10 7/10 7/10 7/10
 1/2 1/2 1/2 1/2       1/2 1/2 1/2 1/2        21/20 21/20 21/20 21/20
 3/5 3/5 3/5 3/5  *    3/5 3/5 3/5 3/5   =    63/50 63/50 63/50 63/50
 2/3 2/3 2/3 2/3       2/3 2/3 2/3 2/3        7/5 7/5 7/5 7/5

C:\book>
```

Figure 9.13 *The program creates two matrices of rational numbers and performs addition and multiplication on them.*

```
1   // TestRationalMatrix.java: Test matrix operations involving
2   // Rational values
3   public class TestRationalMatrix {
4     public static void main(String[] args) {
5       // Declare Rational arrays m1, m2
6       Object[][] m1 = new Rational[4][4];
7       Object[][] m2 = new Rational[4][4];
8
9       // Initialize Rational arrays m1 and m2
10      for (int i = 0; i < m1.length; i++)
11        for (int j = 0; j < m1[0].length; j++) {
12          m1[i][j] = new Rational(i + 1, i + 3);
13          m2[i][j] = new Rational(i + 1, i + 3);
14        }
15
16      // Create RationalMatrix instances
17      RationalMatrix rm1 = new RationalMatrix(m1);
18      RationalMatrix rm2 = new RationalMatrix(m2);
19
20      // Perform Rational matrix addition, and multiplication
21      RationalMatrix rm3 = (RationalMatrix)rm1.addMatrix(rm2);
22      RationalMatrix rm4 = (RationalMatrix)rm1.multiplyMatrix(rm2);
23
24      // Display rm1, rm2, rm3, rm4
25      System.out.println("m1 + m2 is ...");
26      GenericMatrix.printResult(rm1, rm2, rm3, '+');
27
```

continues

361

Example 9.4 continued

```
28          System.out.println("\nm1 * m2 is ...");
29          GenericMatrix.printResult(rm1, rm2, rm4, '*');
30      }
31    }
```

Review

Because the matrix element type in the GenericMatrix class is a generic object, the program doesn't know how to add or multiply two matrix elements and doesn't know what the zero value is for the element (e.g., 0 for int or 0/1 for Rational). Therefore, add, multiply, and zero are defined as abstract methods. These methods are implemented in the subclasses in which the matrix element type is specified.

The matrix element type in GenericMatrix is Object. This enables you to use an object of any class as long as you can implement the abstract add, multiply, and zero methods in subclasses.

The addMatrix and multiplyMatrix methods (Lines 25–79 in the GenericMatrix class) are concrete methods. They are ready to use as long as the add, multiply, and zero methods are implemented in the subclasses.

The createGenericMatrix method creates an instance of GenericMatrix. This method is used in the addMatrix and multiplyMatrix methods for returning instances of the GenericMatrix type. Since GenericMatrix is an abstract class, the createGenericMatrix method must be declared abstract in the GenericMatrix class.

The printResult method (Lines 81–106 in GenericMatrix) displays the matrix on the console. The toString() method is used to display the element.

The addMatrix and multiplyMatrix methods check the bounds of the matrices before performing operations. If the two matrices have incompatible bounds, the program terminates.

IntegerMatrix and RationalMatrix are concrete subclasses of GenericMatrix for integer matrix arithmetic. These classes extend the GenericMatrix class and implement the add, multiply, and zero methods.

Casting the object from type Object to type Integer in the IntegerMatrix class (Lines 16–17, 24–25)is necessary because the program has to use the intValue method for integer addition and multiplication, and it is not available in Object. For the same reason, casting from type Object to type Rational is needed in the RationalMatrix class (Lines 16–17, 24–25).

The TestIntegerMatrix program creates and initializes two matrices: m1 and m2. The statement (Lines 21–22)

```
IntegerMatrix im1 = new IntegerMatrix(m1);
IntegerMatrix im2 = new IntegerMatrix(m2);
```

in `TestIntegerMatrix` creates `im1` as an instance of `IntegerMatrix` for matrix `m1`, so you can use `im1.addMatrix(im2)` and `im1.multiplyMatrix(im2)` to perform matrix addition and multiplication for `im1` and `im2`. The variables `rm1` and `rm2` were created for the same reason in `TestRationalMatrix`.

9.8   Designing Classes for Linked Lists (Optional)

Arrays are useful for storing and managing a set of elements of the same type. Since the length of an array is fixed once the array is created, however, you need to know the length before you create the array. If you don't know the length of the array in advance, you have to estimate it when creating the array. If the estimate is larger than the actual length, valuable memory space may be wasted; if the estimate is smaller than the actual length, your program could run into trouble. Obviously, it would be unwise to use an array to store an unspecified number of elements. You can use a linked list to store a collection of elements. A linked list can grow or shrink dynamically as needed. This section demonstrates designing classes for a generic linked list.

A linked list consists of nodes, as shown in Figure 9.14. Each node contains an element, and each node is linked to its next neighbor. Thus a node can be defined as a class, as follows:

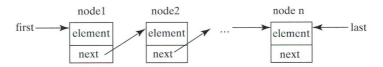

Figure 9.14   *A linked list consists of any number of nodes chained together.*

```
public class Node {
  Object element;
  Node next;

  public Node(Object o) {
    element = o;
  }
}
```

The variable `first` refers to the first node in the list, and the variable `last` refers to the last node in the list. If the list is empty, both are `null`. For example, you can create three nodes to store three circle objects (radius 1, 2, and 3) in a list:

```
Node first;
Node last;

// Create a node to store the first circle object
first = new Node(new Circle(1));
last = first;
```

```
// Create a node to store the second circle object
last.next = new Node(new Circle(2));
last = last.next;

// Create a node to store the third circle object
last.next = new Node(new Circle(3));
last = last.next;
```

The process of creating a new linked list adding three nodes is shown in Figure 9.15.

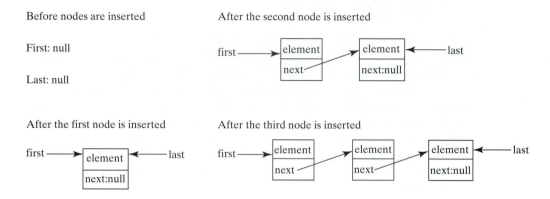

Figure 9.15   *Three nodes are added to a new linked list.*

You can create a linked list to store a collection of objects, add objects to the list, remove objects from the list, search an object, or sort objects in the list. To make it easy to use and reusable, create a class named GenericLinkedList to model all the linked lists, as shown in Figure 9.16.

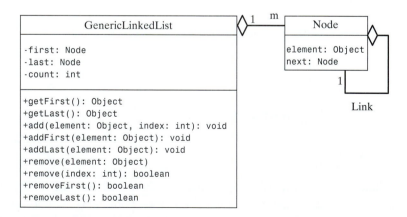

Figure 9.16   *The* GenericLinkedList *class is an abstract superclass for* IntegerMatrix *and* RationalMatrix.

The class source code is given as follows:

```
1  public class GenericLinkedList {
2    private Node first, last;
3    private int count = 0; // The number of elements in the list
4
5    public GenericLinkedList() {
6    }
7
8    /** Return the first element in the list */
9    public Object getFirst() {
10     if (count == 0) return null;
11     else return first.element;
12   }
13
14   /** Return the last element in the list */
15   public Object getLast() {
16     if (count == 0) return null;
17     else return last.element;
18   }
19
20   /** Add an element to the beginning of the list */
21   public void addFirst(Object element) {
22     Node newNode = new Node(element);
23     newNode.next = first;
24     first = newNode;
25     count++;
26
27     if (last == null)
28       last = first;
29   }
30
31   /** Add an element to the end of the list */
32   public void addLast(Object element) {
33     if (last == null) {
34       first = last = new Node(element);
35     }
36     else {
37       last.next = new Node(element);
38       last = last.next;
39     }
40
41     count++;
42   }
43
44   /** Add an element to the location after index in the list
45    * index for the first element in the list is 1.
46    */
47   public void add(Object element, int index) {
48     if (index == 1) addFirst(element);
49     else if (index >= count) addLast(element);
50     else {
51       Node current = first;
52       for (int i = 1; i < index; i++)
53         current = current.next;
54       Node temp = current.next;
55       current.next = new Node(element);
56       (current.next).next = temp;
57       count++;
58     }
59   }
60
61   /** Remove the first node */
62   public boolean removeFirst() {
63     if (count == 0) return false;
```

```
64      else {
65        first = first.next;
66        count--;
67        return true;
68      }
69    }
70
71    /** Remove the last node */
72    public boolean removeLast() {
73      if (count == 0) return false;
74      else {
75        Node current = first;
76
77        for (int i = 1; i <= count - 1; i++) {
78          current = current.next;
79        }
80
81        last = current;
82        last.next = null;
83        count--;
84        return true;
85      }
86    }
87
88    /** Remove the node at the specified index
89     * Return true if the element is removed
90     * Return false if no element is removed
91     */
92    public boolean remove(int index) {
93      if (index == 1) return removeFirst();
94      else if (index == count) return removeLast();
95      else if ((index < 1) || (index > count)) return false;
96      else {
97        Node current = first;
98
99        for (int i = 1; i < index - 1; i++) {
100         current = current.next;
101       }
102
103       current.next = current.next.next;
104       count--;
105       return true;
106     }
107   }
108
109   /** Remove the first node that contains the specified element
110    * Return true if the element is removed
111    * Return false if no element is removed
112    */
113   public boolean remove(Object element) {
114     Node previous = first;
115     Node current;
116
117     if (first != null) {
118       if (element.equals(first.element)) {
119         first = first.next;
120         count--;
121         return true;
122       }
123       else {
124         current = first.next;
125       }
126     }
127     else
128       return false;
129
```

366

```
130       for (int i = 0; i < count - 1; i++) {
131         if (element.equals(current.element)) {
132           previous.next = current.next; // Remove the current element
133           count--;
134           return true;
135         }
136         else {
137           previous = current;
138           current = current.next;
139         }
140       }
141
142       return false;
143     }
144
145     /** Print the list */
146     public void printList() {
147       Node current = first;
148
149       for (int i = 0; i < count; i++) {
150         System.out.print(current.element + " ");
151         current = current.next;
152       }
153
154       System.out.println();
155     }
156   }
```

The variable count tracks the elements in the list. When a new element is added to the list, count is incremented by 1, and when an element is removed from the list, count is decremented by 1. The variables first and last refer to the first and last nodes in the list, respectively. The getFirst() and getLast() methods return the first and last elements in the list, respectively.

The addFirst method adds an element to the beginning of the list. After the insertion, first should refer to this new element node. The addLast method adds an element to the end of the list. After the insertion, last should refer to this new element node. The add(Object element, int index) method adds an element to the list at the specified index. The method first locates where to insert the new element. As shown in Figure 9.17, the new element is to be inserted between the nodes current and temp. The method then assigns the new node to current.next and assigns temp to the new node's next.

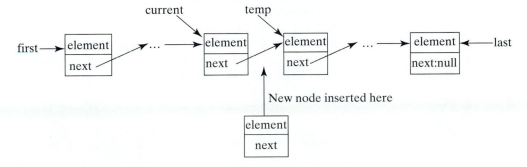

Figure 9.17   *A new element is added to the list.*

367

The `removeFirst` method removes the first element in the list by pointing `first` to the second element. The `removeLast` method removes the last element from the list. Afterwards, `last` should refer to the former second-last element. The `remove(Object element)` method finds the element in the list and then removes it. The method locates the current node for the current element and the node formerly before the current element, as shown in Figure 9.18. The method then assigns `current.next` to `previous.next` to eliminate the current node. The `remove(int index)` method removes the node at the specified index.

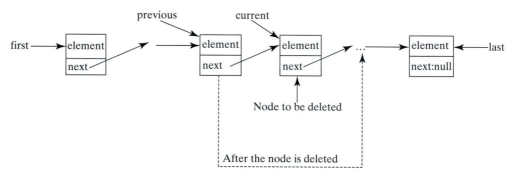

Figure 9.18   *An element is deleted from the list.*

Example 9.5 Using Linked Lists

Problem

Write a program that creates a linked list using `GenericLinkedList`. It then uses the `add` method to add strings to the list and the `remove` method to remove strings from the list.

Solution

The following code gives the solution to the problem. A sample run of the program is shown in Figure 9.19.

Figure 9.19   *The program uses a linked list to store and process strings.*

```
1    public class TestLinkedList {
2      public static void main(String[] args) {
3        // Create a linked list
4        GenericLinkedList list = new GenericLinkedList();
5
6        // Add elements to the list
7        list.addFirst("Tom");
8        list.addFirst("John");
9        list.addLast("George");
10       list.addLast("Michael");
11       list.add("Michelle", 2);
12       list.add("Samantha", 5);
13       list.add("Daniel", 0);
14
15       // Print the list
16       System.out.println("Strings are added to the list");
17       list.printList();
18       System.out.println();
19
20       // Remove elements from the list
21       list.remove("Daniel");
22       list.remove(2);
23       list.removeLast();
24
25       // Print the list
26       System.out.println("The contents of the list after deletions");
27       list.printList();
28     }
29   }
```

Review

The GenericLinkedList class is a typical example of object-oriented software development. The GenericLinkedList class contains a dynamic data structure for storing elements. The data structures are hidden from the user. The class provides public methods to enable the client to add or remove elements. The linked list can hold any objects.

The data structure in GenericLinkedList is one-directional, enabling one-way traversal of the list. You can modify the data structure to bi-directional traversal. See Exercise 9.4.

NOTE

A class for linked list is already provided in Java in the java.util.LiskedList. The purpose of this section is to demonstrate how to design generic classes using linked list as example. The java.util.LinkedList class will be introduced in Java Collections Framework in Chapter 19, "Java Data Structures."

Chapter Summary

This chapter explained the use of the object-oriented approach to develop software. You learned how to analyze the relationships among objects and to represent relationships using classes. You learned how to use wrapper classes to process primitive type values as objects, and how to design reusable classes through examples of a generic sort, a generic matrix, and a generic linked list.

Review Questions

9.1 What are the types of relationships among classes? Describe the graphical notations for modeling the relationships among classes.

9.2 What relationship is appropriate for the following classes?

- Company and Employee
- Course and Faculty
- Student and Person
- House and Window
- Account and Savings Account

9.3 Describe primitive-type wrapper classes. Why do you need these wrapper classes?

9.4 Are the following statements correct?

```
Integer i = new Integer("23");
Integer i = new Integer(23);
Integer i = Integer.valueOf("23");
Integer i = Integer.parseInt("23",8);
Double d = new Double();
Double d = Double.valueOf("23.45");
int i = (Integer.valueOf("23")).intValue();
double d = (Double.valueOf("23.4")).doubleValue();
int i = (Double.valueOf("23.4")).intValue();
String s = (Double.valueOf("23.4")).toString();
```

9.5 How do you convert an integer into a string? How do you convert a numerical string into an integer?

9.6 How do you convert a double number into a string? How do you convert a numerical string into a double value?

9.7 Why do the following two lines of code compile but cause a runtime error?

```
Number numberRef = new Integer(0);
Double doubleRef = (Double)numberRef;
```

9.8 Why do the following two lines of code compile but cause a runtime error?

```
Number[] numberArray = new Integer[2];
numberArray[0] = new Double(1.5);
```

9.9 Analyze the following code:

```
public class Test {
  public static void main(String[] args) {
    Number x = new Integer(3);
    System.out.println(x.intValue());
    System.out.println(x.compareTo(new Integer(4)));
  }
}
```

a. The program has a syntax error because an `Integer` instance cannot be assigned to a `Number` variable.

b. The program has a syntax error because `intValue` is an abstract method in `Number`.

c. The program has a syntax error because `x` does not have the `compareTo` method.

d. The program compiles and runs fine.

e. None of the above.

9.10 Analyze the following code:

```
public class Test {
  public static void main(String[] args) {
    Number x = new Integer(3);
    System.out.println(x.intValue());
    System.out.println((Integer)x.compareTo(new Integer(4)));
  }
}
```

a. The program has a syntax error because an `Integer` instance cannot be assigned to a `Number` variable.

b. The program has a syntax error because `intValue` is an abstract method in `Number`.

c. The program has a syntax error because `x` cannot be cast into `Integer`.

d. The program has a syntax error because the member access operator (.) is executed before the casting operator.

e. The program compiles and runs fine.

Programming Exercises

9.1 Write a program that will compute the following summation series using the `Rational` class.

$$1/1 + 1/2 + 1/3 +...+ 1/n$$
$$1/1 + 1/2 + 1/2^2 +...+ 1/2^n$$

9.2 Rewrite the `Rational` class in Example 9.2 using a new internal representation for numerator and denominator. Declare an array of two integers as follows:

```
private long[] r = new long[2];
```

Use `r[0]` to represent the numerator and `r[1]` to represent the denominator. The signatures of the methods in the `Rational` class are not changed, so a client application that uses the previous `Rational` class can continue to use this new `Rational` class without being recompiled.

9.3 Write a program similar to the one in Example 7.5, "Using Command-Line Parameters." Instead of using integers, use rationals, as shown in Figure 9.20. You will need to use the `StringTokenizer` class, introduced in Chapter 7, "Strings," to retrieve the numerator string and denominator string, and convert strings into integers using the `Integer.parseInt` method.

```
Command Prompt                                    _ □ ×
C:\exercise>java Exercise9_3 + -1/2 1/3
-1/2+1/3=-1/6

C:\exercise>
```

Figure 9.20 *The program takes three parameters (an operator and two rational operands) from the command line and displays the expression and the result of the arithmetic operation.*

9.4 The `GenericLinkedList` class used in Example 9.5 is a one-way directional linked list that enables one-way traversal of the list. Modify the `Node` class to add a new field name `previous` to refer to the previous node in the list, as follows:

```
public class Node {
  Object element;
  Node next;
  Node previous;

  public Node(Object o) {
    element = o;
  }
}
```

Simplify the implementation of the `add(Object element, int index)` method and the `remove(int index)` and `remove(Object element)` to take advantage of the bi-directional linked list.

Add a new method in the class to sort the elements in the list, provided that all the elements are instances of the `Comparable` interface.

9.5 Write a method that summarizes the area of all the geometric objects in an array. The method signature is:

```
public static double sumArea(GeometricObject[] a)
```

Write a test program that creates an array of three objects (a circle, a cylinder, and a rectangle) and computes their total area using the `sumArea` method.

9.6 Write a method that returns the largest object in an array of objects. The method signature is:

```
public static Object max(Object[] a)
```

All the objects are instances of the `Comparable` interface. The order of the objects in the array is determined using the `compareTo` method.

Write a test program that creates an array of ten strings, an array of ten integers, and an array of ten `Comparable` circles, and finds the largest string, integer, and circle in the arrays.

9.7 Create the classes as shown in Figure 9.21. Implement the `compareTo` method to compare persons in alphabetical order of their last name, first name, and middle-name initial. Implement the `compareTo` method to compare students in alphabetical order of their major, last name, first name, and middle-name initial.

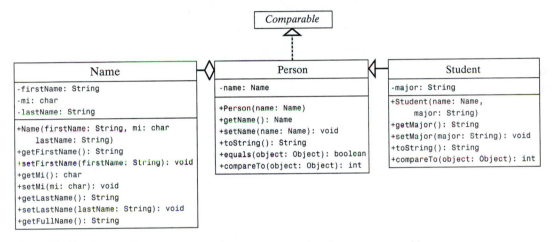

Figure 9.21   *A person has a name, a student is a person, and students are comparable.*

Write a test program with the following three methods:

```
/** Sort an array of comparable objects   */
public static void sort(Object[] list)

/** Return the max object in an array of comparable objects */
public static Object max(Object[] list)
```

main method: Test the `sort` and `max` methods using an array of four students, an array of four strings, an array of one hundred random rationals, and an array of one hundred random integers.

PART III

GUI Programming

In Part II, "Object-Oriented Programming," you learned the basics of object-oriented programming. The design of the API for Java GUI programming is an excellent example of how the object-oriented principle is applied. In the chapters that follow in this part of the book, you will learn the architecture of Java GUI API and use the GUI components to develop user-friendly interfaces for applications and applets.

CHAPTER 10

GETTING STARTED WITH GUI PROGRAMMING

Objectives

- To be able to describe the Java GUI API hierarchy.
- To use frames, panels, and simple UI components.
- To understand the role of layout managers.
- To use the `FlowLayout`, `GridLayout`, and `BorderLayout` managers.
- To become familiar with the `paintComponent` method.
- To become familiar with the `Color`, `Font`, and `FontMetrics` classes.
- To be able to use the drawing methods in the `Graphics` class.
- To understand the concept of event-driven programming.
- To become familiar with the Java event-delegation model: event registration, listening, and handling.

10.1   Introduction

Until now, you have only used dialog boxes and the command window for input and output. You used `JOptionPane.showInputDialog` to obtain input, and `JOptionPane.showMessageDialog` and `System.out.println` to display results. These approaches have limitations and are inconvenient. For example, to read ten numbers, you have to open ten input dialog boxes. Starting with this chapter, you will learn Java GUI programming. You will create custom graphical user interfaces (GUI, pronounced *goo-ee*) to obtain input and display output in the same user interface.

When Java was introduced, the GUI components were bundled in a library known as the Abstract Windows Toolkit (AWT). For every platform on which Java runs, the AWT components are automatically mapped to the platform-specific components through their respective agents, known as *peers*. AWT is fine for developing simple graphical user interfaces, but not for developing comprehensive GUI projects. Besides, AWT is prone to platform-specific bugs because its peer-based approach relies heavily on the underlying platform. With the release of Java 2, the AWT user-interface components were replaced by a more robust, versatile, and flexible library known as *Swing components*. Swing components are painted directly on canvases using Java code, except for components that are subclasses of `java.awt.Window` or `java.awt.Panel`, which must be drawn using native GUI on a specific platform. Swing components are less dependent on the target platform and use less of the native GUI resource. For this reason, Swing components that don't rely on native GUI are referred to as *lightweight components*, and AWT components are referred to as *heavyweight components*. Although AWT components are still supported in Java 2, I recommend that you learn to program using Swing components, because the AWT user-interface components will eventually fade away.

Java provides a rich set of classes to help you build graphical user interfaces. You can use various GUI-building classes—frames, panels, labels, buttons, text fields, text areas, combo boxes, check boxes, radio buttons, menus, scroll bars, scroll panes, and tabbed panes—to construct user interfaces. This chapter introduces the basics of Java GUI programming. Specifically, it discusses GUI components and their relationships, containers and layout managers, colors, fonts, and drawing geometric figures, such as lines, rectangles, ovals, arcs, and polygons, and introduces event-driven programming.

NOTE

The Swing components do not replace all the classes in AWT, only the AWT user-interface components (`Button`, `TextField`, `TextArea`, etc.). The AWT helper classes (`Graphics`, `Color`, `Font`, `FontMetrics`, and `LayoutManager`) remain unchanged. In addition, the Swing components use the AWT event model.

10.2   The Java GUI API

The design of the Java API for GUI programming is an excellent example of the use of classes, inheritance, and interfaces. The API contains the essential classes listed below. Their hierarchical relationships are shown in Figure 10.1.

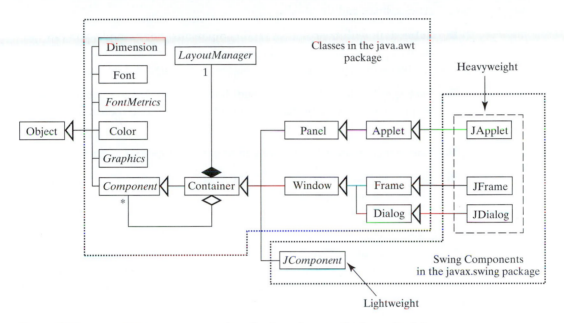

Figure 10.1   *Java GUI programming utilizes the classes shown in this hierarchical diagram.*

- ■ `Component` is a superclass of all user interface classes.

- ■ `Container` is used to group components. A layout manager is used to position and place components in a container in the desired location and style. Frames, panels, and applets are examples of containers.

- ■ `JComponent` is a superclass of all the lightweight Swing components, which are drawn directly on canvases using Java code, rather than on specific platforms using native GUI. Its subclasses (`JButton`, `JCheckBox`, `JMenu`, `JRadioButton`, `JLabel`, `JList`, `JTextField`, `JTextArea`, `JScrollPane`) are the basic elements for constructing the GUI.

- ■ `JFrame` is a window not contained inside another window. It is the container that holds other Swing user-interface components in Java graphical applications.

- ■ `JDialog` is a popup window or message box generally used as a temporary window to receive additional information from the user or to provide notification that an event has occurred.

- ■ `JApplet` is a subclass of `Applet`. You must extend `JApplet` to create a Swing-based Java applet.

- **JPanel** is an invisible container that holds user-interface components. Panels can be nested. You can place panels inside panels and in a frame in Java applications or in an applet in Java applets. JPanel can also be used as a canvas to draw graphics.

- **Graphics** is an abstract class that provides a graphical context for drawing strings, lines, and simple shapes.

- **Color** deals with the colors of GUI components. For example, you can specify background or foreground colors in components like JFrame and JPanel, or you can specify colors of lines, shapes, and strings in drawings.

- **Font** specifice fonts for the text and drawings on GUI components. For example, you can specify the font type (SansSerif), style (bold), and size (24 points) for the text on a button.

- **FontMetrics** is an abstract class used to get the properties of the font.

- **Dimension** encapsulates the width and height of a component (in integer precision) in a single object.

The GUI classes can be classified into three groups: *container classes*, *component classes*, and *helper classes*. The container classes, such as JFrame, JPanel, and JApplet, are used to contain other components. The UI component classes, such as JButton, JTextField, JTextArea, JComboBox, JList, JRadioButton, and JMenu, are subclasses of JComponent. The helper classes, such as Graphics, Color, Font, FontMetrics, Dimension, and LayoutManager, are used by components and containers to draw and place objects.

The JFrame, JApplet, JDialog, and JComponent classes and their subclasses are grouped in the javax.swing package. All the other classes in Figure 10.1 are grouped in the java.awt package. Swing GUI components are named with a prefixed *J*. For example, the Swing version of Button is called JButton to distinguish it from its AWT counterpart.

NOTE

Swing is a comprehensive solution to developing graphical user interfaces. There are more than 250 classes in Swing, some of which are illustrated in Figure 10.2. Since the discussion in this book is only an introduction to Java GUI programming using Swing, the components listed in the dotted rectangle are not covered. For a more detailed treatment of Swing components, including model-view architecture, look-and-feel, and advanced components, please refer to some of the references provided in the companion Web site.

TIP

Do not mix Swing user-interface components like JButton with AWT user-interface components like Button. For example, do not place JButton in java.awt.Panel, and similarly do not place Button in javax.swing.JPanel. Mixing them may cause problems. This book uses Swing user interfaces exclusively.

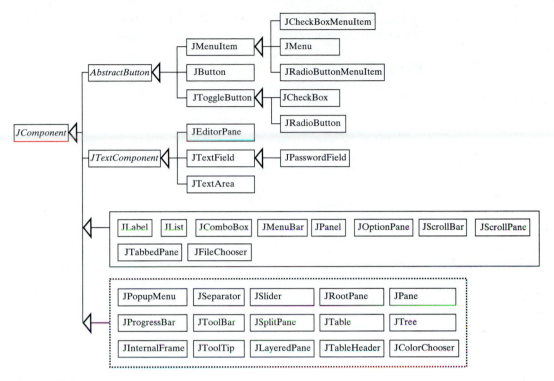

Figure 10.2   `JComponent` *and its subclasses are the basic elements for building graphical user interfaces.*

10.3   Frames

To create a user interface, you need to create either a frame or an applet to hold the user-interface components. Figure 10.3 provides examples of possible user-interface layouts in a frame and an applet.

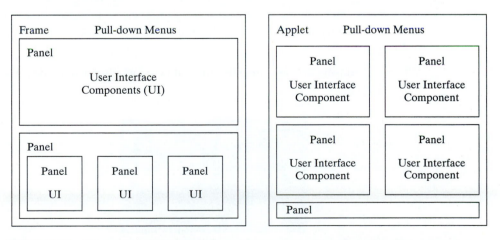

Figure 10.3   *Frames and applets can both contain menus, panels, and user-interface components. Panels are used to group user-interface components. Panels can contain other panels.*

Creating Java applets will be introduced in Chapter 12, "Applets and Advanced GUI." This section introduces the procedure for creating frames.

10.3.1   Creating a Frame

The following program creates a frame:

```
1     // MyFrame.java: Display a frame
2     import javax.swing.*;
3
4     public class MyFrame {
5       public static void main(String[] args) {
6         JFrame frame = new JFrame("Test Frame");
7         frame.setSize(400, 300);
8         frame.setVisible(true);
9         frame.setDefaultCloseOperation(JFrame.EXIT_ON_CLOSE);
10      }
11    }
```

Because JFrame is in the javax.swing package, the statement import javax.swing.* makes available all the classes from the javax.swing package, including JFrame, so that they can be used in the MyFrame class.

The following two constructors are used to create a JFrame object.

■   public JFrame()

Constructs an untitled JFrame object.

■   public JFrame(String title)

Constructs a JFrame object with a specified title. The title appears in the title bar of the frame.

The frame is not displayed *until* the frame.setVisible(true) method is applied. frame.setSize(400, 300) specifies that the frame is 400 pixels wide and 300 pixels high. If the setSize method is not used, the frame will be sized at 0 by 0 pixels, and nothing will be seen except the title bar. Since the setSize and setVisible methods are both defined in the Component class, they are inherited by the JFrame class. Later you will see that these methods are also useful in many other subclasses of Component.

When you run the MyFrame program, the following window will be displayed on-screen (see Figure 10.4).

Figure 10.4   *The program creates and displays a frame with the title* Test Frame.

`frame.setDefaultCloseOperation(JFrame.EXIT_ON_CLOSE)` tells the program to terminate when the frame is closed. If this statement is not used, the program does not terminate when the frame is closed. In that case, you have to stop the program by pressing Ctrl+C at the DOS prompt window in Windows or use the kill command to stop the process in Unix.

10.3.2   Centering a Frame (Optional)

By default, a frame is displayed in the upper-left corner of the screen. To display a frame at a specified location, use the `setLocation(x, y)` method in the `JFrame` class. This method places the upper-left corner of the frame at location (x, y).

To center a frame on the screen, you need to know the width and height of the screen and the frame in order to determine the frame's upper-left coordinates. The screen's width and height can be obtained using the `java.awt.Toolkit` class:

```
Dimension screenSize = Toolkit.getDefaultToolkit().getScreenSize();
int screenWidth = screenSize.width;
int screenHeight = screenSize.height;
```

Therefore, as shown in Figure 10.5, the upper-left x and y coordinates of the centered frame `frame` can be:

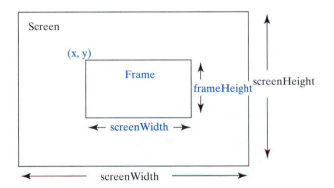

Figure 10.5   *The frame is centered on the screen.*

```
Dimension frameSize = frame.getSize();
int x = (screenWidth - frameSize.width) / 2;
int y = (screenHeight - frameSize.height) / 2;
```

The `getSize` method is defined in the `Component` class. The `java.awt.Dimension` class encapsulates the width and height of a component (in integer precision) in a single object.

To display a centered frame, the program can be modified as follows:

```
1    // CenterFrame.java: Display a frame
2    import javax.swing.*;
3    import java.awt.*;
4
5    public class CenterFrame {
```

```
6     public static void main(String[] args) {
7       JFrame frame = new JFrame("Centered Frame");
8       frame.setSize(400, 300);
9
10      // New in JDK 1.3 to exit the program upon closing
11      frame.setDefaultCloseOperation(JFrame.EXIT_ON_CLOSE);
12
13      // Get the dimension of the screen
14      Dimension screenSize =
15        Toolkit.getDefaultToolkit().getScreenSize();
16      int screenWidth = screenSize.width;
17      int screenHeight = screenSize.height;
18
19      // Get the dimension of the frame
20      Dimension frameSize = frame.getSize();
21      int x = (screenWidth - frameSize.width) / 2;
22      int y = (screenHeight - frameSize.height) / 2;
23
24      frame.setLocation(x, y);
25      frame.setVisible(true);
26    }
27  }
```

10.3.3   Adding Components to a Frame

The frame shown in Figure 10.4 is empty. Using the add method, you can add components into the frame's content pane, as follows:

```
1   // MyFrameWithComponents.java: Add components into a frame
2   import javax.swing.*;
3
4   public class MyFrameWithComponents {
5     public static void main(String[] args) {
6       JFrame frame = new JFrame("Adding Components into the Frame");
7
8       // Add a button into the frame
9       frame.getContentPane().add(new JButton("OK"));
10
11      frame.setSize(400, 300);
12      frame.setVisible(true);
13      frame.setDefaultCloseOperation(JFrame.EXIT_ON_CLOSE);
14    }
15  }
```

The getContentPane method in the JFrame class returns the content pane of the frame. The content pane holds the frame's components. An object of JButton was created using new JButton("OK"), and this object was added to the content pane of the frame. When you run the program MyFrameWithComponents, the following window will be displayed in Figure 10.6.

Figure 10.6 *An OK button is added to the frame.*

The button is always centered in the frame and occupies the entire frame no matter how you resize the frame in Figure 10.6. This is because components are put in the frame by the content pane's layout manager, and the default layout manager for the content pane places the button in the center. In the next section, you will use several different layout managers to place components in other locations as desired.

NOTE

The content pane is a subclass of Container. Line 9 can be replaced by the following two lines:

```
Container container = frame.getContentPane();
container.add(new JButton("OK"));
```

10.4   Layout Managers

In many other window systems, the user-interface components are arranged by using hard-coded pixel measurements. For example, put a button at location (10, 10) in the window. Using hard-coded pixel measurements, the user interface might look fine on one system but be unusable on another. Java's layout managers provide a level of abstraction that automatically maps your user interface on all window systems.

The Java GUI components are placed in containers, where they are arranged by the container's layout manager. In the preceding program, you did not specify where to place the OK button in the frame, but Java knows where to place the button because the layout manager works behind the scenes to place components in the correct locations. The five basic layout managers are FlowLayout, GridLayout, BorderLayout, CardLayout, and GridBagLayout. These classes implement the LayoutManager interface.

Layout managers are set in containers. Here is the syntax to set a layout manager:

```
container.setLayout(new SpecificLayout());
```

To add a component to a container, use the add method. To remove a component from a container, use the remove method. The following statements create a button and add it to a container.

```
JButton jbtOK = new JButton("OK");
container.add(jbtOK);
```

The next statement removes the button from the container:

```
container.remove(jbtOK);
```

The container can be the content pane of a frame or an applet, or an instance of JPanel.

The following sections introduce the FlowLayout, GridLayout, and BorderLayout managers. CardLayout and GridBagLayout are introduced in Chapter 12, "Applets and Advanced GUI."

10.4.1   FlowLayout

FlowLayout is the simplest layout manager. The components are arranged in the container from left to right in the order in which they were added. When one row is filled, a new row is started. You can specify the way the components are aligned by using one of three constants: FlowLayout.RIGHT, FlowLayout.CENTER, or FlowLayout.LEFT. You can also specify the gap between components in pixels. FlowLayout has three constructors:

- public FlowLayout(int align, int hGap, int vGap)

  Constructs a new FlowLayout with the specified alignment, horizontal gap, and vertical gap. The gaps are the distances in pixels between components.

- public FlowLayout(int alignment)

  Constructs a new FlowLayout with a specified alignment and a default gap of 5 pixels horizontally and vertically.

- public FlowLayout()

  Constructs a new FlowLayout with a default center alignment and a default gap of 5 pixels horizontally and vertically.

Example 10.1 Testing the FlowLayout Manager

Problem

Write a program that arranges components in a frame by using the FlowLayout manager with a specified alignment and horizontal and vertical gaps.

Solution

The program uses the following simple code to arrange ten buttons in a frame. The output is shown in Figure 10.7.

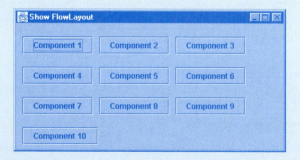

Figure 10.7   *The components are added with the* FlowLayout *manager to fill in the rows in the container one after another.*

```
1    // ShowFlowLayout.java: Demonstrate using FlowLayout
2    import javax.swing.JButton;
3    import javax.swing.JFrame;
4    import java.awt.Container;
5    import java.awt.FlowLayout;
6
7    public class ShowFlowLayout extends JFrame {
8      /** Default constructor */
9      public ShowFlowLayout() {
10        // Get the content pane of the frame
11        Container container = getContentPane();
12
13        // Set FlowLayout, aligned left with horizontal gap 10
14        // and vertical gap 20 between components
15        container.setLayout(new FlowLayout(FlowLayout.LEFT, 10, 20));
16
17        // Add buttons to the frame
18        for (int i = 1; i <= 10; i++)
19          container.add(new JButton("Component " + i));
20      }
21
22      /** Main method */
23      public static void main(String[] args) {
24        ShowFlowLayout frame = new ShowFlowLayout();
25        frame.setTitle("Show FlowLayout");
26        frame.setDefaultCloseOperation(JFrame.EXIT_ON_CLOSE);
27        frame.setSize(200, 200);
28        frame.setVisible(true);
29      }
30    }
```

Review

This example creates a program using a style different from the programs in the preceding section, where frames were created using the JFrame class (Line 7). This example creates a class named ShowFlowLayout that extends the JFrame class. The main method in this program creates an instance of ShowFlowLayout (Line 24). The constructor of ShowFlowLayout constructs and places the components in the frame. This is the preferred style of creating GUI applications for two reasons: (1) creating a GUI application means creating a frame, so it is natural to define a frame to extend JFrame; (2) the new class can be reused if desirable. Using one style consistently makes programs easy to read. From now on, all the GUI main classes will extend the JFrame class. The constructor of the main class constructs the user interface. The main method creates an instance of the main class and then displays the frame.

In this example, the FlowLayout manager is used to place components in a frame. If you resize the frame, the components are automatically rearranged to fit in it.

If you replace the setLayout statement (Line 15) with setLayout(new FlowLayout(FlowLayout.RIGHT, 0, 0)), all the buttons will be right-aligned with no gaps.

continues

Example 10.1 continued

An anonymous `FlowLayout` object was created in the statement (Line 15):

```
container.setLayout(new FlowLayout(FlowLayout.LEFT, 10, 20));
```

This statement is equivalent to the following code:

```
FlowLayout layout = new FlowLayout(FlowLayout.LEFT, 10, 20);
container.setLayout(layout);
```

This code creates an explicit reference to the object `layout` of the `FlowLayout` class. The explicit reference is not necessary, because the object is not directly referenced in the `ShowFlowLayout` class.

The `setTitle` method (Line 25) is defined in the `java.awt.Frame` class. Since `JFrame` is a subclass of `Frame`, you can use it to set a title for an object of `JFrame`.

CAUTION
Do not forget to put the `new` operator before a layout manager class when setting a layout style; for example, `setLayout(new FlowLayout())`.

NOTE
The constructor `ShowFlowLayout()` does not explicitly invoke the constructor `JFrame()`, but the constructor `JFrame()` is invoked implicitly. See the first Note box on Page 283.

10.4.2   GridLayout

The `GridLayout` manager arranges components in a grid (matrix) formation with the number of rows and columns defined by the constructor. The components are placed in the grid from left to right, starting with the first row, then the second, and so on, in the order in which they are added. The `GridLayout` manager has three constructors:

■   `public GridLayout(int rows, int columns, int hGap, int vGap)`

Constructs a new `GridLayout` with the specified number of rows and columns, along with specified horizontal and vertical gaps between components in the container.

■   `public GridLayout(int rows, int columns)`

Constructs a new `GridLayout` with the specified number of rows and columns. The horizontal and vertical gaps are zero.

■   `public GridLayout()`

Constructs a new `GridLayout` with one column in a single row.

You can specify the number of rows and columns in the grid. The basic rule is as follows:

- The number of rows or the number of columns can be zero, but not both. If one is zero and the other is nonzero, the nonzero dimension is fixed, while the zero dimension is determined dynamically by the layout manager. For example, if you specify zero rows and three columns for a grid that has ten components, GridLayout creates three fixed columns of four rows, with the last row containing one component. If you specify three rows and zero columns for a grid that has ten components, GridLayout creates three fixed rows of four columns, with the last row containing two components.

- If both the number of rows and the number of columns are nonzero, the number of rows is the dominating parameter; that is, the number of rows is fixed, and the layout manager dynamically calculates the number of columns. For example, if you specify three rows and three columns for a grid that has ten components, GridLayout creates three fixed rows of four columns, with the last row containing two components.

Example 10.2 Testing the GridLayout Manager

Problem

Write a program that arranges components in a frame with GridLayout.

Solution

The program gives the following code to arrange ten buttons in a grid of four rows and three columns. Its output is shown in Figure 10.8.

Figure 10.8   *The* GridLayout *manager divides the container into grids, then the components are added to fill in the cells row by row.*

```
1    // ShowGridLayout.java: Demonstrate using GridLayout
2    import javax.swing.JButton;
3    import javax.swing.JFrame;
4    import java.awt.GridLayout;
5    import java.awt.Container;
6
7    public class ShowGridLayout extends JFrame {
8      /** Default constructor */
9      public ShowGridLayout() {
10       // Get the content pane of the frame
11       Container container = getContentPane();
12
```

continues

Example 10.2 continued

```
13          // Set GridLayout, 4 rows, 3 columns, and gaps 5 between
14          // components horizontally and vertically
15          container.setLayout(new GridLayout(4, 3, 5, 5));
16
17          // Add buttons to the frame
18          for (int i = 1; i <= 10; i++)
19            container.add(new JButton("Component " + i));
20        }
21
22        /** Main method */
23        public static void main(String[] args) {
24          ShowGridLayout frame = new ShowGridLayout();
25          frame.setTitle("Show GridLayout");
26          frame.setDefaultCloseOperation(JFrame.EXIT_ON_CLOSE);
27          frame.setSize(200, 200);
28          frame.setVisible(true);
29        }
30      }
```

Review

If you resize the frame, the layout of the buttons remains unchanged (i.e., the number of rows and columns does not change, and the gaps don't change either).

All components are given equal size in the container of `GridLayout`.

Replacing the `setLayout` statement (Line 15) with `setLayout(new GridLayout (3, 10))` would yield three rows and *four* columns, with the last row containing two components. The columns parameter is ignored because the rows parameter is nonzero. The actual number of columns is calculated by the layout manager.

NOTE

In `FlowLayout` and `GridLayout`, the order in which the components are added to the container is important. It determines the location of the components in the container.

10.4.3   BorderLayout

The `BorderLayout` manager divides the window into five areas: East, South, West, North, and Center. Components are added to a `BorderLayout` by using `add(Component, index)`, where index is a constant `BorderLayout.EAST`, `Border-Layout.SOUTH`, `BorderLayout.WEST`, `BorderLayout.NORTH`, or `BorderLayout.CENTER`. You can use one of the following two constructors to create a new `BorderLayout`:

■   `public BorderLayout(int hGap, int vGap)`

Constructs a new `BorderLayout` with the specified horizontal and vertical gaps between the components.

■   `public BorderLayout()`

Constructs a new `BorderLayout` without horizontal or vertical gaps.

The components are laid out according to their preferred sizes and where they are placed in the container. The North and South components can stretch horizontally; the East and West components can stretch vertically; the Center component can stretch both horizontally and vertically to fill any empty space.

Example 10.3 Testing the `BorderLayout` Manager

Problem

Write a program that places components in a frame with `BorderLayout`.

Solution

The program uses the following code to place East, South, West, North, and Center buttons in the frame by using `BorderLayout`. The output of the program is shown in Figure 10.9.

Figure 10.9   `BorderLayout` *divides the container into five areas, each of which can hold a component.*

```
1    // ShowBorderLayout.java: Demonstrate using BorderLayout
2    import javax.swing.JButton;
3    import javax.swing.JFrame;
4    import java.awt.Container;
5    import java.awt.BorderLayout;
6
7    public class ShowBorderLayout extends JFrame {
8      /** Default constructor */
9      public ShowBorderLayout() {
10       // Get the content pane of the frame
11       Container container = getContentPane();
12
13       // Set BorderLayout with horizontal gap 5 and vertical gap 10
14       container.setLayout(new BorderLayout(5, 10));
15
16       // Add buttons to the frame
17       container.add(new JButton("East"), BorderLayout.EAST);
18       container.add(new JButton("South"), BorderLayout.SOUTH);
19       container.add(new JButton("West"), BorderLayout.WEST);
```

continues

Example 10.3 continued

```
20          container.add(new JButton("North"), BorderLayout.NORTH);
21          container.add(new JButton("Center"), BorderLayout.CENTER);
22        }
23
24        /** Main method */
25        public static void main(String[] args) {
26          ShowBorderLayout frame = new ShowBorderLayout();
27          frame.setTitle("Show BorderLayout");
28          frame.setDefaultCloseOperation(JFrame.EXIT_ON_CLOSE);
29          frame.setSize(300, 200);
30          frame.setVisible(true);
31        }
32      }
```

Review

The buttons are added to the frame. Note that the add method for BorderLayout is different from the one for FlowLayout and GridLayout. With BorderLayout you specify where to put the components.

It is unnecessary to place components to occupy all the areas. If you remove the East button from the program and rerun it, you will see that the center stretches rightward to occupy the East area.

NOTE

For convenience, BorderLayout interprets the absence of an index specification as BorderLayout.CENTER. For example, add(component) is the same as add(Component, BorderLayout.CENTER). If you add two components into a container of the BorderLayout, as follows:

```
container.add(component1);
container.add(component2);
```

only the last component is displayed.

10.4.4   Properties of Layout Managers (Optional)

Layout managers have properties that can be changed dynamically. FlowLayout has alignment, hGap, and vGap properties. You can use the setAlignment, setHGap, and setVGap methods to specify the alignment, and horizontal and vertical gaps. GridLayout has the rows, columns, hGap, and vGap properties. You can use the setRows, setColumns, setHGap, and setVGap methods to specify the number of rows, number of columns, and horizontal and vertical gaps. BorderLayout has the hGap and vGap properties. You can use the setHGap and setVGap methods to specify the horizontal and vertical gaps.

In the preceding sections, an anonymous layout manager is used because the properties of a layout manager are not changed once a layout manager is created. If you have to change the properties of a layout manager dynamically, the layout manager must be explicitly referenced by a variable. You can then change the properties of the layout manager through the variable. For example, the following code creates a layout manager and sets its properties:

```
// Create a layout manager
FlowLayout flowLayout = new FlowLayout();

// Set layout properties
flowLayout.setAlignment(FlowLayout.RIGHT);
flowLayout.setHGap(10);
flowLayout.setVGap(20);
```

To use these properties, please refer to Exercises 11.15 and 11.16.

10.4.5   The *validate* and *doLayout* Methods (Optional)

A container can have only one layout manager at a time. You can change its layout manager by using the setLayout method and then, using the new layout manager, use the validate method to force the container to re-layout the components in the container.

If you use the same layout manager but change its properties, you need to use the doLayout method to force the container to re-layout the components using the new properties of the layout manager.

To use these methods, please refer to Exercises 11.15 and 11.16.

10.5   Using Panels as Containers

Suppose that you want to place ten buttons and a text field on a frame. The buttons are placed in grid formation, but the text field is placed on a separate row. It is difficult to achieve the desired look by placing all the components in a single container. With Java GUI programming, you can divide a window into panels. Panels act as smaller containers to group user-interface components. You add the buttons in one panel, and then add the panel into the frame.

The Swing version of panel is JPanel. To add a button to panel p, for instance, you can use:

```
JPanel p = new JPanel();
p.add(new JButton("ButtonName"));
```

By default, JPanel uses FlowLayout. Panels can be placed inside a frame or inside another panel. The following statement places panel p into frame f:

```
f.getContentPane().add(p);
```

NOTE
To add a component to JFrame, you actually add it to the content pane of JFrame. To add a component to a panel, you add it directly to the panel using the add method.

Example 10.4 Testing Panels

Problem

Write a program that uses panels to organize components. The program creates a user interface for a microwave oven, as shown in Figure 10.10.

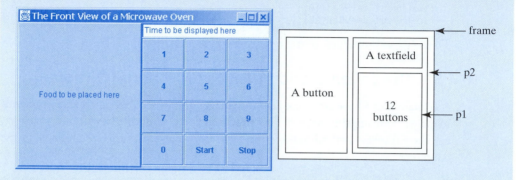

Figure 10.10   *The program uses panels to organize components.*

Solution

The program is given as follows:

```
1    // TestPanels.java: Use panels to group components
2    import java.awt.*;
3    import javax.swing.*;
4
5    public class TestPanels extends JFrame {
6      /** Default constructor */
7      public TestPanels() {
8        // Get the content pane of the frame
9        Container container = getContentPane();
10
11       // Set BorderLayout for the frame
12       container.setLayout(new BorderLayout());
13
14       // Create panel p1 for the buttons and set GridLayout
15       JPanel p1 = new JPanel();
16       p1.setLayout(new GridLayout(4, 3));
17
18       // Add buttons to the panel
19       for (int i = 1; i <= 9; i++) {
20         p1.add(new JButton("" + i));
21       }
22
23       p1.add(new JButton("" + 0));
24       p1.add(new JButton("Start"));
25       p1.add(new JButton("Stop"));
26
27       // Create panel p2 to hold a text field and p1
28       JPanel p2 = new JPanel();
29       p2.setLayout(new BorderLayout());
30       p2.add(new JTextField("Time to be displayed here"),
31         BorderLayout.NORTH);
32       p2.add(p1, BorderLayout.CENTER);
33
```

```
34        // Add p2 and a button to the frame
35        container.add(p2, BorderLayout.EAST);
36        container.add(new Button("Food to be placed here"),
37          BorderLayout.CENTER);
38      }
39
40      /** Main method */
41      public static void main(String[] args) {
42        TestPanels frame = new TestPanels();
43        frame.setTitle("The Front View of a Microwave Oven");
44        frame.setDefaultCloseOperation(JFrame.EXIT_ON_CLOSE);
45        frame.setSize(400, 250);
46        frame.setVisible(true);
47      }
48    }
```

Review

To achieve the desired layout, the program uses panel p1 of GridLayout to group the number buttons, the Stop button, and the Start button, and uses panel p2 of BorderLayout to hold a text field in the north and p1 in the center. The button representing the food is placed in the center of the frame, and p2 is placed in the east of the frame.

The statement (Line 30)

```
p2.add(new JTextField("Time to be displayed here"),
        BorderLayout.NORTH);
```

creates an instance of JTextField and adds it to p2.

Text field is a GUI component that can be used for user input as well as to display values. Text fields will be introduced in Chapter 11, "Creating User Interfaces."

10.6   Drawing Graphics in Panels

Panels are invisible and are used as small containers that group components to achieve a desired layout look. Another important use of JPanel is for drawing strings and graphics.

To draw in a panel, you create a new class that extends JPanel and overrides the paintComponent method to tell the panel how to draw things. You can then display strings, draw geometric shapes, and view images on the panel. Although you can draw things directly in a frame or an applet using the paint method, I recommend that you use JPanel to draw messages and shapes and to show images; this way your drawing will not interfere with other components.

The signature of the paintComponent method is:

```
public void paintComponent(Graphics g)
```

The Graphics object g is created automatically by the Java runtime system. This object controls how information is drawn. You can use various drawing methods defined in the Graphics class to draw strings and geometric figures. For example, you can draw a string using the following method in the Graphics class:

```
drawString(string, x1, y1);
```

The program given below draws a message "Welcome to Java" on the panel, as shown in Figure 10.11.

Figure 10.11   *The message is drawn on a panel and the panel is placed inside the frame.*

```java
// DrawMessage.java: Display a message on a JPanel
import javax.swing.*;
import java.awt.*;

public class DrawMessage extends JPanel {
  /** Main method */
  public static void main(String[] args) {
    JFrame frame = new JFrame("DrawMessage");
    frame.getContentPane().add(new DrawMessage());
    frame.setDefaultCloseOperation(JFrame.EXIT_ON_CLOSE);
    frame.setSize(300, 200);
    frame.setVisible(true);
  }

  /** Paint the message */
  public void paintComponent(Graphics g) {
    super.paintComponent(g);

    g.drawString("Welcome to Java!", 40, 40);
  }
}
```

NOTE

The Swing components use the paintComponent method to draw things. The paintComponent method is invoked to paint the graphics context. This method is invoked when the frame is displayed or whenever you resize the frame. Invoking super.paintComponent(g) is necessary to clear the viewing area before a new drawing is displayed. If this method is not invoked, the previous drawings will not be cleared.

NOTE

The Graphics class is an abstract class for displaying figures and images on the screen on different platforms. The Graphics class is implemented on the native platform in the JVM. When you use the paintComponent method to draw things on a graphics context g, this g is an instance of a concrete subclass of the abstract Graphics class for the specific platform. The Graphics class encapsulates the platform details and enables you to draw things uniformly without concerning specific platforms.

All the drawing methods have arguments that specify the locations of the subjects to be drawn. The Java coordinate system has *x* in the horizontal axis and *y* in the vertical axis, with the origin (0, 0) at the upper-left corner of the window. The *x* coordinate increases to the right, and the *y* coordinate increases downward. All measurements in Java are made in pixels, as shown in Figure 10.12.

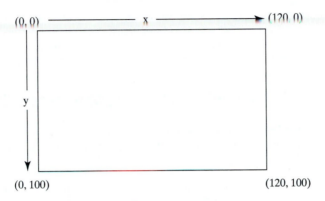

Figure 10.12   *The Java graphics coordinate system is measured in pixels, with* (0, 0) *at its upper-left corner.*

You can draw things using appropriate colors and fonts. The next sections introduce the Color class, the Font class, the FontMetrics class, and drawing methods in the Graphics class.

10.7   The *Color* Class

You can set colors for GUI components by using the java.awt.Color class. Colors are made of red, green, and blue components, each of which is represented by a byte value that describes its intensity, ranging from 0 (darkest shade) to 255 (lightest shade). This is known as the *RGB model*.

The syntax to create a Color object is

```
Color color = new Color(r, g, b);
```

in which r, g, and b specify a color by its red, green, and blue components. For example:

```
Color color = new Color(128, 100, 100);
```

You can use the setBackground(Color c) and setForeground(Color c) methods defined in the Component class to set a component's background and foreground colors. Here is an example of setting the background of a panel:

```
JPanel myPanel = new JPanel();
myPanel.setBackground(c);
```

Alternatively, you can use one of the thirteen standard colors (black, blue, cyan, darkGray, gray, green, lightGray, magenta, orange, pink, red, white, yellow) defined as constants in `java.awt.Color`. The following code, for instance, sets the background color of a panel to yellow:

```
JPanel myPanel = new JPanel();
myPanel.setBackground(Color.yellow);
```

NOTE

The standard color names are constants, but they are named as variables with lowercase for the first word and uppercase for the first letters of subsequent words. Thus the color names violate the Java naming convention.

10.8   The *Font* and *FontMetrics* Classes

You can set fonts for the components or subjects you draw, and use font metrics to measure font size. Fonts and font metrics are encapsulated in the classes `Font` and `FontMetrics`.

Whatever font is current will be used in the subsequent drawing. To set a font, you need to create a `Font` object from the `Font` class. The syntax is:

```
Font myFont = new Font(name, style, size);
```

You can choose a font name from `SansSerif`, `Serif`, `Monospaced`, `Dialog`, or `DialogInput`, and choose a style from `Font.PLAIN`, `Font.BOLD`, and `Font.ITALIC`. The styles can be combined, as in the following code:

```
Font myFont = new Font("SansSerif", Font.BOLD, 16);
Font myFont = new Font("Serif", Font.BOLD + Font.ITALIC, 12);
```

If your system supports other fonts, such as "Times New Roman," you can use it to create a font. To find the fonts available on your system, you need to create an instance of `java.awt.GraphicsEnvironment` using its static method `getLocalGraph-icsEnvironment()`. `GraphicsEnvironment` is an abstract class that describes the graphics environment on a particular system. You can use its `getAllFonts()` method to obtain all the available fonts on the system, and its `getAvailableFont-FamilyNames()` method to obtain the names of all the available fonts. For example, the following statements print all the available font names in the system:

```
GraphicsEnvironment e =
  GraphicsEnvironment.getLocalGraphicsEnvironment();
String[] fontnames = e.getAvailableFontFamilyNames();

for (int i = 0; i < fontnames.length; i++)
  System.out.println(fontnames[i]);
```

`FontMetrics` can be used to compute the exact length and width of a string, which is helpful for measuring the size of a string in order to display it in the right position. For example, you can center strings in the viewing area with the help of the `FontMetrics` class. A `FontMetrics` is measured by the following attributes (see Figure 10.13):

Figure 10.13 *The* `FontMetrics` *class can be used to determine the font properties of characters.*

- **Leading,** pronounced *ledding*, is the amount of space between lines of text.

- **Ascent** is the height of a character, from the baseline to the top.

- **Descent** is the distance from the baseline to the bottom of a descending character, such as *j, y,* and *g.*

- **Height** is the sum of leading, ascent, and descent.

`FontMetrics` is an abstract class. To get a `FontMetrics` object for a specific font, use the following `getFontMetrics` methods defined in the `Graphics` class:

- `public FontMetrics getFontMetrics(Font f)`

  Returns the font metrics of the specified font.

- `public FontMetrics getFontMetrics()`

  Returns the font metrics of the current font.

You can use these instance methods in the `FontMetrics` class to obtain font information:

```
public int getAscent()
public int getDescent()
public int getLeading()
public int getHeight()
public int stringWidth(String str)
```

Example 10.5 Using FontMetrics

Problem

Write a program that displays "Welcome to Java" in SansSerif 20-point bold, centered in the frame, as shown in Figure 10.14.

Solution

Here are the steps for the program:

1. Create a panel named `MessagePanel` to display the message. `MessagePanel` extends `JPanel` to display a message in a specified location or centered. The properties and methods in `MessagePanel` are shown in Figure 10.15.

continues

Example 10.5 continued

Figure 10.14   *The program uses the* FontMetrics *class to measure the string width and height, and displays it at the center of the frame.*

2. Create a frame named `TestFontMetrics` that extends `JFrame`. `TestFont-Metrics` creates an instance of `MessagePanel` and places it in the center of the frame. The relationship between `TestFontMetrics` and `MessagePanel` is shown in Figure 10.15.

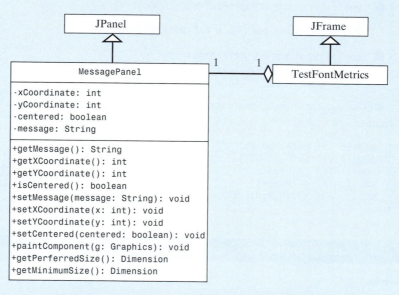

Figure 10.15   `TestFontMetrics` *uses* `MessagePanel` *to display a message.*

```
1    // MessagePanel.java: Display a message on a JPanel
2    import java.awt.Font;
3    import java.awt.FontMetrics;
4    import java.awt.Dimension;
5    import java.awt.Graphics;
6    import javax.swing.JPanel;
7
8    public class MessagePanel extends JPanel {
9      /** The message to be displayed */
10     private String message = "Welcome to Java";
11
```

```
12        /** The x coordinate where the message is displayed */
13        private int xCoordinate = 20;
14
15        /** The y coordinate where the message is displayed */
16        private int yCoordinate = 20;
17
18        /** Indicate whether the message is displayed in the center */
19        private boolean centered;
20
21        /** Default constructor */
22        public MessagePanel() {
23        }
24
25        /** Constructor with a message parameter */
26        public MessagePanel(String message) {
27          this.message = message;
28        }
29
30        /** Return message */
31        public String getMessage() {
32          return message;
33        }
34
35        /** Set a new message */
36        public void setMessage(String message) {
37          this.message = message;
38        }
39
40        /** Return xCoordinator */
41        public int getXCoordinate() {
42          return xCoordinate;
43        }
44
45        /** Set a new xCoordinator */
46        public void setXCoordinate(int x) {
47          this.xCoordinate = x;
48        }
49
50        /** Return yCoordinator */
51        public int getYCoordinate() {
52          return yCoordinate;
53        }
54
55        /** Set a new yCoordinator */
56        public void setYCoordinate(int y) {
57          this.yCoordinate = y;
58        }
59
60        /** Return centered */
61        public boolean isCentered() {
62          return centered;
63        }
64
65        /** Set a new centered */
66        public void setCentered(boolean centered) {
67          this.centered = centered;
68        }
69
70        /** Paint the message */
71        public void paintComponent(Graphics g) {
72          super.paintComponent(g);
73
```

continues

Example 10.5 continued

```
74          if (centered) {
75            // Get font metrics for the current font
76            FontMetrics fm = g.getFontMetrics();
77
78            // Find the center location to display
79            int w = fm.stringWidth(message);  // Get the string width
80            // Get the string height, from top to the baseline
81            int h = fm.getAscent();
82            xCoordinate = getWidth() / 2 - w / 2;
83            yCoordinate = getHeight() / 2 + h / 2;
84          }
85
86          g.drawString(message, xCoordinate, yCoordinate);
87        }
88
89        /** Override get method for preferredSize */
90        public Dimension getPreferredSize() {
91          return new Dimension(200, 100);
92        }
93
94        /** Override get method for minimumSize */
95        public Dimension getMinimumSize() {
96          return new Dimension(200, 100);
97        }
98      }
```

```
1    // TestFontMetrics.java: Draw a message at the center of a panel
2    import java.awt.Font;
3    import java.awt.FontMetrics;
4    import java.awt.Graphics;
5    import javax.swing.*;
6
7    public class TestFontMetrics extends JFrame {
8      /** Default constructor */
9      public TestFontMetrics() {
10       MessagePanel messagePanel = new MessagePanel("Welcome to Java");
11
12       // Set font SansSerif 20-point bold
13       messagePanel.setFont(new Font("SansSerif", Font.BOLD, 20));
14
15       // Center the message
16       messagePanel.setCentered(true);
17
18       getContentPane().add(messagePanel);
19     }
20
21     /** Main method */
22     public static void main(String[] args) {
23       TestFontMetrics frame = new TestFontMetrics();
24       frame.setDefaultCloseOperation(JFrame.EXIT_ON_CLOSE);
25       frame.setSize(300, 200);
26       frame.setTitle("TestFontMetrics");
27       frame.setVisible(true);
28     }
29   }
```

Review

TestFontMetrics creates an instance of MessagePanel to display a message at the center of the panel. The setFont method (Line 13) sets a new font for the message panel. This method is available for all subclasses of Component. The new font is created using new Font("SansSerif", Font.BOLD, 20). It is used to display the message in the panel.

The MessagePanel class has the properties message, xCoordinate, yCoordinate, and centered. xCoordinate and yCoordinate specify where the message is displayed if centered is false. If centered is true, the message is displayed at the center of the panel.

The methods getWidth() and getHeight() (Lines 82–83), defined in the Component class, return the component's width and height, respectively.

Since the centered property is set to true in TestFontMetrics, the message is displayed in the center of the panel. Resizing the frame results in the message always being displayed in the center of the panel.

yCoordinate is height of the baseline for the first character of the string to be displayed. When centered is true, yCoordinate should be getHeight() / 2 + h / 2 (Line 83), where h is the ascent of the string.

The getPreferredSize() method (Lines 90–92), defined in Component, is overridden in MessagePanel to specify a preferred size for the layout manager to consider when laying out a MessagePanel object.

The drawString method draws on the panel (Line 86). The drawString(s, x, y) method draws a string s whose left end of the baseline starts at (x, y).

There are many ways to write Java programs. You can rewrite this example using one class. See Exercise 10.17.

CAUTION
The MessagePanel class uses the properties xCoordinate and yCoordinate to specify the position of the message displayed on the panel. Do not use property names x and y, because they are already defined in the Component class to specify the position of the component in the parent's coordinate system.

NOTE
The Component class has the setBackground, setForeground, and setFont methods. These methods are for setting colors and fonts for the entire component. Suppose you want to draw several messages in a panel with different colors and fonts; you have to use the setColor and setFont methods in the Graphics class to set the color and font for the current drawing.

NOTE
One of the key features of Java programming is the reuse of classes. Throughout the book, you will develop reusable classes and later reuse them. MessagePanel is an example of this. It can be reused whenever you need to display a message on a panel.

10.9   Drawing Geometric Figures

This section introduces the methods in the Graphics class for drawing lines, rectangles, ovals, arcs, and polygons.

10.9.1   Drawing Lines

You can use the method shown below to draw a straight line:

```
drawLine(x1, y1, x2, y2);
```

The parameters x1, y1, x2, and y2 represent the starting point (x1, y1) and the ending point (x2, y2) of the line, as shown in Figure 10.16.

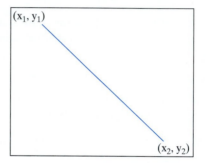

Figure 10.16   *The* drawLine *method draws a line between two specified points.*

10.9.2   Drawing Rectangles

Java provides six methods for drawing rectangles in outline or filled with color. You can draw plain rectangles, rounded rectangles, or 3D rectangles.

To draw a plain rectangle, use the following code:

```
drawRect(x, y, w, h);
```

To draw a rectangle filled with color, use:

```
fillRect(x, y, w, h);
```

The parameters x and y represent the upper-left corner of the rectangle, and w and h are its width and height (see Figure 10.17).

Figure 10.17   *The* drawRect *method draws a rectangle with specified upper-left corner* (x, y), *width, and height.*

To draw a rounded rectangle, use the following method:

```
drawRoundRect(x, y, w, h, aw, ah);
```

To draw a rounded rectangle filled with color, use this method:

```
fillRoundRect(x, y, w, h, aw, ah);
```

Parameters x, y, w, and h are the same as in the drawRect method, parameter aw is the horizontal diameter of the arcs at the corner, and ah is the vertical diameter of the arcs at the corner (see Figure 10.18). In other words, aw and ah are the width and the height of the oval that produces a quarter-circle at each corner.

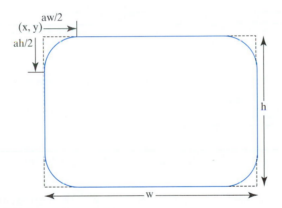

Figure 10.18   *The* drawRoundRect *method draws a rounded rectangle.*

To draw a 3D rectangle, use

```
draw3DRect(x, y, w, h, raised);
```

in which x, y, w, and h are the same as in the drawRect method. The last parameter, a Boolean value, indicates whether the rectangle is raised above the surface or etched into the surface.

The example given below demonstrates these methods. The output is shown in Figure 10.19.

Figure 10.19 *The program draws a rectangle, a rounded rectangle, a raised 3D rectangle, and a plain 3D rectangle.*

```java
// TestRect.java: Demonstrate drawing rectangles
import java.awt.Graphics;
import java.awt.Color;
import javax.swing.JPanel;
import javax.swing.JFrame;

public class TestRect extends JFrame {
  /** Default constructor */
  public TestRect() {
    setTitle("Show Rectangles");
    getContentPane().add(new RectPanel());
  }

  /** Main method */
  public static void main(String[] args) {
    TestRect frame = new TestRect();
    frame.setDefaultCloseOperation(JFrame.EXIT_ON_CLOSE);
    frame.setSize(300, 250);
    frame.setVisible(true);
  }
}

class RectPanel extends JPanel {
  public void paintComponent(Graphics g) {
    super.paintComponent(g);

    // Set new color
    g.setColor(Color.red);

    // Draw a rectangle
    g.drawRect(5, 5, getWidth() / 2 - 10, getHeight() / 2 - 10);

    // Draw a rounded rectangle
    g.drawRoundRect(getWidth() / 2 + 5, 5,
      getWidth() / 2 - 10, getHeight() / 2 - 10, 60, 30);

    // Change the color to cyan
    g.setColor(Color.cyan);

    // Draw a 3D rectangle
    g.fill3DRect(5, getHeight() / 2 + 5, getWidth() / 2 - 10,
      getHeight() / 2 - 10, true);

    // Draw a raised 3D rectangle
    g.fill3DRect(getWidth() / 2 + 5, getHeight() / 2 + 5,
      getWidth() / 2 - 10, getHeight() / 2 - 10, false);
  }
}
```

■■■ NOTE
The RectPanel class will be reused in Exercises 10.15 and 10.16.

10.9.3   Drawing Ovals

Depending on whether you wish to draw an oval in outline or filled solid, you can use either the drawOval method or the fillOval method. Since an oval in Java is drawn based on its bounding rectangle, give the parameters as if you were drawing a rectangle.

Here is the method for drawing an oval:

```
drawOval(x, y, w, h);
```

To draw a filled oval, use the following method:

```
fillOval(x, y, w, h);
```

Parameters x and y indicate the top-left corner of the bounding rectangle, and w and h indicate the width and height, respectively, of the bounding rectangle, as shown in Figure 10.20.

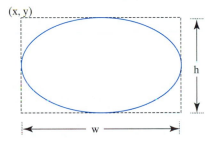

Figure 10.20   *The* drawOval *method draws an oval based on its bounding rectangle.*

The following is an example of how to draw ovals, with the output in Figure 10.21.

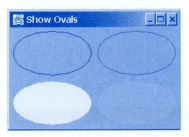

Figure 10.21   *The program draws ovals.*

407

```
// TestOvals.java: Demonstrate drawing ovals
import javax.swing.JFrame;
import javax.swing.JPanel;
import java.awt.Color;
import java.awt.Graphics;

public class TestOvals extends JFrame {
  /** Default constructor */
  public TestOvals() {
    setTitle("Show Ovals");
    getContentPane().add(new OvalsPanel());
  }

  /** Main method */
  public static void main(String[] args) {
    TestOvals frame = new TestOvals();
    frame.setDefaultCloseOperation(JFrame.EXIT_ON_CLOSE);
    frame.setSize(250, 250);
    frame.setVisible(true);
  }
}

// The class for drawing the ovals on a panel
class OvalsPanel extends JPanel {
  public void paintComponent(Graphics g) {
    super.paintComponent(g);

    g.drawOval(5, 5, getWidth() / 2 - 10, getHeight() / 2 - 10);
    g.setColor(Color.red);
    g.drawOval(getWidth() / 2 + 5, 5, getWidth() / 2 - 10,
      getHeight() / 2 - 10);
    g.setColor(Color.yellow);
    g.fillOval(5, getHeight() / 2 + 5, getWidth() / 2 - 10,
      getHeight() / 2 - 10);
    g.setColor(Color.orange);
    g.fillOval(getWidth() / 2 + 5, getHeight() / 2 + 5,
      getWidth() / 2 - 10, getHeight() / 2-10);
  }
}
```

10.9.4   Drawing Arcs

Like an oval, an arc is drawn based on its bounding rectangle. An arc is conceived as part of an oval. The methods to draw or fill an arc are as follows:

```
drawArc(x, y, w, h, angle1, angle2);
fillArc(x, y, w, h, angle1, angle2);
```

Parameters x, y, w, and h are the same as in the drawOval method; parameter angle1 is the starting angle; angle2 is the spanning angle (i.e., the angle covered by the arc). Angles are measured in degrees and follow the usual mathematical conventions (i.e., 0 degrees is at 3 o'clock, and positive angles indicate counterclockwise rotation; see Figure 10.22).

Shown below is an example of how to draw arcs; the output is shown in Figure 10.23.

```
// TestArcs.java: Demonstrate drawing arcs
import javax.swing.JFrame;
import javax.swing.JPanel;
```

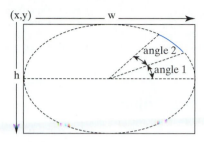

Figure 10.22   *The* drawArc *method draws an arc based on an oval with specified angles.*

   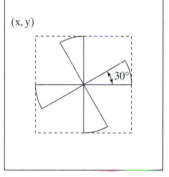

Figure 10.23   *The program draws four filled arcs.*

```
import java.awt.Color;
import java.awt.Graphics;

public class TestArcs extends JFrame {
  /** Default constructor */
  public TestArcs() {
    setTitle("Show Arcs");
    getContentPane().add(new ArcsPanel());
  }

  /** Main method */
  public static void main(String[] args) {
    TestArcs frame = new TestArcs();
    frame.setDefaultCloseOperation(JFrame.EXIT_ON_CLOSE);
    frame.setSize(250, 300);
    frame.setVisible(true);
  }
}

// The class for drawing arcs on a panel
class ArcsPanel extends JPanel {
  // Draw four blazes of a fan
  public void paintComponent(Graphics g) {
    super.paintComponent(g);

    int xCenter = getWidth() / 2;
    int yCenter = getHeight() / 2;
    int radius =
      (int)(Math.min(getWidth(), getHeight()) * 0.4);

    int x = xCenter - radius;
    int y = yCenter - radius;
```

```
            g.fillArc(x, y, 2 * radius, 2 * radius, 0, 30);
            g.fillArc(x, y, 2 * radius, 2 * radius, 90, 30);
            g.fillArc(x, y, 2 * radius, 2 * radius, 180, 30);
            g.fillArc(x, y, 2 * radius, 2 * radius, 270, 30);
      }
  }
```

10.9.5   Drawing Polygons

The Polygon class encapsulates a description of a closed, two-dimensional region within a coordinate space. This region is bounded by an arbitrary number of line segments, each of which is one side (or edge) of the polygon. Internally, a polygon comprises a list of (x, y) coordinate pairs in which each pair defines a vertex of the polygon, and two successive pairs are the endpoints of a line that is a side of the polygon. The first and final pairs of (x, y) points are joined by a line segment that closes the polygon.

Java enables you to draw a polygon in two ways: by using the direct method or by using the Polygon object.

The direct method draws a polygon by specifying all the points, using the following two methods:

```
drawPolygon(x, y, n);
fillPolygon(x, y, n);
```

Parameters x and y are arrays representing x-coordinates and y-coordinates, and n indicates the number of points. For example:

```
int x[] = {40, 70, 60, 45, 20};
int y[] = {20, 40, 80, 45, 60};
g.drawPolygon(x, y, x.length);
g.fillPolygon(x, y, x.length);
```

The drawing method opens the polygon by drawing lines between point (x[i], y[i]) and point (x[i+1], y[i+1]) for i = 0, . . . , length-1; it closes the polygon by drawing a line between the first and last points (see Figure 10.24).

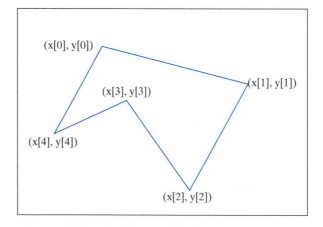

Figure 10.24   *The* drawPolygon *method draws a polygon with specified points.*

You can also draw a polygon by creating a `Polygon` object, adding points to it, and displaying it. To create a `Polygon` object, use

```
Polygon poly = new Polygon();
```

or

```
Polygon poly = new Polygon(x, y, n);
```

Parameters `x`, `y`, and `n` are the same as in the previous `drawPolygon` method. Here is an example of how to draw a polygon in `Graphics g`:

```
Polygon polygon = new Polygon();
polygon.addPoint(20, 30);
polygon.addPoint(40, 40);
polygon.addPoint(50, 50);
g.drawPolygon(poly);
```

The `addPoint` method adds a point to the polygon. The `drawPolygon` method also takes a `Polygon` object as a parameter.

Next is an example of how to draw a polygon, with the output shown in Figure 10.25.

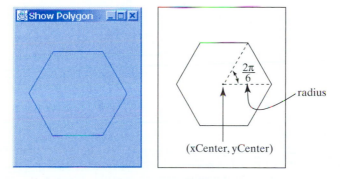

Figure 10.25   *The program uses the* `drawPolygon` *method to draw a polygon.*

```
// TestPolygon.java: Demonstrate drawing polygons
import javax.swing.JFrame;
import javax.swing.JPanel;
import java.awt.Graphics;
import java.awt.Polygon;

public class TestPolygon extends JFrame {
  /** Default constructor */
  public TestPolygon() {
    setTitle("Show Polygon");
    getContentPane().add(new PolygonsPanel());
  }

  /** Main method */
  public static void main(String[] args) {
    TestPolygon frame = new TestPolygon();
    frame.setDefaultCloseOperation(JFrame.EXIT_ON_CLOSE);
    frame.setSize(200, 250);
    frame.setVisible(true);
  }
}
```

```
// Draw a polygon in the panel
class PolygonsPanel extends JPanel {
  public void paintComponent(Graphics g) {
    super.paintComponent(g);

    int xCenter = getWidth() / 2;
    int yCenter = getHeight() / 2;
    int radius =
      (int)(Math.min(getWidth(), getHeight()) * 0.4);

    // Create a Polygon object
    Polygon polygon = new Polygon();

    // Add points to the polygon
    polygon.addPoint(xCenter + radius, yCenter);
    polygon.addPoint((int)(xCenter + radius *
      Math.cos(2 * Math.PI / 6)), (int)(yCenter - radius *
      Math.sin(2 * Math.PI / 6)));
    polygon.addPoint((int)(xCenter + radius *
      Math.cos(2 * 2 * Math.PI / 6)), (int)(yCenter - radius *
      Math.sin(2 * 2 * Math.PI / 6)));
    polygon.addPoint((int)(xCenter + radius *
      Math.cos(3 * 2 * Math.PI / 6)), (int)(yCenter - radius *
      Math.sin(3 * 2 * Math.PI / 6)));
    polygon.addPoint((int)(xCenter + radius *
      Math.cos(4 * 2 * Math.PI / 6)), (int)(yCenter - radius *
      Math.sin(4 * 2 * Math.PI / 6)));
    polygon.addPoint((int)(xCenter + radius *
      Math.cos(5 * 2 * Math.PI / 6)), (int)(yCenter - radius *
      Math.sin(5 * 2 * Math.PI / 6)));

    // Draw the polygon
    g.drawPolygon(polygon);
  }
}
```

NOTE

Prior to JDK 1.1, a polygon was a sequence of lines that were not necessarily closed. But in JDK 1.1, a polygon is always closed. Nevertheless, you can draw an unclosed polygon by using the drawPolyline(int[] x, int[] y, int nPoints) method, which draws a sequence of connected lines defined by arrays of x and y coordinates. The figure is not closed if the first point differs from the last point.

10.10   Case Studies

This case study presents an example that uses several drawing methods and trigonometric methods to draw a clock showing the current time in a frame. To draw a clock, you need to draw a circle and three hands for second, minute, and hour. To draw a hand, you need to specify the two ends of the line. As shown in Figure 10.26, one end is the center of the clock at (xCenter, yCenter); the other end, at (xEnd, yEnd), is determined by the following formula:

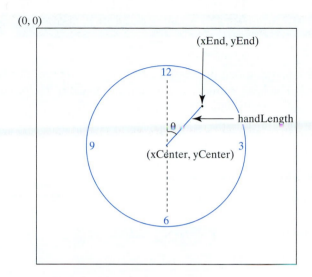

Figure 10.26   *The end point of a clock hand can be determined given the spanning angle, the hand length, and the center point.*

```
xEnd = xCenter + handLength × sin(θ)
yEnd = yCenter - handLength × cos(θ)
```

Angle θ is in radians. Let `second`, `minute`, and `hour` denote the current second, minute, and hour.

Since there are sixty seconds in one minute, the angle for the second hand is

```
second × (2π/60)
```

The position of the minute hand is determined by the minute and second. The exact minute value combined with seconds is `minute + second/60`. For example, if the time is 3 minutes and 30 seconds. The total minutes are 3.5. Since there are sixty minutes in one hour, the angle for the minute hand is

```
(minute + second/60) × (2π/60)
```

Since one circle is divided into twelve hours, the angle for the hour hand is

```
(hour + minute/60 + second/(60 × 60))) × (2π/12)
```

For simplicity, you can omit the seconds in computing the angles of the minute hand and the hour hand, since they are very small and can be neglected. Therefore the end points for the second hand, minute hand, and hour hand can be computed as:

```
xSecond = xCenter + secondHandLength × sin(second × (2π/60))
ySecond = yCenter - secondHandLength × cos(second × (2π/60))
xMinute = xCenter + minuteHandLength × sin(minute × (2π/60))
yMinute = yCenter - minuteHandLength × cos(minute × (2π/60))
xHour = xCenter + hourHandLength × sin((hour + minute/60) × (2π/60)))
yHour = yCenter - hourHandLength × cos((hour + minute/60) × (2π/60)))
```

Example 10.6 Drawing a Clock

Problem

Write a program that displays a clock based on the specified hour, minute, and second. The hour, minute, and second are passed to the program as command-line arguments like this:

```
java DisplayClock hour minute second
```

For example, if you run the program using

```
java DisplayClock 4 30 45
```

the output is shown in Figure 10.27.

Figure 10.27   *The program displays a clock that shows the time with the specified hour, minute, and second.*

Solution

Here are the steps in the program:

1. Create a panel named `DrawClock` to display the clock with the specified hour, minute, and second. The `hour`, `minute`, and `second` are defined as the data fields in `DrawClock`. The `paintComponent` method draws the clock and the hour, minute, and hands on the clock.

2. Create a frame named `DisplayClock` that extends `JFrame`. The `main` method in `DisplayClock` can take three arguments (hour, minute, and second), two arguments (hour and minute), one argument (hour), or no arguments. By default, hour, minute, and second are 0. The values of hour, minute, and second are passed as arguments to the constructor of `DrawClock` to create a `DrawClock` object with the specified hour, minute, and second. The `DrawClock` object is placed in the content pane of `DisplayClock` to display the clock in the frame.

```
1    // DrawClock.java: Display a clock in JPanel
2    import java.awt.*;
3    import javax.swing.*;
4
```

```
5    public class DrawClock extends JPanel {
6      private int hour;
7      private int minute;
8      private int second;
9      protected int xCenter, yCenter;
10     protected int clockRadius;
11
12     /** Construct a clock panel */
13     public DrawClock(int hour, int minute, int second) {
14       this.hour = hour;
15       this.minute = minute;
16       this.second = second;
17     }
18
19     /** Draw the clock */
20     public void paintComponent(Graphics g) {
21       super.paintComponent(g);
22
23       // Initialize clock parameters
24       clockRadius =
25         (int)(Math.min(getWidth(), getHeight()) * 0.8 * 0.5);
26       xCenter = (getWidth()) / 2;
27       yCenter = (getHeight()) / 2;
28
29       // Draw circle
30       g.setColor(Color.black);
31       g.drawOval(xCenter - clockRadius,yCenter - clockRadius,
32         2 * clockRadius, 2 * clockRadius);
33       g.drawString("12", xCenter - 5, yCenter - clockRadius + 12);
34       g.drawString("9", xCenter - clockRadius + 3, yCenter + 5);
35       g.drawString("3", xCenter + clockRadius - 10, yCenter + 3);
36       g.drawString("6", xCenter - 3, yCenter + clockRadius - 3);
37
38       // Draw second hand
39       int sLength = (int)(clockRadius * 0.8);
40       int xSecond = (int)(xCenter + sLength *
41         Math.sin(second * (2 * Math.PI / 60)));
42       int ySecond = (int)(yCenter - sLength *
43         Math.cos(second * (2 * Math.PI / 60)));
44       g.setColor(Color.red);
45       g.drawLine(xCenter, yCenter, xSecond, ySecond);
46
47       // Draw minute hand
48       int mLength = (int)(clockRadius * 0.65);
49       int xMinute = (int)(xCenter + mLength *
50         Math.sin(minute * (2 * Math.PI / 60)));
51       int yMinute = (int)(yCenter - mLength *
52         Math.cos(minute * (2 * Math.PI / 60)));
53       g.setColor(Color.blue);
54       g.drawLine(xCenter, yCenter, xMinute, yMinute);
55
56       // Draw hour hand
57       int hLength = (int)(clockRadius * 0.5);
58       int xHour = (int)(xCenter + hLength *
59         Math.sin((hour + minute / 60.0) * (2 * Math.PI / 12)));
60       int yHour = (int)(yCenter - hLength *
61         Math.cos((hour + minute / 60.0) * (2 * Math.PI / 12)));
62       g.setColor(Color.green);
63       g.drawLine(xCenter, yCenter, xHour, yHour);
64
65       // Display current time in string
66       g.setColor(Color.red);
```

continues

Example 10.6 Drawing a Clock

```
67        String time = "Hour: " + hour + " Minute: " + minute +
68          " Second: " + second;
69        FontMetrics fm = g.getFontMetrics();
70        g.drawString(time, (getWidth() -
71          fm.stringWidth(time)) / 2, yCenter+clockRadius + 30);
72    }
73  }
```

```
1   // DisplayClock.java: Display a clock in a panel
2   import java.awt.*;
3   import javax.swing.*;
4
5   public class DisplayClock extends JFrame {
6     /** Main method to display hour, minute and hour
7         @param args[0] hour
8         @param args[1] minute
9         @param args[2] second
10    */
11    public static void main(String[] args) {
12      // Declare hour, minute, and second values
13      int hour = 0;
14      int minute = 0;
15      int second = 0;
16
17      // Check usage and get hour, minute, second
18      if (args.length > 3) {
19        System.out.println(
20          "Usage: java DisplayClock hour minute second");
21        System.exit(0);
22      }
23      else if (args.length == 3) {
24        hour = new Integer(args[0]).intValue();
25        minute = new Integer(args[1]).intValue();
26        second = new Integer(args[2]).intValue();
27      }
28      else if (args.length == 2) {
29        hour = new Integer(args[0]).intValue();
30        minute = new Integer(args[1]).intValue();
31      }
32      else if (args.length == 1) {
33        hour = new Integer(args[0]).intValue();
34      }
35
36      // Create a frame to hold the clock
37      DisplayClock frame = new DisplayClock();
38      frame.setTitle("Display Clock");
39      frame.getContentPane().add(new DrawClock(hour, minute, second));
40      frame.setDefaultCloseOperation(JFrame.EXIT_ON_CLOSE);
41      frame.setSize(300, 350);
42      frame.setVisible(true);
43    }
44  }
```

Review

The DisplayClock class obtains command-line arguments for hour, minute, and second, and uses this information to create an instance of DrawClock (Line 39). DrawClock is responsible for drawing the clock in a panel.

The program enables the clock size to adjust as the frame resizes. Every time you resize the frame, the paintComponent method is automatically invoked to paint the new frame. The paintComponent method displays the clock in proportion to the frame size (Lines 24–27 in DrawClock).

The numeric time (consisting of hour, minute, and second) is displayed below the clock. The program uses font metrics to determine the size of the time string and display it in the center (Lines 65–71 in DrawClock).

10.11 Event-Driven Programming

All the programs you have written so far are object-oriented but executed in a procedural order. You used decision and loop statements to control the flow of execution, but the program dictated the flow of execution. Java GUI programming is event-driven. In event-driven programming, code is executed when an event occurs—a button click, perhaps, or a mouse movement. This section introduces the Java event model.

10.11.1 Event and Event Source

When you run Java GUI programs, the program interacts with the user and the events drive its execution. An *event* can be defined as a signal to the program that something has happened. The event is generated either by external user actions, such as mouse movements, mouse button clicks, and keystrokes, or by the operating system, such as a timer. The program can choose to respond to or ignore the event.

The GUI component on which an event is generated is called the *source object*. For example, a button is the source object for a button-clicking action event. An event is an instance of an event class. The root class of the event classes is java.util.EventObject. The hierarchical relationships of the event classes used in this book are shown in Figure 10.28.

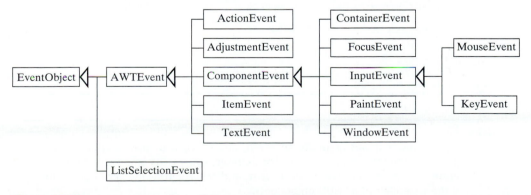

Figure 10.28 *An event is an object of the* EventObject *class.*

An event object contains whatever properties are pertinent to the event. You can identify the source object of the event using the getSource() instance method in the EventObject class. The subclasses of EventObject deal with special types of events, such as button actions, window events, component events, mouse movements, and keystrokes. Table 10.1 lists external user actions, source objects, and event types generated.

TABLE 10.1   User Action, Source Object, and Event Type

User Action	Source Object	Event Type Generated
Click a button	JButton	ActionEvent
Change text	JTextComponent	TextEvent
Press return on a text field	JTextField	ActionEvent
Select a new item	JComboBox	ItemEvent, ActionEvent
Select item(s)	JList	ListSelectionEvent
Click a check box	JCheckBox	ItemEvent, ActionEvent
Click a radio button	JRadioButton	ItemEvent, ActionEvent
Select a menu item	JMenuItem	ActionEvent
Move the scroll bar	JScrollBar	AdjustmentEvent
Window opened, closed, iconified, deiconified, or closing	Window	WindowEvent
Component added or removed from the container	Container	ContainerEvent
Component moved, resized, hidden, or shown	Component	ComponentEvent
Component gained or lost focus	Component	FocusEvent
Key released or pressed	Component	KeyEvent
Mouse pressed, released, clicked, entered, or exited	Component	MouseEvent
Mouse moved or dragged	Component	MouseEvent

NOTE

If a component can generate an event, any subclass of the component can generate the same type of event. For example, every GUI component can generate MouseEvent, KeyEvent, FocusEvent, and ComponentEvent, since Component is the superclass of all GUI components.

> **Note**
>
> All the event classes in Figure 10.28 are included in the `java.awt.event` package except `ListSelectionEvent`, which is in the `javax.swing.event` package. The AWT events were originally designed for AWT components, but many Swing components fire them.

10.11.2   Event Registration, Listening, and Handling

Java uses a delegation-based model for event handling: an external user action on a source object triggers an event, and an object interested in the event receives the event. The latter object is called a *listener*. Not every object can receive events. To become a listener, an object must be registered as a listener by the source object. The source object maintains a list of listeners and notifies all the registered listeners by invoking the event-handling method, known as the *handler*, on the listener object to respond to the event, as shown in Figure 10.29.

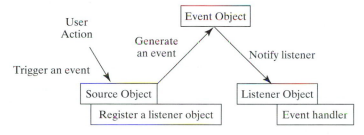

Figure 10.29   *An event is triggered by user actions on the source object; the source object generates the event object and invokes the handler of the listener object to process the event.*

For example, if a `JFrame` object is interested in the external events on a `JButton` source object, it must register with the `JButton` object. The registration is done by invoking a method from the `JButton` object to declare that the `JFrame` object is a listener for the `JButton` object. When you click the button, the `JButton` object generates an `ActionEvent` and notifies the listener by invoking a method defined in the listener to handle the event.

> **Note**
>
> A source object and a listener object may be the same. A source object can listen for its own events. A source object may have many listeners. It maintains a queue for them.

Registration methods are dependent on event type. For `ActionEvent`, the method is `addActionListener`. In general, the method is named `addXListener` for `XEvent`.

To become a listener, the listener must implement the standard handler. The handler is defined in the corresponding event-listener interface. Java provides a listener interface for every type of GUI event. For example, the corresponding listener interface for `ActionEvent` is `ActionListener`; each listener for `ActionEvent` should implement the `ActionListener` interface.

Table 10.2 lists event types, the corresponding listener interfaces, and the methods defined in the listener interfaces.

TABLE 10.2   Events, Event Listeners, and Listener Methods

Event Class	Listener Interface	Listener Method (Handler)
ActionEvent	ActionListener	actionPerformed(ActionEvent e)
ItemEvent	ItemListener	itemStateChanged(ItemEvent e)
WindowEvent	WindowListener	windowClosing(WindowEvent e)
		windowOpened(WindowEvent e)
		windowIconified(WindowEvent e)
		windowDeiconified(WindowEvent e)
		windowClosed(WindowEvent e)
		windowActivated(WindowEvent e)
		windowDeactivated(WindowEvent e)
ContainerEvent	ContainerListener	componentAdded(ContainerEvent e)
		componentRemoved(ContainerEvent e)
ComponentEvent	ComponentListener	componentMoved(ComponentEvent e)
		componentHidden(ComponentEvent e)
		componentResized(ComponentEvent e)
		componentShown(ComponentEvent e)
FocusEvent	FocusListener	focusGained(FocusEvent e)
		focusLost(FocusEvent e)
TextEvent	TextListener	textValueChanged(TextEvent e)
KeyEvent	KeyListener	keyPressed(KeyEvent e)
		keyReleased(KeyEvent e)
		keyTyped(KeyEvent e)
MouseEvent	MouseListener	mousePressed(MouseEvent e)
		mouseReleased(MouseEvent e)
		mouseEntered(MouseEvent e)
		mouseExited(MouseEvent e)
		mouseClicked(MouseEvent e)
	MouseMotionListener	mouseDragged(MouseEvent e)
		mouseMoved(MouseEvent e)
AdjustmentEvent	AdjustmentListener	adjustmentValueChanged
		(AdjustmentEvent e)

> **NOTE**
>
> In general, the listener interface is named *XListener* for *XEvent*, except for MouseMotionListener.

10.11.3   Handling Events

A listener object must implement the corresponding listener interface. For example, a listener for a JButton source object must implement the ActionListener interface. The ActionListener interface contains the actionPerformed(ActionEvent e) method. This method must be implemented in the listener class. Upon receiving notification, it is executed to handle the event.

An event object is passed to the handling method. The event object contains information pertinent to the event type. You can get useful data values from the event object for processing the event. For example, you can use e.getSource() to obtain the source object in order to determine whether it is a button, a check box, a radio button, or a menu item.

Three examples of the use of event handling are given below. The first is for ActionEvent, the second for WindowEvent, and the third involves multiple listeners for a source.

Example 10.7   Handling Simple Action Events

Problem

Write a program that displays two buttons, OK and Cancel, in the window. A message is displayed on the console to indicate which button is clicked, as shown in Figure 10.30.

Figure 10.30   *The program responds to the button action events.*

Solution

Here are the steps in the program:

1. Create a listener class named ButtonListener for handling ActionEvent on the buttons. This class implements the ActionListener interface.

2. Create a test program named TestActionEvent that extends JFrame. Add two buttons to the frame and create a listener object from ButtonListener. Register the listener with the buttons.

continues

Example 10.7 continued

```java
1    // TestActionEvent.java: Test ActionEvent
2    import javax.swing.*;
3    import java.awt.*;
4    import java.awt.event.*;
5
6    public class TestActionEvent extends JFrame {
7      // Create two buttons
8      private JButton jbtOk = new JButton("OK");
9      private JButton jbtCancel = new JButton("Cancel");
10
11     /** Default constructor */
12     public TestActionEvent() {
13       // Set the window title
14       setTitle("TestActionEvent");
15
16       // Set FlowLayout manager to arrange the components
17       // inside the frame
18       getContentPane().setLayout(new FlowLayout());
19
20       // Add buttons to the frame
21       getContentPane().add(jbtOk);
22       getContentPane().add(jbtCancel);
23
24       // Create a listener object
25       ButtonListener btListener = new ButtonListener();
26
27       // Register listeners
28       jbtOk.addActionListener(btListener);
29       jbtCancel.addActionListener(btListener);
30     }
31
32     /** Main method */
33     public static void main(String[] args) {
34       TestActionEvent frame = new TestActionEvent();
35       frame.setDefaultCloseOperation(JFrame.EXIT_ON_CLOSE);
36       frame.setSize(100, 80);
37       frame.setVisible(true);
38     }
39   }
40
41   class ButtonListener implements ActionListener {
42     /** This method will be invoked when a button is clicked */
43     public void actionPerformed(ActionEvent e) {
44       if (e.getActionCommand().equals("OK")) {
45         System.out.println("The OK button is clicked");
46       }
47       else if (e.getActionCommand().equals("Cancel")) {
48         System.out.println("The Cancel button is clicked");
49       }
50     }
51   }
```

Review

The button objects jbtOk and jbtCancel are the source of ActionEvent. The ButtonListener class defines the listeners for the buttons, and its instance btListener is registered with the buttons (Lines 28–29).

Clicking a button causes the `actionPerformed` method in `btListener` to be invoked. The `e.getActionCommand()` method returns the action command from the button. By default, a button's action command is the text of the button. You can use the action event to determine which button has been clicked.

The `TestActionEvent` class itself can be a listener class. You can rewrite the program as follows:

```java
// TestActionEvent.java: Test ActionEvent
import javax.swing.*;
import java.awt.*;
import java.awt.event.*;

public class TestActionEvent extends JFrame
  implements ActionListener {
  // Create two buttons
  private JButton jbtOk = new JButton("OK");
  private JButton jbtCancel = new JButton("Cancel");

  /** Default constructor */
  public TestActionEvent() {
    // Set the window title
    setTitle("TestActionEvent");

    // Set FlowLayout manager to arrange the components
    // inside the frame
    getContentPane().setLayout(new FlowLayout());

    // Add buttons to the frame
    getContentPane().add(jbtOk);
    getContentPane().add(jbtCancel);

    // Register listeners
    jbtOk.addActionListener(this);
    jbtCancel.addActionListener(this);
  }

  /** Main method */
  public static void main(String[] args) {
    TestActionEvent frame = new TestActionEvent();
    frame.setDefaultCloseOperation(JFrame.EXIT_ON_CLOSE);
    frame.setSize(100, 80);
    frame.setVisible(true);
  }

  /** This method will be invoked when a button is clicked */
  public void actionPerformed(ActionEvent e) {
    if (e.getSource() == jbtOk) {
      System.out.println("The OK button is clicked");
    }
    else if (e.getSource() == jbtCancel) {
      System.out.println("The Cancel button is clicked");
    }
  }
}
```

The statements

```java
jbtOk.addActionListener(this);
jbtCancel.addActionListener(this);
```

continues

423

Example 10.7 continued

register this (referring to TestActionEvent) to listen to ActionEvent on jbtOk and jbtCancel.

e.getSource() returns the source of the event and can be used to determine which button is clicked.

CAUTION

Missing listener registration is a common mistake in event handling. If the source object doesn't notify the listener, the listener cannot act on the event.

Example 10.8 Handling Window Events

Problem

Write a program that demonstrates handling window events.

Solution

Any subclass of the Window class can generate the following window events: window opened, closing, closed, activated, deactivated, iconified, and deiconified. This program creates a frame, listens to the window events, and displays a message to indicate the occurring event. Figure 10.31 shows a sample run of the program.

Figure 10.31   *The window events are displayed on the console when you run the program from a DOS prompt.*

```
1    // TestWindowEvent.java: Create a frame to test window events
2    import java.awt.*;
3    import java.awt.event.*;
4    import javax.swing.JFrame;
5
6    public class TestWindowEvent extends JFrame
7      implements WindowListener {
8      // Main method
9      public static void main(String[] args) {
10       TestWindowEvent frame = new TestWindowEvent();
11       frame.setDefaultCloseOperation(JFrame.EXIT_ON_CLOSE);
```

```
12          frame.setTitle("Test Window Event");
13          frame.setSize(100, 80);
14          frame.setVisible(true);
15        }
16
17        /** Default constructor */
18        public TestWindowEvent() {
19          addWindowListener(this);   // Register listener
20        }
21
22        /**
23         * Handler for window deiconified event
24         * Invoked when a window is changed from a minimized
25         * to a normal state.
26         */
27        public void windowDeiconified(WindowEvent event) {
28          System.out.println("Window deiconified");
29        }
30
31        /**
32         * Handler for window iconified event
33         * Invoked when a window is changed from a normal to a
34         * minimized state. For many platforms, a minimized window
35         * is displayed as the icon specified in the window's
36         * iconImage property.
37         * @see Frame#setIconImage
38         */
39        public void windowIconified(WindowEvent event) {
40          System.out.println("Window iconified");
41        }
42
43        /**
44         * Handler for window activated event
45         * Invoked when the window is set to be the user's
46         * active window, which means the window (or one of its
47         * subcomponents) will receive keyboard events.
48         */
49        public void windowActivated(WindowEvent event) {
50          System.out.println("Window activated");
51        }
52
53        /**
54         * Handler for window deactivated event
55         * Invoked when a window is no longer the user's active
56         * window, which means that keyboard events will no longer
57         * be delivered to the window or its subcomponents.
58         */
59        public void windowDeactivated(WindowEvent event) {
60          System.out.println("Window deactivated");
61        }
62
63        /**
64         * Handler for window opened event
65         * Invoked the first time a window is made visible.
66         */
67        public void windowOpened(WindowEvent event) {
68          System.out.println("Window opened");
69        }
70
71        /**
72         * Handler for window closing event
73         * Invoked when the user attempts to close the window
```

continues

Example 10.8 continued

```
74       * from the window's system menu.  If the program does not
75       * explicitly hide or dispose the window while processing
76       * this event, the window close operation will be cancelled.
77       */
78      public void windowClosing(WindowEvent event) {
79        System.out.println("Window closing");
80      }
81
82      /**
83       * Handler for window closed event
84       * Invoked when a window has been closed as the result
85       * of calling dispose on the window.
86       */
87      public void windowClosed(WindowEvent event) {
88        System.out.println("Window closed");
89      }
90    }
```

Review

The WindowEvent can be generated by the Window class or any subclass of Window. Since JFrame is a subclass of Window, it can generate WindowEvent.

TestWindowEvent extends JFrame and implements WindowListener. The WindowListener interface defines several abstract methods (windowActivated, windowClosed, windowClosing, windowDeactivated, windowDeiconified, window-Iconified, windowOpened) for handling window events when the window is activated, closed, closing, deactivated, deiconified, iconified, or opened.

When a window event, such as activation, occurs, the windowActivated method is triggered. Implement the windowActivated method with a concrete response if you want the event to be processed.

Because the methods in the WindowListener interface are abstract, you must implement all of them even if your program does not care about some of the events.

For an object to receive event notification, it must register as an event listener. addWindowListener(this) (Line 19) registers the object of TestWindowEvent as a window-event listener so that it can receive notification about the window event. TestWindowEvent is both a listener and a source object.

Example 10.9 Multiple Listeners for a Single Source

Problem

Write a program that modifies Example 10.7 to add a new listener for each button. This example creates a new listener class as an additional listener for the action events on the buttons. When a button is clicked, both listeners respond to the action event.

Solution

The following code gives the solution to the problem. Figure 10.32 shows a sample run of the program.

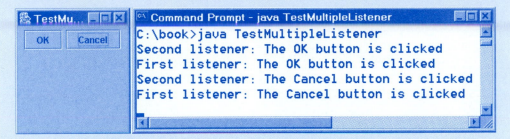

Figure 10.32   *Both listeners respond to the button action events]*

```
1    // TestMultipleListener.java: Test multiple listeners
2    import javax.swing.*;
3    import java.awt.*;
4    import java.awt.event.*;
5
6    public class TestMultipleListener extends JFrame
7      implements ActionListener {
8      // Create two buttons
9      private JButton jbtOk = new JButton("OK");
10     private JButton jbtCancel = new JButton("Cancel");
11
12     /** Default constructor */
13     public TestMultipleListener() {
14       // Set the window title
15       setTitle("TestMultipleListener");
16
17       // Set FlowLayout manager to arrange the components
18       // inside the frame
19       getContentPane().setLayout(new FlowLayout());
20
21       // Add buttons to the frame
22       getContentPane().add(jbtOk);
23       getContentPane().add(jbtCancel);
24
25       // Register the frame as listeners
26       jbtOk.addActionListener(this);
27       jbtCancel.addActionListener(this);
28
29       // Register a second listener for buttons
30       SecondListener secondListener = new SecondListener();
31       jbtOk.addActionListener(secondListener);
32       jbtCancel.addActionListener(secondListener);
33     }
34
35     /** Main method */
36     public static void main(String[] args) {
37       TestMultipleListener frame = new TestMultipleListener();
38       frame.setDefaultCloseOperation(JFrame.EXIT_ON_CLOSE);
39       frame.setSize(100, 80);
40       frame.setVisible(true);
41     }
42
```

continues

Example 10.9 continued

```
43        /** This method will be invoked when a button is clicked */
44        public void actionPerformed(ActionEvent e) {
45          System.out.print("First listener: ");
46
47          if (e.getSource() == jbtOk) {
48            System.out.println("The OK button is clicked");
49          }
50          else if (e.getSource() == jbtCancel) {
51            System.out.println("The Cancel button is clicked");
52          }
53        }
54      }
55
56      /** The class for the second listener */
57      class SecondListener implements ActionListener {
58        /** Handle ActionEvent */
59        public void actionPerformed(ActionEvent e) {
60          System.out.print("Second listener: ");
61
62          // A button has an actionCommand property, which is same as the
63          // text of the button by default.
64          if (e.getActionCommand().equals("OK")) {
65            System.out.println("The OK button is clicked");
66          }
67          else if (e.getActionCommand().equals("Cancel")) {
68            System.out.println("The Cancel button is clicked");
69          }
70        }
71      }
```

Review

Each source object in the preceding two examples has a single listener. Each button in this example has two listeners: one is an instance of TestMultiple-Listener, and the other is an instance of SecondListener.

When a button is clicked, both listeners are notified and their respective actionPerformed methods are invoked. Using this method can detect which button is clicked. If you want to use the getSource method to detect which button is clicked, see Exercise 10.18.

The source object maintains a list of all its listeners. When a listener is registered with the source object, it is added at the top of the list. When an event occurs, the source object notifies the listener objects on the list by invoking each listener's handler. In this case, the handler is the actionPerformed method.

What would happen if you replaced the highlighted code in the example with the following code?

```
// Register a second listener for buttons
jbtOk.addActionListener(new SecondListener(this));
jbtCancel.addActionListener(new SecondListener(this));
```

Two instances of SecondListener would be created. The program would run just as before the change, but the change is obviously not good.

Chapter Summary

In this chapter, you learned Java GUI programming using the container classes, UI component classes, and helper classes.

The container classes (e.g., JFrame, JPanel, JApplet) are used to contain other components. The UI component classes (e.g., JButton, JTextField, JTextArea, JComboBox, JList, JRadioButton, JMenu) are subclasses of JComponent. They are used to facilitate user interactions. These classes are referred to as Swing UI components and are grouped in the javax.swing package.

The helper classes (e.g., Graphics, Color, Font, FontMetrics, Dimension, Layout-Manager) are used by components and containers to draw and place objects. These classes are grouped in the java.awt package.

You learned how to override the paintComponent method to display graphics and to draw strings and simple shapes using the drawing methods in the Graphics class.

Java GUI programming is event-driven. The code is executed when events are activated. An event is generated by user actions, such as mouse movements, keystrokes, or clicking buttons. Java uses a delegation-based model to register listeners and handle events. External user actions on the source object generate events. The source object notifies listener objects of events by invoking the handlers implemented by the listener class.

Review Questions

10.1 Describe the Java GUI class hierarchy.

10.2 Describe the methods in Component, Frame, JFrame, JComponent, and JPanel.

10.3 Explain the difference between AWT UI components, such as java.awt.Button, and Swing components, such as javax.swing.JButton.

10.4 How do you create a frame? How do you set the size for the frame? How do you get the size of a frame? How do you add components to the frame? What would happen if the statements frame.setSize(400, 300) and frame.setVisible(true) were swapped in the MyFrameWithComponents class in Section 10.3.3, "Adding Components to a Frame"?

10.5 Determine whether the following statements are true or false:

- You can add a component to a button.

- You can add a button to a frame.

- You can add a frame to a panel.

- You can add a panel to a frame.

- You can add any number of components to a panel, a frame, or an applet.

- You can derive a class from JPanel, JFrame, or JApplet.

10.6   Why do you need to use the layout managers? What is the default layout manager for the content pane of a frame? What is the default layout manager for a `JPanel`?

10.7   Can you use the `setTitle` method in a panel? What is the purpose of using a panel?

10.8   Describe `FlowLayout`. How do you create a `FlowLayout` manager? How do you add a component to a `FlowLayout` container? Is there a limit to the number of components that can be added to a `FlowLayout` container?

10.9   Describe `GridLayout`. How do you create a `GridLayout` manager? How do you add a component to a `GridLayout` container? Is there a limit to the number of components that can be added to a `GridLayout` container?

10.10   Describe `BorderLayout`. How do you create a `BorderLayout` manager? How do you add a component to a `BorderLayout` container? Can you add multiple components in the same section?

10.11   Suppose that you want to draw a new message below an existing message. Should the x, y coordinate increase or decrease?

10.12   How do you set colors and fonts in a graphics context? How do you find the current color and font style?

10.13   Describe the methods for drawing lines, rectangles, ovals, arcs, and polygons.

10.14   Write a statement to draw the following shapes:

- Draw a thick line from (10, 10) to (70, 30). You can draw several lines next to each other to create the effect of one thick line.

- Draw a rectangle of width 100 and height 50 with the upper-left corner at (10, 10).

- Draw a rounded rectangle with width 100, height 200, corner horizontal diameter 40, and corner vertical diameter 20.

- Draw a circle with radius 30.

- Draw an oval with width 50 and height 100.

- Draw the upper half of a circle with radius 50.

- Draw a polygon connecting the following points: (20, 40), (30, 50), (40, 90), (90, 10), (10, 30).

- Draw a 3D cube like the one in Figure 10.33.

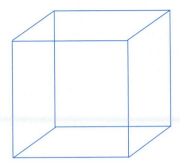

Figure 10.33   *Use the* `drawLine` *method to draw a 3D cube.*

10.15 Can a button generate a `WindowEvent`? Can a button generate a `MouseEvent`? Can a button generate an `ActionEvent`?

10.16 Explain how to register a listener object and how to implement a listener interface.

10.17 What information is contained in an `AWTEvent` object and the objects of its subclasses? Find the variables, constants, and methods defined in these event classes.

10.18 How do you override a method defined in the listener interface? Do you need to override all the methods defined in the listener interface?

10.19 Describe the `paintComponent` method. Where is it defined? How is it invoked? Can you use the `paintComponent` method to draw things directly on a frame?

Programming Exercises

10.1 Write a program that meets the following requirements (see Figure 10.34):

■ Create a frame and set its content pane's layout to `FlowLayout`.

■ Create two panels and add the panels to the frame.

■ Each panel contains three buttons. The panel uses `FlowLayout`.

■ When a button is clicked, display a message on the console indicating that a button has been clicked. (Do this part after finishing Section 10.11, "Event-Driven Programming.")

Figure 10.34   *The first three buttons are placed in one panel, and the remaining three buttons are placed in another panel.*

10.2 Rewrite the preceding program to create the same user interface. Instead of using FlowLayout for the frame's content pane, use BorderLayout. Place one panel in the south of the content pane, and the other panel in the center of the content pane.

10.3 Rewrite the preceding program to create the same user interface. Instead of using FlowLayout for the panels, use a GridLayout of two rows and three columns.

10.4 Rewrite the preceding program to create the same user interface. Instead of creating buttons and panels separately, define the panel class that extends the JPanel class. Place three buttons in your panel class, and create two panels from the user-defined panel class.

10.5 Write a program that uses the MessagePanel class in Example 10.5 to display a centered message in red, SansSerif, italic, and 20-point size.

10.6 Write a program that displays a multiplication table in a panel using the drawing methods, as shown in Figure 10.35.

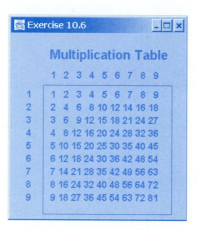

Figure 10.35 *The program displays a multiplication table.*

10.7 Write a program that displays numbers, as shown in Figure 10.36. The number of lines in the display changes to fit the window as the window resizes.

```
Exercise 10.7

1
1 2
1 2 3
1 2 3 4
1 2 3 4 5
1 2 3 4 5 6
1 2 3 4 5 6 7
1 2 3 4 5 6 7 8
1 2 3 4 5 6 7 8 9
1 2 3 4 5 6 7 8 9 10
```

Figure 10.36 *The program displays numbers in a triangle formation.*

10.8 Write a program that draws a diagram for the function $f(x) = x^2$ (see Figure 10.37).

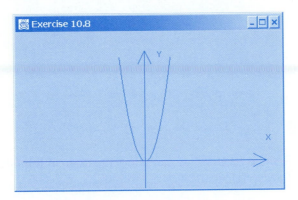

Figure 10.37 *The program draws a diagram for function $f(x) = x^2$.*

HINT

Add points to a polygon p using the following loop:

```
double scaleFactor = 0.1;

for (int x = -100; x <= 100; x++) {
  p.addPoint(x + 200, 200 - (int)(scaleFactor * x * x));
}
```

Use the drawPolyline method in the Graphics class to connect the points.

10.9 Write a program that draws a diagram for the sin function, as shown in Figure 10.38.

HINT

The Unicode for π is \u03c0. To display –2π, use g.drawString("-2\u03c0", x, y). For a trigonometric function like sin(x), x is in radians. Use the following loop to add the points to a polygon p:

```
for (int x = -100; x <= 100; x++) {
  p.addPoint(x + 200,
    100 - (int)(50 * Math.sin((x / 100.0) * 2 * Math.PI)));
}
```

–2π is at (100, 100), the center of the axes is at (200, 100), and 2π is at (300, 100). Connect the points using g.drawPolyline(p.xpoints, p.ypoints, p.npoints) for a Graphics object g. p.xpoints returns an array of x coordinates, p.ypoints returns an array of y coordinates, and p.npoints returns the number of points in Polygon object p.

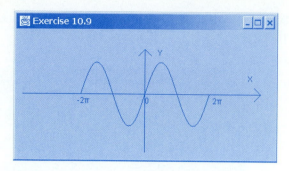

Figure 10.38   *The program draws a diagram for function f(x)= sin(x).*

10.10   Write a generic class that draws the diagram for a function. The class is defined as follows:

```
public abstract class AbstractDrawFunction extends JPanel {
  /** Polygon to hold the points */
  private Polygon p = new Polygon();

  /** Default constructor */
  protected AbstractDrawFunction () {
    drawFunction();
  }

  /** Return the y coordinate */
  abstract double f(double x);

  /** Obtain points for x coordinates 100, 101, ..., 300 */
  public void drawFunction() {
    for (int x = -100; x <= 100; x++) {
      p.addPoint(x + 200, 200 - (int)f(x));
    }
  }

  /** Implement paintComponent to draw axes, labels, and
    *connecting points */
  public void paintComponent(Graphics g) {
    // To be completed by you
  }
}
```

Test the class with the following functions:

```
f(x) = x2;
f(x) = sin(x);
f(x) = cos(x);
f(x) = tan(x);
f(x) = cos(x) + 5sin(x);
f(x) = cos(x) + 5sin(x);
f(x) = log(x) + x²;
```

For each function, create a class that extends the `AbstractDrawFunction` class and implements the `f` method. Figure 10.39 displays the drawings for the sine function and the cosine function.

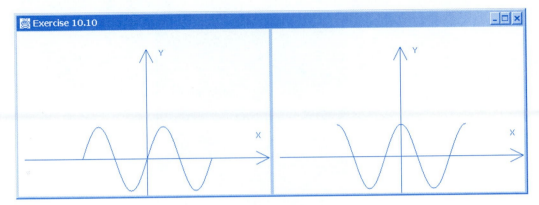

Figure 10.39 *The drawings for the sine and cosine functions are displayed in a frame.*

10.11 Write a program that draws a fan with four blades, as shown in Figure 10.40. Draw the circle in blue and the blades in red. To make the fan reusable, create a panel to display a fan, and place the panel in the frame. The panel can be reused elsewhere; for example, in Exercise 10.13. (Hint: Use the `fillArc` method to draw the blades.)

Figure 10.40 *The drawing methods are used to draw a fan with four blades.*

10.12 Modify Example 10.6 to draw the clock with more details on the hours and minutes, as shown in Figure 10.41.

10.13 Write a program that places four fans in a frame of `GridLayout` with two rows and two columns, as shown in Figure 10.42.

10.14 Write a program that uses a pie chart to display the percentages of the overall grade represented by projects, quizzes, midterm exams, and the final exam, as shown in Figure 10.43. Suppose that projects take 20% and are displayed in red, quizzes take 10% and are displayed in green, midterm exams take 30% and are displayed in blue, and the final exam takes 40% and is displayed in orange.

Figure 10.41   *All the hours are displayed on the clock.*

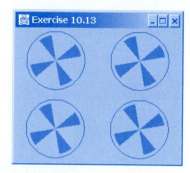

Figure 10.42   *Four fans are placed in a frame.*

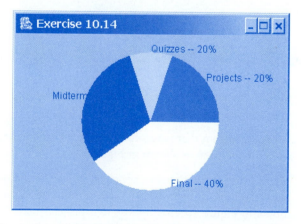

Figure 10.43   *The pie chart displays the percentages of projects, quizzes, midterm exams, and final exam in the overall grade.*

10.15 Write a program that creates four panels using the classes `RectPanel`, `OvalsPanel`, `ArcsPanel`, and `PolygonsPanel` presented in Section 10.9, "Drawing Geometric Figures," and places the panels in the content pane of the frame using a `GridLayout`, as shown in Figure 10.44.

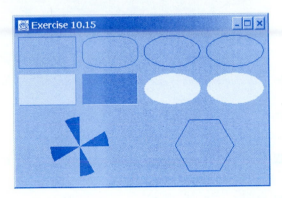

Figure 10.44   *Four panels of geometric figures are displayed in a frame of* `GridLayout`.

10.16 Write a program with four buttons: "Show Rectangle," "Show Oval," "Show Arc," and "Show Polygon." When you click a button, a corresponding panel (`RectPanel`, `OvalsPanel`, `ArcsPanel`, and `PolygonsPanel`) is added to the frame, as shown in Figure 10.45. By default, the `RectPanel` is displayed in the frame.

HINT

You may define a variable named `figurePanel` of the `JPanel` type to reference one of the four figure panels. Initially, `figurePanel` references an object of the `RectPanel` and is placed in the center of the frame's content pane. Whenever a new figure panel is selected, remove `figurePanel` from the content pane, assign the reference of the new figure panel to `figurePanel`, add `figurePanel` to the content pane of the frame, repaint and validate the content pane as follows:

```
public void actionPerformed(ActionEvent e) {
  getContentPane().remove(figurePanel);

  if (e.getSource() == jbtRect)
    figurePanel = rectPanel;
  else if (e.getSource() == jbtOval)
    figurePanel = ovalPanel;
  else if (e.getSource() == jbtArc)
    figurePanel = arcPanel;
  else if (e.getSource() == jbtPolygon)
    figurePanel = polygonPanel;

  getContentPane().add(figurePanel);
  getContentPane().repaint();
  getContentPane().validate();
}
```

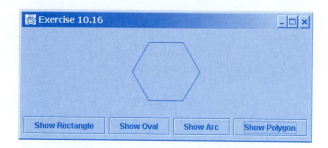

Figure 10.45   *Clicking a button to add a corresponding panel to the frame.*

10.17   Rewrite Example 10.5, "Using FontMetrics," to test `MessagePanel` from a main method inside `MessagePanel`, as follows:

■ Add a `main` method in the `MessagePanel` class. The `main` method creates a `JFrame` instance.

■ Create and add a `MessagePanel` instance to the `JFrame` object. (The solution for this exercise will be found in **exercise\MessagePanel.java** in the CD-ROM.)

10.18   Rewrite Example 10.9, "Multiple Listeners for a Single Source," as follows:

■ Create a method in `TestMultipleListener`:

```
public void processButtons(ActionEvent e) {
  if (e.getSource() == jbtOk) {
    System.out.println("The OK button is clicked");
  }
  else if (e.getSource() == jbtCancel) {
    System.out.println("The Cancel button is clicked");
  }
}
```

■ Invoke `processButtons(e)` from the `actionPerformed(e)` method in `TestMultipleListener`.

■ Modify `SecondListener` to invoke `processButtons(e)` defined in `TestMultipleListener` from the `actionPerformed` method in `SecondListener`. For the `actionPerformed` method in the `SecondListener` class to invoke the `processButtons(e)` method in the `TestMultipleListener` class, you may pass a reference of a `TestMultipleListener` object to `SecondListener` through the constructor of `SecondListener`.

10.19   In Exercise 10.14, you wrote a program that displays data in a pie chart. The program is difficult to reuse. In this exercise you will write a reusable component named `PieChart` to display a pie chart for *any* set of data. Suppose the data are stored in an array of double elements named `data`, and the names for the data are stored in an array of strings named `dataName`. For example, the enrollment data {200, 40, 50, 100, 40} stored in the array `data` are for {"CS", "Math", "Chem", "Biol", "Phys"} in the array `dataName`. The outline of this component is as follows:

```
public class PieChart extends JPanel {
  /** Sample data, and data names */
  private double[] dataValue = {200, 140, 100, 60, 40};
  private String[] dataName = {"CS", "Math", "Chem", "Biol",
    "Phys"};

  /** Display the pie chart */
  public void paintComponent(Graphics g) {
    // Write your code here
  }

  /** Set data */
  public void setData(String[] dataName , double[] dataValue) {
    this.dataName = dataName;
    this.dataValue = dataValue;
    repaint();
  }
}
```

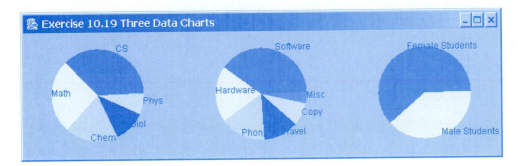

Figure 10.46   *Three pie charts are placed in a frame of GridLayout.*

HINT

Each pie represents a percentage of the total data. Color the pie using the colors from an array named colors, which is {Color.red, Color.yellow, Color.green, Color.blue, Color.cyan, Color.magenta, Color.orange, Color.pink, Color.dark-Gray}. Use colors[i % colors.length] for the *i*th pie. Use black color to display the data names. Figure 10.46 shows three pie charts created using this component.

10.20 Similar to Exercise 10.19, create a new chart component named BarChart to display bar charts, as shown in Figure 10.47. Can you combine the PieChart and BarChart components into one component named Chart? Add a property named chartType to determine which type of chart is displayed.

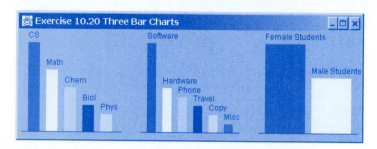

Figure 10.47 *Three bar charts are placed in a frame of* GridLayout.

CHAPTER 11

CREATING USER INTERFACES

Objectives

- To know various user-interface components: JButton, JLabel, JTextField, JTextArea, JComboBox, JList, JCheckBox, JRadioButton, JMenuBar, JMenu, JMenuItem, JCheckBoxMenuItem, JRadioButtonMenuItem, JScrollBar, JScrollPane, and JTabbedPane.

- To use various UI components to create interactive graphical user interfaces.

- To learn how to display images with the ImageIcon class.

- To use borders to visually group user-interface components.

- To know how to use the dialog boxes.

- To create multiple windows in an application.

- To learn how to implement the listener interface for the user-interface components.

11.1   Introduction

A graphical user interface (GUI) makes a system user-friendly and easy to use. Creating a GUI requires creativity and knowledge of how GUI components work. Since the GUI components in Java are very flexible and versatile, you can create a wide assortment of different user interfaces.

Many Java IDEs provide tools for visually designing and programming Java classes. This enables you to rapidly assemble the elements of a user interface (UI) for a Java application or applet with minimum coding. Tools, however, cannot do everything. You have to modify the programs they produce. Consequently, before you begin to use the visual tools, it is imperative that you understand the basic concepts of Java GUI programming.

This chapter concentrates on creating user interfaces. In particular, it discusses the various GUI components that make up a user interface and how to make them work.

11.2   The *Component* and *JComponent* Classes

Once you understand the basics of Java GUI programming, such as containers, layout managers, and event handling, you will be able to learn new components and explore their properties. The `Component` class is the root for all UI components and containers. Here is a list of frequently used properties available in `Component`:

- **`font`** is the font used to display text on the component.

- **`background`** is the background color of the component.

- **`foreground`** is the foreground color of the component.

- **`height`** is the current height of the component.

- **`width`** is the current width of the component.

- **`locale`** is the locale of the component. This topic will be introduced in Chapter 14, "Internationalization."

- **`preferredSize`** specifies the ideal size at which the component looks best. This property may or may not be considered by the layout manager, depending on its rules. For example, a component uses its preferred size in a container with a `FlowLayout` manager, but its preferred size may be ignored if it is placed in a container with a `GridLayout` manager.

- **`minimumSize`** specifies the minimum size for the component to be useful. For most Swing components, `minimumSize` is the same as `preferredSize`. Layout managers generally respect `minimumSize` more than `preferredSize`.

- **`maximumSize`** specifies the maximum size the component needs so that the layout manager won't waste space by giving it to a component that does not need it. For instance, BorderLayout could limit the center component's size to its maximum size, and then either give the space to border components or limit the size of the outer window when resized.

All but a few Swing components, such as JFrame, JApplet, and JDialog, are subclasses of JComponent. Many of the properties of the Swing components are defined in the JComponent class. Here is a list of frequently used properties in JComponent:

- **toolTipText** specifies the text displayed when the mouse points on the component without clicking. This text is generally used to give the user a tip about the component's function.

- **doubleBuffered** specifies whether the component is painted using double-buffering. This is a technique for reducing flickering. In AWT programming, you have to manually implement this technique in the program. With Swing, this capability is automatically supported if the doubleBuffered property is set to true. By default, it is true.

- **border** specifies a border of the component. The border types and styles will be introduced in Section 11.11, "Borders."

All the properties in the Swing components are associated with accessor methods. You can retrieve them using get methods and modify them using set methods.

NOTE

Throughout this book, the prefixes jbt, jlbl, jtf, jta, jcbo, jlst, jchk, jrb, jmi, jchkmi, and jrbmi are used to name objects of JButton, JLabel, JTextField, JTextArea, JComboBox, JList, JCheckBox, JRadioButton, JMenuItem, JCheckBoxMenuItem, and JRadioButtonMenuItem.

11.3 Buttons

A *button* is a component that triggers an action event when clicked. The Swing version of a button is named JButton. Its default constructor creates an empty button. In addition, JButton has the following constructors:

- public JButton(String text)

  Creates a button labeled with the specified text.

- public JButton(Icon icon)

  Creates a button with the specified icon.

- public JButton(String text, Icon icon)

  Creates a button with the specified text and icon.

An icon is a fixed-size picture; typically it is small and used to decorate components. An icon can be obtained from an image file by using the ImageIcon class, such as:

```
Icon icon = new ImageIcon("photo.gif");
```

`javax.swing.ImageIcon` is a subclass of `javax.swing.Icon`.

■ **NOTE**

Java currently supports three image formats: GIF (Graphics Interchange Format), JPEG (Joint Photographic Experts Group), and PNG (Portable Network Graphics). The image filenames for these types end with .gif, .jpg, and .png respectively. If you have a bitmap file or image files in other formats, you can use image-processing utilities to convert them into GIF, JPEG, or PNG format for use in Java. GIF uses a lossless compression algorithm, but JPEG uses a lossy compression algorithm. GIF file size is larger than JPEG. The PNG format was designed to replace GIF. PNG uses a lossless compression algorithm that creates images that are usually a bit smaller than their GIF counterparts.

■ **NOTE**

File names are not case-sensitive on Windows, but are case-sensitive on Unix. To enable your programs to run on all platforms, I recommend that you name all the image files consistently.

Since `JButton` is a subclass of `JComponent`, all the properties in `JComponent` can be used in `JButton`. Additionally, `JButton` has the following useful properties:

■ **text** is the label on the button. For example, to set the label "OK" on the button `jbt`, you can use `jbt.setText("OK")`.

■ **icon** is the image icon on the button. For example, to set the icon on `jbt` using the image file smiley.gif, you can use `jbt.setIcon(new ImageIcon("smiley.gif"))`.

■ **mnemonic** specifies a shortcut key. You can select the button by pressing the ALT key and the mnemonic key at the same time. For example, to set the mnemonic key O on `jbt`, you can use `jbt.setMnemonic('O')`.

■ **horizontalAlignment** is one of the three values (`SwingConstants.LEFT`, `SwingConstants.CENTER`, and `SwingConstants.RIGHT`) that specify how the icon and text are placed horizontally on a button. The default horizontal alignment is `SwingConstants.CENTER`.

■ **NOTE**

`SwingConstants` is an interface that contains the constants used by Swing components. All Swing GUI components implement `SwingConstants`. Therefore, you can reference the constants through `SwingConstants` or a GUI component. For example, `SwingConstants.CENTER` is the same as `JButton.CENTER`.

■ **verticalAlignment** is one of the three values (`SwingConstants.TOP`, `SwingConstants.CENTER`, and `SwingConstants.BOTTOM`) that specify how the icon and text are placed vertically on a button. The default vertical alignment is `SwingConstants.CENTER`.

- **horizontalTextPosition** is one of the three values (`SwingConstants.LEFT`, `SwingConstants.CENTER`, and `SwingConstants.RIGHT`) that specify the horizontal position of the text relative to the icon. The default horizontal text position is `SwingConstants.RIGHT`.

- **verticalTextPosition** is one of the three values (`SwingConstants.TOP`, `SwingConstants.CENTER`, and `SwingConstants.BOTTOM`) that specify the vertical position of the text relative to the icon. The default horizontal text position is `SwingConstants.CENTER`.

NOTE

The `Container` class is the superclass for many GUI component classes, such as `JButton`. In theory, you could use the `setLayout` method to set the layout in a button and add components into a button, because all the public methods in the `Container` class are inherited into `JButton`, but for practical reasons they should not be used in `JButton`.

Buttons can generate many types of events, but often you need to respond to an `ActionEvent`. In order to make a button responsive to an `ActionEvent`, you must implement the `actionPerformed` method in the `ActionListener` interface. The following code is an example of how to handle a button event. The code prints out "Button clicked" on the console when the button is clicked.

```
public void actionPerformed(ActionEvent e) {
  // Make sure the event source is a button.
  if (e.getSource() instanceof JButton)
    System.out.println("Button clicked!");
}
```

Example 11.1 Using Buttons

Problem

Write a program that displays a message on a panel and uses two buttons, <= and =>, to move the message on the panel to the left or right. The layout of the UI and the output of the program are shown in Figure 11.1.

Figure 11.1   *Clicking the <= and => buttons causes the message on the panel to move to the left and right, respectively.*

continues

Example 11.1 continued

Solution

Here are the major steps in the program:

1. Create the user interface.

   Create a MessagePanel object to display the message. The MessagePanel class was created in Example 10.5, "Using FontMetrics." Place it in the center of the frame. Create two buttons, <= and =>, on a panel. Place the panel in the south of the frame.

2. Process the event.

   Implement the actionPerformed handler to move the message left or right according to whether the left or right button was clicked.

```java
1   // ButtonDemo.java: Use buttons to move message in a panel
2   import java.awt.*;
3   import java.awt.event.ActionListener;
4   import java.awt.event.ActionEvent;
5   import javax.swing.*;
6
7   public class ButtonDemo extends JFrame implements ActionListener {
8     // Declare a panel for displaying message
9     private MessagePanel messagePanel;
10
11    // Declare two buttons to move the message left and right
12    private JButton jbtLeft, jbtRight;
13
14    /** Main method */
15    public static void main(String[] args) {
16      ButtonDemo frame = new ButtonDemo();
17      frame.setDefaultCloseOperation(JFrame.EXIT_ON_CLOSE);
18      frame.setSize(200, 200);
19      frame.setVisible(true);
20    }
21
22    /** Default constructor */
23    public ButtonDemo() {
24      setTitle("Button Demo");
25
26      // Create a MessagePanel instance and set colors
27      messagePanel = new MessagePanel("Welcome to Java");
28      messagePanel.setBackground(Color.yellow);
29
30      // Create Panel jpButtons to hold two Buttons "<=" and "right =>"
31      JPanel jpButtons = new JPanel();
32      jpButtons.setLayout(new FlowLayout());
33      jpButtons.add(jbtLeft = new JButton());
34      jpButtons.add(jbtRight = new JButton());
35
36      // Set button text
37      jbtLeft.setText("<=");
38      jbtRight.setText("=>");
39
40      // Set keyboard mnemonics
41      jbtLeft.setMnemonic('L');
42      jbtRight.setMnemonic('R');
43
```

```
44          // Set icons
45          //jbtLeft.setIcon(new ImageIcon("image/left.gif"));
46          //jbtRight.setIcon(new ImageIcon("image/right.gif"));
47
48          // Set toolTipText on the "<=" and "=>" buttons
49          jbtLeft.setToolTipText("Move message to left");
50          jbtRight.setToolTipText("Move message to right");
51
52          // Place panels in the frame
53          getContentPane().setLayout(new BorderLayout());
54          getContentPane().add(messagePanel, BorderLayout.CENTER);
55          getContentPane().add(jpButtons, BorderLayout.SOUTH);
56
57          // Register listeners with the buttons
58          jbtLeft.addActionListener(this);
59          jbtRight.addActionListener(this);
60      }
61
62      /** Handle button events */
63      public void actionPerformed(ActionEvent e) {
64        if (e.getSource() == jbtLeft) {
65          left();
66        }
67        else if (e.getSource() == jbtRight) {
68          right();
69        }
70      }
71
72      /** Move the message in the panel left */
73      private void left() {
74        int x = messagePanel.getXCoordinate();
75        if (x > 10) {
76          // Shift the message to the left
77          messagePanel.setXCoordinate(x - 10);
78          messagePanel.repaint();
79        }
80      }
81
82      /** Move the message in the panel right */
83      private void right() {
84        int x = messagePanel.getXCoordinate();
85        if (x < getSize().width - 20) {
86          // Shift the message to the right
87          messagePanel.setXCoordinate(x + 10);
88          messagePanel.repaint();
89        }
90      }
91    }
```

Review

Each button has a tool-tip text (Lines 49–50), which appears when the mouse is set on the button without clicking, as shown in Figure 11.1.

You can set an icon image on the button by using the setIcon method. If you replace the setText method with the setIcon method (Lines 45–46), as follows:

```
jbtLeft.setIcon(new ImageIcon("image/left.gif"));
jbtRight.setIcon(new ImageIcon("image/right.gif"));
```

continues

Example 11.1 continued

the texts are replaced by the icons, as shown in Figure 11.2. "image/left.gif" is located in "c:\book\image\left.gif." Note that the back slash is the Windows file path notation. In Java, the forward slash should be used.

Figure 11.2   *You can set an icon on a* JButton.

You can set icons and labels on a button at the same time, if you wish. By default, the labels and icons are centered horizontally and vertically.

The button can also be accessed by using the keyboard mnemonics. Pressing ALT+L is equivalent to clicking the <= button, since you set the mnemonic property to 'L' in the left button (Line 41). If you change the left button text to "Left" and the right button to "Right", the L and R in the captions of these buttons will be underlined, as shown in Figure 11.3.

Figure 11.3   *The buttons can be accessed by using the keyboard mnemonics.*

The repaint method is defined in the Component class. Invoking repaint (Lines 78, 88) causes the paintComponent method to be called. The repaint method is invoked to refresh the viewing area. Typically, you call it if you have new things to display.

CAUTION

The paintComponent method should never be invoked directly. It is invoked either by the Java runtime system whenever the viewing area changes or by the repaint method. You should override the paintComponent method to tell the system how to paint the viewing area, but never override the repaint method.

> **NOTE**
>
> The `repaint` method lodges a request to update the viewing area and returns immediately. Its effect is asynchronous, and if several requests are outstanding, it is likely that only the last `paintComponent` will be done.

11.4   Labels

A *label* is a display area for a short text, an image, or both. It is often used to label other components (usually text fields). The default constructor of `JLabel` creates an empty label. Other constructors for `JLabel` are as follows:

■   `public JLabel(String text, int horizontalAlignment)`

Creates a label with the specified string and horizontal alignment (`Swing-Constants.LEFT`, `SwingConstants.RIGHT`, or `SwingConstants.CENTER`).

■   `public JLabel(String text)`

Creates a label with a specified text.

■   `public JLabel(Icon icon)`

Creates a label with an icon.

■   `public JLabel(Icon icon, int horizontalAlignment)`

Creates a label with the specified image and horizontal alignment.

■   `public JLabel(String text, Icon icon, int horizontalAlignment)`

Creates a label with the specified text, image, and horizontal alignment.

For example, the following statement creates a label with the string `"Interest Rate"`:

```
JLabel myLabel = new JLabel("Interest Rate");
```

The following statement creates a label with the specified image in the file "image/map.gif":

```
JLabel mapLabel = new JLabel(new ImageIcon("image/map.gif"));
```

`JLabel` inherits all the properties from `JComponent` and has many properties used in `JButton`, such as `text`, `icon`, `horizontalAlignment`, and `verticalAlignment`.

449

Example 11.2 Using Labels

Problem

Write a program that uses a label as an area for displaying images. There are nine images in image files named flag1.gif, flag2.gif, . . . , fkag9.gif stored in the **image** directory under **c:\book**. You can use two buttons, Prior and Next, to browse the images, as shown in Figure 11.4.

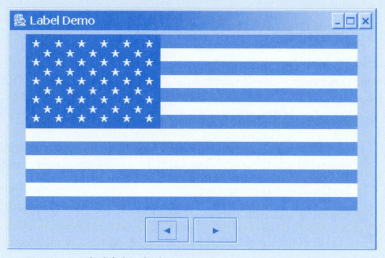

Figure 11.4   *You can use the label to display images.*

Solution

Here are the major steps in the program:

1. Create the user interface.

   Create a JLabel object to display image icons, and place the label in the center of the frame. Create two buttons, Prior and Next, on a panel. Place the panel in the south of the frame.

2. Process the event.

   Implement the actionPerformed handler to set the appropriate image icon in the label according to whether the Prior or Next button was clicked.

```
1   // LabelDemo.java: Use label to display images
2   import java.awt.*;
3   import java.awt.event.*;
4   import javax.swing.*;
5
6   public class LabelDemo extends JFrame implements ActionListener {
7     // Declare an ImageIcon array. There are total 9 images
8     private ImageIcon[] imageIcon = new ImageIcon[9];
9
10    // The current image index
11    private int currentIndex = 0;
12
13    // Buttons for browsing images
14    private JButton jbtPrior, jbtNext;
15
```

```
16      // Label for displaying images
17      private JLabel jlblImageViewer = new JLabel();
18
19      final int TOTAL_NUMBER_OF_IMAGES = 9;
20
21      /** Main method */
22      public static void main(String[] args) {
23        LabelDemo frame = new LabelDemo();
24        frame.setDefaultCloseOperation(JFrame.EXIT_ON_CLOSE);
25        frame.setSize(500, 500);
26        frame.setVisible(true);
27      }
28
29      /** Default Constructor */
30      public LabelDemo() {
31        setTitle("Label Demo");
32
33        // Load images into imageIcon array
34        for (int i = 1; i <= TOTAL_NUMBER_OF_IMAGES; i++) {
35          imageIcon[i - 1] = new ImageIcon("image/flag" + i + ".gif");
36        }
37
38        // Show the first image
39        jlblImageViewer.setIcon(imageIcon[currentIndex]);
40
41        // Set center alignment
42        jlblImageViewer.setHorizontalAlignment(SwingConstants.CENTER);
43        jlblImageViewer.setVerticalAlignment(SwingConstants.CENTER);
44
45        // Panel jpButtons to hold two buttons for browsing images
46        JPanel jpButtons = new JPanel();
47        jpButtons.add(jbtPrior = new JButton());
48        jbtPrior.setIcon(new ImageIcon("image/left.gif"));
49        jpButtons.add(jbtNext = new JButton());
50        jbtNext.setIcon(new ImageIcon("image/right.gif"));
51
52        // Add jpButton and the label to the frame
53        getContentPane().add(jlblImageViewer, BorderLayout.CENTER);
54        getContentPane().add(jpButtons, BorderLayout.SOUTH);
55
56        // Register listeners
57        jbtPrior.addActionListener(this);
58        jbtNext.addActionListener(this);
59      }
60
61      /** Handle ActionEvent from buttons */
62      public void actionPerformed(ActionEvent e) {
63        if (e.getSource() == jbtPrior) {
64          // Make sure index is nonnegative
65          if (currentIndex == 0) currentIndex = TOTAL_NUMBER_OF_IMAGES;
66          currentIndex = (currentIndex - 1) % TOTAL_NUMBER_OF_IMAGES;
67          jlblImageViewer.setIcon(imageIcon[currentIndex]);
68        }
69        else if (e.getSource() == jbtNext) {
70          currentIndex = (currentIndex + 1) % TOTAL_NUMBER_OF_IMAGES;
71          jlblImageViewer.setIcon(imageIcon[currentIndex]);
72        }
73      }
74    }
```

continues

Example 11.2 Using Labels

Review

The images are stored in files flag1.gif, flag2.gif, . . ., and flag9.gif under the \book\image directory, and are loaded to an array of ImageIcon in a for loop (Lines 33–36).

The variable currentIndex (Line 11) tracks which image icon is displayed in the label. When the Prior button or the Next button is clicked, the currentIndex is decremented or incremented by 1.

By default, the icon is centered vertically but left-aligned horizontally. The following statement (Line 42) ensures that the image is displayed in the center of the viewing area.

```
jlblImageViewer.setHorizontalAlignment(SwingConstants.CENTER);
```

11.5   Text Fields

A *text field* can be used to enter or display a string. The default constructor of JTextField creates an empty text field. Other constructors of JTextField are:

- public JTextField(int columns)

  Creates an empty text field with the specified number of columns.

- public JTextField(String text)

  Creates a text field initialized with the specified text.

- public JTextField(String text, int columns)

  Creates a text field initialized with the specified text and the number of columns.

In addition to such properties as text and horizontalAlignment, JTextField has the following properties:

- **editable** is a boolean property indicating whether the text field can be edited by the user.

- **columns** specifies the number of columns in the text field.

JTextField can generate ActionEvent among many other events. Pressing Enter in a text field triggers the ActionEvent.

Here is an example of how to react to an ActionEvent on a text field.

```
public void actionPerformed(ActionEvent e) {
  // Make sure it is a text field
  if (e.getSource() instanceof JTextField)
    // Process the event
    ...
}
```

Example 11.3 Using Text Fields

Problem

Write a program that converts Celsius and Fahrenheit temperatures, as shown in Figure 11.5. If you enter a value in the Celsius-degree text field and press the Enter key, the Fahrenheit temperature is displayed in the Fahrenheit text field. Likewise, if you enter a value in the Fahrenheit-degree text field, and press the Enter key, the corresponding Celsius degree is displayed in the Celsius text field.

Figure 11.5   *The program converts Celsius to Fahrenheit, and vice versa.*

Solution

Here are the major steps in the program:

1. Create the user interface.

   Create a panel of GridLayout with two rows to hold two labels, and create another panel of GridLayout with two rows to hold two text fields. Add the first panel to the west and the second panel to the center of the frame's content pane.

2. Process the event.

   Implement the actionPerformed handler to detect which text field has been entered. If the Celsius-degree text field is entered, retrieve number from the text field, compute its corresponding Fahrenheit value, and display the result in the Fahrenheit-degree text. If the Fahrenheit-degree text field is entered, it can be processed in the same way.

```
1    // TextFieldDemo.java: Convert Celsius to Fahrenheit and vice versa
2    import java.awt.*;
3    import java.awt.event.*;
4    import javax.swing.*;
5
6    public class TextFieldDemo extends JFrame
7      implements ActionListener {
8      private JTextField jtfCelsius = new JTextField(10);
9      private JTextField jtfFahrenheit = new JTextField(10);
10
11     /** Main method */
12     public static void main(String[] args) {
13       TextFieldDemo frame = new TextFieldDemo();
14       frame.pack();
15       frame.setTitle("TextFieldDemo");
16       frame.setDefaultCloseOperation(JFrame.EXIT_ON_CLOSE);
17       frame.setVisible(true);
18     }
19
```

continues

Example 11.3 Using Text Fields

```
20        public TextFieldDemo() {
21          // Panel p1 to hold labels
22          JPanel p1 = new JPanel();
23          p1.setLayout(new GridLayout(2, 1));
24          p1.add(new JLabel("Celsius"));
25          p1.add(new JLabel("Fahrenheit"));
26
27          // Panel p2 to hold text fields
28          JPanel p2 = new JPanel();
29          p2.setLayout(new GridLayout(2, 1));
30          p2.add(jtfCelsius);
31          p2.add(jtfFahrenheit);
32
33          // Add p1 and p3 to the frame
34          getContentPane().add(p1, BorderLayout.WEST);
35          getContentPane().add(p2, BorderLayout.CENTER);
36
37          // Set horizontal alignment to RIGHT for text fields
38          jtfCelsius.setHorizontalAlignment(JTextField.RIGHT);
39          jtfFahrenheit.setHorizontalAlignment(JTextField.RIGHT);
40
41          // Register listener
42          jtfCelsius.addActionListener(this);
43          jtfFahrenheit.addActionListener(this);
44        }
45
46      /** Handle ActionEvent */
47      public void actionPerformed(ActionEvent e) {
48        if (e.getSource() == jtfCelsius) {
49          double celsius =
50            Double.parseDouble(jtfCelsius.getText().trim());
51          double fahrenheit = (9.0 / 5.0) * celsius + 32;
52          jtfFahrenheit.setText(new Double(fahrenheit).toString());
53        }
54        else {
55          double fahrenheit =
56            Double.parseDouble(jtfFahrenheit.getText().trim());
57          double celsius = (5.0 / 9.0) * (fahrenheit - 32);
58          jtfCelsius.setText(new Double(celsius).toString());
59        }
60      }
61    }
```

Review

Instead of using the setSize method to set the size for the frame, the program uses the pack() method (Line 14), which automatically sizes up the frame according to the size of the components placed in it.

The program uses two panels, p1 and p2, to contain the components. Panel p1 is for the labels (Lines 22–25), and p2 is for the text fields (Lines 28–31).

The jtfCelsius.getText() method (Line 50) returns the text in the text field jtfCelsius, and jtfFahrenheit.setText(s) (Line 52) sets the specified string into the text field jtfFahrenheit.

The `trim()` method (Lines 50, 56) is useful for removing blank space from both ends of a string. If you run the program without applying `trim()` to the string, a runtime exception may occur when the string is converted to an integer.

Pressing Enter in a text field triggers an `ActionEvent`. The `actionPerformed` handler (Lines 47–60) checks which text field is the source of the event to process the event accordingly.

11.6   Text Areas

If you want to let the user enter multiple lines of text, you have to create several instances of `JTextField`. A better alternative is to use `JTextArea`, which enables the user to enter multiple lines of text.

The default constructor of `JTextArea` creates an empty text area. Other constructors of `JTextArea` are listed below:

- ■ `public JTextArea(int rows, int columns)`

  Creates a text area with the specified number of rows and columns.

- ■ `public JTextArea(String text, int rows, int columns)`

  Creates a text area with the specified text and the number of rows and columns specified.

In addition to `text`, `editable`, and `columns`, `JTextArea` has the following properties:

- ■ `lineWrap` is a `boolean` property indicating whether the line in the text area is automatically wrapped.

- ■ `wrapStyleWord` is a `boolean` property indicating whether the line is wrapped on words or characters. The default value is `false`, which indicates that the line is wrapped on characters.

- ■ `rows` specifies the number of lines in the text area.

- ■ `lineCount` specifies the number of lines in the text.

- ■ `tabSize` specifies the number of spaces inserted when the Tab key is pressed.

You can use the following methods to insert, append, and replace text:

- ■ `public void insert(String s, int pos)`

  Inserts string `s` in the specified position in the text area.

- ■ `public void append(String s)`

  Appends string `s` to the end of the text.

- ■ `public void replaceRange(String s, int start, int end)`

  Replaces partial texts in the range from position `start` to position `end` with string `s`.

JTextArea does not handle scrolling, but you can create a JScrollPane object to hold an instance of JTextArea and let JScrollPane handle scrolling for JTextArea, as follows:

```
// Create a scroll pane to hold text area
JScrollPane scrollPane = new JScrollPane(jta = new JTextArea());
getContentPane().add(scrollPane, BorderLayout.CENTER);
```

JScrollPane will be discussed further in Section 11.16, "Scroll Panes."

Example 11.4   Using Text Areas

Problem

Write a program that displays an image in a label, a title in a label, and a text in a text area. A sample run of the program is shown in Figure 11.6.

Figure 11.6   *The program displays an image in a label, a title in a label, and a text in the text area.*

Solution

Here are the major steps in the program:

1. Create a class named DescriptionPanel that extends JPanel. This class contains a text area inside a scroll pane, a label for displaying an image icon, and a label for displaying a title. This class is used in this example and will also be used in later examples.

2. Create a class named TextAreaDemo that extends JFrame. Create an instance of DescriptionPanel and add it to the center of the frame. The relationship between DescriptionPanel and TextAreaDemo is shown in Figure 11.7.

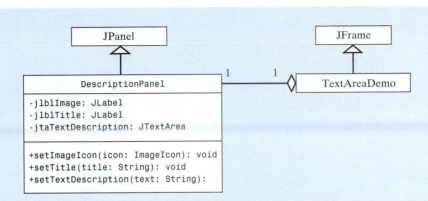

Figure 11.7 `TextAreaDemo` *uses* `DescriptionPanel` *to display an image, title, and text description of a national flag.*

```
1    // TextAreaDemo.java: Display an image in a label, the title for
2    // the image in a label, and the description of the image in a
3    // text area
4    import java.awt.*;
5    import javax.swing.*;
6
7    public class TextAreaDemo extends JFrame {
8      // Declare and create a description panel
9      private DescriptionPanel descriptionPanel = new DescriptionPanel();
10
11     /** Main method */
12     public static void main(String[] args) {
13       TextAreaDemo frame = new TextAreaDemo();
14       frame.pack();
15       frame.setDefaultCloseOperation(JFrame.EXIT_ON_CLOSE);
16       frame.setTitle("Text Area Demo");
17       frame.setVisible(true);
18     }
19
20     /** Default constructor */
21     public TextAreaDemo() {
22       // Set title, text and image in the description panel
23       descriptionPanel.setTitle("Canada");
24       String description = "The Maple Leaf flag \n\n" +
25         "The Canadian National Flag was adopted by the Canadian " +
26         "Parliament on October 22, 1964 and was proclaimed into law " +
27         "by Her Majesty Queen Elizabeth II (the Queen of Canada) on " +
28         "February 15, 1965. The Canadian Flag (colloquially known " +
29         "as The Maple Leaf Flag) is a red flag of the proportions " +
30         "two by length and one by width, containing in its center a " +
31         "white square, with a single red stylized eleven-point " +
32         "mapleleaf centered in the white square.";
33       descriptionPanel.setTextDescription(description);
34       descriptionPanel.setImageIcon(new ImageIcon("image/ca.gif"));
35
36       // Add the description panel to the frame
37       getContentPane().setLayout(new BorderLayout());
38       getContentPane().add(descriptionPanel, BorderLayout.CENTER);
39     }
40   }
41
```

continues

457

Example 11.4 continued

```
42        // Define a panel for displaying image and text
43        class DescriptionPanel extends JPanel {
44          /** Label for displaying an image icon */
45          private JLabel jlblImage = new JLabel();
46
47          /** Label for displaying a title */
48          private JLabel jlblTitle = new JLabel();
49
50          /** Text area for displaying text */
51          private JTextArea jtaTextDescription;
52
53          /** Default constructor */
54          public DescriptionPanel() {
55            // Group image label and title label in a panel
56            JPanel panel = new JPanel();
57            panel.setLayout(new BorderLayout());
58            panel.add(jlblImage, BorderLayout.CENTER);
59            panel.add(jlblTitle, BorderLayout.SOUTH);
60
61            // Create a scroll pane to hold text area
62            JScrollPane scrollPane = new JScrollPane
63              (jtaTextDescription = new JTextArea());
64
65            // Center the title on the label
66            jlblTitle.setHorizontalAlignment(JLabel.CENTER);
67
68            // Set the font for the title and text
69            jlblTitle.setFont(new Font("SansSerif", Font.BOLD, 16));
70            jtaTextDescription.setFont(new Font("Serif", Font.PLAIN, 14));
71
72            // Set lineWrap and wrapStyleWord true for text area
73            jtaTextDescription.setLineWrap(true);
74            jtaTextDescription.setWrapStyleWord(true);
75
76            // Set preferred size for the scroll pane
77            scrollPane.setPreferredSize(new Dimension(200, 100));
78
79            // Set BorderLayout for the whole panel, add panel and scrollpane
80            setLayout(new BorderLayout(5, 5));
81            add(scrollPane, BorderLayout.CENTER);
82            add(panel, BorderLayout.WEST);
83          }
84
85          /** Set the title */
86          public void setTitle(String title) {
87            jlblTitle.setText(title);
88          }
89
90          /** Set the image icon */
91          public void setImageIcon(ImageIcon icon) {
92            jlblImage.setIcon(icon);
93            Dimension dimension = new Dimension(icon.getIconWidth(),
94              icon.getIconHeight());
95            jlblImage.setPreferredSize(dimension);
96          }
97
98          /** Set the text description */
99          public void setTextDescription(String text) {
100            jtaTextDescription.setText(text);
101          }
102        }
```

458

Review

TextAreaDemo simply creates an instance of DescriptionPanel (Line 9), and sets the title (Line 23), image (Line 34), and text in the description panel (Line 33). DescriptionPanel is a subclass of JPanel. DescriptionPanel contains a label for displaying the image icon, a label for displaying title, and a text area for displaying a description of the image.

It is not necessary to create a separate class for DescriptionPanel in this example. Nevertheless, this class was created for reuse in the next example, where you will use it to display a description panel for various images.

The text area is inside a JScrollPane, which provides scrolling functions for the text area. Scrollbars automatically appear if there is more text than the physical size of the text area, and disappear if the text is deleted and the remaining text does not exceed the text area size.

The lineWrap property is set to true (Line 73) so that the line is automatically wrapped when the text cannot fit in one line. The wrapStyleWord property is set to true (Line 74) so that the line is wrapped on words rather than characters.

The text area is editable. It supports editing functions, such as cut, paste, and copy.

The preferredSize property in jlblImage is set to the size of the image icon (Line 77). The getIconWidth() and getIconHeight() methods (Lines 93–94) obtain the width and height of the icon. The preferredSize property (Line 77) in scrollPane is set to 200 in width and 100 in height. The BorderLayout manager respects the preferred size of the components.

11.7   Combo Boxes

A *combo box*, also known as *choice* or *drop-down list*, is a simple list of items from which the user can choose. It is useful in limiting a user's range of choices and avoids the cumbersome validation of data input.

To create a JComboBox, use its default constructor, or use the following constructor to create a list with a set of strings:

```
public JComboBox(Object[] stringItems)
```

where stringItems is an array of String.

The following properties are often useful:

- **selectedIndex** is an int value indicating the index of the selected item in the combo box.

- **selectedItem** holds a selected item whose type is Object.

The following methods are useful for operating a JComboBox object:

- `public void addItem(Object item)`

    Adds the item of any object into the combo box.

■ `public Object getItemAt(int index)`

Gets an item from the combo box at the specified index.

■ `public void removeItem(Object anObject)`

Removes the specified item from the item list.

■ `public void removeAllItems()`

Removes all the items from the item list.

Here is an example of how to create a combo box and add items to the object:

```
JComboBox jcb = new JComboBox();
jcb.addItem("Item 1");
jcb.addItem("Item 2");
jcb.addItem("Item 3");
```

This creates a `JComboBox` with three items in the combo box.

To get data from a `JComboBox` menu, you can use `getSelectedItem()` to return the currently selected item, or `e.getItem()` method to get the item from the `itemStateChanged(ItemEvent e)` handler.

`JComboBox` can generate `ActionEvent` and `ItemEvent`, among many other events. Whenever a new item is selected, `JComboBox` generates `ItemEvent` twice, once for deselecting the previously selected item, and the other for selecting the currently selected item. `JComboBox` generates an `ActionEvent` after generating `ItemEvent`. To respond to an `ItemEvent`, you need to implement the `itemState-Changed(ItemEvent e)` handler for processing a choice. Here is an example of how to get data from the `itemStateChanged(ItemEvent e)` handler:

```
public void itemStateChanged(ItemEvent e) {
  // Make sure the source is a combo box
  if (e.getSource() instanceof JComboBox)
    String s = (String)e.getItem();
}
```

Example 11.5 Using Combo Boxes

Problem

Write a program that lets users view an image and a description of a country's flag by selecting the country from a combo box. Figure 11.8 shows a sample run of the program.

Solution

Here are the major steps in the program:

1. Create the user interface.

   Create a combo box with country names as its selection values. Create a `DescriptionPanel` object. The `DescriptionPanel` class was introduced in the preceding example. Place the combo box in the north of the frame and the description panel in the center of the frame.

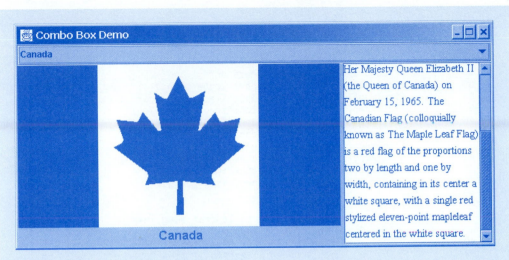

Figure 11.8   *A country's info, including a flag image and a description of the flag, is displayed when the country is selected in the combo box.*

   2. Process the event.

      Implement the `itemStateChanged` handler to set the flag title, image, and text in the description panel for the selected country name.

```
1   // ComboBoxDemo.java: Use a combo box to select a country and
2   // display the selected country's flag information
3   import java.awt.*;
4   import java.awt.event.*;
5   import javax.swing.*;
6
7   public class ComboBoxDemo extends JFrame implements ItemListener {
8     // Declare an array of Strings for flag titles
9     private String[] flagTitle = {"Canada", "China", "Denmark",
10      "France", "Germany", "India", "Norway", "United Kingdom",
11      "United States of America"};
12
13    // Declare an ImageIcon array for the national flags of 9 countries
14    private ImageIcon[] flagImage = new ImageIcon[9];
15
16    // Declare an array of strings for flag descriptions
17    private String[] flagDescription = new String[9];
18
19    // Declare and create a description panel
20    private DescriptionPanel descriptionPanel = new DescriptionPanel();
21
22    // The combo list for selecting countries
23    private JComboBox jcbo;
24
25    /** Main Method */
26    public static void main(String[] args) {
27      ComboBoxDemo frame = new ComboBoxDemo();
28      frame.pack();
29      frame.setTitle("Combo Box Demo");
30      frame.setDefaultCloseOperation(JFrame.EXIT_ON_CLOSE);
31      frame.setVisible(true);
32    }
33
```

continues

461

Example 11.5 continued

```
34          /** Default Constructor */
35          public ComboBoxDemo() {
36            // Load images into flagImage array
37            flagImage[0] = new ImageIcon("image/ca.gif");
38            flagImage[1] = new ImageIcon("image/china.gif");
39            flagImage[2] = new ImageIcon("image/denmark.gif");
40            flagImage[3] = new ImageIcon("image/fr.gif");
41            flagImage[4] = new ImageIcon("image/germany.gif");
42            flagImage[5] = new ImageIcon("image/india.gif");
43            flagImage[6] = new ImageIcon("image/norway.gif");
44            flagImage[7] = new ImageIcon("image/uk.gif");
45            flagImage[8] = new ImageIcon("image/us.gif");
46
47            // Set text description
48            flagDescription[0] = "The Maple Leaf flag \n\n" +
49              "The Canadian National Flag was adopted by the Canadian " +
50              "Parliament on October 22, 1964 and was proclaimed into law " +
51              "by Her Majesty Queen Elizabeth II (the Queen of Canada) on " +
52              "February 15, 1965. The Canadian Flag (colloquially known " +
53              "as The Maple Leaf Flag) is a red flag of the proportions " +
54              "two by length and one by width, containing in its center a " +
55              "white square, with a single red stylized eleven-point " +
56              "mapleleaf centered in the white square.";
57            flagDescription[1] = "Description for China ... ";
58            flagDescription[2] = "Description for Denmark ... ";
59            flagDescription[3] = "Description for France ... ";
60            flagDescription[4] = "Description for Germany ... ";
61            flagDescription[5] = "Description for India ... ";
62            flagDescription[6] = "Description for Norway ... ";
63            flagDescription[7] = "Description for UK ... ";
64            flagDescription[8] = "Description for US ... ";
65
66            // Create items into the combo box
67            jcbo = new JComboBox(flagTitle);
68
69            // Set the first country (Canada) for display
70            setDisplay(0);
71
72            // Add combo box and description panel to the list
73            getContentPane().add(jcbo, BorderLayout.NORTH);
74            getContentPane().add(descriptionPanel, BorderLayout.CENTER);
75
76            // Register listener
77            jcbo.addItemListener(this);
78          }
79
80          /** Handle item selection */
81          public void itemStateChanged(ItemEvent e) {
82            setDisplay(jcbo.getSelectedIndex());
83          }
84
85          /** Set display information on the description panel */
86          public void setDisplay(int index) {
87            descriptionPanel.setTitle(flagTitle[index]);
88            descriptionPanel.setImageIcon(flagImage[index]);
89            descriptionPanel.setTextDescription(flagDescription[index]);
90          }
91        }
```

Review

The frame listens to `ItemEvent` from the `JComboBox` item, so it implements `ItemListener` (Lines 81–83). Instead of using the `ItemEvent`, you can rewrite the program to use `ActionEvent` for handling combo box item selection.

The program stores the flag information in three arrays: `flagTitle`, `flagImage`, and `flagDescription` (Lines 9–17). The array `flagTitle` contains the names of the nine countries, the array `flagImage` contains images of the nine countries' flags, and the array `flagDescription` contains descriptions of the flags.

The program creates an instance of `DescriptionPanel` (Line 20), which was presented in Example 11.4. The program creates a combo box with initial values from `flagTitle` (Line 67). When the user selects an item in the combo box, the `ItemStateChanged` handler is executed, which finds the selected index and sets its corresponding flag title, flag image, and flag description on the panel.

11.8   Lists

A *list* is a component that basically performs the same function as a combo box but enables the user to choose a single value or multiple values. The Swing `JList` is very versatile. Its advanced features are beyond the scope of this book. This section demonstrates selecting string items from a list.

To create a list with a set of strings, use the following constructor:

```
public JList(Object[] stringItems)
```

where `stringItems` is an array of `String`.

The following properties are often useful:

- **selectedIndex** is an `int` value indicating the index of the selected item in the list.

- **selectedIndices** is an array of `int` values representing the indices of the selected items in the list.

- **selectedValue** is the first selected value in the list.

- **selectedValues** is an array of objects representing selected values in the list.

- **selectionMode** is one of the three values (`SINGLE_SELECTION`, `SINGLE_INTERVAL_SELECTION`, `MULTIPLE_INTERVAL_SELECTION`) that indicate whether a single item, single-interval item, or multiple-interval item can be selected. Single selection allows only one item to be selected. Single-interval selection allows multiple selections, but the selected items must be contiguous. Multiple-interval selection allows selections of multiple contiguous items. The default value is `MULTIPLE_INTERVAL_SELECTION`.

- **visibleRowCount** is the preferred number of rows in the list that can be displayed without a scrollbar. The default value is 8.

Lists do not scroll automatically. To make a list scrollable, create a scroll pane and add the list to it. Text areas are made scrollable in the same way.

JList generates javax.swing.event.ListSelectionEvent to notify the listeners of the selections. The listener must implement the valueChanged handler to process the event. Here is an example of how to get a selected item from the valueChanged(ListSelectionEvent e) handler:

```
public void valueChanged(ListSelectionEvent e) {
  String selectedItem = (String)jlst.getSelectedValue();
}
```

Example 11.6 Using Lists

Problem

Write a program that lets users select countries in a list and display the flags of the selected countries in the labels. Figure 11.9 shows a sample run of the program.

Figure 11.9   *When the countries in the list are selected, corresponding images of their flags are displayed in the labels.*

Solution

Here are the major steps in the program:

1. Create the user interface.

   Create a list with nine country names as selection values, and place the list inside a scroll pane. Place the scroll pane in the west of the frame. Create nine labels to be used to display countries' flag images. Place the labels in the panel, and place the panel in the center of the frame.

2. Process the event.

Implement the `valueChanged` method to set the selected countries' flag images in the labels.

```java
1   // ListDemo.java: Use list to select a country and display the
2   // selected country's flag
3   import java.awt.*;
4   import java.awt.event.*;
5   import javax.swing.*;
6   import javax.swing.event.*;
7
8   public class ListDemo extends JFrame
9     implements ListSelectionListener {
10    // Declare an ImageIcon array for the national flags of 9 countries
11    private ImageIcon[] imageIcon = new ImageIcon[9];
12
13    // Arrays of labels for displaying images
14    private JLabel[] jlblImageViewer = new JLabel[9];
15
16    // The list for selecting countries
17    JList jlst;
18
19    /** Main Method */
20    public static void main(String[] args) {
21      ListDemo frame = new ListDemo();
22      frame.setSize(650, 500);
23      frame.setTitle("List Demo");
24      frame.setDefaultCloseOperation(JFrame.EXIT_ON_CLOSE);
25      frame.setVisible(true);
26    }
27
28    /** Default Constructor */
29    public ListDemo() {
30      // Load images into imageIcon array
31      imageIcon[0] = new ImageIcon("image/us.gif");
32      imageIcon[1] = new ImageIcon("image/ca.gif");
33      imageIcon[2] = new ImageIcon("image/uk.gif");
34      imageIcon[3] = new ImageIcon("image/germany.gif");
35      imageIcon[4] = new ImageIcon("image/fr.gif");
36      imageIcon[5] = new ImageIcon("image/denmark.gif");
37      imageIcon[6] = new ImageIcon("image/norway.gif");
38      imageIcon[7] = new ImageIcon("image/china.gif");
39      imageIcon[8] = new ImageIcon("image/india.gif");
40
41      // Create a string of country names
42      String[] countries = {"United States of America", "Canada",
43        "United Kingdom", "Germany", "France", "Denmark", "Norway",
44        "China", "India"};
45
46      // Create a list with the country names
47      jlst = new JList(countries);
48
49      // Create a panel to hold nine labels
50      JPanel p = new JPanel();
51      p.setLayout(new GridLayout(3, 3, 5, 5));
52
53      for (int i = 0; i < 9; i++) {
54        p.add(jlblImageViewer[i] = new JLabel());
55        jlblImageViewer[i].setHorizontalAlignment
56          (SwingConstants.CENTER);
57      }
58
```

continues

Example 11.6 Using Lists

```
59          // Add p and the list to the frame
60          getContentPane().add(p, BorderLayout.CENTER);
61          getContentPane().add(new JScrollPane(jlst), BorderLayout.WEST);
62
63          // Register listeners
64          jlst.addListSelectionListener(this);
65        }
66
67        /** Handle list selection */
68        public void valueChanged(ListSelectionEvent e) {
69          // Get selected indices
70          int[] indices = jlst.getSelectedIndices();
71
72          int i;
73          // Set icons in the labels
74          for (i = 0; i < indices.length; i++) {
75            jlblImageViewer[i].setIcon(imageIcon[indices[i]]);
76          }
77
78          // Remove icons from the rest of the labels
79          for ( ; i < 9; i++) {
80            jlblImageViewer[i].setIcon(null);
81          }
82        }
83      }
```

Review

The frame listens to ListSelectionEvent for handling the selection of country names in the list, so it implements ListSelectionListener (Line 9). ListSelectionEvent and ListSelectionListener are defined in the javax.swing.event package, so this package is imported in the program.

The program creates an array of nine labels for displaying flag images for nine countries. The program loads the images of the nine countries into an image array (Lines 30–39) and creates a list of the nine countries in the same order as in the image array (Line 47). Thus the index 0 of the image array corresponds to the first country in the list.

The list is placed in a scroll pane (Line 61) so that it can be scrolled when the number of items in the list extends beyond the viewing area.

By default, the selection mode of the list is multiple-interval, which allows the user to select multiple items from different blocks in the list. When the user selects countries in the list, the valueChanged handler (Lines 67–82) is executed, which gets the indices of the selected item and sets their corresponding image icons in the label to display the flags.

The example constructs a list with a fixed set of strings. If you want to add new items to the list or delete existing items, you have to use the list model. The use of list models is explained in Advanced Swing Components in the companion Web site.

11.9   Check Boxes

A *check box* is a component that enables the user to toggle a choice on or off, like a light switch.

To create a check box, use the following constructors:

- `public JCheckBox()`

  Creates an unselected empty check box.

- `public JCheckBox(String text)`

  Creates an unselected check box with the specified text.

- `public JCheckBox(String text, boolean selected)`

  Creates a check box with a text and specifies whether the check box is initially selected.

- `public JCheckBox(Icon icon)`

  Creates an unselected check box with an icon.

- `public JCheckBox(Icon icon, boolean selected)`

  Creates a check box with an icon and specifies whether the check box is initially selected.

- `public JCheckBox(String text, Icon icon)`

  Creates an unselected check box with an icon and a text.

- `public JCheckBox (String text, Icon icon, boolean selected)`

  Creates a check box with an icon and a text, and specifies whether the check box is initially selected.

In addition to `text`, `icon`, `mnemonic`, `verticalAlignment`, `horizontalAlignment`, `horizontalTextPosition`, and `verticalTextPosition`, `JCheckBox` has the following property:

- **`selected`** specifies whether the check box is selected.

`JCheckBox` can generate `ActionEvent` and `ItemEvent`, among many other events. The following code shows you how to implement `itemStateChanged` handler to determine whether a box is checked or unchecked in response to an `ItemEvent`:

```
public void itemStateChanged(ItemEvent e) {
  // Make sure the source is a JCheckBox
  if (e.getSource() instanceof JCheckBox)
    if (jchk1.isSelected())
      // Process the selection for jchk1;
    if (jchk2.isSelected())
      // Process the selection for jchk2;
}
```

Example 11.7 Using Check Boxes

Problem

Write a program that can dynamically change the font of a message to be displayed on a panel. The message can be displayed in bold and italic at the same time, or can be displayed in the center of the panel. You can select the font name or font size from combo boxes, as shown in Figure 11.10.

Figure 11.10   *The program uses three* JCheckBox *components to let the user choose the font style for the message displayed and specify whether the message is centered, and uses combo boxes for selecting font names and font sizes.*

Solution

Here are the major steps in the program:

1. Create the user interface.

   Create a panel to hold font name and size combo boxes, and place the panel in the north of the frame. Create a MessagePanel object, and place it in the center of the frame. Create a panel to hold three check boxes for Centered, Bold, and Italic, and place the panel in the south of the frame.

2. Process the event.

   Implement the itemStateChanged method to set appropriate font, size, and style for the message in the MessagePanel based on the item selections from the combo boxes and check boxes.

```
1    // CheckBoxDemo.java: Use check boxes to select one or more choices
2    import java.awt.BorderLayout;
3    import java.awt.Color;
4    import java.awt.Font;
5    import java.awt.GraphicsEnvironment;
6    import java.awt.event.*;
7    import javax.swing.*;
8
9    public class CheckBoxDemo extends JFrame implements ItemListener {
10     // Declare check boxes
11     private JCheckBox jchkCentered, jchkBold, jchkItalic;
12
13     // Declare a combo box to hold font names
14     private JComboBox jcboFontName = new JComboBox();
15
```

```
16      // Declare a combo box to hold font sizes
17      private JComboBox jcboFontSize = new JComboBox();
18
19      // Font name
20      private String fontName = "SansSerif";
21
22      // Font style
23      private int fontStyle = Font.PLAIN;
24
25      // Font Size
26      private int fontSize = 12;
27
28      // Declare a panel for displaying message
29      private MessagePanel messagePanel;
30
31      /** Main method */
32      public static void main(String[] args) {
33        CheckBoxDemo frame = new CheckBoxDemo();
34        frame.setDefaultCloseOperation(JFrame.EXIT_ON_CLOSE);
35        frame.pack();
36        frame.setVisible(true);
37      }
38
39      /** Default constructor */
40      public CheckBoxDemo() {
41        setTitle("Check Box Demo");
42
43        // Find all available font names
44        GraphicsEnvironment e =
45          GraphicsEnvironment.getLocalGraphicsEnvironment();
46        String[] fontnames = e.getAvailableFontFamilyNames();
47        for (int i = 0; i < fontnames.length; i++)
48          jcboFontName.addItem(fontnames[i]);
49        jcboFontName.setSelectedItem("" + fontName);
50
51        // Add font sizes into jcboFontSize
52        for (int i = 1; i <= 100; i++)
53          jcboFontSize.addItem("" + i);
54        jcboFontSize.setSelectedItem("" + fontSize);
55
56        // Create the message panel
57        messagePanel = new MessagePanel();
58        messagePanel.setMessage("Welcome to Java!");
59        messagePanel.setBackground(Color.yellow);
60
61        // Hold font name label and combo box
62        JPanel p1 = new JPanel();
63        p1.setLayout(new BorderLayout());
64        p1.add(new JLabel("Font Name"), BorderLayout.WEST);
65        p1.add(jcboFontName, BorderLayout.CENTER);
66
67        // Hold font size label and combo box
68        JPanel p2 = new JPanel();
69        p2.setLayout(new BorderLayout());
70        p2.add(new JLabel("Font Size"), BorderLayout.WEST);
71        p2.add(jcboFontSize, BorderLayout.CENTER);
72
73        // Add p1 and p2 into p3
74        JPanel p3 = new JPanel();
75        p3.setLayout(new BorderLayout());
76        p3.add(p1, BorderLayout.CENTER);
77        p3.add(p2, BorderLayout.EAST);
78
```

continues

469

Example 11.7 continued

```
79          // Put three check boxes in panel p
80          JPanel p = new JPanel();
81          p.add(jchkCentered = new JCheckBox("Centered"));
82          p.add(jchkBold = new JCheckBox("Bold"));
83          p.add(jchkItalic = new JCheckBox("Italic"));
84
85          // Set keyboard mnemonics
86          jchkCentered.setMnemonic('C');
87          jchkBold.setMnemonic('B');
88          jchkItalic.setMnemonic('I');
89
90          // Place messagePanel, p3, and p in the frame
91          getContentPane().setLayout(new BorderLayout());
92          getContentPane().add(messagePanel, BorderLayout.CENTER);
93          getContentPane().add(p3, BorderLayout.NORTH);
94          getContentPane().add(p, BorderLayout.SOUTH);
95
96          // Register listeners on jcboFontName and jcboFontSize
97          jcboFontName.addItemListener(this);
98          jcboFontSize.addItemListener(this);
99
100         // Register listeners on jchkCentered, jchkBold, and jchkItalic
101         jchkCentered.addItemListener(this);
102         jchkBold.addItemListener(this);
103         jchkItalic.addItemListener(this);
104       }
105
106       /** Handle check box selection */
107       public void itemStateChanged(ItemEvent e) {
108         if (e.getSource() == jcboFontName) {
109           fontName = (String)(jcboFontName.getSelectedItem());
110
111           // Set font for the message
112           messagePanel.setFont(new Font(fontName, fontStyle, fontSize));
113         }
114         else if (e.getSource() == jcboFontSize) {
115           fontSize = Integer.parseInt(
116             (String)(jcboFontSize.getSelectedItem()));
117
118           // Set font for the message
119           messagePanel.setFont(new Font(fontName, fontStyle, fontSize));
120         }
121         else if ((e.getSource() == jchkBold) ||
122           (e.getSource() == jchkItalic)) {
123           fontStyle = Font.PLAIN;
124
125           // Determine a font style
126           if (jchkBold.isSelected())
127             fontStyle = fontStyle + Font.BOLD;
128           if (jchkItalic.isSelected())
129             fontStyle = fontStyle + Font.ITALIC;
130
131           // Set font for the message
132           messagePanel.setFont(new Font(fontName, fontStyle, fontSize));
133         }
134         else if (e.getSource() == jchkCentered) {
135           if (jchkCentered.isSelected())
136             messagePanel.setCentered(true);
```

```
137            else
138               messagePanel.setCentered(false);
139
140            // Repaint the message panel
141            messagePanel.repaint();
142         }
143      }
144   }
```

Review

The program displays the message using the MessagePanel class. The user can choose a font name, style, and size for the font in MessagePanel. The font name and size are selected in the combo boxes. The font styles (Font.BOLD and Font.ITALIC) are specified in the check boxes. If no font style is selected, the font style is Font.PLAIN. You can also specify whether a message is centered in the Centered check box.

The combo boxes and check boxes can all fire ItemEvent. When the itemState-Changed handler is invoked (Line 107), it checks the source of the event and processes the event accordingly. For an event from the font name combo box, the handler stores the selected font name to fontName (Line 109). For an event from the font size, the handler stores the selected font size to fontSize (Lines 115–116). For an event from a check box, the handler determines the state of each check box and combines all selected fonts (Lines 123–129). The font styles are the int constants Font.BOLD and Font.ITALIC, and the default font style is Font.PLAIN. Font styles are combined by adding together the selected integers representing the fonts. When the Centered check box is checked or unchecked, the centered property of the MessagePanel class is set to true or false (Lines 135–138).

The keyboard mnemonics 'C', 'B', and 'I' are set on the check boxes "Centered", "Bold", and "Italic", respectively (Lines 86–88). You can use a mouse gesture or a shortcut key to select a check box.

The setFont method defined in the Component class is inherited in the MessagePanel class. This method automatically invokes the repaint method. Invoking setFont in messagePanel automatically repaints the message (Lines 112, 119, 132).

Since invoking the method setCentered in MessagePanel does not repaint the viewing area in the panel, you must invoke the repaint method to refresh the panel (Line 141).

11.10   Radio Buttons

Radio buttons, also known as *option buttons*, enable you to choose a single item from a group of choices. In appearance radio buttons resemble check boxes, but check boxes display a square that is either checked or blank, whereas radio buttons display a circle that is either filled (if selected) or blank (if not selected).

The constructors of JRadioButton, shown directly below, are similar to the constructors of JCheckBox.

■ public JRadioButton()

Creates an unselected empty radio button.

■ public JRadioButton(String text)

Creates an unselected radio button with the specified text.

■ public JRadioButton(String text, boolean selected)

Creates a radio button with a text and specifies whether the radio button is initially selected.

■ public JRadioButton(Icon icon)

Creates an unselected radio button with an icon.

■ public JRadioButton(Icon icon, boolean selected)

Creates a radio button with an icon and specifies whether the radio button is initially selected.

■ public JRadioButton(String text, Icon icon)

Creates an unselected radio button with an icon and a text.

■ public JRadioButton(String text, Icon icon, boolean selected)

Creates a radio button with an icon and a text, and specifies whether the radio button is initially selected.

Here is how to create a radio button with a text and an icon:

```
JRadioButton jrb = new JRadioButton(
  "My Radio Button", new ImageIcon("imagefile.gif"));
```

Radio buttons are added to a container just like buttons. To group radio buttons, you need to create an instance of java.swing.ButtonGroup and use the add method to add them to it, as follows:

```
ButtonGroup btg = new ButtonGroup();
btg.add(jrb1);
btg.add(jrb2);
```

This code creates a radio button group for radio buttons jrb1 and jrb2 so that jrb1 and jrb2 are selected mutually exclusively. Without grouping, jrb1 and jrb2 would be independent.

JRadioButton has such properties as text, icon, mnemonic, verticalAlignment, horizontalAlignment, selected, horizontalTextPosition, and verticalText-Position.

JRadioButton can generate ActionEvent and ItemEvent among many other events. The following code shows you how to implement the itemStateChanged handler to determine whether a box is checked or unchecked in response to an ItemEvent:

```
public void itemStateChanged(ItemEvent e) {
  // Make sure the source is a JRadioButton
  if (e.getSource() instanceof JRadioButton)
    if (jrb1.isSelected())
      // Process the selection for jrb1
    else if (jrb2.isSelected())
      // Process the selection for jrb2
}
```

Example 11.8 Using Radio Buttons

Problem

Write a program that simulates traffic lights. The program lets the user select one of three lights: red, yellow, or green. When a radio button is selected, the light is turned on, and only one light can be on at a time. No light is on when the program starts. Figure 11.11 contains the output of a sample run of the program.

Figure 11.11 *The radio buttons are grouped to let you select only one color in the group to control traffic lights.*

Solution

Here are the major steps in the program:

1. Define a subclass of JPanel named Light to draw three traffic lights (Red, Green, and Yellow). Create a Light object and place it in the center of the frame. Create three radio buttons for Red, Green, and Yellow, place them in a panel, and place the panel in the south of the frame.

continues

Example 11.8 continued

2. Create a `ButtonGroup` object and use it to group three radio buttons.

3. Implement the `itemStateChanged` method to check which radio button is selected, and set the corresponding light in the `Light` object.

```java
1    // RadioButtonDemo.java: Use radio buttons to select a choice
2    import java.awt.*;
3    import java.awt.event.*;
4    import javax.swing.*;
5
6    public class RadioButtonDemo extends JFrame
7      implements ItemListener {
8      // Declare radio buttons
9      private JRadioButton jrbRed, jrbYellow, jrbGreen;
10
11     // Declare a radio button group
12     private ButtonGroup btg = new ButtonGroup();
13
14     // Declare a traffic light display panel
15     private Light light;
16
17     /** Main method */
18     public static void main(String[] args) {
19       RadioButtonDemo frame = new RadioButtonDemo();
20       frame.setDefaultCloseOperation(JFrame.EXIT_ON_CLOSE);
21       frame.setSize(250, 170);
22       frame.setVisible(true);
23     }
24
25     /** Default constructor */
26     public RadioButtonDemo() {
27       setTitle("RadioButton Demo");
28
29       // Add traffic light panel to panel p1
30       JPanel p1 = new JPanel();
31       p1.setSize(200, 200);
32       p1.setLayout(new FlowLayout(FlowLayout.CENTER));
33       light = new Light();
34       light.setSize(40, 90);
35       p1.add(light);
36
37       // Put the radio button in Panel p2
38       JPanel p2 = new JPanel();
39       p2.setLayout(new FlowLayout());
40       p2.add(jrbRed = new JRadioButton("Red", false));
41       p2.add(jrbYellow = new JRadioButton("Yellow", false));
42       p2.add(jrbGreen = new JRadioButton("Green", false));
43
44       // Set keyboard mnemonics
45       jrbRed.setMnemonic('R');
46       jrbYellow.setMnemonic('Y');
47       jrbGreen.setMnemonic('G');
48
49       // Group radio buttons
50       btg.add(jrbRed);
51       btg.add(jrbYellow);
52       btg.add(jrbGreen);
53
```

```
54        // Place p1 and p2 in the frame
55        getContentPane().setLayout(new BorderLayout());
56        getContentPane().add(p1, BorderLayout.CENTER);
57        getContentPane().add(p2, BorderLayout.SOUTH);
58
59        // Register listeners for check boxes
60        jrbRed.addItemListener(this);
61        jrbYellow.addItemListener(this);
62        jrbGreen.addItemListener(this);
63      }
64
65      /** Handle checkbox events */
66      public void itemStateChanged(ItemEvent e) {
67        if (jrbRed.isSelected())
68          light.turnOnRed(); // Set red light
69        if (jrbYellow.isSelected())
70          light.turnOnYellow(); // Set yellow light
71        if (jrbGreen.isSelected())
72          light.turnOnGreen(); // Set green light
73      }
74    }
75
76  // Three traffic lights shown in a panel
77  class Light extends JPanel {
78    private boolean red;
79    private boolean yellow;
80    private boolean green;
81
82    /** Default constructor */
83    public Light() {
84      turnOnGreen();
85    }
86
87    /** Set red light on */
88    public void turnOnRed() {
89      red = true;
90      yellow = false;
91      green = false;
92      repaint();
93    }
94
95    /** Set yellow light on */
96    public void turnOnYellow() {
97      red = false;
98      yellow = true;
99      green = false;
100     repaint();
101   }
102
103   /** Set green light on */
104   public void turnOnGreen() {
105     red = false;
106     yellow = false;
107     green = true;
108     repaint();
109   }
110
111   /** Display lights */
112   public void paintComponent(Graphics g) {
113     super.paintComponent(g);
114
```

continues

Example 11.8 continued

```
115          if (red) {
116            g.setColor(Color.red);
117            g.fillOval(10, 10, 20, 20);
118            g.setColor(Color.black);
119            g.drawOval(10, 35, 20, 20);
120            g.drawOval(10, 60, 20, 20);
121            g.drawRect(5, 5, 30, 80);
122          }
123          else if (yellow) {
124            g.setColor(Color.yellow);
125            g.fillOval(10, 35, 20, 20);
126            g.setColor(Color.black);
127            g.drawRect(5, 5, 30, 80);
128            g.drawOval(10, 10, 20, 20);
129            g.drawOval(10, 60, 20, 20);
130          }
131          else if (green) {
132            g.setColor(Color.green);
133            g.fillOval(10, 60, 20, 20);
134            g.setColor(Color.black);
135            g.drawRect(5, 5, 30, 80);
136            g.drawOval(10, 10, 20, 20);
137            g.drawOval(10, 35, 20, 20);
138          }
139          else {
140            g.setColor(Color.black);
141            g.drawRect(5, 5, 30, 80);
142            g.drawOval(10, 10, 20, 20);
143            g.drawOval(10, 35, 20, 20);
144            g.drawOval(10, 60, 20, 20);
145          }
146        }
147
148        /** Set preferred size */
149        public Dimension getPreferredSize() {
150          return new Dimension(40, 90);
151        }
152    }
```

Review

The lights are displayed on a panel. The program groups the radio buttons in a panel and places it below the traffic light panel. BorderLayout is used to arrange these components.

The Light class, a subclass of JPanel, contains the methods turnOnRed(), turnOnYellow(), and turnOnGreen() to control the lights. For example, use light.turnOnRed() to turn on the red light, where light is an instance of Light.

The program creates a ButtonGroup btg and puts three JRadioButton instances (jrbRed, jrbYellow, and jrbGreen) in the group (Lines 49–52). When the user checks a box in the group, the handler, itemStateChanged(ItemEvent e), determines which radio button is selected, using the isSelected() method, and turns on the corresponding light (Lines 65–73).

The getPreferredSize() method is overridden to set the preferred size to 40 by 90 (Lines 149–151). This is just the right size for displaying the traffic lights.

11.11   Borders

Borders are an interesting and useful feature. You can set a border on any object of the JComponent class, but often it is useful to set a titled border on a JPanel that groups a set of related user-interface components.

There are several basic types of borders to choose from. The titled border is the most useful. To create a titled border, use the following statement:

```
Border titledBorder = new TitledBorder("A Title");
```

Border is the interface for all types of borders. TitledBorder is an implementation of Border with a title. You can create a border as desired by using the following properties:

- **title** specifies the title of the border.

- **titleColor** specifies the color of the title.

- **titleFont** specifies the font of the title.

- **titleJustification** specifies Border.LEFT, Border.CENTER, or Border.RIGHT for left, center, or right title justification.

- **titlePosition** is one of the six values (Border.ABOVE_TOP, Border.TOP, Border.BELOW_TOP, Border.ABOVE_BOTTOM, Border.BOTTOM, Border.BELOW_ BOTTOM) that specify the title position above the border line, on the border line, or below the border line.

- **border** is a property in TitleBorder for building composite borders. You can have borders inside borders.

The other types of borders can be created by using the following classes:

- **BevelBorder** is a 3D-look border that can be lowered or raised. To construct a BevelBorder, use the following constructor, which creates a BevelBorder with the specified bevelType (BevelBorder.LOWERED or BevelBorder.RAISED):

  ```
  public BevelBorder(int bevelType)
  ```

- **EtchedBorder** is an etched border that can be etched-in or etched-out. You can use its default constructor to construct an EtchedBorder with a lowered border. EtchedBorder has a property etchType with the value LOWERED or RAISED.

- **LineBorder** is a line border of arbitrary thickness and a single color. To create a LineBorder, use the following constructor:

  ```
  public LineBorder(Color c, int thickness)
  ```

- **MatteBorder** is a matte-like border padded with the icon images. To create a MatteBorder, use the following constructor:

  ```
  public MatteBorder(Icon tileIcon)
  ```

- **EmptyBorder** is a border with border space but no drawings. To create an EmptyBorder, use the following constructor:

  ```
  public EmptyBorder(int top, int left, int bottom, int right)
  ```

NOTE

All the border classes and interfaces are grouped in the package `javax.swing.border`.

Swing also provides the `javax.swing.BorderFactory` class, which contains static methods for creating borders. Some of the static methods are:

```
public static TitledBorder createTitledBorder(String title)

public static Border createLoweredBevelBorder()

public static Border createRaisedBevelBorder()

public static Border createLineBorder(Color color)

public static Border createLineBorder(Color color, int thickness)

public static Border createEtchedBorder()

public static Border createEtchedBorder(
    Color highlight, Color shadow)

public static Border createEmptyBorder()

public static Border createEmptyBorder(
    int top, int left, int bottom, int right)

public static MatteBorder createMatteBorder(
    int top, int left, int bottom, int right, Color color)

public static MatteBorder createMatteBorder(
    int top, int left, int bottom, int right, Icon tileIcon)

public static Border createCompoundBorder(
    Border outsideBorder, Border insideBorder)
```

For example, to create an etched border, use the following statement:

```
Border border = BorderFactory.createEtchedBorder();
```

NOTE

Borders and icons can be shared. Thus you can create a border or icon and use it to set the border or icon property for any GUI component. For example, the following statements set a border b for two panels p1 and p2:

```
p1.setBorder(b);
p2.setBorder(b);
```

Example 11.9 Using Borders

Problem

Write a program that creates and displays various types of borders. You can select a border with a title or without a title. For a border without a title, you can choose a border style from Lowered Bevel, Raised Bevel, Etched, Line, Matte, or Empty. For a border with a title, you can specify the title position and justification. You can also embed another border into a titled border. Figure 11.12 displays a sample run of the program.

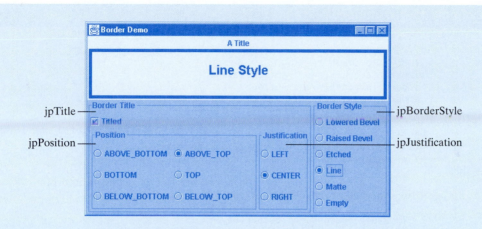

Figure 11.12   *The program demonstrates various types of borders.*

Solution

Here are the major steps in the program:

1. Create the user interface.

   a. Create a MessagePanel object and place it in the center of the frame.

   b. Create a panel named jpPositon to group the radio buttons for selecting the border title position. Set the border of this panel in the titled border with the title "Position".

   c. Create a panel named jpJustification to group the radio buttons for selecting the border title justification. Set the border of this panel in the titled border with the title "Justification".

   d. Create a panel named jpTitleOptions to hold the jpPosition panel and the jpJustification panel.

   e. Create a panel named jpTitle to hold a check box named "Titled" and the jpTitleOptions panel.

   f. Create a panel named jpBorderStyle to group the radio buttons for selecting border styles.

   g. Create a panel named jpAllChoices to hold the panels jpTitle and jpBorderStyle. Place jpAllChoices in the south of the frame.

2. Process the event.

   Implement the actionPerformed handler to set the border for the message panel according to the events from the check box, and all the radio buttons.

   continues

479

Example 11.9 continued

```
1    // BorderDemo.java: Use borders for JComponent components
2    import java.awt.*;
3    import java.awt.event.ActionListener;
4    import java.awt.event.ActionEvent;
5    import javax.swing.*;
6    import javax.swing.border.*;
7
8    public class BorderDemo extends JFrame implements ActionListener {
9      // Declare a panel for displaying message
10     private MessagePanel messagePanel;
11
12     // A check box for selecting a border with or without a title
13     private JCheckBox jchkTitled;
14
15     // Radio buttons for border styles
16     private JRadioButton jrbLoweredBevel, jrbRaisedBevel,
17       jrbEtched, jrbLine, jrbMatte, jrbEmpty;
18
19     // Radio buttons for titled border options
20     private JRadioButton jrbAboveBottom, jrbBottom,
21       jrbBelowBottom, jrbAboveTop, jrbTop, jrbBelowTop,
22       jrbLeft, jrbCenter, jrbRight;
23
24     // TitledBorder for the message panel
25     private TitledBorder messagePanelBorder;
26
27     /** Main method */
28     public static void main(String[] args) {
29       BorderDemo frame = new BorderDemo();
30       frame.setDefaultCloseOperation(JFrame.EXIT_ON_CLOSE);
31       frame.pack();
32       frame.setVisible(true);
33     }
34
35     /** Constructor */
36     public BorderDemo() {
37       setTitle("Border Demo");
38
39       // Create a MessagePanel instance and set colors
40       messagePanel = new MessagePanel("Display the border type");
41       messagePanel.setCentered(true);
42       messagePanel.setBackground(Color.yellow);
43       messagePanel.setBorder(messagePanelBorder);
44
45       // Place title position radio buttons
46       JPanel jpPosition = new JPanel();
47       jpPosition.setLayout(new GridLayout(3, 2));
48       jpPosition.add(
49         jrbAboveBottom = new JRadioButton("ABOVE_BOTTOM"));
50       jpPosition.add(jrbAboveTop = new JRadioButton("ABOVE_TOP"));
51       jpPosition.add(jrbBottom = new JRadioButton("BOTTOM"));
52       jpPosition.add(jrbTop = new JRadioButton("TOP"));
53       jpPosition.add(
54         jrbBelowBottom = new JRadioButton("BELOW_BOTTOM"));
55       jpPosition.add(jrbBelowTop = new JRadioButton("BELOW_TOP"));
56       jpPosition.setBorder(new TitledBorder("Position"));
57
58       // Place title justification radio buttons
59       JPanel jpJustification = new JPanel();
60       jpJustification.setLayout(new GridLayout(3,1));
```

```
61          jpJustification.add(jrbLeft = new JRadioButton("LEFT"));
62          jpJustification.add(jrbCenter = new JRadioButton("CENTER"));
63          jpJustification.add(jrbRight = new JRadioButton("RIGHT"));
64          jpJustification.setBorder(new TitledBorder("Justification"));
65
66          // Create panel jpTitleOptions to hold jpPosition and
67          // jpJustification
68          JPanel jpTitleOptions = new JPanel();
69          jpTitleOptions.setLayout(new BorderLayout());
70          jpTitleOptions.add(jpPosition, BorderLayout.CENTER);
71          jpTitleOptions.add(jpJustification, BorderLayout.EAST);
72
73          // Create Panel jpTitle to hold a check box and title position
74          // radio buttons, and title justification radio buttons
75          JPanel jpTitle = new JPanel();
76          jpTitle.setBorder(new TitledBorder("Border Title"));
77          jpTitle.setLayout(new BorderLayout());
78          jpTitle.add(jchkTitled = new JCheckBox("Titled"),
79            BorderLayout.NORTH);
80          jpTitle.add(jpTitleOptions, BorderLayout.CENTER);
81
82          // Group radio buttons for title position
83          ButtonGroup btgTitlePosition = new ButtonGroup();
84          btgTitlePosition.add(jrbAboveBottom);
85          btgTitlePosition.add(jrbBottom);
86          btgTitlePosition.add(jrbBelowBottom);
87          btgTitlePosition.add(jrbAboveTop);
88          btgTitlePosition.add(jrbTop);
89          btgTitlePosition.add(jrbBelowTop);
90
91          // Group radio buttons for title justification
92          ButtonGroup btgTitleJustification = new ButtonGroup();
93          btgTitleJustification.add(jrbLeft);
94          btgTitleJustification.add(jrbCenter);
95          btgTitleJustification.add(jrbRight);
96
97          // Create Panel jpBorderStyle to hold border style radio buttons
98          JPanel jpBorderStyle = new JPanel();
99          jpBorderStyle.setBorder(new TitledBorder("Border Style"));
100         jpBorderStyle.setLayout(new GridLayout(6, 1));
101         jpBorderStyle.add(jrbLoweredBevel =
102           new JRadioButton("Lowered Bevel"));
103         jpBorderStyle.add(jrbRaisedBevel =
104           new JRadioButton("Raised Bevel"));
105         jpBorderStyle.add(jrbEtched = new JRadioButton("Etched"));
106         jpBorderStyle.add(jrbLine = new JRadioButton("Line"));
107         jpBorderStyle.add(jrbMatte = new JRadioButton("Matte"));
108         jpBorderStyle.add(jrbEmpty = new JRadioButton("Empty"));
109
110         // Group radio buttons for border styles
111         ButtonGroup btgBorderStyle = new ButtonGroup();
112         btgBorderStyle.add(jrbLoweredBevel);
113         btgBorderStyle.add(jrbRaisedBevel);
114         btgBorderStyle.add(jrbEtched);
115         btgBorderStyle.add(jrbLine);
116         btgBorderStyle.add(jrbMatte);
117         btgBorderStyle.add(jrbEmpty);
118
```

continues

Example 11.9 continued

```
119          // Create Panel jpAllChoices to place jpTitle and jpBorderStyle
120          JPanel jpAllChoices = new JPanel();
121          jpAllChoices.setLayout(new BorderLayout());
122          jpAllChoices.add(jpTitle, BorderLayout.CENTER);
123          jpAllChoices.add(jpBorderStyle, BorderLayout.EAST);
124
125          // Place panels in the frame
126          getContentPane().setLayout(new BorderLayout());
127          getContentPane().add(messagePanel, BorderLayout.CENTER);
128          getContentPane().add(jpAllChoices, BorderLayout.SOUTH);
129
130          // Register listeners
131          jchkTitled.addActionListener(this);
132          jrbAboveBottom.addActionListener(this);
133          jrbBottom.addActionListener(this);
134          jrbBelowBottom.addActionListener(this);
135          jrbAboveTop.addActionListener(this);
136          jrbTop.addActionListener(this);
137          jrbBelowTop.addActionListener(this);
138          jrbLeft.addActionListener(this);
139          jrbCenter.addActionListener(this);
140          jrbRight.addActionListener(this);
141          jrbLoweredBevel.addActionListener(this);
142          jrbRaisedBevel.addActionListener(this);
143          jrbLine.addActionListener(this);
144          jrbEtched.addActionListener(this);
145          jrbMatte.addActionListener(this);
146          jrbEmpty.addActionListener(this);
147       }
148
149       /** Handle ActionEvents on check box and radio buttons */
150       public void actionPerformed(ActionEvent e) {
151          // Get border style
152          Border border = new EmptyBorder(2, 2, 2, 2);
153
154          if (jrbLoweredBevel.isSelected()) {
155             border = new BevelBorder(BevelBorder.LOWERED);
156             messagePanel.setMessage("Lowered Bevel Style");
157          }
158          else if (jrbRaisedBevel.isSelected()) {
159             border = new BevelBorder(BevelBorder.RAISED);
160             messagePanel.setMessage("Raised Bevel Style");
161          }
162          else if (jrbEtched.isSelected()) {
163             border = new EtchedBorder();
164             messagePanel.setMessage("Etched Style");
165          }
166          else if (jrbLine.isSelected()) {
167             border = new LineBorder(Color.black, 5);
168             messagePanel.setMessage("Line Style");
169          }
170          else if (jrbMatte.isSelected()) {
171             border = new MatteBorder(20, 20, 20, 20,
172                new ImageIcon("image/swirl.gif"));
173             messagePanel.setMessage("Matte Style");
174          }
175          else if (jrbEmpty.isSelected()) {
176             border = new EmptyBorder(2, 2, 2, 2);
```

482

```
177              messagePanel.setMessage("Empty Style");
178          }
179
180          if (jchkTitled.isSelected()) {
181              // Get the title position and justification
182              int titlePosition = TitledBorder.DEFAULT_POSITION;
183              int titleJustification = TitledBorder.DEFAULT_JUSTIFICATION;
184
185              if (jrbAboveBottom.isSelected())
186                titlePosition = TitledBorder.ABOVE_BOTTOM;
187              else if (jrbBottom.isSelected())
188                titlePosition = TitledBorder.BOTTOM;
189              else if (jrbBelowBottom.isSelected())
190                titlePosition = TitledBorder.BELOW_BOTTOM;
191              else if (jrbAboveTop.isSelected())
192                titlePosition = TitledBorder.ABOVE_TOP;
193              else if (jrbTop.isSelected())
194                titlePosition = TitledBorder.TOP;
195              else if (jrbBelowTop.isSelected())
196                titlePosition = TitledBorder.BELOW_TOP;
197
198              if (jrbLeft.isSelected())
199                titleJustification = TitledBorder.LEFT;
200              else if (jrbCenter.isSelected())
201                titleJustification = TitledBorder.CENTER;
202              else if (jrbRight.isSelected())
203                titleJustification = TitledBorder.RIGHT;
204
205              messagePanelBorder = new TitledBorder("A Title");
206              messagePanelBorder.setBorder(border);
207              messagePanelBorder.setTitlePosition(titlePosition);
208              messagePanelBorder.setTitleJustification(titleJustification);
209              messagePanelBorder.setTitle("A Title");
210              messagePanel.setBorder(messagePanelBorder);
211          }
212          else {
213            messagePanel.setBorder(border);
214          }
215        }
216      }
```

Review

This example uses many panels to group UI components to achieve the desired look. Figure 11.12 illustrates the relationship of the panels. The Border Title panel groups all the options for setting title properties. The position options are grouped in the Position panel. The justification options are grouped in the Justification panel. The Border Style panel groups the radio buttons for choosing Lowered Bevel, Raised Bevel, Etched, Line, Matte, and Empty borders.

The MessagePanel displays the selected border with or without a title, depending on the selection of the title check box. The MessagePanel also displays a message indicating which type of border is being used, depending on the selection of the radio button in the Border Style panel.

continues

Example 11.9 continued

The `TitledBorder` can be mixed with other borders. To do so, simply create an instance of `TitledBorder`, and use the `setBorder` method to embed a new border in `TitledBorder`.

The `MatteBorder` can be used to display icons on the border, as shown in Figure 11.13.

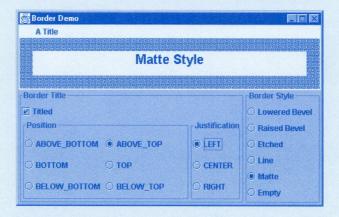

Figure 11.13   `MatteBorder` *can display icons on the border.*

11.12   *JOptionPane* Dialogs

You have used `JOptionPane` to create input and output dialog boxes. This section provides a comprehensive introduction to `JOptionPane` and other dialog boxes. A *dialog box* is normally used as a temporary window to receive additional information from the user or to provide notification that some event has occurred. Java provides the `JOptionPane` class, which can be used to create standard dialogs. You can build custom dialogs by extending the `JDialog` class.

The `JOptionPane` class can be used to create four kinds of standard dialogs:

- **Message dialog** shows a message and waits for the user to click OK.

- **Confirmation dialog** shows a question and asks for confirmation, such as OK or Cancel.

- **Input dialog** shows a question and gets the user's input from a text field, combo box, or list.

- **Option dialog** shows a question and gets the user's answer from a set of options.

These dialogs are created using the static methods `showXxxDialog` and generally appear as shown in Figure 11.14.

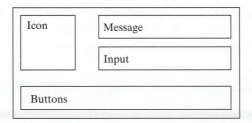

Figure 11.14   *A* JOptionPane *dialog can display an icon, a message, an input, and option buttons.*

For example, you can use the following method to create a message dialog box, as shown in Figure 11.15:

```
JOptionPane.showMessageDialog(this, "SSN not found",
   "For Your Information", JOptionPane.INFORMATION_MESSAGE);
```

Figure 11.15   *The message dialog displays a message and waits for the user to click OK.*

11.12.1 Message Dialogs

A *message dialog* box displays a message that alerts the user and waits for the user to click the OK button to close the dialog. The methods for creating message dialogs are:

```
public static void showMessageDialog(Component parentComponent,
                                     Object message)
public static void showMessageDialog(Component parentComponent,
                                     Object message,
                                     String title,
                                     int messageType)
public static void showMessageDialog(Component parentComponent,
                                     Object message,
                                     String title,
                                     int messageType,
                                     Icon icon)
```

The parentComponent can be any component or null. The message is an object, but often a string is used. These two parameters must always be specified. The title is a string displayed in the title bar of the dialog with default value "Message".

The messageType is one of the following constants:

```
JOptionPane.ERROR_MESSAGE
JOptionPane.INFORMATION_MESSAGE
JOptionPane.PLAIN_MESSAGE
JOptionPane.WARNING_MESSAGE
JOptionPane.QUESTION_MESSAGE
```

By default, messageType is JOptionPane.INFORMATION_MESSAGE. Each type has an associated icon except the PLAIN_MESSAGE type, as shown in Figure 11.16. You can also supply your own icon in the icon parameter.

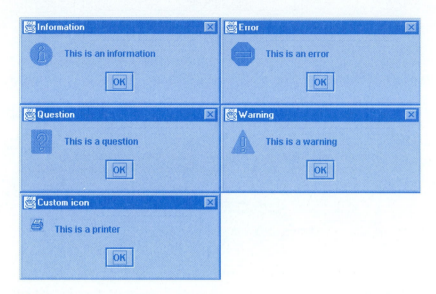

Figure 11.16   *There are five types of message dialog boxes.*

The message parameter is an object. If it is a GUI component, the component is displayed. If it is a non-GUI component, the string representation of the object is displayed. For example, the following statement displays a clock in a message dialog, as shown in Figure 11.17.

```
JOptionPane.showMessageDialog(this, new DrawClock(5, 40, 55),
  "Current Time", JOptionPane.PLAIN_MESSAGE);
```

Figure 11.17   *A clock is displayed in a message dialog.*

486

11.12.2   Confirmation Dialogs

A message dialog box displays a message and waits for the user to click the OK button to dismiss the dialog. The message dialog does not return any value. A *confirmation dialog* asks a question and requires the user to respond with an appropriate button. The confirmation dialog returns a value that corresponds to a selected button.

The methods for creating confirmation dialogs are:

```
public static int showConfirmDialog(Component parentComponent,
                                    Object message)
public static int showConfirmDialog(Component parentComponent,
                                    Object message,
                                    String title,
                                    int optionType)
public static int showConfirmDialog(Component parentComponent,
                                    Object message,
                                    String title,
                                    int optionType,
                                    int messageType)
public static int showConfirmDialog(Component parentComponent,
                                    Object message,
                                    String title,
                                    int optionType,
                                    int messageType,
                                    Icon icon)
```

The parameters `parentComponent`, `message`, `title`, `icon`, and `messageType` are the same as in the `showMessageDialog` method. The default value for `title` is "Select an Option" and for `messageType` is `QUESTION_MESSAGE`. The `optionType` determines which buttons are displayed in the dialog. The possible values are:

```
JOptionPane.YES_NO_OPTION
JOptionPane.YES_NO_CANCEL_OPTION
JOptionPane.OK_CANCEL_OPTION
```

Figure 11.18 shows the confirmation dialogs with these options.

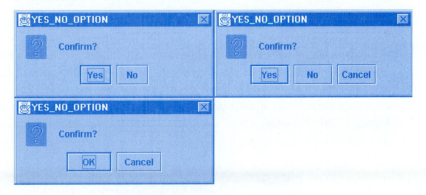

Figure 11.18   *The confirmation dialog displays a question and three types of option buttons, and requires responses from the user.*

The `showConfirmDialog` method returns one of the following `int` values corresponding to the selected option:

```
JOptionPane.YES_OPTION
JOptionPane.NO_OPTION
JOptionPane.CANCEL_OPTION
JOptionPane.OK_OPTION
JOptionPane.CLOSED_OPTION
```

These options correspond to the button that was activated, except for the `CLOSED_OPTION`, which implies that the dialog box is closed without buttons activated.

11.12.3   Input Dialogs

An *input dialog* box is used to receive input from the user. The input can be entered from a text field or selected from a combo box or a list. Selectable values can be specified in an array, and one of them can be designated as the initial selected value. If no selectable value is specified when an input dialog is created, a text field is used for entering input. If fewer than twenty selection values are specified, a combo box is displayed in the input dialog. If twenty or more selection values are specified, a list is used in the input dialog.

The methods for creating input dialogs are shown below:

```
public static String showInputDialog(Object message)
public static String showInputDialog(Component parentComponent,
                                     Object message)
public static String showInputDialog(Component parentComponent,
                                     Object message,
                                     String title,
                                     int messageType)
public static Object showInputDialog(Component parentComponent,
                                     Object message,
                                     int messageType,
                                     Icon icon,
                                     Object[] selectionValues,
                                     Object initialSelectionValue)
```

The first three methods listed above use text field for input, as shown in Figure 11.19. The last method listed above specifies an array of `Object` type as selection values in addition to an object specified as an initial selection. The first three methods return a `String` that is entered from the text field in the input dialog. The last method returns an `Object` selected from a combo box or a list. The input dialog displays a combo box if there are fewer than twenty selection values, as shown in Figure 11.20; it displays a list if there are twenty or more selection values, as shown in Figure 11.21.

Figure 11.19   *When creating an input dialog without specifying selection values, the input dialog displays a text field for data entry.*

Figure 11.20   *When creating an input dialog with selection values, the input dialog displays a combo box if there are fewer than twenty selection values.*

Figure 11.21   *When creating an input dialog with selection values, the input dialog displays a list if there are twenty or more selection values.*

NOTE

The `showInputDialog` method does not have the `optionType` parameter. The buttons for input dialog are not configurable. The OK and Cancel buttons are always used.

11.12.4   Option Dialogs

An *option dialog* allows you to create custom buttons. You can create an option dialog using the following method:

```
public static int showOptionDialog(Component parentComponent,
                                   Object message,
                                   String title,
                                   int optionType,
                                   int messageType,
                                   Icon icon,
                                   Object[] options,
                                   Object intialValue)
```

The buttons are specified using the `options` parameter. The `intialValue` parameter allows you to specify a button to receive initial focus. The `showOptionDialog` method returns an `int` value indicating the button that was activated. For example, here is the code that creates an option dialog, as shown in Figure 11.22:

```
int value =
  JOptionPane.showOptionDialog(this, "Select a button",
    "Option Dialog", JOptionPane.DEFAULT_OPTION,
    JOptionPane.PLAIN_MESSAGE, null,
     new Object[]{"Button 0", "Button 1", "Button 2"}, "Button 1");
```

Figure 11.22   *The option dialog displays the custom buttons.*

Example 11.10 Creating JOptionPane Dialogs

Problem

Write a program that demonstrates the use of JOptionPane dialogs. The program prompts the user to select the annual interest rate from a list in an input dialog, the number of years from a combo box in an input dialog, and the loan amount from an input dialog, and displays the loan payment schedule in a text area inside a JScrollPane in a message dialog, as shown in Figure 11.23.

Solution

Here are the major steps in the program:

1. Display an input dialog box to let the user select an annual interest rate from a list.

2. Display an input dialog box to let the user select the number of years from a combo box.

3. Display an input dialog box to let the user enter loan amount.

4. Compute the monthly payment, total payment and loan payment schedule, and display the result in a text area in a message dialog box.

```
1    // JOptionPaneDemo.java: Using standard dialogs
2    import javax.swing.*;
3
4    public class JOptionPaneDemo {
5      public static void main(String args[]) {
6        // Create an array for annual interest rates
7        Object[] rateList = new Object[25];
8        int i = 0;
9        for (double rate = 5; rate <= 8; rate += 1.0 / 8)
10         rateList[i++] = new Double(rate);
11
12        // Prompt the user to select an annual interest rate
13        Object annualInterstRateObject = JOptionPane.showInputDialog(
14          null, "Select annual interest rate:", "JOptionPane Demo",
15          JOptionPane.QUESTION_MESSAGE, null, rateList, null);
16        double annualInterestRate =
17          ((Double)annualInterstRateObject).doubleValue();
18
```

```
19          // Create an array for number of years
20          Object[] yearList = {new Integer(7), new Integer(15),
21            new Integer(30)};
22
23          // Prompt the user to enter number of years
24          Object numOfYearsObject = JOptionPane.showInputDialog(null,
25            "Select number of years:", "JOptionPane Demo",
26            JOptionPane.QUESTION_MESSAGE, null, yearList, null);
27          int numOfYears = ((Integer)numOfYearsObject).intValue();
28
29          // Prompt the user to enter loan amount
30          String loanAmountString = JOptionPane.showInputDialog(null,
31            "Enter loan amount,\nfor example, 150000 for $150000",
32            "JOptionPane Demo", JOptionPane.QUESTION_MESSAGE);
33          double loanAmount = Double.parseDouble(loanAmountString);
34
35          // Obtain monthly payment and total payment
36          Mortgage mortgage = new Mortgage(
37            annualInterestRate, numOfYears, loanAmount);
38          double monthlyPayment = mortgage.monthlyPayment();
39          double totalPayment = mortgage.totalPayment();
40
41          // Prepare output string
42          String output = "Interest Rate: " + annualInterestRate + "%" +
43            " Number of Years: " + numOfYears + " Loan Amount: $"
44            + loanAmount;
45          output += "\nMonthly Payment: " + "$" +
46            (int)(monthlyPayment * 100) / 100.0;
47          output += "\nTotal Payment: $" +
48            (int)(monthlyPayment * 12 * numOfYears * 100) / 100.0 + "\n";
49
50          // Obtain monthly interest rate
51          double monthlyInterestRate = annualInterestRate / 1200;
52
53          double balance = loanAmount;
54          double interest;
55          double principal;
56
57          // Display the header
58          output += "\nPayment#\tInterest\tPrincipal\tBalance\n";
59
60          for (i = 1; i <= numOfYears * 12; i++) {
61            interest = (int)(monthlyInterestRate * balance * 100) / 100.0;
62            principal = (int)((monthlyPayment - interest) * 100) / 100.0;
63            balance = (int)((balance - principal) * 100) / 100.0;
64            output += i + "\t" + interest + "\t" + principal + "\t" +
65              balance + "\n";
66          }
67
68          // Display monthly payment and total payment
69          JOptionPane.showMessageDialog(null,
70            new JScrollPane(new JTextArea(output)),
71            "JOptionPane Demo", JOptionPane.INFORMATION_MESSAGE, null);
72
73          System.exit(0);
74        }
75      }
```

Review

The JOptionPane dialog boxes are *modal*, which means that no other window can be accessed until a dialog box is dismissed.

continues

491

Example 11.10 continued

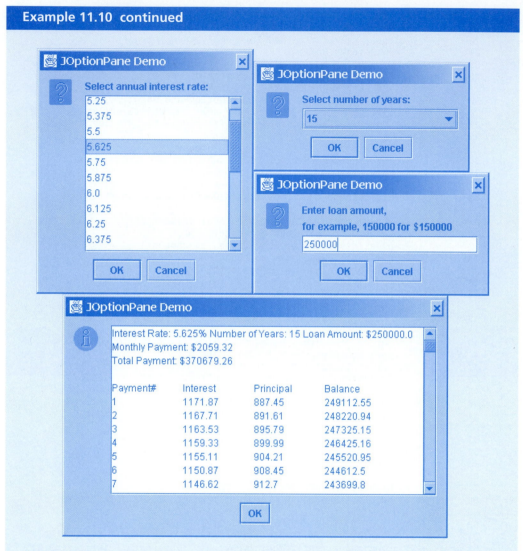

Figure 11.23   *The input dialogs can contain a list or a combo box for selecting input, and the message dialogs can contain GUI objects like* JScrollPane.

You have used the input dialog box to enter input from a text field. This example shows you that the input dialog boxes can also contain a list (Lines 13–15) or a combo box (Lines 24–26) to list input options. The elements of the list are objects. The return value from these input dialog boxes is of the Object type. To obtain a double value or a int value, you have to cast the return object into Double or Integer, then use the doubleValue or intValue method to get the double or int value (See Lines 16–17 and 27).

You have already used the message dialog box to display a string. This example shows that the message dialog box can also contain GUI objects. The output string is contained in a text area, the text area is inside a scroll pane, and the scroll pane is placed in the message dialog box (Lines 69–71).

11.13   Menus

Menus make selection easier and are widely used in window applications. Java provides five classes that implement menus: JMenuBar, JMenu, JMenuItem, JCheckBox-MenuItem, and JRadioButtonMenuItem.

JMenuBar is a top-level menu component used to hold the menus. A menu consists of *menu items* that the user can select (or toggle on or off). A menu item can be an instance of JMenuItem, JCheckBoxMenuItem, or JRadioButtonMenuItem.

11.13.1   Creating Menus

The sequence of implementing menus in Java is as follows:

1. Create a menu bar and associate it with a frame by using the setJMenuBar method.

```java
JFrame frame = new JFrame();
frame.setSize(300, 200);
frame.setVisible(true);
JMenuBar jmb = new JMenuBar();
frame.setJMenuBar(jmb);  // Attach a menu bar to a frame
```

This code creates a frame and a menu bar, and sets the menu bar in the frame.

2. Create menus and associate them with the menu bar.

You can use the following constructor to create a menu:

```java
public JMenu(String label)
```

Here is an example of creating menus:

```java
JMenu fileMenu = new JMenu("File");
JMenu helpMenu = new JMenu("Help");
```

This creates two menus labeled File and Help, as shown in Figure 11.24. The menus will not be seen until they are added to an instance of JmenuBar, as follows:

```java
jmb.add(fileMenu);
jmb.add(helpMenu);
```

Figure 11.24   *The menu bar appears below the title bar on the frame.*

3. Create menu items and add them to menus.

```
fileMenu.add(new JMenuItem("New"));
fileMenu.add(new JMenuItem("Open"));
fileMenu.addSeparator();
fileMenu.add(new JMenuItem("Print"));
fileMenu.addSeparator();
fileMenu.add(new JMenuItem("Exit"));
```

This code adds the menu items New, Open, a separator bar, Print, another separator bar, and Exit, in this order, to the File menu, as shown in Figure 11.25.

Figure 11.25   *Clicking a menu on the menu bar reveals the items under the menu.*

The addSeparator() method adds a separate bar in the menu.

3.1. Creating submenu items.

You can also embed menus inside menus so that the embedded menus become submenus. Here is an example:

```
JMenu softwareHelpSubMenu = new JMenu("Software");
JMenu hardwareHelpSubMenu = new JMenu("Hardware");
helpMenu.add(softwareHelpSubMenu);
helpMenu.add(hardwareHelpSubMenu);
softwareHelpSubMenu.add(new JMenuItem("Unix"));
softwareHelpSubMenu.add(new JMenuItem("NT"));
softwareHelpSubMenu.add(new JMenuItem("Win95"));
```

This code adds two submenus, softwareHelpSubMenu and hardware-HelpSubMenu, in helpMenu. The menu items Unix, NT, and Win95 are added to softwareHelpSubMenu (see Figure 11.26).

Figure 11.26   *Clicking a menu item reveals the secondary items under the menu item.*

3.2.   Creating check box menu items.

You can also add a JCheckBoxMenuItem to a JMenu. JCheckBoxMenuItem is a subclass of JMenuItem that adds a Boolean state to the JMenuItem, and displays a check when its state is true. You can click a menu item to turn it on and off. For example, the following statement adds the check box menu item Check it (see Figure 11.27).

```
helpMenu.add(new JCheckBoxMenuItem("Check it"));
```

Figure 11.27   *A check box menu item lets you check or uncheck a menu item just like a check box.*

3.3.   Creating radio button menu items.

You can also add radio buttons to a menu, using the JRadioButtonMenu-Item class. This is often useful when you have a group of mutually exclusive choices in the menu. For example, the following statements add a submenu named Color and a set of radio buttons for choosing a color (see Figure 11.28):

```
JMenu colorHelpSubMenu = new JMenu("Color");
helpMenu.add(colorHelpSubMenu);

JRadioButtonMenuItem jrbmiBlue, jrbmiYellow, jrbmiRed;
colorHelpSubMenu.add(jrbmiBlue =
  new JRadioButtonMenuItem("Blue"));
colorHelpSubMenu.add(jrbmiYellow =
  new JRadioButtonMenuItem("Yellow"));
colorHelpSubMenu.add(jrbmiRed =
  new JRadioButtonMenuItem("Red"));

ButtonGroup btg = new ButtonGroup();
btg.add(jrbmiBlue);
btg.add(jrbmiYellow);
btg.add(jrbmiRed);
```

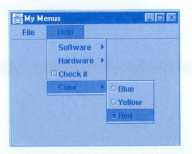

Figure 11.28   *You can use* JRadioButtonMenuItem *to choose among mutually exclusive menu choices.*

495

4. The menu items generate `ActionEvent`. Your program must implement the `actionPerformed` handler to respond to the menu selection. The following is an example:

```
public void actionPerformed(ActionEvent e) {
  String actionCommand = e.getActionCommand();

  // Make sure the source is JMenuItem
  if (e.getSource() instanceof JMenuItem)
    if ("New".equals(actionCommand))
      respondToNew();
}
```

This code executes the method `respondToNew()` when the menu item labeled `New` is selected.

11.13.2   Image Icons, Keyboard Mnemonics, and Keyboard Accelerators

The menu components `JMenu`, `JMenuItem`, `JCheckBoxMenuItem`, and `JRadioButton-MenuItem` have the `icon` and `mnemonic` properties. For example, using the following code, you can set icons for the New and Open menu items, and set keyboard mnemonics for File, Help, New, and Open:

```
JMenuItem jmiNew, jmiOpen;
fileMenu.add(jmiNew = new JMenuItem("New"));
fileMenu.add(jmiOpen = new JMenuItem("Open"));
jmiNew.setIcon(new ImageIcon("image/new.gif"));
jmiOpen.setIcon(new ImageIcon("image/open.gif"));
helpMenu.setMnemonic('H');
fileMenu.setMnemonic('F');
jmiNew.setMnemonic('N');
jmiOpen.setMnemonic('O');
```

The new icons and mnemonics are shown in Figure 11.29. You can also use `JMenuItem` constructors like the ones that follow to construct and set an icon or mnemonic in one statement.

```
public JMenuItem(String label, Icon icon);
public JMenuItem(String label, int mnemonic);
```

Figure 11.29   *You can set image icons, keyboard mnemonics, and keyboard accelerators in menus.*

By default, the text is at the right of the icon. Use the `setHorizontalText-Position(SwingConstants.LEFT)` to set the text to the left of the icon.

To select a menu, press the ALT key and the mnemonic key. For example, press ALT+F to select the File menu, and then press ALT+O to select the Open menu item. Keyboard mnemonics is useful, but it only lets you select menu items from the currently open menu. Key accelerators, however, let you select a menu item directly by pressing the CTRL and accelerator keys. For example, by using the following code, you can attach the accelerator key CTRL+O to the Open menu item:

```
jmiOpen.setAccelerator(KeyStroke.getKeyStroke
  (KeyEvent.VK_O, ActionEvent.CTRL_MASK));
```

The `setAccelerator` method takes a `KeyStroke` object. The static method `getKeyStroke` in the `KeyStroke` class creates an instance of the key stroke. `VK_O` is a constant representing the O key, and `CTRL_MASK` is a constant indicating that the CTRL key is associated with the keystroke.

Example 11.11 Using Menus

Problem

Write a program that creates a user interface to perform arithmetic. The interface contains labels and text fields for Number 1, Number 2, and Result. The Result text field displays the result of the arithmetic operation between Number 1 and Number 2. Figure 11.30 contains a sample run of the program.

Figure 11.30 *Arithmetic operations can be performed by clicking buttons or by choosing menu items from the Operation menu.*

Solution

Here are the major steps in the program:

1. Create a menu bar and set it in the frame. Create the menus Operation and Exit and add them to the menubar. Add the menu items Add, Subtract, Multiply, and Divide under the Operation menu, and add the menu item Close under the Exit menu.

2. Create a panel to hold labels and text fields, and place the panel in the center of the frame.

continues

Example 11.11 continued

3. Create a panel to hold the four buttons labeled Add, Subtract, Multiply, and Divide. Place the panel in the south of the frame.

4. Implement the `actionPerformed` handler to process the events from the menu items and the buttons.

```java
// MenuDemo.java: Use menus to move message in a panel
import java.awt.*;
import java.awt.event.*;
import javax.swing.*;

public class MenuDemo extends JFrame implements ActionListener {
  // Text fields for Number 1, Number 2, and Result
  private JTextField jtfNum1, jtfNum2, jtfResult;

  // Buttons "Add", "Subtract", "Multiply" and "Divide"
  private JButton jbtAdd, jbtSub, jbtMul, jbtDiv;

  // Menu items "Add", "Subtract", "Multiply","Divide" and "Close"
  private JMenuItem jmiAdd, jmiSub, jmiMul, jmiDiv, jmiClose;

  /** Main method */
  public static void main(String[] args) {
    MenuDemo frame = new MenuDemo();
    frame.setDefaultCloseOperation(JFrame.EXIT_ON_CLOSE);
    frame.pack();
    frame.setVisible(true);
  }

  /** Default constructor */
  public MenuDemo() {
    setTitle("Menu Demo");

    // Create menu bar
    JMenuBar jmb = new JMenuBar();

    // Set menu bar to the frame
    setJMenuBar(jmb);

    // Add menu "Operation" to menu bar
    JMenu operationMenu = new JMenu("Operation");
    operationMenu.setMnemonic('O');
    jmb.add(operationMenu);

    // Add menu "Exit" in menu bar
    JMenu exitMenu = new JMenu("Exit");
    exitMenu.setMnemonic('E');
    jmb.add(exitMenu);

    // Add menu items with mnemonics to menu "Operation"
    operationMenu.add(jmiAdd= new JMenuItem("Add", 'A'));
    operationMenu.add(jmiSub = new JMenuItem("Subtract", 'S'));
    operationMenu.add(jmiMul = new JMenuItem("Multiply", 'M'));
    operationMenu.add(jmiDiv = new JMenuItem("Divide", 'D'));
    exitMenu.add(jmiClose = new JMenuItem("Close", 'C'));

    // Set keyboard accelerators
    jmiAdd.setAccelerator(
      KeyStroke.getKeyStroke(KeyEvent.VK_A, ActionEvent.CTRL_MASK));
```

```
54          jmiSub.setAccelerator(
55            KeyStroke.getKeyStroke(KeyEvent.VK_S, ActionEvent.CTRL_MASK));
56          jmiMul.setAccelerator(
57            KeyStroke.getKeyStroke(KeyEvent.VK_M, ActionEvent.CTRL_MASK));
58          jmiDiv.setAccelerator(
59            KeyStroke.getKeyStroke(KeyEvent.VK_D, ActionEvent.CTRL_MASK));
60
61          // Panel p1 to hold text fields and labels
62          JPanel p1 = new JPanel();
63          p1.setLayout(new FlowLayout());
64          p1.add(new JLabel("Number 1"));
65          p1.add(jtfNum1 = new JTextField(3));
66          p1.add(new JLabel("Number 2"));
67          p1.add(jtfNum2 = new JTextField(3));
68          p1.add(new JLabel("Result"));
69          p1.add(jtfResult = new JTextField(4));
70          jtfResult.setEditable(false);
71
72          // Panel p2 to hold buttons
73          JPanel p2 = new JPanel();
74          p2.setLayout(new FlowLayout());
75          p2.add(jbtAdd = new JButton("Add"));
76          p2.add(jbtSub = new JButton("Subtract"));
77          p2.add(jbtMul = new JButton("Multiply"));
78          p2.add(jbtDiv = new JButton("Divide"));
79
80          // Add panels to the frame
81          getContentPane().setLayout(new BorderLayout());
82          getContentPane().add(p1, BorderLayout.CENTER);
83          getContentPane().add(p2, BorderLayout.SOUTH);
84
85          // Register listeners
86          jbtAdd.addActionListener(this);
87          jbtSub.addActionListener(this);
88          jbtMul.addActionListener(this);
89          jbtDiv.addActionListener(this);
90          jmiAdd.addActionListener(this);
91          jmiSub.addActionListener(this);
92          jmiMul.addActionListener(this);
93          jmiDiv.addActionListener(this);
94          jmiClose.addActionListener(this);
95        }
96
97        /** Handle ActionEvent from buttons and menu items */
98        public void actionPerformed(ActionEvent e) {
99          String actionCommand = e.getActionCommand();
100
101          // Handle button events
102          if (e.getSource() instanceof JButton) {
103            if ("Add".equals(actionCommand))
104              calculate('+');
105            else if ("Subtract".equals(actionCommand))
106              calculate('-');
107            else if ("Multiply".equals(actionCommand))
108              calculate('*');
109            else if ("Divide".equals(actionCommand))
110              calculate('/');
111          }
112          else if (e.getSource() instanceof JMenuItem) {
113            // Handle menu item events
114            if ("Add".equals(actionCommand))
115              calculate('+');
```

continues

Example 11.11 continued

```
116              else if ("Subtract".equals(actionCommand))
117                calculate('-');
118              else if ("Multiply".equals(actionCommand))
119                calculate('*');
120              else if ("Divide".equals(actionCommand))
121                calculate('/');
122              else if ("Close".equals(actionCommand))
123                System.exit(0);
124          }
125        }
126
127        /** Calculate and show the result in jtfResult */
128        private void calculate(char operator) {
129          // Obtain Number 1 and Number 2
130          int num1 = (Integer.parseInt(jtfNum1.getText().trim()));
131          int num2 = (Integer.parseInt(jtfNum2.getText().trim()));
132          int result = 0;
133
134          // Perform selected operation
135          switch (operator) {
136            case '+': result = num1 + num2;
137                    break;
138            case '-': result = num1 - num2;
139                    break;
140            case '*': result = num1 * num2;
141                    break;
142            case '/': result = num1 / num2;
143          }
144
145          // Set result in jtfResult
146          jtfResult.setText(String.valueOf(result));
147        }
148      }
```

Review

The program creates a menu bar, jmb, which holds two menus: operationMenu and exitMenu (Liens 28–42). The operationMenu contains four menu items for doing arithmetic: Add, Subtract, Multiply, and Divide. The exitMenu contains the menu item Close for exiting the program. The menu items in the Operation menu are created with keyboard mnemonics and accelerators.

The user enters two numbers in the number fields. When an operation is chosen from the menu, its result, involving two numbers, is displayed in the Result field. The user can also click the buttons to perform the same operation.

The private method calculate(char operator) (Lines 127–147) retrieves operands from the text fields in Number 1 and Number 2, applies the binary operator on the operands, and sets the result in the Result text field.

11.14   Creating Multiple Windows

Occasionally, you may want to create multiple windows in an application. Suppose that your application has two tasks: displaying traffic lights and doing arithmetic calculations. You can design a main frame with two buttons representing the two tasks. When the user clicks one of the buttons, the application opens a new window to perform the specified task. The new windows are called *subwindows,* and the main frame is called the *main window.*

To create a subwindow from an application, you need to create a subclass of `JFrame` that defines the task and tells the new window what to do. You can then create an instance of this subclass in the application and launch the new window by setting the frame instance to be visible.

Example 11.12 Creating Multiple Windows

Problem

Write a program that creates a main window with a text area in the scroll pane and a button named "Show Histogram". When the user clicks the button, a new window appears that displays a histogram to show the occurrence of the letters in the text area. Figure 11.31 contains a sample run of the program.

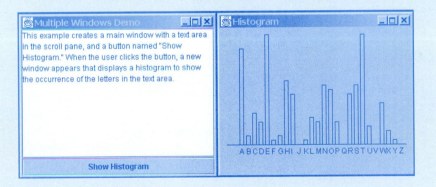

Figure 11.31   *The histogram is displayed in a separate frame.*

Solution

Here are the major steps in the program:

1. Create a main class for the frame named `MultipleWindowsDemo`. Add a text area inside a scroll pane, and place the scroll pane in the center of the frame. Create a button "Show Histogram" and place it in the south of the frame.

2. Create a subclass of `JPanel` named `Histogram`. The class contains a data field named `count` of the `int[][]` type, which counts the occurrece of twenty-six letters. The values in count are displayed in the histogram.

continues

Example 11.12 continued

3. Implement the `actionPerformed` handler in `MultipleWindowsDemo`, as follows:

 a. Create an instance of `Histogram`. Count the letters in the text area and pass the count to the `Histogram` object.

 b. Create a new frame and place the `Histogram` object in the center of frame. Display the frame.

```
1   // MultipleWindowsDemo.java: Display histogram in a separate window
2   import java.awt.*;
3   import java.awt.event.*;
4   import javax.swing.*;
5
6   public class MultipleWindowsDemo extends JFrame
7     implements ActionListener {
8     private JTextArea jta;
9     private JButton jbtShowHistogram = new JButton("Show Histogram");
10    private Histogram histogram = new Histogram();
11
12    // Create a new frame to hold the histogram panel
13    private JFrame histogramFrame = new JFrame();
14
15    /** Default construct */
16    public MultipleWindowsDemo() {
17      // Store text area in a scroll pane
18      JScrollPane scrollPane = new JScrollPane(jta = new JTextArea());
19      scrollPane.setPreferredSize(new Dimension(300, 200));
20      jta.setWrapStyleWord(true);
21      jta.setLineWrap(true);
22
23      // Place scroll pane and button in the frame
24      getContentPane().add(scrollPane, BorderLayout.CENTER);
25      getContentPane().add(jbtShowHistogram, BorderLayout.SOUTH);
26
27      // Register listener
28      jbtShowHistogram.addActionListener(this);
29
30      // Create a new frame to hold the histogram panel
31      histogramFrame.getContentPane().add(histogram);
32      histogramFrame.pack();
33      histogramFrame.setTitle("Histogram");
34    }
35
36    /** Handle the button action */
37    public void actionPerformed(ActionEvent e) {
38      // Count the letters in the text area
39      int[] count = countLetters();
40
41      // Set the letter count to histogram for display
42      histogram.showHistogram(count);
43
44      // Show the frame
45      histogramFrame.setVisible(true);
46    }
47
```

```
48      /** Count the letters in the text area */
49      private int[] countLetters() {
50        // Count for 26 letters
51        int[] count = new int[26];
52
53        // Get contents from the text area
54        String text = jta.getText();
55
56        // Count occurrence of each letter (case insensitive)
57        for (int i = 0; i < text.length(); i++) {
58          char character = text.charAt(i);
59
60          if ((character >= 'A') && (character <= 'Z')) {
61            count[(int)character - 65]++; // The ASCII for 'A' is 65
62          }
63          else if ((character >= 'a') && (character <= 'z')) {
64            count[(int)character - 97]++; // The ASCII for 'a' is 97
65          }
66        }
67
68        return count; // Return the count array
69      }
70
71      /** Main method */
72      public static void main(String[] args) {
73        MultipleWindowsDemo frame = new MultipleWindowsDemo();
74        frame.setDefaultCloseOperation(JFrame.EXIT_ON_CLOSE);
75        frame.setTitle("Multiple Windows Demo");
76        frame.pack();
77        frame.setVisible(true);
78      }
79    }
```

```
1    // Histogram.java: Display a histogram in a panel to show the
2    // occurrence of the letters
3    import javax.swing.*;
4    import java.awt.*;
5
6    public class Histogram extends JPanel {
7      // Count the occurrence of 26 letters
8      private int[] count;
9
10     /** Set the count and display histogram */
11     public void showHistogram(int[] count) {
12       this.count = count;
13       repaint();
14     }
15
16     /** Paint the histogram */
17     public void paintComponent(Graphics g) {
18       if (count == null) return; // No display if count is null
19
20       super.paintComponent(g);
21
22       // Find the panel size and bar width and interval dynamically
23       int width = getSize().width;
24       int height = getSize().height;
25       int interval = (width - 40) / count.length;
26       int individualWidth = (int)(((width - 40) / 24) * 0.60);
27
```

continues

Example 11.12 continued

```
28        // Find the maximum count. The maximum count has the highest bar
29        int maxCount = 0;
30        for (int i = 0; i < count.length; i++) {
31          if (maxCount < count[i])
32            maxCount = count[i];
33        }
34
35        // x is the start position for the first bar in the histogram
36        int x = 30;
37
38        // Draw a horizontal base line
39        g.drawLine(10, height - 45, width - 10, height - 45);
40        for (int i = 0; i < count.length; i++) {
41          // Find the bar height
42          int barHeight =
43            (int)(((double)count[i] / (double)maxCount) * (height - 55));
44
45          // Display a bar (i.e. rectangle)
46          g.drawRect(x, height - 45 - barHeight, individualWidth,
47            barHeight);
48
49          // Display a letter under the base line
50          g.drawString((char)(65 + i) + "", x, height - 30);
51
52          // Move x for displaying the next character
53          x += interval;
54        }
55      }
56
57      /** Override getPreferredSize */
58      public Dimension getPreferredSize() {
59        return new Dimension(300, 300);
60      }
61    }
```

Review

The program contains two classes: `MultipleWindowsDemo` and `Histogram`. Their relationship is shown in Figure 11.32.

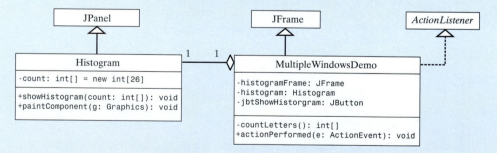

Figure 11.32 `MultipleWindowsDemo` *uses* `Histogram` *to display a histogram of the occurrence of the letters in a text area in the frame.*

`MultipleWindowsDemo` is a frame that holds a text area in a scroll pane and a button. `Histogram` is a subclass of `JPanel` that displays a histogram for the occurrence of letters in the text area.

When the user clicks the "Show Histogram" button, the handler counts the occurrences of letters in the text area. Letters are counted regardless of their case. Non-letter characters are not counted. The count is stored in an `int` array of twenty-six elements. The first element stores the count for letter 'a' or 'A', and the last element in the array stores the count for letter 'z' or 'Z'. The count array is passed to the histogram for display.

The `MultipleWindowsDemo` class contains a `main` method. The `main` method creates an instance of `MultipleWindowsDemo` and displays the frame. The `MultipleWindowsDemo` class also contains an instance of `JFrame`, named `histogramFrame`, which holds an instance of `Histogram`. When the user clicks the "Show Histogram" button, `histogramFrame` is set to visible to display the histogram.

The height and width of the bars in the histogram are determined dynamically according to the window size of the histogram.

You cannot add an instance of `JFrame` to a container. For example, adding `histogramFrame` to the main frame would cause a runtime exception. However, you can create a frame instance and set it visible to launch a new window.

11.15   Scrollbars

A *scrollbar* is a control that enables the user to select from a range of values. Scrollbars appear in two styles, *horizontal* and *vertical*.

You can use the following constructors to create a scrollbar:

- `public JScrollBar()`

  Constructs a new vertical scrollbar.

- `public JScrollBar(int orientation)`

  Constructs a new scrollbar with the specified orientation (`JScrollBar.HORIZONTAL` or `JScrollBar.VERTICAL`).

- `public JScrollbar(int orientation, int value, int visible, int minimum, int maximum)`

  Constructs a new scrollbar with the specified orientation, initial value, visible bubble size, and minimum and maximum values, as shown in Figure 11.33.

`JScrollBar` has the following properties:

- **orientation** specifies horizontal or vertical style, with `JScrollBar.HORIZONTAL` (0) for horizontal and `JScrollBar.VERTICAL` (1) for vertical.

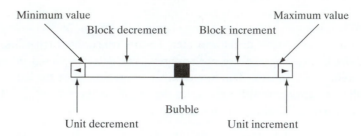

Figure 11.33   *A scrollbar represents a range of values graphically.*

- **maximum** specifies the maximum value the scrollbar represents when the bubble reaches the right end of the scrollbar for horizontal style or the bottom of the scrollbar for vertical style.

- **minimum** specifies the minimum value the scrollbar represents when the bubble reaches the left end of the scrollbar for horizontal style or the top of the scrollbar for vertical style.

- **visibleAmount** specifies the relative width of the scrollbar's bubble. The actual width appearing on the screen is determined by the maximum value and the value of visibleAmount.

- **value** represents the current value of the scrollbar. Normally, a program should change a scrollbar's value by calling the setValue method. The setValue method simultaneously and synchronously sets the minimum, maximum, visible amount, and value properties of a scrollbar, so that they are mutually consistent.

- **blockIncrement** is the value added (subtracted) when the user activates the block-increment (decrement) area of the scrollbar, as shown in Figure 11.33. The blockIncrement property, which is new in JDK 1.1, supersedes the pageIncrement property used in JDK 1.02.

- **unitIncrement** is the value added (subtracted) when the user activates the unit-increment (decrement) area of the scrollbar, as shown in Figure 11.33. The unitIncrement property, which is new in JDK 1.1, supersedes the lineIncrement property used in JDK 1.02.

NOTE

The width of the scrollbar's track corresponds to maximum + visibleAmount. When a scrollbar is set to its maximum value, the left side of the bubble is at maximum, and the right side is at maximum + visibleAmount.

Normally, the user changes the value of the scrollbar by making a gesture with the mouse. For example, the user can drag the scrollbar's bubble up and down, or click in the scrollbar's unit-increment or block-increment areas. Keyboard gestures can also be mapped to the scrollbar. By convention, the Page Up and Page Down keys are equivalent to clicking in the scrollbar's block-increment and block-decrement areas.

When the user changes the value of the scrollbar, the scrollbar generates an instance of `AdjustmentEvent`, which is passed to every registered listener. An object that wishes to be notified of changes to the scrollbar's value should implement the `adjustmentValueChanged` method in the `AdjustmentListener` interface defined in the package `java.awt.event`.

Example 11.13 Using Scrollbars

Problem

Write a program that uses horizontal and vertical scrollbars to control a message displayed on a panel. The horizontal scrollbar is used to move the message to the left or the right, and the vertical scrollbar to move it up and down. A sample run of the program is shown in Figure 11.34.

Figure 11.34   *The scrollbars move the message on a panel horizontally and vertically.*

Solution

Here are the major steps in the program:

1. Create the user interface.

   Create a `MessagePanel` object and place it in the center of the frame. Create a vertical scroll bar and place it in the east of the frame. Create a horizontal scroll bar and place it in the south of the frame.

2. Process the event.

   Implement the `adjustmentValueChanged` handler to move the message according to the bar movement in the scroll bars.

```
1    // ScrollBarDemo.java: Use scrollbars to move the message
2    import java.awt.*;
3    import java.awt.event.*;
4    import javax.swing.*;
5
6    public class ScrollBarDemo extends JFrame
7      implements AdjustmentListener {
8      // Declare scrollbars
9      JScrollBar jscbHort, jscbVert;
10
11     // Declare a MessagePanel
12     MessagePanel messagePanel;
13
```

continues

507

Example 11.13 continued

```
14       /** Main method */
15       public static void main(String[] args) {
16         ScrollBarDemo frame = new ScrollBarDemo();
17         frame.setDefaultCloseOperation(JFrame.EXIT_ON_CLOSE);
18         frame.pack();
19         frame.setVisible(true);
20       }
21
22       /** Default constructor */
23       public ScrollBarDemo() {
24         setTitle("ScrollBar Demo");
25
26         // Create a vertical scrollbar
27         jscbVert = new JScrollBar();
28         jscbVert.setOrientation(Adjustable.VERTICAL);
29
30         // Create a horizontal scrollbar
31         jscbHort = new JScrollBar();
32         jscbHort.setOrientation(Adjustable.HORIZONTAL);
33
34         // Add scrollbars and message panel to the frame
35         messagePanel = new MessagePanel("Welcome to Java");
36         getContentPane().setLayout(new BorderLayout());
37         getContentPane().add(messagePanel, BorderLayout.CENTER);
38         getContentPane().add(jscbVert, BorderLayout.EAST);
39         getContentPane().add(jscbHort, BorderLayout.SOUTH);
40
41         // Register listener for the scrollbars
42         jscbHort.addAdjustmentListener(this);
43         jscbVert.addAdjustmentListener(this);
44       }
45
46       /** Handle scrollbar adjustment actions */
47       public void adjustmentValueChanged(AdjustmentEvent e) {
48         if (e.getSource() == jscbHort) {
49           // getValue() and getMaximumValue() return int, but for better
50           // precision, use double
51           double value = jscbHort.getValue();
52           double maximumValue = jscbHort.getMaximum();
53           double newX =
54             (value * messagePanel.getSize().width / maximumValue);
55           messagePanel.setXCoordinate((int)newX);
56           messagePanel.repaint();
57         }
58         else if (e.getSource() == jscbVert) {
59           // getValue() and getMaximumValue() return int, but for better
60           // precision, use double
61           double value = jscbVert.getValue();
62           double maximumValue = jscbVert.getMaximum();
63           double newY =
64             (value * messagePanel.getSize().height / maximumValue);
65           messagePanel.setYCoordinate((int)newY);
66           messagePanel.repaint();
67         }
68       }
69     }
```

Review

The program creates an instance of MessagePanel (messagePanel) (Line 35) and two scrollbars (jscbVert and jscbHort) (Lines 27, 31). messagePanel is placed in the center of the frame; jscbVert and jscbHort are placed in the east and south sections of the frame (Lines 37–39), respectively.

You can specify the orientation of the scrollbar in the constructor or use the setOrientation method. By default, the property value is 100 for maximum, 0 for minimum, 10 for blockIncrement, and 10 for visibleAmount.

When the user drags the bubble, or clicks the increment or decrement unit, the value of the scrollbar changes. An instance of AdjustmentEvent is generated and passed to the listener by invoking the adjustmentValueChanged handler. Since there are two scrollbars in the frame, the e.getSource() method is used to determine the source of the event. The vertical scrollbar moves the message up and down, and the horizontal bar moves the message to right and left.

The maximum value of the vertical scrollbar corresponds to the height of the panel, and the maximum value of the horizontal scrollbar corresponds to the width of the panel. The ratio between the current and maximum values of the horizontal scrollbar is the same as the ratio between the x value and the width of the panel. Similarly, the ratio between the current and maximum values of the vertical scrollbar is the same as the ratio between the y value and the height of the panel.

11.16   Scroll Panes

Often you need to use a scrollbar to scroll the contents of an object that does not fit completely into the viewing area. JScrollBar can be used for this purpose, but you have to *manually* write the code to implement scrolling with it. JScrollPane is a component that supports *automatic* scrolling without coding. It was used to scroll text area in Example 11.4. In fact, it can be used to scroll any subclass of JComponent.

A JScrollPane can be viewed as a specialized container with a view port for displaying the contained component. In addition to horizontal and vertical scrollbars, a JScrollPane can have a column header, a row header, and corners, as shown in Figure 11.35.

The view port is an instance of JViewport through which a scrollable component is displayed. When you add a component to a scroll pane, you are actually placing it in the scroll pane's view port.

To construct a JScrollPane instance, use the following constructors:

■   public JScrollPane()

Creates an empty scroll pane with a view port and no viewing component where both horizontal and vertical scrollbars appear when needed.

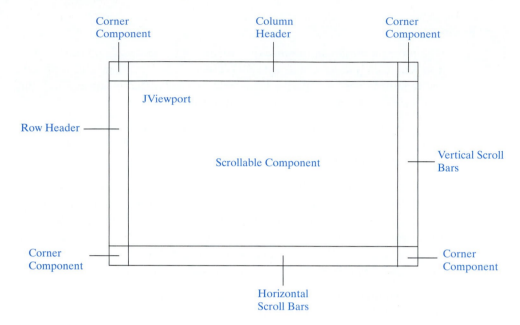

Figure 11.35 *A* `JScrollPane` *has a view port, optional horizontal and vertical bars, optional column and row headers, and optional corners.*

- ■ `public JScrollPane(Component view)`

  Creates a scroll pane and a view port to display the contents of the specified component, where both horizontal and vertical scrollbars appear whenever the component's contents are larger than the view.

- ■ `public JScrollPane(Component view, int vsbPolicy, int hsbPolicy)`

  Creates a scroll pane that displays the view component in a view port whose view position can be controlled with a pair of scrollbars.

- ■ `public JScrollPane(int vsbPolicy, int hsbPolicy)`

  Creates an empty scroll pane with specified scrollbar policies.

The constructor always creates a view port regardless of whether the viewing component is specified. The `vsbPolicy` parameter can be one of the following three values:

```
JScrollPane.VERTICAL_SCROLLBAR_AS_NEEDED
JScrollPane.VERTICAL_SCROLLBAR_NEVER
JScrollPane.VERTICAL_SCROLLBAR_ALWAYS
```

The `hsbPolicy` parameter can be one of the following three values:

```
JScrollPane.HORIZONTAL_SCROLLBAR_AS_NEEDED
JScrollPane.HORIZONTAL_SCROLLBAR_NEVER
JScrollPane.HORIZONTAL_SCROLLBAR_ALWAYS
```

The following properties of `JScrollPane` are often useful:

- **horizontalScrollBarPolicy** specifies when the horizontal scrollbar appears in the scroll pane. The default value is `JScrollPane.HORIZONTAL_SCROLLBAR_AS_NEEDED`.

- **verticalScrollBarPolicy** specifies when the vertical scrollbar appears in the scroll pane. The default value is `JScrollPane.VERTICAL_SCROLLBAR_AS_NEEDED`.

- **viewportView** specifies the component to be viewed in the view port.

- **viewportBorder** specifies a border around the view port in the scroll pane.

- **rowHeaderView** specifies the row header view component to be used in the scroll pane.

- **columnHeaderView** specifies the column header view component to be used in the scroll pane.

To set a corner component, use the following method:

```
public void setCorner(String key, Component corner)
```

The legal values for the key are:

```
JScrollPane.LOWER_LEFT_CORNER
JScrollPane.LOWER_RIGHT_CORNER
JScrollPane.UPPER_LEFT_CORNER
JScrollPane.UPPER_RIGHT_CORNER
```

Example 11.14 Using Scroll Panes

Problem

Write a program that uses a scroll pane to browse a large map. The program lets you choose a map from a combo box and display it in the scroll pane, as shown in Figure 11.36.

Figure 11.36 *The scroll pane can be used to scroll contents automatically.*

continues

Example 11.14 continued

Solution

Here are the major steps in the program:

1. Create the user interface.

    Create a scroll pane and place it in the center of the frame. Set the appropriate row header, column header, and corners for the scroll pane. Create a combo box with the string values "Indiana" and "Ohio", and place it in the south of the frame. Create two labels named lblIndianaMap and lblOhioMap to display maps for Indiana and Ohio.

2. Process the events.

    Implement the itemStateChanged handler to set the label lblIndianaMap or lblOhioMap in the view port of the scroll pane according to whether Indiana or Ohio is selected in the combo box.

```
1    // ScrollPaneDemo.java: Use scroll pane to view large maps
2    import java.awt.*;
3    import java.awt.event.*;
4    import javax.swing.*;
5    import javax.swing.border.*;
6
7    public class ScrollPaneDemo extends JFrame implements ItemListener {
8      // Create images in labels
9      private JLabel lblIndianaMap =
10       new JLabel(new ImageIcon("image/indianaMap.gif"));
11     private JLabel lblOhioMap =
12       new JLabel(new ImageIcon("image/ohioMap.gif"));
13
14     // Declare a scroll pane to scroll map in the labels
15     private JScrollPane jspMap;
16
17     /** Main method */
18     public static void main(String[] args) {
19       ScrollPaneDemo frame = new ScrollPaneDemo();
20       frame.setDefaultCloseOperation(JFrame.EXIT_ON_CLOSE);
21       frame.setSize(300, 300);
22       frame.setVisible(true);
23     }
24
25     /** Default constructor */
26     public ScrollPaneDemo() {
27       setTitle("ScrollPane Demo");
28
29       // Create a scroll pane with northern California map
30       jspMap = new JScrollPane(lblIndianaMap);
31
32       // Create a combo box for selecting maps
33       JComboBox jcboMap = new JComboBox();
34       jcboMap.addItem("Indiana");
35       jcboMap.addItem("Ohio");
36
37       // Panel p to hold combo box
38       JPanel p = new JPanel();
39       p.setLayout(new BorderLayout());
40       p.add(jcboMap);
41       p.setBorder(new TitledBorder("Select a map to display"));
42
```

```
43        // Set row header, column header and corner header
44        jspMap.setColumnHeaderView(
45          new JLabel(new ImageIcon("image/horizontalRuler.gif")));
46        jspMap.setRowHeaderView(
47          new JLabel(new ImageIcon("image/verticalRuler.gif")));
48        jspMap.setCorner(JScrollPane.UPPER_LEFT_CORNER,
49          new CornerPanel(JScrollPane.UPPER_LEFT_CORNER));
50        jspMap.setCorner(ScrollPaneConstants.UPPER_RIGHT_CORNER,
51          new CornerPanel(JScrollPane.UPPER_RIGHT_CORNER));
52        jspMap.setCorner(JScrollPane.LOWER_RIGHT_CORNER,
53          new CornerPanel(JScrollPane.LOWER_RIGHT_CORNER));
54        jspMap.setCorner(JScrollPane.LOWER_LEFT_CORNER,
55          new CornerPanel(JScrollPane.LOWER_LEFT_CORNER));
56
57        // Add the scroll pane and combo box panel to the frame
58        getContentPane().add(jspMap, BorderLayout.CENTER);
59        getContentPane().add(p, BorderLayout.NORTH);
60
61        // Register listener
62        jcboMap.addItemListener(this);
63      }
64
65      /** Show the selected map */
66      public void itemStateChanged(ItemEvent e) {
67        String selectedItem = (String)e.getItem();
68        if (selectedItem.equals("Indiana")) {
69          // Set a new view in the view port
70          jspMap.setViewportView(lblIndianaMap);
71        }
72        else if (selectedItem.equals("Ohio")) {
73          // Set a new view in the view port
74          jspMap.setViewportView(lblOhioMap);
75        }
76
77        // Revalidate the scroll pane
78        jspMap.revalidate();
79      }
80    }
81
82  // A panel displaying a line used for scroll pane corner
83  class CornerPanel extends JPanel implements ScrollPaneConstants {
84    // Line location
85    private String location;
86
87    /** Default constructor */
88    public CornerPanel(String location) {
89      this.location = location;
90    }
91
92    /** Draw a line depending on the location */
93    public void paintComponent(Graphics g) {
94      super.paintComponents(g);
95
96      if (location == "UPPER_LEFT_CORNER")
97        g.drawLine(0, getSize().height, getSize().width, 0);
98      else if (location == "UPPER_RIGHT_CORNER")
99        g.drawLine(0, 0, getSize().width, getSize().height);
100       else if (location == "LOWER_RIGHT_CORNER")
101         g.drawLine(0, getSize().height, getSize().width, 0);
102       else if (location == "LOWER_LEFT_CORNER")
103         g.drawLine(0, 0, getSize().width, getSize().height);
104     }
105   }
```

continues

Example 11.14 continued

Review

The program creates a scroll pane to view image maps. The image maps are created using the `ImageIcon` class and are placed in labels (Lines 9–12). To view an image, the label that contains the image is placed in the scroll pane's view port.

The scroll pane has a main view, a header view, a column view, and four corner views. Each view is a subclass of `Component`. Since `ImageIcon` is not a subclass of `Component`, it cannot be directly used as a view in the scroll pane. Instead the program places an `ImageIcon` to a label and uses the label as a view.

The `CornerPanel` (Lines 83–105) is a subclass of `JPanel`, which is used to display a line. How the line is drawn depends on the `location` of the corner. The `location` is a string, passed in as a parameter in the `CornerPanel`'s constructor. The `CornerPanel` class also implements the `ScrollPaneConstants` interface. The constants representing the location of the four corners are available in `CornerPanel`.

Whenever a new map is selected, the label for displaying the map image is set to the scroll pane's view port. The `validate()` method (Line 78) must be invoked to cause the new image to be displayed. The `validate()` method causes a container to lay out its subcomponents again after the components it contains have been added to or modified.

11.17   Tabbed Panes

`JTabbedPane` is a useful Swing component that provides a set of mutually exclusive tabs for accessing multiple components. Usually you place the panels inside a `JTabbedPane` and associate a tab with each panel. `JTabbedPane` is easy to use, since the selection of the panel is handled automatically by clicking the corresponding tab. You can switch between a group of panels by clicking a tab with a given title and/or icon.

To construct a `JTabbedPane` instance, use the following constructors:

- `public JTabbedPane()`

  Creates an empty tabbed pane.

- `public JTabbedPane(int tabPlacement)`

  Creates an empty `JTabbedPane` with the specified tab placement of either `SwingConstants.TOP`, `SwingConstants.BOTTOM`, `SwingConstants.LEFT`, or `SwingConstants.RIGHT`.

You can also set the tab placement using the following method:

```
public void setTabPlacement(int tabPlacement)
```

By default, the tabs are placed at the top.

To add a component to a JTabbedPane, use the following add method:

```
add(Component component, Object constraints)
```

where component is the component to be displayed when the tab is clicked, and constraints can be a title for the tab.

Example 11.15 Using Tabbed Panes

Problem

Write a program that uses a tabbed pane with four tabs to display four types of figures: Square, Rectangle, Circle, and Oval. You click the corresponding tab to select a figure to be displayed. You can also use the radio buttons to specify the tab placement. A sample run of the program is shown in Figure 11.37.

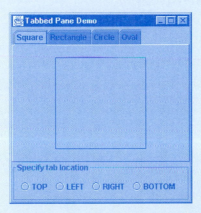

Figure 11.37   *A tabbed pane can be used to access multiple components using tabs.*

Solution

Here are the major steps in the program:

1. Create a subclass of JPanel named FigurePanel to display the figures based on the figureType property in the class.

2. Create the user interface.

   Create a JTabbedPane object and place it in the center of the frame. Create four objects of FigurePanel for square, rectangle, circle, and oval, and add them to the tabbed pane. Create a panel to hold four radio buttons for specifying tab locations. Place the panel in the south of frame.

3. Process the events.

   Implement the itemStateChanged handler to set the location of the tabs according to the selection of the radio buttons.

continues

Example 11.15 continued

```
1   // TabbedPaneDemo.java: Use tabbed pane to select figures
2   import java.awt.*;
3   import java.awt.event.*;
4   import javax.swing.*;
5   import javax.swing.border.TitledBorder;
6
7   public class TabbedPaneDemo extends JFrame implements ItemListener {
8     // Create a tabbed pane to hold figure panels
9     private JTabbedPane jtpFigures = new JTabbedPane();
10
11    // Radio buttons for specifying where tab is placed
12    private JRadioButton jrbTop, jrbLeft, jrbRight, jrbBottom;
13
14    /** Main method */
15    public static void main(String[] args) {
16      TabbedPaneDemo frame = new TabbedPaneDemo();
17      frame.setDefaultCloseOperation(JFrame.EXIT_ON_CLOSE);
18      frame.setSize(200, 300);
19      frame.setVisible(true);
20    }
21
22    /** Default constructor */
23    public TabbedPaneDemo() {
24      setTitle("Tabbed Pane Demo");
25
26      jtpFigures.add(new FigurePanel(FigurePanel.SQUARE), "Square");
27      jtpFigures.add(
28        new FigurePanel(FigurePanel.RECTANGLE), "Rectangle");
29      jtpFigures.add(new FigurePanel(FigurePanel.CIRCLE), "Circle");
30      jtpFigures.add(new FigurePanel(FigurePanel.OVAL), "Oval");
31
32      // Panel p to hold radio buttons for specifying tab location
33      JPanel p = new JPanel();
34      p.add(jrbTop = new JRadioButton("TOP"));
35      p.add(jrbLeft = new JRadioButton("LEFT"));
36      p.add(jrbRight = new JRadioButton("RIGHT"));
37      p.add(jrbBottom = new JRadioButton("BOTTOM"));
38      p.setBorder(new TitledBorder("Specify tab location"));
39
40      // Group radio buttons
41      ButtonGroup btg = new ButtonGroup();
42      btg.add(jrbTop);
43      btg.add(jrbLeft);
44      btg.add(jrbRight);
45      btg.add(jrbBottom);
46
47      // Place tabbed pane and panel p into the frame
48      this.getContentPane().add(jtpFigures, BorderLayout.CENTER);
49      this.getContentPane().add(p, BorderLayout.SOUTH);
50
51      // Register listeners
52      jrbTop.addItemListener(this);
53      jrbLeft.addItemListener(this);
54      jrbRight.addItemListener(this);
55      jrbBottom.addItemListener(this);
56    }
57
58    /** Handle radio button selection */
59    public void itemStateChanged(ItemEvent e) {
60      if (jrbTop.isSelected())
```

```
61              jtpFigures.setTabPlacement(SwingConstants.TOP);
62          else if (jrbLeft.isSelected())
63              jtpFigures.setTabPlacement(SwingConstants.LEFT);
64          else if (jrbRight.isSelected())
65              jtpFigures.setTabPlacement(SwingConstants.RIGHT);
66          else if (jrbBottom.isSelected())
67              jtpFigures.setTabPlacement(SwingConstants.BOTTOM);
68      }
69  }
70
71  // The panel for displaying a figure
72  class FigurePanel extends JPanel {
73    final static int SQUARE = 1;
74    final static int RECTANGLE = 2;
75    final static int CIRCLE = 3;
76    final static int OVAL = 4;
77    private int figureType = 1;
78
79    /** Construct a panel for a specified figure */
80    public FigurePanel(int figureType) {
81      this.figureType = figureType;
82    }
83
84    /** Return figureType */
85    public int getFigureType() {
86      return figureType;
87    }
88
89    /** Set figureType */
90    public void setFigureType(int figureType) {
91      this.figureType = figureType;
92      repaint();
93    }
94
95    /** Draw a figure on the panel */
96    public void paintComponent(Graphics g) {
97      super.paintComponent(g);
98
99      // Get the appropriate size for the figure
100     int width = getSize().width;
101     int height = getSize().height;
102     int side = (int)(0.80 * Math.min(width, height));
103
104     switch (figureType) {
105       case 1:
106         g.drawRect((width - side) / 2, (height - side) / 2,
107           side, side);
108         break;
109       case 2:
110         g.drawRect((int)(0.1 * width), (int)(0.1 * height),
111           (int)(0.8 * width), (int)(0.8 * height));
112         break;
113       case 3:
114         g.drawOval((width - side) /2, (height - side) / 2, side, side);
115         break;
116       case 4:
117         g.drawOval((int)(0.1 * width), (int)(0.1 * height),
118           (int)(0.8 * width), (int)(0.8 * height));
119         break;
120     }
121   }
122 }
```

continues

Example 11.15 continued

Review

The program creates a tabbed pane that holds four panels, each of which displays a figure. A panel is associated with a tab. Tabs are created using the add method and are titled Square, Rectangle, Circle, and Oval.

By default, the tabs are placed at the top of the tabbed pane. You can use the radio buttons to select a different placement, as shown in Figure 11.38.

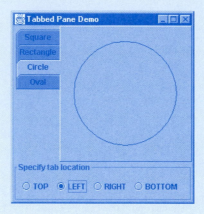

Figure 11.38   *The tabs can be placed at the top, bottom, left, or right of the tabbed pane.*

Chapter Summary

In this chapter, you learned how to create graphical user interfaces using JButton, JLabel, JTextField, JTextArea, JComboBox, JList, JCheckBox, JRadioButton, Border (TitledBorder, BevelBorder, LineBorder, EtchedBorder, MatteBorder, and Empty-Border), JOptionPane dialog boxes, JMenuBar, JMenu, JMenuItem, JCheckBoxMenu-Item, JRadioButtonMenuItem, JScrollBar, JScrollPane, and JTabbedPane.

JButton is used to activate actions. The user expects something to happen when a button is clicked. Clicking a button generates the ActionEvent and invokes the listener to invoke the actionPerformed method.

JLabel is an area for displaying texts or images, or both. JTextField is used to accept user input into a string. JTextArea can accept multiple lines of strings.

JComboBox is a simple list of values to choose from. JList allows multiple selections. JCheckBox is for specifying whether the item is selected or not. JRadioButton is similar to JCheckBox, but is generally used to select a value exclusively.

A dialog box is commonly used to gather information from the user or show information to the user. This chapter introduced using the JOptionPane class to create message dialogs, confirmation dialogs, input dialogs, and option dialogs.

Menus can be placed in a frame or an applet. A menu bar is used to hold the menus. You must use the setJMenuBar method to add a menu bar to the frame or applet, add menus to the menu bar, and add menu items to a menu.

Scrollbars are the controls for selecting from a range of values. You can create scrollbars using the JScrollBar class and specify horizontal or vertical scrollbars using the setOrientation method. JScrollPane provides automatic scrolling, so using it is convenient in most cases.

JTabbedPane can be used to select multiple panels using tabs. The tabs can be placed at the top, left, right, or bottom. Since tab selection is automatically implemented in JTabbedPane, clicking a tab causes the associated panel to be displayed.

To handle events generated by buttons, combo boxes, check boxes, radio buttons, menus, or scrollbars, you must register the listener object with the source object and implement the corresponding listener interface.

Since you cannot add an instance of the Window class to a container, you cannot put a frame into a frame. However, you can create a frame and set it to visible to launch a separate window in the program.

Review Questions

11.1 How do you create a button labeled "OK"? How do you change a label on a button? How do you set an icon in a button?

11.2 How do you create a label named "Address"? How do you change the name on a label? How do you set an icon in a label?

11.3 How do you create a text field with a width of ten characters and the default text "Welcome to Java"?

11.4 How do you create a text area with ten rows and twenty columns? How do you insert three lines into the text area? How do you create a scrollable text area?

11.5 How do you create a combo box, add three items to it, and retrieve a selected item?

11.6 How do you create a check box? How do you determine whether a box is checked?

11.7 How do you create a radio button? How do you group the radio buttons together? How do you determine whether a radio button is selected?

11.8 Can you have a border for any subclass of JComponent? How do you set a titled border for a panel?

11.9 How do you create the menus File, Edit, View, Insert, Format, and Help, and add the menu items Toolbar, Format Bar, Ruler, Status Bar, and Options to the View menu? (See Figure 11.39.)

Figure 11.39   *Create a menu like this in WordPad, with menus and menu items.*

11.10   How do you create a vertical scrollbar? What event can a scrollbar generate?

11.11   How do you create a scroll pane to view an image file?

11.12   Describe how to create a simple message dialog box. Describe the message types used in the JOptionPane class.

11.13   Explain how to create and show multiple frames in an application.

11.14   What method causes the layout manager to lay out the components in a container again? When should a container be laid out again?

11.15   Suppose you want to display the same component named c in the four corners of a scroll pane named jsp. What would be wrong with using the following statements?

```
jsp.setCorner(JScrollPane.UPPER_LEFT_CORNER, c);
jsp.setCorner(JScrollPane.UPPER_RIGHT_CORNER, c);
jsp.setCorner(JScrollPane.LOWER_RIGHT_CORNER, c);
jsp.setCorner(JScrollPane.LOWER_LEFT_CORNER, c);
```

(Since each corner view is an individual component, you need to create four separate objects.)

11.16   Can you share a border or icon for GUI components?

Programming Exercises

11.1   Rewrite Example 11.1 to add a group of radio buttons to select background colors. The available colors are red, yellow, white, gray, and green (see Figure 11.40).

Figure 11.40   *The <= and => buttons move the message on the panel, and you can also set the color for the message.*

11.2 Write a program to perform subtract, multiply, and divide operations (see Figure 11.41).

Figure 11.41 *The program does addition, subtraction, multiplication, and division on double numbers.*

11.3 Write a program that meets the following requirements (see Figure 11.42):

Figure 11.42 *The program stores text from the text field in the text area and combo box, and displays selected items from the combo box in the text field.*

- Create a text field, a text area, and a combo box in a panel using `FlowLayout`.

- Create a button labeled Store and place it in a panel using `FlowLayout`.

- Place the preceding two panels in a frame of `BorderLayout`. Place the first panel in the center, and the second panel in the south.

- The action of the Store button is to retrieve the item from the text field and store it in a text area and in a combo box.

- When an item in the combo box is selected, it is displayed in the text field.

11.4 Write a program that converts miles and kilometers, as shown in Figure 11.43. If you enter a value in the Mile text field and press the Enter key, the corresponding kilometer is displayed in the Kilometer text field. Likewise, if you enter a value in the Kilometer text field, and press the Enter key, the corresponding mile is displayed in the Mile text field.

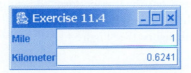

Figure 11.43 *The program converts miles to kilometers, and vice versa.*

11.5   Write a program that draws various figures on a panel. The user selects a figure from a radio button. The selected figure is then displayed on the panel (see Figure 11.44).

Figure 11.44   *The program displays lines, rectangles, ovals, arcs, or polygons when you select a shape type.*

11.6   Write a program that calculates the future value of an investment at a given interest rate for a specified number of years. The formula for the calculation is as follows:

```
futureValue = investmentAmount * (1 + monthlyInterestRate)
```
^{years*12}

Use text fields for interest rate, investment amount, and years. Display the future amount in a text field when the user clicks the Calculate button or chooses Calculate from the Operation menu (see Figure 11.45). Show a message dialog box when the user clicks the About menu item from the Help menu.

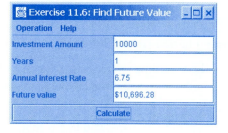

Figure 11.45   *The user enters the investment amount, years, and interest rate to compute future value.*

11.7   Write a program that lets users enter their name, department, university, city, state, and zip code, and store the information in a text area. The state is a JComboBox item. Figure 11.46 shows a sample run of the program.

11.8   Create a main window with two buttons: Simple Calculator and Traffic Lights. When the user clicks Simple Calculator, a new window appears. This new window lets the user perform add, subtract, multiply, and divide operations. When the user clicks Traffic Lights, another window appears that displays traffic lights. (See Figure 11.47.)

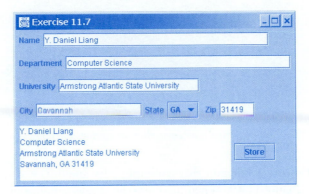

Figure 11.46   *When the Store button is clicked, the name, department, university, city, state, and zip code are displayed in the text area.*

The Simple Calculator frame named `MenuDemo` is given in Example 11.11, and the Traffic Lights frame named `RadioButtonDemo` is given in Example 11.8. They can be used directly in this exercise without modification

When the user clicks the Simple Calculator button, the Calculator window appears, and the name of the button changes to Hide Calculator. When the user clicks the Hide Calculator button, the window is closed, and the name of the button changes back to Simple Calculator. Implement the function of the Traffic Lights button in the same way.

Figure 11.47   *Multiple windows can be displayed simultaneously, as shown in this exercise.*

11.9   Write a program that uses scrollbars to select the foreground color for a label, as shown in Figure 11.48. Three horizontal scrollbars are used for selecting the red, green, and blue components of the color. Use a title border on the panel that holds the scrollbars.

Figure 11.48   *The foreground color changes in the label as you adjust the scrollbars.*

11.10   Write a program that computes sales amount or commission, as shown in Figure 11.49. When the user types a sales amount in the Sales Amount text field and presses the Enter key, the commission is displayed in the Commission text field. Likewise, when the user types a commission, the corresponding sales amount is displayed. The commission rates are the same as in Example 3.7, "Finding Sales Amount." The commission rates are displayed using labels.

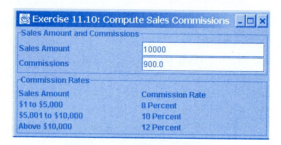

Figure 11.49   *The sales amount and the commission are synchronized. You can compute sales amount given the commission or commission given the sales amount.*

11.11   Write a program that sets the alignment and text position properties of a button dynamically, as shown in Figure 11.50. The program places a button in the center of the frame. The button has a text "Banana", and an image icon for banana. Use combo boxes for the user to select horizontal-position alignment, vertical-position alignment, text horizontal–position alignment, and text vertical–position alignment.

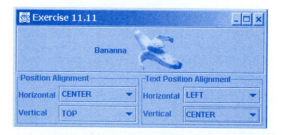

Figure 11.50   *You can set the alignment and text-position properties of a button dynamically.*

11.12 Write a program that sets the horizontal-alignment and column-size properties of a text field dynamically, as shown in Figure 11.51.

Figure 11.51   *You can set the horizontal-alignment and column-size properties of a text field dynamically.*

11.13 Write a program that demonstrates the wrapping styles of the text area. The program uses a check box to indicate whether the text area is wrapped. In the case where the text area is wrapped, you need to specify whether it is wrapped by characters or by words, as shown in Figure 11.52.

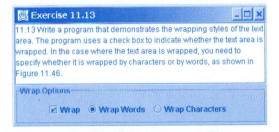

Figure 11.52   *You can set the options to wrap a text area by characters or by words dynamically.*

11.14 Write a program that demonstrates selecting items in a list. The program uses a combo box to specify a selection mode, as shown in Figure 11.53. When you select items, they are displayed in a label below the list.

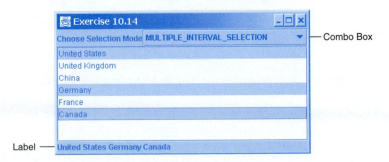

Figure 11.53   *You can choose single selection, single-interval selection, or multiple-interval selection in a list.*

525

11.15 Create a program that enables the user to set the properties of a FlowLayout manager dynamically, as shown in Figure 11.54. The FlowLayout manager is used to place fifteen components in a panel. You can set the alignment, hgap, and vhap properties of the FlowLayout dynamically. (Hint: See Sections 10.4.4 and 10.4.5.)

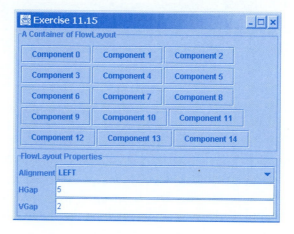

Figure 11.54   *The program enables you to set the properties of a* FlowLayout *manager dynamically.*

11.16 Create a program that enables the user to set the properties of a GridLayout manager dynamically, as shown in Figure 11.55. The GridLayout manager is used to place fifteen components in a panel. You can set the rows, columns, hgap, and vhap properties of the GridLayout dynamically. (Hint: See Sections 10.4.4 and 10.4.5.)

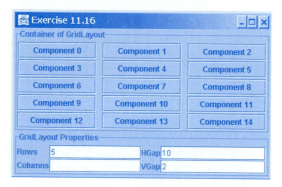

Figure 11.55   *The program enables you to set the properties of a* GridLayout *manager dynamically.*

11.17 Use JTabbedPane to write a program that displays flags for the United States, United Kingdom, Germany, Canada, China, and India (see Figure 11.56).

11.18 Instead of displaying the occurrence of the letters using the Histogram component in Example 11.12, "Creating Multiple Windows," use the BarChart component in Exercise 10.20, so that the display is shown in Figure 11.57.

Figure 11.56   *You can show the flag by selecting a tab in the tabbed pane.*

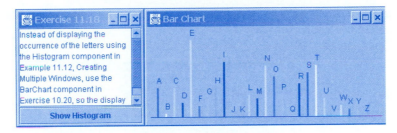

Figure 11.57   *The number of occurrences of each letter is displayed in a bar chart.*

11.19   Rewrite Exercise 3.14 to create a user interface, as shown in Figure 11.58. Your program should let the user enter the loan amount and loan period in number of years from a text field, and should display the monthly and total payments for each interest rate starting from 5% to 8%, with an increment of 1/8 in a text area.

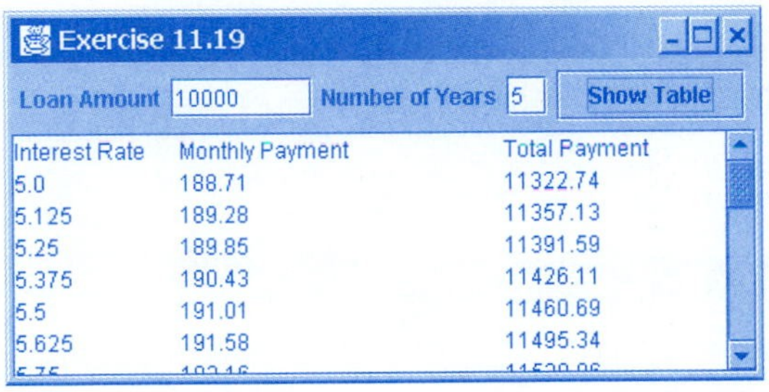

Figure 11.58   *The program displays a table for monthly payments and total payments on a given loan based on various interest rates.*

11.20   Rewrite Example 2.4, "Computing Change," using an input dialog box to enter the amount and a message dialog box to display the result, as shown in Figure 11.59.

11.21   Rewrite Example 3.8, "Displaying a Pyramid of Numbers," to display the pyramid in a message dialog box, as shown in Figure 11.60.

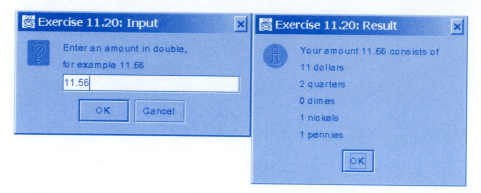

Figure 11.59   *The program prompts the user to enter the amount from an input dialog box and displays the output in a message dialog box.*

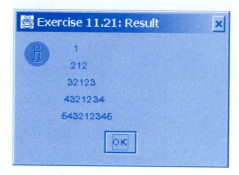

Figure 11.60   *The program prompts the user to enter the amount from an input dialog box and displays the output in a message dialog box.*

NOTE

The numbers are not aligned perfectly in the figure, because numbers are displayed in different widths in graphics.

CHAPTER 12

APPLETS AND ADVANCED GUI

Objectives

- To understand how the Web browser controls and executes applets.
- To become familiar with the init, start, stop, and destroy methods in the Applet class.
- To know how to embed applets in Web pages.
- To know how to pass parameters to applets from HTML.
- To write a Java program that can run as both an application and an applet.
- To learn how to handle mouse events and keystrokes.
- To model dynamic behavior using sequence diagrams and statechart diagrams.
- To become familiar with standard event adapters and anonymous event adapters. (Optional)
- To know how to package and deploy Java projects.(Optional)
- To know how to use CardLayout, GridBagLayout, and no layout managers. (Optional)

12.1 Introduction

Java's early success has been attributed to applets. Running from a Java-enabled Web browser, applets bring dynamic interaction and live animation to an otherwise static HTML page. It is safe to say that Java would be nowhere today without applets. They made Java instantly appealing, attractive, and popular during its infancy stage. Java is now used not only for applets, but also for standalone applications and as a programming language for developing server-side applications and for mobile devices.

In this book so far, you have only used Java applications. Everything you have learned about writing applications, however, also applies to writing applets. Applications and applets share many common programming features, although they differ slightly in some respects. For example, every application must have a `main` method, which is invoked by the Java interpreter. Java applets, on the other hand, do not need a `main` method. They run in the Web browser environment. Because applets are invoked from a Web page, Java provides special features that enable applets to run from a Web browser.

In this chapter, you will learn how to write Java applets, discover the relationship between applets and the Web browser, and explore the similarities and differences between applications and applets. You will also see more complex examples of handling mouse events and keystrokes, and of using advanced layout managers.

12.2 The *Applet* Class

The `Applet` class provides the essential framework that enables applets to be run by a Web browser. While every Java application has a `main` method that is executed when the application starts, applets do not have a `main` method. Instead they depend on the browser to call the methods. Every applet is made up of the following methods:

```
public class MyApplet extends java.applet.Applet {
  ...
  /** The default constructor is called by the browser when the Web
     page containing this applet is initially loaded, or reloaded
   */
  public MyApplet() {
    ...
  }

  /** Called by the browser after the applet is loaded
   */
  public void init() {
    ...
  }

  /** Called by the browser after the init() method, or
     every time the Web page is visited
   */
  public void start() {
    ...
  }
```

```
    /** Called by the browser when the page containing this
       applet becomes inactive
       */
    public void stop() {
       ...
    }

    /** Called by the browser when the Web browser exits */
    public void destroy() {
       ...
    }

    /** Other methods if necessary... */
}
```

When the applet is loaded, the Web browser creates an instance of the applet by invoking the applet's default constructor. The browser uses the `init`, `start`, `stop`, and `destroy` methods to control the applet. By default, these methods do nothing. To perform specific functions, they need to be modified in the user's applet so that the browser can call your code properly. Figure 12.1 shows how the browser calls these methods.

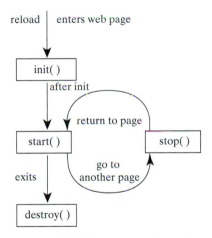

Figure 12.1   *The Web browser uses the* `init`, `start`, `stop`, *and* `destroy` *methods to control the applet.*

12.2.1   The *init* Method

The `init` method is invoked after the applet is created or recreated.

A subclass of `Applet` should override this method if the subclass has an initialization to perform. The functions usually implemented in this method include creating new threads, loading images, setting up user-interface components, and getting parameters from the `<applet>` tag in the HTML page. Chapter 15, "Multithreading," discusses threads in more detail; passing `Applet` parameters is discussed below in Section 12.6, "Enabling Applets to Run as Applications."

12.2.2   The *start* Method

The `start` method is invoked after the `init` method. It is also called whenever the applet becomes active again after the page containing the applet is revisited. The `start` method is called, for example, when the user returns to the Web page containing the applet after surfing other pages.

A subclass of `Applet` overrides this method if it has any operation that needs to be performed whenever the Web page containing the applet is visited. An applet with animation, for example, might use the `start` method to resume animation.

12.2.3   The *stop* Method

The `stop` method is the opposite of the `start` method. The `start` method is called when the user moves back to the page that contains the applet. The `stop` method is invoked when the user leaves the page.

A subclass of `Applet` overrides this method if it has any operation that needs to be performed each time the Web page containing the applet is no longer visible. When the user leaves the page, any threads the applet has started but not completed will continue to run. You should override the `stop` method to suspend the running threads so that the applet does not take up system resources when it is inactive.

12.2.4   The *destroy* Method

The `destroy` method is invoked when the browser exits normally to inform the applet that it is no longer needed and should release any resources it has allocated. The `stop` method is always called before the `destroy` method.

A subclass of `Applet` overrides this method if it has any operation that needs to be performed before it is destroyed. Usually, you won't need to override this method unless you wish to release specific resources, such as threads that the applet created.

12.3   The *JApplet* Class

The `Applet` class is an AWT class and is not designed to work with Swing components. To use Swing components in Java applets, it is necessary to create a Java applet that extends `javax.swing.JApplet`, which is a subclass of `java.applet.Applet`. `JApplet` inherits all the methods from the `Applet` class. In addition, it provides support for laying out Swing components.

To add a component to a `JApplet`, you add it to the content pane of a `JApplet` instance, which is the same as adding a component to a `JFrame` instance. By default, the content pane of `JApplet` uses `BorderLayout`. Here is an example of a simple applet that uses `MessagePanel` to display a message.

```
// WelcomeApplet.java: Applet for displaying a message
import java.awt.*;
import javax.swing.*;
```

```java
public class WelcomeApplet extends JApplet {
  /** Initialize the applet */
  public void init() {
    getContentPane().add(new MessagePanel("Welcome to Java"));
  }
}
```

You cannot run this applet standalone, because it does not have a `main` method. To run this applet, you have to create an HTML file with the applet tag that references the applet. When you write Java GUI applications, you must create a frame to hold graphical components, set the frame size, and make the frame visible. Applets are run from the Web browser. The Web browser automatically places the applet inside it and makes it visible. The following section shows how to create HTML files for applets.

NOTE

You could rewrite the `WelcomeApplet` by moving the code in the `init` method to the default constructor as follows:

```java
// WelcomeApplet.java: Applet for displaying a message
import java.awt.*;
import javax.swing.*;

public class WelcomeApplet extends JApplet {
  /** Construct the applet */
  public WelcomeApplet() {
    getContentPane().add(new MessagePanel("Welcome to Java"));
  }
}
```

12.4   The HTML File and the <applet> Tag

HTML is a markup language that presents static documents on the Web. It uses tags to instruct the Web browser how to render a Web page and contains a tag called <applet> that incorporates applets into a Web page.

The following HTML file named WelcomeApplet.html invokes the **Welcome-Applet.class**:

```html
<html>
<head>
<title>Welcome Java Applet</title>
</head>
<body>
<applet
  code = "WelcomeApplet.class"
  width = 350
  height = 200>
</applet>
</body>
</html>
```

A *tag* is an instruction to the Web browser. The browser interprets the tag and decides how to display or otherwise treat the subsequent contents of the HTML document. Tags are enclosed inside brackets. The first word in a tag, called the *tag name*, describes tag functions. Tags can have additional attributes, sometimes with values after an equals sign, which further define the tag's action. For example, in the preceding HTML file, `<applet>` is the tag name, and `code`, `width`, and `height` are the attributes. The `width` and `height` attributes specify the rectangular viewing area of the applet.

Most tags have a *start tag* and a corresponding *end tag*. The tag has a specific effect on the region between the start tag and the end tag. For example, `<applet . . .> . . . </applet>` tells the browser to display an applet. An end tag is always the start tag's name preceded by a slash.

An HTML document begins with the `<html>` tag, which declares that the document is written in HTML. Each document has two parts, a *head* and a *body*, defined by `<head>` and `<body>` tags, respectively. The head part contains the document title, using the `<title>` tag and other parameters the browser can use when rendering the document, and the body part contains the actual contents of the document. The header is optional. For more information, refer to Appendix F, "An HTML Tutorial."

The complete syntax of the `<applet>` tag is as follows:

```
<applet
  [codebase=applet_url]
  code=classfilename.class
  width=applet_viewing_width_in_pixels
  height=applet_viewing_height_in_pixels
  [archive=archivefile]
  [vspace=vertical_margin]
  [hspace=horizontal_margin]
  [align=applet_alignment]
  [alt=alternative_text]
>
<param name=param_name1 value=param_value1>
<param name=param_name2 value=param_value2>
...
<param name=param_name3 value=param_value3>
</applet>
```

The `code`, `width`, and `height` attributes are required; all the others are optional. The `<param>` tag is introduced in Section 12.5, "Passing Parameters to Applets." The meanings of the other attributes are explained below:

- **codebase** specifies a base where your classes are loaded. If this attribute is not used, the Web browser loads the applet from the directory in which the HTML page is located. If your applet is located in a different directory from the HTML page, you must specify the `applet url` for the browser to load the applet. This attribute enables you to load the class from anywhere on the Internet. The classes used by the applet are dynamically loaded when needed.

- **archive** instructs the browser to load an archive file that contains all the class files needed to run the applet. Archiving allows the Web browser to load all the classes from a single compressed file at one time, thus reducing loading time and improving performance. To create archives, see Section 12.12, "Packaging and Deploying Java Projects."

534

- **vspace** and **hspace** specify the size, in pixels, of the blank margin to pad around the applet vertically and horizontally.

- **align** specifies how the applet will be aligned in the browser. One of nine values is used: left, right, top, texttop, middle, absmiddle, baseline, bottom, or absbottom.

- **alt** attribute specifies the text to be displayed in case the browser cannot run Java.

> **NOTE**
> The W3 consortium (www.w3.org) has introduced the <object> tag as a replacement for the <applet> tag. The <object> tag has more options and is more versatile than the <applet> tag. This book will continue to use the <applet> tag, however, because not all Web browsers support the <object> tag yet.

12.4.1   Viewing Applets Using the Applet Viewer Utility

You can test the applet using the applet viewer utility, which can be invoked from the DOS prompt using the **appletviewer** command from **c:\book**, as shown in Figure 12.2. Its output is shown in Figure 12.3.

```
Command Prompt - appletviewer WelcomeApplet.html

C:\book>dir WelcomeApplet.*
 Volume in drive C has no label.
 Volume Serial Number is F0F9-E7AF

 Directory of C:\book

07/25/2002  02:09p               562 WelcomeApplet.class
10/14/2001  09:39p               159 WelcomeApplet.html
07/25/2002  02:08p               264 WelcomeApplet.java
               3 File(s)           985 bytes
               0 Dir(s)     781,327,360 bytes free

C:\book>appletviewer WelcomeApplet.html
```

Figure 12.2   *The appletviewer command runs a Java applet in the applet viewer utility.*

12.4.2   Viewing Applets from a Web Browser

Applets are eventually displayed in a Web browser. Using the applet viewer, you do not need to start a Web browser. The applet viewer functions as a browser. It is convenient for testing applets during development. However, you should also test the applets from a Web browser before deploying them on a Web site. To display an applet from a Web browser, open the applet's HTML file (i.e., Welcome-Applet.html). Its output is shown in Figure 12.4.

535

Figure 12.3   *The WelcomeApplet program is running from the applet viewer.*

Figure 12.4   *The WelcomeApplet program is displayed in Netscape 6.*

■■■ **NOTE**

You have to view the above applet using a Web browser that supports Java 2. At present, Netscape 6 and Internet Explorer 6 support Java 2. To view applets from other browsers, such as IE 5.0 and Netscape 4.7, you have to use the Java Plug-In. Please see supplements for information on Java Plug-In, at www.prenhall.com/liang/intro4e.html.

To make your applet accessible on the Web, you need to store the Welcome-Applet.class and WelcomeApplet.html on a Web server. You can view the applet from an appropriate URL. For example, I have uploaded these two files on Web server www.cs.armstrong.edu. As shown in Figure 12.5, you can access the applet from www.cs.armstrong.edu/liang/intro4e/book/WelcomeApplet.html.

Figure 12.5   *The WelcomeApplet program is downloaded from the Web server.*

Example 12.1 Using Applets

Problem

Write an applet that computes mortgages. The applet enables the user to enter the interest rate, the number of years, and the loan amount. Clicking the Compute Mortgage button displays the monthly payment and the total payment.

Solution

The applet and the HTML code containing the applet are provided in the following code. Figure 12.6 contains a sample run of the applet.

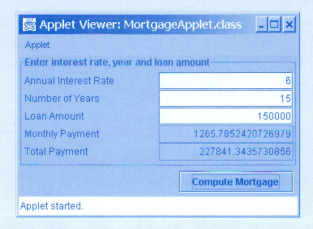

Figure 12.6   *The applet computes the monthly payment and the total payment when provided with the interest rate, number of years, and loan amount.*

```
1  // MortgageApplet.java: Applet for computing mortgage payments
2  import java.awt.*;
3  import java.awt.event.*;
4  import javax.swing.*;
5  import javax.swing.border.TitledBorder;
6
7  public class MortgageApplet extends JApplet
8    implements ActionListener {
9    // Declare and create text fields for interest rate
10   // year, loan amount, monthly payment, and total payment
11   private JTextField jtfAnnualInterestRate = new JTextField();
12   private JTextField jtfNumOfYears = new JTextField();
13   private JTextField jtfLoanAmount = new JTextField();
14   private JTextField jtfMonthlyPayment = new JTextField();
15   private JTextField jtfTotalPayment = new JTextField();
16
17   // Declare and create a Compute Mortgage button
18   private JButton jbtComputeMortgage = new JButton("Compute Mortgage");
19
20   /** Initialize user interface */
21   public void init() {
22     // Set properties on the text fields
23     jtfMonthlyPayment.setEditable(false);
24     jtfTotalPayment.setEditable(false);
25
```

continues

Example 12.1 continued

```
26      // Right align text fields
27      jtfAnnualInterestRate.setHorizontalAlignment(JTextField.RIGHT);
28      jtfNumOfYears.setHorizontalAlignment(JTextField.RIGHT);
29      jtfLoanAmount.setHorizontalAlignment(JTextField.RIGHT);
30      jtfMonthlyPayment.setHorizontalAlignment(JTextField.RIGHT);
31      jtfTotalPayment.setHorizontalAlignment(JTextField.RIGHT);
32
33      // Panel p1 to hold labels and text fields
34      JPanel p1 = new JPanel();
35      p1.setLayout(new GridLayout(5, 2));
36      p1.add(new Label("Annual Interest Rate"));
37      p1.add(jtfAnnualInterestRate);
38      p1.add(new Label("Number of Years"));
39      p1.add(jtfNumOfYears);
40      p1.add(new Label("Loan Amount"));
41      p1.add(jtfLoanAmount);
42      p1.add(new Label("Monthly Payment"));
43      p1.add(jtfMonthlyPayment);
44      p1.add(new Label("Total Payment"));
45      p1.add(jtfTotalPayment);
46      p1.setBorder(new
47        TitledBorder("Enter interest rate, year and loan amount"));
48
49      // Panel p2 to hold the button
50      JPanel p2 = new JPanel();
51      p2.setLayout(new FlowLayout(FlowLayout.RIGHT));
52      p2.add(jbtComputeMortgage);
53
54      // Add the components to the applet
55      getContentPane().add(p1, BorderLayout.CENTER);
56      getContentPane().add(p2, BorderLayout.SOUTH);
57
58      // Register listener
59      jbtComputeMortgage.addActionListener(this);
60    }
61
62    /** Handle the "Compute Mortgage" button */
63    public void actionPerformed(ActionEvent e) {
64      if (e.getSource() == jbtComputeMortgage)
65      {
66
67        // Get values from text fields
68        double interest = (Double.valueOf(
69          jtfAnnualInterestRate.getText())).doubleValue();
70        int year =
71          (Integer.valueOf(jtfNumOfYears.getText())).intValue();
72        double loan =
73          (Double.valueOf(jtfLoanAmount.getText())).doubleValue();
74
75        // Create a mortgage object
76        Mortgage m = new Mortgage(interest, year, loan);
77
78        // Display monthly payment and total payment
79        jtfMonthlyPayment.setText(String.valueOf(m.monthlyPayment()));
80        jtfTotalPayment.setText(String.valueOf(m.totalPayment()));
81      }
82    }
83  }
```

```
1 <!--HTML code, this code is separated from the preceding Java code-->
2 <html>
3 <head>
4 <title>Mortgage Applet</title>
5 </head>
6 <body>
7 This is a mortgage calculator. Enter your input for interest, year, and
     loan amount.
8 Click  "Compute Mortgage" button, you will get the payment
     information.<p>
9 <applet
10   code = "MortgageApplet.class"
11   width = 300
12   height = 150
13   alt="You must have a Java 2-enabled browser to view the applet">
14 </applet>
15 </body>
16 </html>
```

Review

You need to use the `public` modifier for the `MortgageApplet`; otherwise, the Web browser cannot load it.

`MortgageApplet` implements `ActionListener` because it listens for button actions.

The `init` method initializes the user interface. The program overrides this method to create user-interface components (labels, text fields, and a button), and places them in the applet.

The only event handled is the Compute Mortgage button. When this button is clicked, the `actionPerformed` method gets the interest rate, number of years, and loan amount from the text fields. It then creates a `Mortgage` object (Line 76) to obtain the monthly payment and the total payment. Finally, it displays the monthly and total payments in their respective text fields.

The `Mortgage` class is responsible for computing the payments. This class was introduced in Example 6.8, "Using the `Mortgage` Class" (see Chapter 6, "Objects and Classes").

The monthly and total payments are not displayed in currency format. To display a number as currency, see Chapter 14, "Internationalization."

12.5 Passing Parameters to Applets

In Chapter 7, "Strings," you learned how to pass parameters to Java applications from a command line. Parameters are passed to the `main` method as an array of strings. When the application starts, the `main` method can use these strings. There is no `main` method in an applet, however, and applets are not run from the command line by the Java interpreter.

How, then, can applets accept arguments? In this section, you will learn how to pass parameters to Java applets.

To be passed to an applet, a parameter must be declared in the HTML file, and must be read by the applet when it is initialized. Parameters are declared using the <param> tag. The <param> tag must be embedded in the <applet> tag and has no end tag. The syntax for the <param> tag is given below:

```
<param name=parametername value=parametervalue>
```

This tag specifies a parameter and its corresponding value.

NOTE

There is no comma separating the parameter name from the parameter value in the HTML code. The HTML parameter names are not case-sensitive.

Suppose you want to write an applet to display a message. The message is passed as a parameter. In addition, you want the message to be displayed at a specific location. The start location of the message is also passed as a parameter in two values, x coordinate and y coordinate. Assume that the applet is named `DisplayMessage`. The parameters and their values are listed in Table 12.1.

TABLE 12.1   Parameter Names and Values for the `DisplayMessage` Applet

Parameter Name	Parameter Value
MESSAGE	"Welcome to Java"
X	20
Y	30

The HTML source file is given as follows:

```
<html>
<head>
<title>Passing Parameters to Java Applets</title>
</head>
<body>
This applet gets a message from the HTML page and displays it.
<p>
<applet
  code = "DisplayMessage.class"
  width = 200
  height = 50
  alt="You must have a Java 2-enabled browser to view the applet"
>
<param name=MESSAGE value="Welcome to Java">
<param name=X value=20>
<param name=Y value=30>
</applet>
</body>
</html>
```

To read the parameter from the applet, use the following method defined in the `Applet` class:

```
public String getParameter("parametername");
```

This returns the value of the specified parameter.

Example 12.2 Passing Parameters to Java Applets

Problem

Write an applet that displays a message at a specified location. The message and the location (x, y) are obtained from the HTML source.

Solution

The program creates a Java source file named **DisplayMessage.java**, as shown below. The output of a sample run is shown in Figure 12.7.

Figure 12.7   *The applet displays the message Welcome to Java passed from the HTML page.*

```
1   // DisplayMessage.java: Display a message on a panel in the applet
2   import javax.swing.*;
3
4   public class DisplayMessage extends JApplet {
5     private String message = "A default message"; // Message to display
6     private int x = 20; // Default x coordinate
7     private int y = 20; // Default y coordinate
8
9     /** Initialize the applet */
10    public void init() {
11      // Get parameter values from the HTML file
12      message = getParameter("MESSAGE");
13      x = Integer.parseInt(getParameter("X"));
14      y = Integer.parseInt(getParameter("Y"));
15
16      // Create a message panel
17      MessagePanel messagePanel = new MessagePanel(message);
18      messagePanel.setXCoordinate(x);
19      messagePanel.setYCoordinate(y);
20
21      // Add the message panel to the applet
22      getContentPane().add(messagePanel);
23    }
24  }
```

continues

Example 12.2 continued

Review

The program gets the parameter values from the HTML in the `init` method. The values are strings obtained using the `getParameter` method (Lines 12–14). Because x and y are `int`, the program uses `Integer.parseInt(string)` to parse a digital string into an `int` value.

If you change *Welcome to Java* in the HTML file to *Welcome to HTML*, and reload the HTML file in the Web browser, you should see *Welcome to HTML* displayed. Similarly, the x and y values can be changed to display the message in a desired location.

CAUTION

The `Applet`'s `getParameter` method can be invoked only after an instance of the applet is created. Therefore, this method cannot be invoked in the constructor of the applet class. You should invoke this method from the `init` method.

12.6   Enabling Applets to Run as Applications

The `JFrame` class and the `JApplet` class have a lot in common despite some differences. Since they both are subclasses of the `Container` class, all their user-interface components, layout managers, and event-handling features are the same. Applications, however, are invoked by the Java interpreter, and applets are invoked by the Web browser.

For security reasons, the restrictions listed below are imposed on applets to prevent destructive programs from damaging the system on which the browser is running.

- Applets are not allowed to read from, or write to, the file system of the computer. Otherwise, they could damage the files and spread viruses.

- Applets are not allowed to run programs on the browser's computer. Otherwise, they might call destructive local programs and damage the local system on the user's computer.

- Applets are not allowed to establish connections between the user's computer and any other computer, except for the server where the applets are stored. This restriction prevents the applet from connecting the user's computer to another computer without the user's knowledge.

NOTE

A new security protocol was introduced in Java 2. You can use a security policy file to grant applets access to local files.

In general, an applet can be converted to an application without loss of functionality. An application can be converted to an applet as long as it does not violate the security restrictions imposed on applets. You can implement a main method in an applet to enable the applet to run as an application. This feature has both theoretical and practical implications. Theoretically, it blurs the difference between applets and applications. You can write a class that is both an applet and an application. From the standpoint of practicality, it is convenient to be able to run a program in two ways.

It is not difficult to write such programs on your own. Suppose you have an applet named TestApplet. To enable it to run as an application, all you need to do is add a main method in the applet with the implementation, as follows:

```java
public static void main(String[] args) {
  // Create a frame
  JFrame frame = new JFrame (
    "Running a program as applet and frame");

  // Create an instance of TestApplet
  TestApplet applet = new TestApplet();

  // Add the applet instance to the frame
  frame.getContentPane().add(applet, BorderLayout.CENTER);

  // Invoke init and start
  applet.init();
  applet.start();

  // Display the frame
  frame.setSize(300, 300);
  frame.setVisible(true);
}
```

Since the JApplet class is a subclass of Component, it can be placed in a frame. You can invoke the init and start methods of the applet to run a JApplet object in an application.

Example 12.3 Running a Program as an Applet and as an Application

Problem

Write a program that modifies the DisplayMessage applet in Example 12.2 to enable it to run both as an applet and as an application.

Solution

The program is identical to DisplayMessage except for the addition of a new main method and of a variable named isStandalone to indicate whether it is running as an applet or as an application. The following code gives the solution to the problem.

```
1    // DisplayMessageApp.java:
2    // The program can run as an applet or application
3    import javax.swing.*;
4    import java.awt.BorderLayout;
5    import java.awt.Font;
6
```

continues

Example 12.3 continued

```
7    public class DisplayMessageApp extends JApplet {
8      private String message = "A default message"; // Message to display
9      private int x = 20; // Default x coordinate
10     private int y = 20; // Default y coordinate
11
12     /** Determine if it is application */
13     private boolean isStandalone = false;
14
15     /** Initialize the applet */
16     public void init() {
17       if (!isStandalone) {
18         // Get parameter values from the HTML file
19         message = getParameter("MESSAGE");
20         x = Integer.parseInt(getParameter("X"));
21         y = Integer.parseInt(getParameter("Y"));
22       }
23
24       // Create a message panel
25       MessagePanel messagePanel = new MessagePanel(message);
26       messagePanel.setFont(new Font("SansSerif", Font.BOLD, 20));
27       messagePanel.setXCoordinate(x);
28       messagePanel.setYCoordinate(y);
29
30       // Add the message panel to the applet
31       getContentPane().add(messagePanel);
32     }
33
34     /** Main method to display a message
35        @param args[0] x coordinate
36        @param args[1] y coordinate
37        @param args[2] message
38      */
39     public static void main(String[] args) {
40       // Create a frame
41       JFrame frame = new JFrame("DisplayMessageApp");
42
43       // Create an instance of the applet
44       DisplayMessageApp applet = new DisplayMessageApp();
45
46       // It runs as an application
47       applet.isStandalone = true;
48
49       // Get parameters from the command line
50       applet.getCommandLineParameters(args);
51
52       // Add the applet instance to the frame
53       frame.getContentPane().add(applet, BorderLayout.CENTER);
54
55       // Invoke init() and start()
56       applet.init();
57       applet.start();
58
59       // Display the frame
60       frame.setSize(300, 300);
61       frame.setDefaultCloseOperation(JFrame.EXIT_ON_CLOSE);
62       frame.setVisible(true);
63     }
64
65     /** Get command line parameters */
66     private void getCommandLineParameters(String[] args) {
67       // Check usage and get x, y and message
68       if (args.length != 3) {
```

```
69              System.out.println(
70                "Usage: java DisplayMessageApp x y message");
71              System.exit(0);
72          }
73          else {
74            x = Integer.parseInt(args[0]);
75            y = Integer.parseInt(args[1]);
76            message = args[2];
77          }
78        }
79      }
```

Review

When you run the program as an applet, the main method is ignored. When you run it as an application, the main method is invoked. A sample run of the program as an application and as an applet is shown in Figure 12.8.

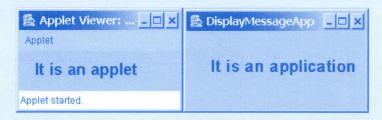

Figure 12.8 *The* DisplayMessageApp *class can run as an application and as an applet.*

The main method creates a JFrame object frame and creates a JApplet object applet, then places the applet applet into the frame frame and invokes its init method. The application runs just like an applet.

The main method sets isStandalone true (Line 47) so that it does not attempt to retrieve HTML parameters when the init method is invoked.

The setVisible(true) method (Line 62) is invoked *after* the components are added to the applet, and the applet is added to the frame to ensure that the components will be visible. Otherwise, the components are not shown when the frame starts.

12.7 Mouse Events

A mouse event is generated whenever a mouse is clicked, released, moved, or dragged on a component. The mouse event object captures the event, such as the number of clicks associated with it or the location (x and y coordinates) of the mouse. Java provides two listener interfaces, MouseListener and MouseMotion-Listener, to handle mouse events. Implement the MouseListener interface to listen for such actions as pressing, releasing, entering, exiting, or clicking the mouse, and implement the MouseMotionListener interface to listen for such actions as dragging or moving the mouse.

The MouseEvent handlers are listed along with the handlers of other events in Table 10.2 in Chapter 10, "Getting Started with GUI Programming." They are also explained below.

- The mouseEntered(MouseEvent e) and mouseExit(MouseEvent e) handlers are invoked when a mouse enters a component or exits the component.

- The mousePressed(MouseEvent e) and mouseReleased(MouseEvent e) handlers are invoked when a mouse is pressed or released. The mouseClicked (MouseEvent e) handler is invoked when a mouse is pressed and then released.

- The mouseMoved(MouseEvent e) handler is invoked when the mouse is moved without a button being pressed. The mouseDragged(MouseEvent e) handler is invoked when the mouse is moved with a button pressed.

The Point class is often used for handling mouse events. The Point class encapsulates a point in a plane. The class contains two instance variables, x and y, for coordinates. To create a point object, use the following constructor:

```
Point(int x, int y)
```

This constructs a Point object with the specified x and y coordinates.

You can use the move(int x, int y) method to move the point to the specified x and y coordinates. You can use the following methods from a MouseEvent object when a mouse event occurs:

- public int getClickCount()

  Returns the number of mouse clicks associated with the event.

- public Point getPoint()

  Returns the x and y coordinates of the event relative to the source component.

- public int getX()

  Returns the x coordinate of the event relative to the source component.

- public int getY()

  Returns the y coordinate of the event relative to the source component.

Since the MouseEvent class inherits InputEvent, you can use the methods defined in the InputEvent class on a MouseEvent object. The following methods in InputEvent are often useful for handling mouse events:

- public long getWhen()

  Returns a time stamp indicating when the event occurred.

- public boolean isAltDown()

  Returns whether the Alt key is down on the event.

- public boolean isControlDown()

Returns whether the Control key is down on the event.

- public boolean isMetaDown()

Returns true if the right mouse button is pressed.

- public boolean isShiftDown()

Returns whether the Shift key is down on the event.

Example 12.4 Moving a Message on a Panel Using a Mouse

Problem

Write a program that displays a message in a panel. You can use the mouse to move the message. The message moves as the mouse drags and is always displayed at the mouse point. A sample run of the program is shown in Figure 12.9.

Figure 12.9   *You can move the message by dragging the mouse.*

Solution

The following code gives the solution to the problem.

```
1    // MoveMessageDemo.java: Move a message in a panel
2    // by dragging the mouse
3    import java.awt.*;
4    import java.awt.event.*;
5    import javax.swing.*;
6
7    public class MoveMessageDemo extends JApplet {
8      /** Initialize the applet */
9      public void init() {
10       // Create a MoveMessagePanel instance for drawing a message
11       MoveMessagePanel p = new MoveMessagePanel("Welcome to Java");
12
13       // Place the message panel in the frame
14       getContentPane().setLayout(new BorderLayout());
15       getContentPane().add(p);
16     }
17
18     /** This main method enables the applet to run as an application */
19     public static void main(String[] args) {
20       // Create a frame
21       JFrame frame = new JFrame("Move Message Using Mouse");
22
```

continues

Example 12.4 continued

```
23          // Create an instance of the applet
24          MoveMessageDemo applet = new MoveMessageDemo();
25
26          // Add the applet instance to the frame
27          frame.getContentPane().add(applet, BorderLayout.CENTER);
28
29          // Invoke init() and start()
30          applet.init();
31          applet.start();
32
33          // Display the frame
34          frame.setSize(300, 300);
35          frame.setDefaultCloseOperation(JFrame.EXIT_ON_CLOSE);
36          frame.setVisible(true);
37      }
38    }
39
40    // MoveMessagePanel draws a message
41    class MoveMessagePanel extends MessagePanel
42      implements MouseMotionListener {
43      /** Construct a panel to draw string s */
44      public MoveMessagePanel(String s) {
45        super(s);
46        this.addMouseMotionListener(this);
47      }
48
49      /** Tell the panel how to draw things */
50      public void paintComponent(Graphics g) {
51        // Invoke the paintComponent method in the MessagePanel class
52        super.paintComponent(g);
53      }
54
55      /** Handle mouse moved event */
56      public void mouseMoved(MouseEvent e) {
57      }
58
59      /** Handle mouse dragged event */
60      public void mouseDragged(MouseEvent e) {
61        // Get the new location and repaint the screen
62        setXCoordinate(e.getX());
63        setYCoordinate(e.getY());
64        repaint();
65      }
66    }
```

Review

The class `MoveMessagePanel` extends `MessagePanel` and implements `Mouse-MotionListener`. The `MessagePanel` class was presented in Example 8.5 to display a message in a panel. The `MoveMessagePanel` class inherits all the features from `MessagePanel`. Additionally, it handles redisplaying the message when the mouse is dragged.

The `MouseMotionListener` interface contains two handlers, `mouseMoved` and `mouseDragged`, for handling mouse-motion events. When you move the mouse with the button pressed, the `mouseDragged` method is invoked to repaint the viewing area and display the message at the mouse point. When you move the mouse without pressing the button, the `mouseMoved` method is invoked.

Because the methods in the MouseMotionListener interface are abstract, you must implement all of them even if your program does not care about some of the events. In MoveMessagePanel, the mouseMoved and mouseDragged event handlers are both implemented, although only the mouseDragged handler is needed.

For an object to receive event notification, it must register as an event listener. addMouseMotionListener(this) registers the object of MoveMessagePanel as a mouse-motion event listener so that the object can receive notification about the mouse-motion event. MoveMessagePanel is both a listener and a source object.

The mouseDragged method is invoked when you move the mouse with a button pressed. This method obtains the mouse location using getX and getY methods in the MouseEvent class. This becomes the new location for the message.

Example 12.5 Scribbling with a Mouse

Problem

Write a program that uses a mouse for scribbling. It can be used to draw things on a panel by dragging with the left mouse button pressed. The drawing can be erased by dragging with the right button pressed. A sample run of the program is shown in Figure 12.10.

Figure 12.10   *The program enables you to scribble using the mouse.*

Solution

The following code gives the solution to the problem.

```
1    // ScribbleDemo.java: Scribble using mouse
2    import java.awt.*;
3    import javax.swing.*;
4    import java.awt.event.*;
5
```

continues

Example 12.5 continued

```
6     public class ScribbleDemo extends JApplet {
7       /** This main method enables the applet to run as an application */
8       public static void main(String[] args) {
9         // Create a frame
10        JFrame frame = new JFrame("Scribbling Demo");
11
12        // Create an instance of the applet
13        ScribbleDemo applet = new ScribbleDemo();
14
15        // Add the applet instance to the frame
16        frame.getContentPane().add(applet, BorderLayout.CENTER);
17
18        // Invoke init() and start()
19        applet.init();
20        applet.start();
21
22        // Display the frame
23        frame.setSize(300, 300);
24        frame.setDefaultCloseOperation(JFrame.EXIT_ON_CLOSE);
25        frame.setVisible(true);
26      }
27
28      /** Initialize the applet */
29      public void init() {
30        // Create a PaintPanel and add it to the applet
31        getContentPane().add(new ScribblePanel(), BorderLayout.CENTER);
32      }
33    }
34
35    // ScribblePanel for scribbling using the mouse
36    class ScribblePanel extends JPanel
37      implements MouseListener, MouseMotionListener {
38      final int CIRCLESIZE = 20; // Circle diameter used for erasing
39      private Point lineStart = new Point(0, 0); // Line start point
40      private Graphics g; // Create a Graphics object for drawing
41
42      public ScribblePanel() {
43        // Register listener for the mouse event
44        addMouseListener(this);
45        addMouseMotionListener(this);
46      }
47
48      public void mouseClicked(MouseEvent e) {
49      }
50
51      public void mouseEntered(MouseEvent e) {
52      }
53
54      public void mouseExited(MouseEvent e) {
55      }
56
57      public void mouseReleased(MouseEvent e) {
58      }
59
60      public void mousePressed(MouseEvent e) {
61        lineStart.move(e.getX(), e.getY());
62      }
63
64      public void mouseDragged(MouseEvent e) {
65        g = getGraphics(); // Get graphics context
66
```

```
67          if (e.isMetaDown()) { // Detect right button pressed
68            // Erase the drawing using an oval
69            g.setColor(getBackground());
70            g.fillOval(e.getX() - (CIRCLESIZE / 2),
71              e.getY() - (CIRCLESIZE / 2), CIRCLESIZE, CIRCLESIZE);
72          }
73          else {
74              g.setColor(Color.black);
75              g.drawLine(lineStart.x, lineStart.y,
76                e.getX(), e.getY());
77          }
78
79          lineStart.move(e.getX(), e.getY());
80          // Dispose this graphics context
81          g.dispose();
82        }
83
84        public void mouseMoved(MouseEvent e) {
85        }
86      }
```

Review

The program creates a `ScribblePanel` instance to capture mouse movements on the panel. Lines are created or erased by dragging the mouse with the left or right button pressed.

When a button is pressed, the `mousePressed` handler is invoked. This handler sets the `lineStart` to the current mouse point as the starting point. Drawing begins when the mouse is dragged with the left button pressed. In this case, the `mouseDragged` handler sets the foreground color to black, and draws a line along the path of the mouse movement.

When the mouse is dragged with the right button pressed, erasing occurs. In this case, the `mouseDragged` handler sets the foreground color to the background color and draws an oval filled with the background color at the mouse pointer to erase the area covered by the oval.

The program does not use the `paintComponent(Graphics g)` method. Instead, it uses `getGraphics()` to obtain a `Graphics` instance and draws on this.

Because the `mousePressed` handler is defined in the `MouseListener` interface, and the `mouseDragged` handler is defined in the `MouseMotionListener` interface, the program implements both interfaces (Line 37).

The `dispose` method (Line 81) disposes of this graphics context and releases any system resources it is using. Although the finalization process of the Java run-time system automatically disposes of the object after it is no longer in use, I recommend that you manually free the associated resources by calling this method rather than rely on a finalization process that may take a long time to run to completion. In this program, a large number of `Graphics` objects can be created within a short time. The program would run fine if these objects were not disposed of manually, but they would consume a lot of memory.

12.8   Keyboard Events

Keyboard events are generated whenever a key is pressed. They enable the use of the keys to control and perform actions or get input from the keyboard.

The keyboard event object describes the nature of the event (namely, that a key is pressed, released, or typed) and the value of the key. The following handlers from the `KeyListener` interface are used to process keyboard events:

- `public void keyPressed(KeyEvent e)`

  Called when a key is pressed.

- `public void keyReleased(KeyEvent e)`

  Called when a key is released.

- `public void keyTyped(KeyEvent e)`

  Called when a key is pressed and then released.

The keys captured in an event are integers representing Unicode character values, which include alphanumeric characters, function keys, the Tab key, the Enter key, and so on. Every keyboard event has an associated key character or key code that is returned by the `getKeyChar()` or `getKeyCode()` method in `KeyEvent`.

Java defines many constants for keys, including function keys in the `KeyEvent` class. Table 10.2 shows the most common ones.

TABLE 10.2   Key Constants

Constant	Description
VK_HOME	The Home key
VK_End	The End key
VK_PGUP	The Page Up key
VK_PGDN	The Page Down key
VK_UP	The up-arrow key
VK_DOWN	The down-arrow key
VK_LEFT	The left-arrow key
VK_RIGHT	The right-arrow key
VK_ESCAPE	The Esc key
VK_TAB	The Tab key
VK_CONTROL	The Control key
VK_SHIFT	The Shift key

TABLE 10.2   continued

Constant	Description
VK_BACK_SPACE	The Backspace key
VK_CAPS_LOCK	The Caps Lock key
VK_NUM_LOCK	The Num Lock key
VK_ENTER	The Enter key
VK_F1 to VK_F12	The function keys from F1 to F12
VK_0 to VK_9	The number keys from 0 to 9
VK_A to VK_Z	The letter keys from A to Z

Example 12.6 Handling Key Events

Problem

Write a program that displays a user-input character. The user can move the character up, down, left, and right, using the arrow keys VK_UP, VK_DOWN, VK_LEFT, and VK_RIGHT. Figure 12.11 contains a sample run of the program.

Figure 12.11   *The program responds to keyboard events by displaying a character and moving it up, down, left, or right.*

Solution

The following code gives the solution to the problem.

```
1    // KeyboardEventDemo.java: Receive key input
2    import java.awt.*;
3    import java.awt.event.*;
4    import javax.swing.*;
5
6    public class KeyboardEventDemo extends JApplet {
7      private KeyboardPanel keyboardPanel = new KeyboardPanel();
8
9      /** Main method used if run as an application */
10     public static void main(String[] args) {
11       // Create a frame
12       JFrame frame = new JFrame("KeyboardEvent Demo");
13
14       // Create an instance of the applet
15       KeyboardEventDemo applet = new KeyboardEventDemo();
16
```

continues

Example 12.6 continued

```
17          // Add the applet instance to the frame
18          frame.getContentPane().add(applet, BorderLayout.CENTER);
19
20          // Invoke init() and start()
21          applet.init();
22          applet.start();
23
24          // Display the frame
25          frame.setSize(300, 300);
26          frame.setDefaultCloseOperation(JFrame.EXIT_ON_CLOSE);
27          frame.setVisible(true);
28
29          // Set focus on the keyboardPanel
30          applet.focus();
31        }
32
33      /** Initialize UI */
34      public void init() {
35        // Add the keyboard panel to accept and display user input
36        getContentPane().add(keyboardPanel);
37
38        // Request focus
39        focus();
40      }
41
42      /** Set focus on the panel */
43      public void focus() {
44        // It is required for receiving key input
45        keyboardPanel.requestFocus();
46      }
47    }
48
49    // KeyboardPanel for receiving key input
50    class KeyboardPanel extends JPanel implements KeyListener {
51      private int x = 100;
52      private int y = 100;
53      private char keyChar = 'A'; // Default key
54
55      public KeyboardPanel() {
56        addKeyListener(this); // Register listener
57      }
58
59      public void keyReleased(KeyEvent e) {
60      }
61
62      public void keyTyped(KeyEvent e) {
63      }
64
65      public void keyPressed(KeyEvent e) {
66        switch (e.getKeyCode()) {
67          case KeyEvent.VK_DOWN: y += 10; break;
68          case KeyEvent.VK_UP: y -= 10; break;
69          case KeyEvent.VK_LEFT: x -= 10; break;
70          case KeyEvent.VK_RIGHT: x += 10; break;
71          default: keyChar = e.getKeyChar();
72        }
73
74        repaint();
75      }
76
```

```
77        /** Draw the character */
78        public void paintComponent(Graphics g) {
79          super.paintComponent(g);
80
81          g.setFont(new Font("TimesRoman", Font.PLAIN, 24));
82          g.drawString(String.valueOf(keyChar), x, y);
83        }
84
85        /** Override this method to enable keyboard focus */
86        public boolean isFocusTraversable() {
87          return true;
88        }
89      }
```

Review

When a non-arrow key is pressed, the key is displayed. When an arrow key is pressed, the character moves in the direction indicated by the arrow key.

Because the program gets input from the keyboard, it listens for `KeyEvent` and implements `KeyListener` to handle key input.

When a key is pressed, the `keyPressed` handler is invoked. The program uses `e.getKeyCode()` to obtain the `int` value for the key and `e.getKeyChar()` to get the character for the key. In fact, `(int)e.getKeyChar()` is the same as `e.getKeyCode()`.

Only a focused component can receive `KeyEvent`. To make a component get the keyboard focus, you need to do two things: (1) override the `isFocusTraversable` method defined in the `Component` class to return true (Lines 86–87); (2) invoke the component's `requestFocus` method to set the focus on this component (Line 45).

> **NOTE**
>
> The `isFocusTraversable` method has been deprecated and replaced by `isFocusable` since JDK 1.4. This example uses `isFocusTraversable` for backward compatibility in case you are using JDK 1.2 or JDK 1.3.

12.9 Modeling Dynamic Behavior Using Sequence Diagrams and Statecharts

The UML diagrams presented so far describe the properties and methods of a class or the static relationships among classes. This section introduces the sequence diagrams and statechart diagrams that model the dynamic behaviors of objects.

12.9.1 Sequence Diagrams

Sequence diagrams describe interactions among objects by depicting the time-ordering of method invocations. A sequence diagram consists of the following elements, as shown in Figure 12.12:

- **Class role** represents the roles the object plays. The objects at the top of the diagram represent class roles.

- **Lifeline** represents the existence of an object over a period of time. A vertical dotted line extending from the object is used to denote a lifeline.

- **Activation** represents the time during which an object is performing an operation. Thin rectangles placed on lifelines are used to denote activations.

- **Method invocation** represents communication between objects. Horizontal arrows labeled with method calls are used to denote method invocations.

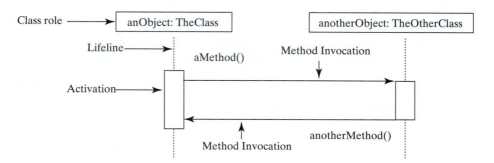

Figure 12.12   *Sequence diagrams describe interactions between objects.*

The interactions between the `ButtonDemo` object and the `MessagePanel` object in Example 11.1, "Using Buttons," are illustrated in Figure 12.13.

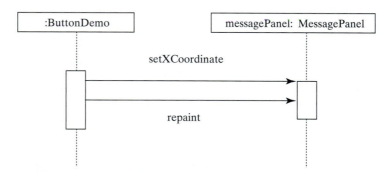

Figure 12.13   *The* `ButtonDemo` *object invokes the* `setXCoordinate` *method to move the message on the* `MessagePanel` *and invokes the repaint method to repaint the message.*

12.9.2   Statechart Diagrams

Statechart diagrams describe the flow of control of an object. A statechart diagram contains the following elements, as shown in Figure 12.14:

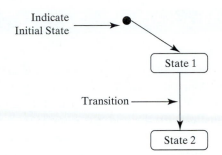

Figure 12.14   *Statechart diagrams describe the flow of control of an object.*

- **State** represents a situation during the life of an object in which it satisfies some condition, performs some action, or waits for some event to occur. All states have names. States are denoted by rectangles with rounded corners, except for the initial state, which is denoted by a small filled circle.

- **Transition** represents the relationship between two states, indicating that an object will perform some action to transfer from one state to the other. A solid arrow with appropriate method invocation denotes a transition.

The statechart diagram in Figure 12.15 can be used to describe the flow of control of an applet. This diagram is much better and clearer than Figure 12.1. The `init` method transfers the applet from the start to the initialized state. The `start` method transfers the applet to the started state. The `stop` method transfers the applet to the stopped state. The `destroy` method transfers the applet to the destroyed state.

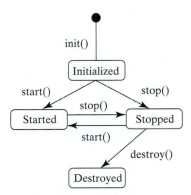

Figure 12.15   *The flow of control of an applet can be described using a statechart diagram.*

12.10   Case Studies (Optional)

You have learned about objects, classes, arrays, class inheritance, GUI, event-driven programming, and applets from the many examples in this chapter and the preceding chapters. Now it is time to put what you have learned to work in developing comprehensive projects. In this section, you will develop a Java applet with which to play the popular game of TicTacToe.

Example 12.7 The TicTacToe Game

Problem

Create a program for playing TicTacToe. In a game of TicTacToe, two players take turns marking an available cell in a 3×3 grid with their respective tokens (either X or O). When one player has placed three tokens in a horizontal, vertical, or diagonal row on the grid, the game is over and that player has won. A draw (no winner) occurs when all the spaces on the grid have been filled with tokens and neither player has achieved a win. Figures 12.16 and 12.17 are representative sample runs of the example.

Figure 12.16   *This sample shows that the X player has won.*

Figure 12.17   *This sample shows a draw with no winner.*

Solution

All the examples you have seen so far show simple behaviors that are easy to model with classes. The behavior of the TicTacToe game is somewhat more complex. To create classes that model the behavior, you need to study and understand the game.

Assume that all the cells are initially empty, and that the first player takes the X token, and the second player takes the O token. To mark a cell, the player points the mouse to the cell and clicks it. If the cell is empty, the token (X or O) is displayed. If the cell is already filled, the player's action is ignored.

From the preceding description, it is obvious that a cell is a GUI object that handles the mouse-click event and displays tokens. Such an object could be either a button or a panel. Drawing on panels is more flexible than on buttons, because the token (X or O) can be drawn on a panel in any size, but on a button it can only be displayed as a text label. Therefore, a panel should be used to model a cell.

Let Cell be a subclass of JPanel. You can declare the 3×3 grid to be an array new Cell[3][3] to model the game. How do you know the state of the cell (empty, X, or O)? You use a property named token of char type in the Cell class. The Cell class is responsible for drawing the token when an empty cell is clicked, so you need to write the code for listening to the MouseEvent and for painting the shape for tokens X and O. To determine which shape to draw, you can introduce a variable named whoseTurn of char type. whoseTurn is initially X, then changes to O, and subsequently changes between X and O whenever a new cell is occupied.

Finally, how do you know whether the game is over, whether there is a winner, and who the winner, if any, is? You can create a method named isWon(char token) to check whether a specified token has won and a method named isFull() to check whether all the cells are occupied.

Clearly, two classes emerge from the foregoing analysis. One is the Cell class, which handles operations for a single cell; and the other is the TicTacToe class, which plays the whole game and deals with all the cells. The relationship between these two classes is shown in Figure 12.18.

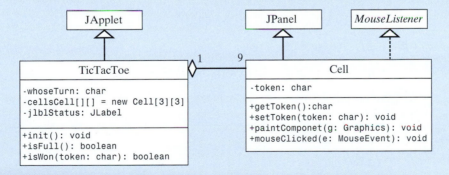

Figure 12.18   *The* TicTacToe *class contains nine cells.*

The Cell class has the following data field and methods:

Data field:

■   char token: This represents the token used in the cell. The initial value is ' ';

continues

Example 12.7 continued

Methods:

- `public char getToken()`

  Returns the token of the cell.

- `public void setToken(char token)`

  Sets the token in the cell.

- `public void paintComponent(Graphics g)`

  Overrides this method to display the token in the cell.

- `public void mouseClicked(MouseEvent e)`

  Implements this method in the `MouseListener` to handle a mouse click on the cell.

The `TicTacToe` class has the following data fields and methods:

Data fields:

- `char whoseTurn`: This indicates which player has the turn. The initial value is 'X', which indicates that it is player X's turn.

- `Cell[][] cells`: This represents the cells.

- `JLabel jlblStatus`: This is a label for displaying game status.

Methods:

- `public void init()`

  Overrides this method to initialize variables and create UI.

- `public boolean isFull()`

  Checks whether all the cells are filled.

- `public boolean isWon(char token)`

  Checks whether the player with the specified token wins.

The interaction between the `TicTacToe` object and a `Cell` object is shown in Figure 12.19.

The program is given below:

```
1    // TicTacToe.java: Play the TicTacToe game
2    import java.awt.*;
3    import java.awt.event.*;
4    import javax.swing.*;
5    import javax.swing.border.LineBorder;
6
7    public class TicTacToe extends JApplet {
8      // Indicate which player has a turn, initially it is the X player
9      private char whoseTurn = 'X';
10
```

```
11        // Create and initialize cells
12        private Cell[][] cells =  new Cell[3][3];
13
14        // Create and initialize a status label
15        private JLabel jlblStatus = new JLabel("X's turn to play");
16
17        /** Initialize UI */
18        public void init() {
19          // Panel p to hold cells
20          JPanel p = new JPanel();
21          p.setLayout(new GridLayout(3, 3, 0, 0));
22          for (int i = 0; i < 3; i++)
23            for (int j = 0; j < 3; j++)
24              p.add(cells[i][j] = new Cell());
25
26          // Set line borders on the cells panel and the status label
27          p.setBorder(new LineBorder(Color.red, 1));
28          jlblStatus.setBorder(new LineBorder(Color.yellow, 1));
29
30          // Place the panel and the label to the applet
31          this.getContentPane().add(p, BorderLayout.CENTER);
32          this.getContentPane().add(jlblStatus, BorderLayout.SOUTH);
33        }
34
35        /** This main method enables the applet to run as an application */
36        public static void main(String[] args) {
37          // Create a frame
38          JFrame frame = new JFrame("Tic Tac Toe");
39
40          // Create an instance of the applet
41          TicTacToe applet = new TicTacToe();
42
43          // Add the applet instance to the frame
44          frame.getContentPane().add(applet, BorderLayout.CENTER);
45
46          // Invoke init() and start()
47          applet.init();
48          applet.start();
49
50          // Display the frame
51          frame.setSize(300, 300);
52          frame.setDefaultCloseOperation(JFrame.EXIT_ON_CLOSE);
53          frame.setVisible(true);
54        }
55
56        /** Determine if the cells are all occupied */
57        public boolean isFull() {
58          for (int i = 0; i < 3; i++)
59            for (int j = 0; j < 3; j++)
60              if (cells[i][j].getToken() == ' ')
61                return false;
62
63          return true;
64        }
65
66        /** Determine if the player with the specified token wins */
67        public boolean isWon(char token) {
68          for (int i = 0; i < 3; i++)
69            if ((cells[i][0].getToken() == token)
70                && (cells[i][1].getToken() == token)
71                && (cells[i][2].getToken() == token)) {
72              return true;
73            }
74
```

continues

561

Example 12.7 continued

```
 75         for (int j = 0; j < 3; j++)
 76           if ((cells[0][j].getToken() ==  token)
 77               && (cells[1][j].getToken() == token)
 78               && (cells[2][j].getToken() == token)) {
 79             return true;
 80           }
 81
 82         if ((cells[0][0].getToken() == token)
 83             && (cells[1][1].getToken() == token)
 84             && (cells[2][2].getToken() == token)) {
 85           return true;
 86         }
 87
 88         if ((cells[0][2].getToken() == token)
 89             && (cells[1][1].getToken() == token)
 90             && (cells[2][0].getToken() == token)) {
 91           return true;
 92         }
 93
 94         return false;
 95       }
 96
 97       // An inner class for a cell
 98       public class Cell extends JPanel implements MouseListener {
 99         // Token used for this cell
100         private char token = ' ';
101
102         public Cell() {
103           setBorder(new LineBorder(Color.black, 1)); // Set cell's border
104           addMouseListener(this);   // Register listener
105         }
106
107         /** Return token */
108         public char getToken() {
109           return token;
110         }
111
112         /** Set a new token */
113         public void setToken(char c) {
114           token = c;
115           repaint();
116         }
117
118         /** Paint the cell */
119         public void paintComponent(Graphics g) {
120           super.paintComponent(g);
121
122           if (token == 'X') {
123             g.drawLine(10, 10, getSize().width-10, getSize().height-10);
124             g.drawLine(getSize().width-10, 10, 10, getSize().height-10);
125           }
126           else if (token == 'O') {
127             g.drawOval(10, 10, getSize().width-20, getSize().height-20);
128           }
129         }
130
131         /** Handle mouse click on a cell */
132         public void mouseClicked(MouseEvent e) {
133           if (token == ' ') { // If cell is not occupied
134             if (whoseTurn == 'X') { // If it is the X player's turn
135               setToken('X');  // Set token in the cell
136               whoseTurn = 'O';  // Change the turn
```

```
137            jlblStatus.setText("O's turn");  // Display status
138            if (isWon('X'))
139               jlblStatus.setText("X won! The game is over");
140            else if (isFull())
141               jlblStatus.setText("Draw! The game is over");
142         }
143         else if (whoseTurn == 'O') { // If it is the O player's turn
144            setToken('O'); // Set token in the cell
145            whoseTurn = 'X';  // Change the turn
146            jlblStatus.setText("X's turn"); // Display status
147            if (isWon('O'))
148               jlblStatus.setText("O won! The game is over");
149            else if (isFull())
150               jlblStatus.setText("Draw! The game is over");
151         }
152      }
153   }
154
155   public void mousePressed(MouseEvent e) {
156      // TODO: implement this java.awt.event.MouseListener method;
157   }
158
159   public void mouseReleased(MouseEvent e) {
160      // TODO: implement this java.awt.event.MouseListener method;
161   }
162
163   public void mouseEntered(MouseEvent e) {
164      // TODO: implement this java.awt.event.MouseListener method;
165   }
166
167   public void mouseExited(MouseEvent e) {
168      // TODO: implement this java.awt.event.MouseListener method;
169   }
170   }
171 }
```

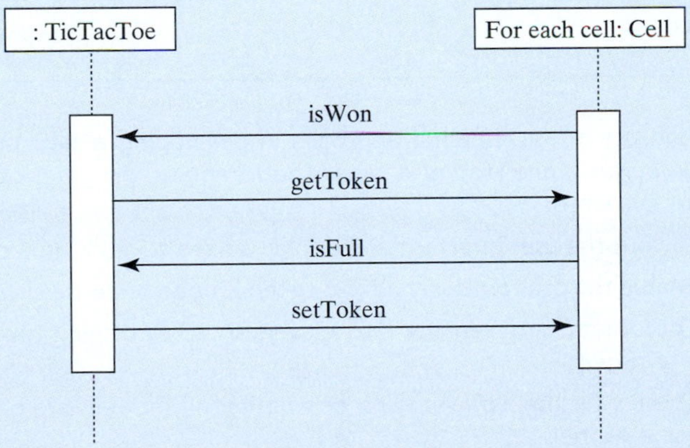

Figure 12.19   *Each* Cell *object communicates with the* TicTacToe *object to play the game.*

continues

Example 12.7 continued

Review

The `TicTacToe` class initializes the user interface with nine cells placed in a panel of `GridLayout` (Lines 20–24). A label named `jlblStatus` is used to show the status of the game (Line 32). The variable `whoseTurn` (Line 9) is used to track the next type of token to be placed in a cell. The methods `isFull` (Line 57) and `isWon` (Line 67) are for checking the status of the game.

It is worth noting that the `Cell` class is declared as an inner class for `TicTacToe`. This is because the `mouseClicked` method in `Cell` references the variable `whoseTurn` and invokes `isFull` and `isWon` in the `TicTacToe` class. Since `Cell` is an inner class in `TicTacToe`, the variable and methods defined in `TicTacToe` can be used directly in it. This approach makes programs simple and concise. If `Cell` were not declared as an inner class of `TicTacToe`, you would have to pass an object of `TicTacToe` to `Cell` in order for the variables and methods in `TicTacToe` to be used in `Cell`. You will rewrite the program without using an inner class in Exercise 12.6.

The `Cell` class implements `MouseListener` to listen for `MouseEvent`. When a cell is clicked, it draws a shape determined by the variable `whoseTurn`, and then checks whether the game is won or all the cells are occupied.

There is a problem in this program in that the user may continue to mark the cells even after the game is over. You will fix this problem in Exercise 12.6.

This program enables two users to play from the same machine. In Chapter 18, "Networking," you will learn how to develop a distributed TicTacToe applet that will enable two users to play on different machines anywhere on the Internet.

TIP

You should use an incremental approach in developing a Java project of this kind, working one step at a time. The foregoing program can be divided into five steps:

1. Lay out the user interface and display a fixed token X on a cell.

2. Enable the cell to display a fixed token X upon a mouse click.

3. Coordinate between the two players so as to display tokens X and O alternately.

4. Check whether a player wins, or whether all the cells are occupied without a winner.

5. Implement displaying a message on the label upon each move by a player.

12.11   Event Adapters (Optional)

The Java event model shown in Figure 10.29 (on page 419) is flexible, allowing modifications and variations. One useful variation of the model is the addition of adapters, as shown in Figure 12.20. When an event occurs, the source object notifies the adapter. The adapter then delegates the handling of the event to the real listener object, which is referred to as a *target*.

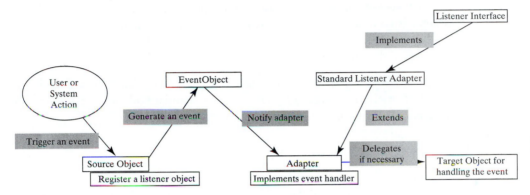

Figure 12.20   *The adapter listens for events and delegates handling to the actual listener (target).*

The adapter is a service object that provides a level of indirection between the source and the target. It is registered as a listener for the source event. Instead of passing the event object to the target, the source passes the event object to the adapter and lets it delegate to the target handler.

At first glance, the advantages of using adapters are not apparent. Adapters seem to make things more complex, but they are valuable in many situations. Here are some examples:

- If you need to hook a source to an existing class that cannot be modified or extended, you can use an adapter as a listener to the source and register it with the source. When an event occurs, the source notifies the adapter, which then invokes the methods in the class.

- You can use an adapter to place all the event notifications from the source in a queue so as to allow the source object to resume execution without blocking. This is particularly useful in a distributed environment, where the target object may be busy or not available when the event occurs.

- You can create a generic adapter to listen for all types of events from all sources, then deliver them to one or multiple targets. The generic adapter can be used as a filter for the events before they are delegated out to the targets. You can apply business rules and logic of all kinds to the delivery of events and sort them by priority.

An adapter usually extends a convenience listener adapter. A *convenience listener adapter* is a support class that provides default implementations for all the methods in the listener interface. The default implementation is usually an empty body. Java provides convenience listener adapters for every AWT listener interface except the `ActionListener`. A convenience listener adapter is named *X*Adapter for *X*Listener. For example, `MouseAdapter` is a standard listener adapter for `MouseListener`.

A listener interface may contain many methods for handling various types of actions of an event. For example, `MouseListener` contains `mouseClicked`, `mousePressed`, `mouseReleased`, `mouseEntered`, and `mouseExited`. The convenience listener adapter is convenient because a listener class may simply extend the adapter and implement only the method for the intended type of action instead of all the methods of the listener interface.

Adapters are an important addition to the Java event model. They are used in the Java IDE tools. Two types of event adapters, standard adapters and anonymous adapters, are introduced in the following sections.

12.11.1 Standard Adapters

A *standard adapter* is a named class that extends a convenience listener adapter or implements a listener interface. The following example demonstrates the use of standard adapters.

Example 12.8 Handling Events Using Standard Adapters

Problem

Rewrite Example 12.5, "Scribbling with a Mouse," using standard adapters. To scribble using a mouse, a mouse-pressed event and mouse-dragged event are used. These events are handled in `MouseListener` and `MouseMotionListener`, respectively.

Solution

The following program creates one standard adapter for handling the mouse-pressed event, and another standard adapter for handling the mouse-dragged event.

```
1    // ScribbleUsingStandardAdapter.java:
2    // Create a frame to test window events
3    import java.awt.*;
4    import java.awt.event.*;
5    import java.applet.*;
6    import javax.swing.*;
7
8    public class ScribbleUsingStandardAdapter extends JApplet {
9      /** Main method */
10     public static void main(String[] args) {
11       // Create a frame
12       JFrame frame = new JFrame("Scribbling Demo");
13
14       // Create an instance of the applet
15       ScribbleUsingStandardAdapter applet =
16         new ScribbleUsingStandardAdapter();
17
```

```
18          // Add the applet instance to the frame
19          frame.getContentPane().add(applet, BorderLayout.CENTER);
20
21          // Invoke init() and start()
22          applet.init();
23          applet.start();
24
25          // Display the frame
26          frame.setSize(300, 300);
27          frame.setDefaultCloseOperation(JFrame.EXIT_ON_CLOSE);
28          frame.setVisible(true);
29        }
30
31        /** Initialize the applet */
32        public void init() {
33          // Create a PaintPanel and add it to the applet
34          getContentPane().add(new ScribblePanelUsingStandardAdapter(),
35            BorderLayout.CENTER);
36        }
37      }
38
39      // ScribblePanelUsingStandardAdapter for scribbling using the mouse
40      class ScribblePanelUsingStandardAdapter extends JPanel {
41        final int CIRCLESIZE = 20; // Circle diameter used for erasing
42        private Point lineStart = new Point(0, 0); // Line start point
43        private Graphics g; // Create a Graphics object for drawing
44
45        public ScribblePanelUsingStandardAdapter() {
46          // Register listener for the mouse event
47          addMouseListener(new MouseListenerAdapter(this));
48          addMouseMotionListener(new MouseMotionListenerAdapter(this));
49        }
50
51        public void mousePressed(MouseEvent e) {
52          lineStart.move(e.getX(), e.getY());
53        }
54
55        public void mouseDragged(MouseEvent e) {
56          g = getGraphics(); // Get graphics context
57
58          if (e.isMetaDown()) { // Detect right button pressed
59            // Erase the drawing using an oval
60            g.setColor(getBackground());
61            g.fillOval(e.getX() - (CIRCLESIZE / 2),
62              e.getY() - (CIRCLESIZE / 2), CIRCLESIZE, CIRCLESIZE);
63          }
64          else {
65            g.setColor(Color.black);
66            g.drawLine(lineStart.x, lineStart.y,
67              e.getX(), e.getY());
68          }
69
70          lineStart.move(e.getX(), e.getY());
71
72          // Dispose this graphics context
73          g.dispose();
74        }
75      }
76
77      /** Standard adapter for mouse pressed */
78      class MouseListenerAdapter extends MouseAdapter {
79        ScribblePanelUsingStandardAdapter adaptee;
80
```

continues

567

Example 12.8 continued

```
81        MouseListenerAdapter(ScribblePanelUsingStandardAdapter adaptee) {
82          this.adaptee = adaptee;
83        }
84
85        public void mousePressed(MouseEvent e) {
86          adaptee.mousePressed(e);
87        }
88      }
89
90      /** Standard adapter for mouse dragged */
91      class MouseMotionListenerAdapter extends MouseMotionAdapter {
92        ScribblePanelUsingStandardAdapter adaptee;
93
94        MouseMotionListenerAdapter(ScribblePanelUsingStandardAdapter
95          adaptee) {
96          this.adaptee = adaptee;
97        }
98
99        public void mouseDragged(MouseEvent e) {
100         adaptee.mouseDragged(e);
101       }
102     }
```

Review

MouseAdapter (Line 78) is a convenience listener adapter that implements MouseListener, and MouseMotionAdapter (Line 91) is a convenience listener adapter that implements MouseMotionListener. MouseListenerAdapter extends MouseAdapter, and MouseMotionListenerAdapter extends MouseMotionAdapter. An instance of MouseListenerAdapter is registered as a listener for mouse events in ScribblePanelUsingStandardAdapter (a subclass of JPanel) using the following statement (Line 47):

```
addMouseListener(new MouseListenerAdapter(this));
```

An instance of MouseMotionListenerAdapter is registered as a listener for mouse-motion events in ScribblePanelUsingStandardAdapter using the following statement (Line 48):

```
addMouseMotionListener(new MouseMotionListenerAdapter(this));
```

ScribblePanelUsingStandardAdapter is passed to the constructor of these adapters to become the adaptee for the adapter. When a mouse-pressed event occurs, the MouseListenerAdapter is notified, and its mousePressed method is invoked. The adapter then delegates the processing to its adaptee by invoking the adaptee's mousePressed method (Line 86). Similarly, when a mouse-dragged event occurs, the MouseMotionListenerAdapter is notified, and its mouseDragged method is invoked. The adapter then delegates the processing to its adaptee by invoking the adaptee's mouseDragged method (Line 100).

12.11.2   Anonymous Adapters

Standard adapters can be shortened using anonymous inner classes. An *anonymous inner class* is an inner class without a name. It combines declaring an inner class and creating an instance of the class in one step. An anonymous inner class is declared as follows:

```
new SuperClassName/InterfaceName() {
  // Implement or override methods in superclass or interface

  // Other methods if necessary
}
```

Since an anonymous inner class is a special kind of inner class, it is treated like an inner class in many ways. In addition, it has the following features:

- An anonymous inner class must always extend a superclass or implement an interface, but it cannot have an explicit `extends` or `implements` clause.

- An anonymous inner class must implement all the abstract methods in the superclass and the interface.

- An anonymous inner class always uses the default constructor from its superclass to create an instance. If an anonymous inner class implements an interface, the default constructor is `Object()`.

Adapters implemented with anonymous inner classes are referred to as *anonymous adapters*. The following example demonstrates the use of anonymous inner adapters.

Example 12.9 Handling Events Using Anonymous Adapters

Problem

Rewrite the preceding example using anonymous inner adapters.

Solution

The following program creates an anonymous adapter for handling the mouse-pressed event, and for handling the mouse-dragged event.

```
1   // ScribbleUsingAnonymousAdapter.java:
2   import java.awt.*;
3   import java.awt.event.*;
4   import java.applet.*;
5   import javax.swing.*;
6
7   public class ScribbleUsingAnonymousAdapter extends JApplet {
8     /** Main method */
9     public static void main(String[] args) {
10      // Create a frame
11      JFrame frame = new JFrame("Scribbling Demo");
12
13      // Create an instance of the applet
14      ScribbleUsingStandardAdapter applet =
15        new ScribbleUsingStandardAdapter();
16
```

continues

Example 12.9 continued

```
17          // Add the applet instance to the frame
18          frame.getContentPane().add(applet, BorderLayout.CENTER);
19
20          // Invoke init() and start()
21          applet.init();
22          applet.start();
23
24          // Display the frame
25          frame.setSize(300, 300);
26          frame.setDefaultCloseOperation(JFrame.EXIT_ON_CLOSE);
27          frame.setVisible(true);
28        }
29
30        /** Initialize the applet */
31        public void init() {
32          // Create a PaintPanel and add it to the applet
33          getContentPane().add(new ScribblePanelUsingAnonymousAdapter(),
34            BorderLayout.CENTER);
35        }
36      }
37
38      // ScribblePanelUsingAnonymousAdapter for scribbling using the mouse
39      class ScribblePanelUsingAnonymousAdapter extends JPanel {
40        final int CIRCLESIZE = 20; // Circle diameter used for erasing
41        private Point lineStart = new Point(0, 0); // Line start point
42        private Graphics g; // Create a Graphics object for drawing
43
44        public ScribblePanelUsingAnonymousAdapter() {
45          // Register listener for the mouse event
46          addMouseListener(
47            // Anonymous adapter
48            new MouseAdapter() {
49              public void mousePressed(MouseEvent e) {
50                // Invoke the outer class's mousePressed method
51                ScribblePanelUsingAnonymousAdapter.this.mousePressed(e);
52              }
53            }
54          );
55
56          addMouseMotionListener(
57            // Anonymous adapter
58            new MouseMotionAdapter() {
59              public void mouseDragged(MouseEvent e) {
60                // Invoke the outer class's mouseDragged method
61                ScribblePanelUsingAnonymousAdapter.this.mouseDragged(e);
62              }
63            }
64          );
65        }
66
67        public void mousePressed(MouseEvent e) {
68          lineStart.move(e.getX(), e.getY());
69        }
70
71        public void mouseDragged(MouseEvent e) {
72          g = getGraphics(); // Get graphics context
73          if (e.isMetaDown()) { // Detect right button pressed
74            // Erase the drawing using an oval
75            g.setColor(getBackground());
76            g.fillOval(e.getX() - (CIRCLESIZE/2),
77              e.getY() - (CIRCLESIZE/2), CIRCLESIZE, CIRCLESIZE);
78          }
```

```
79          else {
80             g.setColor(Color.black);
81             g.drawLine(lineStart.x, lineStart.y,
82                e.getX(), e.getY());
83          }
84
85          lineStart.move(e.getX(), e.getY());
86
87          // Dispose this graphics context
88          g.dispose();
89       }
90    }
```

Review

The anonymous adapters (Lines 48–53 and 58–63) in this example work the same way as the standard adapters in the preceding example. The program is condensed using anonymous adapters.

An inner class can reference the methods defined in its outer class. The `mousePressed` method is defined in both the inner class and the outer class. To reference the `mousePressed` method defined in the outer class from the inner class, use the following statement (Line 51):

```
ScribblePanelUsingAnonymousAdapter.this.mousePressed(e);
```

Inner classes are compiled into `OuterClassName$#.class`, where # starts at 1 and is incremented for each anonymous class encountered by the compiler.

12.12   Packaging and Deploying Java Projects (Optional)

Your project may consist of many classes and supporting files, such as image files and audio files. To make your programs run on the end-user side, you need to provide end-users with all these files. For convenience, Java supports an archive file that can be used to group all the project files in a compressed file.

The Java archive file format (JAR) is based on the popular ZIP file format. Although JAR can be used as a general archiving tool, the primary motivation for its development was to make it possible for Java applications, applets, and their requisite components (.class files, images, and sounds) to be transported in a single file.

This single file can be deployed on an end-user's machine as an application. It also can be downloaded to a browser in a single HTTP transaction, rather than opening a new connection for each piece. This greatly simplifies application deployment and improves the speed with which an applet can be loaded onto a Web page and begin functioning. The JAR format also supports compression, which reduces the size of the file and improves download time still further. Additionally, individual entries in a JAR file can be digitally signed by the applet author to authenticate their origin.

You can use the JDK **jar** command to create an archive file. The following command creates an archive file named TicTacToe.jar for classes TicTacToe.class and TicTacToe$Cell.class.

```
jar -cf TicTacToe.jar TicTacToe.class TicTacToe$Cell.class
```

The **-c** option is for creating a new archive file, and the **-f** option specifies the archive file's name.

NOTE

You can view the contents of a .jar file using WinZip32, a popular compression utility for Windows, as shown in Figure 12.21.

Figure 12.21 *You can view the files contained in the archive file using the WinZip utility.*

12.12.1   The Manifest File

As shown in Figure 12.21, a manifest file was created with the path name `meta-inf\`. The manifest is a special file that contains information about the files packaged in a JAR file. For instance, the manifest file in Figure 10.22 contains the following information:

```
Manifest-Version: 1.0

Name: TicTacToe.class
Java-Bean: True

Name: TioTacToe$Cell.class
Java-Bean: True
```

You can modify the information contained in the manifest file to enable the JAR file to be used for a variety of purposes. For instance, you can add information to specify a `main` class to run an application using the .jar file.

12.12.2   Running Archived Projects

You can package all the class files and dependent resource files in an archive file for distribution to the end-user. If the project is a Java application, the user should have a Java-running environment already installed. If it is not installed, the user can download the Java Runtime Environment (JRE) from JavaSoft at `http://www.javasoft.com/` and install it.

> **NOTE**
>
> The Java Runtime Environment is the minimum standard Java platform for running Java programs. It contains the Java interpreter, Java core classes, and supporting files. The JRE does not contain any development tools (such as Applet Viewer or javac) or classes that pertain only to a development environment. The JRE is a subset of JDK.

To run `TicTacToe` as an application, take the following steps:

1. Update the manifest file to insert an entry for the main class. You need to create a text file containing the following two lines:

```
Main-Class: TicTacToe
Sealed: true
```

   The first line specifies the main class. The second line is necessary to ensure that the first line can be inserted into an existing manifest file in a jar. Assume that these two lines are contained in the file temp.mf.

2. Execute the `jar` command to insert the main class line to the manifest file in TicTacToe.jar, as follows:

```
jar -uvmf temp.mf TicTacToe.jar
```

   The **-u** option is for updating an existing jar file, the **-v** option is for displaying command output, and the **-m** option is for appending the contents in temp.mf to the manifest file in the archive.

3. Run the .jar file using the java command from the directory that contains TicTacToe.jar, as follows:

```
java -jar TicTacToe.jar
```

> **NOTE**
>
> You can write an installation procedure that creates the necessary directories and subdirectories on the end-user's computer. The installation can also create an icon which the end-user can double-click on to start the program. For information on creating Windows desktop icon, please see **www.prenhall.com/liang/intro4e.html**.

To run `TicTacToe` as an applet, modify the <APPLET> tag in the HTML file to include an ARCHIVE attribute. The ARCHIVE attribute specifies the archive file in which the applet is contained. For example, the HTML file for running `TicTacToe` can be modified as shown below:

```
<APPLET
   CODE     = "TicTacToe.class"
   ARCHIVE  = "TicTacToe.jar"
   WIDTH    = 400
   HEIGHT   = 300
   HSPACE   = 0
   VSPACE   = 0
   ALIGN    = Middle
>
</APPLET>
```

12.13   The *CardLayout* Manager (Optional)

Layout managers arrange components in a container. You have already used the FlowLayout manager, GridLayout manager, and BorderLayout manager. Java has other layout managers, like CardLayout and GridBagLayout. Java also enables you to directly place components in specific positions without using a layout manager. This section discusses the CardLayout manager; the following sections discuss the GridBagLayout manager and using no layout manager.

The CardLayout manager arranges components in a queue of cards. You can only see one card at a time. To construct a CardLayout, use the constructor CardLayout().

Cards are usually placed in a container, such as a panel of CardLayout, in the order in which they are added. To add a component to the CardLayout container, use the following method:

```
public void add(Component component, String name)
```

This adds the specified component to the container. The String argument of the method, name, gives an explicit identity to the component in the container.

To make a component visible in the container with CardLayout, use the following instance methods in the CardLayout object:

- public void first(Container container)

   Views the first card in the container.

- public void last(Container container)

   Views the last card in the container.

- public void next(Container container)

   Views the next card in the container.

- public void previous(Container container)

   Views the preceding card in the container.

- public void show(Container container, String name)

   Views the component with the specified name in the container. It can be used to directly display the component.

Example 12.10 Testing CardLayout Manager

Problem

Write a program that creates two panels in a frame. The first panel uses CardLayout to hold nine labels for displaying images. The second panel uses FlowLayout to group four buttons named First, Next, Previous, and Last, and a combo box labeled Image, as shown in Figure 12.22.

These buttons control which image will be shown in the CardLayout panel. When the user clicks the button named First, for example, the first image in the CardLayout panel appears. The combo box enables the user to directly select an image.

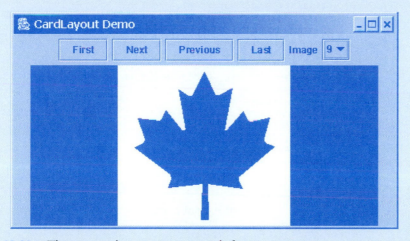

Figure 12.22 *The program shows images in a panel of* CardLayout.

Solution

The following code gives the solution to the program.

```
1    // ShowCardLayout.java: Using CardLayout to display images
2    import java.awt.*;
3    import java.awt.event.*;
4    import javax.swing.*;
5
6    public class ShowCardLayout extends JFrame
7      implements ActionListener, ItemListener {
8      private CardLayout cardLayout = new CardLayout();
9      private JPanel cardPanel = new JPanel();
10     private JButton jbtFirst, jbtNext, jbtPrevious, jbtLast;
11     private JComboBox jcboImage;
12
13     public ShowCardLayout() {
14       // Use CardLayout for cardPanel
15       cardPanel.setLayout(cardLayout);
16
```

continues

Example 12.10 continued

```
17          // Add 9 labels for displaying images into cardPanel
18          for (int i = 1; i <= 9; i++)
19            cardPanel.add
20              (new JLabel(new ImageIcon("image/flag" + i + ".gif")),
21                String.valueOf(i));
22
23          // Panel p to hold buttons and a combo box
24          JPanel p = new JPanel();
25          p.add(jbtFirst = new JButton("First"));
26          p.add(jbtNext = new JButton("Next"));
27          p.add(jbtPrevious= new JButton("Previous"));
28          p.add(jbtLast = new JButton("Last"));
29          p.add(new JLabel("Image"));
30          p.add(jcboImage = new JComboBox());
31
32          // Initialize combo box items
33          for (int i = 1; i <= 9; i++)
34            jcboImage.addItem(String.valueOf(i));
35
36          // Place panels in the frame
37          getContentPane().add(cardPanel, BorderLayout.CENTER);
38          getContentPane().add(p, BorderLayout.SOUTH);
39
40          // Register listeners with the source objects
41          jbtFirst.addActionListener(this);
42          jbtNext.addActionListener(this);
43          jbtPrevious.addActionListener(this);
44          jbtLast.addActionListener(this);
45          jcboImage.addItemListener(this);
46        }
47
48        /** Main method */
49        public static void main(String[] args) {
50          ShowCardLayout frame = new ShowCardLayout();
51          frame.setSize(300, 300);
52          frame.setDefaultCloseOperation(JFrame.EXIT_ON_CLOSE);
53          frame.setTitle("CardLayout Demo");
54          frame.setVisible(true);
55        }
56
57        /** Handle button actions */
58        public void actionPerformed(ActionEvent e) {
59          String actionCommand = e.getActionCommand();
60          if (e.getSource() instanceof JButton)
61            if ("First".equals(actionCommand))
62              // Show the first component in cardPanel
63              cardLayout.first(cardPanel);
64            else if ("Last".equals(actionCommand))
65              // Show the last component in cardPanel
66              cardLayout.last(cardPanel);
67            else if ("Previous".equals(actionCommand))
68              // Show the previous component in cardPanel
69              cardLayout.previous(cardPanel);
70            else if ("Next".equals(actionCommand))
71              // Show the next component in cardPanel
72              cardLayout.next(cardPanel);
73        }
74
```

```
75        /** Handle selection of combo box item */
76        public void itemStateChanged(ItemEvent e) {
77          if (e.getSource() == jcboImage)
78            // Show the component at specified index
79            cardLayout.show(cardPanel, (String)e.getItem());
80        }
81      }
```

Review

The program creates an instance of CardLayout, cardLayout = new Card-Layout() (Line 8). The statement cardPanel.setLayout(cardLayout) (Line 15) sets the cardPanel with the CardLayout; cardPanel is an instance of JPanel. You have already used such statements as setLayout(new FlowLayout()) to create an anonymous layout object and set the layout for a container, instead of declaring and creating a separate instance of the layout manager, as in this program. The cardLayout object, however, is useful later in the program to show components in cardPanel. You have to use cardLayout.first(cardPanel) (Line 63), for example, to view the first component in cardPanel.

The statement cardPanel.add(new JLabel(new ImageIcon("image/flag" + i + ".gif")), String.valueOf(i)) (Lines 19–21) adds the image label with the identity String.valueOf(i). Later, when the user selects an image with number i, the identity String.valueOf(i) is used in the cardLayout.show() method (Line 79) to view the image with the specified identity.

12.14   The *GridBagLayout* Manager (Optional)

The GridBagLayout manager is the most flexible and the most complex. It is similar to the GridLayout manager in the sense that both layout managers arrange components in a grid. The components of GridBagLayout can vary in size, however, and can be added in any order. For example, with GridBagLayout you can create the layout shown in Figure 12.23.

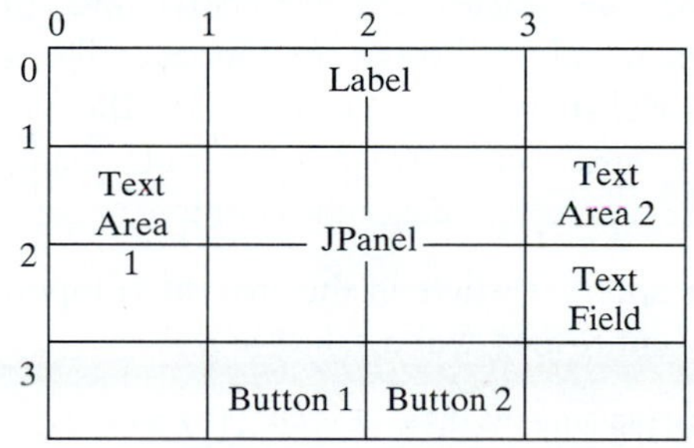

Figure 12.23   *A* GridBagLayout *manager divides the container into cells. A component can occupy several cells.*

The constructor `GridBagLayout()` is used to create a new `GridBagLayout`. In `GridLayout`, the grid size (the number of rows and columns) may be specified in the constructor. It is not specified in `GridBagLayout`.

Each `GridBagLayout` uses a dynamic rectangular grid of cells, with each component occupying one or more cells called its *display area*. Each component managed by a `GridBagLayout` is associated with a `GridBagConstraints` instance that specifies how the component is laid out within its display area. How a `GridBagLayout` places a set of components depends on the `GridBagConstraints` and minimum size of each component, as well as the preferred size of the component's container.

To use `GridBagLayout` effectively, you must customize the `GridBagConstraints` of one or more of its components. You customize a `GridBagConstraints` object by setting one or more of its instance variables.

- **gridx** and **gridy** specify the cell at the upper left of the component's display area, where the upper-leftmost cell has the address `gridx=0`, `gridy=0`. Note that `gridx` specifies the column in which the component will be placed, and `gridy` specifies the row in which it will be placed. In Figure 12.23, Button 1 has a `gridx` value of `1` and a `gridy` value of `3`, and Label has a `gridx` value of 0 and a `gridy` value of 0.

- **gridwidth** and **gridheight** specify the number of cells in a row (for `gridheight`) or column (for `gridwidth`) in the component's display area. The default value is 1. In Figure 12.23, the `JPanel` in the center occupies two columns and two rows, and Text Area 2 occupies one row and one column.

- **weightx** and **weighty** specify the extra horizontal and vertical space to allocate for the component when the window is resized. Unless you specify a weight for at least one component in a row (`weightx`) and a column (`weighty`), all the components clump together in the center of their container. This is because, when the weight is zero (the default), the `GridBagLayout` puts any extra space between its grid of cells and the edges of the container. You will see the effect of these parameters in Example 12.11.

- **fill** specifies how the component should be resized if its viewing area is larger than its current size. Valid values are `GridBagConstraints.NONE` (the default), `GridBagConstraints.HORIZONTAL` (makes the component wide enough to fill its display area horizontally, but doesn't change its height), `GridBagConstraints.VERTICAL` (makes the component tall enough to fill its display area vertically, but doesn't change its width), and `GridBagConstraints.BOTH` (makes the component totally fill its display area).

- **anchor** specifies where in the area the component is placed when it does not fill the entire area. Valid values are:

  `GridBagConstraints.CENTER (the default)`

  `GridBagConstraints.NORTH`

  `GridBagConstraints.NORTHEAST`

```
GridBagConstraints.EAST

GridBagConstraints.SOUTHEAST

GridBagConstraints.SOUTH

GridBagConstraints.SOUTHWEST

GridBagConstraints.WEST

GridBagConstraints.NORTHWEST
```

The `fill` and `anchor` parameters deal with how to fill and place a component when the viewing area is larger than the requested area. The `fill` and `anchor` parameters are class variables, whereas `gridx`, `gridy`, `gridwidth`, `gridheight`, `weightx`, and `weighty` are instance variables.

Example 12.11 Testing the `GridBagLayout` Manager

Problem

Write a program that uses the `GridBagLayout` manager to create a layout for Figure 12.23. The output of the program is shown in Figure 12.24.

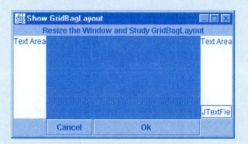

Figure 12.24 *The components are placed in the frame of* `GridBagLayout`.

Solution

The following code gives the solution to the problem.

```
1    // ShowGridBagLayout.java: Using GridBagLayout
2    import java.awt.*;
3    import java.awt.event.*;
4    import javax.swing.*;
5
6    public class ShowGridBagLayout extends JFrame {
7      private JLabel jlbl;
8      private JTextArea jta1, jta2;
9      private JTextField jtf;
10     private JPanel jp;
11     private JButton jbt1, jbt2;
12     private GridBagLayout gbLayout;
13     private GridBagConstraints gbConstraints;
14
```

continues

Example 12.11 continued

```
15        /** Main method */
16        public static void main(String[] args) {
17          ShowGridBagLayout frame = new ShowGridBagLayout();
18          frame.setSize(350,200);
19          frame.setDefaultCloseOperation(JFrame.EXIT_ON_CLOSE);
20          frame.setVisible(true);
21        }
22
23        /** Add a component to the container */
24        private void addComp(Component c, GridBagLayout gbLayout,
25                             GridBagConstraints gbConstraints,
26                             int row, int column, int numRows,
27                             int numColumns, int weightx, int weighty) {
28          // Set parameters
29          gbConstraints.gridx = column;
30          gbConstraints.gridy = row;
31          gbConstraints.gridwidth = numColumns;
32          gbConstraints.gridheight = numRows;
33          gbConstraints.weightx = weightx;
34          gbConstraints.weighty = weighty;
35
36          // Set constraints in the GridBagLayout
37          gbLayout.setConstraints(c, gbConstraints);
38
39          // Add component to the container
40          getContentPane().add(c);
41        }
42
43        /** Default Constructor */
44        public ShowGridBagLayout() {
45          setTitle("Show GridBagLayout");
46
47          // Initialize UI components
48          jlbl = new JLabel("Resize the Window and Study GridBagLayout",
49                    JLabel.CENTER);
50          jp = new JPanel();
51          jta1 = new JTextArea("Text Area", 5, 15 );
52          jta2 = new JTextArea("Text Area", 5, 15 );
53          jtf = new JTextField("JTextField");
54          jbt1 = new JButton("Cancel" );
55          jbt2 = new JButton("Ok" );
56
57          // Create GridBagLayout and GridBagConstraints object
58          gbLayout = new GridBagLayout();
59          gbConstraints = new GridBagConstraints();
60          getContentPane().setLayout(gbLayout);
61
62          // Place JLabel to occupy row 0 (the first row)
63          gbConstraints.fill = GridBagConstraints.BOTH;
64          gbConstraints.anchor = GridBagConstraints.CENTER;
65          addComp(jlbl, gbLayout, gbConstraints, 0, 0, 1, 4, 0, 0);
66
67          // Place text area 1 in row 1 and 2, and column 0
68          addComp(jta1, gbLayout, gbConstraints, 1, 0, 2, 1, 0, 0);
69
70          // Place Panel in row 1 and 2, and column 1 and 2
71          addComp(jp, gbLayout, gbConstraints, 1, 1, 2, 2, 100, 100);
72          jp.setBackground(Color.red);
73
74          // Place text area 2 in row 1 and column 3
75          addComp(jta2, gbLayout, gbConstraints, 1, 3, 1, 1, 0, 100);
76
```

```
77          // Place text field in row 2 and column 3
78          addComp(jtf, gbLayout, gbConstraints, 2, 3, 1, 1, 0, 0);
79
80          // Place JButton 1 in row 3 and column 1
81          addComp(jbt1, gbLayout, gbConstraints, 3, 1, 1, 1, 0, 0);
82
83          // Place JButton 2 in row 3 and column 2
84          addComp(jbt2, gbLayout, gbConstraints, 3, 2, 1, 1, 0, 0);
85      }
86   }
```

Review

The program defines the addComp method (Lines 24–41) to add a component to the GridBagLayout with the specified constraint parameters.

Since the program creates a panel with a weightx of 100 and a weighty of 100 (Line 71), the component has extra space to grow horizontally and vertically up to 100 pixels. If you resize the window, the panel's viewing area will increase or shrink as the window grows or shrinks.

Since the program creates the second text area jta2 with weightx 0 and weighty 100 (Line 75), this text area can grow vertically but not horizontally when the window is resized.

The weightx and weighty for all the other components are 0. Whether the size of these components grows or shrinks depends on the fill and anchor parameters. The program defines fill = BOTH and anchor = CENTER (Lines 63–64).

Because the fill and anchor parameters are class variables, their values are for all components. Consider this scenario: Suppose that you enlarge the window. The panel is expanded, which causes the display area for text area jta1 to increase. Because fill is BOTH for jta1, jta1 fills in its new display area.

12.15   Using No Layout Manager (Optional)

Java enables you to place components in a container without using a layout manager. In this case, the component must be placed using the component's instance method setBounds(), as follows:

```
public void setBounds(int x, int y, int width, int height);
```

This sets the location and size for the component, as in the next example:

```
JButton jbt = new JButton("Help");
jbt.setBounds(10, 10, 40, 20);
```

The upper-left corner of the Help button is placed at (10, 10); the button width is 40, and the height is 20.

You perform the following steps in order not to use a layout manager:

1. Use this statement to specify no layout manager:

```
setLayout(null);
```

2. Add the component to the container:

```
add(component);
```

3. Specify the location where the component is to be placed, using the `setBounds()` method:

```
JButton jbt = new JButton("Help");
jbt.setBounds(10, 10, 40, 20);
```

Example 12.12   Using No Layout Manager

Problem

Write a program that places the same components in the same layout as in the preceding example, but without using a layout manager. Figure 12.25 contains the sample output.

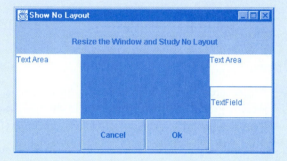

Figure 12.25   *The components are placed in the frame without using a layout manager.*

Solution

The following code gives the solution to the problem.

```
1    // ShowNoLayout.java: Place components without using a layout manager
2    import java.awt.*;
3    import java.awt.event.*;
4    import javax.swing.*;
5
6    public class ShowNoLayout extends JFrame {
7      private JLabel jlbl =
8        new JLabel("Resize the Window and Study No Layout",
9          JLabel.CENTER);
10     private JTextArea jta1 = new JTextArea("Text Area", 5, 10 );
11     private JTextArea jta2 = new JTextArea("Text Area", 5, 10 );
12     private JTextField jtf = new JTextField("TextField");
13     private JPanel jp = new JPanel();
14     private JButton jbt1 = new JButton("Cancel" );
15     private JButton jbt2 = new JButton("Ok" );
16     private GridBagLayout gbLayout;
17     private GridBagConstraints gbConstraints;
18
19     public static void main(String[] args) {
20       ShowNoLayout frame = new ShowNoLayout();
21       frame.setSize(400,200);
```

```
22          frame.setDefaultCloseOperation(JFrame.EXIT_ON_CLOSE);
23          frame.setVisible(true);
24      }
25
26      public ShowNoLayout() {
27          setTitle("Show No Layout");
28
29          // Set background color for the panel
30          jp.setBackground(Color.red);
31
32          // Specify no layout manager
33          getContentPane().setLayout(null);
34
35          // Add components to frame
36          getContentPane().add(jlbl);
37          getContentPane().add(jp);
38          getContentPane().add(jta1);
39          getContentPane().add(jta2);
40          getContentPane().add(jtf);
41          getContentPane().add(jbt1);
42          getContentPane().add(jbt2);
43
44          // Put components in the right place
45          jlbl.setBounds(0, 10, 400, 40);
46          jta1.setBounds(0, 50, 100, 100);
47          jp.setBounds(100, 50, 200, 100);
48          jta2.setBounds(300, 50, 100, 50);
49          jtf.setBounds(300, 100, 100, 50);
50          jbt1.setBounds(100, 150, 100, 50);
51          jbt2.setBounds(200, 150, 100, 50);
52      }
53  }
```

Review

If you run this program on Windows with 640×480 resolution, the layout size is just right. When the program is run on Windows with a higher resolution, the components appear very small and clump together. When it is run on Windows with a lower resolution, they cannot be shown in their entirety.

If you resize the window, you will see that the location and size of the components are not changed, as shown in Figure 12.26.

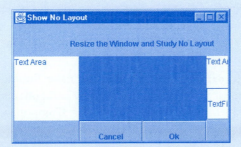

Figure 12.26   *With no layout manager, the size and positions of the components are fixed.*

continues

Example 12.12 continued

 TIP
Do not use the no-layout-manager option to develop platform-indepen-dent applications.

Chapter Summary

In this chapter, you learned about applets and advanced GUI programming using mouse and keyboard events, event adapters, CardLayout manager, GridBagLayout manager, and no layout manager.

The Web browser controls and executes applets through the init, start, stop, and destroy methods in the Applet class. Applets always extend the Applet class and implement these methods, if applicable, so that they can be run by a Web browser. The applet bytecode must be specified, using the <applet> tag in an HTML file to tell the Web browser where to find the applet. The applet can accept parameters from HTML using the <param> tag. JApplet is a subclass of Applet. It should be used for developing Java applets with Swing components.

The procedures for writing applications and writing applets are very similar. An applet can easily be converted into an application, and vice versa. Moreover, an applet can be written with the additional capability of running as an application.

Three examples and a case study demonstrated how to handle mouse events and keyboard events. Mouse events and keyboard events have many uses in GUI pro-gramming. Clicking, pressing, or releasing a mouse button generates a MouseEvent; dragging or moving a mouse generates a MouseMotionEvent. Entering a key gener-ates a KeyEvent. MouseEvent, MouseMotionEvent, and KeyEvent are subclasses of InputEvent, which contains several common methods useful in processing mouse and keyboard events.

The CardLayout manager arranges components in a queue of cards. Only one com-ponent can be seen at a time. To add a component to the container, you need to use add(component, string). You can see the components by using the method first(container), last(container), next(container), previous(container), or show(container, string). The show(container, string) method directly displays the component identified by the string.

The GridBagLayout manager provides the most flexible way to arrange compo-nents. It is similar to GridLayout in that the components are placed in cells, but it enables components to occupy multiple cells. Components can vary in size and can be placed in any order.

Components can be placed without using a layout manager. In such cases, they are placed at a hard-coded location. If you use this approach, your program may look fine on one machine and be useless on others. For this reason, it is advisable to use the layout managers to develop a platform-independent graphical user interface.

Review Questions

12.1 How do you write a Web page to contain an applet?

12.2 Describe the `init()`, `start()`, `stop()`, and `destroy()` methods in the `Applet` class.

12.3 Where is the `getParameter` method defined?

12.4 How do you add components to a `JApplet`?

12.5 Describe the `<applet>` HTML tag. How do you pass parameters to an applet?

12.6 What are the differences between applications and applets? How do you run an application, and how do you run an applet? Is the compilation process different for applications and applets? List some security restrictions on applets.

12.7 Can you place a frame in an applet?

12.8 Can you place an applet in a frame?

12.9 What is the event type for a mouse movement? What is the event type for getting key input?

12.10 What is the listener interface for mouse pressed, released, clicked, entered, and exited? What is the listener interface for mouse moved and dragged?

12.11 What method is used to process key event?

12.12 What methods are used in responding to a mouse-motion event?

12.13 Describe `CardLayout`. How do you create a `CardLayout`? How do you add a component to a `CardLayout` container? How do you show a card in a `CardLayout` container?

12.14 Describe `GridBagLayout`. How do you create a `GridBagLayout`? How do you create a `GridBagConstraints` object? What constraints did you learn in this chapter? Describe their functions. How do you add a component to a `GridBagLayout` container?

12.15 Is the order in which components are added important for certain layout managers? Identify such layout managers.

12.16 Which layout manager allows the components in a container to be moved to other rows when the window is resized?

12.17 Can you place components without using a layout manager? What are the disadvantages of not using a layout manager?

Programming Exercises

12.1 Convert Example 11.8, "Using Radio Buttons," into an applet.

12.2 Rewrite Example 12.2, "Passing Parameters to Java Applets," to display a message with a standard color, font, and size. The message, x, y, color, fontname, and fontsize are parameters in the `<applet>` tag, as shown below:

```
<applet
  code = "Exercise12_2.class"
  width = 200
  height = 50>
  <param name=MESSAGE value="Welcome to Java">
  <param name=X value=40>
  <param name=Y value=50>
  <param name=COLOR value="red">
  <param name=FONTNAME value="Monospaced">
  <param name=FONTSIZE value=20>
You must have a Java-enabled browser to view the applet
</applet>
```

12.3 Rewrite the `MortgageApplet` in Example 12.1, "Using Applets," to enable it to run as an application as well as an applet.

12.4 Write a program that displays the mouse position when the mouse is pressed (see Figure 12.27).

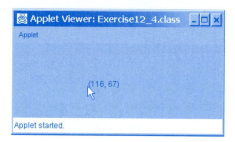

Figure 12.27   *When you click the mouse, the pixel coordinates are shown.*

12.5 Write an applet that will find a path in a maze, as shown in Figure 12.28. The applet should also run as an application. The maze is represented by an 8×8 board. The path must meet the following conditions:

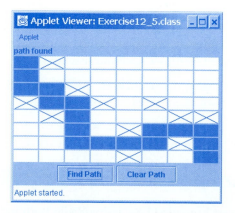

Figure 12.28   *The program finds a path from the upper-left corner to the bottom-right corner.*

■ The path is between the upper-left corner cell and the lower-right corner cell in the maze.

■ The applet enables the user to insert or remove a mark on a cell. A path consists of adjacent unmarked cells. Two cells are said to be adjacent if they are horizontal or vertical neighbors, but not diagonal neighbors.

■ The path does not contain cells that form a square. The path in Figure 12.29, for example, does not meet this condition. (The condition makes a path easy to identify on the board.)

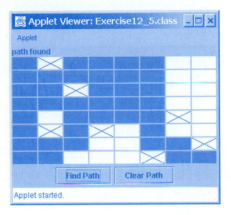

Figure 12.29   *The path does not meet the third condition for this exercise.*

12.6   Rewrite Example 12.7, "The TicTacToe Game," with the following modifications:

■ Declare Cell as a standalone class rather than an inner class.

■ When the game is over, the user cannot click to mark empty cells.

12.7   Modify Example 12.7, "The TicTacToe Game," to add a menu named File with a menu item New, as shown in Figure 12.30. The New menu item starts a new game.

Figure 12.30   *The New menu item starts a new game.*

12.8 Use various panels of FlowLayout, GridLayout, and BorderLayout to lay out the following calculator and to implement addition (+), subtraction (-), division (/), square root (sqrt), and modulus (%) functions (see Figure 12.31).

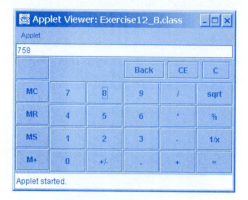

Figure 12.31   *This is a Java implementation of a popular calculator.*

12.9 Use GridBagLayout to lay out the preceding calculator.

12.10 Write a program to get character input from the keyboard and put the characters where the mouse points.

12.11 Write an applet that emulates a paint utility. Your program should enable the user to choose options and, based on them, to draw shapes or get characters from the keyboard (see Figure 12.32). Enable the applet to run as an application.

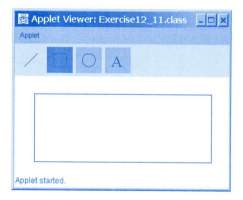

Figure 12.32   *This exercise produces a prototype drawing utility that enables you to draw lines, rectangles, ovals, and characters.*

12.12 Write an applet that does arithmetic on integers and rationals. The program uses two panels in a CardLayout manager, one for integer arithmetic and the other for rational arithmetic.

The program provides a menu labeled Operation that has two menu items, Integer and Rational, for selecting the two panels. When the user chooses the Integer menu item from the Operation menu, the integer panel is activated. When the user chooses the Rational menu item, the rational panel is activated. (See Figure 12.33.)

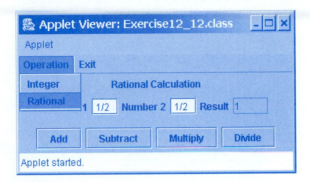

Figure 12.33 *This exercise uses* `CardLayout` *to select panels that perform integer operations and rational number operations.*

12.13 Rewrite the preceding exercise using tabbed panes instead of `CardLayout` (see Figure 12.34).

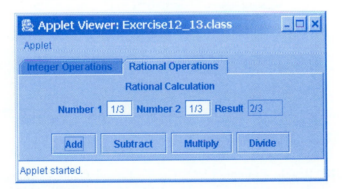

Figure 12.34 *This exercise uses tabbed panes to select panels that perform integer operations and rational number operations.*

12.14 Rewrite Example 10.7, "Handling Simple Action Events," using a standard adapter.

12.15 Rewrite Example 10.7, "Handling Simple Action Events," using an anonymous adapter.

12.16 Rewrite Exercise 10.16 using `CardLayout` manager. Create instances of `RectPanel`, `OvalsPanel`, `ArcsPanel`, and `PolygonsPanel`, and place them in a panel of `CardLayout` manager. Place this panel in the center of the content pane of an applet.

12.17 Write an applet that contains two buttons called Simple Calculator and Mortgage. When you click Simple Calculator, a frame for Example 11.11, "Using Menus," appears in a new window so that you can perform arithmetic (see Chapter 11, "Creating User Interfaces"). When you click Mortgage, a frame for computing mortgages appears in a separate new window so that you can calculate a mortgage (see Figure 12.35).

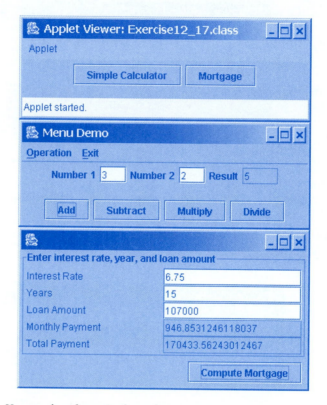

Figure 12.35   *You can show frames in the applets.*

12.18 Rewrite Example 12.7, "The TicTacToe Game," with you as one player and the computer as the other. Add a File menu with two items: New Game and Exit. When you click New Game, it displays a dialog box. From this dialog box, you can decide whether to let the computer go first.

PART IV

DEVELOPING
COMPREHENSIVE PROJECTS

This part of the book is devoted to several advanced features of Java programming. The subjects treated include the use of exception handling to make programs robust, the use of internationalization support to develop projects for international audiences, the use of multithreading to make programs more responsive and inter-active, the incorporation of sound and images to make programs user-friendly, the use of input and output to manage and process large quantities of data, the creation of client/server applications with Java networking support, and the use of Java Collections Framework to support Java data structures. You will learn how to use these features to develop comprehensive programs.

EXCEPTION HANDLING

Objectives

- ◉ To understand the concept of exception handling.
- ◉ To become familiar with exception types.
- ◉ To know how to claim exceptions in a method.
- ◉ To know how to throw exceptions in a method.
- ◉ To use the `try-catch` block to handle exceptions.
- ◉ To create your own exception classes.
- ◉ To know how to rethrow exceptions in a `try-catch` block.
- ◉ To use the `finally` clause in a `try-catch` block.
- ◉ To know when to use exceptions.

13.1   Introduction

Programming errors are unavoidable, even for experienced programmers. In Chapter 2, "Primitive Data Types and Operations," you learned that there are three categories of errors: syntax errors, runtime errors, and logic errors. *Syntax errors* arise because the rules of the language have not been followed. They are detected by the compiler. *Runtime errors* occur while the program is running if the environment detects an operation that is impossible to carry out. *Logic errors* occur when a program doesn't perform the way it was intended to. In general, syntax errors are easy to find and easy to correct because the compiler indicates where they came from and why they occurred. You can use the debugging techniques introduced in Section 2.17, "Debugging," to find logic errors. This chapter deals with runtime errors.

Runtime errors cause *exceptions*: events that occur during the execution of a program and disrupt the normal flow of control. A program that does not provide code to handle exceptions may terminate abnormally, causing serious problems. For example, if your program attempts to transfer money from a savings account to a checking account but, because of a runtime error, is terminated *after* the money is drawn from the savings account and *before* the money is deposited in the checking account, the customer will lose money.

Java provides programmers with the capability to handle runtime errors. With this capability, referred to as *exception handling*, you can develop robust programs for mission-critical computing.

Here is an example. The following program terminates abnormally because the divisor is 0, which causes a numerical error.

```java
public class Test {
  public static void main(String[] args) {
    System.out.println(3 / 0);
  }
}
```

You can handle this error in the following code, using a new construct called the *try-catch block* to enable the program to catch the error and continue to execute.

```java
public class Test {
  public static void main(String[] args) {
    try {
      System.out.println(3 / 0);
    }
    catch (Exception ex) {
      System.out.println("Error: " + ex.getMessage());
    }

    System.out.println("Execution continues");
  }
}
```

This chapter introduces Java's exception-handling model. The chapter covers exception types, claiming exceptions, throwing exceptions, catching exceptions, creating exception classes, rethrowing exceptions, and the `finally` clause.

13.2   Exceptions and Exception Types

Runtime errors occur for various reasons. The user may enter an invalid input, for example, or the program may attempt to open a file that doesn't exist, or the network connection may hang up, or the program may attempt to access an out-of-bounds array element. When a runtime error occurs, Java raises an exception.

Exceptions are handled differently from the events of GUI programming. (In Chapter 10, "Getting Started with GUI Programming," you learned the events used in GUI programming.) An *event* may be ignored in GUI programming, but an *exception* cannot be ignored. In GUI programming, a listener must register with the source object. External user action on the source object generates an event, and the source object notifies the listener by invoking the handlers implemented by the listener. If no listener is registered with the source object, the event is ignored. When an exception occurs, however, the program may terminate if no handler can be used to deal with it.

A Java exception is an instance of a class derived from `Throwable`. The `Throwable` class is contained in the `java.lang` package, and subclasses of `Throwable` are contained in various packages. Errors related to GUI components are included in the `java.awt` package; numeric exceptions are included in the `java.lang` package because they are related to the `java.lang.Number` class. You can create your own exception classes by extending `Throwable` or a subclass of `Throwable`. Figure 13.1 shows some of Java's predefined exception classes.

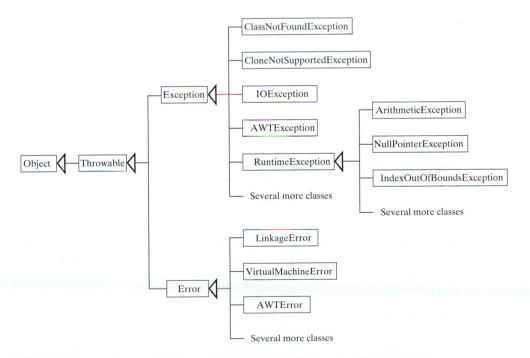

Figure 13.1   *The exceptions are instances of the classes shown in this diagram.*

NOTE

The class names `Error`, `Exception`, and `RuntimeException` are somewhat confusing. All the classes are exceptions. `Exception` is just one of these classes, and all the errors discussed here occur at runtime.

The `Error` class describes internal system errors. Such errors rarely occur. If one does, there is little you can do beyond notifying the user and trying to terminate the program gracefully. Examples of subclasses of `Error` are `LinkageError`, `Virtual-MachineError`, and `AWTError`. Subclasses of `LinkageError` indicate that a class has some dependency on another class, but that the latter class has changed incompatibly after the compilation of the former class. Subclasses of `VirtualMachineError` indicate that the Java Virtual Machine is broken or has run out of the resources necessary for it to continue operating. `AWTError` is caused by a fatal error in the GUI components.

The `Exception` class describes errors caused by your program and external circumstances. These errors can be caught and handled by your program. `Exception` has many subclasses, among them `ClassNotFoundException`, `CloneNotSupported-Exception`, `IOException`, `RuntimeException`, and `AWTException`.

The `ClassNotFoundException` is raised if you attempt to use a class that does not exist. It would occur, for example, if you tried to run a nonexistent class using the **java** command.

The `CloneNotSupportedException` is raised if you attempt to clone an object whose defining class does not implement the `Cloneable` interface. Cloning objects were introduced in Chapter 8, "Class Inheritance and Interfaces."

The `RuntimeException` class describes programming errors, such as bad casting, accessing an out-of-bounds array, and numeric errors. Examples of subclasses of `RuntimeException` are `ArithmeticException`, `NullPointerException`, and `IndexOut-OfBoundsException`.

`ArithmeticException` is for integer arithmetic. Java deals with integer arithmetic differently from floating-point arithmetic. Dividing by zero or modulus by zero is invalid for integer arithmetic and throws `ArithmeticException`. Floating-point arithmetic does not throw exceptions. For floating-point arithmetic, dividing by zero overflows to infinity. See Appendix I, "Special Floating-Point Values," for a discussion of special values for floating-point arithmetic.

The `IOException` class describes errors related to input/output operations, such as invalid input, reading past the end of a file, and opening a nonexistent file. Examples of subclasses of `IOException` are `InterruptedIOException`, `EOFException`, and `FileNotFoundException`.

The `AWTException` class describes exceptions in GUI components.

13.3   Understanding Exception Handling

Java's exception-handling model is based on three operations: *claiming an exception*, *throwing an exception*, and *catching an exception*, as shown in Figure 13.2.

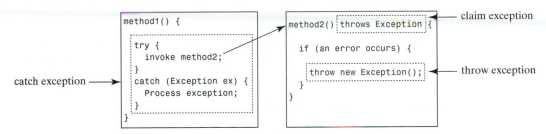

Figure 13.2   *Exception handling in Java consists of claiming exceptions, throwing exceptions, and catching and processing exceptions.*

In Java, the statement currently being executed belongs to a method. The Java interpreter invokes the `main` method for a Java application, and the Web browser invokes the applet's default constructor and then the `init` method for a Java applet. In general, every method must state the types of exceptions it might encounter. This process is called *claiming an exception*, which simply tells the compiler what might go wrong.

When a statement causes errors, the method containing the statement creates an exception object and passes it to the system. The exception object contains information about the exception, including its type and the state of the program when the error occurred. This process is called *throwing an exception*.

After a method throws an exception, the Java runtime system begins the process of finding the code to handle the error. The code that handles the error is called the *exception handler*; it is found by searching backward through a chain of method calls, starting from the current method. The handler must match the type of exception thrown. If no handler is found, the program terminates. The process of finding a handler is called *catching an exception*.

13.3.1   Claiming Exceptions

To claim an exception is to declare in a method what might go wrong when the method is executing. Because system errors and runtime errors can happen to any code, Java does not require that you claim `Error` and `RuntimeException` explicitly in the method. However, all other exceptions must be explicitly claimed in the method declaration if they are thrown by the method.

To claim an exception in a method, you use the `throws` keyword in the method declaration, as in this example:

```
public void myMethod() throws IOException
```

The throws keyword indicates that myMethod might throw an IOException. If the method might throw multiple exceptions, you can add a list of the exceptions, separated by commas, after throws:

```
MethodDeclaration throws Exception1, Exception2, ..., ExceptionN
```

13.3.2   Throwing Exceptions

In the method that has claimed the exception, you can throw an object of the exception if the exception arises. The following is the syntax to throw an exception:

```
throw new TheException();
```

Or if you prefer, you can use the following:

```
TheException ex = new TheException();
throw ex;
```

NOTE

The keyword to claim an exception is throws, and the keyword to throw an exception is throw.

A method can only throw the exceptions claimed in the method declaration or Error, RuntimeException, or subclasses of Error and RuntimeException. For example, a method cannot throw IOException if it is not claimed in the method declaration, but a method can always throw RuntimeException or a subclass of it even if it is not claimed by the method.

RuntimeException and Error are known as *unchecked exceptions*. All other exceptions are known as *checked exceptions*, meaning that the compiler checks your method and only throws the exceptions that have been declared.

13.3.3   Catching Exceptions

You now know how to claim an exception and how to throw an exception. Next, you will learn how to handle exceptions. When calling a method that explicitly claims a checked exception, you must use the try-catch block to wrap the statement, as shown in the next few lines:

```
try {
  statements;  // Statements that may throw exceptions
}
catch (Exception1 ex) {
  handler for exception1;
}
catch (Exception2 ex) {
  handler for exception2;
}
...
catch (ExceptionN ex) {
  handler for exceptionN;
}
```

If no exceptions arise during the execution of the try clause, the catch clauses are skipped.

If one of the statements inside the `try` block throws an exception, Java skips the remaining statements and starts to search for a handler for the exception. If the exception type matches one listed in a `catch` clause, the code in the `catch` clause is executed. If the exception type does not match any exception in the `catch` clauses, Java exits this method, passes the exception to the method that invoked the method, and continues the same process to find a handler. If no handler is found in the chain of methods being invoked, the program terminates and prints an error message on the console.

Consider the scenario in Figure 13.3. Suppose that an exception occurs in the `try-catch` block that contains a call to `method3`. If the exception type is `Exception3`, it is caught by the `catch` clause for handling exception `ex3`. If the exception type is `Exception2`, it is caught by the `catch` clause for handling exception `ex2`. If the exception type is `Exception1`, it is caught by the `catch` clause for handling exception `ex1` in the `main` method. If the exception type is not `Exception1`, `Exception2`, or `Exception3`, the program immediately terminates.

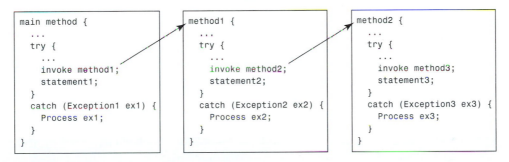

Figure 13.3   *If an exception is not caught in the current method, it is passed to its caller. The process is repeated until the exception is caught or passed to the* main *method.*

If the exception type is `Exception3`, `statement3` is skipped. If the exception type is `Exception2`, `statement2` and `statement3` are skipped. If the exception type is `Exception1`, `statement1`, `statement2`, and `statement3` are skipped.

NOTE

If an exception of a subclass of `Exception` occurs in a GUI component, Java prints the error message on the console, but the program goes back to its user-interface-processing loop to run continuously. The exception is ignored.

An exception object contains valuable information about the exception. You may use the following instance methods in the `java.lang.Throwable` class to get information regarding the exception.

- `public String getMessage()`

  Returns the detailed message of the `Throwable` object.

- `public String toString()`

  Returns a short description of the `Throwable` object, whereas `getMessage()` returns a detailed message.

- **public String getLocalizedMessage()**

  Returns a localized description of the `Throwable` object. Subclasses of `Throwable` can override this method in order to produce a locale-specific message. For subclasses that do not override this method, the default implementation returns the same result as `getMessage()`. Locale-specific issues are addressed in Chapter 14, "Internationalization."

- **public void printStackTrace()**

  Prints the `Throwable` object and its trace information on the console.

NOTE

Various exception classes can be derived from a common superclass. If a `catch` clause catches exception objects of a superclass, it can catch all the exception objects of the subclasses of that superclass.

The order in which the exceptions are specified in a `catch` clause is important. A compilation error will result if you do not specify an exception object of a class before an exception object of the superclass of that class.

NOTE

Java forces you to deal with exceptions. If a method claims a checked exception (i.e., an exception other than `Error` or `RuntimeException`), you must place it in a `try` statement and handle it in order to avoid abnormal termination.

Example 13.1 Claiming, Throwing, and Catching Exceptions

Problem

This example demonstrates claiming, throwing, and catching exceptions by modifying the `Rational` class defined in Example 9.2, "Using the `Rational` Class" (see Chapter 9, "Object-Oriented Software Development") so that it can handle the zero-divisor exception.

Solution

You create a new `Rational` class, which is the same except that the `divide` method throws a zero-divisor exception if the client attempts to call the method with a zero divisor.

```
1    // Rational.java: Define a rational number and its associated
2    // operations such as add, subtract, multiply, and divide
3    // the divide method throws an exception
4    public class Rational extends Number implements Comparable {
5      // Data fields for numerator and denominator
6      private long numerator = 0;
7      private long denominator = 1;
8
9      /** Default constructor */
10     public Rational() {
11       this(0, 1);
12     }
13
```

```
14    /** Construct a rational with specified numerator and denominator */
15    public Rational(long numerator, long denominator) {
16      long gcd = gcd(numerator, denominator);
17      this.numerator = numerator/gcd;
18      this.denominator = denominator/gcd;
19    }
20
21    /** Find GCD of two numbers */
22    private long gcd(long n, long d) {
23      long t1 = Math.abs(n);
24      long t2 = Math.abs(d);
25      long remainder = t1%t2;
26
27      while (remainder != 0) {
28        t1 = t2;
29        t2 = remainder;
30        remainder = t1%t2;
31      }
32
33      return t2;
34    }
35
36    /** Return numerator */
37    public long getNumerator() {
38      return numerator;
39    }
40
41    /** Return denominator */
42    public long getDenominator() {
43      return denominator;
44    }
45
46    /** Add a rational number to this rational */
47    public Rational add(Rational secondRational) {
48      long n = numerator*secondRational.getDenominator() +
49        denominator*secondRational.getNumerator();
50      long d = denominator*secondRational.getDenominator();
51      return new Rational(n, d);
52    }
53
54    /** Subtract a rational number from this rational */
55    public Rational subtract(Rational secondRational) {
56      long n = numerator*secondRational.getDenominator()
57        - denominator*secondRational.getNumerator();
58      long d = denominator*secondRational.getDenominator();
59      return new Rational(n, d);
60    }
61
62    /** Multiply a rational number to this rational */
63    public Rational multiply(Rational secondRational) {
64      long n = numerator*secondRational.getNumerator();
65      long d = denominator*secondRational.getDenominator();
66      return new Rational(n, d);
67    }
68
69    /** Divide a rational number from this rational */
70    public Rational divide(Rational secondRational)
71      throws RuntimeException {
72      if (secondRational.getNumerator() == 0)
73        throw new RuntimeException("Divisor cannot be zero");
74
```

continues

Example 13.1 continued

```
75        long n = numerator*secondRational.getDenominator();
76        long d = denominator*secondRational.getNumerator();
77        return new Rational(n, d);
78      }
79
80      /** Override the toString() method */
81      public String toString() {
82        if (denominator == 1)
83          return numerator + "";
84        else
85          return numerator + "/" + denominator;
86      }
87
88      /** Override the equals method */
89      public boolean equals(Object parm1) {
90        /** @todo: Override this java.lang.Object method */
91        if ((this.subtract((Rational)(parm1))).getNumerator() == 0)
92          return true;
93        else
94          return false;
95      }
96
97      /** Override the intValue method */
98      public int intValue() {
99        /** @todo: implement this java.lang.Number abstract method */
100       return (int)doubleValue();
101     }
102
103     /** Override the floatValue method */
104     public float floatValue() {
105       /** @todo: implement this java.lang.Number abstract method */
106       return (float)doubleValue();
107     }
108
109     /** Override the doubleValue method */
110     public double doubleValue() {
111       /** @todo: implement this java.lang.Number abstract method */
112       return numerator*1.0/denominator;
113     }
114
115     /** Override the longValue method */
116     public long longValue() {
117       /** @todo: implement this java.lang.Number abstract method */
118       return (long)doubleValue();
119     }
120
121     /** Override the compareTo method */
122     public int compareTo(Object o) {
123       /** @todo: Implement this java.lang.Comparable method */
124       if ((this.subtract((Rational)o)).getNumerator() > 0)
125         return 1;
126       else if ((this.subtract((Rational)o)).getNumerator() < 0)
127         return -1;
128       else
129         return 0;
130     }
131   }
```

A test program that uses the new Rational class is given below. Figure 13.4 shows a sample run of the test program.

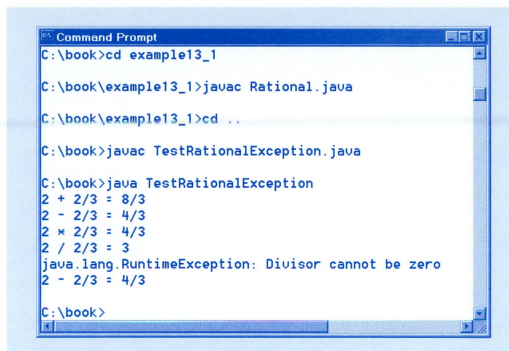

Figure 13.4   *The exception is raised when the divisor is zero.*

```
1    // TestRationalException.java: Catch and handle exceptions
2    public class TestRationalException {
3      /** Main method */
4      public static void main(String[] args) {
5        // Create three rational numbers
6        Rational r1 = new Rational(4, 2);
7        Rational r2 = new Rational(2, 3);
8        Rational r3 = new Rational(0, 1);
9
10       try {
11         System.out.println(r1+" + "+ r2 +" = " + r1.add(r2));
12         System.out.println(r1+" - "+ r2 +" = " + r1.subtract(r2));
13         System.out.println(r1+" * "+ r2 +" = " + r1.multiply(r2));
14         System.out.println(r1+" / "+ r2 +" = " + r1.divide(r2));
15         System.out.println(r1+" / "+ r3 +" = " + r1.divide(r3));
16         System.out.println(r1+" + "+ r2 +" = " + r1.add(r2));
17       }
18       catch (Exception ex) {
19         System.out.println(ex);
20       }
21
22       // Display the result
23       System.out.println(r1 + " - " + r2 + " = " + r1.subtract(r2));
24     }
25   }
```

Review

The original `Rational` class remains intact except for the `divide` method. The
`divide` method now claims an exception and throws it if the divisor is zero.

continues

Example 13.1 continued

The `divide` method claims the exception to be an instance of `RuntimeException` by using `throws RuntimeException` in the method signature. The method throws the exception by using the following statement (Line 77 in Rational.java):

```
throw new RuntimeException("Divisor cannot be zero");
```

The `Rational` class would still compile if the throws `RuntimeException` clause were removed from the method declaration, since every method can throw `RuntimeException`, regardless of whether it is declared in the method header.

The program creates three `Rational` numbers, r1, r2, and r3, to test numeric methods (`add`, `subtract`, `multiply`, and `divide`) on rational numbers.

Invoking the `divide` method with divisor 0 (Line 15 in `TestRationalException`) causes the method to throw an exception object. In the `catch` clause, the type of the object ex is `RuntimeException`, which matches the object thrown by the `divide` method. So this exception is caught by the `catch` clause.

The exception handler simply prints a short message, `ex.toString()` (Line 19), about the exception, using `System.out.println(ex)`.

Note that the execution continues in the event of the zero divisor. If the handlers had not caught the exception, the program would have abruptly terminated.

The test program would still compile if the `try` statement were not used, because the `divide` method throws `RuntimeException`. If a method throws an exception other than `RuntimeException` and `Error`, the method must be invoked within a `try` statement.

Example 13.2 Exceptions in GUI Applications

Problem

Here Example 11.11, "Using Menus" (from Chapter 11, "Creating User Interfaces"), is used to demonstrate the effect of exceptions in GUI applications.

Solution

Run the program and enter any number in the Number 1 field and 0 in the Number 2 field; then click the Divide button (see Figure 13.5). You will see nothing in the `Result` field, but an error message will appear in the Output window, as shown in Figure 13.6. The GUI application continues.

Figure 13.5 *In GUI programs, if an exception of the* Exception *class is not caught, it is ignored, and the program continues.*

```
Command Prompt - java MenuDemo                                    _ □ ×
C:\book>java MenuDemo
java.lang.ArithmeticException: / by zero
        at MenuDemo.calculate(MenuDemo.java:142)
        at MenuDemo.actionPerformed(MenuDemo.java:110)
        at javax.swing.AbstractButton.fireActionPerformed(AbstractBu
67)
        at javax.swing.AbstractButton$ForwardActionEvents.actionPerf
ctButton.java:1820)
        at javax.swing.DefaultButtonModel.fireActionPerformed(Defaul
.java:419)
        at javax.swing.DefaultButtonModel.setPressed(DefaultButtonMo
)
        at javax.swing.plaf.basic.BasicButtonListener.mouseReleased(
istener.java:258)
        at java.awt.Component.processMouseEvent(Component.java:5021)
        at java.awt.Component.processEvent(Component.java:4818)
```

Figure 13.6 *In GUI programs, if an exception of the* Exception *class is not caught, an error message appears in the console window.*

Review

If an exception of the Exception type is not caught when a Java GUI program is running, an error message is displayed on the console, but the program continues to run.

If you rewrite the calculate method in the MenuDemo program of Example 11.11 with a try-catch block to catch RuntimeException, as shown below, the program will display a message dialog box in the case of a numerical error, as shown in Figure 13.7. No errors are reported because they are handled in the program.

```
// Calculate and show the result in jtfResult
private void calculate(char operator) {
  // Obtain Number 1 and Number 2
  int num1 = (Integer.parseInt(jtfNum1.getText().trim()));
  int num2 = (Integer.parseInt(jtfNum2.getText().trim()));
  int result = 0;
```

continues

Example 13.2 continued

```
      try {
        // Perform selected operation
        switch (operator) {
          case '+': result = num1 + num2;
                    break;
          case '-': result = num1 - num2;
                    break;
          case '*': result = num1 * num2;
                    break;
          case '/': result = num1 / num2;
        }

        // Set result in jtfResult
        jtfResult.setText(String.valueOf(result));
      }
      catch (RuntimeException ex) {
        JOptionPane.showMessageDialog(this, ex.getMessage(),
          "Operation error", JOptionPane.ERROR_MESSAGE);
      }
    }
```

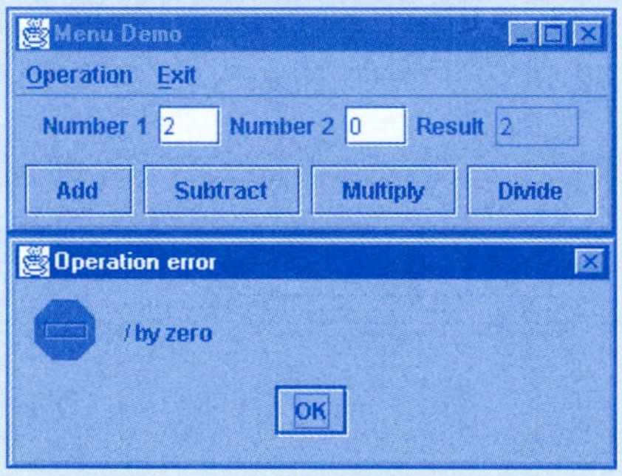

Figure 13.7   *When you click the Divide button to divide a number by 0, a numerical exception occurs. The exception is displayed in the message dialog box.*

13.4   Rethrowing Exceptions

When an exception occurs in a method, the method exits immediately if it does not catch the exception. If the method is required to perform some task before exiting, you can catch the exception in the method and then rethrow it to the real handler in a structure like the one given below:

```
try {
  statements;
}
catch (TheException ex) {
  perform operations before exits;
  throw ex;
}
```

The statement `throw ex` rethrows the exception so that other handlers get a chance to process the exception `ex`.

13.5   The *finally* Clause

Occasionally, you may want some code to be executed regardless of whether an exception occurs or is caught. Java has a `finally` clause that can be used to accomplish this objective. The syntax for the `finally` clause might look like this:

```
try {
  statements;
}
catch (TheException ex) {
  handling ex;
}
finally {
  finalStatements;
}
```

The code in the `finally` block is executed under all circumstances, regardless of whether an exception occurs in the `try` block or whether it is caught. Consider three possible cases:

■ If no exception arises in the `try` block, `finalStatements` is executed, and the next statement after the `try` statement is executed.

■ If one of the statements causes an exception in the `try` block that is caught in a `catch` clause, the other statements in the `try` block are skipped, the `catch` clause is executed, and the `finally` clause is executed. If the `catch` clause does not rethrow an exception, the next statement after the `try` statement is executed. If it does, the exception is passed to the caller of this method.

■ If one of the statements causes an exception that is not caught in any `catch` clause, the other statements in the `try` block are skipped, the `finally` clause is executed, and the exception is passed to the caller of this method.

___

NOTE
The `catch` clause may be omitted when the `finally` clause is used.

___

13.6   Cautions When Using Exceptions

Exception handling separates error-handling code from normal programming tasks, thus making programs easier to read and to modify. Be aware, however, that exception handling usually requires more time and resources because it requires instantiating a new exception object, rolling back the call stack, and propagating the errors to the calling methods.

Exception handling should not be used to replace simple tests. You should test simple exceptions whenever possible, and reserve exception handling for dealing with situations that cannot be handled with `if` statements. Do not use exception handling to validate user input. The input can be validated with simple `if` statements.

In general, common exceptions that may occur in multiple classes in a project are candidates for exception classes. Simple errors that may occur in individual classes are best handled using `if` statements.

13.7   Creating Custom Exception Classes (Optional)

Java provides quite a few exception classes. Use them whenever possible instead of creating your own exception classes. However, if you run into a problem that cannot be adequately described by the predefined exception classes, you can create your own exception class, derived from `Exception` or from a subclass of `Exception`, such as `IOException`. This section shows how to create your own exception class.

Example 13.3 Creating Your Own Exception Classes

Problem

Create a Java applet for handling account transactions. The applet displays the account ID and balance, and lets the user deposit to or withdraw from the account. For each transaction, a message is displayed to indicate the status of the transaction: successful or failed. In case of failure, the reason for the failure is reported. A sample run of the program is shown in Figure 13.8.

Figure 13.8   *The program lets you deposit and withdraw funds, and displays the transaction status on the label.*

If a transaction amount is negative, the program raises a negative-amount exception. If the account's balance is less than the requested transaction amount, an insufficient-funds exception is raised.

The example consists of four classes: `Account`, `NegativeAmountException`, `InsufficientAmountException`, and `AccountApplet`. The `Account` class provides information and operations pertaining to the account. `NegativeAmount-Exception` and `InsufficientAmountException` are the exception classes that deal with transactions of negative or insufficient amounts. The `AccountApplet` class utilizes all these classes to perform transactions, transferring funds among accounts. The relationships among these classes are shown in Figure 13.9.

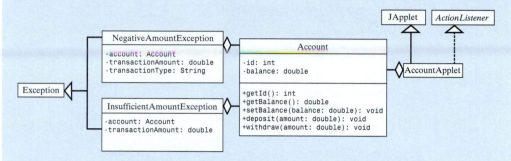

Figure 13.9 NegativeAmountException *and* InsufficientAmountException *are subclasses of* Exception *that contain the account information, transaction amount, and transaction type for the failed transaction.*

Solution

The code for the Account class follows. This class contains two data fields: id (for account ID) and balance (for current balance). The methods for Account are deposit and withdraw. Both methods will throw NegativeAmountException if the transaction amount is negative. The withdraw method will also throw InsufficientFundException if the current balance is less than the requested transaction amount.

```
1   // Account.java: The class for describing an account
2   public class Account {
3     // Two data fields in an account
4     private int id;
5     private double balance;
6
7     /** Construct an account with specified id and balance */
8     public Account(int id, double balance) {
9       this.id = id;
10      this.balance = balance;
11    }
12
13    /** Return id */
14    public int getId() {
15      return id;
16    }
17
18    /** Setter method for balance */
19    public void setBalance(double balance) {
20      this.balance = balance;
21    }
22
23    /** Return balance */
24    public double getBalance() {
25      return balance;
26    }
27
```

continues

Example 13.3 continued

```
28        /** Deposit an amount to this account */
29        public void deposit(double amount)
30          throws NegativeAmountException {
31          if (amount < 0)
32            throw new NegativeAmountException
33              (this, amount, "deposit");
34          balance = balance + amount;
35        }
36
37        /** Withdraw an amount from this account */
38        public void withdraw(double amount)
39          throws NegativeAmountException, InsufficientFundException {
40          if (amount < 0)
41            throw new NegativeAmountException
42              (this, amount, "withdraw");
43          if (balance < amount)
44            throw new InsufficientFundException(this, amount);
45          balance = balance - amount;
46        }
47      }
```

The NegativeAmountException exception class follows. It contains information about the attempted transaction type (deposit or withdrawal), the account, and the negative amount passed from the method.

```
1     // NegativeAmountException.java: Negative amount exception
2     public class NegativeAmountException extends Exception {
3       /** Account information to be passed to the handlers */
4       private Account account;
5       private double amount;
6       private String transactionType;
7
8       /** Construct an negative amount exception */
9       public NegativeAmountException(Account account,
10                                     double amount,
11                                     String transactionType) {
12        super("Negative amount");
13        this.account = account;
14        this.amount = amount;
15        this.transactionType = transactionType;
16      }
17    }
```

The InsufficientFundException exception class follows. It contains information about the account and the amount passed from the method.

```
1     // InsufficientFundException.java: An exception class for describing
2     // insufficient fund exception
3     public class InsufficientFundException extends Exception {
4       /** Information to be passed to the handlers */
5       private Account account;
6       private double amount;
7
8       /** Construct an insufficient exception */
9       public InsufficientFundException(Account account, double amount) {
10        super("Insufficient amount");
11        this.account = account;
12        this.amount = amount;
13      }
14
```

```
15        /** Override the "toString" method */
16        public String toString() {
17          return "Account balance is " + account.getBalance();
18        }
19      }
```

The AccountApplet class is given as follows:

```
1     // AccountApplet.java: Use custom exception classes
2     import java.awt.*;
3     import java.awt.event.*;
4     import javax.swing.*;
5     import javax.swing.border.*;
6
7     public class AccountApplet extends JApplet
8       implements ActionListener {
9       // Declare text fields
10      private JTextField jtfID, jtfBalance, jtfDeposit, jtfWithdraw;
11
12      // Declare Deposit and Withdraw buttons
13      private JButton jbtDeposit, jbtWithdraw;
14
15      // Create an account with initial balance $1000
16      private Account account = new Account(1, 1000);
17
18      // Create a label for showing status
19      private JLabel jlblStatus = new JLabel();
20
21      /** Initialize the applet */
22      public void init() {
23        // Panel p1 to group ID and Balance labels and text fields
24        JPanel p1 = new JPanel();
25        p1.setLayout(new GridLayout(2, 2));
26        p1.add(new JLabel("Account ID"));
27        p1.add(jtfID = new JTextField(4));
28        p1.add(new JLabel("Account Balance"));
29        p1.add(jtfBalance = new JTextField(4));
30        jtfID.setEditable(false);
31        jtfBalance.setEditable(false);
32        p1.setBorder(new TitledBorder("Display Account Information"));
33
34        // Panel p2 to group deposit amount and Deposit button and
35        // withdraw amount and Withdraw button
36        JPanel p2 = new JPanel();
37        p2.setLayout(new GridLayout(2, 3));
38        p2.add(new JLabel("Deposit"));
39        p2.add(jtfDeposit = new JTextField(4));
40        p2.add(jbtDeposit = new JButton("Deposit"));
41        p2.add(new JLabel("Withdraw"));
42        p2.add(jtfWithdraw = new JTextField(4));
43        p2.add(jbtWithdraw = new JButton("Withdraw"));
44        p2.setBorder(new TitledBorder("Deposit or withdraw funds"));
45
46        // Place panels p1, p2, and label in the applet
47        this.getContentPane().add(p1, BorderLayout.WEST);
48        this.getContentPane().add(p2, BorderLayout.CENTER);
49        this.getContentPane().add(jlblStatus, BorderLayout.SOUTH);
50
51        // Refresh ID and Balance fields
52        refreshFields();
53
```

continues

Example 13.3 continued

```
54        // Register listener
55        jbtDeposit.addActionListener(this);
56        jbtWithdraw.addActionListener(this);
57      }
58
59      /** Handle ActionEvent */
60      public void actionPerformed(ActionEvent e) {
61        if (e.getSource() == jbtDeposit) {
62          try {
63            double depositValue = (Double.valueOf(
64              jtfDeposit.getText().trim())).doubleValue();
65            account.deposit(depositValue);
66            refreshFields();
67            jlblStatus.setText("Transaction Processed");
68          }
69          catch (NegativeAmountException ex) {
70            jlblStatus.setText("Negative Amount");
71          }
72        }
73        else if (e.getSource() == jbtWithdraw) {
74          try {
75            double withdrawValue = (Double.valueOf(
76              jtfWithdraw.getText().trim())).doubleValue();
77            account.withdraw(withdrawValue);
78            refreshFields();
79            jlblStatus.setText("Transaction Processed");
80          }
81          catch (NegativeAmountException ex) {
82            jlblStatus.setText("Negative Amount");
83          }
84          catch (InsufficientFundException ex) {
85            jlblStatus.setText("Insufficient Funds");
86          }
87        }
88      }
89
90      /** Update the display for account balance */
91      public void refreshFields() {
92        jtfID.setText(String.valueOf(account.getId()));
93        jtfBalance.setText(String.valueOf(account.getBalance()));
94      }
95    }
```

Review

In the Account class, the deposit method (Line 29) throws NegativeAmount-Exception (Line 32–33) if the amount to be deposited is less than 0. The with-draw method (Line 38) throws a NegativeAmountException if the amount to be withdrawn is less than 0 (Lines 41–42), and throws an InsufficientFund-Exception if the amount to be withdrawn is less than the current balance (Line 44).

The user-defined exception class always extends Exception or a subclass of Exception. Therefore, both NegativeAmountException and InsufficientFund-Exception extend Exception.

Storing relevant information in the exception object is useful, because the han-dler can then retrieve the information from the exception object. For example,

`NegativeAmountException` contains the account, the amount, and the transaction type.

The `AccountApplet` class creates an applet with two panels (`p1` and `p2`) (Lines 24, 36) and a label that displays messages. Panel `p1` contains account ID and balance; panel `p2` contains the action buttons for depositing and withdrawing funds.

With a click of the Deposit button, the amount in the `Deposit` text field is added to the balance. With a click of the Withdraw button, the amount in the `Withdraw` text field is subtracted from the balance.

For each successful transaction, the message `Transaction Processed` is displayed. For a negative amount, the message `Negative Amount` is displayed; for insufficient funds, the message `Insufficient Funds` is displayed.

Chapter Summary

In this chapter, you learned how Java handles exceptions. When an exception occurs, Java creates an object that contains the information for the exception. You can use the information to handle the exception.

A Java exception is an instance of a class derived from `java.lang.Throwable`. You can create your own exception classes by extending `Throwable` or a subclass of `Throwable`. The Java system provides a number of predefined exception classes, such as `Error`, `Exception`, `RuntimeException`, and `IOException`. You can also define your own exception class.

Exceptions occur during the execution of a method. When defining the method, you have to claim an exception if the method might throw that checked exception, thus telling the compiler what can go wrong.

To use the method that claims checked exceptions, you must enclose the method call in a `try` statement. When an exception occurs during the execution of the method, the `catch` clause catches and handles the exception.

Exception handling takes time because it requires the instantiation of a new exception object. Exceptions are not meant to substitute for simple tests. Avoid using exception handling if a simple `if` statement is sufficient.

Review Questions

In the following questions, assume that the divide method in Rational is defined as follows:

```java
public Rational divide(Rational secondRational) throws Exception {
  if (secondRational.getNumerator() == 0)
    throw new Exception("Divisor cannot be zero");

  long n = numerator * secondRational.getDenominator();
  long d = denominator * secondRational.getNumerator();
  return new Rational(n, d);
}
```

The divide method in the Rational class throws Exception if the divisor is 0.

13.1 Describe the Java Throwable class, its subclasses, and the types of exceptions.

13.2 What is the purpose of claiming exceptions? How do you claim an exception, and where? Can you claim multiple exceptions in a method declaration?

13.3 How do you throw an exception? Can you throw multiple exceptions in one throw statement?

13.4 What is the keyword throw used for? What is the keyword throws used for?

13.5 What does the Java runtime system do when an exception occurs?

13.6 How do you catch an exception?

13.7 Does the presence of the try-catch block impose overhead when no exception occurs?

13.8 Suppose that statement2 causes an exception in the following try-catch block:

```java
try {
  statement1;
  statement2;
  statement3;
}
catch (Exception1 ex1) {
}
catch (Exception2 ex2) {
}

statement4;
```

Answer the following questions:

■ Will statement3 be executed?

■ If the exception is not caught, will statement4 be executed?

■ If the exception is caught in the catch clause, will statement4 be executed?

■ If the exception is passed to the caller, will statement4 be executed?

13.9   Suppose that `statement2` causes an exception in the following statement:

```
try {
  statement1;
  statement2;
  statement3;
}
catch (Exception1 ex1) {
}
catch (Exception2 ex2) {
}
catch (Exception3 ex3) {
  throw ex3;
}
finally {
  statement4;
};
statement5;
```

Answer the following questions:

■ Will `statement5` be executed if the exception is not caught?

■ If the exception is of type `Exception3`, will `statement4` be executed, and will `statement5` be executed?

13.10   What is wrong in the following program?

```
class TestRationalWithException {
  public static void main(String[] args) {
    Rational r1 = new Rational(4, 2);
    Rational r2 = new Rational(2, 3);
    Rational r3 = new Rational(0, 1);

    try {
      System.out.println(
        r1 + " + " + r2 + " = " + r1.add(r2));
      System.out.println(
        r1 + " - " + r2 + " = " + r1.subtract(r2));
      System.out.println(
        r1 + " * " + r2 + " = " + r1.multiply(r2));
      System.out.println(
        r1 + " + " + r2 + " = " + r1.add(r2));
    }
  }
}
```

13.11   What is displayed when the following program is run?

```
class Test {
  public static void main(String[] args) {
    try {
      System.out.println("Welcome to Java");
    }
    finally {
      System.out.println("The finally clause is executed");
    }
  }
}
```

13.12 What is displayed when the following program is run?

```java
class Test {
  public static void main(String[] args) {
    try {
      System.out.println("Welcome to Java");
      return;
    }
    finally {
      System.out.println("The finally clause is executed");
    }
  }
}
```

13.13 What is displayed when the following program is run?

```java
class Test {
  public static void main(String[] args) {
    try {
      System.out.println("Welcome to Java");
      int i = 0;
      int y = 2 / i;
      System.out.println("Welcome to HTML");
    }
    finally {
      System.out.println("The finally clause is executed");
    }
  }
}
```

13.14 What is displayed when the following program is run?

```java
class Test {
  public static void main(String[] args) {
    try {
      System.out.println("Welcome to Java");
      int i = 0;
      double y = 2.0 / i;
      System.out.println("Welcome to HTML");
    }
    finally {
      System.out.println("The finally clause is executed");
    }
  }
}
```

13.15 What is displayed when the following program is run?

```java
class Test {
  public static void main(String[] args) {
    try {
      System.out.println("Welcome to Java");
      int i = 0;
      int y = 2 / i;
      System.out.println("Welcome to HTML");
    }
    catch (RuntimeException ex) {
      System.out.println("RuntimeException caught");
    }
    finally {
      System.out.println("The finally clause is executed");
    }
  }
}
```

13.16 What is displayed when the following program is run?

```java
class Test {
  public static void main(String[] args) {
    try {
      System.out.println("Welcome to Java");
      int i = 0;
      int y = 2 / i;
      System.out.println("Welcome to HTML");
    }
    catch (RuntimeException ex) {
      System.out.println("RuntimeException caught");
    }
    finally {
      System.out.println("Finally clause is executed");
    }

    System.out.println("End of the block");
  }
}
```

13.17 What is displayed when the following program is run?

```java
class Test {
  public static void main(String[] args) {
    try {
      System.out.println("Welcome to Java");
      int i = 0;
      int y = 2 / i;
      System.out.println("Welcome to HTML");
    }
    finally {
      System.out.println("The finally clause is executed");
    }

    System.out.println("End of the block");
  }
}
```

13.18 What is wrong with the following code?

```java
class Test {
  public static void main(String[] args) {
    try {
      Rational r1 = new Rational(3, 4);
      Rational r2   = new Rational(0, 1);
      Rational x = r1.divide(r2);

      int i = 0;
      int y = 2 / i;
    }
    catch (Exception ex) {
      System.out.println("Rational operation error ");
    }
    catch (RuntimeException ex) {
      System.out.println("Integer operation error");
    }
  }
}
```

13.19 What is displayed when the following program is run?

```java
class Test {
  public static void main(String[] args) {
    try {
      Rational r1 = new Rational(3, 4);
      Rational r2   = new Rational(0, 1);
      Rational x = r1.divide(r2);

      int i = 0;
      int y = 2 / i;
      System.out.println("Welcome to Java");
    }
    catch (RuntimeException ex) {
      System.out.println("Integer operation error");
    }
    catch (Exception ex) {
      System.out.println("Rational operation error");
    }
  }
}
```

13.20 What is displayed when the following program is run?

```java
class Test {
  public static void main(String[] args) {
    try {
      method();
      System.out.println("After the method call");
    }
    catch (RuntimeException ex) {
      System.out.println("Integer operation error");
    }
    catch (Exception e) {
      System.out.println("Rational operation error");
    }
  }

  static void method() throws Exception {
    Rational r1 = new Rational(3, 4);
    Rational r2   = new Rational(0, 1);
    Rational x = r1.divide(r2);
    int i = 0;
    int y = 2 / i;
    System.out.println("Welcome to Java");
  }
}
```

13.21 What is displayed when the following program is run?

```java
class Test {
  public static void main(String[] args) {
    try {
      method();
      System.out.println("After the method call");
    }
    catch (RuntimeException ex) {
      System.out.println("Integer operation error");
    }
    catch (Exception ex) {
      System.out.println("Rational operation error");
    }
  }
```

```
  static void method() throws Exception {
    try {
      Rational r1 = new Rational(3, 4);
      Rational r2   = new Rational(0, 1);
      Rational x = r1.divide(r2);

      int i = 0;
      int y = 2 / i;
      System.out.println("Welcome to Java");
    }
    catch (RuntimeException ex) {
      System.out.println("Integer operation error");
    }
    catch (Exception ex) {
      System.out.println("Rational operation error");
    }
  }
}
```

13.22 What is displayed when the following program is run?

```
class Test {
  public static void main(String[] args) {
    try {
      method();
      System.out.println("After the method call");
    }
    catch (RuntimeException ex) {
      System.out.println("Integer operation error");
    }
    catch (Exception ex) {
      System.out.println("Rational operation error");
    }
  }

  static void method() throws Exception {
    try {
      Rational r1 = new Rational(3, 4);
      Rational r2   = new Rational(0, 1);
      Rational x = r1.divide(r2);

      int i = 0;
      int y = 2 / i;
      System.out.println("Welcome to Java");
    }
    catch (RuntimeException ex) {
      System.out.println("Integer operation error");
    }
    catch (Exception ex) {
      System.out.println("Rational operation error");
      throw ex;
    }
  }
}
```

13.23 If an exception were not caught in a non-GUI application, what would happen? If an exception were not caught in a GUI application, what would happen?

13.24 What does the method `printStackTrace` do?

Programming Exercises

13.1 Example 7.5, "Using Command-Line Parameters," in Chapter 7, "Strings," is a simple command-line calculator. Note that the program terminates if any operand is non-numeric. Write a program with an exception handler that deals with non-numeric operands; then write another program without using an exception handler to achieve the same objective. Your program should display a message that informs the user of the wrong operand type before exiting (see Figure 13.10).

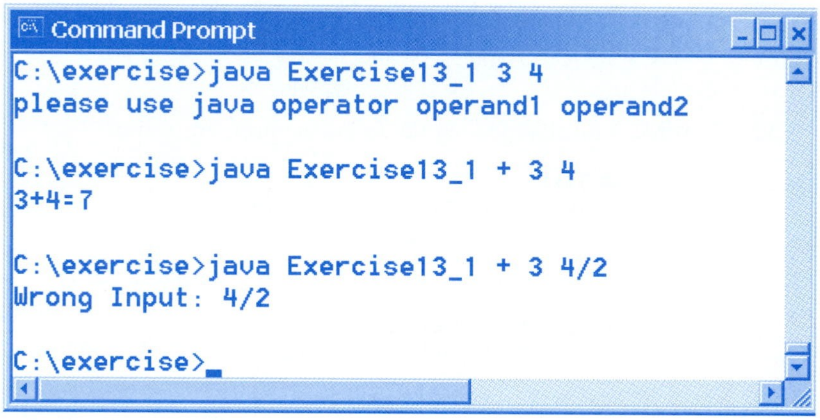

```
Command Prompt                                    _ □ ✕
C:\exercise>java Exercise13_1 3 4
please use java operator operand1 operand2

C:\exercise>java Exercise13_1 + 3 4
3+4=7

C:\exercise>java Exercise13_1 + 3 4/2
Wrong Input: 4/2

C:\exercise>_
```

Figure 13.10 *The program performs arithmetic operations and detects input errors.*

13.2 Example 11.11, "Using Menus," is a GUI calculator. Note that if Number 1 or Number 2 were a non-numeric string, the program would report exceptions. Modify the program with an exception handler to catch Arithmetic-Exception (i.e., divided by 0) and NumberFormatException (i.e., input is not an integer) and display the errors in a message dialog box, as shown in Figure 13.11.

Figure 13.11 *The program displays an error message in the dialog box if the divisor is 0.*

13.3 Write a program that meets the following requirements:

- Create an array with one hundred randomly chosen elements.

- Create a text field to enter an array index and another text field to display the array element at the specified index (see Figure 13.12).

- Create a Show Element button to cause the array element to be displayed. If the specified index is out of bounds, display the message Out of Bound.

Figure 13.12   *The program displays the array element at the specified index or displays the message Out of Bound if the index is out of bounds.*

14

INTERNATIONALIZATION

Objectives

- To understand the concept of Java's internationalization mechanism.
- To know how to construct a locale with language, country, and variant.
- To learn how to process date and time based on locale.
- To learn how to display numbers, currencies, and percentages based on locale.
- To use resource bundles.

14.1   Introduction

Java is an Internet programming language. Since the Internet has no boundaries, your applets may be viewed by people who don't understand English. What is useful for those who can read English may be unusable for those who can only read French. Many Web sites maintain several versions of HTML pages so that readers can choose one written in a language they understand. Because there are so many languages in the world, it would be highly problematic to create and maintain enough different versions to meet the needs of all clients everywhere. Java comes to the rescue. Java is the first language designed from ground up to support internationalization. In consequence, it allows your programs to be customized for any number of countries or languages without requiring cumbersome changes in the code.

Here are the major Java features that support internationalization:

■ Java characters use *Unicode*, a 16-bit encoding scheme established by the Unicode Consortium to support the interchange, processing, and display of written texts in the world's diverse languages. The use of Unicode encoding makes it easy to write Java programs that can manipulate strings in any international language.

■ Java provides the `Locale` class to encapsulate information about a specific locale. A `Locale` object determines how locale-sensitive information, such as date, time, and number, is displayed, and how locale-sensitive operations, such as sorting strings, are performed. The classes for formatting date, time, and numbers, and for sorting strings are grouped in the `java.text` package.

■ Java uses the `ResourceBundle` class to separate locale-specific information, such as status messages and GUI component labels, from the program. The information is stored outside the source code and can be accessed and loaded dynamically at runtime from a `ResourceBundle`, rather than hard-coded into the program.

In this chapter, you will learn how to format dates, numbers, currencies, and percentages for different regions, countries, and languages. You will also learn how to use resource bundles to define which images and strings are used by a component, depending on the user's locale and preferences.

14.2   The *Locale* Class

A `Locale` object represents a geographical, political, or cultural region in which a specific language or custom is used. For example, Americans speak English, and the Chinese speak Chinese. The conventions for formatting dates, numbers, currencies, and percentages may differ from one country to another. The Chinese, for instance, use year/month/day to represent the date, while Americans use month/day/year. It is important to realize that locale is not defined only by country. For example, Canadians speak either Canadian English or Canadian French, depending on which region of Canada they reside in.

624

NOTE

Every Swing user-interface class has a `locale` property inherited from the `Component` class.

To create a `Locale` object, use the following constructors in the `java.util.Locale` class:

```
Locale(String language, String country)
Locale(String language, String country, String variant)
```

The `language` should be a valid language code, that is to say, one of the lowercase two-letter codes defined by ISO-639. For example, zh stands for Chinese, da for Danish, en for English, de for German, and ko for Korean. A complete list can be found at a number of sites, among them:

```
http://www.indigo.ie/egt/standards/iso639/
```

```
http://www.ics.uci.edu/pub/ietf/http/related/iso639.txt
```

The country should be a valid ISO country code, that is to say, one of the upper-case, two-letter codes defined by ISO-3166. For example, CA stands for Canada, CN for China, DK for Denmark, DE for Germany, and US for the United States. A complete list can be found at a number of sites, including:

```
ftp://ftp.ripe.net/iso3166-countrycodes
```

```
http://userpage.chemie.fu-berlin.de/diverse/doc/ISO_3166.html
```

The argument variant is rarely used and is needed only for exceptional or system-dependent situations to designate information specific to a browser or vendor. For example, the Norwegian language has two sets of spelling rules, a traditional one called *bokmål* and a new one called *nynorsk*. The locale for traditional spelling would be created as follows:

```
new Locale("no", "NO", "B");
```

For convenience, the `Locale` class contains many predefined locale constants. `Locale.CANADA` is for the country Canada and language English; `Locale.CANADA_FRENCH` is for the country Canada and language French.

At present Java supports the locales shown in Table 14.1.

Several useful methods contained in the `Locale` class are listed below (note that the default locale is used if no locale is specified):

■ `public static Locale getDefault()`

Returns the default locale as stored on the machine where the program is running.

■ `public static void setDefault(Locale newLocale)`

Sets the default locale.

TABLE 14.1   A List of Supported Locales

Locale	Language	Country
da_DK	Danish	Denmark
de_AT	German	Austria
de_CH	German	Switzerland
de_DE	German	Germany
el_GR	Greek	Greece
en_CA	English	Canada
en_GB	English	United Kingdom
en_IE	English	Ireland
en_US	English	United States
es_ES	Spanish	Spain
fi_FI	Finnish	Finland
fr_BE	French	Belgium
fr_CA	French	Canada
fr_CH	French	Switzerland
fr_FR	French	France
it_CH	Italian	Switzerland
it_IT	Italian	Italy
ja_JP	Japanese	Japan
ko_KR	Korean	Korea
nl_BE	Dutch	Belgium
nl_NL	Dutch	Netherlands
no_NO	Norwegian (*nynorsk*)	Norway
no_NO_B	Norwegian (*bokmål*)	Norway
pt_PT	Portuguese	Portugal
sv_SE	Swedish	Sweden
tr_TR	Turkish	Turkey
zh_CN	Chinese (Simplified)	China
zh_TW	Chinese (Traditional)	Taiwan

■ `public String getLanguage()`

Returns a lowercase two-letter language code.

■ `public String getCountry()`

Returns an uppercase two-letter country code.

■ `public String getVariant()`

Returns the code for the variant.

■ `public final String getDisplayLanguage()`

Returns the name of the language for the current locale.

■ `public String getDisplayLanguage(Locale inLocale)`

Returns the name of the language for the specified locale.

■ `public final String getDisplayCountry()`

Returns the name of the country as expressed in the current locale.

■ `public String getDisplayCountry(Locale inLocale)`

Returns the name of the country as expressed in the specified locale.

■ `public final String getDisplayVariant()`

Returns the variant code.

■ `public String getDisplayVariant(Locale inLocale)`

Returns the variant code for the specified locale.

■ `public String getDisplayName(Locale l)`

Returns the name for the locale. For example, the name is `Chinese (China)` for the locale `Locale.CHINA`.

■ `public String getDisplayName()`

Returns the name for the default locale.

An operation that requires a `Locale` to perform its task is called *locale-sensitive*. Displaying a number as a date or time, for example, is a locale-sensitive operation; the number should be formatted according to the customs and conventions of the user's locale.

Several classes in the Java class libraries contain locale-sensitive methods. `Date`, `Calendar`, `DateFormat`, and `NumberFormat`, for example, are locale-sensitive. All the locale-sensitive classes contain a static method, `getAvailableLocales()`, which returns an array of the locales they support. For example,

```
Locale[] availableLocales = Calendar.getAvailableLocales();
```

returns all the locales for which calendars are installed.

14.3 Processing Date and Time

Applications often need to obtain date and time. Java provides a system-independent encapsulation of date and time in the `java.util.Date` class; it also provides `java.util.TimeZone` for dealing with time zones, and `java.util.Calendar` for extracting detailed information from `Date`. Different locales have different conventions for displaying date and time. Should the year, month, or day be displayed first? Should slashes, periods, or colons be used to separate fields of the date? What are the names of the months in the language? The `java.text.DateFormat` class can be used to format date and time in a locale-sensitive way for display to the user.

14.3.1   The *Date* Class

A `Date` object represents a specific instant in time. You can use its instance method `getTime()` to obtain the number of milliseconds since January 1, 1970, 00:00:00 GMT represented by this date. You can use the `toString()` method to display a string representing this date.

14.3.2   The *Calender* and *GregorianCalendar* Classes

The `Calendar` class contains the overloaded `get` methods to extract year, month, day, hour, minute, and second. For example, you can use `calendar.get(Calendar.YEAR)` to get the year, and `calendar.get(Calendar.MINUTE)` to get the minute from a `Calendar` object `calendar`. You can use the overloaded `set` methods to set year, month, day, hour, minute, and second in this calendar. For example, the following statements set the calendar to December 1, 2000.

```
calendar.set(Calendar.YEAR, 2000);
calendar.set(Calendar.MONTH, 12-1); // Month starts from 0
calendar.set(Calendar.DATE, 1);
```

Note that month starts from 0 in the `Calendar` class.

Subclasses of `Calendar` interpret a `Date` according to the rules of a specific calendar system. `java.util.GregorianCalendar` is currently supported in Java. Future subclasses could represent other types of calendars used in some parts of the world.

14.3.3   The *TimeZone* Class

`TimeZone` represents a time zone offset, and also figures out daylight savings. To set a time zone in a `Calendar` object, use the `setTimeZone` method with a time zone ID. For example, `cal.setTimeZone("CST")` sets the time zone to Central Standard Time. To find all the available time zones supported in Java, use the static method `getAvailableIDs()` in the `TimeZone` class. In general, the international time zone ID is a string in the form of continent/city like Europe/Berlin, Asia/Taipei, and America/Washington. You can also use the static method `getDefault()` in the `TimeZone` class to obtain the default time zone on the host machine.

14.3.4   The *DateFormat* Class

The `DateFormat` class can be used to format date and time in a number of styles. The `DateFormat` class supports several standard formatting styles. To format date and time using the `DateFormat` class, simply create an instance of `DateFormat` using one of the following three static methods:

■   `public static final DateFormat getDateInstance(int dateStyle, Locale aLocale)`

Returns the date formatter with the formatting style for the given locale.

■ `public static final DateFormat getTimeInstance(int timeStyle, Locale aLocale)`

Returns the time formatter with the formatting style for the given locale.

■ `public static final DateFormat getDateTimeInstance(int dateStyle, int timeStyle, Locale aLocale)`

Returns the date/time formatter with the formatting style for the given locale.

If the arguments are not present, the default style or default locale is used. The `dateStyle` and `timeStyle` are one of the following constants: `DateFormat.SHORT`, `DateFormat.MEDIUM`, `DateFormat.LONG`, `DateFormat.FULL`. The exact result depends on the locale, but generally,

■ `SHORT` is completely numeric, such as 7/24/98 (for date) and 4:49 PM (for time);

■ `MEDIUM` is longer, such as 24-Jul-98 (for date) and 4:52:09 PM (for time);

■ `LONG` is even longer, such as July 24, 1998 (for date) and 4:53:16 PM EST (for time);

■ `FULL` is completely specified, such as Friday, July 24, 1998 (for date) and 4:54:13 o'clock PM EST (for time).

The statements given below display current time with a specified time zone (CST), formatting style (full date and full time), and locale (US).

```
GregorianCalendar calendar = new GregorianCalendar();
DateFormat formatter = DateFormat.getDateTimeInstance(
  DateFormat.FULL, DateFormat.FULL, Locale.US);
TimeZone timeZone = TimeZone.getTimeZone("CST");
formatter.setTimeZone(timeZone);
System.out.println("The local time is "+
  formatter.format(calendar.getTime()));
```

14.3.5   The *SimpleDateFormat* Class

The date and time formatting subclass, `SimpleDateFormat`, enables you to choose any user-defined pattern for date and time formatting. The constructor shown below can be used to create a `SimpleDateFormat` object, and the object can be used to convert a `Date` object into a string with the desired format.

```
public SimpleDateFormat(String pattern)
```

The parameter `pattern` is a string consisting of characters with special meanings. For example, y means year, M means month, d means day of the month, G is for era designator, h means hour, m means minute of the hour, s means second of the minute, and z means time zone. Therefore, the following code will display a string like "Current time is 1997.11.12 AD at 04:10:18 PST" because the pattern is "yyyy.MM.dd G 'at' hh:mm:ss z".

```
SimpleDateFormat formatter
  = new SimpleDateFormat ("yyyy.MM.dd G 'at' hh:mm:ss z");
date currentTime = new Date();
String dateString = formatter.format(currentTime);
System.out.println("Current time is " + dateString);
```

The following two examples demonstrate how to display date, time, and calendar based on locale. The first example creates a clock and displays date and time in locale-sensitive format. The second example displays several different calendars with the names of the days shown in the appropriate local language.

Example 14.1   Displaying a Clock

Problem

Write a program that displays a clock to show the current time based on the specified locale and time zone. The language, country, and time zone are passed to the program as parameters. The program can run as an applet or an application. When it runs as an applet, the parameters are passed from HTML tags. When it runs as an application, the parameters are passed as command-line arguments like this:

```
java CurrentTimeApplet en US CST
```

The program is given next, and a sample run is shown in Figure 14.1.

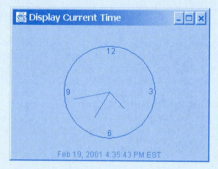

Figure 14.1   *The program displays a clock that shows the current time with specified locale and time zone.*

Solution

Here are the major steps in the program:

1. Create a subclass of `JPanel` named `StillClock` for displaying a clock to show the current time based on the specified locale and time zone.

2. Create an applet named `CurrentTimeApplet` with a main method to enable it to run standalone. Override the `init` method to obtain the parameters for language, country, and time zone from the HTML file, and create a clock in the applet. In the main method, obtain these parameters from the command line. The relationship between `CurrentTimeApplet` and `StillClock` is shown in Figure 14.2.

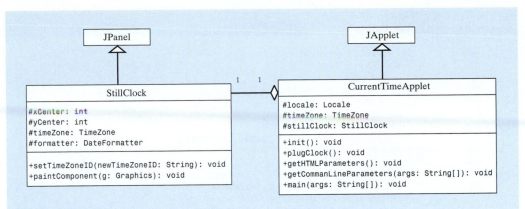

Figure 14.2 *The* `CurrentTimeApplet` *class displays a clock.*

```
1    // CurrentTimeApplet.java: Display a still clock on the applet
2    import java.awt.*;
3    import java.util.*;
4    import javax.swing.*;
5
6    public class CurrentTimeApplet extends JApplet {
7      protected Locale locale;
8      protected TimeZone timeZone;
9      protected StillClock stillClock;
10     private boolean isStandalone = false;
11
12     /** Construct the applet */
13     public CurrentTimeApplet() {
14     }
15
16     /** Initialize the applet */
17     public void init() {
18       if (!isStandalone) {
19         // Get locale and timezone from HTML
20         getHTMLParameters();
21       }
22
23       // Add the clock to the applet
24       plugClock();
25     }
26
27     /** Create a clock and add it to the applet */
28     public void plugClock() {
29       getContentPane().add(stillClock =
30         new StillClock(locale, timeZone));
31     }
32
33     /** Obtain HTML parameters if runs as applet */
34     public void getHTMLParameters() {
35       // Get parameters from the HTML
36       String language = getParameter("language");
37       String country = getParameter("country");
38       String timezone = getParameter("timezone");
39
40       // Set default values if parameters are not given
41       // in the HTML file
42       if (language == null)
43         language = "en";
44
```

continues

Example 14.1 continued

```
45        if (country == null)
46          country = "US";
47
48        if (timezone == null)
49          timezone = "CST";
50
51        // Set locale and timezone
52        locale = new Locale(language, country);
53        timeZone = TimeZone.getTimeZone(timezone);
54    }
55
56    /** Main method with three arguments:
57       @param args[0] language such as en
58       @param args[1] country such as US
59       @param args[2]: timezone such as CST
60     */
61    public static void main(String[] args) {
62      // Create a frame
63      JFrame frame = new JFrame("Display Current Time");
64
65      // Create an instance of the applet
66      CurrentTimeApplet applet = new CurrentTimeApplet();
67
68      // It runs as an application
69      applet.isStandalone = true;
70
71      // Get parameters from the command line
72      applet.getCommandLineParameters(args);
73
74      // Add the applet instance to the frame
75      frame.getContentPane().add(applet, BorderLayout.CENTER);
76
77      // Invoke init() and start()
78      applet.init();
79      applet.start();
80
81      // Display the frame
82      frame.setSize(300, 300);
83      frame.setDefaultCloseOperation(JFrame.EXIT_ON_CLOSE);
84      frame.setVisible(true);
85    }
86
87    /** Get command line parameters if runs standalone */
88    public void getCommandLineParameters(String[] args) {
89      // Declare locale and timezone with default values
90      locale = Locale.getDefault();
91      timeZone = TimeZone.getDefault();
92
93      // Check usage and get language, country and time zone
94      if (args.length > 3) {
95        System.out.println(
96          "Usage: java CurrentTimeApplet language country timezone");
97        System.exit(0);
98      }
99      else if (args.length == 3) {
100        locale = new Locale(args[0], args[1]);
101        timeZone = TimeZone.getTimeZone(args[2]);
102      }
103      else if (args.length == 2) {
104        locale = new Locale(args[0], args[1]);
105        timeZone = TimeZone.getDefault();
106      }
107      else if (args.length == 1) {
```

```
108            System.out.println(
109              "Usage: java DisplayTime language country timezone");
110            System.exit(0);
111          }
112          else {
113            locale = Locale.getDefault();
114            timeZone = TimeZone.getDefault();
115          }
116        }
117      }
```

```
1    // StillClock.java: Display a clock in JPanel
2    import java.awt.*;
3    import java.util.*;
4    import java.text.*;
5    import javax.swing.*;
6
7    public class StillClock extends JPanel {
8      protected TimeZone timeZone;
9      protected int xCenter, yCenter;
10     protected int clockRadius;
11     protected DateFormat formatter;
12
13     /** Default constructor */
14     public StillClock() {
15       this(Locale.getDefault(), TimeZone.getDefault());
16     }
17
18     /** Construct a clock with specified locale and time zone */
19     public StillClock(Locale locale, TimeZone timeZone) {
20       setLocale(locale);
21       this.timeZone = timeZone;
22     }
23
24     /** Set timezone using a time zone id such as "CST" */
25     public void setTimeZoneID(String newTimeZoneID) {
26       timeZone = TimeZone.getTimeZone(newTimeZoneID);
27     }
28
29     /** Override the paintComponent to display a clock */
30     public void paintComponent(Graphics g) {
31       super.paintComponent(g);
32
33       // Initialize clock parameters
34       clockRadius =
35         (int)(Math.min(getSize().width, getSize().height) * 0.7 * 0.5);
36       xCenter = (getSize().width) / 2;
37       yCenter = (getSize().height) / 2;
38
39       // Draw circle and hours
40       g.setColor(Color.black);
41       g.drawOval(xCenter - clockRadius,yCenter - clockRadius,
42         2 * clockRadius, 2 * clockRadius);
43       g.drawString("12", xCenter - 5, yCenter – clockRadius + 12);
44       g.drawString("9", xCenter - clockRadius + 3, yCenter + 5);
45       g.drawString("3", xCenter + clockRadius - 10, yCenter + 3);
46       g.drawString("6", xCenter - 3, yCenter + clockRadius - 3);
47
48       // Get current time using GregorianCalendar
49       GregorianCalendar cal = new GregorianCalendar(timeZone);
50
51       // Draw second hand
52       int second = (int)cal.get(GregorianCalendar.SECOND);
```

continues

633

Example 14.1 continued

```
53          int sLength = (int)(clockRadius * 0.8);
54          int xSecond = (int)(xCenter + sLength *
55            Math.sin(second * (2 * Math.PI / 60)));
56          int ySecond = (int)(yCenter - sLength *
57            Math.cos(second * (2 * Math.PI / 60)));
58          g.setColor(Color.red);
59          g.drawLine(xCenter, yCenter, xSecond, ySecond);
60
61          // Draw minute hand
62          int minute = (int)cal.get(GregorianCalendar.MINUTE);
63          int mLength = (int)(clockRadius * 0.65);
64          int xMinute = (int)(xCenter + mLength *
65            Math.sin(minute * (2 * Math.PI / 60)));
66          int yMinute = (int)(yCenter - mLength *
67            Math.cos(minute * (2 * Math.PI / 60)));
68          g.setColor(Color.blue);
69          g.drawLine(xCenter, yCenter, xMinute, yMinute);
70
71          // Draw hour hand
72          int hour = (int)cal.get(GregorianCalendar.HOUR_OF_DAY);
73          int hLength = (int)(clockRadius * 0.5);
74          int xHour = (int)(xCenter + hLength *
75            Math.sin((hour + minute / 60.0) * (2 * Math.PI / 12)));
76          int yHour = (int)(yCenter - hLength *
77            Math.cos((hour + minute / 60.0) * (2 * Math.PI / 12)));
78          g.setColor(Color.black);
79          g.drawLine(xCenter, yCenter, xHour, yHour);
80
81          // Set display format in specified style, locale and timezone
82          formatter = DateFormat.getDateTimeInstance
83            (DateFormat.MEDIUM, DateFormat.LONG, getLocale());
84          formatter.setTimeZone(timeZone);
85
86          // Display current date
87          g.setColor(Color.red);
88          String today = formatter.format(cal.getTime());
89          FontMetrics fm = g.getFontMetrics();
90          g.drawString(today, (getSize().width -
91            fm.stringWidth(today)) / 2, yCenter + clockRadius + 30);
92        }
93      }
```

Review

The `CurrentTimeApplet` class can run as an applet or as an application. When it runs as an application, it sets `isStandalone` true (Line 69) so that it does not attempt to retrieve HTML parameters.

The program obtains language, country, and time zone as either an HTML parameter or a command-line parameter, and uses this information to create an instance of `StillClock`. `StillClock` is responsible for drawing the clock for the current time. `StillClock` is similar to the `DrawClock` class in Example 10.6, "Drawing a Clock," except that the time (hour, minute, and second) is passed as a parameter to `DrawClock`, but the time in `StillClock` is the current time for the specified locale and time zone.

This program uses the `GregorianCalendar` class to extract the hour, minute, and second from the current time, and the `DateFormat` class to format date and time in a string, with the locale and time zone specified by the user.

The date is displayed below the clock. The program uses font metrics to determine the size of the date/time string and center the display.

The Component class has a variable locale, which can be accessed through the getLocale and setLocale methods. Since StillClock is a JPanel, a subclass of Component, you can use these methods to work with the locale in StillClock.

The variables are purposely declared as protected (Lines 7–9 in CurrentTimeApplet and Lines 8–12 in StillClock) so that they can be accessed by StillClock's subclasses in later chapters. The setTimeZoneID method (Lines 24–27) defined in StillClock is not used here, but it will be used in Example 15.5, "Controlling a Group of Clocks," in Chapter 15, "Multithreading."

The clock is locale-sensitive. If you use the Chinese locale with language (zh) and country (CN), the date and time are displayed in Chinese, as shown in Figure 14.3.

The CurrentTimeApplet class is designed for reuse in future chapters. The plugClock method (Lines 27–31) is purposely defined in such a way as to make it possible to plug different types of clocks to the applet in Chapter 16, "Multimedia," by overriding this method.

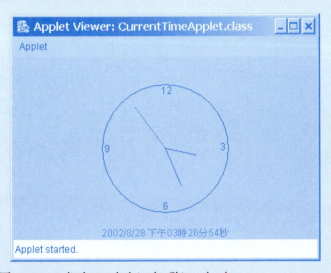

Figure 14.3 *The program displays a clock in the Chinese locale.*

continues

Example 14.1 continued

 TIP

To enable Asian characters, you need to install appropriate fonts, and modify the font.properties file in c:\program files\Java\j2rel.4.0_01\lib and c:\j2sdk1.4.0_01\jre\lib. For example, to make the Chinese fonts work on Windows, install the MingLiU font, and replace font properties with font.properties with font.properties.zh_TW on Windows 98, and replace font.properties with font.properties.zh.NT on Windows NT and 2000.

Example 14.2 Displaying a Calendar

Problem

Write a program that displays a calendar based on the specified locale, as shown in Figures 14 4 and 14.5. The user can specify a locale from a combo box that consists of a list of all the available locales supported by the system. When the program starts, the calendar for the current month of the year is displayed. The user can use the Prior and Next buttons to browse the calendar.

Figure 14.4   *The calendar applet displays a calendar with the Danish locale.*

Solution

Here are the major steps in the program:

1. Create a subclass of `GregorianCalendar` named `MyCalendar`. `MyCalendar` contains the `daysInMonth` method, which returns the number of days in the current month.

2. Create a subclass of `JPanel` named `CalendarPanel` for displaying the calendar for the given year and month based on the specified locale and time zone.

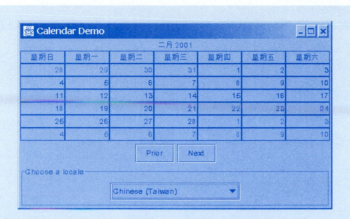

Figure 14.5 *The calendar applet displays a calendar with the Chinese locale.*

3. Create an applet named `CalendarApplet`. Create a panel to hold an instance of `CalendarPanel` and two buttons, Prior and Next. Place the panel in the center of the applet. Create a combo box and place it in the south of the applet. The relationships among these classes are shown in Figure 14.6.

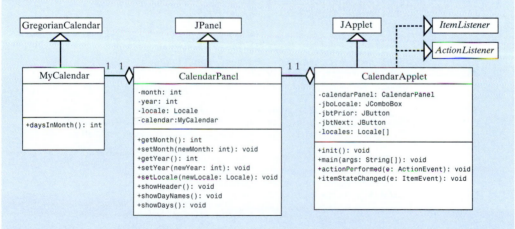

Figure 14.6 `CalendarApplet` *contains* `CalendarPanel`, *and* `CalendarPanel` *contains* `MyCalendar`.

```
1   // CalendarApplet.java: Display a locale-sensitive calendar
2   import java.awt.*;
3   import java.awt.event.*;
4   import javax.swing.*;
5   import javax.swing.border.*;
6   import java.util.*;
7   import java.text.DateFormat;
8
9   public class CalendarApplet extends JApplet
10    implements ItemListener, ActionListener {
11    // Create a CalendarPanel for showing calendars
12    private CalendarPanel calendarPanel = new CalendarPanel();
13
```

continues

Example 14.2 continued

```
14          // Combo box for selecting available locales
15          private JComboBox jcboLocale = new JComboBox();
16
17          // Declare locales to store available locales
18          private Locale locales[] = Calendar.getAvailableLocales();
19
20          // Buttons Prior and Next to displaying prior and next month
21          private JButton jbtPrior = new JButton("Prior");
22          private JButton jbtNext = new JButton("Next");
23
24          /** Initialize the applet */
25          public void init() {
26            // Panel jpLocale to hold the combo box for selecting locales
27            JPanel jpLocale = new JPanel();
28            jpLocale.setBorder(new TitledBorder("Choose a locale"));
29            jpLocale.setLayout(new FlowLayout());
30            jpLocale.add(jcboLocale);
31
32            // Initialize the combo box to add locale names
33            for (int i = 0; i < locales.length; i++)
34              jcboLocale.addItem(locales[i].getDisplayName());
35
36            // Panel jpButtons to hold buttons
37            JPanel jpButtons = new JPanel();
38            jpButtons.setLayout(new FlowLayout());
39            jpButtons.add(jbtPrior);
40            jpButtons.add(jbtNext);
41
42            // Panel jpCalendar to hold calendarPanel and buttons
43            JPanel jpCalendar = new JPanel();
44            jpCalendar.setLayout(new BorderLayout());
45            jpCalendar.add(calendarPanel, BorderLayout.CENTER);
46            jpCalendar.add(jpButtons, BorderLayout.SOUTH);
47
48            // Place jpCalendar and jpLocale to the applet
49            this.getContentPane().add(jpCalendar, BorderLayout.CENTER);
50            this.getContentPane().add(jpLocale, BorderLayout.SOUTH);
51
52            // Register listeners
53            jcboLocale.addItemListener(this);
54            jbtPrior.addActionListener(this);
55            jbtNext.addActionListener(this);
56          }
57
58          /** Main method */
59          public static void main(String[] args) {
60            // Create a frame
61            JFrame frame = new JFrame("Calendar Demo");
62
63            // Create an instance of the applet
64            CalendarApplet applet = new CalendarApplet();
65
66            // Add the applet instance to the frame
67            frame.getContentPane().add(applet, BorderLayout.CENTER);
68
69            // Invoke init() and start()
70            applet.init();
71            applet.start();
72
```

```
73          // Display the frame
74          frame.pack();
75          frame.setDefaultCloseOperation(JFrame.EXIT_ON_CLOSE);
76          frame.setVisible(true);
77        }
78
79      /** Handle locale selection */
80      public void itemStateChanged(ItemEvent e) {
81        // Set a new locale
82        calendarPanel.changeLocale(
83          locales[jcboLocale.getSelectedIndex()]);
84      }
85
86      /** Handle the Prior and Next buttons */
87      public void actionPerformed(ActionEvent e) {
88        int currentMonth = calendarPanel.getMonth();
89
90        if (e.getSource() == jbtPrior) {
91          if (currentMonth==1) {
92            calendarPanel.setMonth(12);
93            calendarPanel.setYear(calendarPanel.getYear()-1);
94          }
95          else
96            calendarPanel.setMonth(currentMonth-1);
97        }
98        else if (e.getSource() == jbtNext) {
99          if (currentMonth == 12) {
100            calendarPanel.setMonth(1);
101            calendarPanel.setYear(calendarPanel.getYear() + 1);
102          }
103          else
104            calendarPanel.setMonth(currentMonth + 1);
105        }
106      }
107    }
```

```
1    // CalendarPanel.java: Display calendar for a month
2    import java.awt.*;
3    import javax.swing.*;
4    import javax.swing.border.LineBorder;
5    import java.util.*;
6    import java.text.*;
7
8    public class CalendarPanel extends JPanel {
9      private int month;
10      private int year;
11
12      // The header label
13      private JLabel jlblHeader = new JLabel(" ", JLabel.CENTER);
14
15      // Labels to display day names and days
16      private JLabel[] jlblDay = new JLabel[49];
17
18      // MyCalendar instance
19      private MyCalendar calendar = new MyCalendar();
20
21      /** Default constructor */
22      public CalendarPanel() {
23        // Panel jpDays to hold day names and days
```

continues

Example 14.2 continued

```
24            JPanel jpDays = new JPanel();
25            jpDays.setLayout(new GridLayout(7, 1));
26            for (int i = 0; i < 49; i++) {
27              jpDays.add(jlblDay[i] = new JLabel());
28              jlblDay[i].setBorder(new LineBorder(Color.black, 1));
29              jlblDay[i].setHorizontalAlignment(JLabel.RIGHT);
30              jlblDay[i].setVerticalAlignment(JLabel.TOP);
31            }
32
33            // Place header and calendar body in the panel
34            this.setLayout(new BorderLayout());
35            this.add(jlblHeader, BorderLayout.NORTH);
36            this.add(jpDays, BorderLayout.CENTER);
37
38            // Set current month, and year
39            calendar = new MyCalendar();
40            month = calendar.get(Calendar.MONTH) + 1;
41            year = calendar.get(Calendar.YEAR);
42
43            // Show calendar
44            showHeader();
45            showDayNames();
46            showDays();
47          }
48
49          /** Update the header based on locale */
50          private void showHeader() {
51            SimpleDateFormat sdf =
52              new SimpleDateFormat("MMMM yyyy", getLocale());
53            String header = sdf.format(calendar.getTime());
54            jlblHeader.setText(header);
55          }
56
57          /** Update the day names based on locale */
58          private void showDayNames() {
59            DateFormatSymbols dfs = new DateFormatSymbols(getLocale());
60            String dayNames[] = dfs.getWeekdays();
61
62            // Set calendar days
63            for (int i = 0; i < 7; i++) {
64              jlblDay[i].setText(dayNames[i + 1]);
65              jlblDay[i].setHorizontalAlignment(JLabel.CENTER);
66            }
67          }
68
69          /** Display days */
70          public void showDays() {
71            // Set the calendar to the first day of the
72            // specified month and year
73            calendar.set(Calendar.YEAR, year);
74            calendar.set(Calendar.MONTH, month-1);
75            calendar.set(Calendar.DATE, 1);
76
77            // Get the day of the first day in a month
78            int startingDayOfMonth = calendar.get(Calendar.DAY_OF_WEEK);
79
80            // Fill the calendar with the days before this month
81            MyCalendar cloneCalendar = (MyCalendar)calendar.clone();
82            cloneCalendar.add(Calendar.DATE, -1);
83
```

```
84        for (int i = 0; i < startingDayOfMonth - 1; i++) {
85          jlblDay[i + 7].setForeground(Color.yellow);
86          jlblDay[i + 7].setText(cloneCalendar.daysInMonth() -
87            startingDayOfMonth + 2 + i + "");
88        }
89
90        // Display days of this month
91        for (int i = 1; i <= calendar.daysInMonth(); i++) {
92          jlblDay[i - 2 + startingDayOfMonth + 7].
93            setForeground(Color.black);
94          jlblDay[i - 2 + startingDayOfMonth + 7].setText(i + "");
95        }
96
97        // Fill the calendar with the days after this month
98        int j = 1;
99        for (int i = calendar.daysInMonth() - 1 + startingDayOfMonth + 7;
100         i < 49; i++) {
101          jlblDay[i].setForeground(Color.yellow);
102          jlblDay[i].setText(j++ + "");
103        }
104
105        showHeader();
106      }
107
108      /** Return month */
109      public int getMonth() {
110        return month;
111      }
112
113      /** Set a new month */
114      public void setMonth(int newMonth) {
115        month = newMonth;
116        showDays();
117      }
118
119      /** Return year */
120      public int getYear() {
121        return year;
122      }
123
124      /** Set a new year */
125      public void setYear(int newYear) {
126        year = newYear;
127        showDays();
128      }
129
130      /** Set a new locale */
131      public void changeLocale(Locale newLocale) {
132        setLocale(newLocale);
133        showHeader();
134        showDayNames();
135      }
136    }
```

```
1   // MyCalendar.java: A subclass of GregorianCalendar
2   import java.awt.*;
3   import java.util.*;
4
5   public class MyCalendar extends GregorianCalendar {
6     /** Find the number of days in a month */
```

continues

Example 14.2 continued

```
 7      public int daysInMonth() {
 8        switch (get(MONTH)) {
 9          case 0: case 2: case 4: case 6: case 7: case 9: case 11:
10            return 31;
11          case 1: if (isLeapYear(get(YEAR))) return 29;
12                  else return 28;
13          case 3: case 5: case 8: case 10: return 30;
14          default: return 0;
15        }
16      }
17    }
```

Review

CalendarApplet creates the user interface and handles the button actions and combo box item selections for locales. The Calendar.getAvailableLocales() method (Line 18) is used to find all available locales that have calendars. Its get-DisplayName() method returns the name of each locale and adds the name to the combo box (Lines 32–34). When the user selects a locale name in the combo box, a new locale is passed to calendarPanel, and a new calendar is displayed based on the new locale (Line 82–83).

CalendarPanel is created to control and display the calendar. It displays the month and year in the header, and the day names and days in the calendar body. The header and day names are locale-sensitive.

The showHeader method (Lines 50–55) displays the calendar title in a form like "MMMM yyyy". The SimpleDateFormat class used in the showHeader method is a subclass of DateFormat. SimpleDateFormat allows you to customize the date format to display the date in various nonstandard styles.

The showDayNames method (Lines 57–67) displays the day names in the calendar. The DateFormatSymbols class used in the showDayNames method is a class for encapsulating localizable date-time formatting data, such as the names of the months, the names of the days of the week, and the time zone data. The getWeekdays method is used to get an array of day names.

The showDays method (Lines 70-105) displays the days for the specified month of the year. As you can see in Figure 14.4, the labels before the current month are filled with the last few days of the preceding month, and the labels after the current month are filled with the first few days of the next month.

To fill the calendar with the days before the current month, a clone of calendar, named cloneCalendar, was created to obtain the days for the preceding month (Line 81). cloneCalendar is a copy of calendar with separate memory space. Thus you can change the properties of cloneCalendar without corrupting the calendar object. The clone() method is defined in the Object class, which was introduced in Chapter 8, "Class Inheritance and Interfaces," on page 288. You can clone any object as long as its defining class implements the Cloneable interface.

14.4   Formatting Numbers

Formatting numbers as currency or percentages is highly locale-dependent. For example, the number 5000.50 is displayed as $5,000.50 in U.S. currency, but as 5 000,50 F in French currency.

Numbers are formatted using the java.text.NumberFormat class, an abstract base class that provides the methods for formatting and parsing numbers. With NumberFormat, you can format and parse numbers for any locale. Your code will be completely independent of locale conventions for decimal points, thousands-separators, or the particular decimal digits used, and even for whether the number format is decimal.

To format a number for the current locale, use one of the factory class methods to get a formatter. Use getInstance or getNumberInstance to get the normal number format. Use getCurrencyInstance to get the currency number format. And use getPercentInstance to get a format for displaying percentages. With this format, a fraction like 0.53 is displayed as 53%.

For example, to display a number in percentages, you can use the following code to create a formatter for the given locale:

```
NumberFormat percentFormatter =
   NumberFormat.getPercentInstance(locale);
```

You can then use percentFormatter to format a number into a string like this:

```
String s = percentFormatter.format(0.075);
```

Conversely, if you want to read a number entered or stored with the conventions of a certain locale, use the parse method of a formatter to convert the formatted number into an instance of java.lang.Number. The parse method throws a ParseException if parsing fails.

You can also control the display of numbers with such methods as setMaximum-FractionDigits and setMinimumFractionDigits. If you want even more control over the format or parsing, or want to give your users more control, try casting the NumberFormat you get from the factory methods to a DecimalFormat, which is a sub-class of NumberFormat. You can then use the applyPattern method of the Decimal-Format class to specify the patterns for displaying the number.

For example, the following statements create an instance of DecimalFormat with the pattern "000.00." A number will be formatted with at least three digits before the decimal point and exactly two digits after the decimal point. If there are more actual digits before the decimal point, all the digits are displayed. If there are more digits after the decimal point, the digits are rounded.

```
NumberFormat numberForm = NumberFormat.getNumberInstance();
DecimalFormat df = (DecimalFormat)numberForm;
df.applyPattern("000.00");
```

For instance, `df.format(30.983)` returns 030.98, `df.format(3000.9856)` returns 3000.99, and `df.format(3.9)` returns 003.90. Note that the `format` method returns a string.

For more information about the formation of the patterns for `DecimalFormat`, please browse the online documentation on `java.text.DecimalFormat`.

Example 14.3 Formatting Numbers

Problem

Create a mortgage calculator similar to the one in Example 12.1, "Using Applets." This new mortgage calculator allows the user to choose locales, and displays numbers in locale-sensitive format. As shown in Figure 14.7, the user enters interest rate, number of years, and loan amount, then clicks the Compute button to display the interest rate in percentage format, the number of years in normal number format, and the loan amount, total payment, and monthly payment in currency format.

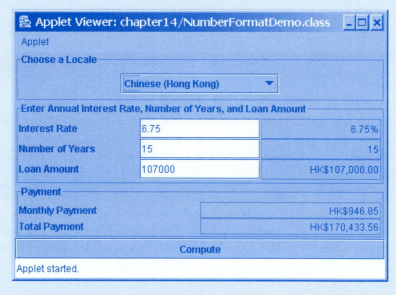

Figure 14.7 *The locale determines the format of the numbers displayed in the mortgage calculator.*

Solution

The following code gives the solution to the problem.

```
1    // NumberFormatDemo.java: Demonstrate formatting numbers
2    import java.awt.*;
3    import java.awt.event.*;
4    import javax.swing.*;
5    import javax.swing.border.*;
6    import java.util.*;
7    import java.text.*;
8
```

```
 9    public class NumberFormatDemo extends JApplet
10      implements ItemListener, ActionListener {
11      // Combo box for selecting available locales
12      JComboBox jcboLocale = new JComboBox();
13
14      // Text fields for interest rate, year, loan amount,
15      JTextField jtfInterestRate = new JTextField(10);
16      JTextField jtfNumOfYears = new JTextField(10);
17      JTextField jtfLoanAmount = new JTextField(10);
18      JTextField jtfFormattedInterestRate = new JTextField(10);
19      JTextField jtfFormattedNumOfYears = new JTextField(10);
20      JTextField jtfFormattedLoanAmount = new JTextField(10);
21
22      // Text fields for monthly payment and total payment
23      JTextField jtfTotalPayment = new JTextField();
24      JTextField jtfMonthlyPayment = new JTextField();
25
26      // Compute Mortgage button
27      JButton jbtCompute = new JButton("Compute");
28
29      // Current locale
30      Locale locale = Locale.getDefault();
31
32      // Declare locales to store available locales
33      Locale locales[] = Calendar.getAvailableLocales();
34
35      /** Initialize the combo box */
36      public void initializeComboBox() {
37        // Add locale names to the combo box
38        for (int i = 0; i < locales.length; i++)
39          jcboLocale.addItem(locales[i].getDisplayName());
40      }
41
42      /** Initialize the applet */
43      public void init() {
44        // Panel p1 to hold the combo box for selecting locales
45        JPanel p1 = new JPanel();
46        p1.setLayout(new FlowLayout());
47        p1.add(jcboLocale);
48        initializeComboBox();
49        p1.setBorder(new TitledBorder("Choose a Locale"));
50
51        // Panel p2 to hold the input
52        JPanel p2 = new JPanel();
53        p2.setLayout(new GridLayout(3, 3));
54        p2.add(new JLabel("Interest Rate"));
55        p2.add(jtfInterestRate);
56        p2.add(jtfFormattedInterestRate);
57        p2.add(new JLabel("Number of Years"));
58        p2.add(jtfNumOfYears);
59        p2.add(jtfFormattedNumOfYears);
60        p2.add(new JLabel("Loan Amount"));
61        p2.add(jtfLoanAmount);
62        p2.add(jtfFormattedLoanAmount);
63        p2.setBorder(new TitledBorder("Enter Annual Interest Rate, " +
64          "Number of Years, and Loan Amount"));
65
```

continues

Example 14.3 continued

```
 66            // Panel p3 to hold the result
 67            JPanel p3 = new JPanel();
 68            p3.setLayout(new GridLayout(2, 2));
 69            p3.setBorder(new TitledBorder("Payment"));
 70            p3.add(new JLabel("Monthly Payment"));
 71            p3.add(jtfMonthlyPayment);
 72            p3.add(new JLabel("Total Payment"));
 73            p3.add(jtfTotalPayment);
 74
 75            // Set text field alignment
 76            jtfFormattedInterestRate.setHorizontalAlignment(JTextField.RIGHT);
 77            jtfFormattedNumOfYears.setHorizontalAlignment(JTextField.RIGHT);
 78            jtfFormattedLoanAmount.setHorizontalAlignment(JTextField.RIGHT);
 79            jtfTotalPayment.setHorizontalAlignment(JTextField.RIGHT);
 80            jtfMonthlyPayment.setHorizontalAlignment(JTextField.RIGHT);
 81
 82            // Set editable false
 83            jtfFormattedInterestRate.setEditable(false);
 84            jtfFormattedNumOfYears.setEditable(false);
 85            jtfFormattedLoanAmount.setEditable(false);
 86            jtfTotalPayment.setEditable(false);
 87            jtfMonthlyPayment.setEditable(false);
 88
 89            // Panel p4 to hold result payments and a button
 90            JPanel p4 = new JPanel();
 91            p4.setLayout(new BorderLayout());
 92            p4.add(p3, BorderLayout.CENTER);
 93            p4.add(jbtCompute, BorderLayout.SOUTH);
 94
 95            // Place panels to the applet
 96            getContentPane().add(p1, BorderLayout.NORTH);
 97            getContentPane().add(p2, BorderLayout.CENTER);
 98            getContentPane().add(p4, BorderLayout.SOUTH);
 99
100            // Register listeners
101            jcboLocale.addItemListener(this);
102            jbtCompute.addActionListener(this);
103        }
104
105        /** Main method */
106        public static void main(String[] args) {
107            // Create a frame
108            JFrame frame = new JFrame("Number Formatting Demo");
109
110            // Create an instance of the applet
111            NumberFormatDemo applet = new NumberFormatDemo();
112
113            // Add the applet instance to the frame
114            frame.getContentPane().add(applet, BorderLayout.CENTER);
115
116            // Invoke init() and start()
117            applet.init();
118            applet.start();
119
120            // Display the frame
121            frame.setSize(300, 300);
122            frame.setDefaultCloseOperation(JFrame.EXIT_ON_CLOSE);
123            frame.setVisible(true);
124        }
125
```

```
126        /** Handle locale selection */
127        public void itemStateChanged(ItemEvent e) {
128          if (e.getSource() == jcboLocale) {
129            locale = locales[jcboLocale.getSelectedIndex()];
130            computeMortgage();
131          }
132        }
133
134        /** Handle button action */
135        public void actionPerformed(ActionEvent e) {
136          if (e.getSource() == jbtCompute)
137            computeMortgage();
138        }
139
140        /** Compute payments and display results locale-sensitive format */
141        private void computeMortgage() {
142          // Retrieve input from user
143          double loan = new Double(jtfLoanAmount.getText()).doubleValue();
144          double interestRate =
145            new Double(jtfInterestRate.getText()).doubleValue() / 1200;
146          int numOfYears = new Integer(jtfNumOfYears.getText()).intValue();
147
148          // Calculate payments
149          double monthlyPayment =
150            loan*interestRate/
151            (1-(Math.pow(1/(1+interestRate),numOfYears*12)));
152          double totalPayment = monthlyPayment*numOfYears*12;
153
154          // Get formatters
155          NumberFormat percentFormatter =
156            NumberFormat.getPercentInstance(locale);
157          NumberFormat currencyForm =
158            NumberFormat.getCurrencyInstance(locale);
159          NumberFormat numberForm = NumberFormat.getNumberInstance(locale);
160          percentFormatter.setMinimumFractionDigits(2);
161
162          // Display formatted input
163          jtfFormattedInterestRate.setText(
164            percentFormatter.format(interestRate*12));
165          jtfFormattedNumOfYears.setText(numberForm.format(numOfYears));
166          jtfFormattedLoanAmount.setText(currencyForm.format(loan));
167
168          // Display results in currency format
169          jtfMonthlyPayment.setText(currencyForm.format(monthlyPayment));
170          jtfTotalPayment.setText(currencyForm.format(totalPayment));
171        }
172    }
```

Review

The computeMortgage method (Lines 141–171) gets the input on interest rate, number of years, and loan amount from the user, computes monthly payment and total payment, and displays annual interest rate in percentage format, number of years in normal number format, and loan amount, monthly payment, and total payment in locale-sensitive format.

The statement percentFormatter.setMinimumFractionDigits(2) (line 160) sets the minimum number of fractional parts to 2. Without this statement, 0.075 would be displayed as 7% rather than 7.5%.

14.5   Resource Bundles (Optional)

The `NumberFormatDemo` in Example 14 3 displays the numbers, currencies, and percentages in local customs, but displays all the message strings, titles, and button labels in English. In this section, you will learn how to use resource bundles to localize message strings, titles, button labels, and so on.

A *resource bundle* is a Java class file or a text file that provides locale-specific information. This information can be accessed by Java programs dynamically. When a locale-specific resource is needed—a message string, for example—your program can load it from the resource bundle appropriate for the desired locale. In this way, you can write program code that is largely independent of the user's locale, isolating most, if not all, of the locale-specific information in resource bundles.

With resource bundles, you can write programs that separate the locale-sensitive part of your code from the locale-independent part. The programs can easily handle multiple locales, and can easily be modified later to support even more locales.

The resources are placed inside the classes that extend the `ResourceBundle` class or a subclass of `ResourceBundle`. Resource bundles contain *key/value* pairs. Each key uniquely identifies a locale-specific object in the bundle. You can use the key to retrieve the object. `ListResourceBundle` is a convenient subclass of `ResourceBundle` that is often used to simplify the creation of resource bundles. Here is an example of a resource bundle that contains four keys using `ListResourceBundle`:

```
// MyResource.java: resource file
public class MyResource extends java.util.ListResourceBundle {
  static final Object[][] contents = {
    {"nationalFlag", "us.gif"},
    {"nationalAnthem", "us.au"},
    {"nationalColor", Color.red},
    {"annualGrowthRate", new Double(7.8)}
  };

  public Object[][] getContents() {
    return contents;
  }
}
```

Keys are case-sensitive strings. In this example, the keys are `nationalFlag`, `nationalAnthem`, `nationalColor`, and `annualGrowthRate`. The values can be any type of `Object`.

If all the resources are strings, they can be placed in a convenient text file with extension .properties. A typical property file would look like this:

```
#Wed Jul 01 07:23:24 EST 1998
nationalFlag=us.gif
nationalAnthem=us.au
```

To retrieve values from a `ResourceBundle` in a program, you first need to create an instance of `ResourceBundle` using one of the following two static methods:

```
public static final ResourceBundle getBundle(String baseName)
  throws MissingResourceException

public static final ResourceBundle getBundle
  (String baseName, Locale locale) throws MissingResourceException
```

The first method returns a `ResourceBundle` for the default locale, and the second method returns a `ResourceBundle` for the specified locale. `baseName` is the base name for a set of classes, each of which describes the information for a given locale. These classes are named in Table 14.2.

TABLE 14.2   Resource Bundle Naming Conventions

1. BaseName_language_country_variant.class

2. BaseName_language_country.class

3. BaseName_language.class

4. BaseName.class

5. BaseName_language_country_variant.properties

6. BaseName_language_country.properties

7. BaseName_language.properties

8. BaseName.properties

For example, MyResource_en_BR.class stores resources specific to the United Kingdom, MyResource_en_US.class stores resources specific to the United States, and MyResource_en.class stores resources specific to all the English-speaking countries.

The `getBundle` method attempts to load the class that matches the specified locale by language, country, and variant by searching the file names in the order shown in Table 14.2. The files searched in this order form a *resource chain*. If no file is found in the resource chain, the `getBundle` method raises a `MissingResourceException`.

Once a resource bundle object is created, you can use the `getObject` method to retrieve the value according to the key. For example,

```
ResourceBundle res = ResourceBundle.getBundle("MyResource");
String flagFile = (String)res.getObject("nationalFlag");
String anthemFile = (String)res.getObject("nationalAnthem");
Color color = (Color)res.getObject("nationalColor");
double growthRate =
  (Double)res.getObject("annualGrowthRate").doubleValue();
```

TIP

If the resource value is a string, a convenient `getString` method can be used to replace the `getObject` method. The `getString` method simply casts the value returned by `getObject` to a string.

What happens if a resource object you are looking for is not defined in the resource bundle? Java employs an intelligent look-up scheme that searches the object in the parent file along the resource chain. This search is repeated until the object is found or all the parent files in the resource chain have been searched. A `Missing-ResourceException` is raised if the search is unsuccessful.

Example 14.4   Using Resource Bundles

Problem

Modify the `NumberFormatDemo` program in Example 14.3 so that it displays messages, title, and button labels in English, Chinese, and French, as shown in Figure 14.8.

Figure 14.8   *The program displays the strings in English, French, or Chinese.*

Solution

The following code gives the solution to the problem.

```
1    // ResourceBundleDemo.java: Demonstrate resource bundle
2    import java.awt.*;
3    import java.awt.event.*;
4    import javax.swing.*;
5    import javax.swing.border.*;
```

```
6    import java.util.*;
7    import java.text.*;
8
9    public class ResourceBundleDemo extends JApplet
10     implements ItemListener, ActionListener {
11     // Combo box for selecting available locales
12     JComboBox jcboLocale = new JComboBox();
13     ResourceBundle res = ResourceBundle.getBundle("MyResource");
14
15     // Create labels
16     JLabel jlblInterestRate =
17       new JLabel(res.getString("Annual_Interest_Rate"));
18     JLabel jlblNumOfYears =
19       new JLabel(res.getString("Number_Of_Years"));
20     JLabel jlblLoanAmount = new JLabel(res.getString("Loan_Amount"));
21     JLabel jlblMonthlyPayment =
22       new JLabel(res.getString("Monthly_Payment"));
23     JLabel jlblTotalPayment = new JLabel(res.getString("Total_Payment"));
24
25     // Create titled borders
26     TitledBorder comboBoxTitle =
27       new TitledBorder(res.getString("Choose_a_Locale"));
28     TitledBorder inputTitle = new TitledBorder
29       (res.getString("Enter_Interest_Rate"));
30     TitledBorder paymentTitle =
31       new TitledBorder(res.getString("Payment"));
32
33     // Text fields for interest rate, year, loan amount,
34     JTextField jtfInterestRate = new JTextField(10);
35     JTextField jtfNumOfYears = new JTextField(10);
36     JTextField jtfLoanAmount = new JTextField(10);
37     JTextField jtfFormattedInterestRate = new JTextField(10);
38     JTextField jtfFormattedNumOfYears = new JTextField(10);
39     JTextField jtfFormattedLoanAmount = new JTextField(10);
40
41     // Text fields for monthly payment and total payment
42     JTextField jtfTotalPayment = new JTextField();
43     JTextField jtfMonthlyPayment = new JTextField();
44
45     // Compute Mortgage button
46     JButton jbtCompute = new JButton(res.getString("Compute"));
47
48     // Current locale
49     Locale locale = Locale.getDefault();
50
51     // Declare locales to store available locales
52     Locale locales[] = Calendar.getAvailableLocales();
53
54     /** Initialize the combo box */
55     public void initializeComboBox() {
56       // Add locale names to the combo box
57       for (int i = 0; i < locales.length; i++)
58         jcboLocale.addItem(locales[i].getDisplayName());
59     }
60
61     /** Initialize the applet */
62     public void init() {
63       // Panel p1 to hold the combo box for selecting locales
64       JPanel p1 = new JPanel();
65       p1.setLayout(new FlowLayout());
66       p1.add(jcboLocale);
```

continues

651

Example 14.4   continued

```
67          initializeComboBox();
68          p1.setBorder(comboBoxTitle);
69
70          // Panel p2 to hold the input for annual interest rate,
71          // number of years and loan amount
72          JPanel p2 = new JPanel();
73          p2.setLayout(new GridLayout(3, 3));
74          p2.add(jlblInterestRate);
75          p2.add(jtfInterestRate);
76          p2.add(jtfFormattedInterestRate);
77          p2.add(jlblNumOfYears);
78          p2.add(jtfNumOfYears);
79          p2.add(jtfFormattedNumOfYears);
80          p2.add(jlblLoanAmount);
81          p2.add(jtfLoanAmount);
82          p2.add(jtfFormattedLoanAmount);
83          p2.setBorder(inputTitle);
84
85          // Panel p3 to hold the payment
86          JPanel p3 = new JPanel();
87          p3.setLayout(new GridLayout(2, 2));
88          p3.setBorder(paymentTitle);
89          p3.add(jlblMonthlyPayment);
90          p3.add(jtfMonthlyPayment);
91          p3.add(jlblTotalPayment);
92          p3.add(jtfTotalPayment);
93
94          // Set text field alignment
95          jtfFormattedInterestRate.setHorizontalAlignment
96            (JTextField.RIGHT);
97          jtfFormattedNumOfYears.setHorizontalAlignment(JTextField.RIGHT);
98          jtfFormattedLoanAmount.setHorizontalAlignment(JTextField.RIGHT);
99          jtfTotalPayment.setHorizontalAlignment(JTextField.RIGHT);
100         jtfMonthlyPayment.setHorizontalAlignment(JTextField.RIGHT);
101
102         // Set editable false
103         jtfFormattedInterestRate.setEditable(false);
104         jtfFormattedNumOfYears.setEditable(false);
105         jtfFormattedLoanAmount.setEditable(false);
106         jtfTotalPayment.setEditable(false);
107         jtfMonthlyPayment.setEditable(false);
108
109         // Panel p4 to hold result payments and a button
110         JPanel p4 = new JPanel();
111         p4.setLayout(new BorderLayout());
112         p4.add(p3, BorderLayout.CENTER);
113         p4.add(jbtCompute, BorderLayout.SOUTH);
114
115         // Place panels to the applet
116         getContentPane().add(p1, BorderLayout.NORTH);
117         getContentPane().add(p2, BorderLayout.CENTER);
118         getContentPane().add(p4, BorderLayout.SOUTH);
119
120         // Register listeners
121         jcboLocale.addItemListener(this);
122         jbtCompute.addActionListener(this);
123       }
124
125     /** Main method */
126     public static void main(String[] args) {
```

```
127        // Create an instance of the applet
128        ResourceBundleDemo applet = new ResourceBundleDemo();
129
130        // Create a frame with a resource string
131        JFrame frame = new JFrame(
132          applet.res.getString("Number_Formatting"));
133
134        // Add the applet instance to the frame
135        frame.getContentPane().add(applet, BorderLayout.CENTER);
136
137        // Invoke init() and start()
138        applet.init();
139        applet.start();
140
141        // Display the frame
142        frame.setSize(300, 300);
143        frame.setDefaultCloseOperation(JFrame.EXIT_ON_CLOSE);
144        frame.setVisible(true);
145      }
146
147      /** Handle locale selection */
148      public void itemStateChanged(ItemEvent e) {
149        if (e.getSource() == jcboLocale) {
150          locale = locales[jcboLocale.getSelectedIndex()];
151          updateStrings();
152          computeMortgage();
153        }
154      }
155
156      /** Handle button action */
157      public void actionPerformed(ActionEvent e) {
158        if (e.getSource() == jbtCompute)
159          computeMortgage();
160      }
161
162      /** Compute payments and display results locale-sensitive format */
163      private void computeMortgage() {
164        // Retrieve input from user
165        double loan = new Double(jtfLoanAmount.getText()).doubleValue();
166        double interestRate =
167          new Double(jtfInterestRate.getText()).doubleValue() / 1200;
168        int numOfYears = new Integer(jtfNumOfYears.getText()).intValue();
169
170        // Calculate payments
171        double monthlyPayment = loan * interestRate/
172          (1 - (Math.pow(1 / (1 + interestRate), numOfYears * 12)));
173        double totalPayment = monthlyPayment * numOfYears * 12;
174
175        // Get formatters
176        NumberFormat percentFormatter =
177          NumberFormat.getPercentInstance(locale);
178        NumberFormat currencyForm =
179          NumberFormat.getCurrencyInstance(locale);
180        NumberFormat numberForm = NumberFormat.getNumberInstance(locale);
181        percentFormatter.setMinimumFractionDigits(2);
182
183        // Display formatted input
184        jtfFormattedInterestRate.setText(
185          percentFormatter.format(interestRate * 12));
```

continues

653

Example 14.4   continued

```
186            jtfFormattedNumOfYears.setText(numberForm.format(numOfYears));
187            jtfFormattedLoanAmount.setText(currencyForm.format(loan));
188
189            // Display results in currency format
190            jtfMonthlyPayment.setText(currencyForm.format(monthlyPayment));
191            jtfTotalPayment.setText(currencyForm.format(totalPayment));
192          }
193
194          /** Update resource strings */
195          private void updateStrings() {
196            res = ResourceBundle.getBundle("MyResource", locale);
197            jlblInterestRate.setText(res.getString("Annual_Interest_Rate"));
198            jlblNumOfYears.setText(res.getString("Number_Of_Years"));
199            jlblLoanAmount.setText(res.getString("Loan_Amount"));
200            jlblTotalPayment.setText(res.getString("Total_Payment"));
201            jlblMonthlyPayment.setText(res.getString("Monthly_Payment"));
202            jbtCompute.setText(res.getString("Compute"));
203            comboBoxTitle.setTitle(res.getString("Choose_a_Locale"));
204            inputTitle.setTitle(res.getString("Enter_Interest_Rate"));
205            paymentTitle.setTitle(res.getString("Payment"));
206
207            // Make sure the new labels are displayed
208            repaint();
209          }
210        }
```

The resource bundle for the English language is given as follows:

```
#MyResource.properties for Chinese language
Number_Of_Years=Years
Total_Payment=French Total\ Payment
Enter_Interest_Rate=Enter\ Interest\ Rate,\ Years,\ and\ Loan\ Amount
Payment=Payment
Compute=Compute
Annual_Interest_Rate=Interest\ Rate
Number_Formatting=Number\ Formatting\ Demo
Loan_Amount=Loan\ Amount
Choose_a_Locale=Choose\ a\ Locale
Monthly_Payment=Monthly\ Payment
=
```

The resource bundle for the Chinese language is given as follows:

```
#MyResource_zh.properties for Chinese language
Choose_a_Locale       = \u9078\u64c7\u570b\u5bb6
Enter_Interest_Rate =
   \u8f38\u5165\u5229\u7387,\u5e74\u9650,\u8cb8\u6b3e\u7e3d\u984d
Annual_Interest_Rate  = \u5229\u7387
Number_Of_Years       = \u5e74\u9650
Loan_Amount           = \u8cb8\u6b3e\u984d\u5ea6
Payment               = \u4ed8\u606f
Monthly_Payment       = \u6708\u4ed8
Total_Payment         = \u7e3d\u984d
Compute               = \u8a08\u7b97\u8cb8\u6b3e\u5229\u606f
=
```

The resource bundle for the French language is given as follows:

```
#MyResourse_fr.properties for French language
Number_Of_Years=annees
Annual_Interest_Rate=le taux d'interet
Loan_Amount=Le montant du pret
```

654

```
Enter_Interest_Rate=inscrire le taux d'interet, les annees, et le
    montant du pret
Payment=paiement
Compute=Calculer l'hypotheque
Number_Formatting=demonstration du formatting des chiffres
Choose_a_Locale=Choisir la localite
Monthly_Payment=versement mensuel
Total_Payment=reglement total
=
```

The resource bundle files MyResource.properties, MyResource_zh.properties, and MyResource_fr.properties should all be placed under c:\book.

Review

Property resource bundles are implemented as text files with a .properties extension, and are placed in the same location as the class files for the application or applet. `ListResourceBundles` are provided as Java class files. Because they are implemented using Java source code, new and modified `ListResourceBundles` need to be recompiled for deployment. With `PropertyResourceBundles`, there is no need for recompilation when translations are modified or added to the application. Nevertheless, `ListResourceBundles` provide considerably better performance than `PropertyResourceBundles`.

If the resource bundle is not found or a resource object is not found in the resource bundle, a `MissingResourceException` is raised. Since `MissingResourceException` is a subclass of `RuntimeException`, you do not need to catch the exception explicitly in the code.

This example is the same as Example 14.3 except that the program contains the code for handling resource strings. The `updateString` method (Lines 195–209) is responsible for displaying the locale-sensitive strings. This method is invoked when a new locale is selected in the combo box. Since the variable `res` of the `ResourceBundle` class is an instance variable in `ResourceBundleDemo`, it cannot be directly used in the `main` method, because the `main` method is static. To fix the problem, create `applet` as an instance of `ResourceBundleDemo` and you will then be able to reference `res` using `applet.res`.

Chapter Summary

This chapter introduced the subject of building Java programs that operate efficiently for an international audience. You learned how to use the `Locale` object to represent a particular locale, how to localize date and time, and how to display numbers in normal format, currency format, and percentage format. You also learned how to create resource bundles and move the locale-specific strings, titles, and labels to them.

Review Questions

14.1 How does Java support international characters in languages like Chinese and Arabic?

14.2 How do you construct a `Locale` object? How do you get all the available locales from a `Calendar` object?

14.3 How do you display current date and time in German?

14.4 How do you format and display numbers and percentages in Chinese?

14.5 How do you limit the number of decimal digits in a fractional number?

14.6 How does the `getBundle` method locate a resource bundle?

14.7 How does the `getObject` method locate a resource?

Programming Exercises

14.1 Develop an applet that displays Unicode characters, as shown in Figure 14.9. The user specifies a Unicode in the text field and presses the Enter key to display a sequence of Unicode characters starting with the specified Unicode. The Unicode characters are displayed in a scrollable text area of twenty lines. Each line contains sixteen characters preceded by the Unicode that is the code for the first character on the line.

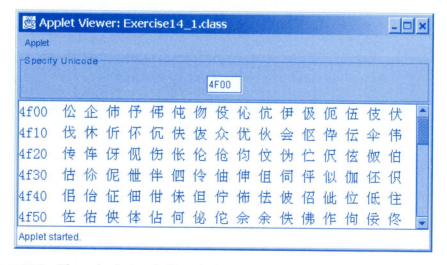

Figure 14.9   *The applet displays the Unicode characters.*

14.2 Write a program that displays a calendar for a specified month, using the `Date`, `Calendar`, and `GregorianCalendar` classes. Your program receives the month and year from the command line. For example:

```
java Exercise14_2 8 2001
```

This displays the calendar shown in Figure 14.10.

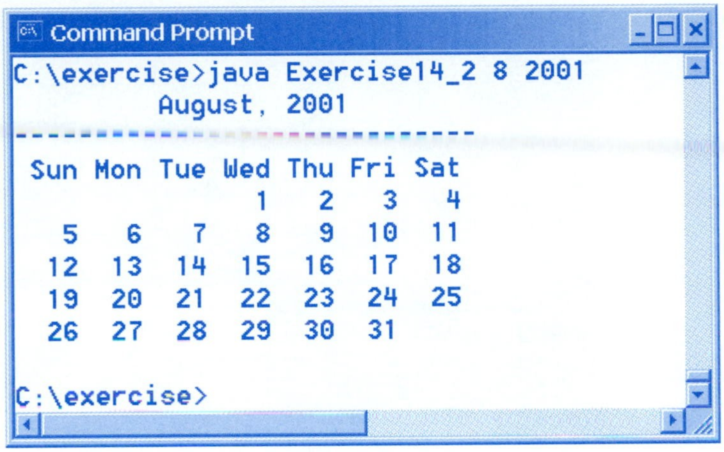

Figure 14.10 *The program displays a calendar for August 2001.*

You also can run the program without the year. In this case, the year is the current year. If you run the program without specifying a month and a year, the month is the current month.

14.3 Modify Example 14.2, "Displaying a Calendar," to localize the labels "Choose a locale" and "Calendar Demo" in French, German, Chinese, or a language of your choice.

14.4 Write a program that converts U.S. dollars to Canadian dollars, German marks, and British pounds, as shown in Figure 14.11. The user enters the U.S. dollar amount and the conversion rate, and clicks the Convert button to display the converted amount.

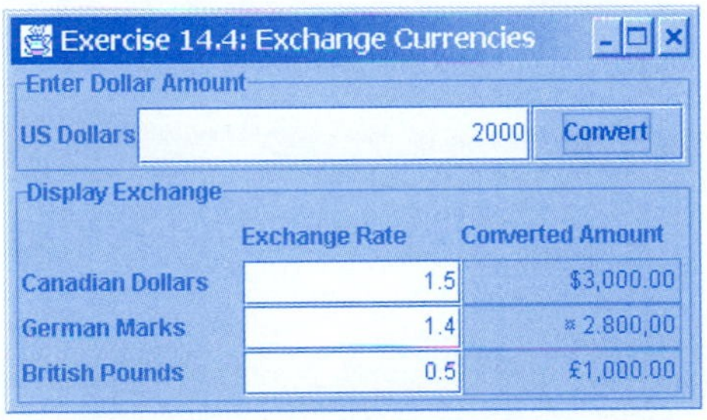

Figure 14.11 *The program converts U.S. dollars to Canadian dollars, German marks, and British pounds.*

14.5 Use a tabbed pane to write a program with two tabs. One, labeled Calendar, displays the calendar, and the other, labeled Clock, displays the current time on a clock (see Figure 14.12).

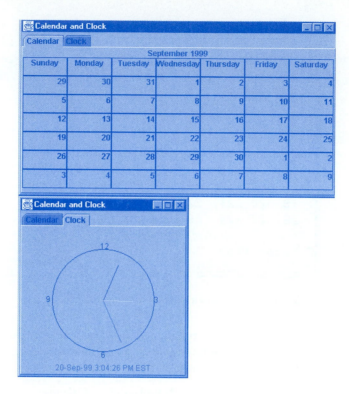

Figure 14.12   *The Calendar tab displays a calendar, and the Clock tab displays a clock.*

14.6   Write two programs to display the available locales and time zone ID. One uses buttons, as shown in Figure 14.13, and the other uses tabs, as shown in Figure 14.14.

Figure 14.13   *The program displays available locales and time zones using the buttons.*

14.7   Rewrite Example 2.3, "Computing Mortgages," to display the monthly payment and total payment in currency.

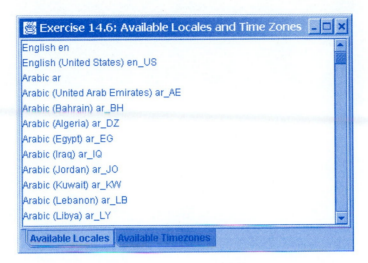

Figure 14.14 *The program displays available locales and time zones using the tabs.*

14.8 Rewrite Exercise 4.4 to display at most two digits after the decimal point for the temperature using the `DecimalFormat` class.

14.9 Rewrite Exercise 3.15 using an applet, as shown in Figure 14.15. The applet allows the user to set the loan amount, loan period, and interest rate, and displays the corresponding interest, principal, and balance in the currency format.

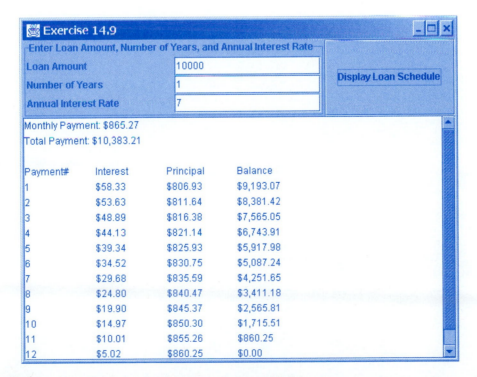

Figure 14.15 *The program displays the loan payment schedule.*

MULTITHREADING

Objectives

- To understand the concept of multithreading and apply it to develop animation.
- To write threads by extending the `Thread` class.
- To write threads by implementing the `Runnable` interface in cases of multiple inheritance.
- To understand the life-cycle of thread states and set thread priorities.
- To know how to control threads.
- To use thread synchronization to avoid resource conflicts.
- To use the `Timer` class to simplify the control of Java animations.

15.1   Introduction

One of the important features of Java is its built-in support for multithreading. Multithreading is the capability of running multiple tasks concurrently within a program. In many programming languages, you have to invoke system-dependent procedures and functions to implement multithreading. This chapter introduces the concepts of threads and how to develop multithreading programs in Java.

15.2   Thread Concepts

A *thread* is the flow of execution, from beginning to end, of a task in a program. With Java, you can launch multiple threads from a program concurrently. These threads can be executed simultaneously in multiprocessor systems, as shown in Figure 15.1.

Figure 15.1   *Here, multiple threads are running on multiple CPUs.*

In single-processor systems, as shown in Figure 15.2, the multiple threads share CPU time, and the operating system is responsible for scheduling and allocating resources to them. This arrangement is practical because most of the time the CPU is idle. It does nothing, for example, while waiting for the user to enter data.

Figure 15.2   *Here, multiple threads share a single CPU.*

Multithreading can make your program more responsive and interactive, as well as enhance performance. For example, a good word processor lets you print or save a file while you are typing. In some cases, multithreaded programs run faster than single-threaded programs even on single-processor systems. Java provides exceptionally good support for creating and running threads and for locking resources to prevent conflicts.

When your program executes as an application, the Java interpreter starts a thread for the main method. When your program executes as an applet, the Web browser starts a thread to run the applet. You can create additional threads to run concurrent tasks in the program. Each new thread is an object of a class that implements the Runnable interface or extends a class that implements the Runnable interface. This new object is referred to as a *runnable object*.

You can create threads either by extending the `Thread` class or by implementing the `Runnable` interface. Both `Thread` and `Runnable` are defined in the `java.lang` package. `Thread` actually implements `Runnable`. In the following sections, you will learn how to use the `Thread` class and the `Runnable` interface to write multithreaded programs.

15.3   Creating Threads by Extending the *Thread* Class

The `Thread` class contains the constructors for creating threads, as well as many useful methods for controlling threads. To create and run a thread, first define a class that extends the `Thread` class. Your thread class must override the `run()` method, which tells the system how the thread will be executed when it runs. You can then create an object running on the thread.

Figure 15.3 illustrates the key elements of a thread class that extends the `Thread` class, and shows how to use it to create a thread in a class. The `thread` is a runnable object created from the `CustomThread` class. The `start` method tells the system that the thread is ready to run.

```
// Custom thread class
public class CustomThread extends Thread {
  ...
  public CustomThread(...) {
    ...
  }

  // Override the run method in Thread
  public void run() {
    // Tell system how to run custom thread
    ...
  }

  ...
}
```

```
// Client class
public class Client {
  ...
  public someMethod() {
    ...
    // Create a thread
    CustomThread thread = new CustomThread(...);

    // Start a thread
    thread.start();
    ...
  }

  ...
}
```

Figure 15.3 *Define a thread class by extending the* `Thread` *class.*

Example 15.1 Using the `Thread` Class to Create and Launch Threads

Problem

Write a program that creates and runs three threads:

- The first thread prints the letter *a* one hundred times.
- The second thread prints the letter *b* one hundred times.
- The third thread prints the integers 1 through 100.

continues

Example 15.1 continued

Solution

The program has three independent threads. To run them concurrently, it needs to create a runnable object for each thread. Because the first two threads have similar functionality, they can be defined in one thread class.

The program is given here, and its output is shown in Figure 15.4.

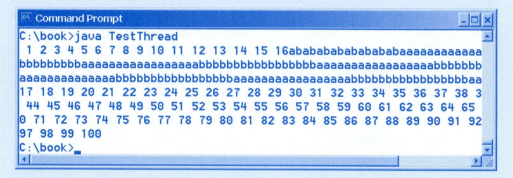

Figure 15.4   *Threads* printA, printB, *and* print100 *are executed simultaneously to display the letter a one hundred times, the letter b one hundred times, and the numbers from 1 to 100.*

```
1     // TestThread.java: Define threads using the Thread class
2     public class TestThread {
3       /** Main method */
4       public static void main(String[] args) {
5         // Create threads
6         PrintChar printA = new PrintChar('a', 100);
7         PrintChar printB = new PrintChar('b', 100);
8         PrintNum  print100 = new PrintNum(100);
9
10        // Start threads
11        print100.start();
12        printA.start();
13        printB.start();
14      }
15    }
16
17    // The thread class for printing a specified character
18    // in specified times
19    class PrintChar extends Thread {
20      private char charToPrint;  // The character to print
21      private int times;  // The times to repeat
22
23      /** Construct a thread with specified character and number of
24          times to print the character
25         */
26      public PrintChar(char c, int t) {
27        charToPrint = c;
28        times = t;
29      }
30
31      /** Override the run() method to tell the system
32          what the thread will do
33         */
34      public void run() {
```

```
35              for (int i = 0; i < times; i++)
36                System.out.print(charToPrint);
37          }
38      }
39
40      // The thread class for printing number from 1 to n for a given n
41      class PrintNum extends Thread {
42        private int lastNum;
43
44        /** Construct a thread for print 1, 2, ... i */
45        public PrintNum(int n) {
46          lastNum = n;
47        }
48
49        /** Tell the thread how to run */
50        public void run() {
51          for (int i = 1; i <= lastNum; i++)
52            System.out.print(" " + i);
53        }
54      }
```

Review

If you run this program on a multiple-CPU system, all three threads will execute simultaneously. If you run the program on a single-CPU system, the three threads will share the CPU and take turns printing letters and numbers on the console. This is known as *time-sharing*.

The program creates thread classes by extending the Thread class. The PrintChar class (Lines 19–38), derived from the Thread class, overrides the run() method (Lines 34–37) with the print-character action. This class provides a framework for printing any single character a given number of times. The runnable objects printA and printB are instances of the user-defined thread class PrintChar.

The PrintNum class (Lines 41–54) overrides the run() method (Lines 50–53) with the print-number action. This class provides a framework for printing numbers from *1* to *n*, for any integer *n*. The runnable object print100 is an instance of the user-defined thread class printNum.

In the client program, the program creates a thread, printA, for printing the letter *a*, and a thread, printB, for printing the letter *b*. Both are objects of the PrintChar class. The print100 thread object is created from the PrintNum class.

The start() method (Lines 11–13) is invoked to start a thread that causes the run() method to execute. When the run() method completes, the threads terminate.

NOTE

On some systems, the program may not terminate or print out all the characters and numbers. The problem has nothing to do with your program. It may be an OS problem or a Java Virtual Machine implementation problem. If the program does not seem to terminate, press Ctrl+C to stop it.

15.4   Creating Threads by Implementing the *Runnable* Interface

In the preceding section, you created and ran a thread by declaring a user thread class that extends the Thread class. This approach works well if the user thread class inherits only from the Thread class, but not if it inherits multiple classes, as in the case of an applet. To inherit multiple classes, you have to implement interfaces. Java provides the Runnable interface as an alternative to the Thread class.

The Runnable interface is rather simple. It contains just the run method. You need to implement this method to tell the system how your thread is going to run. Figure 15.5 illustrates the key elements of a thread class that implements the Runnable interface, and how to use it to create a thread in a class.

```
// Custom thread class
public class CustomThread
  implements Runnable { ............
  ...
  public CustomThread(...) {
    ...
  }

  // Implement the run method in Runnable
  public void run() {
    // Tell system how to run custom thread
    ...
  }

  ...
}
```

```
// Client class
public class Client {
  ...
  public someMethod() {
    ...
    // Create an instance of CustomThread
    CustomThread customThread
      = new CustomThread(...);

    // Create a thread
    Thread thread = new Thread(customThread);

    // Start a thread
    thread.start();
    ...
  }
  ...
}
```

Figure 15.5   *Define a thread class by implementing the* Runnable *interface.*

To start a new thread with the Runnable interface, you must first create an instance of the class that implements the Runnable interface, then use the Thread class constructor to construct a thread.

The following example demonstrates how to create threads using the Runnable interface.

Example 15.2 Using the Runnable Interface to Create and Launch Threads

Problem

Modify Example 15.1 to create and run the same threads using the Runnable interface.

Solution

The following code gives the solution to the problem.

```
1    // TestRunnable.java: Define threads using the Runnable interface
2    public class TestRunnable {
3      /** Main method */
4      public static void main(String[] args) {
5        new TestRunnable();
6      }
7
8      /** Default constructor */
9      public TestRunnable() {
10       // Create threads
11       Thread printA = new Thread(new PrintChar('a', 100));
12       Thread printB = new Thread(new PrintChar('b', 100));
13       Thread print100 = new Thread(new PrintNum(100));
14
15       // Start threads
16       print100.start();
17       printA.start();
18       printB.start();
19     }
20
21     // The thread class for printing a specified character
22     // in specified times
23     class PrintChar implements Runnable {
24       private char charToPrint;  // The character to print
25       private int times;  // The times to repeat
26
27       /** Construct a thread with specified character and number of
28          times to print the character
29        */
30       public PrintChar(char c, int t) {
31         charToPrint = c;
32         times = t;
33       }
34
35       /** Override the run() method to tell the system
36          what the thread will do
37        */
38       public void run() {
39         for (int i = 0; i < times; i++)
40           System.out.print(charToPrint);
41       }
42     }
43
44     // The thread class for printing number from 1 to n for a given n
45     class PrintNum implements Runnable {
46       private int lastNum;
47
48       /** Construct a thread for print 1, 2, ... i */
49       public PrintNum(int n) {
50         lastNum = n;
51       }
52
53       /** Tell the thread how to run */
54       public void run() {
55         for (int i = 1; i <= lastNum; i++)
56           System.out.print(" " + i);
57       }
58     }
59   }
```

continues

Example 15.2 continued

Review

The program creates thread classes by implementing the `Runnable` interface.

This example performs the same task as in Example 15.1. The classes `PrintChar` and `PrintNum` are the same as in Example 15.1 except that they implement the `Runnable` interface rather than extend the `Thread` class.

The `PrintChar` and `PrintNum` classes are implemented as inner classes to avoid naming conflicts with the `PrintChar` and `PrintNum` classes in Example 15.1. Threads `printA`, `printB`, and `print100` are created in the constructor instead of directly in the `main` method. This is because the `main` method is static and the inner classes `PrintChar` and `PrintNum` are nonstatic; you cannot reference non-static members of a class in a static method.

An instance of the class that extends the `Thread` class is a thread, which can be started using the `start()` method in the `Thread` class. But an instance of the class that implements the `Runnable` interface is not yet a thread. You have to wrap it, using the `Thread` class, to construct a thread for the instance, such as

```
Thread printA = new Thread(new PrintChar('a', 100));
```

15.5   Thread Controls and Communications

The `Thread` class contains the following methods for controlling threads:

■ `public void run()`

Invoked by the Java runtime system to execute the thread. You must override this method and provide the code you want your thread to execute in your thread class. This method is never directly invoked by the runnable object in a program, although it is an instance method of a runnable object.

■ `public void start()`

Starts the thread that causes the `run()` method to be invoked. This method is called by the runnable object in the client class.

■ `public void stop()`

Stops the thread. As of Java 2, this method is *deprecated* (or *outdated*) because it is known to be inherently unsafe. You should assign `null` to a `Thread` variable to indicate that it is stopped rather than use the `stop()` method.

■ `public void suspend()`

Suspends the thread. As of Java 2, this method is deprecated because it is known to be deadlock-prone. You should write the code to use the `wait()` method along with a `boolean` variable to indicate whether a thread is suspended rather than use the deprecated `suspend()` method. The code will be introduced in Section 15.9, "Creating Threads for Applets."

- `public void resume()`

  Resumes the thread. As of Java 2, this method, along with the `suspend()` method, is deprecated because it is deadlock-prone. You should write the code to use the `notify()` method along with a `boolean` variable to indicate whether a thread is resumed rather than use the deprecated `resume()` method.

- `public static void sleep(long millis) throws InterruptedException`

  Puts the runnable object to sleep for a specified time in milliseconds. Note that the `sleep` method is a static method.

- `public static void yield(long millis)`

  Causes the currently executing thread object to temporarily pause and allow other threads to execute.

- `public void interrupt()`

  Interrupts a running thread.

- `public static boolean isInterrupted()`

  Tests whether the current thread has been interrupted.

- `public boolean isAlive()`

  Tests whether the thread is currently running.

- `public void setPriority(int p)`

  Sets priority p (ranging from 1 to 10) for this thread.

NOTE

With the release of a Java 2, some methods in the previous version have been deprecated and replaced by new methods. The deprecated methods are still supported for compatibility reasons, but Sun recommends against using them.

The `wait()`, `notify()`, and `notifyAll()` methods in the `Object` class are often used with threads to facilitate communications among them.

- `public final void wait() throws InterruptedException`

  Forces the thread to wait until the `notify` or `notifyAll` method is called for the object to which `wait` is called.

- `public final void notify()`

  Awakens one of the threads that are waiting on this object. Which one is notified depends on the system implementation.

- `public final void notifyAll()`

  Awakens all the threads that are waiting on this object.

Examples of thread communications will be given in Section 15.9, "Creating Threads for Applets."

15.6 Thread States

Threads can be in one of five states: new, ready, running, blocked, or finished (see Figure 15.6).

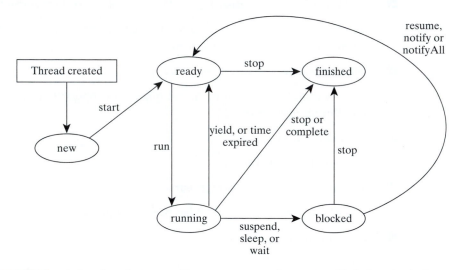

Figure 15.6   *A thread can be in one of five states: new, ready, running, blocked, or finished.*

When a thread is newly created, it enters the *new state*. After a thread is started by calling its `start()` method, it enters the *ready state*. A ready thread is runnable but may not be running yet. The operating system has to allocate CPU time to it.

When a ready thread begins executing, it enters the *running state*. A running thread may enter the ready state if its given CPU time expires or its `yield()` method is called.

A thread can enter the *blocked state* (i.e., become inactive) for several reasons. It may have invoked the `sleep()`, `wait()`, or `suspend()` method, or some other thread may have invoked its `sleep()` or `suspend()` method. It may be waiting for an I/O operation to finish. A blocked thread may be reactivated when the action inactivating it is reversed. For example, if a thread has been put to sleep and the sleep time has expired, the thread is reactivated and enters the ready state.

Finally, a thread is *finished* if it completes the execution of its `run()` method or if its `stop()` method is invoked.

The `isAlive()` method is used to find out the state of a thread. It returns `true` if a thread is in the ready, inactive, or running state; it returns `false` if a thread is new and has not started or if it is finished.

Java assigns every thread a priority. By default, a thread inherits the priority of the thread that spawned it. You can increase or decrease the priority of any thread by using the setPriority method, and you can get the thread's priority by using the getPriority method. Priorities are numbers ranging from 1 to 10. The Thread class has the int constants MIN_PRIORITY, NORM_PRIORITY, and MAX_PRIORITY, representing 1, 5, and 10, respectively. The priority of the main thread is Thread.NORM_PRIORITY.

TIP

The priority numbers may be changed in a future version of Java. To minimize the impact of any changes, use the constants in the Thread class to specify the thread priorities.

The Java runtime system always picks the currently runnable thread with the highest priority. If several runnable threads have equally high priorities, the CPU is allocated to all of them in round-robin fashion. A lower-priority thread can run only when no higher-priority threads are running.

15.7 Thread Groups

A *thread group* is a set of threads. Some programs contain quite a few threads with similar functionality. For convenience, you can group them together and perform operations on the entire group. For example, you can suspend or resume all of the threads in a group at the same time.

Listed below are the guidelines for using thread groups:

1. Use the ThreadGroup constructor to construct a thread group:

```
ThreadGroup g = new ThreadGroup("thread group");
```

This creates a thread group g named "thread group". The name is a string and must be unique.

2. Using the Thread constructor, place a thread in a thread group:

```
Thread t = new Thread(g, new ThreadClass(), "This thread");
```

This statement creates a thread and places it in the thread group g. You can add a thread group under another thread group to form a tree in which every thread group except the initial one has a parent.

3. To find out how many threads in a group are currently running, use the activeCount() method. The following statement displays the active number of threads in group g.

```
System.out.println("The number of runnable threads in the group "
    + g.activeCount());
```

4. Each thread belongs to a thread group. By default, a newly created thread becomes a member of the current thread group that spawned it. To find which group a thread belongs to, use the getThreadGroup() method.

NOTE

You have to start each thread individually. There is no `start()` method in `ThreadGroup`.

In the next section, you will see an example that uses the `ThreadGroup` class.

15.8 Synchronization

A shared resource may be corrupted if it is accessed simultaneously by multiple threads. The following example demonstrates the problem.

Example 15.3 Showing Resource Conflict

Problem

Write a program that demonstrates the problem of resource conflict. Suppose that you create and launch one hundred threads, each of which adds a penny to a piggy bank. Assume that the piggy bank is initially empty. You create a class named `PiggyBank` to model the piggy bank, a class named `AddAPennyThread` to add a penny to the piggy bank, and a main class that creates and launches threads. The relationships of these classes are shown in Figure 15.7.

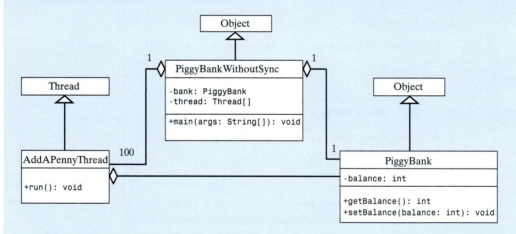

Figure 15.7 `PiggyBankWithoutSync` *contains an instance of* `PiggyBank`, *and one hundred threads of* `AddAPennyThread`.

Solution

The program is given as follows. The output of the program is shown in Figure 15.8.

```
1    // PiggyBankWithoutSync.java: Demonstrate resource conflict
2    public class PiggyBankWithoutSync {
3      private PiggyBank bank = new PiggyBank();
4      private Thread[] thread = new Thread[100];
5
```

```
 6        public static void main(String[] args) {
 7          PiggyBankWithoutSync test = new PiggyBankWithoutSync();
 8          System.out.println("What is balance ? " +
 9            test.bank.getBalance());
10        }
11
12        public PiggyBankWithoutSync() {
13          ThreadGroup g = new ThreadGroup("group");
14          boolean done = false;
15
16          // Create and launch 100 threads
17          for (int i = 0; i < 100; i++) {
18            thread[i] = new Thread(g, new AddAPennyThread(), "t");
19            thread[i].start();
20          }
21
22          // Check if all the threads are finished
23          while(!done)
24            if (g.activeCount() == 0)
25              done = true;
26        }
27
28
29        // A thread for adding a penny to the piggy bank
30        class AddAPennyThread extends Thread {
31          public void run() {
32            int newBalance = bank.getBalance() + 1;
33
34            try {
35              Thread.sleep(5);
36            }
37            catch (InterruptedException ex) {
38              System.out.println(ex);
39            }
40
41            bank.setBalance(newBalance);
42          }
43        }
44      }
45
46      // A class for piggy bank
47      class PiggyBank {
48        private int balance = 0;
49
50        public int getBalance() {
51          return balance;
52        }
53
54        public void setBalance(int balance) {
55          this.balance = balance;
56        }
57      }
```

Review

The program creates one hundred threads in the array thread, and groups all of them into a thread group g (Lines 13–20). The activeCount() method is used to count the active threads. When all the threads are finished, it returns 0.

continues

Example 15.3 continued

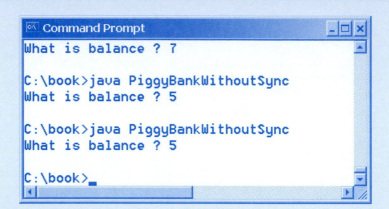

Figure 15.8   *The* `PiggyBankWithoutSync` *program causes data inconsistency.*

The balance of the piggy bank is initially 0 (Line 48). When all the threads are finished, the balance should be 100, but the output is unpredictable. As can be seen in Figure 15.8, the answers are wrong in the sample run. This demonstrates the data-corruption problem that occurs when all the threads have access to the same data source simultaneously.

Interestingly, it is not easy to replicate the problem. The `sleep` method (Line 35) is deliberately added to magnify the data-corruption problem and make it easy to see. If you run the program several times but still do not see the problem, increase the sleep time. This will dramatically increase the chances for resource contention.

What, then, caused the error in Example 15.3? Here is a possible scenario, as shown in Figure 15.9.

Step	balance	thread[i]	thread[j]
1	0	newBalance = bank.getBalance() + 1;	
2	0		newBalance = bank.getBalance() + 1;
3	1	bank.setBalance(newBalance);	
4	1		bank.setBalance(newBalance);

Figure 15.9   `Thread[i]` *and* `thread[j]` *both add 1 to the same balance.*

In Step 1, `thread[i]`, for some `i`, gets the balances from the bank. In Step 2, `thread[j]`, for some `j`, gets the same balances from the bank. In Step 3, `thread[i]` writes a new balance to the bank. In Step 4, `thread[j]` writes a new balance to the bank.

The effect of this scenario is that thread `thread[i]` did nothing, because in Step 4 thread `thread[j]` overrides `thread[i]`'s result. Obviously, the problem is that `thread[i]` and `thread[j]` are accessing a common resource in a way that causes conflict.

15.8.1   The Keyword *synchronized*

To avoid resource conflicts, Java uses the keyword synchronized to synchronize method invocation so that only one thread can access a method at a time. To correct the data-corruption problem in Example 15.3, rewrite the program as follows:

```
1    // PiggyBankWithSync.java: Demonstrate avoiding resource conflict
2    public class PiggyBankWithSync {
3      private PiggyBank bank = new PiggyBank();
4      private Thread[] thread = new Thread[100];
5
6      public static void main(String[] args) {
7        PiggyBankWithSync test = new PiggyBankWithSync();
8        System.out.println("What is balance ? " +
9          test.bank.getBalance());
10     }
11
12     public PiggyBankWithSync() {
13       ThreadGroup g1 = new ThreadGroup("group");
14       boolean done = false;
15
16       for (int i = 0; i < 100; i++) {
17         thread[i] = new Thread(g1, new AddAPennyThread(), "t");
18         thread[i].start();
19       }
20
21       while(!done)
22         if (g1.activeCount() == 0)
23           done = true;
24     }
25
26     // Synchronize: add a penny one at a time
27     private static synchronized void addAPenny(PiggyBank bank) {
28       int newBalance = bank.getBalance() + 1;
29
30       try {
31         Thread.sleep(5);
32       }
33       catch (InterruptedException ex) {
34         System.out.println(ex);
35       }
36
37       bank.setBalance(newBalance);
38     }
39
40     // A thread for adding a penny to the piggy bank
41     class AddAPennyThread extends Thread {
42       public void run()
43       {
44         addAPenny(bank);
45       }
46     }
47   }
```

With the keywords static and synchronized for the method addAPenny, the preceding scenario cannot happen. If thread thread[j] starts to enter the method, and thread thread[i] is already in the method, thread thread[j] is blocked until thread thread[i] finishes the method.

A synchronized method acquires a lock before it executes. In the case of an instance method, the lock is on the object for which the method was invoked. In the case of a static (class) method, the lock is on the class. If one thread invokes a synchronized instance method (respectively, static method) on an object, the lock of that object (respectively, class) is acquired first, then the method is executed, and finally the lock is released. Another thread invoking the same method of that object (respectively, class) is blocked until the lock is released.

You can rewrite the program to add a synchronized instance method named addAPenny in the PiggyBank class. In this case, the lock would be on a single PiggyBank object, which is sufficient to ensure that only one thread can execute the addAPenny method at any given time. See Exercise 15.11.

15.8.2   Synchronized Statements

Invoking a synchronized instance method of an object acquires a lock on the object, and invoking a synchronized static method of a class acquires a lock on the class. A synchronized statement can be used to acquire a lock on any object, not just *this* object, when executing a block of the code in a method. This block is referred to as a synchronized block. The general form of a synchronized statement is as follows:

```
synchronized (expr) {
  statements;
}
```

The expression expr must evaluate to an object reference. If the object is already locked by another thread, the thread is blocked until the lock is released. When a lock is obtained on the object, the statements in the synchronized block are executed, and then the lock is released.

Synchronized statements enable you to synchronize part of the code in a method instead of the entire method. This increases concurrency. Synchronized statements enable you to acquire a lock on any object so that you can synchronize the access to an object instead of to a method. See Exercise 15.12.

NOTE

Any synchronized instance method can be converted into a synchronized statement. Suppose that the following is a synchronized instance method:

```
public synchronized void xMethod() {
  // method body
}
```

This method is equivalent to

```
public void xMethod() {
  synchronized (this) {
    // method body
  }
}
```

15.9   Creating Threads for Applets

In Example 14.1, "Displaying a Clock," you drew a clock to show the current time in an applet. The clock does not tick after it is displayed. What can you do to make the clock display a new current time every second? The key to making the clock tick is to repaint it every second with a new current time. You can use the code given below to override the `start()` method in `CurrentTimeApplet`:

```
public void start() {
  while (true) {
    stillClock.repaint();

    try {
      Thread.sleep(1000);
    }
    catch(InterruptedException ex) {
    }
  }
}
```

The `start()` method is called when the applet begins. The infinite loop repaints the clock every thousand milliseconds (in other words, at one-second intervals). This appears to refresh the clock every second, but if you run the program, the browser hangs up. The problem is that as long as the `while` loop is running, the browser cannot serve any other event that might occur. Therefore, the `paintComponent` method is not called. The solution is to move the `while` loop to another thread that can be executed in parallel with the `paintComponent` method.

To create a new thread for the applet, you need to implement the `Runnable` interface in the applet. Here are the implementation guidelines:

1. Add `implements Runnable` in the applet class declaration:

   ```
   public class MyApplet extends JApplet implements Runnable
   ```

2. Declare a thread in `MyApplet`. For example, the following statement declares a thread instance, `thread`, with the initial value `null`:

   ```
   private Thread thread = null;
   ```

   By default, the initial value is `null`, so assigning `null` in this statement is not necessary.

3. Create a new thread in the applet's `init()` method and start it right away in `MyApplet`:

   ```
   public void init() {
     thread = new Thread(this);  // Create a thread
     thread.start();  // Start the thread
   }
   ```

   The `this` argument in the `Thread` constructor is required; it specifies that the run function of `MyApplet` should be called when the thread executes an instance of `MyApplet`.

4. Override the applet's `start()` method in `MyApplet`, as follows, to resume the thread.

```
public void start() {
  resume();
}
```

5. Create `resume()` and `suspend()` methods, as follows:

```
public synchronized void resume() {
  if (suspended) {
    suspended = false;
    notify();
  }
}

public synchronized void suspend() {
  suspended = true;
}
```

Since the `resume()` and `suspend()` methods in the `Thread` class have been deprecated, you must create new methods for resuming and suspending threads.

The variable `suspended` should be declared as a data member of the class, which indicates the state of the thread. The keyword `synchronized` ensures that the `resume()` and `suspend()` methods are serialized to avoid race conditions that could result in an inconsistent value for the variable `suspended`.

6. Write the code you want the thread to execute in the `run()` method:

```
public void run() {
  while (true) {
    // Repaint the clock to display current time
    stillClock.repaint();

    try {
      thread.sleep(1000);
      waitForNotificationToResume();
    }
    catch (InterruptedException ex) {
    }
  }
}
```

The `run()` method is invoked by the Java runtime system when the thread starts. In the `while` loop body, `stillClock.repaint()` is invoked every second if the thread is not suspended. If `suspended` is true, the `waitForNotification-ToResume()` method causes the thread to suspend and wait for notification by the `notify()` method invoked from the `resume()` method. The `repaint()` method runs on the system default thread, which is separate from the thread on which the `while` loop is running.

7. The `waitForNotificationToResume` method is implemented as follows:

```
private synchronized void waitForNotificationToResume()
  throws InterruptedException {
  while (suspended)
    wait();
}
```

8. Override the `stop()` method in the `Applet` class to suspend the running thread:

```
public void stop() {
  suspend();
}
```

This code suspends the thread so that it does not consume CPU time when the Web page containing the applet becomes inactive.

9. Override the `destroy()` method in the `Applet` class to kill the thread:

```
public void destroy() {
  thread = null;
}
```

This code releases all the resources associated with the thread when the Web browser exits.

> **NOTE**
> The `wait()`, `notify()`, and `notifyAll()` methods are used for thread communications. These methods must be called within a synchronized method or a synchronized block. Otherwise, an `IllegalMonitorStateException` would occur.

> **NOTE**
> When `wait()` is invoked, it pauses the thread and simultaneously releases the lock on the object. When the thread is restarted after being notified, the lock is automatically reacquired.

Example 15.4 Displaying a Running Clock in an Applet

Problem

Write an applet that displays a clock. To simulate the clock running, a separate thread is used to repaint it. The output of the program is shown in Figure 15.10.

Solution

The following code gives the solution to the problem.

```
1   // ClockApplet.java: Display a running clock on the applet
2   import java.applet.*;
3   import java.awt.*;
4   import java.util.*;
5
6   public class ClockApplet extends CurrentTimeApplet
7     implements Runnable {
8     // Declare a thread for running the clock
9     private Thread thread = null;
10
```

continues

Example 15.4 continued

```
11      // Determine if the thread is suspended
12      private boolean suspended = false;
13
14      /** Initialize applet */
15      public void init() {
16        super.init();
17
18        // Create the thread
19        thread = new Thread(this);
20
21        // Start the thread
22        thread.start();
23      }
24
25      /** Implement the start() method to resume the thread */
26      public void start() {
27        resume();
28      }
29
30      /** Implement the run() method to dictate what the thread will do */
31      public void run() {
32        while (true) {
33          // Repaint the clock to display current time
34          stillClock.repaint();
35
36          try {
37            thread.sleep(1000);
38            waitForNotificationToResume();
39          }
40          catch (InterruptedException ex) {
41          }
42        }
43      }
44
45      private synchronized void waitForNotificationToResume()
46        throws InterruptedException {
47        while (suspended)
48          wait();
49      }
50
51      /** Implement the stop method to suspend the thread */
52      public void stop() {
53        suspend();
54      }
55
56      /** Destroy the thread */
57      public void destroy() {
58        thread = null;
59      }
60
61      /** Resume the suspended thread */
62      public synchronized void resume() {
63        if (suspended) {
64          suspended = false;
65          notify(); // Notify the waiting object
66        }
67      }
68
```

```
69        /** Suspend the thread */
70        public synchronized void suspend() {
71           suspended = true;
72        }
73     }
```

Figure 15.10   *The control of how to paint the clock runs a thread separately from the* paintComponent *method that draws the clock.*

Review

The CurrentTimeApplet class is presented in Example 14.1, "Displaying a Clock," to display the current time. The ClockApplet class extends CurrentTimeApplet with a control loop running on a separate thread to make the clock tick.

The run method (Lines 31–43) comes from the Runnable interface and is modified to specify what the separate thread will do. The paintComponent method defined in CurrentTimeApplet is called every second by the repaint method (Line 34) to display the current time.

The init, start, stop, and destroy methods in the Applet class are modified for this program to work with the Web browser. The init method (Lines 15–23) is invoked to start the thread when the Web page is loaded. The stop method (Lines 52–54) is invoked to suspend the thread when the Web page containing the applet becomes inactive. The start method (Lines 26–29) is invoked to resume the thread when the Web page containing the applet becomes active. The destroy method (Lines 57–59) is invoked to terminate the thread when the Web browser exits.

The separate thread named thread is created and started in the applet's init method:

```
thread = new Thread(this);
thread.start();
```

continues

Example 15.4 continued

The ClockApplet's init() method calls super.init() defined in the Current-TimeApplet class, which gets parameters for country, language, and time zone from HTML. Therefore, the ClockApplet class can get these parameters from HTML.

The resume() method (Lines 62–67) sets the variable suspended to false and awakens the thread that is waiting on the notification by invoking the notify() method. The suspend() method sets the variable suspended to true, which causes the thread to suspend and wait for notification to resume.

NOTE
The start() method in thread.start() is different from the start() method in the applet. The former starts the thread and causes the run() method to execute, whereas the latter is executed by the Web browser when the applet starts for the first time or is reactivated.

TIP
I recommend that you suspend the threads in the applet's stop method so that the applet does not consume CPU time when the Web page is inactive.

CAUTION
The ClockApplet class does not define the main method, but its subclass CurrentTimeApplet has a main method. Therefore, while you can run ClockApplet as an application, you would not see the clock running, because the main method is for running the CurrentTimeApplet class.

15.10   Using the *Timer* Class to Control Animation

The preceding example creates a thread to run a while loop that repaints the clock in a panel every thousand milliseconds. Java animations frequently repaints panels at a predefined rate. For this reason, Java provides the javax.swing.Timer class, which can be used to control repainting a panel at a predefined rate. Using the Timer class dramatically simplifies the program. A Timer object serves as the source of an ActionEvent. It fires an ActionEvent at a fixed rate. The listeners for the event are registered with the Timer object. When you create a Timer object, you have to specify the delay and a listener using the following constructor:

```
public Timer(int delay, ActionListener listener)
```

where delay specifies the number of milliseconds between two action events. You can add additional listeners using the addActionListener method, and adjust the delay using the setDelay method. To start the timer, use the start method. To stop the timer, use the stop method. In the action listener class, you can implement the actionPerformed handler by invoking the repaint method to repaint the panel. This actionPerformed method is invoked at a rate determined by the delay.

Using the Timer class, the preceding program can be modified as follows:

```java
// NewClockApplet.java: Display a running clock on the applet
import java.awt.event.*;
import javax.swing.Timer;

public class NewClockApplet extends CurrentTimeApplet
  implements ActionListener {
  protected Timer timer;

  /** Initialize applet */
  public void init() {
    super.init();

    // Create a timer with delay 1000 ms and listener NewClockApplet
    timer = new Timer(1000, this);
  }

  /** Override the start method in the Applet class */
  public void start() {
    timer.start();
  }

  /** Override the stop method in the Applet class */
  public void stop() {
    timer.stop();
  }

  /** Handle the action event */
  public void actionPerformed(ActionEvent e) {
    repaint();
  }
}
```

NOTE

Using a thread to control animations and using a timer to control animations are two entirely different approaches. The thread approach places the animation control on a separate thread so that it does not interfere with the drawing. The timer approach uses the action event to control the drawing. If your drawings are painted at a fixed rate, use the timer approach, because it can greatly simplify programming.

15.11 Case Studies

The preceding examples show how to override init, start, and stop in the Applet class to enable threads to work correctly with Java applets using the thread approach and using the timer approach. The ClockApplet class and NewClockApplet class work correctly to display a running clock. However, reusing these classes is difficult because they are subclasses of JApplet, which is a heavyweight component. A heavyweight component is not suitable for placement inside a lightweight container such as JPanel. To make reusing it easier, you can create a Clock component to be a subclass of JPanel. Since the StillClock class is a subclass of JPanel, you can create Clock by extending the StillClock class, as follows:

```java
// Clock.java: Show a running clock on the panel
import java.util.*;
import java.awt.event.*;
import javax.swing.Timer;

public class Clock extends StillClock implements ActionListener {
  protected Timer timer;

  /** Default constructor */
  public Clock() {
    this(Locale.getDefault(), TimeZone.getDefault());
  }

  /** Construct a clock with specified locale and time zone */
  public Clock(Locale locale, TimeZone timeZone) {
    super(locale, timeZone);

    // Create a timer with delay 1000 ms and listener Clock
    timer = new Timer(1000, this);

    // Start the timer
    timer.start();
  }

  /** Resume the clock */
  public void resume() {
    timer.start();
  }

  /** Suspend the clock */
  public void suspend() {
    timer.stop();
  }

  /** Handle the action event */
  public void actionPerformed(ActionEvent e) {
    repaint();
  }
}
```

The Clock class extends StillClock and implements ActionListener. The Clock class is the listener for timer, which fires an action event every second. When an action event occurs, the actionPerformed method is invoked, which invokes the repaint method. The repaint method causes the paintComponent method to be called to redraw the clock with the new current time. The paintComponent method is defined in StillClock.

The following example uses the Clock class to create a group of clocks.

Example 15.5 Controlling a Group of Clocks

Problem

Write a program that displays three clocks in a group. Each clock has individual Resume and Suspend control buttons. You can also resume or suspend all the clocks by using the group-control Resume All and Suspend All buttons. Figure 15.11 contains the output of a sample run of the program.

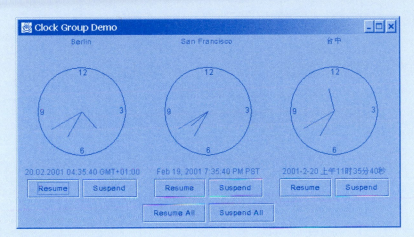

Figure 15.11   *Three clocks run independently with individual control and group control.*

Solution

Here are the major steps in the program:

1. Create a subclass of JPanel named ClockPanel to hold a clock with two control buttons, Resume and Suspend.

2. Create an applet named ClockGroup. Create a panel with GridLayout, add three instances of ClockPanel into the panel, and place the panel in the center of the applet. Create two control buttons, Resume and Suspend, to control all the clocks in the group. The relationship of these classes is shown in Figure 15.12.

```
1    // ClockGroup.java: Display a group of international clocks
2    import java.awt.*;
3    import java.awt.event.*;
4    import java.util.*;
5    import javax.swing.*;
6
7    public class ClockGroup extends JApplet implements ActionListener {
8      // Declare three clock panels
9      private ClockPanel clockPanel1, clockPanel2, clockPanel3;
10
11     // Declare group control buttons
12     private JButton jbtResumeAll, jbtSuspendAll;
13
```

continues

Example 15.5 continued

```
14        /** This main method enables the applet to run as an application */
15        public static void main(String[] args) {
16          // Create a frame
17          JFrame frame = new JFrame("Clock Group Demo");
18
19          // Create an instance of the applet
20          ClockGroup applet = new ClockGroup();
21
22          // Add the applet instance to the frame
23          frame.getContentPane().add(applet, BorderLayout.CENTER);
24
25          // Invoke init() and start()
26          applet.init();
27          applet.start();
28
29          // Display the frame
30          frame.setSize(600, 300);
31          frame.setVisible(true);
32        }
33
34        /** Initialize the applet */
35        public void init() {
36          // Panel p1 for holding three clocks
37          JPanel p1 = new JPanel();
38          p1.setLayout(new GridLayout(1, 3));
39
40          // Create a clock for Berlin
41          p1.add(clockPanel1 = new ClockPanel());
42          clockPanel1.setTitle("Berlin");
43          clockPanel1.clock.setTimeZoneID("ECT");
44          clockPanel1.clock.setLocale(Locale.GERMAN);
45
46          // Create a clock for San Francisco
47          p1.add(clockPanel2 = new ClockPanel());
48          clockPanel2.clock.setLocale(Locale.US);
49          clockPanel2.clock.setTimeZoneID("PST");
50          clockPanel2.setTitle("San Francisco");
51
52          // Create a clock for Taichung
53          p1.add(clockPanel3 = new ClockPanel());
54          clockPanel3.setTitle("\u53f0\u4e2d");
55          clockPanel3.clock.setLocale(Locale.CHINESE);
56          clockPanel3.clock.setTimeZoneID("CTT");
57
58          // Panel p2 for holding two group control buttons
59          JPanel p2 = new JPanel();
60          p2.setLayout(new FlowLayout());
61          p2.add(jbtResumeAll = new JButton("Resume All"));
62          p2.add(jbtSuspendAll = new JButton("Suspend All"));
63
64          // Add panel p1 and p2 into the applet
65          getContentPane().setLayout(new BorderLayout());
66          getContentPane().add(p1, BorderLayout.CENTER);
67          getContentPane().add(p2, BorderLayout.SOUTH);
68
69          // Register listeners
70          jbtResumeAll.addActionListener(this);
71          jbtSuspendAll.addActionListener(this);
72        }
73
```

```
74       /** Handle group control buttons */
75       public void actionPerformed(ActionEvent e) {
76         if (e.getSource() == jbtResumeAll) {
77           // Start all clocks
78           clockPanel1.resume();
79           clockPanel2.resume();
80           clockPanel3.resume();
81         }
82         else if (e.getSource() == jbtSuspendAll) {
83           // Stop all clocks
84           clockPanel1.suspend();
85           clockPanel2.suspend();
86           clockPanel3.suspend();
87         }
88       }
89     }
90
91   // ClockPanel for holding a header, a clock, and control buttons
92   class ClockPanel extends JPanel implements ActionListener {
93     // Header title of the clock panel
94     private JLabel jlblTitle;
95
96     protected Clock clock  = null;
97
98     // Individual clock Resume and Suspend control buttons
99     private JButton jbtResume, jbtSuspend;
100
101    /** Constructor */
102    public ClockPanel() {
103      // Panel jpButtons for grouping buttons
104      JPanel jpButtons = new JPanel();
105      jpButtons.add(jbtResume = new JButton("Resume"));
106      jpButtons.add(jbtSuspend = new JButton("Suspend"));
107
108      // Set BorderLayout for the ClockPanel
109      setLayout(new BorderLayout());
110
111      // Add title label to the north of the panel
112      add(jlblTitle = new JLabel(), BorderLayout.NORTH);
113      jlblTitle.setHorizontalAlignment(JLabel.CENTER);
114
115      // Add the clock to the center of the panel
116      add(clock = new Clock(), BorderLayout.CENTER);
117
118      // Add jpButtons to the south of the panel
119      add(jpButtons, BorderLayout.SOUTH);
120
121      // Register ClockPanel as a listener to the buttons
122      jbtResume.addActionListener(this);
123      jbtSuspend.addActionListener(this);
124    }
125
126    /** Set label on the title */
127    public void setTitle(String title) {
128      jlblTitle.setText(title);
129    }
130
131    /** Handle buttons "Resume" and "Suspend" */
132    public void actionPerformed(ActionEvent e) {
133      if (e.getSource() == jbtResume) {
134        clock.resume();
135      }
```

Example 15.5 continued

```
136            else if (e.getSource() == jbtSuspend) {
137              clock.suspend();
138            }
139          }
140
141          /** Resume the clock */
142          public void resume() {
143            if (clock != null) clock.resume();
144          }
145
146          /** Resume the clock */
147          public void suspend() {
148            if (clock != null) clock.suspend();
149          }
150        }
```

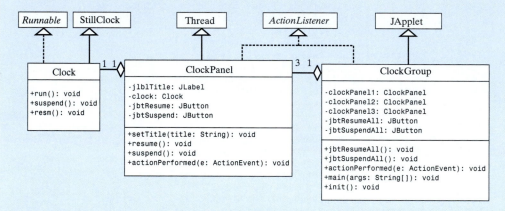

Figure 15.12 ClockGroup *contains three instances of* ClockPanel *for international clocks with control buttons and titles.*

Review

ClockPanel contains a title, a clock, and its control buttons, Resume and Suspend. You can use these two buttons to resume or suspend an individual clock.

The ClockGroup class creates and places three clock panels above two group-control buttons, Resume All and Suspend All, in the applet. You can use these two buttons to resume or suspend all the clocks. The three clocks are for Berlin, San Francisco, and Taichung. The titles and times displayed in the panel are locale-sensitive. The Unicode "\u53f0\u4e2d" consists of the Chinese characters for Taichung, and time is automatically displayed in Chinese because you have set the locale for the clock to Locale.CHINESE (Line 55). If your machine does not support Chinese fonts, you will not see the Chinese characters.

Chapter Summary

In this chapter, you learned how to develop multithreaded programs, using the Thread class and the Runnable interface. You can derive your thread class from the Thread class and create a thread instance to run a task on a separate thread. If your class needs to inherit multiple classes, you can implement the Runnable interface to run multiple tasks in the program simultaneously.

After a thread object is created, you can use the start method to start a thread, and the sleep method to put a thread to sleep so that other threads get a chance to run. Since the stop, suspend, and resume methods are deprecated in Java 2, you need to implement these methods to stop, suspend, and resume a thread.

A thread object never directly invokes the run method. The Java runtime system invokes the run method when it is time to execute the thread. Your class must override the run method to tell the system what the thread will do when it runs.

Threads can be assigned priorities. The Java runtime system always executes the ready thread with the highest priority. You can use a thread group to put relevant threads together for group control. To prevent threads from corrupting a shared resource, put the keyword synchronized into the method that may cause corruption.

You can use either the thread approach or the timer approach to control Java animations.

Review Questions

15.1 Why do you need multithreading capability in applications? How can multiple threads run simultaneously in a single-processor system?

15.2 What are two ways to create threads? When do you use the Thread class, and when do you use the Runnable interface? What are the differences between the Thread class and the Runnable interface?

15.3 How do you create a thread and launch a thread object? Which of the following methods are instance methods? Which of them are deprecated in Java 2?

run, start, stop, suspend, resume, sleep, isInterrupted

15.4 Will the program behave differently if Thread.sleep(1000) is replaced by thread.sleep(1000) in Example 15.4?

15.5 Explain the life-cycle of a thread object.

15.6 How do you set a priority for a thread? What is the default priority?

15.7 Describe a thread group. How do you create a thread group? Can you control an individual thread in a thread group (suspend, resume, stop, etc.)?

15.8 Give some examples of possible resource corruption when running multiple threads. How do you synchronize conflict threads?

15.9 Why does the following class have a runtime error?

```
class Test extends Thread {
  public static void main(String[] args) {
    Test t = new Test();
    t.start();
    t.start();
  }

  public void run() {
    System.out.println("test");
  }
}
```

15.10 Why does the following class have a syntax error?

```
import javax.swing.*;

class Test extends JApplet implements Runnable {
  public void init() throws InterruptedException {
    Thread thread = new Thread(this);
    thread.sleep(1000);
  }

  public synchronized void run() {
  }
}
```

15.11 How do you override the methods `init`, `start`, `stop`, and `destroy` in the `Applet` class to work well with the threads in the applets?

15.12 How do you use the `Timer` class to control Java animations?

Programming Exercises

15.1 Write an applet that displays a flashing label. Enable it to run as an application.

HINT
To make the label flash, you need to repaint the window alternately with the label and without the label (blank screen). Use a `boolean` variable to control the alternation.

15.2 Write an applet that displays a moving label. The label continuously moves from right to left in the applet's viewing area. Whenever the label disappears at the far left of the viewing area, it reappears again on the right-hand side. The label freezes when the mouse is pressed, and moves again when the button is released. Enable it to run as an application.

HINT
Repaint the window with a new x coordinate.

15.3 Rewrite Example 15.1, "Using the `Thread` Class to Create and Launch Threads," to display the output in a text area, as shown in Figure 15.13.

Figure 15.13 *The output from three threads is displayed in a text area.*

15.4 Write a program that launches one hundred threads. Each thread adds 1 to a variable sum that initially is zero. You need to pass sum by reference to each thread. In order to pass it by reference, define an Integer wrapper object to hold sum. Run the program with and without synchronization to see its effect.

15.5 Modify Example 15.3, "Showing Resource Conflict," as follows:

■ Create two panels with the titles "Synchronized Threads" and "Unsynchronized Threads," as shown in Figure 15.14. The Synchronized Threads panel displays a piggy bank balance after a penny has been added one hundred times using synchronized threads. The Unsynchronized Threads panel displays a piggy bank balance after a penny has been added one hundred times using unsynchronized threads.

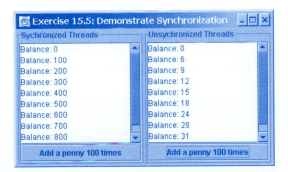

Figure 15.14 *The program shows the effect of executing the threads with and without synchronization.*

■ Since the two panels are very similar, you can create a class to model them uniformly, as shown in Figure 15.15. Use a variable named mode to indicate whether synchronized threads or unsynchronized threads are used in the panel. Invoke the method addAPennyWithSync or addAPennyWithoutSync, depending on the mode.

691

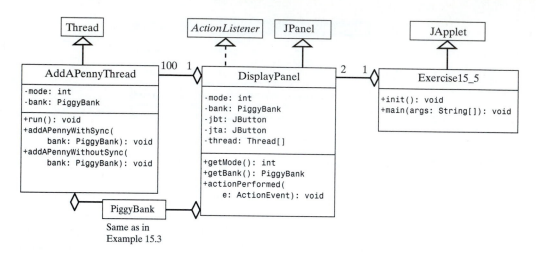

Figure 15.15   `DisplayPanel` *displays the balance in the text area after a penny is added to the balance one hundred times.*

15.6   Write a Java applet that displays a stock index ticker (see Figure 15.16). The stock index information is passed from the <param> tag in the HTML file. Each index has four parameters: Index Name (e.g., S&P 500), Current Time (e.g., 15:54), the index from the previous day (e.g., 919.01), and Change (e.g., 4.54). Enable the applet to run standalone.

Use at least five indexes, such as Dow Jones, S&P 500, NASDAQ, NIKKEI, and Gold & Silver Index. Display positive changes in green, and negative changes in red. The indexes move from right to left in the applet's viewing area. The applet freezes the ticker when the mouse button is pressed; it moves again when the mouse button is released.

Figure 15.16   *The program displays a stock index ticker.*

15.7   Write a Java applet that simulates a running fan, as shown in Figure 15.17. The buttons Start, Stop, and Reverse control the fan. The scrollbar controls the fan's speed. Create a class named `Fan`, a subclass of `JPanel`, to display the fan. This class also contains the methods to suspend and resume the fan, set its speed, and reverse its direction. Create a class named `FanControlPanel` that contains a fan, and three buttons and a scroll bar to control the fan. Create a Java applet that contains an instance of `FanControlPanel`. Enable the applet to run standalone. The relationships of these classes are shown in Figure 15.18.

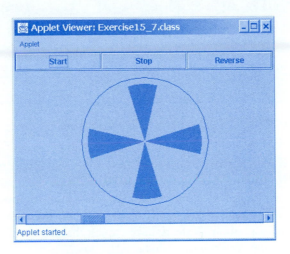

Figure 15.17   *The program simulates a running fan.*

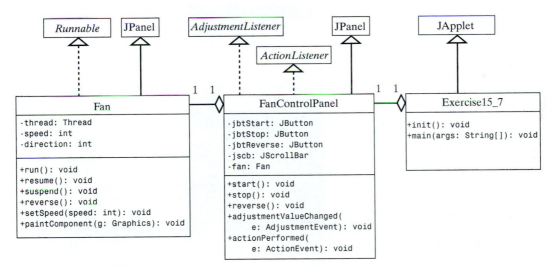

Figure 15.18   *The* `FanControlPanel` *class contains a fan, three buttons, and a scroll bar to control the fan; and the* `Fan` *class displays a running fan.*

15.8   Write a Java applet that displays three fans in a group with control buttons to start and stop all of them, as shown in Figure 15.19. Use the `FanControlPanel` to control and display a single fan. Enable the applet to run standalone.

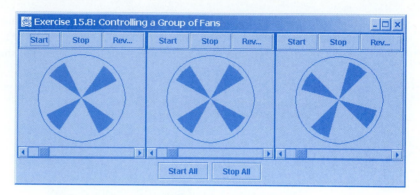

Figure 15.19   *The program runs and controls a group of fans.*

15.9 Write an applet that simulates an elevator going up and down (see Figure 15.20). The buttons on the left indicate the floor where the passenger is now located. The passenger must click a button on the left to request that the elevator move to his or her floor. On entering the elevator, the passenger clicks a button on the right to request that it go to the specified floor. Enable the applet to run standalone.

Figure 15.20   *The program simulates elevator operations.*

15.10 The `Clock` class in Section 15.11, "Case Studies," uses the timer approach to redraw the clock. Use the thread approach to rewrite the `Clock` class.

15.11 Add the following method in the `PiggyBank` class.

```
public synchronized void addAPenny() {
  int newBalance = getBalance() + 1;

  try {
    Thread.sleep(5);
  }
```

```
      catch (InterruptedException ex) {
        System.out.println(ex);
      }

      setBalance(newBalance);
    }
```

Modify Example 15.3 to create one hundred threads, each of which runs this method to add a penny to the piggy bank.

Test your program by removing the keyword synchronized from the method. You will see that the balance is corrupted.

15.12 Modify Example 15.3 using a synchronized statement to synchronize access to the PiggyBank object.

CHAPTER 16

MULTIMEDIA

Objectives

- To develop multimedia applications with audio and images.
- To get audio files and play sound in Java applets.
- To get image files and display images in Java applets.
- To display images and play audio in Java applications.
- To use `MediaTracker` to ensure that images are completely loaded before they are displayed.

16.1   Introduction

Welcome to the fascinating world of *multimedia*. You have seen computer animation used every day in TV and movies. When surfing the Web, you have seen sites with text, images, sounds, animation, and movie clips. These are examples of multimedia at work.

Multimedia is a broad term that encompasses making, storing, retrieving, transferring, and presenting various types of information, such as text, graphics, pictures, videos, and sound. Multimedia involves a complex weave of communications, electronics, and computer technologies. It is beyond the scope of this book to cover multimedia in great detail. This chapter concentrates on the presentation of multimedia in Java.

Whereas most programming languages have no built-in multimedia capabilities, Java was designed with multimedia in mind. It provides extensive built-in support that makes it easy to develop powerful multimedia applications. Java's multimedia capabilities include animation that uses drawings, audio, and images.

You have already used animation with drawings in the examples that simulated a clock, and you used the icons in the Swing components. In this chapter, you will learn how to develop Java programs with audio and images.

16.2   Playing Audio

Audio is stored in files. There are several formats of audio files. Prior to Java 2, sound files in the AU format used on the UNIX operating system were the only ones Java was able to play. With Java 2, you can play sound files in the WAV, AIFF, MIDI, AU, and RMF formats, with better sound quality.

To play an audio file in an applet, you use the following `play` method in the `Applet` class:

```
public void play(URL url, String filename);
```

This method downloads the audio file from the `url` and plays the audio in the file. Nothing happens if the audio file cannot be found.

The URL (Universal Resource Locator) describes the location of a resource on the Internet. Java provides a class that is used to manipulate URLs: `java.net.URL`. Java's security mechanism restricts all files read via a browser to the directory where the HTML file is stored or to the subdirectory of that location. You can use `getCodeBase()` to get the URL of the applet (.class file), or `getDocumentBase()` to get the URL of the HTML file that contains the applet. These two methods, `getCodeBase()` and `getDocumentBase()`, are defined in the `Applet` class:

```
play(getCodeBase(), "soundfile.au");
play(getDocumentBase(), "soundfile.au");
```

The former method plays the sound file soundfile.au, which is located in the code base directory specified by the `codebase` attribute in the `<applet>` tag. The latter method plays the sound file soundfile.au, which is located in the HTML file's directory.

The statement play(url, filename) downloads the audio file every time you play the audio. If you want to play the audio many times, you can create an *audio clip object* for the file. The audio clip is created once and can be played repeatedly without reloading the file. To create an audio clip, use either of the following methods:

```
public AudioClip getAudioClip(URL url);
public AudioClip getAudioClip(URL url, String name);
```

In order to specify a sound file, the former requires an absolute URL address; the latter lets you use a relative URL with the filename. Using the absolute URL address will be introduced in Chapter 18, "Networking." The relative URL is obtained by using getCodeBase() or getDocumentBase(). For example, the following statement creates an audio clip for the file soundfile.au that is stored in the same directory as the applet that contains the statement.

```
AudioClip ac = getAudioClip(getCodeBase(), "soundfile.au");
```

To manipulate a sound for an audio clip, use the following instance methods of java.applet.AudioClip:

■ public void play()

Plays the clip once. The clip is restarted from the beginning every time the method is called.

■ public void loop()

Plays the clip repeatedly.

■ public void stop()

Stops playing the clip.

Example 16.1 Incorporating Sound in Applets

Problem

Write a program that displays a running clock, as shown in Example 15.4, "Displaying a Running Clock in an Applet." In addition, the program plays sound files that announce the time at one-minute intervals. For example, if the current time is 6:30:00, the applet announces, "The time is six-thirty A.M." If the current time is 20:20:00, the applet announces, "The time is eight-twenty P.M."

Solution

Here are the major steps in the program:

1. Create a class named ClockWithAudio that extends Clock. The Clock class was given in Example 15.5, "Controlling a Group of Clocks." The relationships of these classes are shown in Figure 16.1. Override the paintComponent method in the Clock class to announce time whenever it repaints the clock.

continues

Example 16.1 continued

2. Create an applet named `ClockAppletWithAudio` that extends the `Current-TimeApplet` class with the capability to announce time. `CurrentTimeApplet` was given in Example 14.1. Override the init method to load the audio files. The relationship of these classes is shown in Figure 16.1.

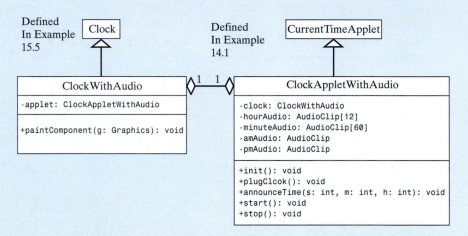

Figure 16.1 `ClockWithAudio` *extends the Clock class with audio, and* `ClockAppletWithAudio` *is an applet that contains an instance of* `ClockWithAudio`.

```
1    // ClockAppletWithAudio.java: Display a running clock on the applet
2    // with audio
3    import java.applet.*;
4
5    public class ClockAppletWithAudio extends CurrentTimeApplet {
6      // Declare audio files
7      protected AudioClip[] hourAudio = new AudioClip[12];
8      protected AudioClip minuteAudio;
9      protected AudioClip amAudio;
10     protected AudioClip pmAudio;
11
12     // Declare a clock
13     ClockWithAudio clock;
14
15     /** Initialize the applet */
16     public void init() {
17       super.init();
18
19       // Create audio clips for pronouncing hours
20       for (int i = 0; i < 12; i++)
21         hourAudio[i] = getAudioClip(getCodeBase(),
22           "timeaudio/hour" + i + ".au");
23
24       // Create audio clips for pronouncing am and pm
25       amAudio = getAudioClip(getCodeBase(), "timeaudio/am.au");
26       pmAudio = getAudioClip(getCodeBase(), "timeaudio/pm.au");
27     }
28
```

```
29        /** Override the plugClock method defined in
30           CurrentTimeApplet and plug a new kind of clock to
31           CurrentTimeApplet
32        */
33        public void plugClock() {
34          getContentPane().add(clock =
35            new ClockWithAudio(locale, timeZone, this));
36        }
37
38        /** Announce the current time at every minute */
39        public void announceTime(int s, int m, int h) {
40          if (s == 0) {
41            // Announce hour
42            hourAudio[h % 12].play();
43
44            // Load the minute file
45            minuteAudio = getAudioClip(getCodeBase(),
46              "timeaudio/minute" + m + ".au");
47
48            // Time delay to allow hourAudio play to finish
49            try {
50              Thread.sleep(1500);
51            }
52            catch(InterruptedException ex) {
53            }
54
55            // Announce minute
56            minuteAudio.play();
57
58            // Time delay to allow minuteAudio play to finish
59            try {
60              Thread.sleep(1500);
61            }
62            catch(InterruptedException ex) {
63            }
64
65            // Announce am or pm
66            if (h < 12)
67              amAudio.play();
68            else
69              pmAudio.play();
70          }
71        }
72
73        /** Implement Applet's start method to resume the thread */
74        public void start() {
75          clock.resume();
76        }
77
78        /** Implement Applet's stop method to suspend the thread */
79        public void stop() {
80          clock.suspend();
81        }
82      }
```

```
1     // ClockWithAudio.java: Display a clock and announce time
2     import java.awt.*;
3     import java.util.*;
4     public class ClockWithAudio extends Clock {
5
6       protected ClockAppletWithAudio applet;
7
```

continues

Example 16.1 continued

```
8        /** Construct a clock with specified locale, timezone, and applet */
9        public ClockWithAudio(Locale locale, TimeZone timeZone,
10         ClockAppletWithAudio applet) {
11         // Invoke the Clock class's constructor
12         super(locale, timeZone);
13
14         this.applet = applet;
15       }
16
17       /** Modify the paintComponent() method to play sound */
18       public void paintComponent(Graphics g) {
19         // Invoke the paintComponent method in the Clock class
20         super.paintComponent(g);
21
22         // Get current time using GregorianCalendar
23         GregorianCalendar calendar = new GregorianCalendar(timeZone);
24
25         // Get second, minute and hour
26         int s = (int)calendar.get(GregorianCalendar.SECOND);
27         int m = (int)calendar.get(GregorianCalendar.MINUTE);
28         int h = (int)calendar.get(GregorianCalendar.HOUR_OF_DAY);
29
30         // Announce current time
31         applet.announceTime(s, m, h);
32       }
33     }
```

Review

Let us first review ClockAppletWithAudio.java.

The hourAudio is an array of twelve audio clips that are used to announce the twelve hours of the day (Line 7); the minuteAudio is an audio clip that is used to announce the minute in an hour (Line 8). The amAudio announces A.M. (Line 9); the pmAudio announces P.M (Line 10).

The init() method invokes super.init() (Line 17) defined in the CurrentTimeApplet class, and creates audio clips for announcing time. super.init() gets country, language, and time zone parameters from HTML, creates a clock, and places it in the applet.

All of the audio files are stored in the directory timeaudio, a subdirectory of the applet's directory. The twelve audio clips that are used to announce the hours are stored in the files **hour0.au**, **hour1.au**, and so on, to **hour11.au**. They are loaded using the following loop (Lines 20–22):

```
for (int i = 0; i < 12; i++)
  hourAudio[i] = getAudioClip(getCodeBase(),
    "timeaudio/hour" + i + ".au");
```

Similarly, the amAudio clip is stored in the file **am.au**, and the pmAudio clip is stored in the file **pm.au**; they are loaded along with the hour clips in the init() method (Lines 25–26).

The program created an array of twelve audio clips to announce each of the twelve hours, but did not create sixty audio clips to announce each of the minutes. Instead, it created and loaded the minute audio clip (Lines 45–46) when needed in the announceTime method. The audio files are very large. Loading all sixty audio clips at once may cause an OutOfMemoryError exception.

In the announceTime method (Lines 39–71), the sleep() method (Lines 50, 60) is purposely invoked to ensure that one clip finishes before the next clip starts, so that the clips do not interfere with each other.

Now let us look at ClockWithAudio.java.

The constructor of ClockWithAudio (Lines 9–15) contains an argument that points to ClockAppletWithAudio, which enables the paintComponent method in ClockWithAudio to invoke announceTime defined in ClockAppletWithAudio. This is a common programming technique for an object to reference methods and data from another class. You might declare ClockWithAudio as an inner class inside ClockAppletWithAudio to avoid passing ClockAppletWithAudio as a parameter. This is fine if ClockWithAudio is not reused elsewhere.

The paintComponent method (Lines 18–32) invokes super.paintComponent(g) and announceTime(h, m, s). super.paintComponent(g), defined in Clock, draws a clock for the current time. announceTime(h, m, s) announces the current hour, minute, and A.M. or P.M. if the second s is 0.

NOTE

Another feature demonstrated in this example is *plugging objects*, a technique for substituting objects. The plugClock method plugs a clock into the applet. In Example 14.1, an instance of StillClock was added to the applet using the plugClock method. In this example, the plugClock method creates an instance of ClockWithAudio and places it in the applet (Lines 33–36 in ClockAppletWithAudio.java).

16.3 Running Audio on a Separate Thread

If you ran the preceding program, you noticed that the second hand did not display at the first, second, and third seconds of the minute. This is because sleep(1500) was invoked twice in the announceTime() method, which takes three seconds to announce the time at the beginning of each minute.

As a result of this delay, the paintComponent method does not have time to draw the clock during the first three seconds of each minute. Clearly, the announceTime method for playing audio interferes with repainting the clock. To avoid the conflict, you should announce the time on a separate thread. This problem is fixed in the following program.

Example 16.2 Announcing the Time on a Separate Thread

Problem

To avoid a conflict between painting the clock and announcing the time, write a program that runs these tasks on separate threads.

Solution

The following code gives the solution to the problem.

```
1    // ClockAppletWithAudioOnSeparateThread.java: Display a
2    // running clock on the applet with audio on a separate thread
3    import java.applet.*;
4
5    public class ClockAppletWithAudioOnSeparateThread
6      extends ClockAppletWithAudio {
7      // Declare a thread for announcing time
8      AnnounceTime announceTime;
9
10     /** Initialize the applet */
11     public void init() {
12       super.init();
13     }
14
15     /** Override this method defined in ClockAppletWithAudio
16        to announce the current time at every minute */
17     public void announceTime(int s, int m, int h) {
18       // Load the minute file
19       minuteAudio = getAudioClip(getCodeBase(),
20         "timeaudio/minute" + m + ".au");
21
22       // Announce current time
23       if (s == 0) {
24         if (h < 12)
25           announceTime = new AnnounceTime(hourAudio[h % 12],
26             minuteAudio, amAudio);
27         else
28           announceTime = new AnnounceTime(hourAudio[h % 12],
29             minuteAudio, pmAudio);
30
31         announceTime.start();
32       }
33     }
34   }
35
36   // Define a thread class for announcing time
37   class AnnounceTime extends Thread {
38     private AudioClip hourAudio, minuteAudio, amPM;
39
40     /** Get Audio clips */
41     public AnnounceTime(AudioClip hourAudio,
42                         AudioClip minuteAudio,
43                         AudioClip amPM) {
44       this.hourAudio = hourAudio;
45       this.minuteAudio = minuteAudio;
46       this.amPM = amPM;
47     }
48
49     public void run() {
50       // Announce hour
51       hourAudio.play();
52
```

```
53          // Time delay to allow hourAudio play to finish
54          // before playing the clip
55          try {
56            Thread.sleep(1500);
57          }
58          catch(InterruptedException ex) {
59          }
60
61          // Announce minute
62          minuteAudio.play();
63
64          // Time delay to allow minuteAudio play to finish
65          try {
66            Thread.sleep(1500);
67          }
68          catch(InterruptedException ex) {
69          }
70
71          // Announce am or pm
72          amPM.play();
73        }
74      }
```

Review

The program extends ClockAppletWithAudio (Lines 5–6) with the capability to announce time without interfering with the paintComponent method. The program defines a new thread class, AnnounceTime (Lines 37–73), which is derived from the Thread class. This new class plays audio.

To create an instance of the AnnounceTime class, you need to pass the three audio clips used to announce the hour, the minute, and A.M. or P.M (Lines 25–26, 28–29). This instance is created only when s equals 0 at the beginning of each minute.

When running this program, you will discover that the audio does not interfere with the clock animation because an instance of AnnounceTime starts on a separate thread to announce the current time. This thread is independent of the thread on which the paintComponent method runs.

An object of AnnounceTime is created every minute to announce the current time. The program can be improved to run more efficiently by creating one such object in advance and passing hour audio, minute audio, and am/pm audio to the object when it is time to announce the current time. See Exercise 16.12.

16.4   Displaying Images

In Example 11.2, "Using Labels," and Example 11.14, "Using a Scroll Pane," you used the `ImageIcon` class to create an icon from an image file and the `setIcon` method to place the image in a UI component, such as a label. These examples are only applicable to Java applications and are not suitable for Java applets, because the image files are directly accessed from the local file system.

To display an image in Java applets, you need to load the image from an Internet source, using the `getImage` method in the `Applet` class. This method returns a `java.awt.Image` object. Two versions of the `getImage` method are shown below:

- `public Image getImage(URL url)`

  Loads the image from the specified URL.

- `public Image getImage(URL url, String filename)`

  Loads the image file from the specified file at the given URL.

Note

When the `getImage` method is invoked, it launches a separate thread to load the image, which enables the program to continue while the image is being retrieved.

Once you have an `Image` instance for the image file, you can create an `ImageIcon` using the following method:

```
ImageIcon imageIcon = new ImageIcon(image);
```

You can now convert Examples 11.2 and 11.14 to Java applets and use the `getImage` method to load the image files.

Using a label as an area for displaying images is simple and convenient, but you don't have much control over how the image is displayed. A more flexible way to display images is to use the `drawImage` method of the `Graphics` class on a panel.

Here are four versions of the `drawImage` method:

- `drawImage(Image img, int x, int y, Color bgcolor, ImageObserver observer)`

  Draws the image in a specified location. The image's top-left corner is at (`x`, `y`) in the graphics context's coordinate space. Transparent pixels in the image are drawn in the specified color `bgcolor`. The `observer` is the object on which the image is displayed. The image is cut off if it is larger than the area it is being drawn on.

- `drawImage(Image img, int x, int y, ImageObserver observer)`

  This is the same as the preceding method except that it does not specify a background color.

■ drawImage(Image img, int x, int y, int width, int height, Image-
Observer observer)

Draws a scaled version of the image that can fill all of the available space in
the specified rectangle.

■ drawImage(Image img, int x, int y, int width, int height, Color
bgcolor, ImageObserver observer)

This is the same as the preceding method except that it provides a solid background color behind the image being drawn.

ImageObserver is an asynchronous update interface that receives notifications of
image information as the image is constructed. The Component class implements
ImageObserver. Therefore, every GUI component is an instance of ImageObserver.
To draw images using the drawImage method in a Swing component, such as
JPanel, override the paintComponent method to tell the component how to display
the image in the panel.

Example 16.3 Displaying Images in an Applet

Problem

Write a program that displays an image in an applet. The image is stored in a
file located in the same directory as the applet. The user enters the filename in a
text field and displays the image on a panel. Figure 16.2 shows a sample run of
the program.

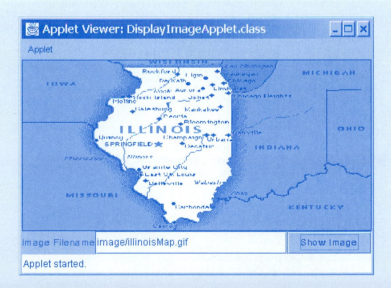

Figure 16.2   *Given the image filename, the applet displays an image.*

continues

Example 16.3 continued

Solution

The following code gives the solution to the problem.

```
1    // DisplayImageApplet.java: Display an image on a panel in the applet
2    import java.awt.*;
3    import java.awt.event.*;
4    import javax.swing.*;
5    import javax.swing.border.LineBorder;
6
7    public class DisplayImageApplet extends JApplet
8      implements ActionListener {
9      // The panel for displaying the image  private
10     private ImagePanel imagePanel = new ImagePanel();
11
12     // The text field for entering the name of the image file
13     private JTextField jtfFilename = new JTextField(20);
14
15     // The button for displaying the image
16     private JButton jbtShow = new JButton("Show Image");
17
18     /** Initialize the applet */
19     public void init() {
20       // Panel p1 to hold a text field and a button
21       JPanel p1 = new JPanel();
22       p1.setLayout(new BorderLayout());
23       p1.add(new JLabel("Image Filename"), BorderLayout.WEST);
24       p1.add(jtfFilename, BorderLayout.CENTER);
25       p1.add(jbtShow, BorderLayout.EAST);
26
27       // Place an ImagePanel object and p1 in the applet
28       getContentPane().add(imagePanel, BorderLayout.CENTER);
29       getContentPane().add(p1, BorderLayout.SOUTH);
30
31       // Set line border on the image panel
32       imagePanel.setBorder(new LineBorder(Color.black, 1));
33
34       // Register listener
35       jbtShow.addActionListener(this);
36       jtfFilename.addActionListener(this);
37     }
38
39     /** Handle the ActionEvent */
40     public void actionPerformed(ActionEvent e) {
41       if ((e.getSource() instanceof JButton) ||
42         (e.getSource() instanceof JTextField))
43         displayImage();
44     }
45
46     /** Display image on the panel */
47     private void displayImage() {
48       // Retrieve image
49       Image image = getImage(getCodeBase(),
50         jtfFilename.getText().trim());
51
52       // Show image in the panel
53       imagePanel.showImage(image);
54     }
55   }
56
```

```
57  // Define the panel for showing an image
58  class ImagePanel extends JPanel {
59    // Image instance
60    private Image image = null;
61
62    /** Default constructor */
63    public ImagePanel() {
64    }
65
66    /** Set image and show it */
67    public void showImage(Image image) {
68      this.image = image;
69      repaint();
70    }
71
72    /** Draw image on the panel */
73    public void paintComponent(Graphics g) {
74      super.paintComponent(g);
75
76      if (image != null)
77        g.drawImage(image, 0, 0, getWidth(), getHeight(), this);
78    }
79  }
```

Review

The image is loaded by using the `getImage` method (Lines 49–50) from the file in the same directory as the applet. The `showImage` method defined in `ImagePanel` sets the image so that it can be drawn in the `paintComponent` method.

The statement `g.drawImage(image, 0, 0, getWidth(), getHeight(), this)` (Line 77) displays the image in the `Graphics` context g on the `ImagePanel` object. To display the image, you enter the filename in the text field, then press the Enter key or click the Show Image button. The filename you enter must be located in the same directory as the applet or in one of its subdirectories.

16.5   Loading Image and Audio Files in Java Applications

The `getImage` method used in Example 16.3 is defined in the `Applet` class, and thus is only available with the applet. The audio files in Example 16.1 "Incorporating Sound in Applets," are loaded through the URL specified by the `getCodeBase()` method, and thus this method of retrieving audio files cannot be used with Java applications.

To write code that can be used to load resource files for both applications and applets, use the `java.lang.Class` class. Whenever Java VM loads a class or an interface, it creates an instance of a special class named `Class`. The `Class` class provides access to useful information about the class, such as the data fields and methods. It also contains the `getResource(filename)` method, which can be used to obtain the

URL of a given file name in the same directory with the class or in its subdirectory. Thus, you can use the following code to get the URL of an image or audio file:

```
Class class = this.getClass();
URL url = class.getResource(filename);
```

To get an audio clip, use a new static method `newAudioClip()` in the `java.applet.Applet` class in Java 2:

```
AudioClip audioClip = Applet.newAudioClip(url);
```

You might attempt to use the `getImage` method to obtain an `Image` object like this:

```
Image image = getImage(url);
```

This method would work fine for Java applets, but not for Java applications. To get an `Image` object from the URL in a Java application, construct an `ImageIcon` object using the new `ImageIcon(url)`, and obtain an image using the `getImage()` method in the `ImageIcon` class, as follows:

```
// Obtain an image icon
ImageIcon imageIcon = new ImageIcon(url);

// Get the image from the image icon
Image image = imageIcon.getImage();
```

Example 16.4 Using Image and Audio in Applications and in Applets

Problem

Write a program that uses the `Class` class to obtain the URL of the image and audio resource, which are located in the program's class directory. The program enables you to select a country from a combo box and then displays the country's flag. You can play the selected country's national anthem by clicking the Play Anthem button, as shown in Figure 16.3.

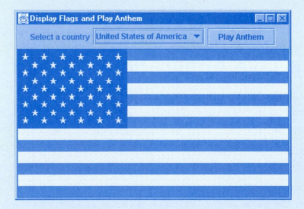

Figure 16.3   *The program displays the flag of the selected country and plays its national anthem.*

Solution

The following code gives the solution to the problem.

```
1    // ResourceLocatorDemo.java: Demonstrate using resource locator to
2    // load image files and audio files to applets and applications
3    import java.awt.*;
4    import java.awt.image.*;
5    import java.awt.event.*;
6    import javax.swing.*;
7    import javax.swing.border.*;
8    import java.net.URL;
9    import java.applet.*;
10
11   public class ResourceLocatorDemo extends JApplet
12     implements ActionListener, ItemListener {
13     // Image panel for displaying an image
14     private ImagePanel imagePanel = new ImagePanel();
15
16     // Combo box for selecting a country
17     private JComboBox jcboCountry = new JComboBox();
18
19     // Button to play an audio
20     private JButton jbtPlayAnthem = new JButton("Play Anthem");
21
22     // Selected country
23     private String country = "United States of America";
24
25     /** Initialize the applet */
26     public void init() {
27       // Panel p to hold a label combo box and a button for play audio
28       JPanel p = new JPanel();
29       p.add(new JLabel("Select a country"));
30       p.add(jcboCountry);
31       p.add(jbtPlayAnthem);
32
33       // Initialize the combo box
34       jcboCountry.addItem("United States of America");
35       jcboCountry.addItem("United Kingdom");
36       jcboCountry.addItem("Denmark");
37       jcboCountry.addItem("Norway");
38       jcboCountry.addItem("China");
39       jcboCountry.addItem("India");
40       jcboCountry.addItem("Germany");
41
42       // By default, the US flag is displayed
43       imagePanel.showImage(createImage("us.gif"));
44       imagePanel.setPreferredSize(new Dimension(300, 300));
45
46       // Place p and an image panel in the applet
47       getContentPane().add(p, BorderLayout.NORTH);
48       getContentPane().add(imagePanel, BorderLayout.CENTER);
49       imagePanel.setBorder(new LineBorder(Color.black, 1));
50
51       // Register listener
52       jbtPlayAnthem.addActionListener(this);
53       jcboCountry.addItemListener(this);
54     }
55
```

continues

Example 16.4 continued

```
 56      /** Handle ActionEvent */
 57      public void actionPerformed(ActionEvent e) {
 58        // Get the file name
 59        String filename = null;
 60
 61        // The .mid audio files are stored in the anthem folder
 62        if (country.equals("United States of America"))
 63          filename = "us.mid";
 64        else if (country.equals("United Kingdom"))
 65          filename = "uk.mid";
 66        else if (country.equals("Denmark"))
 67          filename = "denmark.mid";
 68        else if (country.equals("Norway"))
 69          filename = "norway.mid";
 70        else if (country.equals("China"))
 71          filename = "china.mid";
 72        else if (country.equals("India"))
 73          filename = "india.mid";
 74        else if (country.equals("Germany"))
 75          filename = "germany.mid";
 76
 77        // Create an audio clip and play it
 78        createAudioClip(filename).play();
 79      }
 80
 81      /** Handle ItemEvent */
 82      public void itemStateChanged(ItemEvent e) {
 83        // Get selected country
 84        country = (String)jcboCountry.getSelectedItem();
 85
 86        // Get the file name
 87        String filename = null;
 88
 89        // The .gif files are stored in the image folder
 90        if (country.equals("United States of America"))
 91          filename = "us.gif";
 92        else if (country.equals("United Kingdom"))
 93          filename = "uk.gif";
 94        else if (country.equals("Denmark"))
 95          filename = "denmark.gif";
 96        else if (country.equals("Norway"))
 97          filename = "norway.gif";
 98        else if (country.equals("China"))
 99          filename = "china.gif";
100        else if (country.equals("India"))
101          filename = "india.gif";
102        else if (country.equals("Germany"))
103          filename = "germany.gif";
104
105        // Load image from the file and show it on the panel
106        imagePanel.showImage(createImage(filename));
107      }
108
109      /** Create an audio from the specified file */
110      public AudioClip createAudioClip(String filename) {
111        // Get the URL for the file name
112        URL url = this.getClass().getResource("anthem/" + filename);
113
```

```
114            // Return the audio clip
115            return Applet.newAudioClip(url);
116        }
117
118        /** Create an image from the specified file */
119        public Image createImage(String filename) {
120            // Get the URL for the file name
121            URL url = this.getClass().getResource("image/" + filename);
122
123            // Obtain an image icon
124            ImageIcon imageIcon = new ImageIcon(url);
125
126            // Return the image
127            return imageIcon.getImage();
128        }
129
130        /** Main method */
131        public static void main(String[] args) {
132            // Create a frame
133            JFrame frame = new JFrame("Display Flags and Play Anthem");
134
135            // Create an instance of the applet
136            ResourceLocatorDemo applet = new ResourceLocatorDemo();
137
138            // Add the applet instance to the frame
139            frame.getContentPane().add(applet, BorderLayout.CENTER);
140
141            // Invoke init() and start()
142            applet.init();
143            applet.start();
144
145            // Display the frame
146            frame.pack();
147            frame.setVisible(true);
148        }
149    }
```

Review

The program can run as an applet or an application. Obtaining the URL using the Class class works not only for standalone applications, but also for Java applets.

The createAudioClip(filename) method (Lines 110–116) obtains the URL instance for the filename and creates an AudioClip for the URL using the newAudioClip static method, which is a new method introduced in Java 2 to support playing audio in applications.

The createImage(filename) method (Lines 119–128) obtains the URL instance for the filename, creates an image icon for the URL, and obtains an Image object, using the getImage method in the ImageIcon class.

The program is not efficient if the user repeatedly chooses the same country and plays the same anthem, because a new Image instance is created for every newly selected country, and a new AudioClip instance is created every time an audio is played. To improve efficiency, load the image and audio files once and store them in the memory using an array.

There is an annoying problem in the program. If you play a new anthem before the preceding anthem is finished, the two audio clips play concurrently. To fix it, stop the first audio clip before playing the new one. See Exercise 16.11.

16.6   Displaying a Sequence of Images

In the preceding section, you learned how to display a single image. Now you will learn how to display a sequence of images that simulates a movie. As in the clock example in the previous chapter, you can use the thread approach or the timer approach to control the animation. Since the timer approach makes programs shorter and simpler, this example uses a timer to trigger repainting of the viewing area with different images.

Example 16.5 Using Image Animation

Problem

Write a program that displays a sequence of images in order to create a movie. The images are files stored in the **image** directory that are named **L1.gif**, **L2.gif**, and so on, to **L52.gif**. When you run the program, you will see a phrase entitled "Learning Java" rotate, as shown in Figure 16.4.

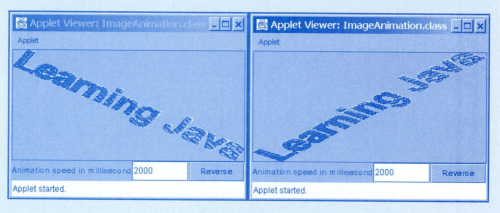

Figure 16.4   *The applet displays a sequence of images.*

Solution

The following code gives the solution to the problem.

```
1    // ImageAnimation.java: Display a sequence of images
2    import java.awt.*;
3    import java.awt.event.*;
4    import javax.swing.*;
5    import javax.swing.border.*;
6
7    public class ImageAnimation extends JApplet
8      implements ActionListener {
9      private Image imageToDisplay;
10     protected Image imageArray[]; // Hold images
11     protected int numOfImages = 52, // Total number of images
12                   currentImageIndex = 0, // Current image subscript
13                   sleepTime = 100; // Milliseconds to sleep
14     protected int direction = 1; // Image rotating direction
15
```

```
16        // Image display panel
17        protected PlayImage imagePanel = new PlayImage();
18
19        // Text field for receiving speed
20        protected JTextField jtfSpeed = new JTextField(5);
21
22        // Button for reversing direction
23        JButton jbtReverse = new JButton("Reverse");
24
25        /** Initialize the applet */
26        public void init() {
27          // Load the image, the image files are named
28          // L1 - L52 in image directory
29          imageArray = new Image[numOfImages];
30          for (int i = 0; i < imageArray.length; i++ ) {
31            imageArray[i] = getImage(getCodeBase(),
32              "image/L" + (i + 1) + ".gif" );
33          }
34
35          // Panel p to hold animation control
36          JPanel p = new JPanel();
37          p.setLayout(new BorderLayout());
38          p.add(new JLabel("Animation speed in millisecond"),
39            BorderLayout.WEST);
40          p.add(jtfSpeed, BorderLayout.CENTER);
41          p.add(jbtReverse, BorderLayout.EAST);
42
43          // Add the image panel and p to the applet
44          getContentPane().add(imagePanel, BorderLayout.CENTER);
45          getContentPane().add(p, BorderLayout.SOUTH);
46
47          // Register listener
48          jtfSpeed.addActionListener(this);
49          jbtReverse.addActionListener(this);
50        }
51
52        /** Handle ActionEvent */
53        public void actionPerformed(ActionEvent e) {
54          if (e.getSource() == jtfSpeed) {
55            sleepTime = Integer.parseInt(jtfSpeed.getText());
56            imagePanel.setSpeed(sleepTime);
57          }
58          else if (e.getSource() == jbtReverse) {
59            direction = -direction;
60          }
61        }
62
63        /** Override the start method in the Applet class */
64        public void start() {
65          imagePanel.start();
66        }
67
68        /** Override the stop method in the Applet class */
69        public void stop() {
70          imagePanel.stop();
71        }
72
73        protected class PlayImage extends JPanel
74          implements ActionListener {
75          protected Timer timer;
76
```

continues

Example 16.5 continued

```
77              /** Constructor */
78              public PlayImage() {
79                // Start with the first image
80                currentImageIndex = 0;
81
82                // Set line border on the panel
83                setBorder(new LineBorder(Color.red, 1));
84
85                // Create a timer with delay 1000 ms and listener Clock
86                timer = new Timer(1000, this);
87
88                // Start the timer
89                timer.start();
90              }
91
92              public void setSpeed(int sleepTime) {
93                timer.setDelay(sleepTime);
94              }
95
96              public void start() {
97                timer.start();
98              }
99
100             public void stop() {
101               timer.stop();
102             }
103
104             // Choose a new image to display
105             public void actionPerformed(ActionEvent e) {
106               imageToDisplay =
107                 imageArray[currentImageIndex % numOfImages];
108
109               // Make sure currentImageIndex is nonnegative
110               if (currentImageIndex == 0) currentImageIndex = numOfImages;
111               currentImageIndex = currentImageIndex + direction;
112               repaint();
113             }
114
115             /** Display an image */
116             public void paintComponent(Graphics g) {
117               super.paintComponent(g);
118
119               if (imageToDisplay != null) {
120                 g.drawImage(imageToDisplay, 0, 0, getSize().width,
121                   getSize().height, this);
122               }
123             }
124           }
125         }
```

Review

Fifty-two image files are located in the **image** directory, which is a subdirectory of the code base directory. The images in these files are loaded to `imageArray` (Lines 30–33) and then painted continuously on the applet at a fixed rate using a timer.

The image is drawn to occupy the entire applet viewing area in a rectangle. It is scaled to fill in the area.

The `timer` is created and started in the `PlayImage` class's constructor (Lines 86–89). `PlayImage` is an inner class in `ImageAnimation`. `PlayImage` controls the display of the images. An instance `imagePanel` of `PlayImage` is created in Line 17 and placed into the applet in Line 44.

You can adjust `sleepTime` to control animation speed by entering a value in milliseconds and pressing the Enter key for the change to take place.

The display sequence can be reversed by clicking the Reverse button.

You can add a simple function to suspend a `timer` when the mouse is pressed. You can resume a suspended `timer` when the mouse is released (see Exercise 16.4).

NOTE

The `JComponent` class has a property named `doubleBuffered`. By default, this property is set to `true`. Double buffering is a technique for reducing animation flickering. It creates a graphics context off-screen and does all the drawings in the off-screen context. When the drawing is complete, it displays the whole context on the real screen. Thus, there is no flickering within an image because all the drawings are displayed at the same time. To see the effect of double buffering, set the `doubleBuffered` property to `false`. You will be stunned by the difference.

16.7   Using MediaTracker

One problem you may face if you run the preceding example is that images are only partially displayed while being loaded. This occurs because the image has not yet been loaded completely. The problem is particularly annoying when you are downloading an image over a slow modem.

To resolve the problem, Java provides the `MediaTracker` class to track the status of a number of media objects. Media objects include audio clips as well as images, though currently only images are supported.

You can use `MediaTracker` to determine whether an image has been completely loaded. To use it, you must first create an instance of `MediaTracker` for a specific graphics component. The following is an example of creating a `MediaTracker`:

```
MediaTracker imageTracker = new MediaTracker(this);
```

To enable `imageTracker` (in order to determine whether the image has been loaded), use the `addImage` method to register the image with `imageTracker`. The following statement registers `anImage` of the `Image` type with `imageTracker`:

```
imageTracker.addImage(anImage, id);
```

The second argument, `id`, is an integer ID that controls the priority order in which the images are fetched. Images with a lower ID number are loaded in preference to those with a higher ID number. The ID can be used to query `imageTracker` about the status of the registered image. To query, use the `checkID` method. For example, the following method returns `true` if the image with the `id` is completely loaded:

```
checkID(id)
```

Otherwise, it returns `false`.

You can use the `waitForID(id)` method to force the program to wait until the image registered with the `id` is completely loaded, or you can use the `waitForAll()` method to wait for all of the registered images to be loaded completely. The methods shown below block the program until the image is completely loaded.

```
waitForID(int id) throws InterruptedException
waitForAll() throws InterruptedException
```

TIP

To track multiple images as a group, register them with a media tracker using the same ID.

Example 16.6 Using `MediaTracker`

Problem

This example uses `MediaTracker` to improve upon the preceding example. With `MediaTracker`, the user of the program can ensure that all of the images are fully loaded before they are displayed.

Solution

The following code gives the solution to the problem.

```
1    // ImageAnimationUsingMediaTracker.java: Monitor loading images
2    // using MediaTracker
3    import java.awt.*;
4    import javax.swing.*;
5
6    public class ImageAnimationUsingMediaTracker
7      extends ImageAnimation {
8      private MediaTracker imageTracker = new MediaTracker(this);
9
10     /** Initialize the applet */
11     public void init() {
12       // Load the image, the image files are named
13       // L1 - L52 in image directory
14       imageArray = new Image[numOfImages];
15       for (int i = 0; i < imageArray.length; i++) {
16         imageArray[i] = getImage(getCodeBase(),
17           "image/L" + (i + 1) + ".gif" );
18
```

```
19              // Register images with the imageTracker
20              imageTracker.addImage(imageArray[i], i);
21          }
22
23          // Wait for all the images to be completely loaded
24          try {
25              imageTracker.waitForAll();
26          }
27          catch (InterruptedException ex) {
28            System.out.println(ex);
29          }
30
31          // Dispose of imageTracker since it is no longer needed
32          imageTracker = null;
33
34          // Panel p to hold animation control
35          JPanel p = new JPanel();
36          p.setLayout(new BorderLayout());
37          p.add(new JLabel("Animation speed in millisecond"),
38            BorderLayout.WEST);
39          p.add(jtfSpeed, BorderLayout.CENTER);
40          p.add(jbtReverse, BorderLayout.EAST);
41
42          // Add the image panel and p to the applet
43          getContentPane().add(new PlayImage(), BorderLayout.CENTER);
44          getContentPane().add(p, BorderLayout.SOUTH);
45
46          // Register listener
47          jtfSpeed.addActionListener(this);
48          jbtReverse.addActionListener(this);
49        }
50      }
```

Review

The `ImageAnimationUsingMediaTracker` class extends `ImageAnimation`, which was created in Example 16.5. The `ImageAnimationUsingMediaTracker` uses `MediaTracker` to monitor loading images.

The program creates an instance of `MediaTracker`, `imageTracker`, and registers images with `imageTracker` in order to track image loading (Line 20). The program uses `imageTracker` to ensure that all the images are completely loaded before they are displayed.

The `waitForAll()` method (Line 25) forces the program to wait for all the images to be loaded before displaying any of them. Because the program needs to load fifty-two images, using `waitForAll()` results in a long delay before images are displayed. You should display something while the image is being loaded in order to keep the user attentive and/or informed. A simple approach is to use the `showStatus()` method in the `Applet` class to display some information on the Web browser's status bar. Here is a possibility:

```
showStatus("Please wait while loading images");
```

Put this statement before the `try-catch` block for `waitForAll()` in the program.

continues

Example 16.6 continued

The `imageTracker` object is no longer needed after the images are loaded. The statement `imageTracker = null` (Line 32) notifies the garbage collector of the Java runtime system to reclaim the memory space previously occupied by the `imageTracker` object.

You can rewrite this example to enable it to run as an application (see Exercise 16.4).

Chapter Summary

In this chapter, you learned how to play audio and display images in Java multimedia programming. You learned how to use the `Class` class to find the URL of the class and to load image and audio files through the URL. You also learned to use the media tracking mechanism to track loading images.

Audio and images files are accessible through a URL. The `getDocumentBase()` method returns the URL of the HTML file that contains the applet. The `getCodeBase()` method returns the URL of the applet. The `Class` class can be used to obtain the URL of an image or audio file for Java applications as well as Java applets. You can obtain an audio clip using `Applet.newAudioClip(url)`. You can construct an image icon using `new ImageIcon(url)`, and obtain an image using `getImage()`.

The `MediaTracker` class is used to determine whether one image or all of the images are completely loaded. The `MediaTracker` obtains this information in order to ensure that the images will be fully displayed.

Review Questions

16.1 What types of audio files are used in Java?

16.2 How do you get an audio file? How do you play, repeatedly play, and stop an audio clip?

16.3 The `getAudioClip` method is defined in the `Applet` class. If you want to use audio in Java applications, what options do you have?

16.4 What is the difference between `getDocumentBase` and `getCodeBase`?

16.5 What is the difference between the `getImage` method in the `Applet` class and the `getImage` method in the `ImageIcon` class?

16.6 How do you get the URL of an image or audio file for both Java applications and Java applets?

16.7 Describe the `drawImage` method in the `Graphics` class.

16.8 Can you create image icons and use the `setIcon` method to set an icon in a `JLabel` instance in Java applets?

16.9 Explain the differences between displaying images in a JLabel instance and in a JPanel instance.

16.10 How do you get an audio clip in Java applications?

16.11 Why do you use MediaTracker? How do you add images to a media tracker? How do you know that an image or all of the images are completely loaded? Can you assign images the same ID in order to register them with a media tracker?

Programming Exercises

16.1 Write an applet that meets the following requirements:

■ Get an audio file from the URL of the HTML base code.

■ Place three buttons labeled Play, Loop, and Stop, as shown in Figure 16.5.

■ If you click the Play button, the audio file is played once. If you click the Loop button, the audio file keeps playing repeatedly. If you click the Stop button, the playing stops.

■ The applet can run as an application.

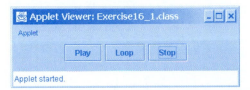

Figure 16.5 *Click Play to play an audio clip once, click Loop to play an audio repeatedly, and click Stop to terminate playing.*

16.2 Sometimes, when you repaint the entire viewing area of a panel, only a tiny portion of the viewing area is changed. You can improve the performance by repainting the affected area only, but do not invoke super.paintComponent(g) when repainting the panel, because this will cause the entire viewing area to be cleared. Use this approach to write an applet to display the temperatures of each hour during the last twenty-four hours in a histogram. Suppose that the temperatures between 50 and 90 degrees Fahrenheit are obtained randomly and are updated every hour. The temperature of the current hour needs to be redisplayed, while the others remain unchanged. Use a unique color to highlight the temperature for the current hour (see Figure 16.6).

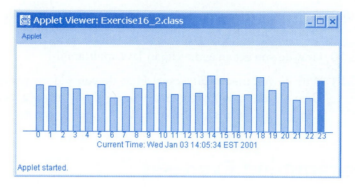

Figure 16.6   *The histogram displays the average temperature of every hour in the last twenty-four hours.*

16.3   Modify the elevator program in Exercise 15.9 of Chapter 15, "Multithreading," to add sound to the program. When the elevator stops on a floor, announce which floor it is on.

16.4   Rewrite Example 16.6, "Using MediaTracker," to add the following new functions:

■   The animation is suspended when the mouse is pressed and resumed when the mouse is released. To implement this feature, add the code in the `PlayImage` inner class of the `ImageAnimation` class to handle the mouse event for `mousePressed` and `mouseReleased` actions.

■   Sound is incorporated into the applet so that it is played while images are displayed.

■   Enable the applet to run standalone.

16.5   Write an applet that will display a digital clock with a large display panel that shows hour, minute, and second. This clock should allow the user to set an alarm. Figure 16.7 shows an example of such a clock. To turn on the alarm, check the Alarm check box. To specify the alarm time, click the "Set alarm" button to display a new frame, as shown in Figure 16.8. You can set the alarm time in the frame. Enable the applet to run standalone.

Figure 16.7   *The program displays current hour, minute, and second, and enables you to set an alarm.*

Figure 16.8   *You can set the alarm time by specifying hour, minute, and second.*

16.6   Create animation using the applet (see Figure 16.9) to meet the following requirements:

■   Allow the user to specify the animation speed. The user can enter the speed in a text field.

■   Get the number of frames and the image filename prefix from the user. For example, if the user enters **n** for the number of frames and **L** for the image prefix, then the files are **L1**, **L2**, and so on, to **Ln**. Assume that the images are stored in the **image** directory, a subdirectory of the applet's directory.

■   Allow the user to specify an audio filename. The audio file is stored in the same directory as the applet. The sound is played while the animation runs.

■   Enable the applet to run standalone.

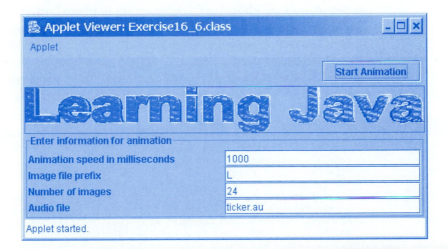

Figure 16.9   *This applet lets the user select image files, audio file, and animation speed.*

16.7   Write an applet that will display a sequence of images from a single image file in different sizes. Initially, the viewing area for this image has a width of 300 and a height of 300. Your program should continuously shrink the viewing area by 1 in width and 1 in height until it reaches a width of 50 and a height of 50. At that point, the viewing area should continuously enlarge by 1 in width and 1 in height until it reaches a width of 300 and a height of 300. The viewing area should shrink and enlarge (alternately) to create animation for the single image. Enable the applet to run standalone.

16.8 Write an applet that introduces national flags, one after the other, by presenting each one's photo, name, and description (see Figure 16.10) along with audio that reads the description.

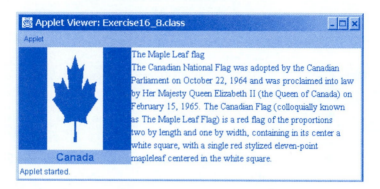

Figure 16.10 *This applet shows each country's flag, name, and description, one after another, and reads the description that is currently shown.*

Suppose your applet displays the flags of eight countries. Assume that the audio files, named **a0.au**, **a1.au**, and so on, up to **a7.au**, are stored in a subdirectory named **audio** in the applet's directory, and the photo image files, named **photo0.gif**, **photo1.gif**, and so on, up to **photo7.gif**, are stored in a subdirectory named **photo** in the applet's directory. The length of each audio is less than 10 seconds. Assume that the name and description of each country's flag are passed from the HTML using the parameter `name0`, `name1`, . . . , `name7`, and `description0`, `description1`, . . . , and `description7`. Pass the number of the countries as an HTML parameter using `numOfCountries`. Here is an example:

```
<param name="numOfCountries" value=8>
<param name="name0" value="Canada">
<param name="description0" value=
"The Maple Leaf flag
The Canadian National Flag was adopted by the Canadian
Parliament on October 22, 1964 and was proclaimed into law
by Her Majesty Queen Elizabeth II (the Queen of Canada) on
February 15, 1965. The Canadian Flag (colloquially known
as The Maple Leaf Flag) is a red flag of the proportions
two by length and one by width, containing in its center a
white square, with a single red stylized eleven-point
mapleleaf centered in the white square.">
```

Hint

Use the `DescriptionPanel` class to display the image, name, and the text. The `DescriptionPanel` class was introduced in Example 11.4, "Using Text Area,"

16.9 Rewrite Example 16.4, "Using Image and Audio in Applications and in Applets." Use the resource bundle to retrieve image and audio files.

HINT

When a new country is selected, set an appropriate locale for it. Have your program look for the flag and audio file from the resource file for the locale.

16.10 Rewrite Exercise 16.8 to display an image to fit in a panel of fixed size. In Exercise 16.8, you used the `DescriptionPanel` class to display an image icon in a label. The image icon is not scalable. If the label dimension is smaller than the image icon, you will see only part of the image. In this exercise, use the `ImagePanel` class, introduced in Example 16.3, "Displaying Images in an Applet," to display an image in a panel. You can modify the `Description-Panel` class to use `ImagePanel` to replace the label for displaying images.

16.11 In Example 16.4, if you play a new audio before the preceding audio played to its completion, the new audio overlaps the preceding audio. Rewrite Example 16.4 to avoid this.

HINT

Use the `stop` method to terminate the audio clip.

16.12 In Example 16.2, an object of `AnnounceTime` is created every minute to announce the current time. Rewrite the program by creating one such object in advance and passing hour audio, minute audio, and am/pm audio to the object when it is time to announce the current time.

CHAPTER 17

INPUT AND OUTPUT

Objectives

- ⊚ To understand input and output streams, and learn how to create them.

- ⊚ To discover the uses of byte and character streams.

- ⊚ To become familiar with the `File` class.

- ⊚ To know how to read from or write to external files using file streams.

- ⊚ To employ data streams for cross-platform data format compatibility.

- ⊚ To use print streams to output data of primitive types in text format.

- ⊚ To learn how to use `JFileChooser` to display open and save file dialog boxes.

- ⊚ To use text input and output on the console.

- ⊚ To store and restore objects using object streams.

- ⊚ To use `RandomAccessFile` for both read and write.

- ⊚ To parse text files using `StreamTokenizer`. (Optional)

17.1   Introduction

Often you need to save output in a file that can be read later in the program. In this chapter, you will learn about many forms of input and output as well as how they work together.

In Java, all I/O is handled in streams. A *stream* is an abstraction of the continuous one-way flow of data. Imagine a swimming pool with pipes that connect it to another pool. Let's consider the water in the first pool as the data, and the water in the second pool as your program. The flow of water through the pipes is called a *stream*. If you want input, just open the valve that lets water out of the data pool and into the program pool. If you want output, just open the valve that lets water out of the program pool and into the data pool.

It's a very simple concept, and a very efficient one. Since Java streams can be applied to any source of data, it is as easy for a programmer to input from a keyboard or output to a console as it is to input from a file or output to a file. Figure 17.1 shows the input and output streams between a program and an external file. Java streams are used liberally. There can even be input and output streams between two programs.

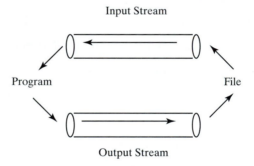

Input Stream

Program   File

Output Stream

Figure 17.1   *The program receives data through the input stream and sends data through the output stream.*

In general, all streams except random-access file streams flow in only one direction; therefore, if you want to input and output, you need two separate stream objects. In Java, streams can be *layered*; that is, connected to one another in pipeline fashion. The output of one stream may become the input of another stream.

This layering capability makes it possible to filter data along the pipeline of streams so that you can get data in the desired format. For instance, suppose you want to get integers from an external file. Use a file input stream to get raw data in binary format, then use a data input stream to extract integers from the output of the file input stream.

Streams are objects. Stream objects have methods that read and write data or do other useful things, such as flushing the stream, closing the stream, and counting the number of bytes in the stream.

17.2   Stream Classes

Java offers stream classes for processing all kinds of data. Figures 17.2 and 17.3 show the hierarchical relationships of these classes.

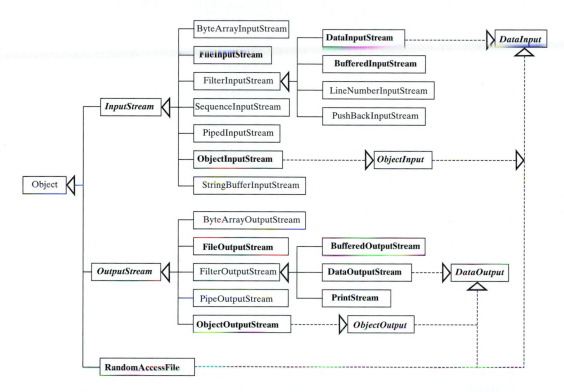

Figure 17.2   `InputStream`, `OutputStream`, `RandomAccessFile`, *and their subclasses deal with streams of bytes.*

NOTE

As shown in Figures 17.2 and 17.3, there are many stream classes in Java. Each stream has its intended application. This chapter introduces the most frequently used streams. These stream classes appear in bold in the figures.

Stream classes can be categorized either as *byte streams* or as *character streams*. The `InputStream/OutputStream` class is the root of all byte stream classes, and the `Reader/Writer` class is the root of all character stream classes.

The `RandomAccessFile` class extends `Object` and implements the `DataInput` and `DataOutput` interfaces. It can be used to open a file that allows both reading and writing. The `StreamTokenizer` class that extends `Object` can be used for parsing text files.

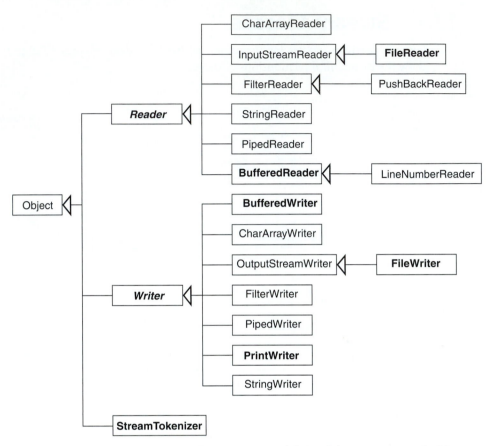

Figure 17.3   Reader, Writer, StreamTokenizer, *and their subclasses are concerned with streams of characters.*

17.2.1   *InputStream and Reader*

The abstract InputStream and Reader classes, extending Object, are the base classes for all of the input streams of bytes and characters, respectively. These classes and their subclasses are very similar, except that InputStream uses bytes for its fundamental unit of information, and Reader uses characters. InputStream and Reader have many common methods with identical signatures. These methods have similar functionality, but InputStream is designed to read bytes, and Reader is designed to read characters.

The following methods, defined in InputStream, are often useful:

- public abstract int read() throws IOException

  Reads the next byte and returns its value. The value of the byte is returned as an int in the range from 0 to 255. At the end of the stream, it returns -1. This method blocks the program from executing until input data are available, the end of the stream is detected, or an exception is thrown. A concrete subclass of InputStream must provide an implementation of this method.

- `public int read(byte[] b) throws IOException`

  Reads up to `b.length` bytes into array `b`, returns `b.length` if the number of available bytes is more than or equal to `b.length`, returns the number of bytes read if the number of available bytes is less than `b.length`, and returns -1 at the end of the stream. This method reads all available bytes to `b` if `b` is large enough.

- `public void close() throws IOException`

  Closes the input stream.

- `public void int available() throws IOException`

  Returns the number of bytes that can be read from the input stream without blocking.

- `public long skip(long n) throws IOException`

  Skips over and discards `n` bytes of data from the input stream. The actual number of bytes skipped is returned.

NOTE

The `read()` method reads a byte from the stream. If no data are available, it blocks the thread from executing the next statement. The thread that invokes the `read()` method is suspended until the data become available.

The `Reader` class contains all of the methods listed previously except `available()`. These methods have the same functionality in `Reader` as in `InputStream`, but they are subject to character stream interpretation. For example, `read()` returns an integer in the range from 0 to 16,383, which represents a Unicode character.

17.2.2   *OutputStream and Writer*

Like `InputStream` and `Reader`, `OutputStream` and `Writer` are counterparts. They are the base classes for all the output streams of bytes and characters, respectively. The following instance methods are in both `OutputStream` and `Writer`:

- `public abstract void write(int b) throws IOException`

  Writes a byte (for `OutputStream`) or a character (for `Writer`).

- `public void write(byte[] b) throws IOException`

  Writes all the bytes in array `b` to the output stream (for `OutputStream`) or the characters in the array of characters (for `Writer`).

- `public void close() throws IOException`

  Closes the output stream.

- `public void flush() throws IOException`

  Flushes the output stream (i.e., sends any buffered data in the stream to their destination).

17.3   The *File* Class

Each file is placed in a directory in the file system. The complete file name consists of the directory path and the file name. For example, c:\book\Welcome.java is the complete file name for the file Welcome.java on the Windows operating system. Here c:\book is referred to as the *directory path* for the file. The directory path and complete file name are machine-dependent. On Unix, the complete file name may be /home/liang/book/Welcome.java, where /home/liang/book is the directory path for the file Welcome.java.

The File class is intended to provide an abstraction that deals with most of the machine-dependent complexities of files and path names in a machine-independent fashion. The filename is a string. The File class is a wrapper class for the file name and its directory path.

You can create a File object using the following constructors:

■   `public File(String pathname)`

Creates a File object for the specified pathname. The pathname may be a directory or a file. For example, new File("c:\\book") creates a File object for the directory c:\book, and new File("c:\\book\\test.dat") creates a File object for the file c:\book\test.dat, both on Windows. You can use the File class's isDirectory() method to check whether the object represents a directory and the isFile() method to check whether the object represents a file name.

Caution

The directory separator for Windows is a backslash (\). The backslash is a special character and should be written as \\ (See Table 2.3 on Page 41).

■   `public File(String parent, String child)`

Creates a File object for the child under the directory parent. child may be a filename or a subdirectory.

■   `public File(File parent, String child)`

Creates a File object for the child under the directory parent. parent is a File object. In the preceding constructor, the parent is a string.

The File class contains the following methods for obtaining file properties and for deleting and renaming files:

■   `public boolean exists()`

Returns true if the file or the directory represented by the File object exists.

■ public boolean canRead()

Returns true if the file represented by the File object exists and can be read.

■ public boolean canWrite()

Returns true if the file represented by the File object exists and can be written.

■ public boolean isDirectory()

Returns true if the File object represents a directory.

■ public boolean isFile()

Returns true if the File object represents a file.

■ public boolean isAbsolute()

Returns true if the File object is created using an absolute path name. An absolute path name is system-dependent. For example, if you create a File object using new File("c:\\book\\test.dat"), it is an absolute path name. If you create a File object using new File("test.dat"), it refers to the file in the current class path directory. This path is not absolute because no system-specific path separators are used.

■ public boolean isHidden()

Returns true if the file represented in the File object is hidden. The exact definition of *hidden* is system-dependent. On Windows, you can mark a file hidden in the File Properties dialog box. On Unix systems, a file is hidden if its name begins with a period character '.'.

■ public String getAbsolutePath()

Returns the complete absolute file or directory name represented by the File object.

■ public String getCanonicalPath() throws IOException

Returns the same as getAbsolutePath() except that it removes redundant names, such as "." and "..", from the pathname, resolves symbolic links (on Unix platforms), and converts drive letters to standard uppercase (on Win32 platforms).

■ public String getName()

Returns the last name of the complete directory and file name represented by the File object. For example, new File("c:\\book\\test.dat").getName() returns test.dat.

■ public String getPath()

Returns the complete directory and file name represented by the File object. For example, new File("c:\\book\\test.dat").getName() returns c:\book\test.dat.

■ `public String getParent()`

Returns the complete parent directory of the current directory or the file represented by the `File` object. For example, `new File("c:\\book\\ test.dat").getParent()` returns c:\book.

■ `public boolean delete()`

Deletes this file. The methods returns `true` if deletion succeeds.

■ `public boolean renameTo(File dest)`

Renames this file. The methods returns `true` if the operation succeeds.

The `File` class has four constants: `pathSeparator`, `pathSeparatorChar`, `separator`, and `separatorChar`. These constants are platform-dependent path separators and name separators. `separatorChar` is `'\'` on Windows and `'/'` on Unix. `separatorChar` is a char and `separator` is a string representation of `separatorChar`. Likewise, `pathSeparator` is a string representation for `pathSeparatorChar`. `pathSeparator` is `';'` on Windows and `':'` on Unix.

■ **NOTE**

`pathSeparator`, `pathSeparatorChar`, `separator`, and `separatorChar` are constants, but they are named as variables with lowercase for the first word and uppercase for the first letters of subsequent words. Thus these names violate the Java naming convention.

Do not use the absolute directory and file name literals in your program. If you use a literal such as `"c:\\book\\test.dat"`, it will work on Windows, but not on other platforms. To enable the program to run correctly on different platforms, use the following string to replace `"c:\\book\\test.dat"`:

```
new File(".").getCanonicalPath() + "book" + File.separator +
"test.dat";
```

Here `"."` denotes the current directory. If you run the Java program from the command line, the current directory is where the java command is issued. If you run the program from an IDE, the current directory is dependent on the IDE settings.

Example 17.1 Using the `File` Class

Problem

Write a program that demonstrates how to create files in a platform-independent way and use the methods in the `File` class to obtain their properties. Figure 17.4 shows a sample run of the program on Windows, and Figure 17.5 a sample run on Unix.

```
Command Prompt                                          _ □ ×
C:\book>java TestFileClass
Does it exist? true
Can it be read? true
Can it be written? true
Is it a directory? false
Is it a file? true
Is it absolute? false
Is it hidden? false
What is its absolute path? C:\book\.\image\us.gif
What is its canonical path? C:\book\image\us.gif
What is its name? us.gif
What is its path? .\image\us.gif
When was it last modified? Sat May 08 14:00:34 EDT 1999
What is the path separator? ;
What is the name separator? \

C:\book>
```

Figure 17.4   *The program creates a* File *object and displays file properties on Windows.*

```
Command Prompt - telnet panda                          _ □ ×
$ pwd
/home/liang/book
$ java TestFileClass
Does it exist? true
Can it be read? true
Can it be written? true
Is it a directory? false
Is it a file? true
Is it absolute? false
Is it hidden? false
What is its absolute path? /home/liang/book/./image/us.gif
What is its canonical path? /home/liang/book/image/us.gif
What is its name? us.gif
What is its path? ./image/us.gif
When was it last modified? Wed Jan 23 11:00:14 EST 2002
What is the path separator? :
What is the name separator? /
$
```

Figure 17.5   *The program creates a* File *object and displays file properties on Unix.*

continues

Example 17.1 continued

Solution

The following code gives the solution to the problem.

```
1   // TestFileClass.java: Demonstrate the File class
2   import java.io.*;
3   import java.util.*;
4
5   public class TestFileClass {
6     public static void main(String[] args) {
7       // Create a File object
8       File file = new File(".", "image" + File.separator + "us.gif");
9       System.out.println("Does it exist? " + file.exists());
10      System.out.println("Can it be read? " + file.canRead());
11      System.out.println("Can it be written? " + file.canRead());
12      System.out.println("Is it a directory? " + file.isDirectory());
13      System.out.println("Is it a file? " + file.isFile());
14      System.out.println("Is it absolute? " + file.isAbsolute());
15      System.out.println("Is it hidden? " + file.isHidden());
16      System.out.println("What is its absolute path? " +
17        file.getAbsolutePath());
18
19      try {
20        System.out.println("What is its canonical path? " +
21          file.getCanonicalPath());
22      }
23      catch (IOException ex) { }
24
25      System.out.println("What is its name? " + file.getName());
26      System.out.println("What is its path? " + file.getPath());
27      System.out.println("When was it last modified? " +
28        new Date(file.lastModified()));
29
30      System.out.println("What is the path separator? " +
31        File.pathSeparatorChar);
32      System.out.println("What is the name separator? " +
33        File.separatorChar);
34    }
35  }
```

Review

The program creates a File object for the file us.gif. This file is stored under the \book\image directory. The statement in Line 8 creates the object in a platform-independent fashion without using the platform-specific name separator and drive letter.

The getCanonicalPath() method can throw an IOException, so it is put in a try-catch block in Lines 19–23.

The lastModified() method returns the date and time when the file was last modified , measured in milliseconds since the epoch (00:00:00 GMT, January 1, 1970). The Date class is used to display it in a readable format in Lines 27–28.

TIP

To develop platform-independent applications, it is imperative not to use absolute directory and file names.

17.4   Processing External Files

The `File` class represents a file, but it does not provide operations for data I/O. You must use file streams to read from or write to a disk file. `FileInputStream` or `FileOutputStream` is used for byte streams, and `FileReader` or `FileWriter` for character streams. To create a file stream, use the following constructors:

```
public FileInputStream(String filenameString)
public FileInputStream(File file)
public FileOutputStream(String filenameString)
public FileOutputStream(File file)
public FileReader(String filenameString)
public FileReader(File file)
public FileWriter(String filenameString)
public FileWriter(File file)
```

The following statements create `infile` and `outfile` streams for the input file in.dat and the output file out.dat, respectively:

```
FileInputStream infile = new FileInputStream("in.dat");
FileOutputStream outfile = new FileOutputStream("out.dat");
```

The abstract method `read(byte b)` in `InputStream` is implemented in `FileInputStream`, and the abstract `write(int b)` method in the `OutputStream` class is implemented in `FileOutputStream`.

Example 17.2 Processing External Files

Problem

Write a program that uses `FileInputStream` and `FileOutputStream` to copy a file, and the `File` class to check the properties of the file. The user needs to provide a source file and a target file as command-line arguments. The program copies the source file to the target file and displays the number of bytes in the file. A sample run of the program is shown in Figure 17.6.

```
Command Prompt                                                _ □ ×
C:\book>java CopyFileUsingByteStream Temp.java t.java
File not found: Temp.java

C:\book>java CopyFileUsingByteStream ButtonDemo.java t.java
The file ButtonDemo.java has 2636 bytes

C:\book>java CopyFileUsingByteStream ButtonDemo.java t.java
file t.java already exists

C:\book>
```

Figure 17.6   *The program copies a file using byte streams.*

continues

Example 17.2 continued

Solution

The following code gives the solution to the problem.

```
1    // CopyFileUsingByteStream.java: Copy files
2    import java.io.*;
3
4    public class CopyFileUsingByteStream {
5      /** Main method
6         @param args[0] for sourcefile
7         @param args[1] for target file
8      */
9      public static void main(String[] args) {
10       // Declare input and output file streams
11       FileInputStream fis = null;
12       FileOutputStream fos = null;
13
14       // Check usage
15       if (args.length != 2) {
16         System.out.println(
17           "Usage: java CopyFileUsingByteStream fromfile tofile");
18         System.exit(0);
19       }
20
21       try {
22         // Create file input stream
23         fis = new FileInputStream(new File(args[0]));
24
25         // Create file output stream if the file does not exist
26         File file = new File(args[1]);
27         if (file.exists()) {
28           System.out.println("file " + args[1] + " already exists");
29           return;
30         }
31         else
32           fos = new FileOutputStream(args[1]);
33
34         // Display the file size
35         System.out.println("The file " + args[0] + " has "+
36           fis.available() + " bytes");
37
38         // Continuously read a byte from fis and write it to fos
39         int r;
40         while ((r = fis.read()) != -1) {
41           fos.write((byte)r);
42         }
43       }
44       catch (FileNotFoundException ex) {
45         System.out.println("File not found: " + args[0]);
46       }
47       catch (IOException ex) {
48         System.out.println(ex.getMessage());
49       }
50       finally {
51         try {
52           // Close files
53           if (fis != null) fis.close();
54           if (fos != null) fos.close();
55         }
```

continues

```
56              catch (IOException ex) {
57                 System.out.println(ex);
58              }
59           }
60        }
61     }
```

Review

The program creates the `fis` (Line 23) and `fos` (Line 32) streams for the input file `args[0]` and the output file `args[1]` (see Figure 17.7).

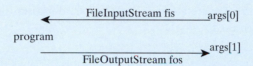

Figure 17.7 *The program uses* `FileInputStream` *to read data from the file and* `FileOutput-Stream` *to write data to the file.*

If the input file `args[0]` does not exist, new `FileInputStream(new File(args[0]))` (Line 23) will raise the exception `FileNotFoundException`. By contrast, new `FileOutputStream(new File(args[1]))` (Line 32) will always create a file output stream, whether or not the file `args[1]` exists.

To avoid writing into an existing file, the program uses the `exists()` method (Line 27) in the `File` class to determine whether `args[1]` exists. If the file already exists, the user will be notified; if not, the file will be created.

The program continuously reads bytes from the `fis` stream and sends them to the `fos` stream until all of the bytes have been read. (The condition `(fis.read() == -1)` (Line 40) signifies the end of a file.)

The program closes any open file streams in the `finally` clause (Lines 53–54). The statements in the `finally` clause are always executed, whether or not exceptions occur.

The program could be rewritten using `FileReader` and `FileWriter`. The new program would be almost exactly the same (see Exercise 17.1).

TIP

When files are no longer needed, always close them using the `close()` method. In some cases, not closing files will cause programming errors. Files are usually closed in the `finally` clause.

17.5   Filter Streams

Filter streams are streams that filter bytes or characters for some purpose. The basic input stream provides a read method that can only be used for reading bytes or characters. If you want to read integers, doubles, or strings, you need a filter class to wrap the input stream. Using a filter class enables you to read integers, doubles, and strings instead of bytes and characters.

When you need to process primitive numeric types, use `FilterInputStream` and `FilterOutputStream` to filter bytes. When you need to process strings, use `BufferedReader` and `PushbackReader` to filter characters. `FilterInputStream` and `FilterOutputStream` are abstract classes; their subclasses (listed in Tables 17.1 and 17.2) are often used.

TABLE 17.1   `FilterInputStream` Subclasses

Class	Usage
`DataInputStream`	Handles binary formats of all the primitive data types.
`BufferedInputStream`	Gets data from the buffer and then reads them from the stream if necessary.
`LineNumberInputStream`	Keeps track of how many lines are read.
`PushbackInputStream`	Allows single-byte lookahead. After a byte is looked at, this stream pushes it back to the stream so that the next read can read it.

TABLE 17.2   FilterOutputStream Subclasses

Class	Usage
`DataOutputStream`	Outputs the binary format of all the primitive types, which is useful if another program uses the output.
`BufferedOutputStream`	Outputs to the buffer first and then, if necessary, to the stream. Programmers can also call the `flush()` method to write the buffer to the stream.
`PrintStream`	Outputs the Unicode format of all the primitive types, which is useful if the format is output to the console.

17.6   Data Streams

The `DataInputStream` and `DataOutputStream` read and write Java primitive types in a machine-independent fashion, thereby enabling you to write a data file on one machine and read it on another machine that has a different operating system or file structure. An application uses a data output stream to write data that can later be read by a data input stream.

`DataInputStream` extends `FilterInputStream` and implements the `DataInput` interface. `DataOutputStream` extends `FilterOutputStream` and implements the

DataOutput interface. The DataInput and DataOutput interfaces are also implemented by the RandomAccessFile class, which is discussed in Section 17.12, "Random Access Files," later in this chapter.

The following methods are defined in the DataInput interface:

```
public int readByte() throws IOException
public int readShort() throws IOException
public int readInt() throws IOException
public int readLong() throws IOException
public float readFloat() throws IOException
public double readDouble() throws IOException
public char readChar() throws IOException
public boolean readBoolean() throws IOException
public String readUTF() throws IOException
```

The following methods are defined in the DataOutput interface:

```
public void writeByte(byte b) throws IOException
public void writeShort(short s) throws IOException
public void writeInt(int i) throws IOException
public void writeLong(long l) throws IOException
public void writeFloat(float f) throws IOException
public void writeDouble(double d) throws IOException
public void writeChar(char c) throws IOException
public void writeBoolean(boolean b) throws IOException
public void writeBytes(String string) throws IOException
public void writeChars(String string) throws IOException
public void writeUTF(String string) throws IOException
```

NOTE

UTF stands for Unicode Transformation Format. The writeUTF method converts a string into a series of bytes in the UTF-8 format and writes them into a binary stream. The readUTF method reads a string that has been written using the writeUTF method. The UTF-8 format has the advantage of saving a byte for each character, since a Unicode character takes up two bytes and a UTF-8 character takes up only one byte. If your characters are regular ASCII code, using UFT-8 is more efficient.

Data streams are used as wrappers on existing input and output streams to filter data in the original stream. They are created using the following constructors:

```
public DataInputStream(InputStream instream)
public DataOutputStream(OutputStream outstream)
```

The statements given below create data streams. The first statement creates an input stream for file in.dat; the second statement creates an output stream for file out.dat.

```
DataInputStream infile =
  new DataInputStream(new FileInputStream("in.dat"));

DataOutputStream outfile =
  new DataOutputStream(new FileOutputStream("out.dat"));
```

Example 17.3 Using Data Streams

Problem

Write a program that creates ten random integers, stores them in a data file, retrieves data from the file, and then displays the integers on the console. Figure 17.8 contains a sample run of the program.

```
Command Prompt                                          _ □ ×
C:\book>java TestDataStream
   246   797   15   393   446   231   642   318   91   328
C:\book>type mytemp.dat
   ÷   ♥↔     ¤   ☺ë  ☺◄     γ  ☻é  ☺>     [   ☺H
C:\book>del mytemp.dat

C:\book>
```

Figure 17.8   *The program creates ten random numbers and stores them in a file named* ***mytemp.dat****. It then reads the data from the file and displays them on the console.*

Solution

The following code gives the solution to the problem.

```
1    // TestDataStream.java: Create a file, store it in binary form, and
2    // display it on the console
3    import java.io.*;
4
5    public class TestDataStream {
6      /** Main method */
7      public static void main(String[] args) {
8        // Declare data input and output streams
9        DataInputStream dis = null;
10       DataOutputStream dos = null;
11
12       // Construct a temp file
13       File tempFile = new File("mytemp.dat");
14
15       // Check if the temp file exists
16       if (tempFile.exists()) {
17         System.out.println("The file mytemp.dat already exists,"
18           + " delete it, rerun the program");
19         System.exit(0);
20       }
21
22       // Write data
23       try {
24         // Create data output stream for tempFile
25         dos = new DataOutputStream(new FileOutputStream(tempFile));
26         for (int i = 0; i < 10; i++)
27           dos.writeInt((int)(Math.random() * 1000));
28       }
29       catch (IOException ex) {
30         System.out.println(ex.getMessage());
31       }
```

```
32        finally {
33          try {
34            // Close files
35            if (dos != null) dos.close();
36          }
37          catch (IOException ex) {
38          }
39        }
40
41        // Read data
42        try {
43          // Create data input stream
44          dis = new DataInputStream(new FileInputStream(tempFile));
45          for (int i = 0; i < 10; i++)
46            System.out.print("  " + dis.readInt());
47        }
48        catch (FileNotFoundException ex) {
49          System.out.println("File not found");
50        }
51        catch (IOException ex) {
52          System.out.println(ex.getMessage());
53        }
54        finally {
55          try {
56            // Close files
57            if (dis != null) dis.close();
58          }
59          catch (IOException ex) {
60            System.out.println(ex);
61          }
62        }
63      }
64    }
```

Review

The program creates a `DataInputStream` object dis wrapped on `FileInputStream` (Line 44) and a `DataOutputStream` object dos wrapped on `FileOutputStream` (Line 25) (see Figure 17.9).

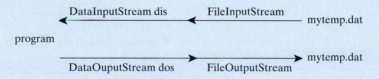

Figure 17.9 *The program uses* `DataOutputStream` *to write data to a file and* `DataInputStream` *to read the data from the file.*

The program uses a temporary file to store data. The temporary file is named mytemp.dat. The program first creates mytemp.dat if it does not exist. Then it writes ten random integers into mytemp.dat using the data output stream, and closes the stream.

The program creates a data input stream for mytemp.dat, reads integers from it, and displays it.

continues

Example 17.3 Using Data Streams

 NOTE

The data stored in **mytemp.dat** are in binary format, which is machine-independent and portable. If you need to transport data between different systems, use data input and data output streams.

17.7   Print Streams

A data output stream outputs a binary representation of data, so you cannot view its contents as text. As shown in Figure 17.8, when you attempt to view the file mytemp.dat on the console, strange symbols are displayed. In Java, you can use print streams to output data into files. These files can be viewed as text.

The `PrintStream` and `PrintWriter` classes provide this functionality. You have already used `System.out.println` to display data on the console. An instance of `PrintStream`, `out`, is defined in the `java.lang.System` class. `PrintStream` and `PrintWriter` have similar methods, listed below:

```
public void print(Object o)
public void print(String s)
public void print(char c)
public void print(char[] cArray)
public void print(int i)
public void print(long l)
public void print(float f)
public void print(double d)
public void print(boolean b)
```

You can replace `print` with `println`. The `println` method, which prints the object, is followed by a new line. When an object is passed to `print` or `println`, the object's `toString()` method converts it to a `String` object.

 NOTE

The print methods do not throw an `IOException`. So when the `System.out.print` method is invoked, it does not need to be inside a `try-catch` block.

`PrintStream` is for byte streams, whereas `PrintWriter` is for character streams. Since printing is clearly character-related output, `PrintWriter` should be used rather than `PrintStream`. However, there is a historical reason why `System.out` and `System.err` have been used for printing to the console: `PrintStream` (in JDK 1.0) was introduced before `PrintWriter` (in JDK 1.1). So you can continue to use these two objects for output to the console.

This section gives an example using `PrintWriter`, but `PrintStream` can be used in the same way. `PrintWriter` has the following constructors:

```
public PrintWriter(Writer out)
public PrintWriter(Writer out, boolean autoFlush)
public PrintWriter(OutputStream out)
public PrintWriter(OutputStream out, boolean autoFlush)
```

Example 17.4 Using Print Streams

Problem

Write a program that creates ten random integers and stores them in a text data file. The file can be viewed on the console by using an OS command, such as type on Windows or cat on UNIX.

Solution

The following code gives the solution to the problem. Figure 17.10 contains the output of a sample run of the program.

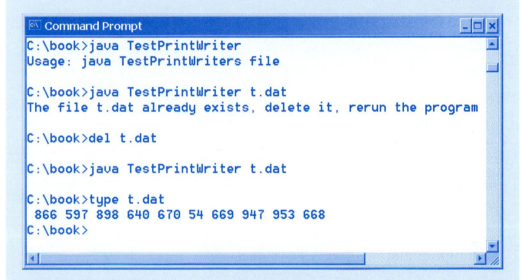

```
C:\book>java TestPrintWriter
Usage: java TestPrintWriters file

C:\book>java TestPrintWriter t.dat
The file t.dat already exists, delete it, rerun the program

C:\book>del t.dat

C:\book>java TestPrintWriter t.dat

C:\book>type t.dat
 866 597 898 640 670 54 669 947 953 668
C:\book>
```

Figure 17.10   *The program creates ten random numbers and stores them in a text file.*

```
1    // TestPrintWriter.java: Create a text file using PrintWriter
2    import java.io.*;
3
4    public class TestPrintWriter {
5      /** Main method: args[0] is the output file */
6      public static void main(String[] args) {
7        // Declare print stream
8        PrintWriter pw = null;
9
10       // Check usage
11       if (args.length != 1) {
12         System.out.println("Usage: java TestPrintWriters file");
13         System.exit(0);
14       }
15
16       File tempFile = new File(args[0]);
17
18       if (tempFile.exists()) {
19         System.out.println("The file " + args[0] +
20           " already exists, delete it, rerun the program");
21         System.exit(0);
22       }
23
```

continues

Example 17.4 continued

```
24            // Write data
25            try {
26              // Create data output stream for tempFile
27              pw = new PrintWriter(new FileOutputStream(tempFile), true);
28              for (int i = 0; i < 10; i++)
29                pw.print(" " + (int)(Math.random() * 1000));
30            }
31            catch (IOException ex) {
32              System.out.println(ex.getMessage());
33            }
34            finally {
35              // Close files
36              if (pw != null) pw.close();
37            }
38          }
39        }
```

Review

The program creates a print stream, `pw`, of `PrintWriter`, wrapped in `FileOutput-Stream`, for text format (Line 27) (see Figure 17.11).

Figure 17.11   *The program uses the* `PrintWriter` *stream, which is wrapped in* `FileOutput-Stream`, *to write data in text format.*

The program creates the file named in args[0] if it does not already exist, writes ten random integers into the file by using the data output stream, and then closes the stream.

The output into the file is in text format. The data can be seen using the type command in DOS.

17.8   Buffered Streams

Java introduces buffered streams that speed input and output by reducing the number of reads and writes. Buffered streams employ a buffered array of bytes or characters that acts as a cache. In the case of input, the array reads a chunk of bytes or characters into the buffer before the individual bytes or characters are read. In the case of output, the array accumulates a block of bytes or characters before writing the entire block to the output stream.

The use of buffered streams enables you to read and write a chunk of bytes or characters at once instead of reading or writing the bytes or characters one at a time. The `BufferedInputStream`, `BufferedOutputStream`, `BufferedReader`, and `BufferedWriter` classes provide this functionality.

The following constructors are used to create a buffered stream:

```
public BufferedInputStream(InputStream in)
public BufferedInputStream(InputStream in, int bufferSize)
public BufferedOutputStream(OutputStream in)
public BufferedOutputStream(OutputStream in, int bufferSize)
public BufferedReader(Reader in)
public BufferedReader(Reader in, int bufferSize)
public BufferedWriter(Writer out)
public BufferedWriter(Writer out, int bufferSize)
```

If no buffer size is specified, the default size is 512 bytes or characters. A buffered input stream reads as many data as possible into its buffer in a single read call. By contrast, a buffered output stream calls the write method only when its buffer fills up or when the `flush()` method is called.

The buffered stream classes inherit methods from their superclasses. In addition to using the methods from their superclasses, `BufferedReader` has a `readLine()` method to read a line, and `BufferedWriter` has a `newLine()` method to write a line separator.

■■■■ **NOTE**

The `readLine()` method return a line without the line separator. The line separator string is defined by the system, and is not necessarily a single ('\n') character. To get the system line separator, use

```
static String lineSeparator = (String)java.security.
  AccessController.doPrivileged(
  new sun.security.action.GetPropertyAction("line.separator"));
```

Example 17.5   Displaying a File in a Text Area

Problem

Write a program that views a file in a text area. The user enters a filename in a text field and clicks the View button; the file is then displayed in a text area. Figure 17.12 contains the output of a sample run of the program.

Figure 17.12   *The program displays the specified file in the text area.*

continues

Example 17.5 continued

Solution

The following code gives the solution to the problem.

```
1    // ViewFile.java: Read a text file and store it in a text area
2    import java.awt.*;
3    import java.awt.event.*;
4    import java.io.*;
5    import javax.swing.*;
6
7    public class ViewFile extends JFrame implements ActionListener {
8      // Button to view view
9      private JButton jbtView = new JButton("View");
10
11     // Text field to receive file name
12     private JTextField jtfFilename = new JTextField(12);
13
14     // Text area to display file
15     private JTextArea jtaFile = new JTextArea();
16
17     /** Main method */
18     public static void main(String[] args) {
19       ViewFile frame = new ViewFile();
20       frame.setTitle("View File");
21       frame.setSize(400, 300);
22       frame.setVisible(true);
23     }
24
25     /**  Default constructor */
26     public ViewFile() {
27       // Panel p to hold a label, a text field, and a button
28       Panel p = new Panel();
29       p.setLayout(new BorderLayout());
30       p.add(new Label("Filename"), BorderLayout.WEST);
31       p.add(jtfFilename, BorderLayout.CENTER);
32       jtfFilename.setBackground(Color.yellow);
33       jtfFilename.setForeground(Color.red);
34       p.add(jbtView, BorderLayout.EAST);
35
36       // Add jtaFile to a scroll pane
37       JScrollPane jsp = new JScrollPane(jtaFile);
38
39       // Add jsp and p to the frame
40       getContentPane().add(jsp, BorderLayout.CENTER);
41       getContentPane().add(p, BorderLayout.SOUTH);
42
43       // Register listener
44       jbtView.addActionListener(this);
45     }
46
47     /** Handle the "View" button */
48     public void actionPerformed(ActionEvent e) {
49       if (e.getSource() == jbtView)
50         showFile();
51     }
52
53     /** Display the file in the text area */
54     private void showFile() {
55       // Use a BufferedReader to read text from the file
56       BufferedReader infile = null;
57
```

```
58          // Get file name from the text field
59          String filename = jtfFilename.getText().trim();
60
61          String inLine;
62
63          try {
64            // Create a buffered stream
65            infile = new BufferedReader(new FileReader(filename));
66
67            // Read a line and append the line to the text area
68            while ((inLine = infile.readLine()) != null)
69            {
70              jtaFile.append(inLine + '\n');
71            }
72          }
73          catch (FileNotFoundException ex) {
74            System.out.println("File not found: " + filename);
75          }
76          catch (IOException ex) {
77            System.out.println(ex.getMessage());
78          }
79          finally {
80            try {
81              if (infile != null) infile.close();
82            }
83            catch (IOException ex) {
84              System.out.println(ex.getMessage());
85            }
86          }
87        }
88      }
```

Review

The user enters a filename into the Filename text field. When the View button is pressed, the program gets the input filename from the text field; it then creates a data input stream. The data are read one line at a time and appended to the text area for display.

The program uses a `BufferedReader` stream (Line 65) to read lines from a buffer. Instead of the `BufferedReader` and `Reader` classes, `BufferedInputStream` and `FileInputStream` can also be used in this example.

You are encouraged to rewrite the program without using buffers and then compare the performance of the two programs. This will show you the improvement in performance obtained by using buffers when reading from a large file.

This program reads a file from the local machine, so you have to write it as a Java application. Example 18.6, "Retrieving Remote Files," in Chapter 18, "Networking," gives another program that allows reading from a file on a remote host.

TIP

Since physical input and output involving I/O devices are typically very slow compared with CPU processing speeds, you should use buffered input/output streams to improve performance.

17.9   File Dialogs

Swing provides `javax.swing.JFileChooser`, which displays a dialog box from which the user can navigate through the file system and select files to load or save, as shown in Figure 17.13.

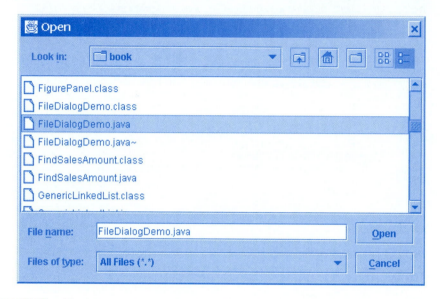

Figure 17.13   *The Swing* `JFileChooser` *shows files and directories, and enables the user to navigate through the file system visually.*

The file dialog box is modal; when displayed, it blocks the rest of the application until it disappears. The file dialog box can appear in two types: open and save. The *open type* is for opening a file, and the *save type* is for storing a file.

There are several ways to construct a file dialog box. The simplest is to use `JFileChooser`'s default constructor.

The `JFileChooser` class is a subclass of `JComponent`. In addition to the properties inherited from `JComponent`, `JFileChooser` has the following useful properties:

- `dialogType` specifies the type of the dialog. Use `OPEN_DIALOG` when you want to bring up a filechooser that the user can use to open a file. Likewise, use `SAVE_DIALOG` to let the user choose a file to save.

- `dialogTitle` specifies the string displayed in the title bar of the dialog box.

- `currentDirectory` specifies the current directory of the file. The type of this property is `java.io.File`. If you want the current directory to be used, use `setCurrentDirectory(new File("."))`.

- `selectedFile` specifies the selected file. You can use `getSelectedFile()` to return the selected file from the dialog box. The type of this property is `java.io.File`. If you have a default file name that you expect to use, use `setSelectedFile(new File(filename))`.

- `selectedFiles` specifies a list of selected files if the filechooser is set to allow multi-selection. The type of this property is `File[]`.

- `multiSelectionEnabled` specifies a `boolean` value indicating whether multiple files can be selected. By default, it is `false`.

To display the dialog box, use the following two methods:

```
public int showOpenDialog(Component parent)
public int showSaveDialog(Component parent)
```

The first method displays an "Open" dialog, and the second displays a "Save" dialog. Both methods return an `int` value, `APPROVE_OPTION` or `CANCEL_OPTION`, which indicates whether the OK button or the Cancel button was clicked.

Example 17.6 Using File Dialogs

Problem

Create a simple notepad using `JFileChooser` to open and save files. The notepad enables the user to open an existing file, edit the file, and save the note to the current file or a specified file. You can display and edit the file in a text area.

A sample run of the program is shown in Figure 17.14. When you open a file, a file dialog box with the default title "Open" appears on-screen to let you select a file for loading, as shown in Figure 17.13. When you save a file, a file dialog box with the default title "Save" appears to let you select a file for saving, as shown in Figure 17.15. The status label below the text area displays the status of the file operations.

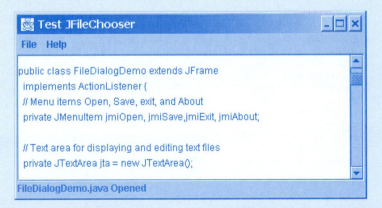

Figure 17.14   *The program enables you to open, save, and edit files.*

Solution

The following code gives the solution to the problem.

continues

Example 17.6 continued

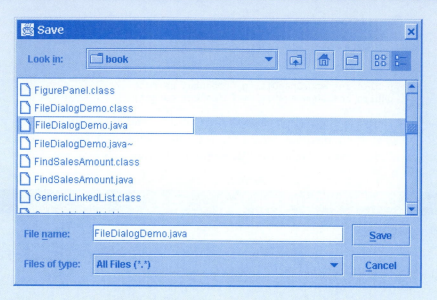

Figure 17.15   *The Save dialog box enables you to save to a new file or an existing file.*

```
1      // FileDialogDemo.java: Demonstrate using JFileDialog to display
2      // file dialog boxes for opening and saving files
3      import java.awt.*;
4      import java.awt.event.*;
5      import java.io.*;
6      import javax.swing.*;
7
8      public class FileDialogDemo extends JFrame
9        implements ActionListener {
10       // Menu items Open, Save, exit, and About
11       private JMenuItem jmiOpen, jmiSave,jmiExit, jmiAbout;
12
13       // Text area for displaying and editing text files
14       private JTextArea jta = new JTextArea();
15
16       // Status label for displaying operation status
17       private JLabel jlblStatus = new JLabel();
18
19       // File dialog box
20       private JFileChooser jFileChooser = new JFileChooser();
21
22       /** Main method */
23       public static void main(String[] args) {
24         FileDialogDemo frame = new FileDialogDemo();
25         frame.setSize(300, 150);
26         frame.setVisible(true);
27       }
28
29       public FileDialogDemo() {
30         setTitle("Test JFileChooser");
31
32         // Create a menu bar mb and attach to the frame
33         JMenuBar mb = new JMenuBar();
34         setJMenuBar(mb);
35
```

```
36          // Add a "File" menu in mb
37          JMenu fileMenu = new JMenu("File");
38          mb.add(fileMenu);
39
40          //add a "Help" menu in mb
41          JMenu helpMenu = new JMenu("Help");
42          mb.add(helpMenu);
43
44          // Create and add menu items to the menu
45          fileMenu.add(jmiOpen = new JMenuItem("Open"));
46          fileMenu.add(jmiSave = new JMenuItem("Save"));
47          fileMenu.addSeparator();
48          fileMenu.add(jmiExit = new JMenuItem("Exit"));
49          helpMenu.add(jmiAbout = new JMenuItem("About"));
50
51          // Set default directory to the current directory
52          jFileChooser.setCurrentDirectory(new File("."));
53
54          // Set BorderLayout for the frame
55          getContentPane().add(new JScrollPane(jta),
56            BorderLayout.CENTER);
57          getContentPane().add(jlblStatus, BorderLayout.SOUTH);
58
59          // Register listeners
60          jmiOpen.addActionListener(this);
61          jmiSave.addActionListener(this);
62          jmiAbout.addActionListener(this);
63          jmiExit.addActionListener(this);
64        }
65
66        /** Handle ActionEvent for menu items */
67        public void actionPerformed(ActionEvent e) {
68          String actionCommand = e.getActionCommand();
69
70          if (e.getSource() instanceof JMenuItem) {
71            if ("Open".equals(actionCommand))
72              open();
73            else if ("Save".equals(actionCommand))
74              save();
75            else if ("About".equals(actionCommand))
76              JOptionPane.showMessageDialog(this,
77                "Demonstrate Using File Dialogs",
78                "About This Demo",
79                JOptionPane.INFORMATION_MESSAGE);
80            else if ("Exit".equals(actionCommand))
81              System.exit(0);
82          }
83        }
84
85        /** Open file */
86        private void open() {
87          if (jFileChooser.showOpenDialog(this) ==
88            JFileChooser.APPROVE_OPTION) {
89            open(jFileChooser.getSelectedFile());
90          }
91        }
92
93        /** Open file with the specified File instance */
94        private void open(File file) {
95          try {
96            // Read from the specified file and store it in jta
```

continues

Example 17.6 continued

```
97          BufferedInputStream in = new BufferedInputStream(
98            new FileInputStream(file));
99          byte[] b = new byte[in.available()];
100         in.read(b, 0, b.length);
101         jta.append(new String(b, 0, b.length));
102         in.close();
103
104         // Display the status of the Open file operation in jlblStatus
105         jlblStatus.setText(file.getName() + " Opened");
106       }
107       catch (IOException ex) {
108         jlblStatus.setText("Error opening " + file.getName());
109       }
110     }
111
112     /** Save file */
113     private void save() {
114       if (jFileChooser.showSaveDialog(this) ==
115         JFileChooser.APPROVE_OPTION) {
116         save(jFileChooser.getSelectedFile());
117       }
118     }
119
120     /** Save file with specified File instance */
121     private void save(File file) {
122       try {
123         // Write the text in jta to the specified file
124         BufferedOutputStream out = new BufferedOutputStream(
125           new FileOutputStream(file));
126         byte[] b = (jta.getText()).getBytes();
127         out.write(b, 0, b.length);
128         out.close();
129
130         // Display the status of the save file operation in jlblStatus
131         jlblStatus.setText(file.getName()  + " Saved ");
132       }
133       catch (IOException ex) {
134         jlblStatus.setText("Error saving " + file.getName());
135       }
136     }
137   }
```

Review

The program creates the File and Help menus. The File menu contains the menu commands Open for loading a file, Save for saving a file, and Exit for terminating the program. The Help menu contains the menu command About to display a message about the program, as shown in Figure 17.16.

jFileChooser, an instance of JFileChooser, is created (Line 20) for displaying the file dialog box to open and save files. The setCurrentDirectory(new File(".")) method (Line 52) is used to set the current directory to the directory where the class is stored.

The open() method (Line 72) is invoked when the user clicks the Open menu command. The showOpenDialog() method (Line 87) displays an Open dialog box, as shown in Figure 17.13. Upon receiving the selected file, the method

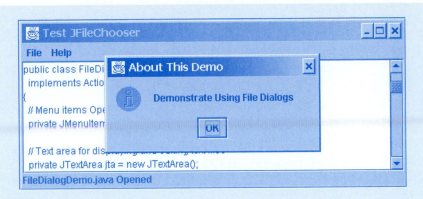

Figure 17.16 *Clicking the About menu item displays a message dialog box.*

open(file) (Line 89) is invoked to load the file to the text area, using a BufferedInputStream wrapped on a FileInputStream.

The save() method (Line 74) is invoked when the user clicks the Save menu command. The showSaveDialog() method (Line 114) displays a Save dialog box, as shown in Figure 17.15. Upon receiving the selected file, the method save(file) (Line 116) is invoked to save the contents from the text area to the file, using a BufferedOutputStream wrapped on a FileOutputStream.

17.10 Text Input and Output on the Console (Optional)

There are two types of *interactive I/O*. One involves simple input from the keyboard and simple output in a pure text form. The other involves input and output in a graphical environment. The former is referred to as *text interactive I/O*, and the latter as *graphical interactive I/O*.

Graphical interactive I/O takes an entirely different approach from text interactive I/O. In the graphical environment, input can be received from a UI component, such as a text field, text area, list, combo box, check box, or radio button. It can also be received from a keystroke or a mouse movement. Output is usually displayed in the panel, in text fields, or in text areas.

Now turn your attention to text I/O. To perform console output, you can use any of the methods for PrintStream in System.out. However, keyboard input is not directly supported in Java. In order to get input from the keyboard, you first use the following statements to read a string from the keyboard:

```
BufferedReader br
  = new BufferedReader(new InputStreamReader(System.in), 1);

// Declare and initialize the string
String string = " ";
```

DEVELOPING COMPRENHENSIVE PROJECTS

```
// Get the string from the keyboard
try {
  string = br.readLine();
}
catch (IOException ex) {
  System.out.println(ex);
}
```

You then parse the string into byte, short, int, long, float, double, char, or boolean. Here is the class that contains the methods for reading primitive data type values and strings from the keyboard:

```
// MyInput.java: Contain the methods for reading int, double, and
// values and string
import java.io.*;

public class MyInput {
  static BufferedReader br
    = new BufferedReader(new InputStreamReader(System.in), 1);

  /** Read a string from the keyboard */
  public static String readString() {
    // Declare and initialize the string
    String string = " ";

    // Get the string from the keyboard
    try {
      string = br.readLine();
    }
    catch (IOException ex) {
      System.out.println(ex);
    }

    // Return the string obtained from the keyboard
    return string;
  }

  /** Read an int value from the keyboard */
  public static int readInt() {
    return Integer.parseInt(readString());
  }

  /** Read a double value from the keyboard */
  public static double readDouble() {
    return Double.parseDouble(readString());
  }

  /** Read a byte value from the keyboard */
  public static byte readByte() {
    return Byte.parseByte(readString());
  }

  /** Read a short value from the keyboard */
  public static short readShort() {
    return Short.parseShort(readString());
  }

  /** Read a long value from the keyboard */
  public static long readLong() {
    return Long.parseLong(readString());
  }
```

```java
/** Read a float value from the keyboard */
public static float readFloat() {
  return Float.parseFloat(readString());
}

/** Read a character from the keyboard */
public static char readChar() {
  return readString().charAt(0);
}

/** Read a boolean value from the keyboard */
public static boolean readBoolean() {
  return new Boolean(readString()).booleanValue();
}
}
```

NOTE

Some brands of PCs running Windows 95 are prone to cause input problems if the buffer size for the `BufferedReader` stream `br` is not set to 1. Therefore, the buffer size of 1 is purposely chosen to help eliminate input problems.

NOTE

`System.out` is a standard output object, and `System.in` is a standard input object. If you run the program from the command window, the output is displayed in the command window and input from the keyboard is echo printed in the command window.

Below is an example that uses the methods in `MyInput`. A sample run of this program is shown in Figure 17.17.

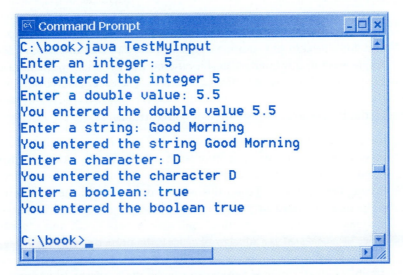

Figure 17.17   *You can enter input from a command window.*

```
// TestMyInput.java: Demo for using MyInput
public class TestMyInput {
  public static void main(String args[]) {
    // Prompt the user to enter an integer
    System.out.print("Enter an integer: ");
    int intValue = MyInput.readInt();
    System.out.println("You entered the integer " + intValue);

    // Prompt the user to enter a double value
    System.out.print("Enter a double value: ");
    double doubleValue = MyInput.readDouble();
    System.out.println("You entered the double value "
      + doubleValue);

    // Prompt the user to enter a string
    System.out.print("Enter a string: ");
    String string = MyInput.readString();
    System.out.println("You entered the string " + string);

    // Prompt the user to enter a character
    System.out.print("Enter a character: ");
    char charValue = MyInput.readChar();
    System.out.println("You entered the character " + charValue);

    // Prompt the user to enter a boolean
    System.out.print("Enter a boolean: ");
    boolean booleanValue = MyInput.readBoolean();
    System.out.println("You entered the boolean " + booleanValue);
  }
}
```

17.11   Object Streams

Thus far, this chapter has covered input and output of bytes, characters, and primitive data types. Object streams enable you to perform input and output at the object level. To enable an object to be read or written, the object's defining class has to implement the java.io.Serializable interface or the java.io.Externalizable interface. The Serializable interface is a marker interface. It has no methods, so you don't need to add additional code in your class that implements Serializable. Implementing this interface enables the Java serialization mechanism to automate the process of storing the objects and arrays. The Externalizable interface extends the Serializable interface and defines the readExternal and writeExternal methods to enable customization of object streams.

To appreciate this automation feature and understand how an object is stored, consider what you need to do in order to store an object without using this feature. Suppose you want to store an object of the MessagePanel class in Example 10.5, "Using FontMetrics." To do this you need to store all the current values of the properties in a MessagePanel object. The properties defined in MessagePanel are message (String), centered (boolean), xCoordinate (int), and yCoordinate (int). Since MessagePanel is a subclass of JPanel, the property values of JPanel have to be stored as well as the properties of all the superclasses of JPanel. If a property is of an object type, storing it requires storing all the property values inside this object.

As you can see, this is a very tedious process. Fortunately, you don't have to go through it manually. Java provides a built-in mechanism to automate the process of writing objects. This process is referred to as *object serialization*. In contrast, the process of reading objects is referred to as *object deserialization*.

17.11.1   The *ObjectOutputStream* and *ObjectInputStream* classes

The `ObjectOutputStream` class is used for storing objects, and the `ObjectInput-Stream` class for restoring objects. These two classes are built upon several other classes. Figure 17.18 shows the hierarchical relationship of these related classes.

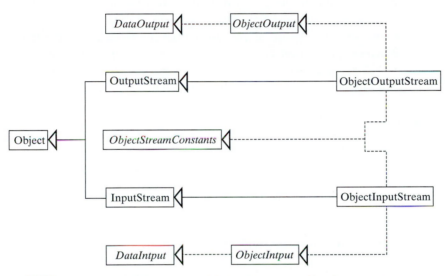

Figure 17.18   `ObjectOutputStream` *extends* `OutputStream` *and implements* `ObjectOutput` *and* `ObjectStreamConstants`. `ObjectInputStream` *extends* `InputStream` *and implements* `ObjectInput` *and* `ObjectStreamConstants`.

`ObjectOutputStream` implements `ObjectOutput`, which inherits `DataOutput`. `DataOutput` provides methods for writing Java primitive-data-type values. `Object-Output` extends `DataOutput` to include output of objects, arrays, and strings. An `ObjectOutputStream` writes Java primitive-data-type values and objects to an `OutputStream`. Persistent storage can be accomplished using a file for the stream. The format of the output is platform-independent. The `OutputStream` can also be a network socket stream, which will be introduced in Chapter 18, "Networking."

`ObjectInputStream` is the inverse of `ObjectOutputStream`. `ObjectInputStream` implements `ObjectInput`, which inherits `DataInput`. `DataInput` provides methods for reading primitive-data-type values. `ObjectInput` extends `DataInput` to include input of objects, arrays, and strings. An `ObjectInputStream` reads the data previously written using an `ObjectOutputStream` with a file stream or a network socket stream.

Only objects that implement the `java.io.Serializable` interface can use `ObjectOutputStream` and `ObjectInputStream`. The `Serializable` interface provides complete automation for serializing and deserializing an object. The `Externalizable` interface gives you the option of customizing how an object should be serialized and deserialized.

All user-interface classes implement `Serializable`, so they are serializable. The method `writeObject(obj)` is used to write an object to the `ObjectOutputStream`, and `readObject()` is used to read an object from the `ObjectInputStream`. Attempting to store an object that does not support the `Serializable` interface would cause `NotSerializableException`.

When a serializable object is stored, the class of the object is encoded; this includes the class name and the signature of the class, the values of the object's fields and arrays, and the closure of any other objects referenced from the initial object. When a primitive-data-type value is stored, appropriate methods, such as `writeInt()`, `writeBoolean()` in the `DataOutput` interface, are used. Multiple objects or primitives can be written to the stream. The objects must be read back from the corresponding `ObjectInputStream` with the same types and in the same order as they were written. Java's safe casting should be used to get the desired type. For instance, when reading an object of the `MessagePanel` class, the object should be cast to `MessagePanel`.

Here is an example of creating an `ObjectOutputStream` and storing a `MessagePanel` object (messagePanel) and an `int` value to the file named object.dat.

```
ObjectOutputStream out = new ObjectOutputStream(
  new FileOutputStream("object.dat"));
out.writeObject(messagePanel);
out.writeInt(5);
```

The corresponding code to restore the object and the `int` value is shown below.

```
ObjectInputStream in = new ObjectInputStream(
  new FileInputStream("object.dat"));
MessagePanel c = (MessagePanel)in.readObject();
int x = in.readInt();
```

Example 17.7 Testing Object Streams

Problem

Write a program that manipulates `MessagePanel`, as shown in Figure 17.19. You will use radio buttons to set the background color, and two buttons, <= and =>, to move the message to left and right. The Store button is provided to save a `MessagePanel` object, and the Restore button is used to reload the saved `MessagePanel` object.

Solution

The following code gives the solution to the problem.

Figure 17.19   *You can use the Store button to save the* `MessagePanel` *object shown in the middle of the window, and the Restore button to reload the saved object later.*

```java
1    // ObjectStreamDemo.java: Demonstrate store and restore objects
2    import java.awt.*;
3    import java.awt.event.*;
4    import javax.swing.*;
5    import java.io.*;
6    import java.util.Date;
7
8    public class ObjectStreamDemo extends JFrame
9      implements ActionListener {
10     // Radio buttons for selecting a color for the message
11     JRadioButton jrbRed = new JRadioButton("Red");
12     JRadioButton jrbGreen = new JRadioButton("Green");
13     JRadioButton jrbYellow = new JRadioButton("Yellow");
14
15     // Buttons for Store, Restore, Left, and Right
16     JButton jbtStore = new JButton("Store");
17     JButton jbtRestore = new JButton("Restore");
18     JButton jbtLeft = new JButton("<=");
19     JButton jbtRight = new JButton("=>");
20
21     // Status label to display date when the object is stored
22     JLabel jlbStatusBar = new JLabel();
23
24     // Create a MessagePanel instance
25     MessagePanel messagePanel = new MessagePanel();
26
27     // Panel for holding radio buttons, message panel, and buttons
28     JPanel jpSerialization = new JPanel();
29
30     /** Construct the frame */
31     public ObjectStreamDemo() {
32       // Create a panel to group radio buttons
33       JPanel jpRadioButtons = new JPanel();
34       jpRadioButtons.add(jrbRed);
35       jpRadioButtons.add(jrbGreen);
36       jpRadioButtons.add(jrbYellow);
37
38       // Group radio buttons
39       ButtonGroup btg = new ButtonGroup();
40       btg.add(jrbRed);
41       btg.add(jrbGreen);
42       btg.add(jrbYellow);
43
```

continues

Example 17.7 continued

```
44            // Create a panel to group buttons
45            JPanel jpButtons = new JPanel();
46            jpButtons.add(jbtStore);
47            jpButtons.add(jbtRestore);
48            jpButtons.add(jbtLeft);
49            jpButtons.add(jbtRight);
50
51            // Group jpRadioButtons, messagePanel, and jpButtons
52            jpSerialization.setLayout(new BorderLayout());
53            jpSerialization.add(jpRadioButtons, BorderLayout.NORTH);
54            jpSerialization.add(messagePanel, BorderLayout.CENTER);
55            jpSerialization.add(jpButtons, BorderLayout.SOUTH);
56
57            // Set borders
58            jpRadioButtons.setBorder(BorderFactory.createEtchedBorder());
59            jpButtons.setBorder(BorderFactory.createEtchedBorder());
60            messagePanel.setBorder(BorderFactory.createRaisedBevelBorder());
61
62            // Add jpSerialization and jlbStatusBar to the frame
63            Container container = getContentPane();
64            container.add(jlbStatusBar, BorderLayout.SOUTH);
65            container.add(jpSerialization, BorderLayout.CENTER);
66
67            // Register listeners
68            jrbRed.addActionListener(this);
69            jrbGreen.addActionListener(this);
70            jrbYellow.addActionListener(this);
71            jbtStore.addActionListener(this);
72            jbtRestore.addActionListener(this);
73            jbtLeft.addActionListener(this);
74            jbtRight.addActionListener(this);
75          }
76
77          /** Handle action events */
78          public void actionPerformed(ActionEvent e) {
79            if (e.getSource() == jrbRed)
80              messagePanel.setBackground(Color.red);
81            else if (e.getSource() == jrbGreen)
82              messagePanel.setBackground(Color.green);
83            else if (e.getSource() == jrbYellow)
84              messagePanel.setBackground(Color.yellow);
85            else if (e.getSource() == jbtStore) {
86              try {
87                ObjectOutputStream out =
88                  new ObjectOutputStream(new FileOutputStream("object.dat"));
89                out.writeObject(messagePanel);
90                out.writeObject(new Date());
91                out.close();
92                jlbStatusBar.setText("The object is stored in object.dat");
93              }
94              catch (IOException ex) {
95                System.out.println(ex);
96              }
97            }
98            else if (e.getSource() == jbtRestore) {
99              try {
100               ObjectInputStream in =
101                 new ObjectInputStream(new FileInputStream("object.dat"));
```

```
102              MessagePanel c = (MessagePanel)in.readObject();
103              Date d = (Date)in.readObject();
104              jpSerialization.remove(messagePanel);
105              messagePanel = c;
106              jpSerialization.add(messagePanel, BorderLayout.CENTER);
107              jpSerialization.repaint();
108              in.close();
109              jlbStatusBar.setText("The object saved at " + d.toString()
110                + " is restored");
111            }
112          catch (IOException ex1) {
113            System.out.println(ex1);
114          }
115          catch (ClassNotFoundException ex2) {
116            System.out.println(ex2);
117          }
118        }
119        else if (e.getSource() == jbtLeft)
120          left();
121        else if (e.getSource() == jbtRight)
122          right();
123      }
124
125      /** Move the message in the panel left */
126      private void left() {
127        int x = messagePanel.getXCoordinate();
128        if (x > 10) {
129          // Shift the message to the left
130          messagePanel.setXCoordinate(x - 10);
131          messagePanel.repaint();
132        }
133      }
134
135      /** Move the message in the panel right */
136      private void right() {
137        int x = messagePanel.getXCoordinate();
138        if (x < getSize().width - 20) {
139          // Shift the message to the right
140          messagePanel.setXCoordinate(x + 10);
141          messagePanel.repaint();
142        }
143      }
144
145      /** Main method */
146      public static void main(String[] args) {
147        ObjectStreamDemo frame = new ObjectStreamDemo();
148        frame.setTitle("Test Object Serialization");
149        frame.setDefaultCloseOperation(JFrame.EXIT_ON_CLOSE);
150        frame.pack();
151        frame.setVisible(true);
152      }
153    }
```

Review

When you click the Store button, the current state of the `messagePanel` and the current time (`new Date()`) are saved to file object.dat using `ObjectOutputStream` (Lines 89–90). When you click the Restore button, these objects are read back from the same file (Lines 102–103). They must be read back in the same order as they were stored. Explicit type casting must be used to ensure that the objects read are of the right type.

continues

Example 17.7 continued

In the handler for the Restore button, `messagePanel` was removed from `jpSerialization` (Line 104), and then a new `messagePanel` was created and added to `jpSerialization` (Lines 105–106) This is necessary to ensure that the newly restored `messagePanel`, and not the old copy, is used in the windows.

Like many Java classes, `java.awt.Component` and `java.util.Date` implement `java.io.Serializable`, so the objects of these classes or their subclasses can be stored using object streams.

17.11.2   The *transient* Keyword

By default, all the nonstatic variables of a serialized object are written to the object stream. However, not all nonstatic variables can be serialized. For example, since the `java.awt.Thread` class does not implement `Serializable`, a `Thread` object cannot be serialized. You can use the `transient` keyword to mark a data field so that it will not be serialized. Consider the following class:

```java
public class Foo {
  private int v1;
  private static double v2;
  transient Thread v3;
}
```

When an object of the `Foo` class is serialized, only variable `v1` is serialized. Variable `v2` is not serialized because it is a static variable, and variable `v3` is not serialized because it is marked `transient`. If `v3` were not marked `transient`, a `java.io.NotSerializableException` would occur.

17.12   Random Access Files

All of the streams you have used so far are known as *read-only* or *write-only* streams. The external files of these streams are sequential files that cannot be updated without creating a new file. It is often necessary to modify files or to insert new records into files. Java provides the `RandomAccessFile` class to allow a file to be read and updated at the same time.

The `RandomAccessFile` class extends `Object` and implements the `DataInput` and `DataOutput` interfaces. Because `DataInputStream` implements the `DataInput` interface, and `DataOutputStream` implements the `DataOutput` interface, many methods in `RandomAccessFile` are the same as those in `DataInputStream` and `DataOutputStream`. For example, `readInt()`, `readLong()`, `readDouble()`, `readUTF()`, `writeInt`, `writeLong`, `writeDouble`, and `writeUTF` can be used in data input streams or data output streams as well as in `RandomAccessFile` streams since `readInt()`, `readLong()`, `readDouble()`, and `readUTF()` are defined in the `DataInput` interface and `writeInt`, `writeLong`, `writeDouble`, and `writeUTF` are defined in the `DataOutput` interface.

Additionally, `RandomAccessFile` provides the following methods to deal with random access:

■ `public void seek(long pos) throws IOException`

Sets the offset (in bytes specified in pos) from the beginning of the `Random-AccessFile` to where the next read or write occurs.

■ `public long getFilePointer() throws IOException`

Returns the offset, in bytes, from the beginning of the file to where the next read or write occurs.

■ `public long length() throws IOException`

Returns the length of the file.

■ `public final void writeChar(int v) throws IOException`

Writes a character to the file as a two-byte Unicode, with the higher byte written first.

■ `public final void writeChars(String s) throws IOException`

Writes a string to the file as a sequence of characters.

When creating a `RandomAccessFile`, you can specify one of two modes (`"r"` or `"rw"`). Mode `"r"` means that the stream is read-only, and mode `"rw"` indicates that the stream allows both read and write. For example, the following statement creates a new stream, `raf`, that allows the program to read from and write to the file test.dat:

```
RandomAccessFile raf = new RandomAccessFile("test.dat", "rw");
```

If test.dat already exists, `raf` is created to access it; if test.dat does not exist, a new file named test.dat is created, and `raf` is created to access the new file. The method `raf.length()` returns the number of bytes in test.dat at any given time. If you append new data into the file, `raf.length()` increases.

NOTE

When you use the `writeChar` method to write a character or the `writeChars` method to write characters, a character occupies two bytes.

TIP

Open the file with the `"r"` mode if the file is not intended to be modified. This prevents unintentional modification of the file.

Random access files are often used to process files of records. For convenience, fixed-length records are used in random access files so that a record can be located easily. A record consists of a fixed number of fields. A field can be a string or a primitive data type. A string in a fixed-length record has a maximum size. If a string is smaller than the maximum size, the rest of the string is padded with blanks.

Example 17.8 Using Random Access Files

Problem

Write a program that registers students and displays student information. The user interface consists of a tabbed pane with two tabs: Register Student and View Student. The Register Student tab enables you to store a student in the file, as shown in Figure 17.20. The View Student tab enables you to browse through student information, as shown in Figure 17.21.

Figure 17.20   *The Register Student tab registers a student.*

Figure 17.21   *The View Student tab displays student information.*

Solution

The following code gives the solution to the problem.

```
1    // TestRandomAccessFile.java: Store and read data
2    // using RandomAccessFile
3    import java.io.*;
4    import java.awt.*;
5    import java.awt.event.*;
6    import javax.swing.*;
7    import javax.swing.border.*;
8
9    public class TestRandomAccessFile extends JFrame {
10     // Create a tabbed pane to hold two panels
11     private JTabbedPane jtpStudent = new JTabbedPane();
12
13     // Random access file for access the student.dat file
14     private RandomAccessFile raf;
15
```

```
16        /** Main method */
17        public static void main(String[] args) {
18          TestRandomAccessFile frame = new TestRandomAccessFile();
19          frame.pack();
20          frame.setTitle("Test RandomAccessFile");
21          frame.setVisible(true);
22        }
23
24        /** Default constructor */
25        public TestRandomAccessFile() {
26          // Open or create a random access file
27          try {
28            raf = new RandomAccessFile("student.dat", "rw");
29          }
30          catch(IOException ex) {
31            System.out.print("Error: " + ex);
32            System.exit(0);
33          }
34
35          // Place buttons in the tabbed pane
36          jtpStudent.add(new RegisterStudent(raf), "Register Student");
37          jtpStudent.add(new ViewStudent(raf), "View Student");
38
39          // Add the tabbed pane to the frame
40          getContentPane().add(jtpStudent);
41        }
42      }
43
44      // Register student panel
45      class RegisterStudent extends JPanel implements ActionListener {
46        // Button for registering a student
47        private JButton jbtRegister;
48
49        // Student information panel
50        private StudentPanel studentPanel;
51
52        // Random access file
53        private RandomAccessFile raf;
54
55        public RegisterStudent(RandomAccessFile raf) {
56          // Pass raf to RegisterStudent Panel
57          this.raf = raf;
58
59          // Add studentPanel and jbtRegister in the panel
60          setLayout(new BorderLayout());
61          add(studentPanel = new StudentPanel(),
62            BorderLayout.CENTER);
63          add(jbtRegister = new JButton("Register"),
64            BorderLayout.SOUTH);
65
66          // Register listener
67          jbtRegister.addActionListener(this);
68        }
69
70        /** Handle button actions */
71        public void actionPerformed(ActionEvent e) {
72          if (e.getSource() == jbtRegister) {
73            Student student = studentPanel.getStudent();
74
75            try {
76              raf.seek(raf.length());
77              student.writeStudent(raf);
78            }
```

continues

767

Example 17.8 continued

```
79              catch(IOException ex) {
80                System.out.print("Error: " + ex);
81              }
82            }
83          }
84        }
85
86        // View student panel
87        class ViewStudent extends JPanel implements ActionListener {
88          // Buttons for viewing student information
89          private JButton jbtFirst, jbtNext, jbtPrevious, jbtLast;
90
91          // Random access file
92          private RandomAccessFile raf = null;
93
94          // Current student record
95          private Student student = new Student();
96
97          // Create a student panel
98          private StudentPanel studentPanel = new StudentPanel();
99
100         // File pointer in the random access file
101         private long lastPos;
102         private long currentPos;
103
104         public ViewStudent(RandomAccessFile raf) {
105           // Pass raf to ViewStudent
106           this.raf = raf;
107
108           // Panel p to hold four navigator buttons
109           JPanel p = new JPanel();
110           p.setLayout(new FlowLayout(FlowLayout.LEFT));
111           p.add(jbtFirst = new JButton("First"));
112           p.add(jbtNext = new JButton("Next"));
113           p.add(jbtPrevious = new JButton("Previous"));
114           p.add(jbtLast = new JButton("Last"));
115
116           // Add panel p and studentPanel to ViewPanel
117           setLayout(new BorderLayout());
118           add(studentPanel, BorderLayout.CENTER);
119           add(p, BorderLayout.SOUTH);
120
121           // Register listeners
122           jbtFirst.addActionListener(this);
123           jbtNext.addActionListener(this);
124           jbtPrevious.addActionListener(this);
125           jbtLast.addActionListener(this);
126         }
127
128         /** Handle navigation button actions */
129         public void actionPerformed(ActionEvent e) {
130           String actionCommand = e.getActionCommand();
131           if (e.getSource() instanceof JButton) {
132             try {
133               if ("First".equals(actionCommand)) {
134                 if (raf.length() > 0)
135                   retrieve(0);
136               }
137               else if ("Next".equals(actionCommand)) {
138                 currentPos = raf.getFilePointer();
```

```
139                    if (currentPos < raf.length())
140                       retrieve(currentPos);
141                  }
142               else if ("Previous".equals(actionCommand)) {
143                  currentPos = raf.getFilePointer();
144                  if (currentPos > 0)
145                     retrieve(currentPos - 2 * 2 * Student.RECORD_SIZE);
146               }
147               else if ("Last".equals(actionCommand)) {
148                  lastPos = raf.length();
149                  if (lastPos > 0)
150                     retrieve(lastPos - 2 * Student.RECORD_SIZE);
151               }
152            }
153            catch(IOException ex) {
154               System.out.print("Error: " + ex);
155            }
156         }
157      }
158
159      /** Retrieve a record at specified position */
160      public void retrieve(long pos) {
161         try {
162            raf.seek(pos);
163            student.readStudent(raf);
164            studentPanel.setStudent(student);
165         }
166         catch(IOException ex) {
167            System.out.print("Error: " + ex);
168         }
169      }
170   }
171
172   // This class contains static methods for reading and writing
173   // fixed length records
174   class FixedLengthStringIO {
175      // Read fixed number of characters from a DataInput stream
176      public static String readFixedLengthString(int size,
177         DataInput in) throws IOException {
178         char c[] = new char[size];
179
180         for (int i = 0; i < size; i++)
181            c[i] = in.readChar();
182
183         return new String(c);
184      }
185
186      // Write fixed number of characters (string s with padded spaces)
187      // to a DataOutput stream
188      public static void writeFixedLengthString(String s, int size,
189         DataOutput out) throws IOException {
190         char cBuffer[] = new char[size];
191         s.getChars(0, s.length(), cBuffer, 0);
192         for (int i = s.length(); i < cBuffer.length; i++)
193            cBuffer[i] = ' ';
194         String newS = new String(cBuffer);
195         out.writeChars(newS);
196      }
197   }
```

continues

Example 17.8 continued

```
1    // StudentPanel.java: Panel for displaying student information
2    import javax.swing.*;
3    import javax.swing.border.*;
4    import java.awt.*;
5
6    public class StudentPanel extends JPanel {
7      JTextField jtfName = new JTextField(32);
8      JTextField jtfStreet = new JTextField(32);
9      JTextField jtfCity = new JTextField(20);
10     JTextField jtfState = new JTextField(2);
11     JTextField jtfZip = new JTextField(5);
12
13     /** Construct a student panel */
14     public StudentPanel() {
15       // Set the panel with line border
16       setBorder(new BevelBorder(BevelBorder.RAISED));
17
18       // Panel p1 for holding labels Name, Street, and City
19       JPanel p1 = new JPanel();
20       p1.setLayout(new GridLayout(3, 1));
21       p1.add(new JLabel("Name"));
22       p1.add(new JLabel("Street"));
23       p1.add(new JLabel("City"));
24
25       // Panel jpState for holding state
26       JPanel jpState = new JPanel();
27       jpState.setLayout(new BorderLayout());
28       jpState.add(new JLabel("State"), BorderLayout.WEST);
29       jpState.add(jtfState, BorderLayout.CENTER);
30
31       // Panel jpZip for holding zip
32       JPanel jpZip = new JPanel();
33       jpZip.setLayout(new BorderLayout());
34       jpZip.add(new JLabel("Zip"), BorderLayout.WEST);
35       jpZip.add(jtfZip, BorderLayout.CENTER);
36
37       // Panel p2 for holding jpState and jpZip
38       JPanel p2 = new JPanel();
39       p2.setLayout(new BorderLayout());
40       p2.add(jpState, BorderLayout.WEST);
41       p2.add(jpZip, BorderLayout.CENTER);
42
43       // Panel p3 for holding jtfCity and p2
44       JPanel p3 = new JPanel();
45       p3.setLayout(new BorderLayout());
46       p3.add(jtfCity, BorderLayout.CENTER);
47       p3.add(p2, BorderLayout.EAST);
48
49       // Panel p4 for holding jtfName, jtfStreet, and p3
50       JPanel p4 = new JPanel();
51       p4.setLayout(new GridLayout(3, 1));
52       p4.add(jtfName);
53       p4.add(jtfStreet);
54       p4.add(p3);
55
56       // Place p1 and p4 into StudentPanel
57       setLayout(new BorderLayout());
58       add(p1, BorderLayout.WEST);
59       add(p4, BorderLayout.CENTER);
60     }
61
```

```
62        /** Get student information from the text fields */
63        public Student getStudent() {
64          return new Student(jtfName.getText().trim(),
65                             jtfStreet.getText().trim(),
66                             jtfCity.getText().trim(),
67                             jtfState.getText().trim(),
68                             jtfZip.getText().trim());
69        }
70
71        /** Set student information on the text fields */
72        public void setStudent(Student s) {
73          jtfName.setText(s.getName());
74          jtfStreet.setText(s.getStreet());
75          jtfCity.setText(s.getCity());
76          jtfState.setText(s.getState());
77          jtfZip.setText(s.getZip());
78        }
79      }
```

```
1   // Student.java: Student class encapsulates student information
2   import java.io.*;
3
4   public class Student implements Serializable {
5     private String name;
6     private String street;
7     private String city;
8     private String state;
9     private String zip;
10
11    // Specify the size of five string fields in the record
12    final static int NAME_SIZE = 32;
13    final static int STREET_SIZE = 32;
14    final static int CITY_SIZE = 20;
15    final static int STATE_SIZE = 2;
16    final static int ZIP_SIZE = 5;
17
18    // the total size of the record in bytes, a Unicode
19    // character is 2 bytes size
20    final static int RECORD_SIZE =
21      (NAME_SIZE + STREET_SIZE + CITY_SIZE + STATE_SIZE + ZIP_SIZE);
22
23    /** Default constructor */
24    public Student() {
25    }
26
27    /** Construct a Student with specified name, street, city, state,
28      and zip
29      */
30    public Student(String name, String street, String city,
31      String state, String zip) {
32      this.name = name;
33      this.street = street;
34      this.city = city;
35      this.state = state;
36      this.zip = zip;
37    }
38
39    /** Return name */
40    public String getName() {
41      return name;
42    }
43
```

Example 17.8 continued

```
44      /** Return street */
45      public String getStreet() {
46        return street;
47      }
48
49      /** Return city */
50      public String getCity() {
51        return city;
52      }
53
54      /** Return state */
55      public String getState() {
56        return state;
57      }
58
59      /** Return zip */
60      public String getZip() {
61        return zip;
62      }
63
64      /** Write a student to a data output stream */
65      public void writeStudent(DataOutput out) throws IOException {
66        FixedLengthStringIO.writeFixedLengthString(
67          name, NAME_SIZE, out);
68        FixedLengthStringIO.writeFixedLengthString(
69          street, STREET_SIZE, out);
70        FixedLengthStringIO.writeFixedLengthString(
71          city, CITY_SIZE, out);
72        FixedLengthStringIO.writeFixedLengthString(
73          state, STATE_SIZE, out);
74        FixedLengthStringIO.writeFixedLengthString(
75          zip, ZIP_SIZE, out);
76      }
77
78      /** Read a student from data input stream */
79      public void readStudent(DataInput in) throws IOException {
80        name = FixedLengthStringIO.readFixedLengthString(
81          NAME_SIZE, in);
82        street = FixedLengthStringIO.readFixedLengthString(
83          STREET_SIZE, in);
84        city = FixedLengthStringIO.readFixedLengthString(
85          CITY_SIZE, in);
86        state = FixedLengthStringIO.readFixedLengthString(
87          STATE_SIZE, in);
88        zip = FixedLengthStringIO.readFixedLengthString(
89          ZIP_SIZE, in);
90      }
91    }
```

Review

A random file, student.dat, is created to store student information if the file does not yet exist. If it does exist, the file is opened. A random file object, raf, is used in both the registration and the viewing part of the program. The user can add a new student record to the file in the Register Student panel and view it immediately in the View Student panel.

Several classes are used in this example. Their relationships are shown in Figure 17.22.

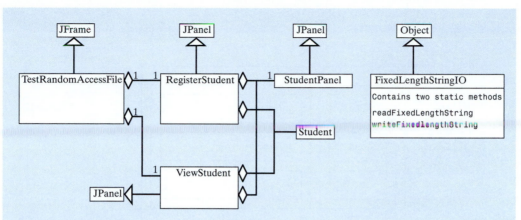

Figure 17.22 *Example 17.8 uses the* `TestRandomAccessFile`, `RegisterStudent`, `ViewStudent`, `StudentPanel`, `Student`, *and* `FixedLengthIO` *classes*.

The main class, `TestRandomAccessFile`, is a subclass of `JFrame`. It creates an instance of the `RegisterStudent` class and an instance of the `ViewStudent` class. These two instances are added to a tabbed pane with two tabs: Register Student and View Student. When the Register Student tab is clicked, the registration panel is shown. When the View Student tab is clicked, the viewing panel is shown.

The `RegisterStudent` class and the `ViewStudent` class have many things in common. They both extend the `JPanel` class, and they both use the `StudentPanel` and `Student` classes.

The student information panels for registering and viewing student information are identical. Therefore, the program creates one class, `StudentPanel`, to lay out the labels and text fields, as shown in Figure 17.23. The `StudentPanel` class also provides the `getStudent` method for getting text fields and the `setStudent` method for setting text fields.

The `Student` class defines the student record structure and provides methods for reading and writing a record into the file. Each field in a student record has a fixed length. The `FixedLengthStringIO` class defines the methods for reading and writing fixed-length strings. The `Student` class implements `Serializable` so that it can be serialized in Example 18.4, "Passing Objects in Network Programs," in Chapter 18, "Networking."

The size of each field in the student record is fixed. For example, zip code is set to a maximum of five characters. If you entered a zip code of more than five characters by mistake, the `ArrayIndexOutofBounds` runtime error would occur when the program attempted to write the zip code into the file using the `writeFixedLengthString` method defined in the `FixedLengthStringIO` class.

continues

Example 17.8 continued

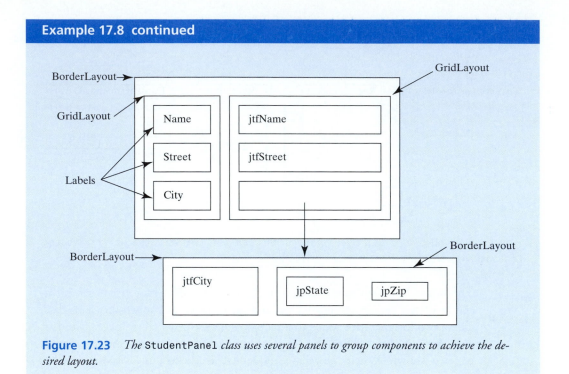

Figure 17.23   *The* StudentPanel *class uses several panels to group components to achieve the desired layout.*

17.13   Parsing Text Files (Optional)

Occasionally you need to process a text file. For example, the Java source file is a text file. The compiler reads the source file and translates it into bytecode, which is a binary file. Java provides the StreamTokenizer class so that you can take an input stream and parse it into words, which are known as *tokens*. The tokens are read one at a time.

To construct an instance of StreamTokenizer, you can use StreamTokenizer(Reader is) on a given character input stream. The StreamTokenizer class contains the useful constants listed in Table 17.3.

TABLE 17.3   StreamTokenizer **Constants**

Constant	Description
TT_WORD	The token is a word.
TT_NUMBER	The token is a number.
TT_EOL	The end of the line has been read.
TT_EOF	The end of the file has been read.

The StreamTokenizer class also contains the useful variables listed in Table 17.4.

TABLE 17.4   `StreamTokenizer` **Variables**

Variable	Description
`int ttype`	Contains the current token type, which matches one of the constants listed previously.
`double nval`	Contains the value of the current token if the token is a number.
`String sval`	Contains a string that gives the characters of the current token if the token is a word.

Typically, the `nextToken()` method is used to retrieve tokens one by one in a loop until `TT_EOF` is returned. The following method parses the next token from the input stream of a `StreamTokenizer`:

```
public int nextToken() throws IOException
```

The type of the next token is returned in the `ttype` field. If `ttype == Stream-Tokenizer.TT_WORD`, the token is stored in `sval`; if `ttype == StreamTokenizer.TT_NUMBER`, the token is stored in `nval`.

Example 17.9 Using `StreamTokenizer`

Problem

Write a program that demonstrates parsing text files. The program reads a text file containing students' exam scores. Each record in the input file consists of a student's name, two midterm exam scores, and a final exam score. The program reads the fields for each record and computes the total score. It then stores the result in a new file. The formula for computing the total score is:

```
total score = midterm1 * 0.3 + midterm2 * 0.3 + final * 0.4;
```

Each record in the output file consists of a student's name and total score.

Solution

The following code gives the solution to the problem. Figure 17.24 shows a sample run of the program.

```
1   // ParsingTextFile.java: Process text file using StreamTokenizer
2   import java.io.*;
3
4   public class ParsingTextFile {
5     /** Main method */
6     public static void main(String[] args) {
7       // Declare file reader and writer streams
8       FileReader frs = null;
9       FileWriter fws = null;
10
11      // Declare streamTokenizer
12      StreamTokenizer in = null;
13
14      // Declare a print stream
15      PrintWriter out = null;
16
```

continues

Example 17.9 continued

```
17          // Four input file fields: student name, midterm1,
18          // midterm2, and final exam score
19          String sname = null;
20          double midterm1 = 0;
21          double midterm2 = 0;
22          double finalScore = 0;
23
24          // Computed total score
25          double total = 0;
26
27          try {
28            // Create file input and output streams
29            frs = new FileReader("in.dat");
30            fws = new FileWriter("out.dat");
31
32            // Create a stream tokenizer wrapping file input stream
33            in = new StreamTokenizer(frs);
34            out = new PrintWriter(fws);
35
36            // Read first token
37            in.nextToken();
38
39            // Process a record
40            while (in.ttype != StreamTokenizer.TT_EOF) {
41              // Get student name
42              if (in.ttype == StreamTokenizer.TT_WORD)
43                sname = in.sval;
44              else
45                System.out.println("Bad file format");
46
47              // Get midterm1
48              if (in.nextToken() == StreamTokenizer.TT_NUMBER)
49                midterm1 = in.nval;
50              else
51                System.out.println("Bad file format");
52
53              // Get midterm2
54              if (in.nextToken() == StreamTokenizer.TT_NUMBER)
55                midterm2 = in.nval;
56              else
57                System.out.println("Bad file format");
58
59              // Get final score
60              if (in.nextToken() == StreamTokenizer.TT_NUMBER)
61                finalScore = in.nval;
62
63              total = midterm1*0.3 + midterm2*0.3 + finalScore*0.4;
64              out.println(sname + " " + total);
65
66              in.nextToken();
67            }
68          }
69          catch (FileNotFoundException ex) {
70            System.out.println("File not found: in.dat");
71          }
72          catch (IOException ex) {
73            System.out.println(ex.getMessage());
74          }
75          finally {
76            try {
77              if (frs != null) frs.close();
78              if (fws != null) fws.close();
79            }
```

```
80              catch (IOException ex) {
81                 System.out.println(ex);
82              }
83           }
84        }
85     }
```

```
Command Prompt                                    _ □ ×

C:\book>type in.dat
James 32 60 30
George 100 100 100
John 90 94 100

C:\book>java ParsingTextFile

C:\book>type out.dat
James 39.6
George 100.0
John 95.2

C:\book>
```

Figure 17.24   *The program uses* StreamTokenizer *to parse the text file into strings and numbers.*

Review

Before running this program, make sure you have created the text file in.dat. To parse the text file in.dat, the program uses StreamTokenizer to wrap a FileReader stream. The nextToken() method is used on a StreamTokenizer object to get one token at a time. The token value is stored in the nval field if the token is numeric, and in the sval field if the token is a string. The token type is stored in the ttype field.

For each record, the program reads the name and the three exam scores and then computes the total score. A FileWriter stream is used to store the name and the total score in the text file out.dat (see Figure 17.25).

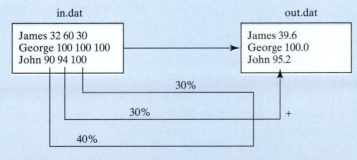

Figure 17.25   *The program reads two midterm scores and a final exam score, and then computes a total score.*

17.14   Array Streams, Piped Streams, String Streams, Pushback Streams, and Line Number Streams (Optional)

You have learned many I/O streams in this chapter. Each stream has its intended application. Streams were first used for file input/output in the C language, but Java streams are not limited to this function. There are several other stream classes that you might find useful. A brief discussion of them follows:

- Array streams like `ByteArrayInputStream`, `CharArrayReader`, `ByteArrayOutputStream`, and `CharArrayWriter` are used to read and write bytes or characters from arrays.

- Piped streams can be thought of as pipes that connect two processes. One process sends data out through the pipe, and the other receives data from the pipe. Piped streams are used in interprocess communication (IPC). Two processes running on separate threads can exchange data. Java provides `PipedInputStream`, `PipedOutputStream`, `PipedReader`, and `PipedWriter` to support piped streams.

- String streams (`StringReader` and `StringWriter`) are exactly like character array streams, except that the source of a string stream is a string, and the destination of a string stream is a string buffer.

- Pushback streams are commonly used in parsers to "push back" a single byte or character in the input stream after reading from the input stream. A pushback stream previews the input to determine what to do next. The number of bytes or characters pushed can be specified when the stream is constructed. By default, a single byte or a single character is pushed back. Java provides the `PushbackInputStream` and `PushbackReader` classes to support pushback streams.

- Line-number streams allow you to track the current line number of an input stream. Java provides the `LineNumberReader` class for this purpose. This class is useful for such applications as editing and debugging. You can use the `getLineNumber()` method to get the current line number of the input, and the `getLine()` method to retrieve a line into a string.

Chapter Summary

In this chapter, you learned about Java input and output. Java handles all I/O in streams. It offers many stream classes for processing all kinds of data.

Streams can be categorized as byte streams and character streams. The `InputStream` and `OutputStream` classes are the root of all byte stream classes, and the `Reader` and `Writer` classes are the root of all character stream classes. The subclasses of `InputStream` and `OutputStream` are analogous to the subclasses of `Reader` and `Writer`. Many of them have similar method signatures, and you can use them in the same way.

File streams (`FileInputStream` and `FileOutputStream` for byte streams, `FileReader` and `FileWriter` for character streams) are used to read data from or write data to external files. Data streams (`DataInputStream` and `DataOutputStream`) read or write Java primitive-data-type values in machine-independent fashion, which enables you to write a data file on one machine and read it on a machine that has a different OS or file structure.

Since the data output stream outputs a binary representation of data, you cannot view its content as text. The `PrintStream` and `PrintWriter` classes allow you to print streams in text format. `System.out`, `System.in`, and `System.err` are examples of `PrintStream` objects.

The `BufferedInputStream`, `BufferedOutputStream`, `BufferedReader`, and `BufferedWriter` classes can be used to speed input and output by reducing the number of reads and writes. Typical physical input/output involving I/O devices is very slow compared with CPU processing, so using buffered I/O can greatly improve performance.

The `JFileChooser` class is used to display standard file dialog boxes from which the user can navigate through the file systems and select files to open or save.

The `ObjectOutputStream` and `ObjectInputStream` classes are used to store and restore objects. To enable object serialization, the object's defining class must implement the `java.io.Serializable` marker interface.

The `RandomAccessFile` class enables you to read and write data to a file at the same time. You can open a file with the `"r"` mode to indicate that it is read-only, or with the `"rw"` mode to indicate that it is updateable. Since the `RandomAccessFile` class implements `DataInput` and `DataOutput` interfaces, many methods in `RandomAccessFile` are the same as those in `DataInputStream` and `DataOutputStream`.

The `StreamTokenizer` class is useful in processing text files. This class enables you to parse an input stream into tokens and read them one at a time.

Review Questions

17.1 Which streams must always be used to process external files?

17.2 What types of data are read or written by `InputStream` and `OutputStream`? Can you use `read()` or `write(byte b)` in these streams?

17.3 `InputStream` reads bytes. Why does the `read()` method return an `int` instead of a byte?

17.4 What types of data are read or written by `Reader` and `Writer`? Can you use `read()` or `write(char c)` in these streams?

17.5 What are the differences between byte streams and character streams?

17.6 What types of data are read or written by file streams? Can you use `read()` or `write(byte b)` in file streams?

17.7 How are data input and output streams used to read and write data?

17.8 What are the differences between `DataOutputStream` and `PrintStream`?

17.9 Is `JFileChooser` modal? What is the return type for `getSelectedFile()` and `getSelectedDirectory()`? How do you set the current directory as the default directory for a `JFileChooser` dialog?

17.10 What are the data types for `System.in`, `System.out`, and `System.err`?

17.11 What types of objects can be stored using the `ObjectOutput` stream? What is the method for writing an object? What is the method for reading an object? What is the return type of the method that reads an object from the `ObjectInputStream`?

17.12 Can `RandomAccessFile` streams read a data file created by `DataOutputStream`?

17.13 Create a `RandomAccessFile` stream for the file student.dat to allow the updating of student information in the file. Create a `DataOutputStream` for the file student.dat. Explain the differences between these two statements.

17.14 What happens if the file test.dat does not exist when you attempt to compile and run the following code?

```
import java.io.*;

class Test {
  public static void main(String[] args) {
    try {
      RandomAccessFile raf =
        new RandomAccessFile("test.dat", "r");
      int i = raf.readInt();
    }
    catch(IOException ex) {
      System.out.println("IO exception");
    }
  }
}
```

17.16 Answer the following questions regarding `StreamTokenizer`:

- When do you use `StreamTokenizer`?

- How do you read data using `StreamTokenizer`?

- Where is the token stored when you are using the `nextToken()` method?

- How do you find the data type of the token?

17.17 Can you close a `StreamTokenizer`?

Programming Exercises

17.1 Rewrite Example 17.2, "Processing External Files," using `FileReader` and `FileWriter` streams. Write another program with buffered streams to boost performance. Test the performance of these two programs (one with buffered streams and the other without buffered streams), as shown in Figure 17.26.

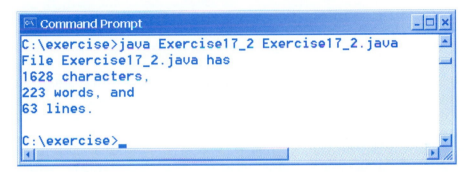

Figure 17.26   *Buffered streams can significantly boost performance.*

17.2   Write a program that will count the number of characters, including blanks, words, and lines, in a file. The filename should be passed as a command-line argument, as shown in Figure 17.27.

```
Command Prompt
C:\exercise>java Exercise17_2 Exercise17_2.java
File Exercise17_2.java has
1628 characters,
223 words, and
63 lines.

C:\exercise>
```

Figure 17.27   *The program displays the number of characters, words, and lines in the given file.*

17.3   Suppose that a text file score.txt contains an unspecified number of scores. Write a program that reads the scores from the file, displays the scores in a text area, and displays the average of the scores. Scores are separated by blanks.

HINT

Read the scores one line at a time until all the lines are read. For each line, use `StringTokenizer` to extract the scores, and convert them into double values using the `Double.parseDouble` method.

17.4   Example 11.5, "Using Combo Boxes," gives a program that lets users view a country's flag image and description by selecting the country from a combo box. The description is a string coded in the program. Rewrite the program to read the text description from a file. Suppose that the descriptions are stored in the file description0.txt, . . ., and description8.txt for the nine countries Canada, China, Denmark, France, Germany, India, Norway, the United Kingdom, and the United States, in this order.

17.5 Rewrite Example 17.5, "Displaying a File in a Text Area," to enable the user to view the file by opening it from a file open dialog box, as shown in Figure 17.28. A file open dialog box is displayed when the Browse button is clicked. The file is displayed in the text area, and the filename is displayed in the text field when the OK button is clicked in the file open dialog box. You can also enter the filename in the text field and press the Enter key to display the file in the text area.

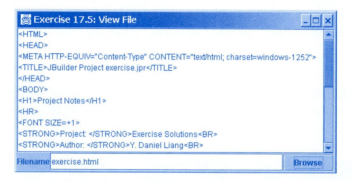

Figure 17.28   *The program enables the user to view a file by selecting it from a file open dialog box.*

17.6 Write a program to select an audio file using the file dialog box, and use three buttons, Play, Loop, and Stop, to control the audio, as shown in Figure 17.29. If you click the Play button, the audio file is played once. If you click the Loop button, the audio file keeps playing repeatedly. If you click the Stop button, the playing stops. The selected audio files are stored in the folder named anthems under the exercise directory. The exercise directory contains the class file for this exercise.

Figure 17.29   *The program allows you to choose an audio file from a dialog box, and use the buttons to play, repeatedly play, or stop the audio.*

17.7 Write a Java application that will display a stock index ticker, as shown in Figure 15.16 for Exercise 15.6. In that exercise, the stock index information is passed from the `<param>` tag in the HTML file.

Your program will get index information from an external text file. The first line in the file contains an integer that indicates the number of stock indices given in the file. Each subsequent line should consist of four fields: Index Name, Current Time, Previous Day Index, and Index Change. The fields are separated by the pound sign (#). The file could contain three lines, such as the following:

```
2
S&P 500#15:54#919.01#4.54
NIKKEI#04:03#1865.17#-7.00
```

17.8 In Example 11.12, "Creating Multiple Windows," you developed a program that displays a histogram to show the occurrences of each letter in a text area. Reuse the `Histogram` class created in Example 11.12 to write a program that will display a histogram on a panel. The histogram should show the occurrences of each letter in a text file, as in Figure 17.30. Assume that the letters are not case-sensitive.

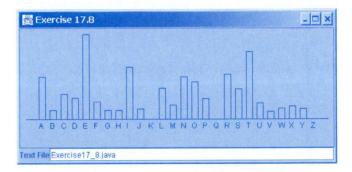

Figure 17.30 *The program displays a histogram that shows the occurrences of each letter in the file.*

■ Place a panel that will display the histogram in the center of the frame.

■ Place a label and a text field in a panel, and put the panel in the south side of the frame. The text file will be entered from this text field.

■ Pressing the Enter key on the text field causes the program to count the occurrences of each letter and display the count in a histogram.

17.9 Modify the View Student panel in Example 17.8, "Using Random Access Files," to add an Update button for updating the student record that is being displayed, as shown in Figure 17.31. The Tab "View Student" is now changed to "View and Update Student."

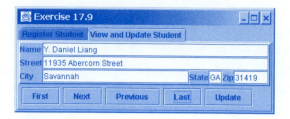

Figure 17.31   *You can browse student records and update the student record that is currently displayed.*

17.10   Use `StreamTokenizer` to write a program that will add all of the integers in a data file. Suppose that the integers are delimited by spaces. Display the result on the console. Rewrite the program, assuming this time that the numbers are `double`.

17.11   Rewrite Example 17.9, "Using `StreamTokenizer`," so that it reads a line as a string in a `BufferedReader` stream, and then use `StringTokenizer` to extract the fields.

17.12   Write a program that converts the Java source code from the next-line brace style to the end-of-line brace style. For example, the following Java source uses the next-line brace style:

```
public class Test
{
  public static void main(String[] args)
  {
      System.out.println("Welcome to Java!");
  }
}
```

Your program converts it to the end-of-line brace style, as follows:

```
public class Test {
  public static void main(String[] args) {
      System.out.println("Welcome to Java!");
  }
}
```

Your program can be invoked from the command line with the Java source code file as the argument. It converts the Java source code to a new format. For example, the following command converts the Java source code file Test.java into the end-of-line brace style.

```
java Exercise17_12 Test.java
```

NETWORKING

Objectives

- To comprehend socket-based communication in Java.
- To understand client/server computing.
- To implement Java networking programs.
- To produce servers for multiple clients.
- To send and receive objects on the network.
- To develop applets that communicate with the server.
- To use the URL class and view Web pages from the applet.
- To create applications or applets to retrieve files from the network.
- To view HTML files from the JEditorPane class.

18.1   Introduction

Networking is tightly integrated in Java. *Socket-based communication* is provided that enables programs to communicate through designated sockets. A *socket* is an abstraction that facilitates communication between a server and a client. Java treats socket communications much as it treats I/O operations; thus programs can read from or write to sockets as easily as they can read from or write to files.

Java supports stream sockets and datagram sockets. *Stream sockets* use TCP (Transmission Control Protocol) for data transmission, whereas *datagram sockets* use UDP (User Datagram Protocol). Since TCP can detect lost transmissions and resubmit them, transmissions are lossless and reliable. UDP, in contrast, cannot guarantee lossless transmission. Because of this, stream sockets are used in most areas of Java programming, and that is why the discussion in this chapter is based on stream sockets. For examples of when and how to use datagrams, please see "Networking Programming Using Datagrams" at www.prenhall.edu/liang/intro4e.html.

18.2   Client/Server Computing

Network programming usually involves a server and one or more clients. The client sends requests to the server, and the server responds to the requests. The client begins by attempting to establish a connection to the server. The server can accept or deny the connection. Once a connection is established, the client and the server communicate through sockets.

The server must be running when a client starts. The server waits for a connection request from a client. The statements needed to create a server and a client are shown in Figure 18.1.

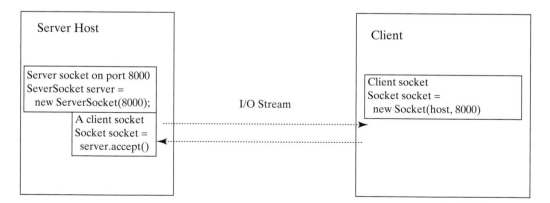

Figure 18.1   *The server creates a server socket and, once a connection to a client is established, connects to the client with a client socket.*

To establish a server, you need to create a server socket and attach it to a port, which is where the server listens for connections. The port identifies the TCP service on the socket. Port numbers between 0 and 1023 are reserved for privileged processes. For instance, the e-mail server runs on port 25, and the Web server usually runs on port 80. You can choose any port number that is not currently used by any other process. The following statement creates a server socket s:

```
ServerSocket s = new ServerSocket(port);
```

> **NOTE**
> Attempting to create a server socket on a port already in use would cause the
> `java.net.BindException`.

After a server socket is created, the server can use the following statement to listen for connections:

```
Socket connectToClient = s.accept();
```

This statement waits until a client connects to the server socket. The client issues the following statement to request a connection to a server:

```
Socket connectToServer = new Socket(ServerName, port);
```

This statement opens a socket so that the client program can communicate with the server. `ServerName` is the server's Internet host name or IP address. The following statement creates a socket at port 8000 on the client machine to connect to the host `drake.armstrong.edu`:

```
Socket connectToServer = new Socket("drake.armstrong.edu", 8000);
```

Alternatively, you can use the IP address to create a socket, as follows:

```
Socket connectToServer = new Socket("130.254.204.36", 8000)
```

An IP address, consisting of four dotted decimal numbers between 0 and 255, such as 130.254.204.36, is a computer's unique identity on the Internet. Since it is not easy to remember so many numbers, they are often mapped to meaningful names called *host names*, such as

```
drake.armstrong.edu.
```

A program can use the host name `localhost` or the IP address 127.0.0.1 to refer to the machine on which a client is running.

> **NOTE**
> There are special servers on the Internet that translate host names into IP addresses. These servers are called Domain Name Servers (DNS). The translation is done behind the scenes. When you create a socket with a host name, the Java Runtime System asks the DNS to translate the host name into the IP address.

After the server accepts the connection, communication between server and client is conducted the same as for I/O streams. The statements needed to create the streams and to exchange data between them are shown in Figure 18.2.

To get an input stream and an output stream, use the `getInputStream()` and `getOutputStream()` methods on a socket object. For example, the following

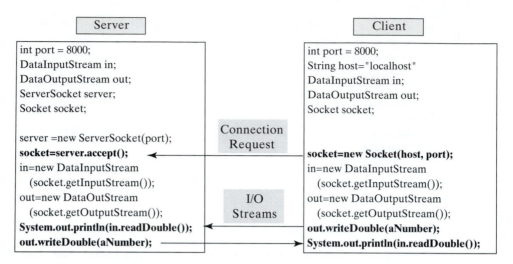

Figure 18.2   *The server and client exchange data through I/O streams on top of the socket.*

statements create an `InputStream` stream, `isFromServer`, and an `OutputStream` stream, `osToServer`, from the socket `connectToServer`:

```
InputStream isFromServer = connectToServer.getInputStream();
OutputStream osToServer = connectToServer.getOutputStream();
```

The `InputStream` and `OutputStream` streams are used to read or write bytes. You can use `DataInputStream`, `DataOutputStream`, `BufferedReader`, and `PrintWriter` to wrap on the `InputStream` and `OutputStream` to read or write data, such as `int`, `double`, or `String`. The following statements, for instance, create a `DataInputStream` stream, `isFromClient`, and a `DataOutput` stream, `osToClient`, to read and write primitive data values:

```
DataInputStream isFromClient = new DataInputStream
  (connectToClient.getInputStream());

DataOutputStream osToClient = new DataOutputStream
  (connectToClient.getOutputStream());
```

The server can use `isFromClient.readDouble()` to receive a double value from the client, and `osToClient.writeDouble(d)` to send double value `d` to the client.

Example 18.1 A Client/Server Example

Problem

This example presents a client program and a server program. The client sends data to a server. The server receives the data, uses them to produce a result, and then sends the result back to the client. The client displays the result on the console. In this example, the data sent from the client comprise the radius of a circle, and the result produced by the server is the area of the circle (see Figure 18.3).

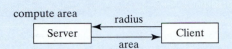

Figure 18.3   *The client sends the radius to the server; the server computes the area and sends it to the client.*

Solution

The server program follows. A sample run of the program is shown in Figure 18.4.

Figure 18.4   *The server receives a radius from the client, computes the area, and sends the area to the client.*

```
1    // Server.java: The server accepts data from the client, processes it
2    // and returns the result back to the client
3    import java.io.*;
4    import java.net.*;
5    import java.util.*;
6    import java.awt.*;
7    import java.awt.event.*;
8    import javax.swing.*;
9
10   public class Server extends JFrame {
11     // Text area for displaying contents
12     private JTextArea jta = new JTextArea();
13
14     public static void main(String[] args) {
15       new Server();
16     }
17
18     public Server() {
19       // Place text area on the frame
20       getContentPane().setLayout(new BorderLayout());
21       getContentPane().add(new JScrollPane(jta), BorderLayout.CENTER);
22
23       setTitle("Server");
24       setSize(500, 300);
25       setDefaultCloseOperation(JFrame.EXIT_ON_CLOSE);
26       setVisible(true); // It is necessary to show the frame here!
27
28       try {
29         // Create a server socket
```

continues

Example 18.1 continued

```
30              ServerSocket serverSocket = new ServerSocket(8000);
31              jta.append("Server started at " + new Date() + '\n');
32
33              // Listen for a connection request
34              Socket connectToClient = serverSocket.accept();
35
36              // Create data input and output streams
37              DataInputStream isFromClient = new DataInputStream(
38                connectToClient.getInputStream());
39              DataOutputStream osToClient = new DataOutputStream(
40                connectToClient.getOutputStream());
41
42              while (true) {
43                // Receive radius from the client
44                double radius = isFromClient.readDouble();
45
46                // Compute area
47                double area = radius*radius*Math.PI;
48
49                // Send area back to the client
50                osToClient.writeDouble(area);
51
52                jta.append("radius received from client: " + radius + '\n');
53                jta.append("Area found: " + area + '\n');
54              }
55            }
56          catch(IOException ex) {
57            System.err.println(ex);
58          }
59        }
60      }
```

The client program follows. A sample run of the program is shown in Figure 18.5.

Figure 18.5   *The client sends the radius to the server and receives the area from the server.*

```
1       // Client.java: The client sends the input to the server and receives
2       // result back from the server
3       import java.io.*;
4       import java.net.*;
5       import java.util.*;
6       import java.awt.*;
7       import java.awt.event.*;
8       import javax.swing.*;
9
```

```
10    public class Client extends JFrame implements ActionListener {
11      // Text field for receiving radius
12      private JTextField jtf = new JTextField();
13
14      // Text area to display contents
15      private JTextArea jta = new JTextArea();
16
17      // IO streams
18      DataOutputStream osToServer;
19      DataInputStream isFromServer;
20      public static void main(String[] args) {
21        new Client();
22      }
23
24      public Client() {
25        // Panel p to hold the label and text field
26        JPanel p = new JPanel();
27        p.setLayout(new BorderLayout());
28        p.add(new JLabel("Enter radius"), BorderLayout.WEST);
29        p.add(jtf, BorderLayout.CENTER);
30        jtf.setHorizontalAlignment(JTextField.RIGHT);
31
32        getContentPane().setLayout(new BorderLayout());
33        getContentPane().add(p, BorderLayout.NORTH);
34        getContentPane().add(new JScrollPane(jta), BorderLayout.CENTER);
35
36        jtf.addActionListener(this); // Register listener
37
38        setTitle("Client");
39        setSize(500,300);
40        setDefaultCloseOperation(JFrame.EXIT_ON_CLOSE);
41        setVisible(true); // It is necessary to show the frame here!
42
43        try {
44          // Create a socket to connect to the server
45          Socket connectToServer = new Socket("localhost", 8000);
46          //Socket connectToServer = new Socket("130.254.204.36", 8000);
47          //Socket connectToServer = new Socket(
48          //   "drake.Armstrong.edu", 8000);
49
50          // Create an input stream to receive data from the server
51          isFromServer = new DataInputStream(
52            connectToServer.getInputStream());
53
54          // Create an output stream to send data to the server
56          osToServer =
57            new DataOutputStream(connectToServer.getOutputStream());
58        }
59        catch (IOException ex) {
60          jta.append(ex.toString() + '\n');
61        }
62      }
63
64      public void actionPerformed(ActionEvent e) {
65        String actionCommand = e.getActionCommand();
66        if (e.getSource() instanceof JTextField) {
67          try {
68            // Get the radius from the text field
69            double radius = Double.parseDouble(jtf.getText().trim());
70
71            // Send the radius to the server
```

Example 18.1 continued

```
72                osToServer.writeDouble(radius);
73                osToServer.flush();
74                // Get area from the server
75                double area = isFromServer.readDouble();
76
77                // Display to the text area
78                jta.append("Radius is " + radius + "\n");
79                jta.append("Area received from the server is "
80                  + area + '\n');
81            }
82          catch (IOException ex) {
83            System.err.println(ex);
84          }
85        }
86      }
87    }
```

Review

You start the server program first, then start the client program. In the client program, enter a radius in the text field and press Enter to send the radius to the server. The server computes the area and sends it back to the client. This process is repeated until one of the two programs terminates.

The networking classes are in the package `java.net`. This should be imported when writing Java network programs.

The `Server` class creates a `ServerSocket serverSocket` and attaches it to port 8000, using the following statement (Line 30 in Server.java):

```
ServerSocket serverSocket = new ServerSocket(8000);
```

The server then starts to listen for connection requests, using the following statement (Line 34 in Server.java):

```
Socket connectToClient = serverSocket.accept();
```

The server waits until a client requests a connection. After it is connected, the server reads the radius from the client through an input stream, computes the area, and sends the result to the client through an output stream.

The `Client` class uses the following statement to create a socket that will request a connection to the server on the same machine (localhost) at port 8000 (Line 45 in Client.java).

```
Socket connectToServer = new Socket("localhost", 8000);
```

If you run the server and the client on different machines, replace `localhost` with the server machine's host name or IP address. In this example, the server and the client are running on the same machine.

If the server is not running, the client program terminates with a `java.net.ConnectException`. After it is connected, the client gets input and output streams—wrapped by data input and output streams—in order to receive and send data to the server.

If you receive a `java.net.BindException` when you start the server, the server port is currently in use. You need to terminate the process that is using the server port and then restart the server.

What happens if the `setVisible(true)` statement in Line 26 in Server.java is moved after the `try/catch` block in Line 59 in Server.java? The frame would not be displayed because the `while` loop in the `try/catch` block will not finish until the program terminates.

18.3 Serving Multiple Clients and the *InetAddress* class

Multiple clients are quite often connected to a single server at the same time. Typically, a server runs constantly on a server computer, and clients from all over the Internet may want to connect to it. You can use threads to handle the server's multiple clients simultaneously. Simply create a thread for each connection. Here is how the server handles the establishment of a connection:

```
while (true) {
  Socket connectToClient = serverSocket.accept();
  Thread thread = new ThreadClass(connectToClient);
  thread.start();
}
```

The server socket can have many connections. Each iteration of the `while` loop creates a new connection. Whenever a connection is established, a new thread is created to handle communication between the server and the new client; and this allows multiple connections to run at the same time.

Occasionally, you would like to know who is connecting to the server. You can use the `InetAddress` class to find the client's host name and IP address. The `InetAddress` class models an IP address. You can use the statement shown below to create an instance of `InetAddress` for the client on the socket `connectToClient`.

```
InetAddress clientInetAddress = connectToClient.getInetAddress();
```

Next, you can display the client's host name and IP address, as follows:

```
System.out.println("Client's host name is " +
  clientInetAddress.getHostName());
System.out.println("Client's IP Address is " +
  clientInetAddress.getHostAddress());
```

Example 18.2 Serving Multiple Clients

Problem

Write a server that serves multiple clients simultaneously. For each connection, the server starts a new thread. This thread continuously receives input (the radius of a circle) from clients and sends the results (the area of the circle) back to corresponding clients (see Figure 18.6).

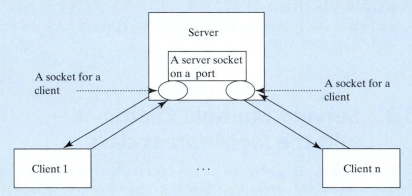

Figure 18.6 *Multithreading enables a server to handle multiple independent clients.*

Solution

The new server program follows. A sample run of the server is shown in Figure 18.7, and sample runs of two clients are shown in Figures 18.8 and 18.9.

Figure 18.7 *The server spawns a thread in order to serve a client.*

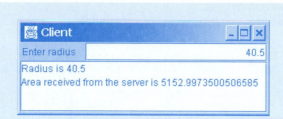

Figure 18.8   *The first client communicates to the server on thread 1.*

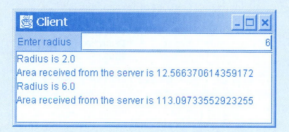

Figure 18.9   *The second client communicates to the server on thread 2.*

```
1    // MultiThreadServer.java: The server can communicate with
2    // multiple clients concurrently using the multiple threads
3    import java.io.*;
4    import java.net.*;
5    import java.util.*;
6    import java.awt.*;
7    import java.awt.event.*;
8    import javax.swing.*;
9
10   public class MultiThreadServer extends JFrame {
11     // Text area for displaying contents
12     private JTextArea jta = new JTextArea();
13
14     public static void main(String[] args) {
15       new MultiThreadServer();
16     }
17
18     public MultiThreadServer() {
19       // Place text area on the frame
20       getContentPane().setLayout(new BorderLayout());
21       getContentPane().add(new JScrollPane(jta), BorderLayout.CENTER);
22
23       setTitle("MultiThreadServer");
24       setSize(500, 300);
25       setDefaultCloseOperation(JFrame.EXIT_ON_CLOSE);
26       setVisible(true); // It is necessary to show the frame here!
27
28       try {
29         // Create a server socket
30         ServerSocket serverSocket = new ServerSocket(8000);
31         jta.append("MultiThreadServer started at " + new Date() + '\n');
32
33         // Number a client
34         int clientNo = 1;
35
```

continues

Example 18.2 continued

```
36          while (true) {
37            // Listen for a new connection request
38            Socket connectToClient = serverSocket.accept();
39
40            // Display the client number
41            jta.append("Starting thread for client " + clientNo +
42              " at " + new Date() + '\n');
43
44            // Find the client's host name, and IP address
45            InetAddress clientInetAddress =
46              connectToClient.getInetAddress();
47            jta.append("Client " + clientNo + "'s host name is "
48              + clientInetAddress.getHostName() + "\n");
49            jta.append("Client " + clientNo + "'s IP Address is "
50              + clientInetAddress.getHostAddress() + "\n");
51
52            // Create a new thread for the connection
53            HandleAClient thread = new HandleAClient(connectToClient);
54            // Start the new thread
55            thread.start();
56
57            // Increment clientNo
58            clientNo++;
59          }
60        }
61      catch(IOException ex) {
62        System.err.println(ex);
63      }
64    }
65
66    // Inner class
67    // Define the thread class for handling new connection
68    class HandleAClient extends Thread {
69      private Socket connectToClient; // A connected socket
70
71      /** Construct a thread */
72      public HandleAClient(Socket socket) {
73        connectToClient = socket;
74      }
75
76      /** Run a thread */
77      public void run() {
78        try {
79          // Create data input and output streams
80          DataInputStream isFromClient = new DataInputStream(
81            connectToClient.getInputStream());
82          DataOutputStream osToClient = new DataOutputStream(
83            connectToClient.getOutputStream());
84
85          // Continuously serve the client
86          while (true) {
87            // Receive radius from the client
88            double radius = isFromClient.readDouble();
89
90            // Compute area
91            double area = radius*radius*Math.PI;
92
93            // Send area back to the client
94            osToClient.writeDouble(area);
95
```

```
96              jta.append("radius received from client: " +
97                radius + '\n');
98              jta.append("Area found: " + area + '\n');
99            }
100         }
101         catch(IOException e) {
102           System.err.println(e);
103         }
104       }
105     }
106   }
```

Review

The server creates a server socket at port 8000 and waits for a connection. When a connection with a client is established, the server creates a new thread to handle the communication. It then waits for another connection.

The threads, which run independently of one another, communicate with designated clients. Each thread creates data input and output streams that receive and send data to the client.

This server accepts an unlimited number of clients. To limit the number of concurrent connections, you can use a thread group to monitor the number of active threads and modify the while loop (Lines 36–59), as follows:

```
ThreadGroup group = new ThreadGroup("serving clients");

while (true) {
  if (group.activeCount() >= maxThreadLimit) {
    try {
      Thread.sleep(1000);
    }
    catch (InterruptedException ex) {
    }

    continue;
  }

  // Listen for a new connection request
  Socket connectToClient = serverSocket.accept();

  // Display the client number
  jta.append("Starting thread for client " + clientNo +
    " at " + new Date() + '\n');

  // Create a new thread for the connection
  Thread thread = new Thread(group,
    new HandleAClient(connectToClient));

  // Start the new thread
  thread.start();

  // Increment clientNo to label the next connection
  clientNo++;
}
```

18.4   Applet Clients

Because of security constraints, applets can only connect to the host from which they were loaded. Therefore, the HTML file must be located on the machine on which the server is running. Below is an example of how to use an applet to connect to a server.

Example 18.3 Creating Applet Clients

Problem

This example, which is similar to Example 17.8, "Using Random Access Files," in Chapter 17, "Input and Output," shows how to use an applet to register students. The client collects and sends registration information to the server. The server appends the information to a data file using a random access file stream.

Solution

The server program follows. A sample run of the program is shown in Figure 18.10.

Figure 18.10   *The server receives information from a client (name, street, city, state, and zip code) and stores it in a file.*

```
1    // RegistrationServer.java: The server for the applet responsible for
2    // writing on the server side
3    import java.io.*;
4    import java.net.*;
5    import javax.swing.*;
6    import java.awt.*;
7    import java.util.Date;
8
9    public class RegistrationServer extends JFrame {
10     private static JTextArea jtaLog;
11
12     // The file to store the records
13     private static RandomAccessFile raf = null;
14
15     /** Main method */
16     public static void main(String[] args) {
17       RegistrationServer server = new RegistrationServer();
18     }
19
20     public RegistrationServer() {
21       // Create a scroll pane to hold text area
```

```
22          JScrollPane scrollPane = new JScrollPane(
23            jtaLog = new JTextArea());
24
25          // Add the scroll pane to the frame
26          getContentPane().add(scrollPane, BorderLayout.CENTER);
27
28          setDefaultCloseOperation(JFrame.EXIT_ON_CLOSE);
29          setSize(300, 300);
30          setTitle("Registration Server");
31          setVisible(true);
32
33          // Open the local file on the server side
34          try {
35            // Open the file if the file exists, create a new file
36            // if the file does not exist
37            raf = new RandomAccessFile("student.dat", "rw");
38          }
39          catch(IOException ex) {
40            jtaLog.append(new Date() + ": Error: " + ex);
41            System.exit(0);
42          }
43
44          // Establish server socket
45          try {
46            // Create a server socket
47            ServerSocket serverSocket = new ServerSocket(8000);
48            jtaLog.append(new Date() + ": Start a new server\n");
49
50            // Count the number of threads started
51            int count = 1;
52
53            while (true) {
54              // Connect to a client
55              Socket socket = serverSocket.accept();
56              jtaLog.append(new Date() + ": A client at " +
57                socket.getInetAddress().getHostAddress() + " connected\n");
58
59              // Start a new thread to register a client
60              new RegistrationThread(socket, count++).start();
61            }
62          }
63          catch (IOException ex) {
64          }
65        }
66
67        /** Write student information to the file */
68        private synchronized static void writeToFile(Student student) {
69          try {
70            // Append it to "student.dat"
71            raf.seek(raf.length());
72            student.writeStudent(raf);
73
74            // Display data saved
75            jtaLog.append("The following info saved in the file\n");
76            jtaLog.append(student.toString());
77          }
78          catch (Exception ex) {
79            jtaLog.append(new Date() + ": " + ex);
80          }
81        }
82
```

continues

Example 18.3 continued

```
83      // Define a thread to process the client registration
84    class RegistrationThread extends Thread {
85      // The socket to serve a client
86      private Socket socket;
87
88      private int clientNo; // The thread number
89
90      // Buffered reader to get input from the client
91      private BufferedReader in;
92
93      // Create a registration thread
94      public RegistrationThread(Socket socket, int clientNo) {
95        this.socket = socket;
96        this.clientNo = clientNo;
97
98        jtaLog.append(new Date() + ": Thread " + clientNo
99          + " started\n");
100
101       // Create an input stream to receive data from a client
102       try {
103         in = new BufferedReader
104           (new InputStreamReader(socket.getInputStream()));
105       }
106       catch(IOException ex) {
107         jtaLog.append(new Date() + ": " + ex);
108       }
109     }
110
111     public void run() {
112       String name;
113       String street;
114       String city;
115       String state;
116       String zip;
117
118       try {
119         // Receive data from the client
120         name = new String(in.readLine());
121         street = new String(in.readLine());
122         city = new String(in.readLine());
123         state = new String(in.readLine());
124         zip = new String(in.readLine());
125
126         // Create a student instance
127         Student student =
128           new Student(name, street, city, state, zip);
129
130         writeToFile(student);
131       }
132       catch (IOException ex) {
133         System.out.println(ex);
134       }
134     }
136   }
137   }
```

The applet client follows, and a sample run is shown in Figure 18.11.

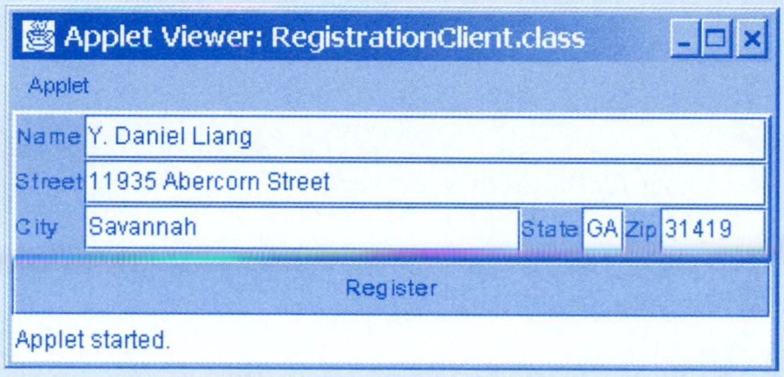

Figure 18.11 *The client gathers the name and address and sends them to the server.*

```
1    // RegistrationClient.java: The applet client for gathering student
2    // informationthe and passing it to the server
3    import java.io.*;
4    import java.net.*;
5    import java.awt.BorderLayout;
6    import java.awt.event.*;
7    import javax.swing.*;
8
9    public class RegistrationClient extends JApplet
10     implements ActionListener {
11     // Button for registering a student in the file
12     private JButton jbtRegister = new JButton("Register");
13
14     // Create student information panel
15     private StudentPanel studentPanel = new StudentPanel();
16
17     // Indicate if it runs as application
18     private boolean isStandAlone = false;
19
20     // Host name or ip
21     private String host = "localhost";
22
23     public void init() {
24       // Add the student panel and button to the applet
25       getContentPane().add(studentPanel, BorderLayout.CENTER);
26       getContentPane().add(jbtRegister, BorderLayout.SOUTH);
27
28       // Register listener
29       jbtRegister.addActionListener(this);
30     }
31
32     /** Handle button action */
33     public void actionPerformed(ActionEvent e) {
34       if (e.getSource() == jbtRegister) {
35         try {
36           // Establish connection with the server
37           Socket socket;
38           if (isStandAlone)
39             socket = new Socket(host, 8000);
40           else
41             socket = new Socket(getCodeBase().getHost(), 8000);
42
43           // Create an output stream to the server
44           PrintWriter toServer =
45             new PrintWriter(socket.getOutputStream(), true);
46
```

continues

Example 18.3 continued

```
47                // Get text field
48                Student s = studentPanel.getStudent();
49
50                // Get data from text fields and send it to the server
51                toServer.println(s.getName());
52                toServer.println(s.getStreet());
53                toServer.println(s.getCity());
54                toServer.println(s.getState());
55                toServer.println(s.getZip());
56            }
57          catch (IOException ex) {
58            System.err.println(ex);
59          }
60        }
61      }
62
63      /** Run the applet as an application */
64      public static void main(String[] args) {
65        // Create a frame
66        JFrame frame = new JFrame("Register Student Client");
67
68        // Create an instance of the applet
69        RegistrationClient applet = new RegistrationClient();
70        applet.isStandAlone = true;
71
72        // Get host
73        if (args.length == 1) applet.host = args[0];
74
75        // Add the applet instance to the frame
76        frame.getContentPane().add(applet, BorderLayout.CENTER);
77
78        // Invoke init() and start()
79        applet.init();
80        applet.start();
81
82        // Display the frame
83        frame.pack();
84        frame.setVisible(true);
85      }
86    }
```

Review

Let us first review RegistrationServer.java:

The server handles multiple clients. It waits for a connection request from a client in the `while` loop (Line 55). After a connection with a client is established, the server creates a thread to serve the client. The server then stays in the `while` loop to listen for the next connection request.

The server passes `socket` (connection socket) and `clientNo` (thread number) to the thread (Line 60). The `clientNo` argument is nonessential; its only use is to identify the thread. The thread receives student information from the client through the `BufferedReader` stream and appends a student record to **student.dat**, using the random-access file `raf`.

The `StudentPanel` and `Student` classes were defined in Example 17.8, "Using Random Access Files." The statement (Lines 127–128) given below creates an instance of `Student`:

```
Student student = new Student(name, street, city, state, zip);
```

The next code (Line 130) writes the student record into the file:

```
s.writeStudent(raf);
```

Now let us review RegistrationClient.java:

The client is an applet and can run standalone. When it runs as an applet, it uses `getCodeBase().getHost()` (Line 41) to return the IP address for the server. When it runs as an application, it passes the URL from the command line. If the URL is not passed from the command line, by default "localhost" is used for the URL.

The data are entered into text fields (name, street, city, state, and zip). When the Register button is clicked, the data from the text fields are collected and sent to the server. Each time the Register button is clicked from a client, the server creates a new thread to store the student information. Obviously, this is not efficient. In Exercise 18.3, you will modify the program to enable one thread to handle all the registration requests from a single client.

When multiple clients register students simultaneously, data may be corrupted. To avoid this, the `writeToFile()` method (Line 68) is synchronized and defined as a static method. The synchronization is at the class level, meaning that only one object of the `RegistrationThread` at a time can execute the `writeToFile()` method to write a student to the file.

18.5   Sending and Receiving Objects

In the preceding examples, you learned to pass data of primitive types. You can also pass objects. To enable passing, the objects must be serializable. The following example demonstrates how to pass objects.

Example 18.4 Passing Objects in Network Programs

Problem

This example rewrites Example 18.3, "Creating Applet Clients," using object streams on the socket. Instead of passing name, street, state, and zip separately, the program passes the student object as a whole object.

Solution

The client uses the `writeObject` method in the `ObjectOutputStream` class to send a student to the server, and the server receives the student using the `readObject` method in the `ObjectInputStream` class. The server and client programs are given as follows:

continues

Example 18.4 continued

```
1    // RegistrationServerUsingObjectStream.java: The server for the
2    // applet responsible for writing on the server side
3    import java.io.*;
4    import java.net.*;
5    import javax.swing.*;
6    import java.awt.*;
7    import java.util.Date;
8
9    public class RegistrationServerUsingObjectStream extends JFrame {
10     private static JTextArea jtaLog;
11
12     // The file to store the records
13     private static RandomAccessFile raf = null;
14
15     /** Main method */
16     public static void main(String[] args) {
17       RegistrationServerUsingObjectStream server =
18         new RegistrationServerUsingObjectStream();
19     }
20
21     public RegistrationServerUsingObjectStream() {
22       // Create a scroll pane to hold text area
23       JScrollPane scrollPane = new JScrollPane(
24         jtaLog = new JTextArea());
25
26       // Add the scroll pane to the frame
27       getContentPane().add(scrollPane, BorderLayout.CENTER);
28
29       setDefaultCloseOperation(JFrame.EXIT_ON_CLOSE);
30       setSize(300, 300);
31       setTitle("Registration Server Using Object Streams");
32       setVisible(true);
33
34       // Open the local file on the server side
35       try {
36         // Open the file if the file exists, create a new file
37         // if the file does not exist
38         raf = new RandomAccessFile("student.dat", "rw");
39       }
40       catch(IOException ex) {
41         jtaLog.append(new Date() + ": Error: " + ex);
42         System.exit(0);
43       }
44
45       // Establish server socket
46       try {
47         // Create a server socket
48         ServerSocket serverSocket = new ServerSocket(8000);
49         jtaLog.append(new Date() + ": Start a new server\n");
50
51         // Count the number of threads started
52         int count = 1;
53
54         while (true) {
55           // Connect to a client
56           Socket socket = serverSocket.accept();
57           jtaLog.append(new Date() + ": A client at " +
58             socket.getInetAddress().getHostAddress() + " connected\n");
59
60           // Start a new thread to register a client
61           new RegistrationThread(socket, count++).start();
62         }
63       }
```

```
64              catch (IOException ex) {
65                jtaLog.append(new Date() + ": " + ex);
66              }
67          }
68
69          /** Write student information to the file */
70          private synchronized static void writeToFile(Student student) {
71            try {
72              // Append it to "student.dat"
73              raf.seek(raf.length());
74              student.writeStudent(raf);
75
76              // Display data saved
77              jtaLog.append("The following info is saved in the file\n");
78              jtaLog.append(student.toString());
79            }
80            catch (Exception ex) {
81              jtaLog.append(new Date() + ": " + ex);
82            }
83          }
84
85          /** Define a thread to process the client registration */
86          class RegistrationThread extends Thread {
87            // The socket to serve a client
88            private Socket socket;
89
90            private int clientNo; // The thread number
91
92            // Object input stream to get input from the client
93            private ObjectInputStream in;
94
95            // Create a registration thread
96            public RegistrationThread(Socket socket, int clientNo) {
97              this.socket = socket;
98              this.clientNo = clientNo;
99              jtaLog.append(new Date() + ": Thread " + clientNo
100                 + " started\n");
101
102             // Create an input stream to receive data from a client
103             try {
104               in = new ObjectInputStream(socket.getInputStream());
105             }
106             catch(IOException ex) {
107               jtaLog.append(new Date() + ": " + ex);
108             }
109           }
110
111           public void run() {
112             try {
113               // Receive data from the client
114               Student student = (Student)in.readObject();
115
116               writeToFile(student);
117             }
118             catch (Exception ex) {
119               System.out.println(ex);
120             }
121           }
122         }
123     }
```

continues

Example 18.4 continued

```
1    // RegistrationClientUsingObjectStream.java: The applet client for
2    // gathering student informationthe and passing it to the server
3    import java.io.*;
4    import java.net.*;
5    import java.awt.BorderLayout;
6    import java.awt.event.*;
7    import javax.swing.*;
8
9    public class RegistrationClientUsingObjectStream extends JApplet
10     implements ActionListener {
11     // Button for registering a student in the file
12     private JButton jbtRegister = new JButton("Register");
13
14     // Create student information panel
15     private StudentPanel studentPanel = new StudentPanel();
16
17     // Indicate if it runs as application
18     private boolean isStandAlone = false;
19
20     // Host name or ip
21     String host = "localhost";
22
23     public void init() {
24       // Add the student panel and button to the applet
25       getContentPane().add(studentPanel, BorderLayout.CENTER);
26       getContentPane().add(jbtRegister, BorderLayout.SOUTH);
27
28       // Register listener
29       jbtRegister.addActionListener(this);
30
31       // Find the IP address of the Web server
32       if (!isStandAlone)
33         host = getCodeBase().getHost();
34     }
35
36     /** Handle button action */
37     public void actionPerformed(ActionEvent e) {
38       if (e.getSource() == jbtRegister) {
39         try {
40           // Establish connection with the server
41           Socket socket = new Socket(host, 8000);
42
43           // Create an output stream to the server
44           ObjectOutputStream toServer =
45             new ObjectOutputStream(socket.getOutputStream());
46
47           // Get text field
48           Student s = studentPanel.getStudent();
49
50           // Get data from text fields and send it to the server
51           toServer.writeObject(s);
52         }
53         catch (IOException ex) {
54           System.err.println(ex);
55         }
56       }
57     }
58
59     /** Run the applet as an application */
60     public static void main(String[] args) {
61       // Create a frame
62       JFrame frame = new JFrame("Register Student Client");
63
```

```
64          // Create an instance of the applet
65          RegistrationClientUsingObjectStream applet =
66            new RegistrationClientUsingObjectStream();
67          applet.isStandAlone = true;
68
69          // Get host
70          if (args.length == 1) applet.host = args[0];
71
72          // Add the applet instance to the frame
73          frame.getContentPane().add(applet, BorderLayout.CENTER);
74
75          // Invoke init() and start()
76          applet.init();
77          applet.start();
78
79          // Display the frame
80          frame.pack();
81          frame.setVisible(true);
82        }
83      }
```

Review

The client collects student information from the text fields and creates an instance of the Student class. The client then serializes the object and sends it to the server using the object output stream through the socket. The server restores the object using the object input stream on the socket.

The Student class in Example 17.8 implements the Serializable interface. Therefore, it can be sent and received using the object output and input streams.

18.6   The *URL* class and Viewing Web Pages from Applets

Given a URL, a Web browser can view an HTML page (e.g., http://www.sun.com). HTTP is the common standard used for communication between Web servers and the Internet. You can open a URL and view a Web page in a Java applet. A URL is a description of a resource location on the Internet. Java provides a class, java.net.URL, to manipulate URLs. The following code can be written to create a URL:

```
try {
  URL url = new URL(URLString);
}
catch(MalformedURLException ex) {
}
```

The next statement creates a Java URL object:

```
try {
  URL url = new URL("http://www.sun.com");
}
catch(MalformedURLException ex) {
}
```

A MalformedURLException is thrown if the URL string has a syntax error. For example, the URL string "http:/www.sun.com" would cause the MalformedURLException runtime error because two slashes (//) are required.

To actually view the contents of an HTML page, you would need to write the following code:

```
AppletContext context = getAppletContext();
context.showDocument(url);
```

The java.applet.AppletContext class provides the environment for displaying Web page contents. The showDocument method displays the Web page in the environment.

Example 18.5 Viewing HTML Pages from Java

Problem

Write a program that demonstrates using an applet to view Web pages. The Web page's URL is entered, the Go button is clicked, and the Web page is displayed (see Figures 18.12 and 18.13).

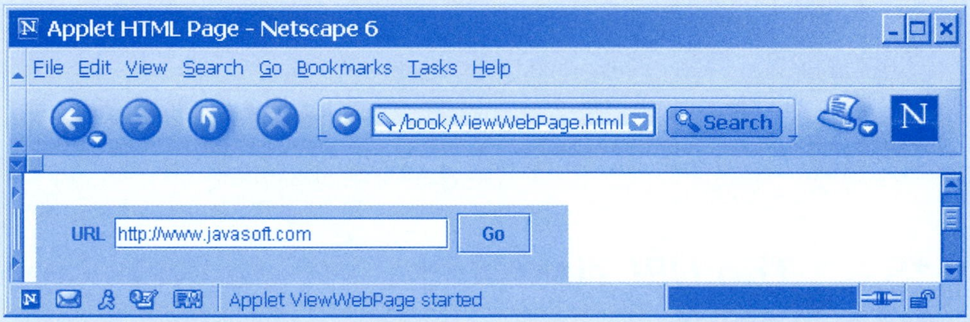

Figure 18.12   *Given the URL, the applet can display a Web page.*

Solution

The following code gives the solution to the problem.

```
1    // ViewWebPage.java: Access HTML pages through applets
2    import java.net.*;
3    import java.awt.*;
4    import java.awt.event.*;
5    import javax.swing.*;
6    import java.applet.*;
7
8    public class ViewWebPage extends JApplet implements ActionListener {
9      // Button to display an HTML page on the applet
10     private JButton jbtGo = new JButton("Go");
11
12     // Text field for receiving the URL of the HTML page
13     private JTextField jtfURL = new JTextField(20);
14
```

```
15        /** Initialize the applet */
16        public void init() {
17          // Add URL text field and Go button
18          getContentPane().setLayout(new FlowLayout());
19          getContentPane().add(new JLabel("URL"));
20          getContentPane().add(jtfURL);
21          getContentPane().add(jbtGo);
22
23          // Register listener
24          jbtGo.addActionListener(this);
25        }
26
27        /** Handle the ActionEvent */
28        public void actionPerformed(ActionEvent evt) {
29          if (evt.getSource() == jbtGo)
30            try {
31              AppletContext context = getAppletContext();
32
33              // Get the URL from text field
34              URL url = new URL(jtfURL.getText());
35              context.showDocument(url);
36            }
37            catch(Exception ex) {
38              showStatus("Error " + ex);
39            }
40        }
41      }
```

Figure 18.13   *The Web page specified in the applet is displayed in the browser.*

Review

When the URL of a publicly available HTML file is entered and the Go button is clicked, a new HTML page is displayed. The page containing the applet becomes the preceding page. A user could return to the preceding page to enter a new URL and then view the new page.

Anyone using this program would have to run it from a Web browser, not from the Applet Viewer utility.

18.7   Retrieving Files from Web Servers

You can display an HTML page from an applet, as shown in the preceding section. But sometimes it is necessary for the Web server to give you access to the contents of a file. This access allows you to pass dynamic information from the server to the applet clients or the standalone application clients, as shown in Figure 18.14. To access the file, you would use the openStream() method defined in the URL class to open a stream to the file's URL.

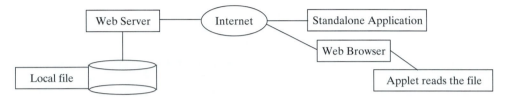

Figure 18.14   *The applet client or application client retrieves files from a Web server.*

The method shown below opens a connection to the file's URL and returns an InputStream so that you can read from the connection.

```
public final InputStream openStream() throws IOException
```

The following statements, for example, open an input stream for the URL http://www.cs.armstrong.edu/liang/index.html for the file **index.html**, which is stored on the author's Web server.

```
try {
  String urlString = "http://www.cs.armstrong.edu/liang/index.html";
  url = new URL(urlString);
  InputStream is = url.openStream();
}
catch (MalformedURLException ex) {
  System.out.println("Bad URL : " + url);
}
catch (IOException ex) {
  System.out.println("IO Error : " + ex.getMessage());
}
```

Example 18.6 Retrieving Remote Files

Problem

This example, which is similar to Example 17.5, "Displaying a File in a Text Area," in Chapter 17, "Input and Output," demonstrates how to retrieve a file from a Web server. The program can run as an application or an applet. The user interface includes a text field in which to enter the URL of the filename, a text area in which to show the file, and a button that can be used to submit an action. A label is added at the bottom of the applet to indicate the status, such as File loaded successfully or Network connection problem. A sample run of the program is shown in Figure 18.15.

Figure 18.15   *The program displays the contents of a specified file on the Web server.*

Solution

The following code gives the solution to the problem.

```
1    // ViewRemoteFile.java: Retrieve remote files
2    import java.awt.*;
3    import java.awt.event.*;
4    import java.io.*;
5    import java.net.*;
6    import javax.swing.*;
7
8    public class ViewRemoteFile extends JApplet
9      implements ActionListener {
10     // Button to view the file
11     private JButton jbtView = new JButton("View");
12
13     // Text field to receive file name
14     private JTextField jtfURL = new JTextField(12);
15
16     // Text area to store file
17     private JTextArea jtaFile = new JTextArea();
18
19     // Label to display status
20     private JLabel jlblStatus = new JLabel();
21
22     /** Initialize the applet */
23     public void init() {
24       // Create a panel to hold a label, a text field, and a button
25       JPanel p1 = new JPanel();
26       p1.setLayout(new BorderLayout());
27       p1.add(new JLabel("Filename"), BorderLayout.WEST);
28       p1.add(jtfURL, BorderLayout.CENTER);
29       p1.add(jbtView, BorderLayout.EAST);
30
31       // Place text area and panel p to the applet
32       getContentPane().setLayout(new BorderLayout());
33       getContentPane().add(new JScrollPane(jtaFile),
34         BorderLayout.CENTER);
35       getContentPane().add(p1, BorderLayout.NORTH);
36       getContentPane().add(jlblStatus, BorderLayout.SOUTH);
37
38       // Register listener
39       jbtView.addActionListener(this);
40     }
41
```

continues

Example 18.6 continued

```
42      /** Handle the "View" button */
43      public void actionPerformed(ActionEvent e) {
44        if (e.getSource() == jbtView)
45          showFile();
46      }
47
48      private void showFile() {
49        // Declare buffered stream
50        BufferedReader infile = null;
51
52        // Get file name from the text field
53        String inLine;
54
55        URL url = null;
56
57        try {
58          // Sample URL
59          String urlString =
60            "http://www.cs.armstrong.edu/liang/index.html";
61          //"file:/C:\\book\\ViewRemoteFile.java";
62          //"http://www.cs.armstrong.edu/liang/intro3e" + filename;
63
64          urlString = jtfURL.getText().trim();
65          url = new URL(urlString);
66          InputStream is = url.openStream();
67
68          // Create a buffered stream
69          infile = new BufferedReader(new InputStreamReader(is));
70
71          // Read a line and append the line to the text area
72          while ((inLine = infile.readLine()) != null) {
73            jtaFile.append(inLine + '\n');
74          }
75
76          jlblStatus.setText("File loaded successfully");
77        }
78        catch (FileNotFoundException e) {
79          jlblStatus.setText("URL not found: " + url);
80        }
81        catch (IOException e) {
82          jlblStatus.setText(e.getMessage());
83        }
84        finally {
85          try {
86            if (infile != null) infile.close();
87          }
88          catch (IOException e) {}
89        }
90      }
91
92      /** Main method */
93      public static void main(String[] args) {
94        // Create a frame
95        JFrame frame = new JFrame("View File From a Web Server");
96
97        // Create an instance of MortgageApplet
98        ViewRemoteFile applet = new ViewRemoteFile();
99
100       // Add the applet instance to the frame
101       frame.getContentPane().add(applet, BorderLayout.CENTER);
102
```

```
103        // Invoke init() and start()
104        applet.init();
105        applet.start();
106
107        // Display the frame
108        frame.setSize(300, 300);
109        frame.setVisible(true);
110      }
111    }
```

Review

This program can run either as an applet or as an application. In order for it to run as an applet, the user would need to place two files on the Web server:

ViewRemoteFile.class

ViewRemoteFile.html

ViewRemoteFile.html can be browsed from any Java 2–enabled Web browser.

The `url = new URL(urlString)` statement creates a URL. The `InputStream is = url.openStream()` opens an input stream to read the remote file. After the input stream is established, reading data from the remote file is just like reading data locally.

The URL for a local file on Windows is different from the one on Unix. For example, on Windows the URL for ViewRemoteFile.java is **file:/C:\\book\\ViewRemoteFile.java**, but on Unix it is **file:/home/liang/book/ViewRemote-File.java**.

18.8   Viewing HTML Files Using *JEditorPane*

Swing provides a new component named `javax.swing.JEditorPane` that can be used to display HTML files. `JEditorPane` is a subclass of `JTextComponent`. Thus it inherits all the behavior and properties of `JTextComponent`. Additionally, it is capable of rendering an HTML file with a given URL. The URL is specified in the `page` property, whose set method is defined as follows:

```
public void setPage(URL url) throws IOException
```

`JEditorPane` generates `javax.swing.event.HyperlinkEvent` when a hyperlink in the editor pane is clicked. Through this event, you can get the URL of the hyperlink and display the content again using the `setPage(url)` method.

Example 18.7 Creating a Web Browser

Problem

Create a simple Web browser to render HTML files. The program lets the user enter an HTML file in a text field and press the Enter key to display it in an editor pane, as shown in Figure 18.16.

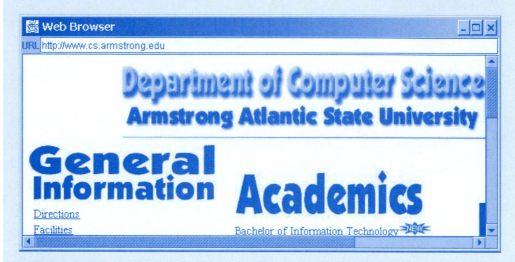

Figure 18.16 *You can specify a URL in the text field and display the HTML file in an editor pane.*

Solution

The following code gives the solution to the problem.

```
1    // WebBrowser.java: Display HTML file in JEditorPane
2    import java.awt.*;
3    import java.awt.event.*;
4    import java.applet.*;
5    import javax.swing.*;
6    import java.net.URL;
7    import javax.swing.event.*;
8    import java.io.*;
9
10   public class WebBrowser extends JApplet
11     implements ActionListener, HyperlinkListener {
12     // JEditor pane to view HTML files
13     private JEditorPane jep = new JEditorPane();
14
15     // Label for URL
16     private JLabel jlblURL = new JLabel("URL");
17
18     // Text field for entering URL
19     private JTextField jtfURL = new JTextField();
20
21     /** Initialize the applet */
22     public void init() {
23       // Create a panel jpURL to hold the label and text field
24       JPanel jpURL = new JPanel();
25       jpURL.setLayout(new BorderLayout());
```

814

```
26           jpURL.add(jlblURL, BorderLayout.WEST);
27           jpURL.add(jtfURL, BorderLayout.CENTER);
28
29           // Create a scroll pane to hold JEditorPane
30           JScrollPane jspViewer = new JScrollPane();
31           jspViewer.getViewport().add(jep, null);
32
33           // Place jpURL and jspViewer in the applet
34           this.getContentPane().add(jspViewer, BorderLayout.CENTER);
35           this.getContentPane().add(jpURL, BorderLayout.NORTH);
36
37           // Set jep noneditable
38           jep.setEditable(false);
39
40           // Register listener
41           jep.addHyperlinkListener(this);
42           jtfURL.addActionListener(this);
43         }
44
45       public void actionPerformed(ActionEvent e) {
46         // TODO: Implement this java.awt.event.ActionListener method
47         try {
48           // Get the URL from text field
49           URL url = new URL(jtfURL.getText().trim());
50
51           // Display the HTML file
52           jep.setPage(url);
53         }
54         catch (IOException ex) {
55           System.out.println(ex);
56         }
57       }
58
59       public void hyperlinkUpdate(HyperlinkEvent e) {
60         // TODO: Implement HyperlinkListener method
61         try {
62           jep.setPage(e.getURL());
63         }
64         catch (IOException ex) {
65           System.out.println(ex);
66         }
67       }
68
69       /** Main method */
70       public static void main(String[] args) {
71         // Create a frame
72         JFrame frame = new JFrame("Web Browser");
73
74         // Create an instance of the applet
75         WebBrowser applet = new WebBrowser();
76
77         // Add the applet instance to the frame
78         frame.getContentPane().add(applet, BorderLayout.CENTER);
79
80         // Invoke init() and start()
81         applet.init();
82         applet.start();
83
84         // Display the frame
85         frame.setSize(600, 600);
86         // frame.setDefaultCloseOperation(JFrame.EXIT_ON_CLOSE);
87         frame.setVisible(true);
88       }
89     }
```

continues

Example 18.7 continued

Review

In this example, a simple Web browser is created using the JEditorPane class. JEditorPane is capable of displaying files in HTML format. To enable scrolling, the editor pane is placed inside a scroll pane.

The user enters a URL of the HTML file in the text field and presses the Enter key to fire an action event to display the URL in the editor pane. To display the URL in the editor pane, simply set the URL in the page property of the editor pane.

The editor pane does not have all the functions of a commercial Web browser, but it is convenient for displaying HTML files, including embedded images.

This program cannot view a local HTML file. To view a remote HTML file, you have to enter a URL beginning with http://. In Exercise 18.8, you will modify the program so that it can also view an HTML file from the local host and accept URLs beginning with either http:// or www.

18.9   Cases Studies (Optional)

In the "Case Studies" section of Chapter 12, "Applets and Advanced GUI," you developed an applet for the TicTacToe game that enables two players to play from the same machine. In this section, you will learn how to develop a distributed TicTacToe game using multithreads and networking with socket streams.

Example 18.8 Distributed TicTacToe Game

Problem

Create a distributed TicTacToe game that enables users to play on different machines from anywhere on the Internet.

Soultion

The example consists of a server for multiple clients. The server creates a server socket, and accepts connections from every two players to form a session. Each session is a thread that communicates with the two players and determines the status of the game. The server can establish any number of sessions, as shown in Figure 18.17.

For each session, the first client connecting to the server is identified as player 1 with token 'X', and the second client connecting to the server is identified as player 2 with token 'O'. The server notifies the players of their respective tokens. Once two clients are connected to it, the server starts a thread to facilitate the game between the two players by performing the steps repeatedly, as shown in Figure 18.18.

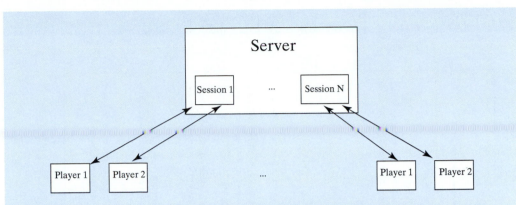

Figure 18.17 *The server can create many sessions, each of which facilitates a TicTacToe game for two players.*

The server does not have to be a graphical component, but creating it as a frame in which game information can be viewed is user-friendly. You can create a scroll pane to hold a text area in the frame and display game information in the text area. The server creates a thread to handle a game session when two players are connected to the server.

The client is responsible for interacting with the players. It creates a user interface with nine cells, and displays the game title and status to the players in the labels. The client class is very similar to the TicTacToe class presented in Example 12.7, "The TicTacToe Game." However, the client in this example does not determine the game status (win or draw), it simply passes the moves to the server and receives game status from the server.

Based on the foregoing analysis, you can create the following classes:

- ■ **TicTacToeServer** serves all the clients.

- ■ **HandleASession** facilitates the game for two players.

- ■ **TicTacToeClient** models a player.

- ■ **Cell** models a cell in the game.

- ■ **TicTacToeConstants** is an interface that defines the constants shared by all the classes in the example.

The relationships of these classes are shown in Figure 18.19.

The program is given as follows:

continues

Example 18.8 continued

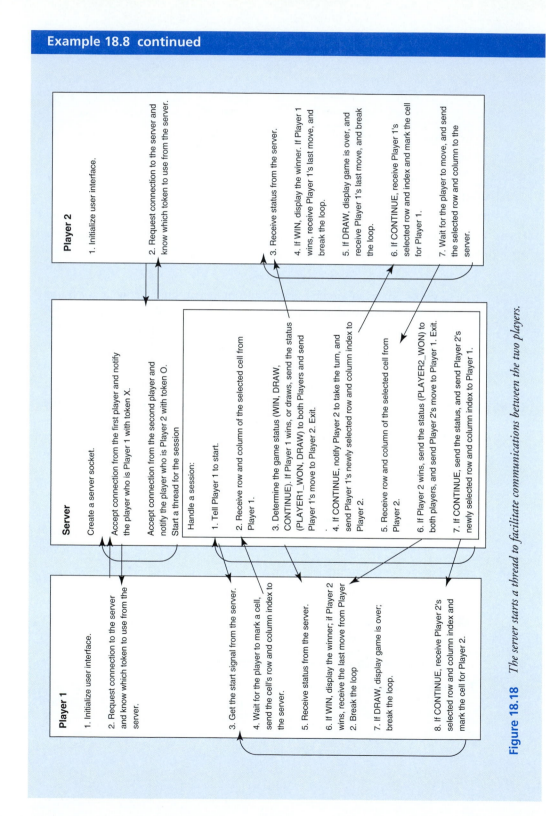

Figure 18.18   *The server starts a thread to facilitate communications between the two players.*

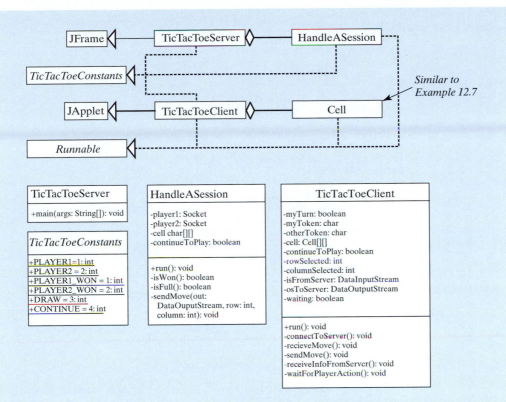

Figure 18.19 `TicTacToeServer` *creates an instance of* `HandleASession` *for each session of two players.* `TicTacToeClient` *creates nine cells in the UI.*

```
1    // TicTacToeConstants.java: Define constants for the classes
2    public interface TicTacToeConstants {
3      public static int PLAYER1 = 1; // Indicate player 1
4      public static int PLAYER2 = 2; // Indicate player 2
5      public static int PLAYER1_WON = 1; // Indicate player 1 won
6      public static int PLAYER2_WON = 2; // Indicate player 2 won
7      public static int DRAW = 3; // Indicate a draw
8      public static int CONTINUE = 4; // Indicate to continue
9    }
```

```
1    // TicTacToeServer.java: Server for the TicTacToe game
2    import java.io.*;
3    import java.net.*;
4    import javax.swing.*;
5    import java.awt.*;
6    import java.util.Date;
7
8    public class TicTacToeServer extends JFrame
9      implements TicTacToeConstants {
10     // Main method
11     public static void main(String[] args) {
12       TicTacToeServer frame = new TicTacToeServer();
13     }
14
15     public TicTacToeServer() {
16       JTextArea jtaLog;
18
```

continues

Example 18.8 continued

```
19        // Create a scroll pane to hold text area
20        JScrollPane scrollPane = new JScrollPane(
21          jtaLog = new JTextArea());
22
23        // Add the scroll pane to the frame
24        getContentPane().add(scrollPane, BorderLayout.CENTER);
25
26        setDefaultCloseOperation(JFrame.EXIT_ON_CLOSE);
27        setSize(300, 300);
28        setTitle("TicTacToeServer");
29        setVisible(true);
30        try {
31          // Create a server socket
32          ServerSocket serverSocket = new ServerSocket(8000);
33          jtaLog.append(new Date() +
34            ": Server started at socket 8000\n");
35
36          // Number a session
37          int sessionNo = 1;
38
39          // Ready to create a session for every two players
40          while (true) {
41            jtaLog.append(new Date() +
42              ": Wait for players to join session " + sessionNo + '\n');
43
44            // Connect to player 1
45            Socket player1 = serverSocket.accept();
46
47            jtaLog.append(new Date() + ": Player 1 joined session " +
48              sessionNo + '\n');
49            jtaLog.append("Player 1's IP address" +
50              player1.getInetAddress().getHostAddress() + '\n');
51
52            // Notify that the player is Player 1
53            new DataOutputStream(
54              player1.getOutputStream()).writeInt(PLAYER1);
55
56            // Connect to player 2
57            Socket player2 = serverSocket.accept();
58
59            jtaLog.append(new Date() +
60              ": Player 2 joined session " + sessionNo + '\n');
61            jtaLog.append("Player 2's IP address" +
62              player2.getInetAddress().getHostAddress() + '\n');
63
64            // Notify that the player is Player 2
65            new DataOutputStream(
66              player2.getOutputStream()).writeInt(PLAYER2);
67
68            // Display this session and increment session number
69            jtaLog.append(new Date() + ": Start a thread for session " +
70              sessionNo++ + '\n');
71
72            // Create a new thread for this session of two players
73            HandleASession thread = new HandleASession(player1, player2);
74
75            // Start the new thread
76            thread.start();
77          }
78        }
```

```
79              catch(IOException ex) {
80                System.err.println(ex);
81              }
82            }
83          }
84
85          // Define the thread class for handling a new session for two players
86          class HandleASession extends Thread implements TicTacToeConstants {
87            private Socket player1;
88            private Socket player2;
89
90            // Create and initialize cells
91            private char[][] cell =  new char[3][3];
92
93            private DataInputStream isFromPlayer1;
94            private DataOutputStream osToPlayer1;
95            private DataInputStream isFromPlayer2;
96            private DataOutputStream osToPlayer2;
97
98            // Continue to play
99            private boolean continueToPlay = true;
100
101           /** Construct a thread */
102           public HandleASession(Socket player1, Socket player2) {
103             this.player1 = player1;
104             this.player2 = player2;
105
106             // Initialize cells
107             for (int i = 0; i < 3; i++)
108               for (int j = 0; j < 3; j++)
109                 cell[i][j] = ' ';
110           }
111
112           /** Implement the run() method for the thread */
113           public void run() {
114             try {
115               // Create data input and output streams
116               DataInputStream isFromPlayer1 = new DataInputStream(
117                 player1.getInputStream());
118               DataOutputStream osToPlayer1 = new DataOutputStream(
119                 player1.getOutputStream());
120               DataInputStream isFromPlayer2 = new DataInputStream(
121                 player2.getInputStream());
122               DataOutputStream osToPlayer2 = new DataOutputStream(
123                 player2.getOutputStream());
124
125               // Write anything to notify player 1 to start
126               // This is just to let player 1 know to start
127               osToPlayer1.writeInt(1);
128
129               // Continuously serve the players and determine and report
130               // the game status to the players
131               while (true) {
132                 // Receive a move from player 1
133                 int row = isFromPlayer1.readInt();
134                 int column = isFromPlayer1.readInt();
135                 cell[row][column] = 'X';
136
137                 // Check if Player 1 wins
138                 if (isWon('X')) {
139                   osToPlayer1.writeInt(PLAYER1_WON);
140                   osToPlayer2.writeInt(PLAYER1_WON);
```

continues

Example 18.8 continued

```
141                  sendMove(osToPlayer2, row, column);
142              break; // Break the loop
143            }
144            else if (isFull()) { // Check if all cells are filled
145              osToPlayer1.writeInt(DRAW);
146              osToPlayer2.writeInt(DRAW);
147              sendMove(osToPlayer2, row, column);
148              break;
149            }
150            else {
151              // Notify player 2 to take the turn
152              osToPlayer2.writeInt(CONTINUE);
153
154              // Send player 1's selected row and column to player 2
155              sendMove(osToPlayer2, row, column);
156            }
157
158            // Receive a move from Player 2
159            row = isFromPlayer2.readInt();
160            column = isFromPlayer2.readInt();
161            cell[row][column] = 'O';
162
163            // Check if Player 2 wins
164            if (isWon('O')) {
165              osToPlayer1.writeInt(PLAYER2_WON);
166              osToPlayer2.writeInt(PLAYER2_WON);
167              sendMove(osToPlayer1, row, column);
168              break;
169            }
170            else {
171              // Notify player 1 to take the turn
172              osToPlayer1.writeInt(CONTINUE);
173
174              // Send player 2's selected row and column to player 1
175              sendMove(osToPlayer1, row, column);
176            }
177          }
178        }
179        catch(IOException ex) {
180          System.err.println(ex);
181        }
182      }
183
184      /** Send the move to other player */
185      private void sendMove(DataOutputStream out, int row, int column)
186        throws IOException {
187        out.writeInt(row); // Send row index
188        out.writeInt(column); // Send column index
189      }
190
191      /** Determine if the cells are all occupied */
192      private boolean isFull() {
193        for (int i = 0; i < 3; i++)
194          for (int j = 0; j < 3; j++)
195            if (cell[i][j] == ' ')
196              return false; // At least one cell is not filled
197
198        // All cells are filled
199        return true;
200      }
201
```

```
202         /** Determine if the player with the specified token wins */
203         private boolean isWon(char token) {
204           // Check all rows
205           for (int i = 0; i < 3; i++)
206             if ((cell[i][0] == token)
207                 && (cell[i][1] == token)
208                 && (cell[i][2] == token)) {
209               return true;
210             }
211
212           /** Check all columns */
213           for (int j = 0; j < 3; j++)
214             if ((cell[0][j] == token)
215                 && (cell[1][j] == token)
216                 && (cell[2][j] == token)) {
217               return true;
218             }
219
220           /** Check major diagonal */
221           if ((cell[0][0] == token)
222               && (cell[1][1] == token)
223               && (cell[2][2] == token)) {
224             return true;
225           }
226
227           /** Check subdiagonal */
228           if ((cell[0][2] == token)
229               && (cell[1][1] == token)
230               && (cell[2][0] == token)) {
231             return true;
232           }
233
234           /** All checked, but no winner */
235           return false;
236         }
237       }
```

```
1    // TicTacToeClient.java: Play the TicTacToe game
2    import java.awt.*;
3    import java.awt.event.*;
4    import javax.swing.*;
5    import javax.swing.border.LineBorder;
6    import java.io.*;
7    import java.net.*;
8
9    public class TicTacToeClient extends JApplet
10     implements Runnable, TicTacToeConstants {
11     // Indicate whether the player has the turn
12     private boolean myTurn = false;
13
14     // Indicate the token for the player
15     private char myToken = ' ';
16
17     // Indicate the token for the other player
18     private char otherToken = ' ';
19
20     // Create and initialize cells
21     private Cell[][] cell = new Cell[3][3];
22
23     // Create and initialize a title label
24     private JLabel jlblTitle = new JLabel();
25
```

continues

Example 18.8 continued

```
26        // Create and initialize a status label
27        private JLabel jlblStatus = new JLabel();
28
29        // Indicate selected row and column by the current move
30        private int rowSelected;
31        private int columnSelected;
32
33        // Input and output streams from/to server
34        private DataInputStream isFromServer;
35        private DataOutputStream osToServer;
36
37        // Continue to play?
38        private boolean continueToPlay = true;
39
40        // Wait for the player to mark a cell
41        private boolean waiting = true;
42
53        /** Initialize UI */
44        public void init() {
45          // Panel p to hold cells
46          JPanel p = new JPanel();
47          p.setLayout(new GridLayout(3, 3, 0, 0));
48          for (int i = 0; i < 3; i++)
49            for (int j = 0; j < 3; j++)
50              p.add(cell[i][j] = new Cell(i, j));
51
52          // Set properties for labels and borders for labels and panel
53          p.setBorder(new LineBorder(Color.black, 1));
54          jlblTitle.setHorizontalAlignment(JLabel.CENTER);
56          jlblTitle.setFont(new Font("SansSerif", Font.BOLD, 16));
57          jlblTitle.setBorder(new LineBorder(Color.black, 1));
58          jlblStatus.setBorder(new LineBorder(Color.black, 1));
59
60          // Place the panel and the labels to the applet
61          this.getContentPane().add(jlblTitle, BorderLayout.NORTH);
62          this.getContentPane().add(p, BorderLayout.CENTER);
63          this.getContentPane().add(jlblStatus, BorderLayout.SOUTH);
64
65          // Connect to the server
66          connectToServer();
67        }
68
69        private void connectToServer() {
70          try {
71            // Create a socket to connect to the server
72            Socket connectToServer = new Socket("localhost", 8000);
73
74            // Create an input stream to receive data from the server
75            isFromServer = new DataInputStream(
76              connectToServer.getInputStream());
77
78            // Create an output stream to send data to the server
79            osToServer =
80              new DataOutputStream(connectToServer.getOutputStream());
81          }
82          catch (Exception ex) {
83            System.err.println(ex);
84          }
85
```

```
 86          // Control the game on a separate thread
 87          Thread thread = new Thread(this);
 88          thread.start();
 89        }
 90
 91        /** This main method enables the applet to run as an application */
 92        public static void main(String[] args) {
 93          // Create a frame
 94          JFrame frame = new JFrame("Tic Tac Toe Client");
 95
 96          // Create an instance of the applet
 97          TicTacToeClient applet = new TicTacToeClient();
 98
 99          // Add the applet instance to the frame
100          frame.getContentPane().add(applet, BorderLayout.CENTER);
101
102          // Invoke init() and start()
103          applet.init();
104          applet.start();
105
106          // Display the frame
107          frame.setSize(320, 300);
108          frame.setDefaultCloseOperation(JFrame.EXIT_ON_CLOSE);
109          frame.setVisible(true);
110        }
111
112        public void run() {
113          try {
114            // Get notification from the server
115            int player = isFromServer.readInt();
116
117            // Am I player 1 or 2?
118            if (player == PLAYER1) {
119              myToken = 'X';
120              otherToken = 'O';
121              jlblTitle.setText("Player 1 with token 'X'");
122              jlblStatus.setText("Waiting for player 2 to join");
123
124              // Receive startup notification from the server
125              isFromServer.readInt(); // Whatever read is ignored
126
127              // The other player has joined
128              jlblStatus.setText("Player 2 has joined. I start first");
129
130              // It is my turn
131              myTurn = true;
132            }
133            else if (player == PLAYER2) {
134              myToken = 'O';
135              otherToken = 'X';
136              jlblTitle.setText("Player 2 with token 'O'");
137              jlblStatus.setText("Waiting for player 1 to move");
138            }
139
140            // Continue to play
141            while (continueToPlay) {
142              if (player == PLAYER1) {
143                waitForPlayerAction(); // Wait for player 1 to move
144                sendMove(); // Send the move to the server
145                receiveInfoFromServer(); // Receive info from the server
146              }
```

continues

825

Example 18.8 continued

```
147            else if (player == PLAYER2) {
148                receiveInfoFromServer(); // Receive info from the server
149                waitForPlayerAction(); // Wait for player 2 to move
150                sendMove(); // Send player 2's move to the server
151            }
152          }
153        }
154      catch (Exception ex) {
155      }
156    }
157
158    /** Wait for the player to mark a cell */
159    private void waitForPlayerAction() throws InterruptedException {
160      while (waiting) {
161        Thread.sleep(100);
162      }
163
164      waiting = true;
165    }
166
167    /** Send this player's move to the server */
168    private void sendMove() throws IOException {
169      osToServer.writeInt(rowSelected); // Send the selected row
170      osToServer.writeInt(columnSelected); // Send the selected column
171    }
172
173    /** Receive info from the server */
174    private void receiveInfoFromServer() throws IOException {
175      // Receive game status
176      int status = isFromServer.readInt();
177
178      if (status == PLAYER1_WON) {
179        // Player 1 won, stop playing
180        continueToPlay = false;
181        if (myToken == 'X') {
182          jlblStatus.setText("I won! (X)");
183        }
184        else if (myToken == 'O') {
185          jlblStatus.setText("Player 1 (X) has won!");
186          receiveMove();
187        }
188      }
189      else if (status == PLAYER2_WON) {
190        // Player 2 won, stop playing
191        continueToPlay = false;
192        if (myToken == 'O') {
193          jlblStatus.setText("I won! (O)");
194        }
195        else if (myToken == 'X') {
196          jlblStatus.setText("Player 2 (O) has won!");
197          receiveMove();
198        }
199      }
200      else if (status == DRAW) {
201        // No winner, game is over
202        continueToPlay = false;
203        jlblStatus.setText("Game is over, no winner!");
204
205        if (myToken == 'O') {
206          receiveMove();
207        }
208      }
```

```
209          else {
210            receiveMove();
211            jlblStatus.setText("My turn");
212            myTurn = true; // It is my turn
213          }
214        }
215
216        private void receiveMove() throws IOException {
217          // Get the other player's move
218          int row = isFromServer.readInt();
219          int column = isFromServer.readInt();
220          cell[row][column].setToken(otherToken);
221        }
222
223        // An inner class for a cell
224        public class Cell extends JPanel implements MouseListener {
225          // Indicate the row and column of this cell in the board
226          private int row;
227          private int column;
228
229          // Token used for this cell
230          private char token = ' ';
231
232          public Cell(int row, int column) {
233            this.row = row;
234            this.column = column;
235            setBorder(new LineBorder(Color.black, 1)); // Set cell's border
236            addMouseListener(this);  // Register listener
237          }
238
239          /** Return token */
240          public char getToken() {
241            return token;
242          }
243
244          /** Set a new token */
245          public void setToken(char c) {
246            token = c;
247            repaint();
248          }
249
250          /** Paint the cell */
251          public void paintComponent(Graphics g) {
252            super.paintComponent(g);
253
254            if (token == 'X') {
255              g.drawLine(10, 10, getSize().width-10, getSize().height-10);
256              g.drawLine(getSize().width-10, 10, 10, getSize().height-10);
257            }
258            else if (token == 'O') {
259              g.drawOval(10, 10, getSize().width-20, getSize().height-20);
260            }
261          }
262
263          /** Handle mouse click on a cell */
264          public void mouseClicked(MouseEvent e) {
265            // If cell is not occupied and the player has the turn
266            if ((token == ' ') && myTurn) {
267              setToken(myToken);  // Set the player's token in the cell
268              myTurn = false;
269              rowSelected = row;
```

continues

Example 18.8 continued

```
270              columnSelected = column;
271              jlblStatus.setText("Waiting for the other player to move");
272              waiting = false; // Just completed a successful move
273            }
274          }
275
276          public void mousePressed(MouseEvent e) {
277            // TODO: implement this java.awt.event.MouseListener method;
278          }
279
280          public void mouseReleased(MouseEvent e) {
281            // TODO: implement this java.awt.event.MouseListener method;
282          }
283
284          public void mouseEntered(MouseEvent e) {
285            // TODO: implement this java.awt.event.MouseListener method;
286          }
287
288          public void mouseExited(MouseEvent e) {
289            // TODO: implement this java.awt.event.MouseListener method;
290          }
291        }
292      }
```

Review

The server can serve any number of sessions. Each session takes care of two players. The client can be a Java applet or a Java application. To run a client as a Java applet from a Web browser, the server must run from a Web server. Figures 18.20 and 18.21 show sample runs of the server and the clients.

Figure 18.20   `TicTacToeServer` *accepts connection requests and creates sessions to serve pairs of players.*

The `TicTacToeConstants` interface defines the constants shared by all the classes in the project. Each class that uses the constants needs to implement the interface. Centrally defining constants in an interface is a common practice in Java. For example, all the constants shared by Swing classes are defined in `java.swing.SwingConstants`.

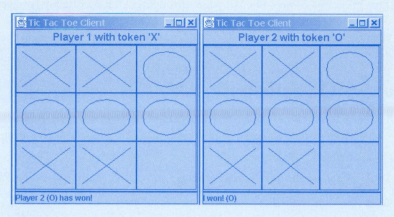

Figure 18.21   `TicTacToeClient` *can run as an applet or an application.*

Once a session is established, the server receives moves from the players in alternation. Upon receiving a move from a player, the server determines the status of the game. If the game is not finished, the server sends the status (`CONTINUE`) and the player's move to the other player. If the game is won or drawn, the server sends the status (`PLAYER1_WON`, `PLAYER2_WON`, or `DRAW`) to both players.

The implementation of Java network programs at the socket level is tightly synchronized. An operation to send data from one machine requires an operation to receive data from the other machine. As shown in this example, the server and the client are tightly synchronized to send or receive data.

Chapter Summary

This chapter introduced socket-level network programming in Java. You learned how to write client/server applications.

To create a server, you must first obtain a server socket, using `new ServerSocket(port)`. After a server socket is created, the server can start to listen for connections, using the `accept()` method on the server socket. The client requests a connection to a server by using `new socket(ServerName, port)` to create a client socket.

Stream socket communication is very much like input/output stream communication after the connection between a server and a client is established. You can obtain an input stream using the `getInputStream` method and an output stream using the `getOutputStream` method on the socket.

A server must often work with multiple clients at the same time. You can use threads to handle the server's multiple clients simultaneously by creating a thread for each connection.

Applets are good for deploying multiple clients. They can be run anywhere with a single copy of the program. However, because of security restrictions, an applet client can only connect to the server where the applet is loaded.

Java programs can get HTML pages through HTTP by directly connecting with a Web server. The URL can be used to view a Web page in a Java applet. To retrieve data files on the Web server from applets, you can open a stream on the file's URL on the Web server.

Review Questions

18.1 How do you create a server socket? What port numbers can be used? What happens if a requested port number is already in use? Can a port connect to multiple clients?

18.2 What are the differences between a server socket and a client socket?

18.3 How does a client program initiate a connection?

18.4 How does a server accept a connection?

18.5 How are data transferred between a client and a server? Can objects be transferred?

18.6 How do you make a server serve multiple clients?

18.7 Can an application retrieve a file from a remote host? Can an application update a file on a remote host?

Programming Exercises

18.1 Write a server for multiple clients. The client sends mortgage information (annual interest rate, number of years, and loan amount) to the server (see Figure 18.22). The server computes monthly payment and total payment and sends them back to the client (see Figure 18.23). Name the client Exercise18_1Client and the server Exercise18_1Server.

Figure 18.22 *The client sends the annual interest rate, number of years, and loan amount to the server and receives the monthly payment and total payment from the server.*

18.2 Rewrite Example 18.1, "A Client/Server Example," using buffered reader for input and print stream for output. Use the readLine() method to read a string from the input stream, and use the Double.parseDouble(string) to convert the string into a double value. Name the client Exercise18_2Client and the server Exercise18_2Server.

Figure 18.23 *The server receives the annual interest rate, number of years, and loan amount from the client, then computes monthly payment and total payment and sends them back to the client.*

18.3 Modify Example 18.3, "Creating Applet Clients," by adding the following features:

■ Add a View button to the user interface that allows the client to view a record for a specified name. The user will be able to enter a name in the Name field and click the View button to display the record for the student, as shown in Figure 18.24.

Figure 18.24 *You can view or register students in this applet.*

■ Limit the concurrent connections to two clients.

■ Display the status of the submission, such as Successful, Failed, Record found, or Record not found, on a label.

■ Use one thread to handle all requests from a client. The thread terminates when the client exits.

■ Name the client Exercise18_3Client and the server Exercise18_3Server.

18.4 Example 17.9, "Using StreamTokenizer," in Chapter 17, "Input and Output," computes total scores from the exam scores stored in a text file. Rewrite this example as an applet to read the file from a Web server. The exercise reads the file from a Web server rather than from the local system. The file contains student exam scores. Each record in the input file consists of a student name, two midterm exam scores, and a final exam score. The program reads the fields for each record, computes the total score, and displays the result in a text area. Figure 18.25 contains the output of a sample run of the program.

Figure 18.25 *The applet retrieves the file from the Web server and processes it.*

18.5 Rewrite Example 18.6, "Retrieving Remote Files," to use JEditorPane instead of JTextArea.

18.6 Write an applet that shows the number of visits made to a Web page. The count should be stored in a file on the server side. Every time the page is visited or reloaded, the applet sends a request to the server, and the server increases the count and sends it to the applet. The applet then displays the new count in a message, such as You are visitor number: 1000, as shown in Figure 18.26. Name the client Exercise18_6Client and the server Exercise18_6Server.

Figure 18.26 *The applet displays how many times this Web page has been accessed. The server stores the count.*

HINT

Use a random-access file stream to read or write the count to the file. To improve performance, read the count from the file when the server starts, and save the count to the file when the server exits. When the server is alive, use a variable to store the count. When a client applet starts, it connects to the server; the server increases the count by 1 and sends it to the client for display.)

18.7 Write an applet like the ones in Exercise 17.7. Ensure that the applet gets the stock index from a file stored on the Web server. Enable the applet to run standalone.

18.8 Modify Example 18.7, "Creating a Web Browser," as follows:

■ It accepts an HTML file from a local host. Assume that a local HTML filename begins neither with http:// nor with www.

■ It accepts a remote HTML file. A remote HTML filename begins with either http:// or www.

Java Data Structures

Objectives

- To understand the limitations of arrays.
- To become familiar with the Java Collections Framework hierarchy.
- To use the `Iterator` interface to traverse a collection.
- To know the `Set` interface, and know when to use `HashSet` or `TreeSet` to store elements.
- To understand the `List` interface, and know whether to use `ArrayList` or `LinkedList` to store elements.
- To understand the differences between `Vector` and `ArrayList`, and know how to use `Vector` and `Stack`.
- To understand the differences between `Collection` and `Map`, and know how to use `Map` to store values associated with keys.
- To use the static methods in the `Collections` and `Arrays` classes.

19.1   Introduction

In Chapter 5, "Arrays," you learned how to store and process elements in arrays. Arrays can be used to store a group of primitive type values or a group of objects. Once an array is created, its size cannot be altered. Arrays are a useful data structure for representing collections of elements, but they do not provide adequate support for inserting, deleting, sorting, and searching operations. The Java 2 platform introduced several new interfaces and classes that can be used to organize and manipulate data efficiently. These new interfaces and classes are known as the *Java Collections Framework.*

A *collection* is an object that represents a group of objects, often referred to as *elements*. The Java Collections Framework supports two types of collections, named *collections* and *maps*. They are defined in the interfaces `Collection` and `Map`. An instance of `Collection` represents a group of objects. An instance of `Map` represents a group of objects, each of which is associated with a key. You can get an object from a map using a key, and you have to use a key to put the object into the map. A collection can be a set or a list, defined in the interfaces `Set` and `List`, which are subinterfaces of `Collection`. An instance of `Set` stores a group of nonduplicate elements. An instance of `List` is an ordered collection of elements. The relationships of the interfaces and classes in the Java Collections Framework are shown in Figures 19.1 and 19.2. These interfaces and classes provide a unified API for efficiently storing and processing a collection of objects. You will learn how to use these interfaces and classes in this chapter.

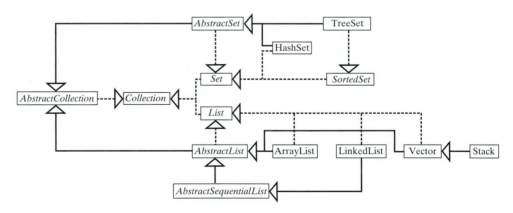

Figure 19.1   *An instance of* `Collection` *stores a group of objects.*

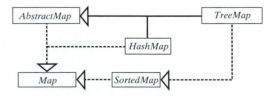

Figure 19.2   *An instance of* `Map` *stores a group of objects and their associated keys.*

NOTE
All the interfaces and classes defined in the Java Collections Framework are grouped in the `java.util` package.

19.2 The *Collection* Interface and the *AbstractCollection* Class

The `Collection` interface is the root interface for storing and processing a collection of objects. Its public methods are listed in Figure 19.3.

Collection
+add(element: Object): boolean *+addAll(collection: Collection): boolean* *+clear(): void* *+contains(elment: Object): boolean* *+containsAll(collection: Collection): boolean* *+equals(object: Object): boolean* *+hashcode(): int* *+iterator(): Iterator* *+remove(element: Object): boolean* *+removeAll(collection: Collection): boolean* *+retainAll(collection: Collection): boolean* *+size(): int* *+toArray(): Object[]* *+toArray(array: Object[]): Object[]*

Figure 19.3 *The* `Collection` *interface is the root for the* `Set` *and* `List` *interfaces.*

19.2.1 The Methods in the *Collection* Interface

The `Collection` interface provides the basic operations for adding and removing elements in a collection. The `add` method adds an element to the collection. The `addAll` method adds the specified collection to this collection. The `remove` method removes an element from the collection. The `removeAll` method removes the elements from this collection that are present in the specified collection. The `retainAll` method retains the elements in this collection that are also present in the specified collection. All these methods return `boolean`. The return value is true if the collection is changed as a result of the method execution. The `clear()` method simply removes all the elements from the collection.

The `Collection` interface provides various query operations. The `size` method returns the number of elements in the collection. The `contains` method checks whether the collection contains the specified element. The `containsAll` method checks whether the collection contains all the elements in the specified collection. The `isEmpty` method returns true if the collection is empty.

The `Collection` interface provides two overloaded methods to convert the collection into an array. The `toArray()` method returns an array representation for the collection. The `toArray(Object[] a)` method returns an array containing all of the elements in this collection whose runtime type is that of the specified runtime type.

The `iterator` method in the `Collection` interface returns an instance of `Iterator`, which can be used to traverse the collection using the `next()` method. You can also use the `hasNext()` method to check whether there are more elements in the iterator, and the `remove()` method to remove the last element returned by the iterator.

The `AbstractCollection` class is a convenience class that provides partial implementation for the `Collection` interface. It implements all the methods in `Collection` except the `size` and `iterator` methods. These are implemented in appropriate subclasses.

NOTE

Some of the methods in the `Collection` interface are optional. If an optional method is not supported by a concrete subclass, it should throw `java.lang.UnsupportedOperationException`. Since this exception is a subclass of `RuntimeException`, you don't have to place the method in a try-catch block.

19.2.2   The *hashCode* Method and the *equals* Method

The `hashCode` method and the `equals` method are defined in the `Object` class as well as in the `Collection` interface. The contract of the two methods in the `Object` class remains the same in the `Collection` interface. A class that implements the `Collection` interface does not have to implement the `hashCode` method and the `equals` method, because both methods have default implementation in the `Object` class. What are the benefits of defining `hashCode` and `equals` in both the `Object` class and the `Collection` interface? It is essentially for facilitating generic programming. For instance, you may have a method with a parameter of the `Collection` type. This parameter can use the `hashCode` method and the `equals` method, because they are in the `Collection` interface.

The `equals(Object o)` method is for checking whether an object has the same contents as another object. The `hashCode` method returns an `int` value known as the *hash code*. The hash code is used to store information in a hash table for quick lookup. The hash code is used to store objects in a `HashSet` and a `HashMap`. Every object has a hash code. An object's reference can be stored in a hash table. The location of an object's reference in a hash table is determined by the object's hash code. The object's reference can be retrieved from a hash table through the hash code.

19.3   The *Set* Interface, and the *AbstractSet* and *HashSet* Classes

The `Set` interface extends the `Collection` interface. It does not introduce new methods or constants, but it stipulates that an instance of `Set` contains no duplicate elements. The concrete classes that implement `Set` must ensure that no duplicate elements can be added to the set. That is, no two elements e1 and e2 can be in the set such that `e1.equals(e2)` is true.

The AbstractSet class is a convenience class that extends AbstractCollection and implements Set. The AbstractSet class provides concrete implementations for the equals method and the hashCode method. The hash code of a set is the sum of the hash codes of all the elements in the set. Since the size method and iterator method are not implemented in the AbstractSet class, AbstractSet is an abstract class.

The HashSet class is a concrete class that implements Set. It can be used to store duplicate-free elements. For efficiency, objects added to a hash set need to implement the hashCode method in a manner that properly disperses the hash code. Most of the classes in the Java API implement the hashCode method. For example, the hashCode in the String class is implemented as follows:

```
public int hashCode() {
   int h = 0;
   int off = offset;
   char val[] = value;
   int len = count;

   for (int i = 0; i < len; i++)
     h = 31 * h + val[off++];

   return h;
}
```

The hashCode in the Integer class simply returns its int value.

Example 19.1   Using HashSet and Iterator

Problem

Write a program that finds all the words used in a text. The program creates a hash set to store the words extracted from the text, and uses an iterator to traverse the elements in the set.

Solution

The following code gives the solution to the problem. The output of the program is shown in Figure 19.4.

```
C:\book>java TestHashSet
[fun, good, day, visit, class, Have, a]
fun good day visit class Have a
C:\book>
```

Figure 19.4   *The program adds string elements to a hash set, displays the elements using the* toString *method, and traverses the elements using an iterator.*

continues

Example 19.1   continued

```
1     import java.util.*;
2
3     public class TestHashSet {
4       public static void main(String[] args) {
5
6         // Create a hash set
7         Set set = new HashSet();
8
9         // Text in a string
10        String text = "Have a good day. Have a good class. " +
11          "Have a good visit. Have fun!";
12
12        // Extract words from text
13        StringTokenizer st = new StringTokenizer(text, " .!?");
14        while (st.hasMoreTokens())
15          set.add(st.nextToken());
16
17        System.out.println(set);
18
19        // Obtain an iterator for the hash set
20        Iterator iterator = set.iterator();
21
22        // Display the elements in the hash set
23        while (iterator.hasNext()) {
24          System.out.print(iterator.next() + " ");
25        }
26      }
27    }
```

Review

The words are extracted using `StringTokenizer` and are added to the set (Lines 7, 15). If a word like "good" is added to the set more than once, only one is stored, because a set does not allow duplicates.

As shown in Figure 19.4, the words are not stored in the order in which they are added. There is no particular order for the elements in a hash set. To impose an order on them, you need to use the `TreeSet` class, which is introduced in the next section.

NOTE

The iterator is *fail-fast*. This means that if you are using an iterator to traverse a collection while the underlying collection is being modified by another thread, then the iterator fails immediately by throwing `java.util.ConcurrentModificationException`. Since this exception is a subclass of `RuntimeException`, you don't have to place the methods of `Iterator` in a try-catch block. In Exercise 19.1, you will write a program that creates a situation in which an iterator throws `Concurrent-ModificationException`.

19.4   The *SortedSet* Interface and the *TreeSet* Class

SortedSet is a subinterface of Set, which guarantees that the elements in the set are sorted. TreeSet is a concrete class that implements the SortedSet interface. To create a TreeSet, use its default constructor or use new TreeSet(Collection). You can add objects into a tree set as long as they can be compared with each other. There are two ways to compare objects.

■   Use the Comparable interface. If the objects added to the set are instances of Comparable, they can be compared using the compareTo method. The Comparable interface was introduced in Chapter 8, "Class Inheritance and Interfaces." Several classes in the Java API, such as the String class and all the wrapper classes for the primitive types, implement the Comparable interface. This approach is referred to as *natural order*.

■   If the class for the elements does not implement the Comparable interface or if you don't want to use the compareTo method in the class that implements the Comparable interface, specify a comparator for the elements in the set. This approach is referred to as *order by comparator*. It will be introduced in Section 19.5, "The Comparator Interface."

Example 19.2   Using TreeSet to Sort Elements in a Set

Problem

The preceding example displays all the words used in a text. The words are displayed in no particular order. This example rewrites the preceding example to display the words in alphabetical order using the TreeSet class.

Solution

The following code gives the solution to the problem.

```
1    import java.util.*;
2
3    public class TestTreeSet {
4      public static void main(String[] args) {
5        // Create a hash set
6        Set set = new HashSet();
7
8        // Text in a string
9        String text = "Have a good day. Have a good class. " +
10         "Have a good visit. Have fun!";
11
12       // Extract words from text
13       StringTokenizer st = new StringTokenizer(text, " .!?");
14       while (st.hasMoreTokens())
15         set.add(st.nextToken());
16
17       TreeSet treeSet = new TreeSet(set);
18       System.out.println(treeSet);
19
```

continues

Example 19.2   continued

```
20        // Obtain an iterator for the hash set
21        Iterator iterator = treeSet.iterator();
22
23        // Display the elements in the hash set
24        while (iterator.hasNext()) {
25          System.out.print(iterator.next() + " ");
26        }
27      }
28    }
```

Figure 19.5   *The program demonstrates the differences between hash sets and tree sets.*

Review

The example creates a hash set filled with strings, and then creates a tree set for the same strings. The strings are sorted in the tree set using the `compareTo` method in the `Comparable` interface.

The elements in the set are sorted once when you create a `TreeSet` object from a `HashSet` object using `new TreeSet(hashSet)` (Line 17). You may rewrite the program to create an instance of `TreeSet` using its default constructor, and add the strings into the `TreeSet` object. Then, every time a string is added to the `TreeSet` object, the elements in it will be reordered. The approach used in the example is generally more efficient because it requires only a one-time sorting.

NOTE

All the classes in Figure 19.1 have at least two constructors. One is the default constructor that constructs an empty collection. The other constructs instances from a collection. Thus the `TreeSet` class has the constructor `TreeSet(Collection c)` for constructing a `TreeSet` from a collection `c`. In this example, `new TreeSet(hashSet)` creates an instance of `TreeSet` from the collection `hashSet`.

TIP

If you don't need to maintain a sorted set when updating a set, you can use a hash set, because it takes less time to insert and remove elements in a hash set. When you need a set to be sorted, you can convert the set into a tree set.

19.5   The *Comparator* Interface.

Sometimes you want to insert elements of different types into a tree set. The elements may not be instances of `Comparable` or are not comparable. You can define a comparator to compare these elements. To do so, create a class that implements the `java.util.Comparator` interface. The `Comparator` interface has two methods, `compare` and `equals`.

■ `public int compare(Object element1, Object element2)`

Returns a negative value if `element1` is less than `element2`, a positive value if `element1` is greater than `element2`, and zero if they are equal.

■ `public boolean equals(Object element)`

Returns true if the specified object is also a comparator and imposes the same ordering as this comparator.

NOTE

The `equals` method is also defined in the `Object` class. Therefore, you will not get a compilation error if you don't implement the `equals` method in your custom comparator class. However, in some cases implementing this method may improve performance by allowing programs to determine that two distinct comparators impose the same order.

For example, you can provide the following comparator to compare two elements of the `GeometricObject` class, defined in Section 8.7, "Abstract Classes," in Chapter 8.

```
import java.util.Comparator;

public class GeometricObjectComparator implements Comparator {
  public int compare(Object o1, Object o2) {
    double area1 = ((GeometricObject)o1).findArea();
    double area2 = ((GeometricObject)o2).findArea();

    if (area1 < area2)
      return -1;
    else if (area1 == area2)
      return 0;
    else
      return 1;
  }
}
```

If you create a TreeSet using its default constructor, the compareTo method is used to compare the elements in the set, assuming that the class of the elements implements the Comparable interface. To use a comparator, you have to use the constructor TreeSet(Comparator comparator) to create a sorted set that uses the compare method in the comparator to order the elements in the set.

Example 19.3 Using Comparator to Sort Elements in a Set

Problem

Write a program that demonstrates how to sort elements in a tree set using the Comparator interface. The example creates a tree set of geometric objects. The geometric objects are sorted using the compare method in the Comparator interface.

Solution

The following code gives the solution to the problem. The output of the program is shown in Figure 19.6.

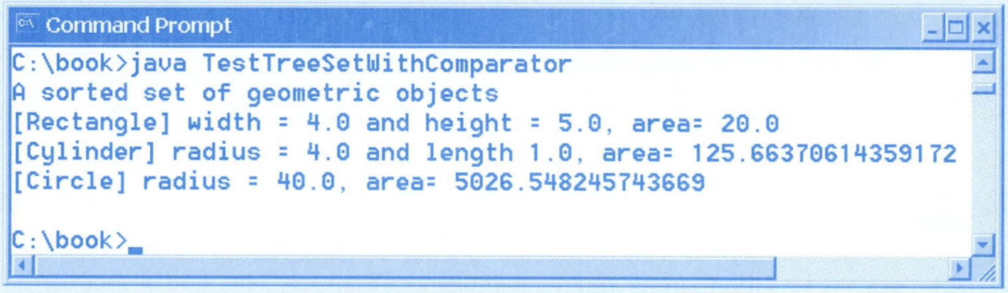

```
Command Prompt                                                    _ □ ×
C:\book>java TestTreeSetWithComparator
A sorted set of geometric objects
[Rectangle] width = 4.0 and height = 5.0, area= 20.0
[Cylinder] radius = 4.0 and length 1.0, area= 125.66370614359172
[Circle] radius = 40.0, area= 5026.548245743669

C:\book>
```

Figure 19.6   *The program demonstrates the use of the* Comparator *interface.*

```
1    import java.util.*;
2
3    public class TestTreeSetWithComparator {
4      public static void main(String[] args) {
5        // Create a tree set for geometric objects using a comparator
6        Set geometricObjectSet =
7          new TreeSet(new GeometricObjectComparator());
8        geometricObjectSet.add(new Rectangle(4, 5));
9        geometricObjectSet.add(new Circle(40));
10       geometricObjectSet.add(new Circle(40));
11       geometricObjectSet.add(new Cylinder(4, 1));
12
13       // Obtain an iterator for the tree set of geometric objects
14       Iterator iterator = geometricObjectSet.iterator();
15
16       // Display geometric objects in the tree set
17       System.out.println("A sorted set of geometric objects");
18       while (iterator.hasNext()) {
19         GeometricObject object = (GeometricObject)iterator.next();
20         System.out.println(object + ", area= " + object.findArea());
21       }
22     }
23   }
```

19.6 The *List* Interface, the *AbstractList* Class, and the *AbstractSequentialList* Class

A set stores nonduplicate elements. To allow duplicate elements to be stored in a collection, you need to use a list. A list can not only store duplicate elements, but also allows the user to specify where they are stored. The user can access elements by an index. The List interface extends Collection to define an ordered collection with duplicates allowed. The List interface adds position-oriented operations, as well as a new list iterator that enables the user to traverse the list bi-directionally. The new methods in the List interface are shown in Figure 19.7.

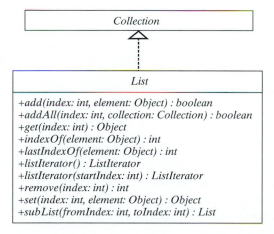

Figure 19.7   *The* List *interface stores elements in sequence, permitting duplicates.*

The add(index, element) method is used to insert an element at a specified index, and the addAll(index, collection) method to insert a collection at a specified index. The remove(index) method is used to remove an element at the specified index from the list. A new element can be set at the specified index using the set(index, element) method.

The indexOf(element) method is used to obtain the index of the first occurrence of the specified element in the list, and the lastIndexOf(element) method to obtain the index of the last occurrence of the specified element in the list. A sublist can be obtained by using the subList(fromIndex, toIndex) method.

The listIterator() or listIterator(startIndex) method returns an instance of ListIterator. The ListIterator interface extends the Iterator interface to add bi-directional traversal of the list. The methods in ListIterator are listed in Figure 19.8.

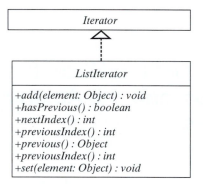

Figure 19.8   ListIterator *enables traversal of a list bi-directionally.*

The add(element) method inserts the specified element into the list. The element is inserted immediately before the next element that would be returned by the next() method defined in the Iterator interface, if any, and after the element that would be returned by the previous() method, if any. If the list contains no elements, the new element becomes the sole element on the list. The set(element) method can be used to replace the last element returned by the next method or the previous method with the specified element.

The hasNext() method defined in the Iterator interface is used to check whether the iterator has more elements when traversed in the forward direction, and the hasPrevious() method to check whether the iterator has more elements when traversed in the backward direction.

The next() method defined in the Iterator interface returns the next element in the iterator, and the previous() method returns the previous element in the iterator. The nextIndex() method returns the index of the next element in the iterator, and the previousIndex() returns the index of the previous element in the iterator.

The AbstractList class provides a partial implementation for the List interface. The AbstractSequentialList class extends AbstractList to provide support for linked lists.

19.7   The *ArrayList* and *LinkedList* Classes

The ArrayList class and the LinkedList class are concrete implementations of the List interface. Which of the two classes you use depends on your specific needs. If you need to support random access through an index without inserting or removing elements except at the end, `ArrayList` offers the most efficient collection, since `ArrayList` is implemented using an array. If, however, your application requires the insertion or deletion of elements anywhere in the list, you should choose `LinkedList`. A list can grow or shrink dynamically. An array is fixed once it is created. If your application does not require the insertion or deletion of elements, an array is the most efficient data structure.

`ArrayList` is a resizable-array implementation of the `List` interface. In addition to implementing the `List` interface, this class provides methods for manipulating the size of the array that is used internally to store the list. Each `ArrayList` instance has a capacity. The capacity is the size of the array used to store the elements in the list. It is always at least as large as the list size. As elements are added to an `ArrayList`, its capacity grows automatically.

`LinkedList` is a linked list implementation of the `List` interface. In addition to implementing the `List` interface, this class provides the methods for retrieving, inserting, and removing elements from both ends of the list, as shown in Figure 19.9. The implementation of `LinkedList` is similar to the implementation of `GenericLinkedList` in Section 9.8, "Designing Clsasses for Linked Lists."

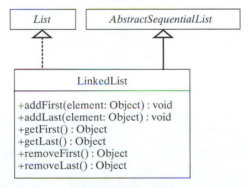

Figure 19.9 `LinkedList` *provides methods for adding and inserting elements at both ends of the list.*

Example 19.4 Using `ArrayList` and `LinkedList`

Problem

Write a program that creates an array list filled with numbers and inserts new elements into specified locations in the list. The example also creates a linked list from the array list, and inserts and removes elements from the list. Finally, the example traverses the list forward and backward.

Solution

The following code gives the solution to the problem. The output of the program is shown in Figure 19.10.

continues

Example 19.4   continued

```
Command Prompt                                    _ □ ×
C:\book>java TestList
A list of integers in the array list:
[10, 1, 2, 30, 3, 1, 4]
Display the linked list forward:
green 10 red 1 2 30 3 1
Display the linked list backward:
1 3 30 2 1 red 10 green
C:\book>
```

Figure 19.10   *The program uses the array list and linked lists.*

```
1      import java.util.*;
2
3      public class TestList {
4        public static void main(String[] args) {
5          ArrayList arrayList = new ArrayList();
6          arrayList.add(new Integer(1));
7          arrayList.add(new Integer(2));
8          arrayList.add(new Integer(3));
9          arrayList.add(new Integer(1));
10         arrayList.add(new Integer(4));
11         arrayList.add(0, new Integer(10));
12         arrayList.add(3, new Integer(30));
13
12         System.out.println("A list of integers in the array list:");
13         System.out.println(arrayList);
14
15         LinkedList linkedList = new LinkedList(arrayList);
16         linkedList.add(1, "red");
17         linkedList.removeLast();
18         linkedList.addFirst("green");
19
20         System.out.println("Display the linked list forward:");
21         ListIterator listIterator = linkedList.listIterator();
20         while (listIterator.hasNext()) {
22           System.out.print(listIterator.next() + " ");
23         }
24         System.out.println();
25
26         System.out.println("Display the linked list backward:");
27         listIterator = linkedList.listIterator(linkedList.size());
28         while (listIterator.hasPrevious()) {
29           System.out.print(listIterator.previous() + " ");
30         }
31       }
30     }
```

Review

A list can hold identical elements. Integer 1 is stored twice in the list (Lines 6, 9). ArrayList and LinkedList are operated similarly. The critical difference between them pertains to internal implementation, which affects their performance. ArrayList is efficient for retrieving elements, and for inserting and removing elements from the end of the list. LinkedList is efficient for inserting and removing elements anywhere in the list.

You can use TreeSet to store sorted elements. But there is no sorted list. However, the Java Collections Framework provides static methods in the Collections class that can be used to sort a list. The Collections class is introduced in Section 19.10, "The Collections Class."

19.8   The *Vector* and *Stack* Classes

The Java Collections Framework was introduced with Java 2. Several data structures were supported prior to Java 2. Among them were the Vector class and the Stack class. These classes were redesigned to fit into the Java Collections Framework, but their old-style methods are retained for compatibility. This section introduces the Vector class and the Stack class.

In Java 2, Vector is the same as ArrayList, except that it contains synchronized methods for accessing and modifying the vector. None of the new collection data structures introduced so far are synchronized. If synchronization is required, you can use the synchronized versions of the collection classes. These classes are introduced in Section 19.10, "The Collections Class."

The Vector class implements the List interface. It also has the methods contained in the original Vector class defined prior to Java 2, as shown in Figure 19.11.

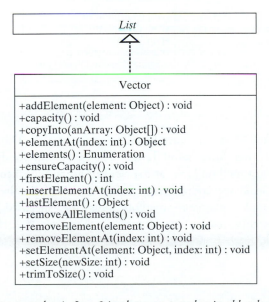

Figure 19.11   *The* Vector *class in Java 2 implements* List*, but its old-style methods are retained.*

Most of the old-style methods in the Vector class listed in the UML diagram in Figure 19.11 are similar to the methods in the List interface. These methods were introduced before the Java Collections Framework. For example, addElement(Object element) is the same as the add(Object element) method, except that addElement method is synchronized. Use the ArrayList class if you don't need synchronization. It works much faster than Vector.

NOTE
The elements() method returns an Enumeration. The Enumeration interface was introduced prior to Java 2 and was superseded by the Iterator interface.

NOTE
Vector is widely used in Java programming because it was the Java resizable array implementation before Java 2. Many of the Swing data models use vectors.

The Stack class represents a last-in/first-out stack of objects. The elements are accessed only from the top of the stack. You can retrieve, insert, or remove an element from the top of the stack. The Stack class extends the Vector class and provides several methods, as shown in Figure 19.12.

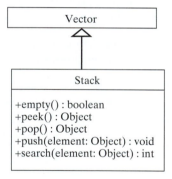

Figure 19.12   *The* Stack *class extends* Vector *to provide a last-in/first-out data structure.*

The Stack class was introduced prior to Java 2. The methods shown in Figure 19.12 were used before Java 2. The empty() method is the same as isEmpty(). The peek() method looks at the element at the top of the stack without removing it. The pop() method removes the top element from the stack and returns it. The push(Object element) method adds the specified element to the stack. The search(Object element) method checks whether the specified element is in the stack.

Example 19.5 Using `Vector` and `Stack`

Problem

This example presents two programs that rewrite Example 5.2, "Assigning Grades," the first using a vector instead of an array, and the second using a stack. The programs read student scores from the keyboard, store the scores in the vector, find the best scores, and then assign grades for all the students. A negative score signals the end of the input.

Solution

The program that uses a vector is given below. A sample run of the program is shown in Figure 19.13.

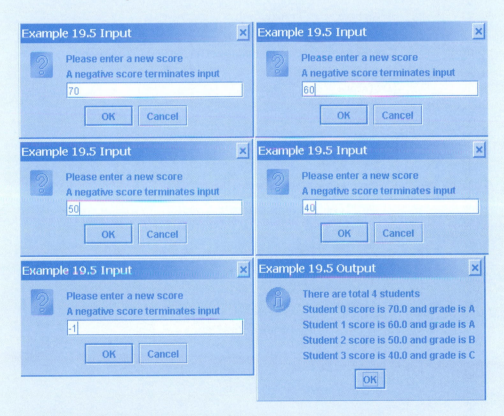

Figure 19.13   *The program receives scores, stores them in a vector, and assigns grades.*

```
1     // AssignGradeUsingVector.java: Assign grade
2     import java.util.*;
3
4     import java.util.*;
5     import javax.swing.JOptionPane;
6
7     public class AssignGradeUsingVector {
8       // Main method
```

continues

Example 19.5 continued

```
 9      public static void main(String[] args) {
10        Vector scoreVector = new Vector(); // Vector to hold scores
11        double best = 0; // The best score
12        char grade; // The grade
13
14        do {
15          // Read scores and find the best score
16          String scoreString = JOptionPane.showInputDialog(null,
17            "Please enter a new score"  +
18            "\nA negative score terminates input", "Example 19.5 Input",
19            JOptionPane.QUESTION_MESSAGE);
20
21          // Convert string into int
22          double score = Integer.parseInt(scoreString);
23
24          if (score < 0) break;
25
26          // Add the score into the vector
27          scoreVector.addElement(new Double(score));
28
29          // Find the best score
30          if (score > best)
31            best = score;
32        } while (true);
33
34        // Prepare the output string
35        String output = "There are total " + scoreVector.size() +
36          " students";
37
38        // Assign and display grades
39        for (int i = 0; i < scoreVector.size(); i++) {
40          // Retrieve an element from the vector
41          Double doubleObject = (Double)(scoreVector.elementAt(i));
42
43          // Get the score
44          double score = doubleObject.doubleValue();
45
46          if (score >= best - 10)
47            grade = 'A';
48         else if (score >= best - 20)
49            grade = 'B';
50          else if (score >= best - 30)
51            grade = 'C';
52          else if (score >= best - 40)
53            grade = 'D';
54          else
55            grade = 'F';
56
57          output += "\nStudent " + i + " score is " + score +
58          " and grade is " + grade;
59        }
60
61        JOptionPane.showMessageDialog(null, output,
62          "Example 19.5 Output", JOptionPane.INFORMATION_MESSAGE);
63
64        System.exit(0);
65      }
66    }
```

Since Stack is a subclass of Vector, the preceding program would work if you replaced all the occurrences of Vector by Stack. However, you can rewrite it using stack operations that operate elements only from the top of the stack. The revision of the program using the Stack class is given as follows:

```java
1   import java.util.*;
2   import javax.swing.JOptionPane;
3
4   public class AssignGradeUsingStack {
5     // Main method
6     public static void main(String[] args) {
7       Stack scoreStack = new Stack(); // Stack to hold scores
8       double best = 0; // The best score
9       char grade; // The grade
10
11      do {
12        // Read scores and find the best score
13        String scoreString = JOptionPane.showInputDialog(null,
14          "Please enter a new score"  +
15          "\nA negative score terminates input", "Example 19.5 Input",
16          JOptionPane.QUESTION_MESSAGE);
17
18        // Convert string into int
19        double score = Integer.parseInt(scoreString);
20
21        if (score < 0) break;
22
23        // Add the score into the Stack
24        scoreStack.push(new Double(score));
25
26        // Find the best score
27        if (score > best)
28          best = score;
29      } while (true);
30
31      // Prepare the output string
32      String output = "There are total " + scoreStack.size() +
33        " students";
34
35      int i = scoreStack.size();
36
37      // Assign and display grades
38      while (!scoreStack.isEmpty()) {
39        // Retrieve an element from the Stack
40        Double doubleObject = (Double)(scoreStack.pop());
41
42        // Get the score
43        double score = doubleObject.doubleValue();
44
45        if (score >= best - 10)
46          grade = 'A';
47        else if (score >= best - 20)
48          grade = 'B';
49        else if (score >= best - 30)
50          grade = 'C';
51        else if (score >= best - 40)
52          grade = 'D';
53        else
54          grade = 'F';
55
```

continues

Example 19.5 continued

```
56              output += "\nStudent " + i-- + " score is " + score +
57                " and grade is " + grade;
58          }
59
60          JOptionPane.showMessageDialog(null, output,
61            "Example 19.5 Output", JOptionPane.INFORMATION_MESSAGE);
62
63          System.exit(0);
64      }
65    }
```

Review

Example 5.2, "Assigning Grades," uses an array to store scores. The size of an array is fixed once the array is created. You should use array lists, linked lists, vectors, or stacks to store an unspecified number of elements.

The element type in an array can be primitive type values or objects, but the element type in the Java Collections Framework must be the Object type.

19.9   The *Map* Interface, the *AbstractMap* class, the *SortedMap* interface, the *HashMap* class, and the *TreeMap* class

The Collection interface represents a set of elements stored in HashSet, TreeSet, ArrayList, LinkedList, Vector, or Stack. The Map interface maps keys to the elements. The keys are like indexes. In List, the indexes are integers. In Map, the keys can be any objects. A map cannot contain duplicate keys. Each key can map to at most one value. The Map interface provides the methods for querying, updating, and obtaining a collection of values and a set of keys, as shown in Figure 19.14.

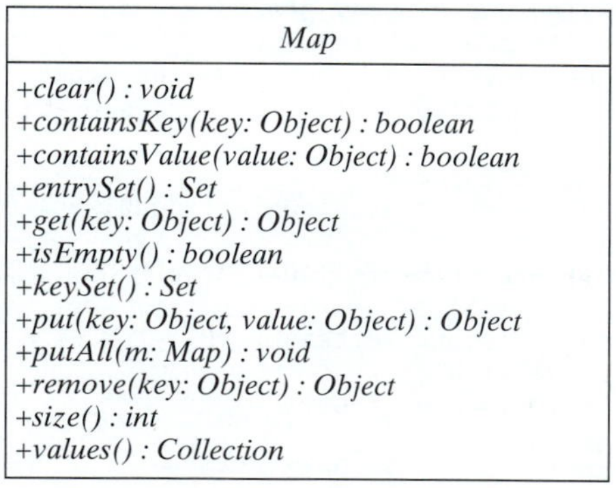

Map
+clear() : void
+containsKey(key: Object) : boolean
+containsValue(value: Object) : boolean
+entrySet() : Set
+get(key: Object) : Object
+isEmpty() : boolean
+keySet() : Set
+put(key: Object, value: Object) : Object
+putAll(m: Map) : void
+remove(key: Object) : Object
+size() : int
+values() : Collection

Figure 19.14   *The* Map *interface maps keys to values.*

The update methods include `clear`, `put`, `putAll`, and `remove`. The `clear()` method removes all mappings from the map. The `put(Object key, Object value)` method associates the specified value with the specified key in the map. If the map formerly contained a mapping for this key, the old value associated with the key is returned. The `putAll(Map m)` method adds the specified map to the map. The `remove(Object key)` method removes the mapping for the specified key from the map.

The query methods include `containsKey`, `containsValue`, `isEmpty`, and `size`. The `containsKey(Object key)` method checks whether the map contains a mapping for the specified key. The `containsValue(Object value)` method checks whether the map contains a mapping for this value. The `isEmpty()` method checks whether the map contains any mappings. The `size()` method returns the number of mappings in the map.

You can obtain a set of keys in the map using the `keySet()` method, and a collection of values in the map using the `values()` method. The `entrySet()` method returns a set of objects that implement the `Map.Entry` interface, where `Entry` is an inner interface for the `Map` interface. Each object in the set is a specific key-value pair in the underlying map.

The `AbstractMap` class is a convenience class that implements all the methods in the `Map` interface except the `entrySet()` method.

The `SortedMap` interface extends the `Map` interface to maintain the mapping in an ascending order of keys.

The `HashMap` and `TreeMap` classes are two concrete implementations of the `Map` interface. The `HashMap` class is efficient for locating a value, inserting a mapping, and deleting a mapping. The `TreeMap` class, implementing `SortedMap`, is efficient for traversing the keys in a sorted order. The keys can be sorted using the `Comparable` interface or the `Comparator` interface. If you create a `TreeMap` using its default constructor, the `compareTo` method in the `Comparable` interface is used to compare the elements in the set, assuming that the class of the elements implements the `Comparable` interface. To use a comparator, you have to use the `TreeMap (Comparator comparator)` constructor to create a sorted map that uses the `compare` method in the comparator to order the elements in the set based on the keys.

NOTE

`Hashtable` was introduced prior to Java 2, and it was redesigned to fit into the Java Collections Framework, but its old-style methods are retained for compatibility. `Hashtable` implements the `Map` interface and is used in the same way as `HashMap` except that `Hashtable` is synchronized.

Example 19.6 Using HashMap and TreeMap

Problem

This example creates a hash map that maps borrowers to mortgages. The Mortgage class, introduced in Chapter 6, "Objects and Classes," was used to model mortgages. Recall that you can create a mortgage using the following constructor:

```
public Mortgage(double annualInterestRate, int numOfYears,
    double loanAmount)
```

The program first creates a hash map with the borrower's name as its key and the mortgage as its value. The program then creates a tree map from the hash map and displays the mappings in ascending order of the keys.

Solution

The following code gives the solution to the problem. The output of the program is shown in Figure 19.15.

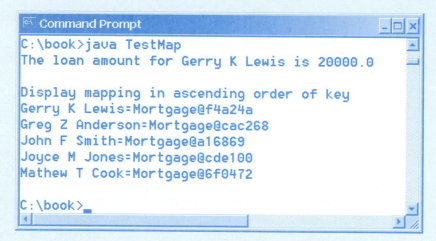

```
C:\book>java TestMap
The loan amount for Gerry K Lewis is 20000.0

Display mapping in ascending order of key
Gerry K Lewis=Mortgage@f4a24a
Greg Z Anderson=Mortgage@cac268
John F Smith=Mortgage@a16869
Joyce M Jones=Mortgage@cde100
Mathew T Cook=Mortgage@6f0472

C:\book>
```

Figure 19.15   *The program demonstrates the use of* HashMap *and* TreeMap.

```
1     import java.util.*;
2
3     public class TestMap {
4       public static void main(String[] args) {
5         // Create a hash set
6         HashMap hashMap = new HashMap();
7         hashMap.put("John F Smith", new Mortgage(7, 15, 150000));
8         hashMap.put("Greg Z Anderson", new Mortgage(7.5, 30, 150000));
9         hashMap.put("Joyce M Jones", new Mortgage(7, 15, 250000));
10        hashMap.put("Gerry K Lewis", new Mortgage(7.85, 30, 20000));
11        hashMap.put("Mathew T Cook", new Mortgage(7, 15, 100000));
12
13        // Display the loan amount for Gerry K Lewis
14        System.out.println("The loan amount for " + "Gerry K Lewis is " +
15          ((Mortgage)(hashMap.get("Gerry K Lewis"))).getLoanAmount());
16
```

```
17        // Create a tree map from the previous hash map
18        TreeMap treeMap = new TreeMap(hashMap);
19
20        // Get an entry set for the tree map
21        Set entrySet = treeMap.entrySet();
22
23        // Get an iterator for the entry set
24        Iterator iterator = entrySet.iterator();
25        // Display mappings
26        System.out.println("\nDisplay mapping in ascending order of key");
27        while (iterator.hasNext()) {
28          System.out.println(iterator.next());
29        }
30      }
31    }
```

Review

All the concrete classes that implement the Map interface have at least two constructors. One is the default constructor that constructs an empty map, and the other constructs a map from an instance of Map. So new TreeMap(hashMap) constructs a tree map from a hash map.

Unlike the Collection interface, the Map interface does not provide an iterator. To traverse the map, you create an entry set of the mappings using the entrySet() method in the Map interface. Each element in the entry set is a string that consists of the string representation of the key object and its counterpart connected by the = sign. As shown in Figure 19.15, the first element in the entry set is Gerry K Lewis-Mortgage@f4a24a.

> **TIP**
> If you don't need to maintain a sorted map when updating the map, use a hash map, because less time is needed to insert and remove mappings in a hash map. When you need the map to be sorted, you can convert it into a tree map.

Example 19.7 Counting the Occurrences of Words in a Text

Problem

Write a program that counts the occurrences of words in a text and displays the words and their occurrences in ascending order of the number of occurrences. The program uses a hash map to store a pair consisting of a word and its count. For each word, check whether it is already a key in the map. If not, add the key and value 1 to the map. Otherwise, increase the value for the word (key) by 1 in the map. To sort the map, convert it to a tree map.

Solution

The following code gives the solution to the problem. The output of the program is shown in Figure 19.16.

continues

Example 19.7 continued

```
Command Prompt                                                    _ □ ×
C:\book>java CountOccurrenceOfWords
Display words and their count in ascending order of the words
Have=4
a=3
class=1
day=1
fun=1
good=3
visit=1

C:\book>
```

Figure 19.16   *The program finds the occurrences of each word in a text.*

```java
1    import java.util.*;
2
3    public class CountOccurrenceOfWords {
4      public static void main(String[] args) {
5        // Text in a string
6        String text = "Have a good day. Have a good class. " +
7          "Have a good visit. Have fun!";
8
9        // Create a hash map to hold words and key and count as value
10       HashMap hashMap = new HashMap();
11
12       StringTokenizer st = new StringTokenizer(text, " .!?");
13       while (st.hasMoreTokens()) {
14         String key = st.nextToken();
15
16         if (hashMap.get(key) != null) {
17           int value = ((Integer)hashMap.get(key)).intValue();
18           value++;
19           hashMap.put(key, new Integer(value));
20         }
21         else {
22           hashMap.put(key, new Integer(1));
23         }
24       }
25
26       // Create a tree map from the hash map
27       TreeMap treeMap = new TreeMap(hashMap);
28
30       Set entrySet = treeMap.entrySet();
31
32       // Get an iterator for the entry set
33       Iterator iterator = entrySet.iterator();
34
35       // Display mappings
36       System.out.println("Display words and their count in " +
37         "ascending order of the words");
38       while (iterator.hasNext()) {
39         System.out.println(iterator.next());
40       }
41     }
42   }
```

Review

The pairs of words and their occurrence counts are stored in the map. The words serve as the keys. Since all elements must be stored as objects in the map, the count is wrapped in an `Integer` object.

The program extracts a word from a text and checks whether it is already stored as a key in the map. If not, a new pair consisting of the word and a zero count (`new Integer(0)`) is stored to the map. Otherwise, the count for the word is incremented by 1.

The program first stores the pairs to a hash map, then creates a tree map from the hash map. It then creates an entry set and displays all the entries in the set. Each entry consists of a word and its count connected by the = sign in ascending order of words. To display them in ascending order of the occurrence counts, see Exercise 19.9.

19.10   The *Collections* Class

The `Collections` class contains static methods for operating on collections and maps, creating synchronized collection classes, and creating read-only collection classes, as shown in Figure 19.17.

Most of the methods in the `Collections` class deal with lists. The sort methods can be used to sort a list using the `Comparable` interface or the `Comparator` interface. The `binarySearch` methods can be used to find an element in a presorted list. In order to use the `binarySearch(list, key)` method, the list must first be sorted through the `Comparable` interface. To use the `binarySearch(list, key, comparator)` method, the list must first be sorted through the `Comparator` interface. The `binarySearch` method returns the index of the search key if it is contained in the list. Otherwise, it returns –(insertion point) – 1. The insertion point is the point at which the key would be inserted into the list.

Use the `copy(src, des)` method to copy a source list to a destination list. Use the `fill(list, object)` method to fill a list with a specified object. Use the `nCopy(n, object)` method to create a list with n number of a specified `object`.

The `min` and `max` methods are generic for all the collections. You can use them to find the minimum and maximum elements in a collection.

The `Collections` class defines three constants: one for an empty set, one for an empty list, and one for an empty map (`EMPTY_SET`, `EMPTY_LIST`, and `EMPTY_MAP`). The class also provides the `singleton(Object o)` method for creating an immutable set containing only a single item, the `singletonList(Object o)` method for creating an immutable list containing only a single item, and the `singleton-Map(Object key, Object value)` method for creating an immutable map containing only a single mapping.

Collections
+binarySearch(list: List, key: Object) : int
+binarySearch(list: List, key: Object, c: Comparator) : int
+copy(src: List, des: List) : void
+enumeration(c: final Collection) : Enumeration
+fill(list: List, o: Object) : void
+max(c: Collection) : Object
+max(c: Collection, c: Comparator) : Object
+min(c: Collection) : Object
+min(c: Collection, c: Comparator) : Object
+nCopies(n: int, o: Object) : List
+reverse(list: List) : void
+reverseOrder() : Comparator
+shuffle(list: List) : void
+shuffle(list: List, rnd: Random) : void
+singleton(o: Object) : Set
+singletonList(o: Object) : List
+singletonMap(key: Object, value: Object) : Map
+sort(list: List) : void
+sort(list: List, c: Comparator) : void
+synchronizedCollection(c: Collection) : Collection
+synchronizedList(list: List) : List
+synchronizedMap(m: Map) : Map
+synchronizedSet(s: Set) : Set
+synchronizedSortedMap(s: SortedMap) : SortedMap
+synchronizedSortedSet(s: SortedSet) : SortedSet
+unmodifiableCollection(c: Collection) : Collection
+unmodifiableList(list: List) : List
+unmodifiableMap(m: Map) : Map
+unmodifiableSet(s: Set) : Set
+unmodifiableSortedMap(s: SortedMap) : SortedMap
+unmodifiableSortedSet(s: SortedSet) : SortedSet

Figure 19.17   *The* `Collections` *class contains static methods for supporting the Java Collections Framework.*

The methods in the `Collection` and `Map` interfaces are not thread-safe, so the `Collections` class provides six static methods for wrapping a collection into a synchronized version: `synchronizedCollection(Collection c)`, `synchronizedList (List list)`, `synchronizedMap(Map m)`, `synchronizedSet(Set set)`, `synchronized-SortedMap(SortedMap m)`, and `synchronizedSortedSet(SortedSet s)`. The synchronized collections can be safely accessed and modified by multiple threads concurrently. It is, however, imperative that a thread acquires a lock on the synchronized list, set, or map when traversing it through an iterator, as shown in the following code:

```
Set hashSet = Collections.synchronizedSet(new HashSet());

synchronized (hashSet) { // Must synchronize it
  Iterator iterator = hashSet.iterator();
  while (iterator.hasNext()) {
    System.out.println(iterator.next());
  }
}
```

Failure to do so may result in nondeterministic behavior, such as `ConcurrentModi-ficationException`. See Exercise 19.2.

The `Collections` class also provides six static methods for creating read-only collections:

`unmodifiableCollection(Collection c)`, `unmodifiableList(List list)`, `unmodifiableMap(Map m)`, `unmodifiableSet(Set set)`, `unmodifiableSortedMap(Sorted-Map m)`, and `unmodifiableSortedSet(SortedSet s)`. The read-only collections prevent the data in the collections from being modified, and, as well, offer better performance for read-only operations.

Example 19.8 Using the `Collections` Class

Problem

Write a program that demonstrates the use of the methods in the `Collections` class. The example creates a list, sorts it, and searches for an element. The example wraps the list into a synchronized and read-only list.

Solution

The following code gives the solution to the problem. The output of the program is shown in Figure 19.18.

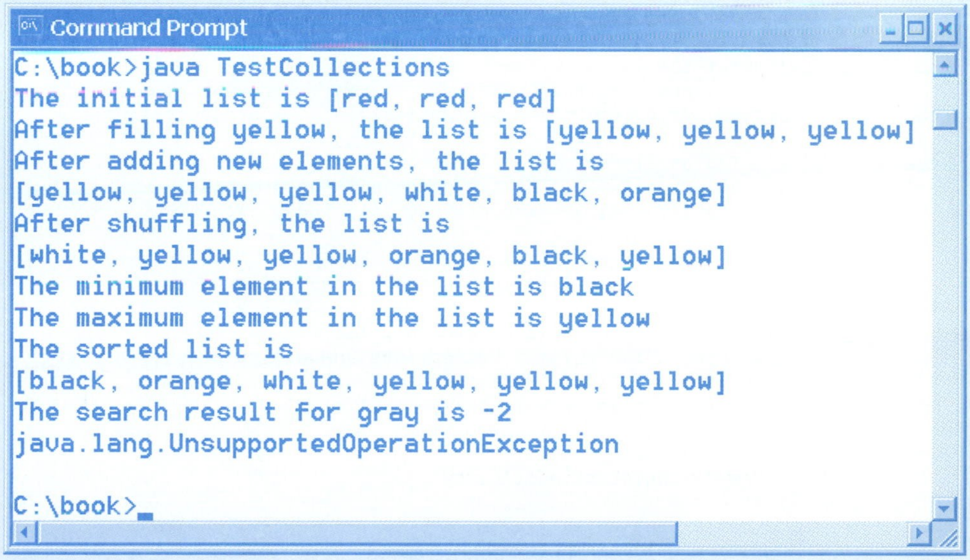

```
C:\book>java TestCollections
The initial list is [red, red, red]
After filling yellow, the list is [yellow, yellow, yellow]
After adding new elements, the list is
[yellow, yellow, yellow, white, black, orange]
After shuffling, the list is
[white, yellow, yellow, orange, black, yellow]
The minimum element in the list is black
The maximum element in the list is yellow
The sorted list is
[black, orange, white, yellow, yellow, yellow]
The search result for gray is -2
java.lang.UnsupportedOperationException

C:\book>
```

Figure 19.18   *The program demonstrates the use of Collections.*

```
1    import java.util.*;
2
3    public class TestCollections {
4      public static void main(String[] args) {
```

continues

Example 19.8 continued

```
5          // Create a list of three strings
6          List list = Collections.nCopies(3, "red");
7
8          // Create an array list
9          ArrayList arrayList = new ArrayList(list);
10         System.out.println("The initial list is " + arrayList);
11         list = null; // Release list
12
13         // Fill in "yellow" to the list
14         Collections.fill(arrayList, "yellow");
15         System.out.println("After filling yellow, the list is " +
16           arrayList);
17
18         // Add three new elements to the list
19         arrayList.add("white");
20         arrayList.add("black");
21         arrayList.add("orange");
22         System.out.println("After adding new elements, the list is\n"
23           + arrayList);
24
25         // Shuffle the list
26         Collections.shuffle(arrayList);
27         System.out.println("After shuffling, the list is\n"
28           + arrayList);
29
30         // Find the minimum and maximum elements in the list
31         System.out.println("The minimum element in the list is "
32           + Collections.min(arrayList));
33         System.out.println("The maximum element in the list is "
34           + Collections.max(arrayList));
35
36         // Sort the list
37         Collections.sort(arrayList);
38         System.out.println("The sorted list is\n" + arrayList);
39
40         // Find an element in the list
41         System.out.println("The search result for gray is " +
42           Collections.binarySearch(arrayList, "gray"));
43
44         // Create a synchronized list
45         List syncList = Collections.synchronizedList(arrayList);
46
48         // Create a synchronized read-only list
48         List unmodifiableList = Collections.unmodifiableList(syncList);
49         arrayList = null; // Release arrayList
50         syncList = null; // Release syncList
51
52         try {
53           unmodifiableList.add("black");
54         }
55         catch (Exception ex) {
56           System.out.println(ex);
57         }
59       }
59     }
```

The program first creates a list filled with the same elements three times using `nCopies(3, "red")` (Line 6). This list is an instance of `List`, but it is not an array list or a linked list. The program creates an array list from the list in Line 9.

The program uses `Collections.fill(arrayList, "yellow")` (Line 14) to replace each element in the list with "yellow."

After adding three new elements into `arrayList`, `Collections.shuffle-(arrayList)` (Line 26) rearranges them in `arrayList`.

The program uses `Collections.min(arrayList)` (Line 32) to find the minimum element in `arrayList`, and `Collections.max(arrayList)` (Line 34) to find the maximum element in `arrayList`.

`Collections.sort(arrayList)` (Line 37) is invoked to sort `arrayList`. `Collections.binarySearch(arrayList, "gray")` (Line 42) is invoked to find "gray" in `arrayList`. This method returns −2 because −(insertion point) − 1 = -2, where insertion point is 1.

The program finally uses `Collections.synchronizedList(arrayList)` (Line 45) to create a synchronized list for `arrayList`, and then creates a synchronized read-only list by wrapping the synchronized list using the `unmodifiableList`. As shown in Figure 19.18, an `UnsupportedOperationException` is thrown when the program attempts to add a new element to the read-only list.

19.11 The *Arrays* Class

The `Arrays` class contains various static methods for sorting and searching arrays, comparing arrays, and filling array elements. It also contains a method for converting an array to a list. Figure 19.19 shows the methods in `Arrays`.

An array must be sorted before the `binarySearch` method is used. The `fill` method can be used to fill part of the array or the whole array with the same value. The `sort` method can be used to sort part of the array or the whole array. `fill (a, fromIndex, toIndex, val)` fills `val` into `a[fromIndex],..., a[toIndex - 1]` and `sort(a, fromIndex, toIndex, val)` sorts `a[fromIndex],..., a[toIndex - 1]`.

```
                          Arrays

+asList(a: Object[]) : List
+binarySearch(a: byte[],key: byte) : int
+binarySearch(a: char[], key: char) : int
+binarySearch(a: double[], key: double) : int
+binarySearch(a,: float[]  key: float) : int
+binarySearch(a: int[], key: int) : int
+binarySearch(a: long[], key: long) : int
+binarySearch(a: Object[], key: Object) : int
+binarySearch(a: Object[], key: Object, c: Comparator) : int
+binarySearch(a: short[], key: short) : int
+equals(a: boolean[], a2: boolean[]) : boolean
+equals(a: byte[], a2: byte[]) : boolean
+equals(a: char[], a2: char[]) : boolean
+equals(a: double[], a2: double[]) : boolean
+equals(a: float[], a2: float[]) : boolean
+equals(a: int[], a2: int[]) : boolean
+equals(a: long[], a2: long[]) : boolean
+equals(a: Object[], a2: Object[]) : boolean
+equals(a: short[], a2: short[]) : boolean
+fill(a: boolean[], val: boolean) : void
+fill(a: boolean[], fromIndex: int, toIndex: int, val: boolean) : void

Overloaded fill method for char, byte, short, int, long, float,
double, and Object.

+sort(a: byte[]) : void
+sort(a: byte[], fromIndex: int, toIndex: int) : void

Overloaded sort method for char, short, int, long, float, double,
and Object.
```

Figure 19.19   *The* `Arrays` *class contains static methods for arrays.*

Example 19.9 Using the `Arrays` Class

Problem

Write a program that demonstrates how to use the methods in the `Arrays` class. The example creates an array of `int` values, fills part of the array with 50, sorts it, searches for an element, and compares the array with another one.

Solution

The following code gives the solution to the problem. The output of the program is shown in Figure 19.20.

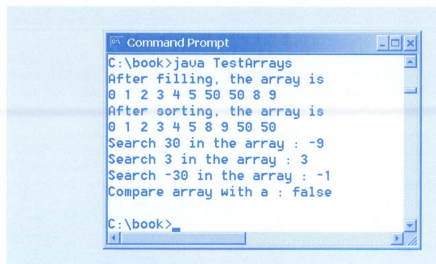

Figure 19.20   *The program demonstrates the use of* Arrays.

```java
1    import java.util.*;
2
3    public class TestArrays {
4      public static void main(String[] args) {
5        // Create an array of 10 int values
6        int[] array = {0, 1, 2, 3, 4, 5, 6, 7, 8, 9};
7
8        // Fill array from index 6 to index 8-1 with 50
9        Arrays.fill(array, 6, 8, 50);
10       System.out.println("After filling, the array is");
11       for (int i = 0; i < 10; i++) {
12         System.out.print(array[i] + " ");
13       }
14       System.out.println();
15
16       // Sort the array
17       Arrays.sort(array);
18       System.out.println("After sorting, the array is");
19       for (int i = 0; i < 10; i++) {
20         System.out.print(array[i] + " ");
21       }
22       System.out.println();
23
24       // Search for 30 in the array
25       System.out.println("Search 30 in the array : " +
26         Arrays.binarySearch(array, 30));
27
28       // Search for 3 in the array
29       System.out.println("Search 3 in the array : " +
30         Arrays.binarySearch(array, 3));
31
32       // Search for -30 in the array
33       System.out.println("Search -30 in the array : " +
34         Arrays.binarySearch(array, -30));
35
36       // Test if two arrays are the same
37       int[] a = new int[10];
38       System.out.println("Compare array with a : " +
39         Arrays.equals(array, a));
40     }
41   }
```

continues

Example 19.9 continued

Review

The program first creates an array of ten int values (Line 6), then fills 50 in the array at index 6 and 7 (Line 9). The sort method (Line 17) is used to sort the entire array.

The program uses the binarySearch method to search for 30, 3, and −30 in the array (Lines 26, 30, 34). The return value is −9 for searching 30, because 30 is not in the list and the insertion point for 30 is at 8. The return value is 3 for searching 3, because 3 is in the list and its index is 3. The return value is −1 for searching −30, because −30 is not in the list and the insertion point for −30 is at 0.

The program also uses the equals method (Line 39) to compare two arrays.

Chapter Summary

This chapter introduced data structures using the Java Collections Framework. You learned how to use Set to store nonduplicate elements, List to store sequenced elements, and Map to store elements mapped with keys. Set, List, and Map are interfaces.

HashSet and TreeSet are concrete implementation classes for Set. Elements are not ordered in a HashSet, but are ordered in a TreeSet. The elements in a sorted collection can be compared using the Comparable or Comparator interface.

ArrayList and LinkedList are the concrete implementation classes for List. ArrayList uses a resizable array to store elements, and LinkedList uses a linked list to store elements. ArrayList is efficient for retrieving elements, and for inserting and removing elements from the end of a list. LinkedList is efficient for inserting and removing elements anywhere in a list. Vector is similar to ArrayList except that all the methods in Vector are synchronized. Stack is a subclass of Vector that provides methods for stack operations.

HashMap and TreeMap are concrete implementation classes for Map. Use HashMap if the elements are not ordered, use TreeMap to order elements in a map.

The Collections class provides static methods for operating on collections and maps, creating synchronized collection classes, and creating read-only collection classes.

The Arrays class contains static methods for sorting and searching arrays, comparing arrays, and filling array elements.

Review Questions

9.1 Describe the Java Collections Framework.

9.2 The hashCode method and the equals method are defined in the Object class. Why are they redefined in the Collection interface?

9.3 Find the default implementation for the `equals` method and the `hashCode` method in the `Object` class from the source code of Object.java.

9.4 How do you create an instance of `Set`? How do you insert a new element in a set? How do you remove an element from a set? How do you find the size of a set? How do you traverse the elements in a set?

9.5 What are the differences between `HashSet` and `TreeSet`? How do you sort the elements in a set using the `compareTo` method in the `Comparable` interface? How do you sort the elements in a set using the `Comparator` interface? What would happen if you added an element that cannot be compared with the existing elements in the tree set?

9.6 How do you add and remove elements from a list? How do you traverse a list in both directions?

9.7 What are the differences between `ArrayList` and `LinkedList`?

9.8 How do you create an instance of `Vector`? How do you add or insert a new element into a vector? How do you remove an element from a vector? How do you find the size of a vector?

9.9 How do you create an instance of `Stack`? How do you add a new element into a stack? How do you remove an element from a stack? How do you find the size of a stack?

19.10 How do you create an instance of `Map`? How do you add a pair of element and key into a map? How do you remove an entry from a map? How do you find the size of a map? How do you traverse entries in a map?

19.11 Describe the static methods in the `Collections` class and the `Arrays` class.

Programming Exercises

19.1 Create a program with two threads concurrently accessing and modifying a set. The first thread creates a hash set filled with numbers, and adds a new number to the set every second. The second thread obtains an iterator for the set and traverses the set back and forth through the iterator every second. You will receive a `ConcurrentModificationException`, because while traversing the set in the second thread, the underlying set is being modified in the first thread.

19.2 Correct the problem in the preceding exercise using synchronization so that the second thread does not throw `ConcurrentModificationException`. You will have to use the `Collections.synchronizedSet(set)` method to obtain a synchronized set and acquire a lock on the returned set when traversing it.

19.3 Rewrite Example 19.5 using an `ArrayList`.

19.4 Rewrite Example 19.7 to read the text from a text file. The text file is passed as a command-line argument.

19.5 Write a program that reads in ten double numbers and uses the sort method in the Arrays class to sort them.

19.6 Rewrite Exercise 19.2 using a vector. You still have to synchronize the vector when traversing it.

19.7 Write a program that reads an unspecified number of integers and finds the one that has the most occurrences. Your input ends when the input is 0. For example, if you entered 2 3 40 3 5 4 −3 3 3 2 0, the number 3 occurred most often. Please enter one number at a time. If not one but several numbers have the most occurrences, all of them should be reported. For example, since 9 and 3 appear twice in the list 9 30 3 9 3 2 4, both should be reported.

19.8 Write a program that reads a Java source code file and reports the number of keywords in the file. Pass the Java file name from the command line.

HINT

Create a set to store all the Java keywords.

19.9 Rewrite Example 19.7 to display the words in ascending order of occurrence counts.

HINT

Create a class named WordOccurrence that implements the Comparable interface. The class contains two fields, word and count. The compareTo method compares the count. For each pair in the entry set in Example 19.7, create an instance of WordOccurrence and store it in an array list. Sort the array list using Collections.sort method.

APPENDIXES

The appendixes cover a mixed bag of topics. Appendix A lists Java keywords. Appendix B gives tables of ASCII characters and their associated codes in decimal and in hex. Appendix C shows the operator precedence. Appendix D summarizes Java modifiers and their usage. Appendix E introduces number systems, conversions among binary, decimal, and hex numbers, and bit operations. Appendix F introduces HTML basics. Appendix G lists UML graphical notations for describing classes and their relationships. Appendix H introduces packages for grouping classes. Appendix I covers special floating-point values. Appendix J provides a glossary of key terms used in the text.

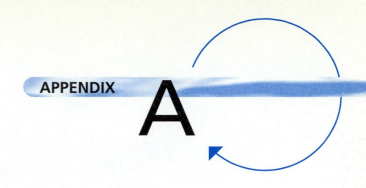

APPENDIX

A

JAVA KEYWORDS

The following 48 keywords are reserved for use by the Java language:

abstract	final	protected
assert*	finally	public
boolean	float	return
break	for	short
byte	goto	static
case	if	super
catch	implements	switch
char	import	synchronized
class	instanceof	this
const	int	throw
continue	interface	throws
default	long	transient
do	native	try
double	new	void
else	package	volatile
extends	private	while

The keywords goto and const are C++ keywords reserved, but not currently used, in Java. This enables Java compilers to identify them and to produce better error messages if they appear in Java programs.

The Boolean literal values true and false are not keywords. Similarly, the null object value is not classified as a keyword. You cannot use them for other purposes, however.

---

*assert is the new keyword introduced since JDK 1.4. For information on how to use it, please see java.sun.com/j2se/1.4/docs/guide/lang/assert.html.

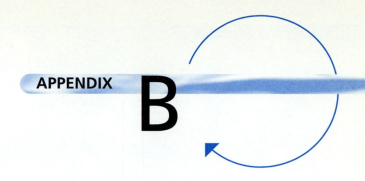

THE ASCII CHARACTER SET

Tables B.1 and B.2 show ASCII characters and their respective decimal and hexadecimal codes. The decimal or hexadecimal code of a character is a combination of its row index and column index. For example, in Table B.1, the letter A is at row 6 and column 5, so its decimal equivalent is 65; in Table B.2, letter A is at row 4 and column 1, so its hexadecimal equivalent is 41.

TABLE B.1 ASCII Character Set in the Decimal Index

	0	1	2	3	4	5	6	7	8	9
0	nul	soh	stx	etx	eot	enq	ack	bel	bs	ht
1	nl	vt	ff	cr	so	si	dle	dc1	dc2	dc3
2	dc4	nak	syn	etb	can	em	sub	esc	fs	gs
3	rs	us	sp	!	"	#	$	%	&	'
4	(	)	*	+	,	-	.	/	0	1
5	2	3	4	5	6	7	8	9	:	;
6	<	=	>	?	@	A	B	C	D	E
7	F	G	H	I	J	K	L	M	N	O
8	P	Q	R	S	T	U	V	W	X	Y
9	Z	[	\	]	^	_	`	a	b	c
10	d	e	f	g	h	i	j	k	l	m
11	n	o	p	q	r	s	t	u	v	w
12	x	y	z	{			}	~	del		

TABLE B.2   ASCII Character Set in the Hexadecimal Index

	0	1	2	3	4	5	6	7	8	9	A	B	C	D	E	F
0	nul	soh	stx	etx	eot	enq	ack	bel	bs	ht	nl	vt	ff	cr	so	si
1	dle	dc1	dc2	dc3	dc4	nak	syn	etb	can	em	sub	esc	fs	gs	rs	us
2	sp	!	"	#	$	%	&	'	(	)	*	+	,	-	.	/
3	0	1	2	3	4	5	6	7	8	9	:	;	<	=	>	?
4	@	A	B	C	D	E	F	G	H	I	J	K	L	M	N	O
5	P	Q	R	S	T	U	V	W	X	Y	Z	[	\	]	<	_
6	`	a	b	c	d	e	f	g	h	i	j	k	l	m	n	o
7	p	q	r	s	t	u	v	w	x	y	z	{			}	~	del

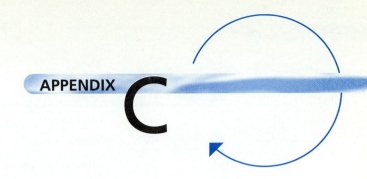

OPERATOR PRECEDENCE CHART

The operators are shown in decreasing order of precedence from top to bottom. Operators in the same group have the same precedence, and their associativity is shown in the table.

Operator	Name	Associativity
()	Parentheses	Left to right
()	Function call	Left to right
[]	Array subscript	Left to right
.	Object member access	Left to right
++	Postincrement	Right to left
--	Postdecrement	Right to left
++	Preincrement	Right to left
--	Predecrement	Right to left
+	Unary plus	Right to left
-	Unary minus	Right to left
!	Unary logical negation	Right to left
(type)	Unary casting	Right to left
new	Creating object	Right to left
*	Multiplication	Left to right
/	Division	Left to right
%	Remainder	Left to right
+	Addition	Left to right
-	Subtraction	Left to right
<<	Left shift	Left to right
>>	Right shift with sign extension	Left to right
>>>	Right shift with zero extension	Left to right
<	Less than	Left to right
>=	Less than or equal to	Left to right
>	Greater than	Left to right
>=	Greater than or equal to	Left to right
instanceof	Checking object type	Left to right
==	Equal comparison	Left to right
!=	Not equal	Left to right
&	(Unconditional AND)	Left to right
^	(Exclusive OR)	Left to right
¦	(Unconditional OR)	Left to right

Operator	Name	Associativity
&&	Conditional AND	Left to right
¦¦	Conditional OR	Left to right
? :	Ternary condition (Conditional expression)	Right to left
=	Assignment	Right to left
+=	Addition assignment	Right to left
-=	Subtraction assignment	Right to left
*=	Multiplication assignment	Right to left
/=	Division assignment	Right to left
%=	Remainder assignment	Right to left

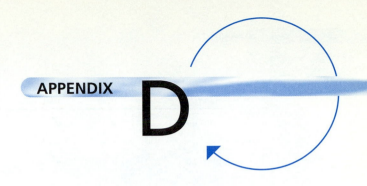

APPENDIX **D**

JAVA MODIFIERS

Modifiers are used on classes and class members (methods and data), but the `final` modifier can also be used on local variables in a method. A modifier that can be applied to a class is called a *class modifier*. A modifier that can be applied to a method is called a *method modifier*. A modifier that can be applied to a data field is called a *data modifier*. The following table gives a summary of the Java modifiers.

Modifier	class	method	data	Explanation
(default)	✓	✓	✓	A class, method, or data field is visible in this package.
public	✓	✓	✓	A class, method, or data field is visible to all the programs in any package.
private		✓	✓	A method or data field is only visible in this class.
protected		✓	✓	A method or data field is visible in this package and in subclasses of this class in any package.
static		✓	✓	Defines a class method or a class data field.
final	✓	✓	✓	A final class cannot be extended. A final method cannot be modified in a subclass. A final data field is a constant.
abstract	✓	✓		An abstract class must be extended. An abstract method must be implemented in a concrete subclass.
native		✓		A native method indicates that the method is implemented using a language other than Java.
synchronized		✓		Only one thread at a time can execute this method.

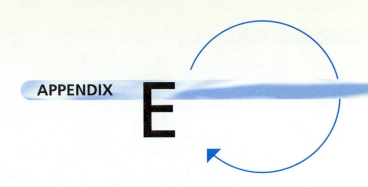

E

NUMBER SYSTEMS
AND BIT MANIPULATIONS

Introduction

This appendix introduces binary numbers, decimal numbers, and hexadecimal numbers, and the methods for converting among them. A related topic on bit manipulations will also be introduced.

The binary number system has two digits, 0 and 1. Computers use binary numbers internally because storage devices like memory and disk are made to store 0s and 1s. A number inside a computer is stored as a sequence of 0s and 1s. Each 0 and 1 is called a *bit*, short for binary digit.

Binary numbers are not intuitive, since we use decimal numbers in our daily life. When you write a number like 20 in a Java program, it is assumed to be a decimal number. The digits in the decimal number system are 0, 1, 2, 3, 4, 5, 6, 7, 8, and 9. Internally, computer software is used to convert decimal numbers into binary numbers, and vice versa.

In this book you write programs using decimal number systems. However, if you write programs to deal with a system like an operating system, you need to use binary numbers to reach down to the "machine-level." Binary numbers tend to be very long and cumbersome. Hexadecimal numbers are often used to abbreviate binary numbers. The hexadecimal number system has sixteen digits: 0, 1, 2, 3, 4, 5, 6, 7, 8, 9, A, B, C, D, E, and F. The letters A, B, C, D, E, and F correspond to the decimal numbers 10, 11, 12, 13, 14, and 15.

Conversions Between Binary Numbers and Decimal Numbers

Given a binary number $b_n b_{n-1} b_{n-2} \ldots b_2 b_1 b_0$, the equivalent decimal value is simply $b_n \times 2^n + b_{n-1} \times 2^{n-1} + b_{n-2} \times 2^{n-2} + \ldots + b_2 \times 2^2 + b_1 \times 2^1 + b_0 \times 2^0$.

For example, the binary number 10101001 is 169 in decimal, since $1 \times 2^7 + 0 \times 2^6 + 1 \times 2^5 + 0 \times 2^4 + 1 \times 2^3 + 0 \times 2^2 + 0 \times 2^1 + 1 \times 2^0 = 169$.

To convert a decimal number d to a binary number is to find the bits b_n, b_{n-1}, b_{n-2}, ... , b_2, b_1, and b_0 such that $d = b_n \times 2^n + b_{n-1} \times 2^{n-1} + b_{n-2} \times 2^{n-2} + ... + b_2 \times 2^2 + b_1 \times 2^1 + b_0 \times 2^0$. These bits can be found by successively dividing d by 2 until the quotient is 0. The remainders are b_0, b_1, b_2, ... , b_{n-2}, b_{n-1}, and b_n.

For example, the decimal number 123 is 1111011 in binary. The conversion is conducted as follows:

61	30	15	7	3	1	0
2 ⌐ 123	2 ⌐ 61	2 ⌐ 30	2 ⌐ 15	2 ⌐ 7	2 ⌐ 3	2 ⌐ 1
122	60	30	14	6	2	0
1	1	0	1	1	1	1
↓	↓	↓	↓	↓	↓	↓
b_0	b_1	b_2	b_3	b_4	b_5	b_6

1. $123\%2 = 1$ (b_0).

2. The quotient of 123 divided by 2 is 61. $61\%2 = 1$ (b_1).

3. The quotient of 61 divided by 2 is 30. $30\%2 = 0$ (b_2).

4. The quotient of 30 divided by 2 is 15. $15\%2 = 1$ (b_3).

5. The quotient of 15 divided by 2 is 7. $7\%2 = 1$ (b_4).

6. The quotient of 7 divided by 2 is 3. $3\%2 = 1$ (b_5).

7. The quotient of 3 divided by 2 is 1. $1\%2 = 1$ (b_6).

8. The quotient of 1 divided by 2 is 0. The conversion is completed.

Conversions Between Hexadecimal Numbers and Decimal Numbers

Given a hexadecimal number $h_n h_{n-1} h_{n-2} ... h_2 h_1 h_0$, the equivalent decimal value is simply $h_n \times 16^n + h_{n-1} \times 16^{n-1} + h_{n-2} \times 16^{n-2} + ... + h_2 \times 16^2 + h_1 \times 16^1 + h_0 \times 16^0$.

For example, the hexadecimal number 43A is 1082 in decimal, since $4 \times 16^2 + 3 \times 16^1 + 10 = 1082$.

To convert a decimal number d to a hexadecimal number is to find the hexadecimal digits h_n, h_{n-1}, h_{n-2}, ... , h_2, h_1, and h_0 such that $d = h_n \times 16^n + h_{n-1} \times 16^{n-1} + h_{n-2} \times 16^{n-2} + ... + h_2 \times 16^2 + h_1 \times 16^1 + h_0 \times 16^0$. These numbers can be found by successively dividing d by 16 until the quotient is 0. The remainders are h_0, h_1, h_2, ... , h_{n-2}, h_{n-1}, and h_n.

For example, the decimal number 123 is 7B in hexadecimal. The conversion is conducted as follows:

```
        7                    0
      ┌──────            ┌──────
16    │  123       16    │  7
      │  112             │  0
      └──────            └──────
         11                 7
          │                 │
          ▼                 ▼
         h₀                h₁
```

1. $123 \% 16 = 11$ (h_0).

2. The quotient of 123 divided by 16 is 7. $7 \% 16 = 7$ (h_1).

3. The quotient of 7 divided by 16 is 0. The conversion is completed.

Conversions Between Binary Numbers and Hexadecimal Numbers

To convert a hexadecimal number to a binary number, simply convert each digit in the hexadecimal number into a four-digit binary number using Table E.1.

TABLE E.1

Hexadecimal	Binary	Decimal
0	0	0
1	1	1
2	10	2
3	11	3
4	100	4
5	101	5
6	110	6
7	111	7
8	1000	8
9	1001	9
A	1010	10
B	1011	11
C	1100	12
D	1101	13
E	1110	14
F	1111	15

For example, the hexadecimal number 7B is 1111011, where 7 is 111 in binary, and B is 1011 in binary.

To convert a binary number to a hexadecimal, convert every four binary digits from left to right in the binary number into a hexadecimal number.

For example, the binary number 1110001101 is 38D, since 1101 is D, 1000 is 8 and 11 is 3 as shown below.

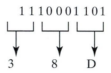

NOTE

Octal numbers are also useful. The octal number system has eight digits, 0 to 7. A decimal number 8 is represented as 10 in the octal system.

NOTE

By default, an integer literal is a decimal number. To denote a hexadecimal integer literal, use a leading 0x or 0X. For example, the following statement assigns FA1D to a variable x.

```
int x = 0xFA1D;
```

Java also provides a notation for writing octal integer literals using prefix O (letter o). For example, O34 denotes an octal number, which is equivalent to 3*8+4 = 28 in decimal.

Bit Manipulations

To write programs at the machine-level, often you need to deal with binary numbers directly and perform operations at the bit-level. Java provides the bitwise operators and shift operators defined in Table E.2.

TABLE E.2

Operator	Name	Example (using bytes in the example)	Description
&	Bitwise AND	10101110 & 10010010 yields 10000010	The AND of two corresponding bits yields a 1 if both bits are 1.
¦	Bitwise inclusive OR	10101110 | 10010010 yields 10101110	The OR of two corresponding bits yields a 1 if either bit is 1.
^	Bitwise exclusive OR	10101110 ^ 10010010 yields 00111100	The XOR of two corresponding bits yields a 1 only if two bits are different.
~	One's complement	~10101110 yields 01010001	The operator toggles each bit from 0 to 1 and from 1 to 0
<<	Left shift	10101110 << 2 yields 10111000	Shift bits in the first operand left by the number of the bits specified in the second operand, filling with 0s on the right.
>>	Right shift with sign extension	10101110 >> 2 yields 11101011 00101110 >> 2 yields 00001011	Shift bit in the first operand right by the number of the bits specified in the second operand, filling with the highest (sign) bit on the left.
>>>	Right shift with zero extension	10101110 >>> 2 yields 00101011 00101110 >>> 2 yields 00001011	Shift bit in the first operand right by the number of the bits specified in the second operand, filling with 0s on the left.

The bit operators apply only to integer types (byte, short, int and long). A character involved in a bit operation is converted to an integer. All the bitwise operators can form bitwise assignment operator such as ^=, ¦=, <<=, >>=, and >>>=.

Review Questions

E.1 Convert the following decimal numbers into hex and binary numbers.
100; 4340; 2000

E.2 Convert the following binary numbers into hex numbers and decimal numbers.
1000011001; 100000000; 100111

E.3 Convert the following hex numbers into binary and decimal numbers.
FEFA9; 93; 2000

E.4 Show the result of the following operations.

0xFFFA9 & 0xABCD

0xFFFA9 | 0xABCD

0xFFFA9 ^ 0xABCD

~0xFFFA9

0xFFFA9 << 3

0xFFFA9 >> 3

0xFFFA9 >>> 2

Programming Exercises

E.1 Write a static method that converts a decimal number into a binary string.

```
public static String binary(long number)
```

E.2 Write a static method that converts a decimal number into a hexadecimal string.

```
public static String hexadecimal(long number)
```

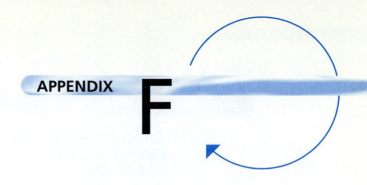

AN HTML TUTORIAL

Java applets are embedded in HTML files. HTML (HyperText Markup Language) is a markup language used to design Web pages for creating and sharing multimedia-enabled, integrated electronic documents over the Internet. HTML allows documents on the Internet to be hyperlinked and presented using fonts, image, and line justification appropriate for the systems on which they are displayed. The World Wide Web is a network of static and dynamic documents, including texts, sound, and images. The Internet has been around for more than thirty years, but has only recently become popular. The Web is the major reason for its popularity.

HTML documents are displayed by a program called a *Web browser*. When a document is coded in HTML, a Web browser interprets the HTML to identify the elements of the document and render it. The browser has control over the document's look-and-feel. At present there are no absolute, unifying HTML standards. Different vendors have rushed to introduce their own features, interpretable by their proprietary browsers. However, the differences aren't significant. This tutorial introduces some frequently used HTML features that have been adopted by most browsers.

There are many easy-to-use authoring tools for creating Web pages. For example, you can create HTML files using Microsoft Word. The Internet Explorer and Netscape Navigator have simple authoring tools to let you create and edit HTML files. Microsoft FrontPage is a comprehensive and fully loaded tool that enables you to design more sophisticated Web pages. Authoring tools greatly simplify the task of creating Web pages but do not support all features of HTML. Since you will probably end up editing the source text produced by whatever tool you adopt, it is imperative to know the basic concept of HTML. In this tutorial, you will learn how to use HTML to create your own Web pages.

Getting Started

Let us begin with an example that demonstrates the structure and syntax of an HTML document.

Example F.1 An HTML Example

The following HTML document displays a message and a list of Web browsers: Netscape, Internet Explorer, and Mosaic. You may use any text editor, such as Microsoft NotePad on Windows, to create HTML documents, as long as it can save the file in ACSII text format.

```
<html>
<head>
<title>My First Web Page</title>
</head>
<body>
<i>Welcome to</i> <b>HTML</b>. Here is a list of popular Web
browsers.
<ul>
  <li>Netscape
  <li>Internet Explorer
  <li>Mosaic
</ul>
<hr size=3>
Created by <A HREF=www.cs.armstrong.edu/liang>Y. Daniel Liang</A>.
</body>
</html>
```

Assume that you have created a file named **ExampleF1.html** for this HTML document. You may use any Web browser to view the document. To view it on Internet Explorer, start up your browser and choose Open from the File menu. A popup window opens to accept the filename. Type the full name of the file (including path), or click the Browser button to locate the file. Click OK to load and display the HTML file. Your document should be displayed as shown in Figure F.1.

Figure F.1 *The HTML page is rendered by a Web browser.*

NOTE
HTML filenames are case-sensitive on UNIX but not on other operating systems. HTML files end with .html or .htm.

> **NOTE**
>
> The same document may be rendered differently depending on the capabilities of the Web browser. Regardless of the differences, the power of HTML is that your document can be viewed on a variety of browsers and on most platforms, and can be formatted to suit any reader. This tutorial uses Internet Explorer 5.0 for illustrations.

What makes *Welcome to* appear in italic in Figure F.1? What makes the document appear in a desired style? HTML is a document-layout and hyperlink-specification language; that is, it tells the Web browser how to display the contents of the document, including text, images, and other media, using instructions called *tags*. The browser interprets the tags and decides how to display or otherwise treat the subsequent contents of the HTML document. Tags are enclosed in brackets; `<html>`, `<i>`, `<b>`, and `</html>` are tags that appear in the preceding HTML example. The first word in a tag, called the *tag name*, describes tag functions. Tags may have additional attributes, sometimes with a value after an equals sign, which further define their action. For example, in Example F.1, the attribute size in the tag `<hr>` defines the size of the bar as 3 inches.

Most tags have a *start tag* and a corresponding *end tag*. A tag has a specific effect on the region between the start tag and the end tag. For example, `<b>text</b>` advises the browser to display the word "text" in bold. `<b>` and `</b>` are the start and end tags for displaying boldface text. An end tag is always the start tag's name preceded by a forward slash (/). A few tags do not have end tags. For example, `<hr>`, a tag to draw a line, has no corresponding end tag.

A tag can be embedded inside another tag; for example, all tags are embedded within `<html>` and `</html>`. However, tags cannot overlap; it would be wrong, for instance, to use `<b>bold  and  <i>italic</b></i>`; the correct use should be `<b><i>bold and italic</i></b>`.

> **TIP**
>
> Tags are not case-sensitive, but it is good practice to use case consistently for clarity and readability. This tutorial uses lowercase for tags.

The following types of tags are introduced in the upcoming sections:

- **Structure tags** defines the structure of documents.
- **Text appearance tags** defines the appearance of text.
- **Paragraph tags** defines headings, paragraphs, and line breaks.
- **Font tags** specifies font sizes and colors.
- **List tags** defines ordered or unordered lists and definition lists.
- **Table tags** defines tables.
- **Link tags** specifies navigation links to other documents.
- **Image tags** specifies where to get images and how to display them.

Structure Tags

An HTML document begins with the `<html>` tag, which declares that the document is written with HTML. Every document has two parts, a *head* and a *body*, defined, respectively, by a `<head>` tag and a `<body>` tag. The head part contains the document title (using the `<title>` tag) and other parameters the browser may use when rendering the document; the body part contains the actual contents of the document. An HTML document may have the following structure:

```
<html>
<head>
<title>My First Web Page</title>
</head>
<body>
<!-- document body-->
</body>
</html>
```

Here the special starting tag `<!--` and ending tag `-->` are used to enclose comments in the HTML documents. The comments are not displayed.

NOTE

Your documents may be displayed properly even if you don't use `<html>`, `<head>`, `<title>`, and `<body>` tags. However, use of these tags is strongly recommended because they communicate certain information to the browser about the properties of a document; the information they provide helps in using the document effectively.

Text Appearance Tags

HTML provides tags to advise about the appearance of text. At present, some text tags have the same effect. For example, `<em>`, `<cite>`, and `<i>` will all display the text in italic. However, a future version of HTML may make these tags distinct. Text tag names are fairly descriptive. Text tags can be classified into two categories: *content-based tags* and *physical tags*.

Content-Based Tags

Content-based tags inform the browser to display the text based on semantic meaning, such as citation, program code, and emphasis. Here is a summary of the content-based tags:

- **`<cite>`** indicates that the enclosed text is a bibliographic citation, displayed in italic.

- **`<code>`** indicates that the enclosed text is a programming code, displayed in monospace font.

- **`<em>`** indicates that the enclosed text should be displayed with emphasis, displayed in italic.

- **`<strong>`** indicates that the enclosed text should be strongly emphasized, displayed in bold.

- **`<var>`** indicates that the enclosed text is a computer variable, displayed in italic.

- **`<address>`** indicates that the enclosed text is an address, displayed in italic.

Table F.1 lists the content-based tags and provides examples of their use.

TABLE F.1   Using Content-Based Tags

Tag	Example	Display
`<cite> . . . </cite>`	`<cite>bibliographic </cite>`	*bibliographic*
`<code> . . . </code>`	`<code>source code </code>`	source code
`<em> . . . </em>`	`<em>emphasis</em>`	*emphasis*
`<strong> . . . </strong>`	`<strong>strongly emphasized</strong>`	**strongly emphasized**
`<var> . . . </var>`	`<var>programming variable</var>`	*programming variable*
`<address> . . . </address>`	`<address>Computer Dept</address>`	*Computer Dept*

Physical Tags

Physical tags explicitly ask the browser to display text in bold, italic, or other ways. Following are six commonly used physical tags:

- **`<i>`** (italic)

- **`<b>`** (bold)

- **`<u>`** (underline)

- **`<tt>`** (monospace)

- **`<strike>`** (strike-through text)

- **`<blink>`** (blink)

Table F.2 lists the physical tags and provides examples of their use.

Paragraph-Style Tags

There are many tags in HTML for dealing with paragraph styles. There are six heading tags (`<h1>`, `<h2>`, `<h3>`, `<h4>`, `<h5>`, `<h6>`) for different sizes of headings, a

TABLE F.2 Using Physical Tags

Tag	Example	Display
`<i> . . . </i>`	`<i>italic</i>`	*italic*
`<b> . . . </b>`	`<b>bold</b>`	**bold**
`<u> . . . </u>`	`<u>underline</u>`	underline
`<tt> . . . </tt>`	`<tt>monospace</tt>`	`monospace`
`<strike> . . . </strike>`	`<strike>strike </strike>`	~~strike~~
`<blink> . . .</blink>`	`<blink>blink </blink>`	blink (causes it to blink)

line-break tag *(<br>)*, a paragraph start tag (<p>), a preformat tag (<pre>), and a block-quote tag (<blockquote>).

The six heading tags indicate the highest (<h1>) and lowest (<h6>) precedence a heading may have in the document. Heading tags may be used with an align attribute to place the heading toward *left*, *center*, or *right*. The default alignment is left. For example, `<h3 align=right>Heading</h3>` tells the browser to right-align the heading.

The line-break tag <br> tells the browser to start displaying from the next line. This tag has an optional end tag <br>.

The paragraph-start tag <p> signals the start of a paragraph. This tag has an optional end tag </p>.

The <pre> tag and its required end tag (</pre>) define the enclosed segment to be displayed in monospaced font by the browser.

The <blockquote> tag is used to contain text quoted from another source. The quote will be indented from both left and right.

Example F.2 HTML Source Code Using Structure Tags

The following HTML source code illustrates the use of paragraph tags. The text the code creates is displayed in Figure F.2.

```
<html>
<head>
<title>Demonstrating Paragraph Tags</title>
</head>
<body>
<!-- Example F.2 -->
<h1 align=right>h1: Heading 1</h1>
<h3 align=center>h3: Heading 3</h3>
<h6 align=left>h6: Heading 6</h6>
<p>
<pre>preformat tag</pre>
```

```
<blockquote>
block quote tag
<br>
and line break
</blockquote>
</body>
</html>
```

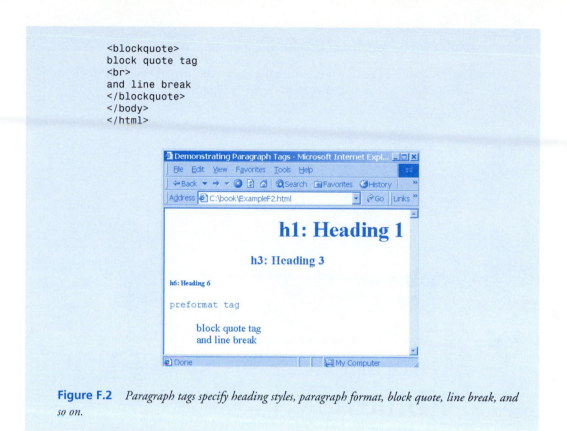

Figure F.2   *Paragraph tags specify heading styles, paragraph format, block quote, line break, and so on.*

Font, Size, and Color Tags

With HTML you can specify font size and colors using font tags. There are two font tags: `<basefont>` and `<font>`.

The `<basefont>` tag is typically placed in the head of an HTML document, where it sets the base font size for the entire document. However, it may appear anywhere in the document, and it may appear many times, each time with a new size attribute. Many browsers use a relative model for sizing fonts, ranging from 1 to 7; the default base font size is 3. Each successive size is 20 percent larger than its predecessor in the range.

The `<font>` tag allows you to specify the size and color of the enclosed text, using size and color attributes. The size attribute is the same as the one for `<basefont>` tag. The color attribute sets the color for the enclosed text between `<font>` and `</font>`. The value of the attribute is a six-digit hex number preceded by a pound sign (#). The first two digits are the red component, the next two digits are the green component, and the last two digits are the blue component. The digits are from 00 to FF. Alternatively, you may set the color by using standard names like red, yellow, blue, or orange.

Example F.3 Testing Font Tags

The following HTML source code illustrates the use of the `<basefont>` and `<font>` tags. The text it creates is displayed in Figure F.3.

```
<html>
<head>
<title>Demonstrating Fonts, Size and Color</title>
</head>
<basefont size=6>
<body bgcolor=white>
<!-- Example F.3 -->
basefont<br>
<font size=7 color=blue>blue7</font><br>
<font size=3 color=#FF0000>red3</font><br>
</body>
</html>
```

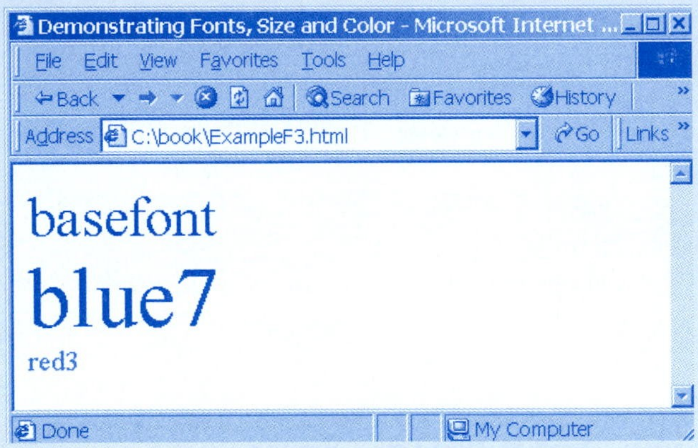

Figure F.3 *Font and color tags specify fonts and colors in HTML pages.*

List Tags

HTML allows you to define three kinds of lists: *ordered lists*, *unordered lists,* and *definition lists*. You can also build nested lists. Example F.1 contains an unordered list of three Web browsers.

Ordered Lists

Ordered lists label the items they contain. An ordered list is used when the sequence of the listed items is important. For example, chapters are listed in order. An ordered list starts with the tag `<ol>` and ends with `</ol>`, and items are placed in between. Each item begins with an `<li>` tag. The browser automatically numbers list items, starting from numeric 1. Instead of using the default numeric numbers for labeling, you may associate the tag `<ol>` with a type attribute. The value of the type determines the style of the label.

■ Type value A for uppercase letter labels A, B, C, . . .

■ Type value a for lowercase letter labels a, b, c, . . .

■ Type value I for capital roman numerals I, II, III, . . .

■ Type value i for lowercase roman numerals i, ii, iii, . . .

■ Type value 1 for arabic numerals 1, 2, 3, . . .

Unordered Lists

When the sequence of the listed items is not important, use an unordered list. For example, a list of Web browsers can be given in any order. An unordered list starts with the tag <ul> and ends with </ul>. Inside, you use <li> tags for items. By default, the browser uses bullets to mark each item. You may use disc, circle, or square as type values to indicate the use of markers other than bullets.

Definition Lists

A definition list is used to define terms. The list is enclosed between <dl> and </dl> tags. Inside the tags are the terms and their definitions. The term and definition have the leading tags <dt> and <dd>, respectively. Browsers typically render the term name at the left margin and the definition below it and indented.

Example F.4 Using Various List Tags

This example illustrates the use of tags for ordered lists, unordered lists, definition lists, and nested lists. The output of the following code is displayed in Figure F.4.

```
<html>
<head>
<title>Demonstrating List Tags</title>
</head>
<body bgcolor=white>
<!-- Example F.4 List Tags -->
<center><b>List Tags</b></center>
An ordered List
<ol type=A>
  <li>Chapter 1: Introduction to Java
  <li>Chapter 2: Java Building Elements
  <li>Chapter 3: Control Structures
</ol>
An unordered List
<ul type=square>
  <li>Apples
  <li>Oranges
  <li>Peaches
</ul>
Definition List
<dl>
   <dt>What is Java?
   <dd>An Internet programming language.
</dl>
</body>
</html>
```

continues

Example F.4 continued

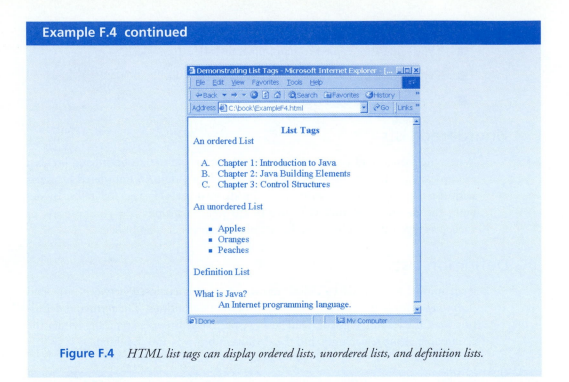

Figure F.4 *HTML list tags can display ordered lists, unordered lists, and definition lists.*

Table Tags

Tables are collections of numbers and words arranged in rows and columns of cells. In HTML, table elements, including data items, row and column headers, and captions, are enclosed between `<table>` and `</table>` tags. Several table tags may be used to specify the layout of a table. Each row in the table is wrapped by `<tr>` and `</tr>`. Inside the row, data or words in a cell are enclosed by `<td>` and `</td>`. You may use `<caption>`...`</caption>` to display a caption for the table, and `<th>`...`</th>` to display column headers.

Table tags may be used with attributes to obtain special effects. Here are some useful attributes:

- **border** can appear in the `<table>` tag to specify that all cells are surrounded with a border.

- **align** can appear in the `<caption>`, `<tr>`, `<th>`, or `<td>` tag. If it appears in `<caption>`, it specifies whether the caption appears above or below the table, using the values `top` or `bottom`. The default is `align=top`. If it appears in `<tr>`, `<th>`, or `<td>`, `align` specifies whether the text is aligned to the left, the right, or centered inside the table cell(s).

- **valign** can appear in `<tr>`, `<th>`, or `<td>`. The values of the attribute are `top`, `middle`, and `bottom` to specify whether the text is aligned to the top, the bottom, or centered inside the table cell(s).

896

■ **colspan** can appear in any table cell to specify how many columns of the table the cell should span. The default value is 1.

■ **rowspan** can appear in any column to specify how many rows of the table the cell should span. The default value is 1.

Example F.5 Illustration of Table Tags

This example creates an HTML table. The output of the code is displayed in Figure F.5.

```
<html>
<head>
<title>Demonstrating Table Tags</title>
</head>
<body bgcolor=white>
<!-- Example F.5 Table Tags -->
<center>Table Tags</center>
<br>
<table border=2>
<caption>This is a Table</caption>
<tr>
  <th>Table heading</th>
  <td>Table data</td>
</tr>
<tr>
  <th valign=bottom>Second row
  <td>Embedded Table
      <table border=3>
      <tr>
        <th>Table heading</th>
        <td align=right>Table data</td>
      </tr>
      </table>
  </td>
</tr>
</table>
</body>
</html>
```

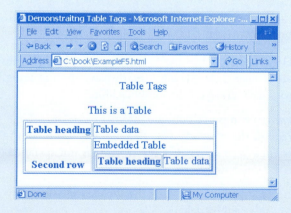

Figure F.5 *Table tags are useful for displaying tables in HTML pages.*

897

Hyperlink Tags

The true power of HTML lies in its capability to join collections of documents together into a full electronic library of information, and to link documents with other documents over the Internet. This is called *hypertext linking*, which is the key feature that makes the Web appealing and popular. By adding hypertext links, called *anchors*, to your HTML document, you create a highly intuitive information flow and guide users directly to the information they want. You can link documents on different computers or on the same computer, and can jump within the same document using anchor tags.

Linking Documents on Different Computers

Every document on the Web has a unique address, known as its *Uniform Resource Locator* (URL). To navigate from a source document to a target document, you need to reference the target's URL inside the anchor tags `<a>` and `</a>` using attribute `href`. The following example displays a list of database vendors:

```
<ul>
 <li><a href="http://www.oracle.com">Oracle</a>
 <li><a href="http://www.sybase.com">Sybase</a>
 <li><a href="http://www.microsoft.com">Microsoft</a>
</ul>
```

In this example, clicking on Oracle will display the Oracle homepage. The URL of Oracle's home page Internet address is **http://www.oracle.com**. The general format of a URL is:

```
method://servername:port/pathname/fullfilename
```

method is the name of the operation that is performed to interpret this URL. The most common methods are `http`, `ftp`, and `file`.

■ **http** accesses a page over the network using the HTTP protocol. For example, **http://www.microsoft.com** links to Microsoft's homepage. **http://** can be omitted.

■ **ftp** downloads a file using anonymous FTP service from a server; for example, **ftp://hostname/directory/fullfilename**.

■ **file** reads a file from the local disk. For example, `file://home/liang/liang.html` displays the file **liang.html** from the directory `/home/liang` on the local machine.

servername is a computer's unique Internet name or Internet Protocol (IP) numerical address on the network. For example, **www.sun.com** is the hostname of Sun Microsystem's Web server. If a server name is not specified, it is assumed that the file is on the same server.

port is the TCP port number that the Web server is running on. Most Web servers use port number 80 by default.

pathname is optional and indicates the directory under which the file is located.

fullfilename is optional and indicates the target filename. Web servers generally use **index.html** on UNIX and **default.htm** on Windows for a default filename. For example, `<a href="http://www.oracle.com">Oracle</a>` is equivalent to `<a href="http://www.oracle.com/index.html">Oracle</a>`.

Linking Documents on the Same Computer

To link documents on the same computer, use the `file` method rather than the `http` method in the target URL. There are two types of links: *absolute links* and *relative links*.

When linking to a document on a different machine, you must use an absolute link to identify the target document. An absolute link uses a URL to indicate the complete path to the target file.

When you are linking to a document on the same computer, it is better to use a relative link. A relative URL omits method and server name and directories. For instance, assume that the source document is under directory `liang/teaching` on the server `www.cs.armstrong.edu`. The URL

```
file://www.cs.armstrong.edu/liang/teaching/teaching.html
```

is equivalent to

```
file://teaching.html
```

Here, `file://` can be omitted. An obvious advantage of using a relative URL is that you can move the entire set of documents to another directory or even another server and never have to change a single link.

Jumping Within the Same Document

HTML offers navigation within the same document. This is helpful for direct browsing of interesting segments of the document.

Example F.6 Navigation Within the Same Document

This example shows a document with three sections. The output of the following code is shown in Figure F.6. When the user clicks Section 1: Introduction on the list, the browser jumps to Section 1 of the document. The `name` attribute within the `<a>` tag labels the section. The label is used as a link to the section. This feature is also known as *using bookmarks*.

When you test this example, make the window small so that you can see the effects of jumping to each reference through the link tags.

```
<html>
<head>
<title>Demonstrating Link Tags</title>
</head>
<body>
```

continues

Example F.6 continued

```
<ol>
  <li><a href="#introduction">Section 1: Introduction</a>
  <li><a href="#methodology">Section 2: Methodology</a>
  <li><a href="#summary">Section 3: Summary</a>
</ol>

<h3><a name="introduction"><b>Section 1</b>: Introduction</a></h3>
an introductory paragraph

<h3><a name="methodology"><b>Section 2</b>: Methodology</a></h3>
a paragraph on methodology

<h3><a name="summary"><b>Section 3</b>: Summary</a></h3>
a summary paragraph
</body>
</html>
```

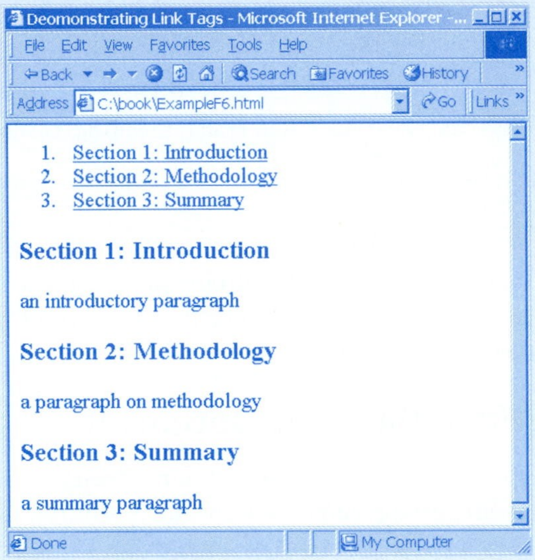

Figure F.6 *Hyperlink tags link documents.*

Embedding Graphics

One of the most compelling features of the Web is its ability to embed graphics in a document. Graphics can be used for icons, pictures, illustrations, drawings, and so on. They bring a live dimension to your documents. You may use an image as a visual map of hyperlinks. This section introduces the use of *horizontal bar tags* and *image tags*.

Horizontal Bar Tags

The horizontal bar tag (`<hr>`) is used to display a rule. It is useful in separating sections of your document with horizontal rules. The attributes size, width, and align can be associated to achieve the desired effect. The rule can be thickened using the size attribute with values in pixels. The width attribute specifies the length of the bar with values in either absolute number of pixels or extension across a certain percentage of the page. The align attribute specifies whether the bar is left-aligned, centered, or right-aligned.

Example F.7   Illustration of Horizontal Bar Tags

This example illustrates the use of the size, width, and align attributes in horizontal bar tags. The output of the following code is shown in Figure F.7.

```
<html>
<head>
<title>Demonstrating Horizontal Rules</title>
</head>
<body bgcolor=white>
<!-- Example F.7 Horizontal Rule -->
<center>Horizontal Rules</center>
<hr size=3 width=80% align=left>
<hr size=2 width=20% align=right noshade>
<hr>
</body>
</html>
```

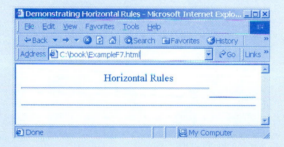

Figure F.7   *Horizontal bar tags are often used to separate contents in documents.*

Image Tags

The image tag, <img>, lets you reference and insert images into the current text. The syntax for the tag is:

```
<img src=URL alt=text align = [top ¦ middle ¦ bottom ¦ texttop ]>
```

Most browsers support GIF and JPEG image format. Format is an encoding scheme to store images. The attribute src specifies the source of the image. The attribute alt specifies an alternative text message to be displayed in case the client's browser cannot display the image. The attribute alt is optional; if it is omitted, no message is displayed. The attribute align tells the browser where to place the image.

Example F.8 Illustration of Image Tags

This example creates a document with image tags. The output of the code is shown in Figure F.8.

```
<html>
<head>
<title>Demonstrating Image Tags</title>
</head>
<body bgcolor=white>
<!-- Example F.8 Image Tags -->
<center>Image Tags</center>
<img src="illinoisMap.gif" align=middle>
</body>
</html>
```

Figure F.8.   *Image tags display images in HTML pages.*

More on HTML

This tutorial is not intended to be a complete reference manual on HTML. It does not mention many interesting features, such as *forms* and *frames*. You will find dozens of books on HTML in your local bookstore. *Special Edition Using HTML* by Mark Brown and John Jung, published by QUE, is a comprehensive reference; it covers all the new HTML features supported by Netscape Navigator and Microsoft Internet Explorer. *HTML Quick Reference* by Robert Mullen, also published by QUE, contains all the essential information you need to build Web pages with HTML in 100 pages. Please refer to these and other books for more information. You can also get information online at the following Web sites:

www.ncsa.uiuc.edu/General/Internet/WWW/HTMLPrimer.html
www.w3.org/pub/WWW/MarkUp/
www.mcli.dist.maricopa.edu/tut/lessons.html
www.netscape.com/assist/net_sites/frames.html

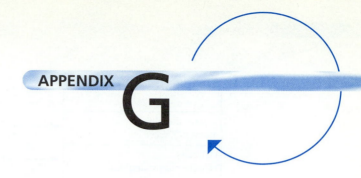

APPENDIX

G

UML GRAPHICAL NOTATIONS

This appendix summarizes the UML notations used in this book.

Classes and Objects

A class is described using a rectangle box with three sections.

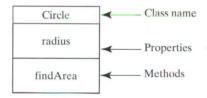

The top section gives the class name, the middle section describes the fields, and the bottom section describes the methods. The middle and bottom sections are optional, but the top section is required.

An object is described using a rectangle box with two sections.

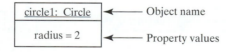

The top section is required. It gives the object's name and its defining class. The second section is optional; it indicates the object's field values.

The Modifiers *public, private, protected,* and *static*

The symbols +, -, and # are used to denote, respectively, `public`, `private`, and `protected` modifiers in the UML. The static fields and methods are underlined.

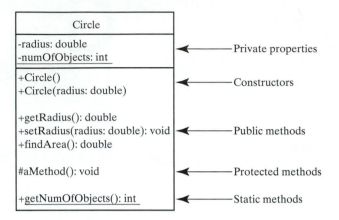

Class Relationships

The relationships of the classes are association, aggregation, and inheritance.

An *association* is illustrated using a solid line between the two classes with an optional label that describes their relationship.

Each class involved in an association may specify a multiplicity. A multiplicity is a number or an interval that specifies the number of objects of the class that are involved in the relationship. The character * means that the number of objects is unlimited, and an interval 1..u means that the number of objects should be between 1 and u, inclusive.

A filled diamond is attached to the composed class to denote the composition relationship, and a hollow diamond is attached to the aggregated class to denote the *aggregation* relationship, as shown below.

Inheritance models the is-a relationship between two classes, as shown below. An open triangle pointing to the superclass is used to denote the inheritance relationship between the two classes involved.

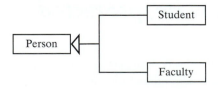

Abstract Classes and Interfaces

Abstract class names, interface names, and abstract methods are italicized. Dashed lines are used to link to the interface, as shown below:

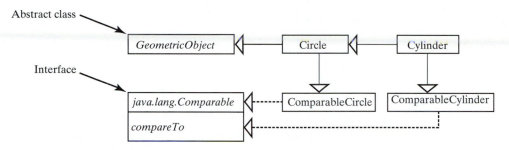

Sequence Diagrams

Sequence diagrams describe interactions among objects by depicting the time ordering of method invocations. The sequence diagram shown below consists of the following elements:

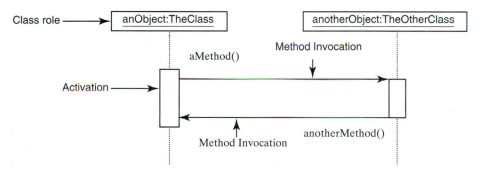

- ■ Class role represents the role an object plays. The objects at the top of the diagram represent class roles.

- ■ Lifeline represents the existence of an object over a period of time. A vertical dashed line extending from the object is used to denote a lifeline.

- ■ Activation represents the time during which an object is performing an operation. Thin rectangles placed on lifelines are used to denote activations.

- ■ Method invocation represents communications between objects. Horizontal arrows labeled with method calls are used to denote method invocations.

Statechart Diagrams

Statechart diagrams describe the flow of control of an object. The statechart diagram shown below contains the following elements:

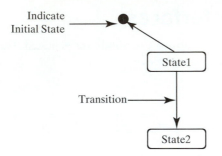

- State represents a situation during the life of an object in which it satisfies some condition, performs some action, or waits for some event to occur. Every state has a name. Rectangles with rounded corners are used to represent states. The small filled circle is used to denote the initial state.

- Transition represents the relationship between two states, indicating that an object will perform some action to transfer from one state to the other. A solid arrow with appropriate method invocation is used to denote a transition.

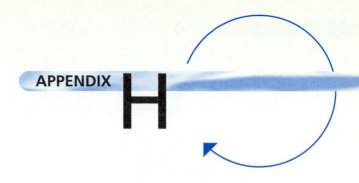

APPENDIX H

PACKAGES

Packages are used to group classes and interfaces. There are three reasons for using packages.

1. *To avoid naming conflicts*. When you develop reusable classes and interfaces to be shared by other programmers, naming conflicts often occur. To prevent this, put your classes and interfaces into packages so that they can be referenced through package names.

2. *To distribute software*. Packages group related classes and interfaces so that they can be easily distributed.

3. *To protect classes*. Packages provide protection so that the protected members of the classes are accessible to the classes in the same package, but not to the external classes.

This appendix introduces Java package-naming conventions, creating packages, and using packages.

Package-Naming Conventions

Packages are hierarchical, and you can have packages within packages. For example, `java.lang.Math` indicates that `Math` is a class in the package `lang` and that `lang` is a package in the package `java`. Levels of nesting can be used to ensure the uniqueness of package names.

Choosing a unique name is important because your package may be used on the Internet by other programs. Java designers recommend that you use your Internet domain name in reverse order as a package prefix. Since Internet domain names are unique, this prevents naming conflicts. Suppose you want to create a package named `mypackage` on a host machine with the Internet domain name `prenhall.com`. To follow the naming convention, you would name the entire package `com.prenhall.mypackage`. By convention, package names are all in lowercase.

Java expects one-to-one mapping of the package name and the file system directory structure. For the package named `com.prenhall.mypackage`, you must create a di-

907

rectory, as shown in Figure H.1. In other words, a package is actually a directory that contains the bytecode of the classes.

Figure H.1   *The package* com.prenhall.mypackage *is mapped to a directory structure in the file system.*

The *classpath* Environment Variable

The com directory does not have to be the root directory. In order for Java to know where your package is in the file system, you must modify the environment variable classpath so that it points to the directory in which your package resides. Suppose the com directory is under c:\myprograms, as shown in Figure H.2. The following line adds c:\myprograms into the classpath:

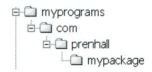

Figure H.2   *The package* com.prenhall.mypackage *is under c:\myprograms.*

```
classpath=.;c:\myprograms;
```

The period (.) indicating the current directory is always in classpath. The directory c:\myprograms is in classpath so that you can use the package com.prenhall.mypackage in the program.

You can add as many directories as necessary in classpath. The order in which the directories are specified is the order in which the classes are searched. If you have two classes of the same name in different directories, Java uses the first one it finds.

The classpath variable is set differently in Windows and UNIX, as outlined below.

- Windows 95 and Windows 98: Edit autoexec.bat using a text editor, such as Microsoft Notepad.

- **Windows NT and Windows 2000:** Go to the Start button and choose Control Panel, select the System icon, then modify classpath in the environment.

- **UNIX:** Use the setenv command to set classpath, such as setenv classpath .:/home/myprograms

  If you insert this line into the .cshrc file, the classpath variable will be automatically set when you log on.

On Windows 95 and Window 98, you must restart the system in order for the `classpath` variable to take effect. On Windows NT and Windows 2000, however, the settings are stored permanently, and affect any new command-line windows, but not the existing command-line windows.

Putting Classes into Packages

Every class in Java belongs to a package. The class is added to the package when it is compiled. All the classes that you have used so far in this book were placed in the current directory (a default package) when the Java source programs were compiled. To put a class in a specific package, you need to add the following line as the first noncomment and nonblank statement in the program:

```
package packagename;
```

Example H.1 Putting Classes into Packages

Problem

This example creates a class and places it in the package com.prenhall.mypackage.

Solution

The following code gives the solution to the problem.

```java
// Appendix.java: Store information on an appendix.
// The class is placed in the package com.prenhall.mypackage
package com.prenhall.mypackage;

public class Appendix {
  private String title;
  private int pageLength;

  /** Default constructor */
  public Appendix() {
    this("Appendix Title");
  }

  /** Construct a Appendix with specified title */
  public Appendix(String title) {
    this.title = title;
  }

  /** Set pageLength */
  public void setPageLength(int pageLength) {
    this.pageLength = pageLength;
  }
}
```

Review

A class must be defined as public in order to be accessed by other programs. Since the directory for the package is not automatically created using the **javac** compiler in JDK, you have to manually create it before compiling it.

continues

Example H.1 continued

You may place the .java file in the package directory and then compile it using the **javac** command. If the .java file is not in the package directory, you can use the following command with the -d option to specify the destination of the .class file in order for the .class file to be placed in the c:\myprograms\com\prenhall\mypackage directory:

```
javac Appendix.java -d c:\myprograms\com\prenhall\mypackage
```

> **NOTE**
> If you want to put several classes into the package, you have to create separate source files for them because one file can have only one public class.

> **NOTE**
> Class files can be archived into a single file for convenience. For instance, you may compress all the class files in the folder mypackage into a single zip file named mypackage.zip with subfolder information kept as shown in Figure H.3. To make the classes in the zip file available for use, add the zip file to the classpath like this:
> ```
> classpath=%classpath%;c:\mypackage.zip
> ```

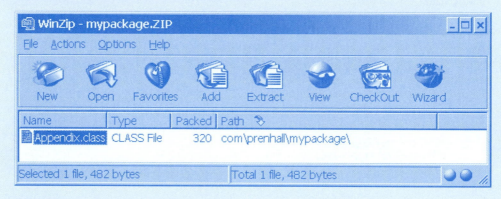

Figure H.3 *The class files can be archived into a single compressed file.*

Using Classes/Interfaces from Packages

There are two ways to use classes/interfaces from a package. One way is to use the fully qualified name of the class/interface. For example, the fully qualified name for Date is java.util.Date. For Appendix in the preceding example it is com.prenhall.mypackage.Appendix. This is convenient if the class/interface is used a few times in the program. The other way is to use the import statement. For example, to import all classes/interfaces in the java.util package, you can use

```
import java.util.*;
```

An import that uses a * is called *an import on demand* declaration. You can also import a specific class/interface. For example, the following statement imports `java.util.Date`:

```
import java.util.Date;
```

The information for the classes/interfaces in an imported package is not read in at compile time or runtime unless the class/interface is used in the program. The import statement simply tells the compiler where to locate the classes/interfaces.

Example H.2 Using Your Own Packages

Problem

This example shows a program that uses the `Appendix` class in the `com.prenhall.mypackage` package.

Solution

The following code gives the solution to the problem.

```
// TestAppendixClass.java: Demonstrate using the Appendix class
// from the com.prenhall.mypackage package
import com.prenhall.mypackage.Appendix;

public class TestAppendixClass {
  /** Main method */
  public static void main(String[] args) {
    // Create and initialize two Appendix objects
    Appendix a1 = new Appendix();
    Appendix a2 = new Appendix("Appendix H");
  }
}
```

Review

Before compiling this program, make sure that the environment variable `classpath` is properly set so that the `Appendix` class can be found. Also, please note that `Appendix` is defined as public so that it can be used by classes in other packages.

The program uses the `import` statement to get the class `Appendix`. You cannot import entire packages, such as `com.prenhall.*.*`. Only one asterisk (*) can be used in the `import` statement.

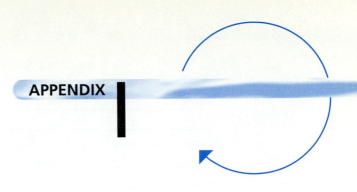

SPECIAL FLOATING-POINT VALUES

Dividing an integer by zero is invalid and throws `ArithmeticException`, but dividing a floating-point value by zero does not cause an exception. Floating-point arithmetic can overflow to infinity if the result of the operation is too large for a `double` or a `float`, or underflow to zero if the result is too small for a `double` or a `float`. Java provides the special floating-point values `POSITIVE_INFINITY`, `NEGATIVE_INFINITY`, and `NaN` (Not a Number) to denote these results. These values are defined as special constants in the `Float` class and the `Double` class.

If a positive floating-point number is divided by zero, the result is `POSITIVE_INFINITY`. If a negative floating-point number is divided by zero, the result is `NEGATIVE_INFINITY`. If a floating-point zero is divided by zero, the result is `NaN`, which means that the result is undefined mathematically. The string representation of these three values are Infinity, -Infinity, and NaN. For example,

```
System.out.print(1.0 / 0); // Print Infinity
System.out.print(-1.0 / 0); // Print -Infinity
System.out.print(0.0 / 0); // Print NaN
```

These special values can also be used as operands in computations. For example, a number divided by `POSITIVE_INFINITY` yields a positive zero. Table I.1 summarizes various combinations of the /, *, %, +, and - operators.

Table I.1   Shortcut Operators

x	y	x/y	x*y	x%y	x+y	x-y
Finite	±0.0	±∞	±0.0	NaN	Finite	Finite
Finite	±∞	±0.0	±∞	x	±∞	∞
±0.0	±0.0	NaN	±∞	NaN	±0.0	±0.0
±∞	Finite	±∞	±∞	NaN	±∞	±∞
±∞	±∞	NaN	±∞	NaN	±∞	∞
±0.0	±∞	±0.0	NaN	±0.0	±∞	±0.0
NaN	Any	NaN	NaN	NaN	NaN	NaN
Any	NaN	NaN	NaN	NaN	NaN	NaN

NOTE

If one of the operands is NaN, the result is NaN.

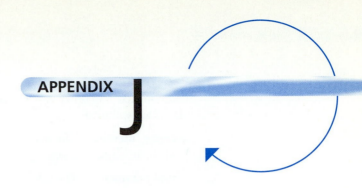

GLOSSARY

This glossary lists and defines the key terms used in the book.

.class file The output of the Java compiler. A .class file contains the byte code for the class.

.java file The source code of a Java program. It may contain one or more Java classes and interfaces. A .java file can be created using a text editor or a Java IDE such as Sun ONE Studio and JBuilder.

.html or .htm file The source code of an HTML file. It contains HTML tags and text. It is the input for a Web browser. A Web browser displays the contents of a .html or .htm file.

abstract class When you are designing classes, a superclass should contain common features that are shared by subclasses. Sometimes the superclass is so abstract that it cannot have any specific instances. These classes are called abstract classes and are declared using the abstract modifier. Abstract classes are like regular classes with data and methods, but you cannot create instances of abstract classes using the new operator.

abstraction A technique in software development that hides detailed implementation. Java supports method abstraction and class abstraction. Method abstraction is defined as separating the use of a method from its implementation. The client can use a method without knowing how it is implemented. If you decide to change the implementation, the client program will not be affected. Similarly, class abstraction hides the implementation of the class from the client.

abstract method A method signature without implementation. Its implementation is provided by its subclasses. An abstract method is denoted with an abstract modifier and must be contained in an abstract class. In a nonabstract subclass extended from an abstract class, all abstract methods must be implemented, even if they are not used in the subclass.

Abstract Window Toolkit (AWT) The set of components for developing simple graphics applications that was in use before the introduction of Swing components. The AWT user interface components have now been replaced by the Swing components, but other AWT classes such as helper classes, and event-handling classes are still used.

accessor method   The get and set methods for retrieving and setting private fields in an object.

actual parameter   The value passed to a method when it is invoked. Actual parameters should match formal parameters in type, order, and number.

algorithm   Describes how a problem is solved in terms of the actions to be executed, and specifies the order in which these actions should be executed. Algorithms can help the programmer plan a program before writing it in a programming language.

aggregation   A special form of association that represents an ownership relationship between two classes.

ambiguous invocation   There are two or more possible methods to match an invocation of a method, neither is more specific than the other(s). Therefore, the invocation is ambiguous.

applet   A special kind of Java program that can run directly from a Web browser or an applet viewer. Various security restrictions are imposed on applets. For example, they cannot perform input/output operations on a user's system and therefore cannot read or write files or transmit computer viruses.

application   A standalone program, such as any program written using a high-level language. Applications can be executed from any computer with a Java interpreter. Applications are not subject to the security restrictions imposed on Java applets. An application class must contain a main method.

API (Application Program Interface)   A set of classes and interfaces that can be used to develop Java programs.

argument   Same as actual parameter.

array   A container object that stores an indexed sequence of the same types of data. Typically, the individual elements are referenced by an index value. The index is an int value starting with 0 for the first element, 1 for the second, and so on.

assignment statement   A simple statement that assigns a value to a variable using an assignment operator (=).

assignment operator (=)   Assigns a value to a variable.

association   A general binary relationship that describes an activity between two classes.

backslash (\)   A character that precedes another character to denote the following character has a special meaning. For example, '\t' denotes a tab character. The backslash character is also used to denote a Unicode character like '\u00FF'.

binary search   An efficient method to search a key in an array. Binary search first compares the key with the element in the middle of the array and reduces the search range by half. For binary search to work, the array must be pre-sorted.

bit   A binary digit 0 or 1.

block   A sequence of statements enclosed in braces ({}).

boolean   A primitive data type for Boolean values (true or false).

boolean expression   An expression that evaluates to a Boolean value.

byte   A unit of storage. Each byte consists of 8 bits. The size of hard disk and memory is measured in bytes. A megabyte is roughly a million bytes.

byte type   Primitive data type that represents an integer in a byte. The range of a byte value is from -2^7 (-128) to 2^7-1 (127).

bytecode   The result of compiling Java source code. Bytecode is machine-independent and can run on any machine that has a Java runtime environment.

call-by-value   Same as pass-by-value.

casting   The process of converting a primitive data type value into another primitive type or converting an object of one object type into another object type. For example, `(int)3.5` converts 3.5 into an `int` value, and `(Cylinder)c` converts an object `c` into the `Cylinder` type. For the object casting to be successful, the object to be casted must be instance of the target class.

char type   A primitive data type that represents a Unicode character.

child class   Same as subclass.

class   An encapsulated collection of data and methods that operate on data. A class may be instantiated to create an object that is an instance of the class.

class hierarchy   A collection of classes organized in terms of superclass and subclass relationships.

class method   A method that can be invoked without creating an instance of the class. To define class methods, put the modifier `static` in the method declaration.

class variable   A data member declared using the `static` modifier. A class variable is shared by all instances of that class. Class variables are used to communicate between different objects of the same class and to handle global states among these objects.

class's contract   Refers to the collection of methods and fields that are accessible from outside a class, together with the description of how these members are expected to behave.

comment   Comments document what a program is and how it is constructed. They are not programming statements and are ignored by the compiler. In Java, comments are preceded by two slashes (`//`) in a line or enclosed between `/*` and `*/` in multiple lines. The javadoc comments are enclosed between `/**` and `*/`.

compiler   A software program that translates Java source code into bytecode.

composition   A form of relationship that represents exclusive ownership of the class by the aggregated class.

constant A variable declared `final` in Java. Since a class constant is usually shared by all objects of the same class, a class constant is often declared `static`. A local constant is a constant declared inside a method.

constructor A special method for initializing objects when creating objects using the `new` operator. The constructor has exactly the same name as its defining class. Constructors can be overloaded, making it easier to construct objects with different initial data values.

data type Data type is used to define variables. Java supports primitive data types and object data types.

debugger A program that facilitates debugging. It enables the program to be executed one statement at a time and enables the contents of the variable to be examined during execution.

debugging The process of finding and fixing errors in a program.

declaration Defines variables, methods, and classes in a program.

decrement operator (--) Subtracts one from a numeric variable or a char variable.

default constructor A constructor that has no parameters. A default constructor is required for a JavaBeans component.

definition Alternative term for a declaration.

deserialization The process of restoring an object that was previously serialized.

design To plan how a program can be structured and implemented by coding.

double buffering A technique to reduce flickering in image animation in Java.

double type A primitive data type to represent double precision floating-point numbers with 14 to 15 significant digits of accuracy.

dot operator (.) An operator used to access members of an object. If the member is static, it can be accessed through the class name using the dot operator.

dynamic binding An object of a subclass can be used by any code designed to work with an object of its superclass. For example, if a method expects a parameter of the `GeometricObject` type, you can invoke it with a `Circle` object. A `Circle` object can be used as both a `Circle` object and a `GeometricObject` object. This feature is known as Polymorphism (a Greek word meaning "many forms.") A method may be defined in a superclass, but is overridden in a subclass. Which implementation of the method is used on a particular call will be determined dynamically by the JVM at runtime. This capability is known as dynamic binding.

encapsulation Combining of methods and data into a single data structure. In Java, this is known as a class.

event A signal to the program that something has happened. Events are generated by external user actions, such as mouse movements, mouse button clicks, and keystrokes, or by the operating system, such as a timer. The program can choose to respond to an event or to ignore it.

event adapter   A class used to filter event methods and only handle specified ones.

event delegation   In Java event-driven programming, events are assigned to the listener object for processing. This is referred to as event delegation.

event-driven programming   Java GUI programming is event-driven. In event-driven programming, codes are executed upon the activation of events, such as clicking a button or moving the mouse.

event handler   A method in the listener's object that is designed to do some specified processing when a particular event occurs.

event listener   The object that receives and handles the event.

event listener interface   An interface implemented by the listener class to handle the specified events.

event registration   To become a listener, an object must be registered as a listener by the source object. The source object maintains a list of listeners and notifies all the registered listeners when an event occurs.

event source   The object that generates the event.

exception   An unexpected event indicating that a program has failed in some way. Exceptions are represented by exception objects in Java. Exceptions can be handled in a `try-catch` block.

expression   represents a computation involving values, variables, and operators, which evaluates to a value.

final   A modifier for classes, data, methods, and local variables. A final class cannot be extended, a final data or local variable is a constant, and a final method cannot be overridden in a subclass.

float type   A primitive data type to represent single precision floating-point numbers with 6 to 7 significant digits of accuracy. The double type is used to represent double precisions with 14 to 15 significant digits of accuracy.

floating-point number   A decimal number with an optional fractional part.

formal parameter   The parameters defined in the method signature.

garbage collection   A JVM feature that automatically detects and reclaims the space occupied by unreferenced objects.

get method   For retrieving private data in a class.

graphical user interface (GUI)   An interface to a program that is implemented using AWT or Swing components, such as frames, buttons, labels, text fields, and so on.

HTML (Hypertext Markup Language)   A script language to design Web pages for creating and sharing multimedia-enabled, integrated electronic documents over the Internet.

increment operator (++)   Adds one to a numeric variable or a char variable.

identifier   A name of a variable, method, class, interface, or package.

indentation   The use of tabs and spaces to indent the source code to make it easy to read and understand.

index   An integer value used to specify the position of an element in the array.

infinite loop   A loop that runs indefinitely due to a bug in the loop.

information hiding   A software engineering concept for hiding and protecting an object's internal features and structure.

inheritance   In object-oriented programming, the use of the extends keyword to derive new classes from existing classes.

initialization block   A block of statements that appears in the class declaration, not inside a method. A non-static initialization block is executed as if it were placed at the beginning of every constructor in the class. A static initialization block is executed when the class is loaded.

inner class   A class embedded in another class. Inner classes enable you to define small auxiliary objects and pass units of behavior, thus making programs simple and concise.

instance   An object of a class.

instance method   A nonstatic method in a class. Instance methods belong to instances and can only be invoked by them.

instance variable   A nonstatic data member of a class. An instance variable belongs to an instance of the class.

instantiation   The process of creating an object of a class.

int type   A primitive data type to represent an integer in the range from -2^{31} (-2147483648) to $2^{31}-1$ (2147483647).

Integrated Development Environment (IDE)   Software that helps programmers write code efficiently. IDE tools integrate editing, compiling, building, debugging, and online help in one graphical user interface.

interface   An interface is treated like a special class in Java. Each interface is compiled into a separate bytecode file, just like a regular class. You cannot create an instance for an interface. The structure of a Java interface is similar to that of an abstract class in that it can have data and methods. The data, however, must be constants, and the methods can have only declarations without implementation. Single inheritance is the Java restriction wherein a class can inherit from a single superclass. This restriction is eased by the use of an interface.

interpreter Software for interpreting and running Java bytecode.

iteration One time execution of the loop body.

Java Virtual Machine (JVM) A machine that run Java byte-code. It is called virtual because it is usually implemented in software rather than in hardware.

java The command to run a Java program from the command line.

javac The command to compile a Java program from the command line.

Java Development Toolkit (JDK) Defines the Java API and contains a set of command-line utilities, such as javac (compiler) and java (interpreter). With Java 2, Sun renamed JDK 1.2 to Java 2 SDK v 1.2. SDK stands for Software Development Toolkit.

Just-in-Time compiler Capable of compiling each bytecode once, and then reinvoking the compiled code repeatedly when the bytecode is executed.

keyword A reserved word defined as part of Java language. (See Appendix A, "Java Keywords," for a full list of keywords.)

linear search A method to search an element in an array. Linear search compares the key with the element in the array sequentially.

literal A constant value that appears directly in the program. A literal may be numeric, character, boolean, or null for object type.

local variable A variable defined inside a method.

logic error An error that causes the program to produce incorrect results.

main class A class that contains a main method.

marker interface An empty interface that is used to signify that all the classes implementing the interface share certain properties.

method A collection of statements grouped together to perform an operation. See class method; instance method.

method overloading Method overloading means that you can define methods with the same name in a class as long as there is enough difference in their parameter profiles.

method overriding Method overriding means that you can modify a method in a subclass that was originally defined in a superclass.

method signature The combination of the name of a method and the list of its parameters.

modal dialog box A dialog box that prevents the user from using other windows before it is dismissed.

modifier A Java keyword that specifies the properties of data, methods, and classes and how they can be used. Examples of modifiers are public, private, and static.

multidimensional array   An array with more than one dimension.

multithreading   The capability of a program to perform several tasks simultaneously within a program.

mutator   A set method that changes the value of an instance variable.

narrowing (of types)   Casting a variable of a type with a larger range to a variable of a type with a smaller range.

null   A literal of an object variable that does not reference any concrete object.

object   Same as instance.

object-oriented programming (OOP)   An approach to programming that involves organizing objects and their behavior into classes of reusable components.

operand evaluation order   Defines the order in which individual operands are evaluated.

operating system   Software that manages computer resources and provides services to programs.

operator   Operations for primitive data type values and on objects. Examples of operators are +, -, *, /, %, <, <=, ==, !=, >, >=, &&, &, ¦¦, ¦, !, and ^.

operator associativity   Defines the order in which operators will be evaluated in an expression if the operators has the same precedence order.

operator precedence   Defines the order in which operators will be evaluated in an expression.

overloading   Making more than one method or constructor the same name with different signatures in the same class.

override   Implement the method in a subclass that is declared in a superclass.

package   A collection of classes.

parameter   Refers to a value passed to a method.

parameter profile   Refers to the type of the parameters, the order of parameters, and the number of parameters.

parent class   Same as superclass.

pass-by-value   A term used when a copy of an argument is passed as a method parameter. For a parameter of a primitive type, the actual value is passed; for a parameter of a reference type, the reference for the object is passed.

polymorphism   See dynamic binding.

primitive data type   The primitive data types are byte, short, int, long, float, double, boolean, and char.

private   A modifier for members of a class. A private member can only be referenced inside the class.

protected   A modifier for members of a class. A protected member of a class can be used in the class in which it is declared or any subclass derived from that class.

public   A modifier for classes, data, and methods that can be accessed by all programs.

ragged array   A multi-dimensional array with different length in the subarrays.

recursive method   A method that invokes itself, directly or indirectly.

reference type   A data type that is a class or an interface.

reference   A value that references an object.

reserved word   Same as keyword.

runtime error   An error that causes the program to terminate abnormally.

return type   The data type for the return value in a method.

return value   A value returned from a method using the return statement.

sentinel value   A special input value that signifies the end of the input.

sequence diagram   A UML diagram that describes interactions among objects by depicting the time-ordering of method invocations.

serialization   The process of writing an object to a stream.

set method   For updating private data in a class.

short type   A primitive data type that represents an integer in the range from -2^{15} (-32768) to $2^{15}-1$ (32767).

short-circuit evaluation   Evaluation that stops when the result of the expression has been determined, even if not all the operands are evaluated. The evaluation involving && or ¦¦ are examples of short-circuit evaluation.

socket   The facilitation of communication between a server and a client.

source code   A program written in a programming language such as Java.

source file   A file that stores the source code.

statechart   A UML diagram that describes the flow of control of an object.

statement   A unit of code that represents an action or a sequence of actions.

static method   Same as class method.

static variable   Same as class variable.

stub   A simple, but not a complete version of the method. The use of stubs enables you to test invoking the method from a caller.

stream   The continuous one-way flow of data between a sender and a receiver.

subclass   A class that inherits from or extends a superclass.

superclass   A class inherited from a subclass.

Swing component   The Swing GUI components are painted directly on canvases using Java code except for components that are subclasses of `java.awt.Window` or `java.awt.Panel`, which must be drawn using native GUI on a specific platform. Swing components are less dependent on the target platform and use less resource of the native GUI. Swing components are more flexible and versatile than their AWT counterparts.

syntax error   An error in the program that violates syntax rules of the language.

tag   An HTML instruction that tells a Web browser how to display a document. Tags are enclosed in brackets, such as `<html>`, `<i>`, `<b>`, and `</html>`.

this   Refers to the object itself.

thread   A flow of execution of a task, with a beginning and an end, in a program.

throw   Causes an exception.

throws   A keyword used to declare a method that may throw an exception.

type   Specifies a range of values.

Unicode   A code system for international characters managed by the Unicode Consortium. Java supports Unicode.

Unified Modeling Language (UML)   A graphical notation for describing classes and their relationships.

Universal Resource Locator (URL)   A mechanism that uniquely identifies resources on the Internet.

widening (of types)   Casting a variable of a type with a smaller range to a variable of a type with a larger range.

wrapper class   A class that provides an object representation for primitive data type values. Java provides wrapper classes `Byte`, `Short`, `Integer`, `Long`, `Float`, `Double`, `Character`, and `Boolean` for primitive data types `byte`, `short`, `int`, `long`, `float`, `double`, `char`, and `boolean`.

INDEX

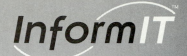

Terms and conditions of the license & export for Java(TM) 2 SDK, Standard Edition 1.4.0

Sun Microsystems, Inc.

BINARY CODE LICENSE AGREEMENT

READ THE TERMS OF THIS AGREEMENT AND ANY PROVIDED SUPPLEMENTAL LICENSE TERMS (COL-LECTIVELY "AGREEMENT") CAREFULLY BEFORE OPENING THE SOFTWARE MEDIA PACKAGE. BY OPENING THE SOFTWARE MEDIA PACKAGE, YOU AGREE TO THE TERMS OF THIS AGREEMENT. IF YOU ARE ACCESSING THE SOFTWARE ELECTRONICALLY, INDICATE YOUR ACCEPTANCE OF THESE TERMS BY SELECTING THE "ACCEPT" BUTTON AT THE END OF THIS AGREEMENT. IF YOU DO NOT AGREE TO ALL THESE TERMS, PROMPTLY RETURN THE UNUSED SOFTWARE TO YOUR PLACE OF PUR-CHASE FOR A REFUND OR, IF THE SOFTWARE IS ACCESSED ELECTRONICALLY, SELECT THE "DE-CLINE" BUTTON AT THE END OF THIS AGREEMENT.

1. LICENSE TO USE. Sun grants you a non-exclusive and non-transferable license for the internal use only of the accompanying software and documentation and any error corrections provided by Sun (collectively "Software"), by the number of users and the class of computer hardware for which the corresponding fee has been paid.

2. RESTRICTIONS. Software is confidential and copyrighted. Title to Software and all associated intellectual property rights is retained by Sun and/or its licensors. Except as specifically authorized in any Supplemental License Terms, you may not make copies of Software, other than a single copy of Software for archival purposes. Unless enforcement is prohibited by applicable law, you may not modify, decompile, or reverse engineer Software. You acknowledge that Software is not de-signed, licensed or intended for use in the design, construction, operation or maintenance of any nuclear facility. Sun dis-claims any express or implied warranty of fitness for such uses. No right, title or interest in or to any trademark, service mark, logo or trade name of Sun or its licensors is granted under this Agreement.

3. LIMITED WARRANTY. Sun warrants to you that for a period of ninety (90) days from the date of purchase, as evi-denced by a copy of the receipt, the media on which Software is furnished (if any) will be free of defects in materials and workmanship under normal use. Except for the foregoing, Software is provided "AS IS". Your exclusive remedy and Sun's entire liability under this limited warranty will be at Sun's option to replace Software media or refund the fee paid for Soft-ware.

4. DISCLAIMER OF WARRANTY. UNLESS SPECIFIED IN THIS AGREEMENT, ALL EXPRESS OR IMPLIED CONDITIONS, REPRESENTATIONS AND WARRANTIES, INCLUDING ANY IMPLIED WARRANTY OF MER-CHANTABILITY, FITNESS FOR A PARTICULAR PURPOSE OR NON-INFRINGEMENT ARE DISCLAIMED, EXCEPT TO THE EXTENT THAT THESE DISCLAIMERS ARE HELD TO BE LEGALLY INVALID.

5. LIMITATION OF LIABILITY. TO THE EXTENT NOT PROHIBITED BY LAW, IN NO EVENT WILL SUN OR ITS LICENSORS BE LIABLE FOR ANY LOST REVENUE, PROFIT OR DATA, OR FOR SPECIAL, INDIRECT, CONSEQUENTIAL, INCIDENTAL OR PUNITIVE DAMAGES, HOWEVER CAUSED REGARDLESS OF THE THEORY OF LIABILITY, ARISING OUT OF OR RELATED TO THE USE OF OR INABILITY TO USE SOFT-WARE, EVEN IF SUN HAS BEEN ADVISED OF THE POSSIBILITY OF SUCH DAMAGES. In no event will Sun's liability to you, whether in contract, tort (including negligence), or otherwise, exceed the amount paid by you for Software under this Agreement. The foregoing limitations will apply even if the above stated warranty fails of its essential purpose.

6. Termination. This Agreement is effective until terminated. You may terminate this Agreement at any time by destroying all copies of Software. This Agreement will terminate immediately without notice from Sun if you fail to comply with any provision of this Agreement. Upon Termination, you must destroy all copies of Software.

7. Export Regulations. All Software and technical data delivered under this Agreement are subject to US export control laws and may be subject to export or import regulations in other countries. You agree to comply strictly with all such laws and regulations and acknowledge that you have the responsibility to obtain such licenses to export, re-export, or import as may be required after delivery to you.

8. U.S. Government Restricted Rights. If Software is being acquired by or on behalf of the U.S. Government or by a U.S. Government prime contractor or subcontractor (at any tier), then the Government's rights in Software and accompanying documentation will be only as set forth in this Agreement; this is in accordance with 48 CFR 227.7201 through 227.7202-4 (for Department of Defense (DOD) acquisitions) and with 48 CFR 2.101 and 12.212 (for non-DOD acquisitions).

9. Governing Law. Any action related to this Agreement will be governed by California law and controlling U.S. federal law. No choice of law rules of any jurisdiction will apply.

10. Severability. If any provision of this Agreement is held to be unenforceable, this Agreement will remain in effect with the provision omitted, unless omission would frustrate the intent of the parties, in which case this Agreement will immediately terminate.

11. Integration. This Agreement is the entire agreement between you and Sun relating to its subject matter. It supersedes all prior or contemporaneous oral or written communications, proposals, representations and warranties and prevails over any conflicting or additional terms of any quote, order, acknowledgment, or other communication between the parties relating to its subject matter during the term of this Agreement. No modification of this Agreement will be binding, unless in writing and signed by an authorized representative of each party.

JAVA™ 2 SOFTWARE DEVELOPMENT KIT (J2SDK), STANDARD EDITION, VERSION 1.4.X
SUPPLEMENTAL LICENSE TERMS

These supplemental license terms ("Supplemental Terms") add to or modify the terms of the Binary Code License Agreement (collectively, the "Agreement"). Capitalized terms not defined in these Supplemental Terms shall have the same meanings ascribed to them in the Agreement. These Supplemental Terms shall supersede any inconsistent or conflicting terms in the Agreement, or in any license contained within the Software.

1. Software Internal Use and Development License Grant. Subject to the terms and conditions of this Agreement, including, but not limited to Section 4 (Java Technology Restrictions) of these Supplemental Terms, Sun grants you a non-exclusive, non-transferable, limited license to reproduce internally and use internally the binary form of the Software complete and unmodified for the sole purpose of designing, developing and testing your Java applets and applications intended to run on the Java platform ("Programs").

2. License to Distribute Software. Subject to the terms and conditions of this Agreement, including, but not limited to Section 4 (Java Technology Restrictions) of these Supplemental Terms, Sun grants you a non-exclusive, non-transferable, limited license to reproduce and distribute the Software, provided that (i) you distribute the Software complete and unmodified (unless otherwise specified in the applicable README file) and only bundled as part of, and for the sole purpose of running, your Programs, (ii) the Programs add significant and primary functionality to the Software, (iii) you do not distribute additional software intended to replace any component(s) of the Software (unless otherwise specified in the applicable README file), (iv) you do not remove or alter any proprietary legends or notices contained in the Software, (v) you only distribute the Software subject to a license agreement that protects Sun's interests consistent with the terms contained in this Agreement, and (vi) you agree to defend and indemnify Sun and its licensors from and against any damages, costs, liabilities, settlement amounts and/or expenses (including attorneys' fees) incurred in connection with any claim, lawsuit or action by any third party that arises or results from the use or distribution of any and all Programs and/or Software. (vi) include the following statement as part of product documentation (whether hard copy or electronic), as a part of a copyright page or proprietary rights notice page, in an "About" box or in any other form reasonably designed to make the statement visible to users of the Software: "This product includes code licensed from RSA Security, Inc.", and (vii) include the statement, "Some portions licensed from IBM are available at http://oss.software.ibm.com/icu4j/".

3. License to Distribute Redistributables. Subject to the terms and conditions of this Agreement, including but not limited to Section 4 (Java Technology Restrictions) of these Supplemental Terms, Sun grants you a non-exclusive, non-transferable, limited license to reproduce and distribute those files specifically identified as redistributable in the Software "README" file ("Redistributables") provided that: (i) you distribute the Redistributables complete and unmodified (unless otherwise specified in the applicable README file), and only bundled as part of Programs, (ii) you do not distribute additional software intended to supersede any component(s) of the Redistributables (unless otherwise specified in the applicable README file), (iii) you do not remove or alter any proprietary legends or notices contained in or on the Redistributables, (iv) you only distribute the Redistributables pursuant to a license agreement that protects Sun's interests consistent with the terms contained in the Agreement, (v) you agree to defend and indemnify Sun and its licensors from and against any damages, costs, liabilities, settlement amounts and/or expenses (including attorneys' fees) incurred in connection with any claim, lawsuit or action by any third party that arises or results from the use or distribution of any and all Programs and/or Software, (vi) include the following statement as part of product documentation (whether hard copy or electronic), as a part of a copyright page or proprietary rights notice page, in an "About" box or in any other form reasonably designed to make the statement visible to users of the Software: "This product includes code licensed from RSA Security, Inc.", and (vii) include the statement, "Some portions licensed from IBM are available at http://oss.software.ibm.com/icu4j/".

4. Java Technology Restrictions. You may not modify the Java Platform Interface ("JPI", identified as classes contained within the "java" package or any subpackages of the "java" package), by creating additional classes within the JPI or otherwise causing the addition to or modification of the classes in the JPI. In the event that you create an additional class and associated API(s) which (i) extends the functionality of the Java platform, and (ii) is exposed to third party software developers for the purpose of developing additional software which invokes such additional API, you must promptly publish broadly an accurate specification for such API for free use by all developers. You may not create, or authorize your licensees to create, additional classes, interfaces, or subpackages that are in any way identified as "java", "javax", "sun" or similar convention as specified by Sun in any naming convention designation.

5. Notice of Automatic Software Updates from Sun. You acknowledge that the Software may automatically download, install, and execute applets, applications, software extensions, and updated versions of the Software from Sun ("Software Updates"), which may require you to accept updated terms and conditions for installation. If additional terms and conditions are not presented on installation, the Software Updates will be considered part of the Software and subject to the terms and conditions of the Agreement.

6. Notice of Automatic Downloads. You acknowledge that, by your use of the Software and/or by requesting services that require use of the Software, the Software may automatically download, install, and execute software applications from sources other than Sun ("Other Software"). Sun makes no representations of a relationship of any kind to licensors of Other Software. TO THE EXTENT NOT PROHIBITED BY LAW, IN NO EVENT WILL SUN OR ITS LICENSORS BE LIABLE FOR ANY LOST REVENUE, PROFIT OR DATA, OR FOR SPECIAL, INDIRECT, CONSEQUENTIAL, INCIDENTAL OR PUNITIVE DAMAGES, HOWEVER CAUSED REGARDLESS OF THE THEORY OF LIABILITY, ARISING OUT OF OR RELATED TO THE USE OF OR INABILITY TO USE OTHER SOFTWARE, EVEN IF SUN HAS BEEN ADVISED OF THE POSSIBILITY OF SUCH DAMAGES.

7. Trademarks and Logos. You acknowledge and agree as between you and Sun that Sun owns the SUN, SOLARIS, JAVA, JINI, FORTE, and iPLANET trademarks and all SUN, SOLARIS, JAVA, JINI, FORTE, and iPLANET-related trademarks, service marks, logos and other brand designations ("Sun Marks"), and you agree to comply with the Sun Trademark and Logo Usage Requirements currently located at http://www.sun.com/policies/trademarks. Any use you make of the Sun Marks inures to Sun's benefit.

8. Source Code. Software may contain source code that is provided solely for reference purposes pursuant to the terms of this Agreement. Source code may not be redistributed unless expressly provided for in this Agreement.

9. Termination for Infringement. Either party may terminate this Agreement immediately should any Software become, or in either party's opinion be likely to become, the subject of a claim of infringement of any intellectual property right.

For inquiries please contact: Sun Microsystems, Inc. 901 San Antonio Road, Palo Alto, California 94303 (LFI#109998/Form ID#011801)

Copyright (c) 1995-2002
Sun Microsystems, Inc.
All Rights Reserved.

Sun(TM) ONE Studio 4, Community Edition License

Sun Microsystems, Inc. Binary Code License Agreement

READ THE TERMS OF THIS AGREEMENT AND ANY PROVIDED SUPPLEMENTAL LICENSE TERMS (COLLECTIVELY "AGREEMENT") CAREFULLY BEFORE OPENING THE SOFTWARE MEDIA PACKAGE. BY OPENING THE SOFTWARE MEDIA PACKAGE, YOU AGREE TO THE TERMS OF THIS AGREEMENT. IF YOU ARE ACCESSING THE SOFTWARE ELECTRONICALLY, INDICATE YOUR ACCEPTANCE OF THESE TERMS BY SELECTING THE "ACCEPT" BUTTON AT THE END OF THIS AGREEMENT. IF YOU DO NOT AGREE TO ALL THESE TERMS, PROMPTLY RETURN THE UNUSED SOFTWARE TO YOUR PLACE OF PURCHASE FOR A REFUND OR, IF THE SOFTWARE IS ACCESSED ELECTRONICALLY, SELECT THE "DECLINE" BUTTON AT THE END OF THIS AGREEMENT.

1. LICENSE TO USE. Sun grants you a non-exclusive and non-transferable license for the internal use only of the accompanying software and documentation and any error corrections provided by Sun (collectively "Software"), by the number of users and the class of computer hardware for which the corresponding fee has been paid.

2. RESTRICTIONS. Software is confidential and copyrighted. Title to Software and all associated intellectual property rights is retained by Sun and/or its licensors. Except as specifically authorized in any Supplemental License Terms, you may not make copies of Software, other than a single copy of Software for archival purposes. Unless enforcement is prohibited by

applicable law, you may not modify, decompile, or reverse engineer Software. You acknowledge that Software is not designed, licensed or intended for use in the design, construction, operation or maintenance of any nuclear facility. Sun disclaims any express or implied warranty of fitness for such uses. No right, title or interest in or to any trademark, service mark, logo or trade name of Sun or its licensors is granted under this Agreement.

3. LIMITED WARRANTY. Sun warrants to you that for a period of ninety (90) days from the date of purchase, as evidenced by a copy of the receipt, the media on which Software is furnished (if any) will be free of defects in materials and workmanship under normal use. Except for the foregoing, Software is provided "AS IS". Your exclusive remedy and Sun's entire liability under this limited warranty will be at Sun's option to replace Software media or refund the fee paid for Software.

4. DISCLAIMER OF WARRANTY. UNLESS SPECIFIED IN THIS AGREEMENT, ALL EXPRESS OR IMPLIED CONDITIONS, REPRESENTATIONS AND WARRANTIES, INCLUDING ANY IMPLIED WARRANTY OF MERCHANTABILITY, FITNESS FOR A PARTICULAR PURPOSE OR NON-INFRINGEMENT ARE DISCLAIMED, EXCEPT TO THE EXTENT THAT THESE DISCLAIMERS ARE HELD TO BE LEGALLY INVALID.

5. LIMITATION OF LIABILITY. TO THE EXTENT NOT PROHIBITED BY LAW, IN NO EVENT WILL SUN OR ITS LICENSORS BE LIABLE FOR ANY LOST REVENUE, PROFIT OR DATA, OR FOR SPECIAL, INDIRECT, CONSEQUENTIAL, INCIDENTAL OR PUNITIVE DAMAGES, HOWEVER CAUSED REGARDLESS OF THE THEORY OF LIABILITY, ARISING OUT OF OR RELATED TO THE USE OF OR INABILITY TO USE SOFTWARE, EVEN IF SUN HAS BEEN ADVISED OF THE POSSIBILITY OF SUCH DAMAGES. In no event will Sun's liability to you, whether in contract, tort (including negligence), or otherwise, exceed the amount paid by you for Software under this Agreement. The foregoing limitations will apply even if the above stated warranty fails of its essential purpose.

6. Termination. This Agreement is effective until terminated. You may terminate this Agreement at any time by destroying all copies of Software. This Agreement will terminate immediately without notice from Sun if you fail to comply with any provision of this Agreement. Upon Termination, you must destroy all copies of Software.

7. Export Regulations. All Software and technical data delivered under this Agreement are subject to US export control laws and may be subject to export or import regulations in other countries. You agree to comply strictly with all such laws and regulations and acknowledge that you have the responsibility to obtain such licenses to export, re-export, or import as may be required after delivery to you.

8. U.S. Government Restricted Rights. If Software is being acquired by or on behalf of the U.S. Government or by a U.S. Government prime contractor or subcontractor (at any tier), then the Government's rights in Software and accompanying documentation will be only as set forth in this Agreement; this is in accordance with 48 CFR 227.7201 through 227.7202-4 (for Department of Defense (DOD) acquisitions) and with 48 CFR 2.101 and 12.212 (for non-DOD acquisitions).

9. Governing Law. Any action related to this Agreement will be governed by California law and controlling U.S. federal law. No choice of law rules of any jurisdiction will apply.

10. Severability. If any provision of this Agreement is held to be unenforceable, this Agreement will remain in effect with the provision omitted, unless omission would frustrate the intent of the parties, in which case this Agreement will immediately terminate.

11. Integration. This Agreement is the entire agreement between you and Sun relating to its subject matter. It supersedes all prior or contemporaneous oral or written communications, proposals, representations and warranties and prevails over any conflicting or additional terms of any quote, order, acknowledgment, or other communication between the parties relating to its subject matter during the term of this Agreement. No modification of this Agreement will be binding, unless in writing and signed by an authorized representative of each party.

PEARSON EDUCATION LICENSE AGREEMENT AND LIMITED WARRANTY

READ THE FOLLOWING TERMS AND CONDITIONS CAREFULLY BEFORE OPENING THIS DISK PACKAGE. THIS LEGAL DOCUMENT IS AN AGREEMENT BETWEEN YOU AND PEARSON EDUCATION, INC. (THE "COMPANY"). BY OPENING THIS SEALED DISK PACKAGE, YOU ARE AGREEING TO BE BOUND BY THESE TERMS AND CONDITIONS. IF YOU DO NOT AGREE WITH THESE TERMS AND CONDITIONS, DO NOT OPEN THE DISK PACKAGE. PROMPTLY RETURN THE UNOPENED DISK PACKAGE AND ALL ACCOMPANYING ITEMS TO THE PLACE YOU OBTAINED THEM FOR A FULL REFUND OF ANY SUMS YOU HAVE PAID.

1. GRANT OF LICENSE: In consideration of your payment of the license fee, which is part of the price you paid for this product, and your agreement to abide by the terms and conditions of this Agreement, the Company grants to you a nonexclusive right to use and display the copy of the enclosed software program (hereinafter the "SOFTWARE") on a single computer (i.e., with a single CPU) at a single location so long as you comply with the terms of this Agreement. The Company reserves all rights not expressly granted to you under this Agreement.

2. OWNERSHIP OF SOFTWARE: You own only the magnetic or physical media (the enclosed disks) on which the SOFTWARE is recorded or fixed, but the Company retains all the rights, title, and ownership to the SOFTWARE recorded on the original disk copy(ies) and all subsequent copies of the SOFTWARE, regardless of the form or media on which the original or other copies may exist. This license is not a sale of the original SOFTWARE or any copy to you.

3. COPY RESTRICTIONS: This SOFTWARE and the accompanying printed materials and user manual (the "Documentation") are the subject of copyright. You may not copy the Documentation or the SOFTWARE, except that you may make a single copy of the SOFTWARE for backup or archival purposes only. You may be held legally responsible for any copying or copyright infringement which is caused or encouraged by your failure to abide by the terms of this restriction.

4. USE RESTRICTIONS: You may not network the SOFTWARE or otherwise use it on more than one computer or computer terminal at the same time. You may physically transfer the SOFTWARE from one computer to another provided that the SOFTWARE is used on only one computer at a time. You may not distribute copies of the SOFTWARE or Documentation to others. You may not reverse engineer, disassemble, decompile, modify, adapt, translate, or create derivative works based on the SOFTWARE or the Documentation without the prior written consent of the Company.

5. TRANSFER RESTRICTIONS: The enclosed SOFTWARE is licensed only to you and may not be transferred to any one else without the prior written consent of the Company. Any unauthorized transfer of the SOFTWARE shall result in the immediate termination of this Agreement.

6. TERMINATION: This license is effective until terminated. This license will terminate automatically without notice from the Company and become null and void if you fail to comply with any provisions or limitations of this license. Upon termination, you shall destroy the Documentation and all copies of the SOFTWARE. All provisions of this Agreement as to warranties, limitation of liability, remedies or damages, and our ownership rights shall survive termination.

7. MISCELLANEOUS: This Agreement shall be construed in accordance with the laws of the United States of America and the State of New York and shall benefit the Company, its affiliates, and assignees.

8. LIMITED WARRANTY AND DISCLAIMER OF WARRANTY: The Company warrants that the SOFTWARE, when properly used in accordance with the Documentation, will operate in substantial conformity with the description of the SOFTWARE set forth in the Documentation. The Company does not warrant that the SOFTWARE will meet your requirements or that the operation of the SOFTWARE will be uninterrupted or error-free. The Company warrants that the media on which the SOFTWARE is delivered shall be free from defects in materials and workmanship under normal use for a period of thirty (30) days from the date of your purchase. Your only remedy and the Company's only obligation under these limited warranties is, at the Company's option, return of the warranted item for a refund of any amounts paid by you or replacement of the item. Any replacement of SOFTWARE or media under the warranties shall not extend the original warranty period. The limited warranty set forth above shall not apply to any SOFTWARE which the Company determines in good faith has been subject to misuse, neglect, improper installation, repair, alteration, or damage by you. EXCEPT FOR THE EXPRESSED WARRANTIES SET FORTH ABOVE, THE COMPANY DISCLAIMS ALL WARRANTIES, EXPRESS OR IMPLIED, INCLUDING WITHOUT LIMITATION, THE IMPLIED WARRANTIES OF

MERCHANTABILITY AND FITNESS FOR A PARTICULAR PURPOSE. EXCEPT FOR THE EXPRESS WARRANTY SET FORTH ABOVE, THE COMPANY DOES NOT WARRANT, GUARANTEE, OR MAKE ANY REPRESENTATION REGARDING THE USE OR THE RESULTS OF THE USE OF THE SOFTWARE IN TERMS OF ITS CORRECTNESS, ACCURACY, RELIABILITY, CURRENTNESS, OR OTHERWISE.

IN NO EVENT, SHALL THE COMPANY OR ITS EMPLOYEES, AGENTS, SUPPLIERS, OR CONTRACTORS BE LIABLE FOR ANY INCIDENTAL, INDIRECT, SPECIAL, OR CONSEQUENTIAL DAMAGES ARISING OUT OF OR IN CONNECTION WITH THE LICENSE GRANTED UNDER THIS AGREEMENT, OR FOR LOSS OF USE, LOSS OF DATA, LOSS OF INCOME OR PROFIT, OR OTHER LOSSES, SUSTAINED AS A RESULT OF INJURY TO ANY PERSON, OR LOSS OF OR DAMAGE TO PROPERTY, OR CLAIMS OF THIRD PARTIES, EVEN IF THE COMPANY OR AN AUTHORIZED REPRESENTATIVE OF THE COMPANY HAS BEEN ADVISED OF THE POSSIBILITY OF SUCH DAMAGES. IN NO EVENT SHALL LIABILITY OF THE COMPANY FOR DAMAGES WITH RESPECT TO THE SOFTWARE EXCEED THE AMOUNTS ACTUALLY PAID BY YOU, IF ANY, FOR THE SOFTWARE.

SOME JURISDICTIONS DO NOT ALLOW THE LIMITATION OF IMPLIED WARRANTIES OR LIABILITY FOR INCIDENTAL, INDIRECT, SPECIAL, OR CONSEQUENTIAL DAMAGES, SO THE ABOVE LIMITATIONS MAY NOT ALWAYS APPLY. THE WARRANTIES IN THIS AGREEMENT GIVE YOU SPECIFIC LEGAL RIGHTS AND YOU MAY ALSO HAVE OTHER RIGHTS WHICH VARY IN ACCORDANCE WITH LOCAL LAW.

ACKNOWLEDGMENT

YOU ACKNOWLEDGE THAT YOU HAVE READ THIS AGREEMENT, UNDERSTAND IT, AND AGREE TO BE BOUND BY ITS TERMS AND CONDITIONS. YOU ALSO AGREE THAT THIS AGREEMENT IS THE COMPLETE AND EXCLUSIVE STATEMENT OF THE AGREEMENT BETWEEN YOU AND THE COMPANY AND SUPERSEDES ALL PROPOSALS OR PRIOR AGREEMENTS, ORAL, OR WRITTEN, AND ANY OTHER COMMUNICATIONS BETWEEN YOU AND THE COMPANY OR ANY REPRESENTATIVE OF THE COMPANY RELATING TO THE SUBJECT MATTER OF THIS AGREEMENT.

Should you have any questions concerning this Agreement or if you wish to contact the Company for any reason, please contact in writing at the address below.

Robin Short
Pearson Education
One Lake Street
Upper Saddle River, New Jersey 07458